LONGMAN

Pocket

PHRASAL VERBS
DICTIONARY

Longman

Pearson Education Limited
Edinburgh Gate, Harlow, Essex CM20 2JE, England
and associated companies throughout the world

Visit our website: http://www.longman.com/dictionaries

First published 2001
005   006   008   007   004

ISBN 0 582 77642 2

Set in 7pt MetaPlus Normal by Peter Wray
Printed in China
NPCC/03

ACKNOWLEDGEMENTS

Director Della Summers
Editorial Director & Publisher Pierre-Henri Cousin
Editor & Project Manager Wendy Lee
Lexicographer Stella O'Shea
Illustrator Chris Simpson
Design Alex Ingr
Cover design Abbey Design, Harlow, Essex
Proofreader Irene Lakhani

and the Longman Dictionaries team

How do I find the phrasal verb I am looking for?

First look for the main (one-word) verb – the 'keyword' – in its alphabetical position; these keywords are shown in big CAPITAL LETTERS. Under each keyword, phrasal verbs are listed alphabetically according to their particles. They are shown in small CAPITAL LETTERS. For example, if you are looking for *get up*, first look for GET in big capital letters. When you have found GET, look for GET UP in small capital letters; you will find it in its alphabetical position, towards the end of the entry for GET.

When you have found the phrasal verb you want, you may discover that it has more than one sense; the most common meanings are listed first.

How can the dictionary help me with grammar?

Your dictionary explains what each phrasal verb means. It also shows you clearly how each is used. It does this in two ways: by giving example sentences, and by giving grammatical information ('grammar patterns') at each sense. The grammar patterns show whether a verb takes an object, where the object goes, and whether the object is a person or a thing.

▶ For example, at *turn on* (=make something start working), there are two grammar patterns: *turn on* sth, *turn* sth *on*. They show that the object can come either after the phrasal verb, or between the main verb and the particle. The examples also help you to understand how the phrasal verb is used, and how the position of the object can vary:

> ▶ *I turned on the radio and listened to the six o' clock news.* ▶ *Could you turn the oven on, if you're going in the kitchen?*

▶ At *nod off*, there is only one grammar pattern: *nod off*. This is because the verb does not take an object, and you can see this again in the example: *I missed the end of her lecture – I think I must have nodded off.*

▶ At *join in* (=take part in an activity with other people), the grammar patterns are: *join in, join in sth*. They show that *join in* can be used without an object, or with an object immediately after the phrasal verb. The examples also help you to see this: *When we get to the chorus, I want everybody to join in.* ▶ *Politely, he joined in the laughter.*

▶ At *talk into* (=persuade someone to do something, especially something they are unwilling to do), this grammar pattern is given: *talk sb into sth*. This shows that *talk into* must have two objects. The first is a person ('sb' = somebody/someone), and the second is a thing ('sth' = something). The example shows the verb in a typical sentence: *I should never have let you talk me into this crazy scheme.*

Phrasal verbs such as *turn on*, *put off*, and *rip off* can all take an object between the main verb and the particle, or after the phrasal verb. They are called 'separable' phrasal verbs because their two parts can be separated:

turn on *Can you turn <u>the oven</u> on for me? Can you turn on <u>the oven</u> for me?*

Remember, though, that with this type of verb, two more rules apply:

▶ If the object is a pronoun (a word such as 'it', 'her', 'them', 'me', 'you' etc which is used instead of a noun so that you do not have to repeat the noun), the pronoun must come between the verb and the adverb. For example:

turn off *If you're not listening to the radio, I'll turn <u>it</u> off* (not *I'll turn off <u>it</u>*).

▶ If the object is a long phrase, it should come after the phrasal verb. For example:

carry out ▶ *The French carried out <u>a series of six nuclear tests</u>.*

What other information does the dictionary give me?

Nouns and adjectives which are related to a phrasal verb are shown after the meaning of the phrasal verb that they come from. For example, the noun *blackout* appears after the phrasal verb *black out* (=suddenly become unconscious), and the adjective *made-up* appears after the phrasal verb *make up* (=invent a story, name etc).

Sometimes you will find that an entry for a phrasal verb is followed by a **bold** preposition. These prepositions are frequently used with the phrasal verb, and the example sentence which follows the preposition shows how this works. For example:

> **back out**: to decide not to do something that you have agreed to do ▶ *The couple who were going to buy our house backed out at the last minute.* **+ of** ▶ *She's made a promise and she can't back out of it now.*

▶ Common phrases which use a particular phrasal verb are also shown in **bold**:

> **bet on** sth: to feel sure that something will happen, especially so that it influences what you decide to do ▶ *Traders who had bet on a rise in share prices lost money.* **don't bet on it/I wouldn't bet on it** ▶ *"Do you think they'll let me work for them again?" "I wouldn't bet on it."*

Abbreviations used in this dictionary

ADJ	adjective
etc	etcetera
N	noun
PL N	plural noun
sb	somebody, someone
sth	something
V	verb

Aa

ABANDON

ABANDON TO →

abandon yourself to sth: to not try to control a strong feeling ► *She abandoned herself entirely to grief.*

ABIDE +

ABIDE BY →

abide by sth: to obey or agree to the conditions of a rule, law, or agreement ► *The President has to abide by the same rules as everyone else.*

ABSORB +

ABSORBED IN →

be absorbed in sth: to be very interested in what you are doing, so that you do not notice what is happening around you ► *I was so absorbed in my work that I didn't notice the time.*

ABSTAIN +

ABSTAIN FROM →

abstain from sth: to not do something you would like to do, especially for health or religious reasons ► *Women are usually advised to abstain from alcohol during pregnancy.*

ACCOUNT

ACCOUNT FOR →

1 account for sth: to form a particular part or amount of something ► *Exports account for over 80 per cent of sales.*

2 account for sth: to give a satisfactory explanation for something ► *How do you account for his sudden disappearance?*

3 account for sth: to be the reason for something ► *social factors that account for high crime rates*

4 account for sb/sth: to know where someone is or what happened to something ► *At last, all the children were accounted for.* ► *Every penny has to be accounted for.*

ACE

ACE OUT →

ace out sb/sth: to easily defeat someone or something ► *She aced out her closest rival for the top job.*

ACHE +

ACHE FOR →

ache for sb/sth: to want someone or something very much ► *I was aching for some time alone with her.* ► *He ached for her.*

ACQUAINT

ACQUAINT WITH →

1 acquaint sb **with** sb/sth: to learn about or to tell someone about someone or something ► *Are you acquainted with my old friend, Simon?* ► *She took the trouble to acquaint herself with her students.*

2 acquaint sb **with** sth: to tell someone about something ► *He decided to use this opportunity to acquaint her with the true facts.*

ACT

ACT OUT →

1 act out sth, **act** sth **out**: to perform the events in a story or situation ► *The students are asked to act out the role of a young person who is being bullied.*

2 act out sth, **act** sth **out**: to express your emotions by doing something ► *teenagers who act out their frustrations through drinking*

ACT UP →

act up: to behave badly ► *He always used to act up in class when he was young.*

ADD

ADD IN →
add in sth, **add** sth **in**: to include something in a total ▶ *If you add in all the other costs, we made very little money.*

ADD ON →
add on sth, **add** sth **on**, **add on**: to increase a number or cost, or add a part to something ▶ *a tour of East Asia, where you could add on an extra week in Bali* ▶ *an extension added on to the back of the house*

ADD TO →
add to sth: to make something bigger or greater ▶ *This will only add to the cost of getting it fixed.* ▶ *The report will only add to the public's fears about genetically modified foods.*

ADD UP →
1 add up sth, **add** sth **up**, **add up**: to calculate the total of several numbers

▶ *The waiter added up the bill again.* ▶ *The kids are all taught how to read, write, and add up.*

2 add up: to be likely to be true or correct ▶ *The sums just didn't add up - £300 seemed to be missing.* ▶ *It all adds up – he's the only person who could possibly have committed the crime.*

3 add up: if small amounts or numbers add up, the total gradually gets to be surprisingly big ▶ *If you snack between meals, the calories soon add up.*

ADD UP TO →
add up to sth: to have a particular result or effect ▶ *All their work adds up to a remarkable achievement.*

ADDRESS

ADDRESS TO →
address yourself to sth: to deal with a subject or problem ▶ *The committee will address itself to three main issues.*

ADHERE

ADHERE TO →
adhere to sth: to obey a rule, law, or agreement ▶ *Both sides are expected to adhere to the rules.*

ADMIT

ADMIT TO →
admit to sth: to say that you have done something wrong or that you have a feeling that you think you should not have. **admit to doing** sth ▶ *He'd never admit to being scared.* ▶ *The three prisoners finally admitted to kidnapping the ambassador.*

ADVISE

ADVISE OF →
advise sb **of** sth: to tell someone about a fact or situation ▶ *Patients were not advised of the risks of the operation.*

AGREE

AGREE WITH →
1 not agree with sb: if a type of food or drink does not agree with you, it makes you feel slightly ill ▶ *I like red wine, but it doesn't really agree with me.*

2 agree with sb: if something agrees with you, it makes you feel good ▶ *She looks really well – the country air obviously agrees with her.*

AIM

AIM AT →
1 aim at sth: to try to achieve something ▶ *We're aiming at a growth rate of 25%.*

2 be aimed at sb: to be intended for a particular type of person or group to use, buy, or watch ▶ *a new TV series aimed at women in their 30s*

3 be aimed at sb: if a remark is aimed at someone, especially a criticism, it is intended to be about them ▶ *I hope that last comment wasn't aimed at me.*

ALLOW

ALLOW FOR →

1 allow for sth: to include or consider something when you are making a plan or decision ▶ *Make sure you allow for possible delays on the way to the airport.*

2 allow for sth: to make it possible for something to happen ▶ *The system allows for photos to be sent via email.*

ALLUDE

ALLUDE TO →

allude to sb/sth: to mention someone or something indirectly ▶ *He seemed to be alluding to recent events in Europe.*

AMOUNT

AMOUNT TO →

1 amount to sth: to be the same or have the same effect as something else ▶ *Pleasure and happiness do not necessarily amount to the same thing.*

2 not amount to much also **not amount to a great deal etc**: to not seem very important, good, successful etc ▶ *She felt that her own academic achievements didn't amount to much.*

3 amount to sth: to result in a particular total ▶ *Total bank lending to farmers in the region amounts to about £300m.*

ANGLE

ANGLE FOR →

angle for sth: to try to get something in an indirect way ▶ *We all knew she was angling for promotion.*

ANSWER

ANSWER BACK →

answer back, answer sb **back**: to answer someone rudely, especially a parent or teacher ▶ *Just do as your mother tells you, and don't answer back!*

ANSWER FOR →

1 answer for sth: to be considered responsible for something bad and possibly be punished for it. **have to answer for** sth ▶ *One day the general will have to answer for his crimes in a court of law.*

2 have a lot to answer for also **have a good deal to answer for**: to be responsible for causing a lot of trouble ▶ *I think that television has a great deal to answer for.*

ANSWER TO →

answer to sb: to have to explain the reasons for your actions to someone and accept what they think about them ▶ *Politicians have to answer to the voters at the general election.*

APPEAL

APPEAL TO →

appeal to sb: to be attractive or interesting to someone ▶ *The movie will appeal to children of all ages.*

APPROVE

APPROVE OF →

approve of sth/sb: to think that something or someone is good, right, or suitable ▶ *His parents didn't really approve of the marriage.*

APPROXIMATE

APPROXIMATE TO →

approximate to sth: to be almost the same as a particular amount or a particular situation ▶ *This figure approximates to the total population of Western Europe.*

ARGUE

ARGUE OUT →
argue sth **out, argue out** sth: to argue about or discuss every part of something in order to make a final decision ► *They spent months arguing out the details of the divorce.*

ARRIVE

ARRIVE AT →
arrive at sth: to make a decision or agreement about something after carefully considering it ► *The jury took five hours to arrive at a verdict.*

ASCRIBE

ASCRIBE TO →
ascribe sth **to** sth: to say what something is caused by ► *Her death was ascribed to natural causes.*

ASK

ASK AFTER →
ask after sb: to ask how someone is or what they have been doing ► *I saw Jan the other day – she asked after you.*

ASK ALONG →
ask sb **along, ask along** sb: to invite someone to go somewhere with you ► *Why don't you ask some of your friends along?*

ASK AROUND, *also* **ASK ROUND →**
ask around/round: to ask several people about something in order to find the information that you need ► *I'll ask around and see if there's a room available.*

ASK FOR →
1 ask for sb: to say that you would like to speak to someone ► *He called the police station and asked for Inspector Tennison.*

2 I/you couldn't ask for a better...: used to say that someone or something is the best of their kind ► *You couldn't ask for a more romantic place for a holiday.*

3 sb is asking for trouble: used to say that someone is doing something that is clearly going to make something bad happen to them ► *Anyone who walks around that area after dark is asking for trouble.*

4 sb was asking for it: used to say that someone deserved to be attacked or deserved something bad that happened to them ► *"Why did you hit him?" "He was asking for it."*

ASK IN →
ask sb **in**: to invite someone to come into a room or building ► *I asked him in for a cup of coffee.*

ASK OUT →
ask sb **out**: to ask someone to go to a restaurant, film etc with you, especially because you want to start a romantic relationship with them ► *At first he was too shy to ask her out.*
+ for ► *She rang me up that same evening and asked me out for a drink.*

ASK OVER, *also* **ASK ROUND →**
ask sb **over/round**: to invite someone to come to your house for a meal, a drink etc ► *You must ask him over for dinner some time.*

ASK ROUND *see* **ASK AROUND, ASK OVER**

ASPIRE

ASPIRE TO →
aspire to sth: to want and try hard to achieve something ► *She had always aspired to a career in politics.*

ASSOCIATE

ASSOCIATE WITH →
1 be associated with sth/sb: to be connected with something or someone ► *We all know the risks that are*

associated with smoking.

2 associate sth/ sb **with** sth/ sb: to make a connection in your mind between one thing or person and another ▶ *People usually associate Japan with high tech consumer products.*

3 associate with sb: to spend time with someone, especially someone other people disapprove of ▶ *My parents didn't want me to associate with the family from across the street.*

ATONE

ATONE FOR →

atone for sth: to do something to show that you are sorry for doing something wrong and want to make the situation you have caused better ▶ *They were anxious to atone for all they had done during the war.*

ATTEND

ATTEND TO →

1 attend to sth: to deal with something ▶ *Tom left early, saying he had some important business to attend to.*

2 attend to sb: to help or look after someone ▶ *Army medics were busy attending to the wounded.*

ATTRIBUTE

ATTRIBUTE TO →

1 attribute sth **to** sth: to think that something was caused or made by a particular person, event, or situation ▶ *Global warming has been attributed to an increase in pollution from cars.* ▶ *The painting was originally attributed to Picasso.*

2 attribute sth **to** sb/ sth: to believe that someone or something has a particular quality ▶ *We must be careful not to attribute human motives to animals.*

AUCTION

AUCTION OFF →

auction off sth, **auction** sth **off**: to sell something valuable to the person who offers the most money. ▶ *The entire contents of the family home had to be auctioned off.*

AVERAGE

AVERAGE OUT →

average out at *also average out to* sth: to have a particular amount as the average ▶ *"How much do you spend on groceries?" "It averages out at around £150 a week."*

Bb

B

BACK

BACK AWAY →

1 back away: to move backwards so that you are further away from someone or something ► *"Are you crazy?" she cried, backing away in horror.*

2 back away: to become unwilling to do something that you originally said you would do. **+ from** ► *The government has been accused of backing away from a promise to increase tax allowances.*

BACK DOWN →

back down: to accept that you cannot win an argument or that you are wrong about something ► *The union refused to back down and called for immediate strike action.*

BACK OFF →

1 back off: to move backwards so that you are further away from someone or something ► *He backed off immediately when I told him I had a gun.*

2 back off: to stop trying to influence someone or trying to make someone do something ► *You should back off for a while and let Alan make his own decisions.*

3 back off: to become unwilling to do something that you originally said you would do. **+ from** ► *The President is backing off from his promise to hold free elections.*

4 back off!: used to tell someone to go away and stop annoying or criticizing you ► *Hey, back off, buddy! Can't you see it's none of your business?*

BACK ONTO,
also **BACK ON TO →**
back onto/on to sth: if a building backs onto a river, field, road, etc the back of the building faces it ► *The house backs onto a field and a nature reserve.*

BACK OUT →

back out: to decide not to do something that you have agreed to do ► *The couple who were going to buy our house backed out at the last minute.* **+ of** ► *She's made a promise and she can't back out of it now.*

BACK UP →

1 back up sth, **back** sth **up**: to prove that something is true ► *There was no scientific evidence to back up their claims.*

2 back sb **up, back up** sb: to support someone by saying that they are telling the truth ► *Peggy was there too. She'll be able to back me up.*

3 back up sb/sth, **back** sb/sth **up**: to provide additional help or support ► *Officials discussed the possibility of using the army to back up the police.*

  back-up N additional help or support ► *Several police cars provided back-up for the officers.*

  back-up ADJ back-up systems, services, or equipment are designed to be used if the main one does not work effectively ► *Nuclear reactors have superbly efficient back-up systems in case of emergencies.*

4 back up sth, **back** sth **up**: to copy computer information onto a separate disk so that the information is safe if there is a problem with the computer ► *You should back up your data at least once a week.*

  back-up N a copy of information on a

computer ▶ *Remember to keep back-ups of all your important files.*
back-up ADJ produced when you make a copy of information on a computer ▶ *a back-up copy*

5 back up, back up sth, **back** sth **up**: to drive a vehicle backwards ▶ *The driver backed the taxi up to the hotel door.*

BAIL

BAIL OUT →
1 bail sb **out, bail out** sb: to help someone with their financial problems by giving them money ▶ *Richard has run up huge debts at college and his parents have refused to bail him out.*

2 bail sb **out, bail out** sb: to leave a sum of money with a law court so that someone can be let out of prison until their trial ▶ *Clarke's family paid £50,000 to bail him out.*

3 bail out, bail out sth, **bail** sth **out**: to use a container to remove water from the bottom of a boat ▶ *We were bailing out as fast as we could, but it was no use.*

4 bail out: to jump out of a plane in order to escape, because it is going to crash ▶ *The aircraft was hit, but the pilot managed to bail out just in time.*

BAIL OUT ON →
bail out on sb: to stop supporting someone ▶ *A lot of people eventually bailed out on the president.*

BALANCE

BALANCE AGAINST →
balance sth **against** sth: to consider the importance of one thing in relation to another ▶ *The cost of treatment has to be balanced against the health benefits.*

BALANCE OUT →
balance out: if two or more things balance out, the final result is that they are equal ▶ *Sometimes I look*

after the kids and sometimes John does – so in the end it all balances out.

BALE see BAIL

BAND

BAND TOGETHER →
band together: to work with other people as a group in order to achieve something ▶ *Local residents banded together to demand more police officers on the streets.*

BANDAGE

BANDAGE UP →
bandage up sth/sb, **bandage** sth/sb **up**: to tie a long narrow piece of material around a part of the body that is injured ▶ *The nurse bandaged me up and sent me home to rest.*

BANDY

BANDY ABOUT, *also* BANDY AROUND →
bandy about/around sth, **bandy** sth **about/around**: to mention a word, name, idea etc often ▶ *Names like Brad Pitt and Anthony Hopkins are being bandied about for starring roles in the show.*

BANG

BANG AROUND, *also* BANG ABOUT →
bang around/about: to move around a place, doing things and making a lot of noise ▶ *Michael was banging about in the garage, hunting for his tools.*

B

BANG AWAY →
bang away: to work hard at something.
+ at/on ► *Marcel banged away on his report all night.*

BANG DOWN →
bang down sth, **bang** sth **down**: to put something down violently and noisily because you are annoyed ► *"That's enough!" Laura said, banging down the iron.*

BANG ON →
bang on: to talk a lot about the same thing especially in order to make people take notice of what you are saying. **+ about** ► *I'm sorry to keep banging on about this, but our safety rules really are very important.*

BANG UP →
1 bang sb **up**: to put someone in prison ► *Their father had been banged up in jail for more than a year.*

2 bang up sth/sb, **bang** sth/sb **up**: to seriously damage something or injure someone ► *My car got pretty banged up, but I'm okay.*
  banged-up ADJ old and damaged ► *She drives a banged-up old jeep.*

BANK

BANK ON →
bank on sth/sb: to depend on something happening or on someone doing something ► *They're banking on a win tonight to take them through to the final.* **I wouldn't bank on it** (=used to emphasize that you cannot depend on something happening) ► *It looks as if the weather will be good on the day, but I wouldn't bank on it.*

BARGAIN

BARGAIN FOR →
more than you bargained for: not expected and not wanted ► *It was a wonderful holiday but it cost a lot more than we'd bargained for.*

BARGAIN FOR, *also* BARGAIN ON
not bargain for/on sth: to not expect something to happen, especially something that causes problems ► *I hadn't bargained on being stuck in traffic for two hours.*

BARGE

BARGE IN, *also* BARGE INTO →
1 barge in, **barge into** sth: to rudely enter a building or room without being asked ► *I wish you wouldn't barge into the bathroom without knocking.*

2 barge in, **barge into** sth: to rudely interrupt what someone else is saying or doing ► *Gordon had an annoying habit of sitting down and barging into other people's conversations.*

BASE

BASE ON, *also* BASE UPON →
base sth **on/upon** sth: to use facts, ideas, records etc that you already have in order to decide something or produce something else ► *I based my decision on what I thought would be best for the children.* ► *The movie was based on a novel by Sinclair Lewis.*

BASH

BASH ABOUT →
bash sb/sth **about**: to treat someone or something roughly or violently ► *Sam came home covered in bruises, saying he'd been bashed about at school.*

BASH AWAY →
bash away: to work hard and continuously at something. **+ at** ► *Mike spent the weekend bashing away at his latest novel.*

BASH IN →
bash in sth, **bash** sth **in**: to break, damage, or seriously injure something ► *I'll bash your head in if you say that again!*

B

BASH UP →
bash up sb/sth, **bash** sb/sth **up**: to badly injure someone or seriously damage something ▶ *They said they'd bash me up if I said anything to the teachers.*

BASK
BASK IN →
bask in sth: to enjoy very much the attention or admiration that you are getting from other people ▶ *The band basked in the admiration of a whole generation.*

BAT
BAT AROUND →
bat around sth, **bat** sth **around**: to discuss ideas in order to decide whether or not they are good ▶ *We batted around several suggestions, but none of them seemed quite right.*

BATHE
BE BATHED IN →
be bathed in sunshine/moonlight etc: if a place is bathed in sunshine or moonlight, the light shines very brightly into or onto it ▶ *The hillside was suddenly bathed in sunshine as the clouds parted.*

BATTEN
BATTEN DOWN →
batten down sth, **batten** sth **down**: to firmly fasten a window, door etc in order to prevent damage from strong winds ▶ *Stephen was busy battening down all the shutters before the hurricane arrived.*

BATTER
BATTER DOWN →
batter down sth, **batter** sth **down**: to hit a door or wall very hard until it breaks and falls down ▶ *Armed police battered the front door down and dragged the men into the street.*

BATTLE
BATTLE OUT →
battle it out: if people, teams etc battle it out, they compete or argue with each other until one person or team wins ▶ *On Sunday, the professionals will be battling it out for a top prize of £100,000.*

BAWL
BAWL OUT →
bawl sb **out**, **bawl out** sb: to speak angrily to someone because they have done something wrong ▶ *My dad really bawled me out for coming home so late.*

BEAR
BEAR DOWN →
1 bear down: to use all your strength to push or press down on something ▶ *The men all bore down, but the stone wouldn't budge.*

2 bear down: to use all your effort to do something ▶ *The home team have to bear down again and get serious if they want to win the game.*

BEAR DOWN ON, also BEAR DOWN UPON →
bear down on/upon sb/sth: to move quickly towards someone or something in a threatening or determined way ▶ *The ship bore down on us and there seemed to be no escape.*

BEAR OUT →
bear out sth/sb, **bear** sth/sb **out**: to support what someone has said and help to prove that it is true ▶ *Recent research bears out the idea that women are safer drivers than men.*

B

BEAR UP →
bear up: to remain cheerful and not be badly affected by a bad situation, illness etc ▶ *It's been a very difficult year for my father, but he's bearing up quite well.*

BEAR WITH →
bear with me: used to politely ask someone to wait or be patient while you do something ▶ *I hope you will bear with me if I tell you a little about my own situation.*

BEAT

BEAT DOWN →
1 the sun beats down: if the sun beats down, it shines very strongly ▶ *The sun was beating down on our backs and our throats were dry.*

2 the rain beats down: if the rain beats down, it rains very hard ▶ *At that moment the sky darkened and the rain began to beat down.*

3 beat sb down: to persuade someone to reduce the price of something you are buying ▶ *They wanted £250,000 for the house but we beat them down to £200,000.*

BEAT OFF →
1 beat off sb/sth, beat sb/sth off: to succeed in stopping someone from attacking you, by hitting them ▶ *The old man managed to beat off his attackers using his walking stick.*

2 beat off sth/sb, beat sth/sb off: to defeat something or someone who is competing with you or opposing you ▶ *an attempt to beat off a rival bid from a mobile phone company*

BEAT OUT →
1 beat out sth, beat sth out: to produce a regular pattern of sounds, especially by hitting something ▶ *Someone began to beat out a rhythm on the drums.*

2 beat out sth, beat sth out: to make a

fire stop burning by hitting it with something ▶ *She tried to beat out the flames with a wet towel.*

3 beat sb out, beat out sb: to defeat someone or do better than them in a competition ▶ *The Raiders beat out their rivals, the Kansas City Chiefs.*

BEAT UP →
beat sb up, beat up sb: to attack and seriously hurt someone, by hitting or kicking them many times ▶ *They beat him up so badly he was in hospital for a month.*

BEAT UP ON →
beat up on sb: to attack someone or criticize them unfairly ▶ *Kerry accused politicians of beating up on the poorest citizens in order to get votes.*

BEAVER

BEAVER AWAY →
beaver away: to work hard at something ▶ *The mechanics have been beavering away all night, trying to get the car ready for the race.*

BECOME

BECOME OF →
what became of sb *also* **whatever became of sb:** used to ask about someone you used to know and about what they are doing now ▶ *Whatever became of Phil Goddard? I haven't heard from him for years.*

BED

BED DOWN →
bed down: to lie down to sleep somewhere, especially not in your usual bed ▶ *About twenty people had bedded down outside the store, waiting for the sale to start.*

BEEF

BEEF UP →
beef up sth, beef sth up: to improve something by making it stronger, more powerful, more effective etc ▶ *Security*

has been beefed up for the Queen's visit.

beefed-up ADJ stronger, more powerful, more effective etc than before ▶ *a beefed-up version of the classic model*

BELIEVE

BELIEVE IN →

1 believe in sth: to believe that a god exists or that a particular religion or belief is true ▶ *Most British people still believe in God, even if they don't go to church.*

2 believe in sth: to think that something is good or right ▶ *I don't believe in all these silly diets.* **believe in doing** sth ▶ *My grandfather was a strict vegetarian – he didn't believe in killing anything.*

3 believe in sb: to be confident that someone will be able to do something successfully ▶ *The people want a president that they can believe in.* **believe in yourself** (=be confident that you are good at something or that you can succeed) ▶ *If you want to be an artist, you have to believe in yourself.*

BELONG

BELONG TO →

1 belong to sb: if something belongs to you, it is yours ▶ *The boat belonged to one of the local fishermen.* ▶ *Who does that house belong to now?*

2 belong to sth: to be a member of a particular group or organization ▶ *Did you belong to any clubs when you were at university?*

3 belong to sth: to come from or be connected with a particular time, place, or style ▶ *The old lady seemed to belong to a different era.*

BELT

BELT OUT →

belt out sth, **belt** sth **out**: to sing or

play something on a musical instrument very loudly ▶ *Downstairs a band was belting out a deafening selection of their early hits.*

BELT UP →

1 belt up!: used to rudely tell someone to stop talking ▶ *"For Christ's sake, belt up!" Barton said.*

2 belt up: to fasten your seatbelt in a car or a plane ▶ *The government have introduced a £500 fine for drivers who don't belt up.*

BEND

BE BENT ON →

be bent on sth: to be very determined to do something, especially something bad. **be bent on doing** sth ▶ *The protesters seem bent on causing as much disruption as possible.*

BET

BET ON →

bet on sth: to feel sure that something will happen, especially so that it influences what you decide to do ▶ *Traders who had bet on a rise in share prices lost money.* **don't bet on it/ I wouldn't bet on it** ▶ *"Do you think they'll let me work for them again?" "I wouldn't bet on it."*

BILL

BILL AS →

bill sb/ sth **as** sth: to publicly describe someone or something in a particular way in order to advertise them ▶ *The festival is being billed as the biggest of its kind in Europe.*

BIND

BIND OVER →

1 bind over sb, **bind** sb **over**: if a court or judge binds someone over, they order that person to cause no more trouble and will punish them if they do. **be bound over to keep the peace** ▶ *Campbell was arrested and bound*

B

over to keep the peace for three months.

2 be bound over for trial: to be taken to a court of law in order to be judged to see if you are guilty of a crime ▶ *Davies, 35, was bound over for trial on charges of aiding an escaped criminal.*

BE BOUND TO →
be bound to sb/sth: to have made a formal agreement or promise to obey someone or something ▶ *I'm afraid that you have signed a contract and therefore you are bound to it.*

BE BOUND UP IN, *also* BE BOUND UP WITH →
be bound up in/with sth: to be very involved in a particular situation ▶ *Joanna's too bound up in her own problems to be able to help at the moment.*

BE BOUND UP WITH →
be bound up with sth: to be closely connected with something ▶ *The history of the company is closely bound up with that of the family who founded it.*

BITE

BITE BACK →
1 bite back sth, **bite** sth **back**: to deliberately stop yourself from saying something or from showing what you really feel ▶ *Carrie had a strong desire to say what she really thought, but she bit back the words.*

2 bite back: to criticize someone strongly and angrily because they have criticized or done something unpleasant to you ▶ *The*

prime minister angrily bit back at government critics today.

BITE INTO →
1 bite into sth: to press so hard against someone's skin that it hurts or cuts them ▶ *Callum tightened his grip and she felt his fingers biting into her wrist.*

2 bite into sth: to use a large part of the money, time etc that you have available ▶ *Share prices have fallen as the recession has bitten into profits.*

BLACK

BLACK OUT →
1 black out: to suddenly become unconscious ▶ *The driver of the car had apparently blacked out at the wheel.*
   blackout N when you suddenly become unconscious ▶ *You'll have to go to the doctor if you keep having these blackouts.*

2 be blacked out: if a room, building, or city is blacked out during a war, all the lights are turned off or hidden at night so that it cannot be seen by enemy planes ▶ *During the bombing, the city was blacked out and the cafes closed at 8 pm.*
   blackout N a period of time at night during a war when all lights are turned off or hidden so that buildings cannot be seen by enemy planes ▶ *Kitty had had enough of the blackout, the bombings and the shortages.*

3 be blacked out: to have no lights on because the electricity has stopped working ▶ *From time to time the whole country was blacked out by power cuts.*
   blackout N when lights cannot be turned on because the electricity is not working ▶ *Due to a power blackout, their hotel was in total darkness.*

B

4 black out sth, **black** sth **out**: to cover something with dark material so that it cannot be seen ▸ *The car's licence plate had been blacked out with tape.*

5 black out sth, **black** sth **out**: to prevent a television or radio programme from being broadcast, or a news report from being seen or read ▸ *The former Soviet authorities tried to black out all broadcasts from the West.*

> **blackout** N when a radio or television programme is officially prevented from being broadcast, or a news report from being printed ▸ *Police ordered a news blackout while the negotiations to free the hostages were in progress.*

BLANK

BLANK OUT →

1 blank out sth/sb, **blank** sth/sb **out**: to deliberately try to stop yourself from thinking about something or someone ▸ *I tried to completely blank her out of my mind.*

2 blank out sth, **blank** sth **out**: to cover or remove something that is written, so that it cannot be read ▸ *The whole of the last paragraph had been blanked out.*

3 blank out, blank out sth: if information or writing on a computer screen blanks out, it disappears or is hidden ▸ *Suddenly the file I was working on blanked out.*

4 blank out: to be unable to remember what to say or do ▸ *Melissa took one look at the exam paper and completely blanked out.*

BLANKET

BLANKET WITH →

be blanketed with snow/mist etc: to be covered with snow, mist etc ▸ *Virtually all of Surrey was blanketed with snow overnight.*

BLARE

BLARE OUT →

blare out: if music, a radio etc is blaring out, it is very loud ▸ *Military music was blaring out from the loudspeaker system.*

BLAST

BLAST AWAY →

1 blast away, blast away sb/sth, **blast** sb/sth **away**: to keep firing a gun or explosives at someone or something. **+ at** ▸ *The farmer started blasting away at the crows with his shotgun.*

2 blast away: to play music very loudly, especially for a long period of time ▸ *At 2am, the band was still blasting away.*

3 blast away: to strongly criticize someone or something. **+ at** ▸ *He blasted away at city officials, blaming them for the housing shortage.*

BLAST OFF →

blast off: if a spacecraft blasts off, it leaves the ground at the beginning of its journey into space ▸ *Next week, a rocket carrying the first Austrian into space will blast off from Cape Canaveral.*

> **blast-off** N the moment when a spacecraft leaves the ground to begin its journey into space ▸ *We have 10 seconds until blast-off.*

BLAST OUT →

blast out sth, **blast** sth **out, blast out**: if music blasts out or something blasts it out, it is very loud ▸ *Rap music was blasting out from the car stereo.*

BLAZE

BLAZE AWAY →

1 blaze away: if a fire blazes away, it burns strongly and brightly ▸ *Soon the campfire was blazing away.*

2 blaze away: to keep firing a gun continuously. **+ at** ▸ *He pulled out a*

B

gun and started blazing away at the oncoming soldiers.

BLEND

BLEND IN, *also* BLEND INTO →

1 blend in, blend into sth: to have the same colour or pattern as surrounding objects and therefore not look very different from them ▶ *Military vehicles are painted green or brown so that they blend into the surroundings.*
+ with ▶ *The house is made of local stone, which blends in well with the surrounding countryside.*

2 blend in, blend into sth: if someone blends in, they seem similar to the other people around them, and do not seem different or unusual ▶ *In Los Angeles, it doesn't matter where you came from – after a while you just blend in.* **+ with** ▶ *Philippe did his best to blend in with the other students.*

BLIMP

BLIMP OUT →

blimp out: to become fat ▶ *During my first year in college I totally blimped out from eating so much junk food.*

BLISS

BLISS OUT →

bliss out, bliss sb out: to feel very happy and relaxed, or to make someone feel this way ▶ *After exercising, bliss out in our relaxing sauna.*

BLOCK

BLOCK IN →

block in sth, **block** sth **in**: to write or draw something that covers a space on a piece of paper ▶ *She'd drawn the swimming pool, then blocked in a blue-green colour.*

BLOCK OFF →

block off sth, **block** sth **off**: to put something across a road, path, entrance etc in order to prevent people from passing through ▶ *Police blocked off the whole area after the shooting, looking for witnesses.*

BLOCK OUT →

1 block out sth, **block** sth **out**: to prevent light, sound, radio waves etc from reaching somewhere ▶ *The new lenses are supposed to block out harmful rays that can damage your eyes.* ▶ *Huge skyscrapers blocked out the view.*

2 block out sth, **block** sth **out**: to stop yourself from thinking about something unpleasant ▶ *Amy didn't tell anyone about the attack, and just tried to block it out of her mind.*

BLOCK UP →

block up sth, **block** sth **up**: to fill a narrow space or the entrance to something so that nothing can pass through ▶ *Crowds of people were blocking up the street in front of the council building.*

BLOT

BLOT OUT →

1 blot out sth, **blot** sth **out**: to cover something and prevent it from being seen ▶ *Clouds of thick black smoke blotted out the sky.*

2 blot out sth, **blot** sth **out**: to stop yourself from thinking about something, especially something unpleasant or painful ▶ *He immersed himself in his work to blot out the pain.*

BLOT UP →

blot up sth, **blot** sth **up**: to remove liquid from a surface by gently pressing a cloth, paper etc on it ▶ *Use a kitchen towel to blot up any excess liquid.*

BLOW

BLOW AWAY →

1 blow sb **away, blow away** sb: to be extremely good and impressive and have a powerful effect on someone ▶ *When I first heard this track, I was blown away.*

2 blow sb **away, blow away** sb: to kill someone or something by shooting them ▶ *Don't move or I'll blow you away!*

3 blow away sb, **blow** sb **away**: to defeat someone or something completely ▶ *The Italian team blew them away in a thrilling game.*

BLOW IN →

blow in: to arrive unexpectedly ▶ *Jim blew in about an hour ago – did you see him?*

BLOW OFF →

1 blow off sth, **blow** sth **off**: if an explosion or bullet blows something off, it removes it with a lot of force ▶ *The bullet blew off three of his fingers.*

2 blow off sb/sth, **blow** sb/sth **off**: to treat someone or something as unimportant ▶ *Parker blew off the sexist remarks he made about female reporters.*

3 blow sth **off, blow off** sth: to not do something that you had planned to do ▶ *We blew off the tennis game and went out to dinner instead.*

BLOW OUT →

1a. blow out sth, **blow** sth **out**: to make a flame or a fire stop burning by blowing air on it ▶ *Helen lit a cigarette and then blew out the match.*
b. blow out: if a flame or fire blows out, it stops burning because of the wind, or because someone has blown air on it ▶ *The candles had blown out in the wind.*

2 blow out: if a tyre blows out all the air suddenly goes out of it because it is damaged ▶ *One of her tyres blew out and she lost control of the car.*

blowout N when all the air suddenly goes out of a tyre because it is damaged ▶ *A blowout at this speed could be really dangerous.*

3 blow out sb/sth, **blow** sb/sth **out**: to easily defeat someone or something ▶ *Our team blew out the Cubs 28-3.*

4 blow itself out: if a storm blows itself out, it ends ▶ *The hurricane moved along the coast before blowing itself out over the North Atlantic.*

5 blow sb **out, blow out** sb: to disappoint someone by not meeting them or not doing what you have agreed to do ▶ *If he blows you out again, tell him you don't want to see him any more.*

BLOW OVER →

1 blow over: if an argument or unpleasant situation blows over, it is forgotten or no longer seems important ▶ *I know she's angry now, but it'll soon blow over.*

2 blow over: if a storm blows over, it ends ▶ *The Weather Centre predicts that the snowstorm will quickly blow over.*

BLOW UP →

1 blow up sth, **blow** sth **up**: to destroy something using a bomb ▶ *An army bus carrying 10 soldiers was blown up by a land mine.*

2 blow up: to be destroyed in an explosion ▶ *Investigators are trying to find out what caused the rocket to blow up in midair.*

B

3 blow up sth, **blow** sth **up**: to fill something with air or gas ▶ *Come and help me blow up the balloons.*

> **blow-up** ADJ a blow-up object is one that you fill with air and is usually made of plastic or rubber ▶ *a blow-up doll*

4 blow up: to suddenly become very angry and start shouting ▶ *She used to blow up over the slightest little thing.*

> **blow-up** N a sudden angry argument ▶ *After our blow-up, Larry didn't speak to me for a week.*

5 blow up sth, **blow** sth **up**: to make a much larger copy of something, especially a photograph ▶ *You should get this photo blown up and framed.*

> **blow-up** N a photograph or picture that has been made much larger ▶ *The evening news showed a blow-up of a spy satellite picture.*

6 blow up: if an angry argument or a difficult situation blows up, it suddenly starts ▶ *A diplomatic crisis has blown up over the accidental bombing of the embassy.*

7 blow up sth, **blow** sth **up**: to talk about something in a way that makes it seem more important or more serious than it really is. **+ into** ▶ *I don't know why you've blown this up into such a big deal – it was just a joke!* **blow** sth **up out of proportion** ▶ *The whole thing is being blown up out of all proportion by the Western media.*

8 blow up: if a storm or strong wind blows up, it suddenly starts ▶ *The sky's getting dark – it looks like there's a storm blowing up.*

BLUFF

BLUFF OUT →

bluff it out: to lie or pretend that you do not know something, in order to avoid being punished or blamed ▶ *If she asks him who took the money, he'll just bluff it out and say he doesn't know anything about it.*

BLUNDER

BLUNDER INTO →

blunder into sth: to get into a difficult or dangerous situation by mistake ▶ *The men took a wrong turn and blundered into a group of enemy soldiers.*

BLURT

BLURT OUT →

blurt out sth, **blurt** sth **out**: to suddenly say something without thinking about it, usually because you are nervous or excited ▶ *"I have to tell you, Mark," she blurted out, "I'm in love with you."*

BOARD

BOARD UP →

board up sth, **board** sth **up**: to cover a window or door with wooden boards, especially in order to make a building safe ▶ *Residents are boarding up their windows before the hurricane strikes.*

BOB

BOB UP →

bob up: if the price or level of something bobs up, it suddenly increases a little ▶ *Fuel prices bobbed up before the holiday weekend.*

BOG

BOG DOWN →

1 get bogged down: to become so involved in unimportant things that you cannot make progress with the main thing you are trying to do. **+ in**

▶ *The peace talks quickly got bogged down in petty regional differences.*

2 bog down sth, **bog** sth **down**, **bog down**: to make something move, work, or happen less quickly and easily ▶ *Snow and freezing rain have been bogging down traffic on highland roads this week.*

BOIL

BOIL DOWN TO →

boil down to sth: if a situation, problem, discussion etc boils down to something, that is the main or basic part of it ▶ *In the end, it all boiled down to whether we could afford to move house or not.*

BOIL OVER →

1 boil over: if a liquid boils over, it rises and flows over the sides of the container it is being heated in because it has become too hot ▶ *The milk's boiling over – quick, turn it off!*

2 boil over: if a situation in which people are angry boils over, they become angry and violent. **boil over into** sth ▶ *Protests by the unemployed boiled over into violence in the city's streets last night.*

BOIL UP →

1 boil up: if angry feelings boil up inside you, you suddenly feel very angry ▶ *She stared at him for a moment, anger boiling up inside her.*

2 boil up: if a quarrel or an unpleasant situation boils up, it suddenly starts to happen ▶ *A price war was boiling up between the US and Japan.*

BOLSTER

BOLSTER UP →

1 bolster up sb/sth, **bolster** sb/sth **up**: to make someone feel more confident, especially by praising them ▶ *He relies on Clare because she bolsters him up and tells him he's wonderful.*

2 bolster up sth, **bolster** sth **up**: to use additional facts or information to try to prove that something is true ▶ *There's plenty of evidence available to bolster up this theory.*

BOLT

BOLT DOWN →

bolt down sth, **bolt** sth **down**: to eat food very quickly ▶ *Charlie bolted down his breakfast and ran out of the house.*

BOMB

BE BOMBED OUT →

1 be bombed out: if people are bombed out, their homes have been destroyed by bombs ▶ *Many families were completely bombed out and had nothing except the clothes they stood up in.*

2 be bombed out: if a building or town is bombed out, it has been destroyed by bombs ▶ *People still remember that night, when half the city was bombed out.*

   bombed-out ADJ a bombed-out building or town has been destroyed by bombs ▶ *the bombed-out capital city*

BOMBARD

BOMBARD WITH →

bombard sb **with** sth: to ask someone a lot of questions, give them a lot of advice, send them a lot of letters etc all at once, expecially in an annoying way ▶ *These days we are bombarded with advice on what to eat and what not to eat.*

B

BONE

BONE UP →

bone up: to learn as much as you can about something, in order to prepare for an examination, meeting etc.
+ on ▸ *I'm very weak in my science subjects, so I'll really have to bone up on them.*

BOOK

BOOK IN, *also* **BOOK INTO** →

1 book in, book into sth: to go to a hotel where you intend to stay and tell them that you have arrived ▸ *We booked into the Savoy and then went out to a restaurant.*

2 book sb **into** sth, **book** sb **in**: to arrange for someone to stay at a hotel, have treatment at a hospital etc ▸ *I can't cancel the room now – I've already booked us in!* **book** sb **in at** sth ▸ *The doctor's booked you in at the West London Clinic.*

BE BOOKED UP →

be booked up: if a trip, concert, course etc is booked up, there are no more seats or places available ▸ *The popular plays are always booked up well in advance.*

BOOM

BOOM OUT →

boom out: if someone's voice or music booms out, it is very loud and deep ▸ *"Come in," a voice boomed out from behind the door.* ▸ *Music boomed out of a loudspeaker.*

BOOT

BOOT OUT →

boot out sb, **boot** sb **out**: to force someone to leave a place, job,

organization etc. **+ of** ▸ *Stephen's just been booted out of his apartment for not paying his rent.* **get booted out** ▸ *The military president got booted out in 1962.*

BOOT UP →

1 boot up: if a computer boots up, it starts working and becomes ready to use ▸ *The PC took a couple of minutes to boot up.*

2 boot up sth, **boot** sth **up**: to make a computer start working so that it is ready to use ▸ *You'll have to shut down the computer and then boot it up again.*

BORDER

BORDER ON →

border on sth: to be almost the same as something very bad ▸ *His behaviour with some female members of staff bordered on sexual harassment.* **be bordering on the ridiculous/the absurd etc** (=seem ridiculous, absurd etc) ▸ *Sometimes, government censorship borders on the absurd.*

BORE

BORE INTO →

bore into sb: if someone's eyes bore into you, they look at you very directly in a way that makes you feel uncomfortable ▸ *The young man's cold angry eyes bored into her.*

BORNE *see* BEAR OUT

—see BEAR OUT

BOSS

BOSS AROUND, *also* **BOSS ABOUT** →

boss sb **around/about**: to keep telling someone what to do in an annoying way ▸ *I can't stand the way James bosses everyone around!*

BOTCH

BOTCH UP →
botch sth **up, botch up** sth: to do something badly and carelessly ▶ *The first lot of builders botched it up so badly that we had to start again.*
   botched-up ADJ done badly and carelessly ▶ *The decorating was a real botched-up job.*

BOTTLE

BOTTLE OUT →
bottle out: to suddenly decide not to do something that you had agreed to do, because you are too nervous ▶ *You said you wanted a fight – it's too late to bottle out now!*

BOTTLE UP →
1 bottle up sth, **bottle** sth **up**: to not show or talk about a strong feeling such as anger or unhappiness, even though it still affects you ▶ *Writing the book was a way of expressing all the anger I'd been bottling up for years.*
2 bottle up sth, **bottle** sth **up** sth: to be unable to move forwards or make progress, or make it difficult for something to do this ▶ *The bill has been bottled up in the Senate since September.*

BOTTOM

BOTTOM OUT →
bottom out: to stop decreasing or getting worse, especially before starting to increase or improve again ▶ *A lot of jobs have been lost, but there are now signs that the recession is bottoming out.*

BOUNCE

BOUNCE AROUND →
1 bounce sth **around, bounce around** sth: to discuss an idea with other people ▶ *I wanted to have a meeting so that we could bounce a few ideas around.*

2 bounce around: to move frequently to different cities or towns ▶ *My family bounced around a lot because my dad was in the army.*

BOUNCE BACK →
1 bounce back: to become successful again after failing or being defeated ▶ *The company's had a lot of problems in the past but it's always managed to bounce back.*

2 bounce back: to feel well or cheerful again after being ill, or after an unpleasant experience ▶ *Suzie's been quite depressed*  *since her illness, but I'm sure she'll soon bounce back.*

BOUNCE INTO →
bounce sb **into (doing)** sth: to make someone do something they do not want to or before they have time to think about it carefully ▶ *She feels that she wasn't really ready to get married, but she was bounced into it by her family.*

BOUNCE OFF →
bounce ideas/suggestions etc off sb: to talk about your ideas, suggestions etc with someone as a way of helping you to make a decision ▶ *We used to bounce ideas off each other and share all our problems.*

BOUND

BE BOUND UP WITH →
be bound up with sth: to be closely connected with a particular problem, situation etc ▶ *Mark's problems are all bound up with his mother's death when he was ten.*

BOW

BOW DOWN →

1 bow down: to bend forward from your waist, especially when you are already kneeling. **+ before** ▶ *Maria bowed down before the statue in the church.*

2 bow down: to do what someone is trying to make you do, especially because you are afraid of them. **+ to** ▶ *The government refuses to bow down to terrorists.*

BOW OUT →

bow out: to give up an important job so that someone can take your place, or to stop taking part in an event ▶ *He later bowed out and left the stage to the Socialist leader.*

BOW TO →

1 bow to sth/sb: to agree to do what someone else wants you to do, especially when this is not what you want. **bow to pressure** ▶ *The Prime Minister reluctantly bowed to pressure from his advisers, and agreed to delay the tax cuts.* **bow to sb's demands/wishes** ▶ *In the end the government was forced to bow to demands from environmental groups.*

2 bow to the inevitable: to accept that something is going to happen and cannot be avoided ▶ *When the recession hit, the company bowed to the inevitable and ceased trading.*

BOWL

BOWL ALONG →

bowl along, bowl along sth: to travel quickly and smoothly, especially in a car ▶ *She looked like a film star, bowling along in her open-topped car.*

BOWL OVER →

bowl sb **over, bowl over** sb: if you are bowled over by someone or something, you are extremely impressed by them ▶ *When she first met Mario, she was bowled over by his good looks and charm.*

BOX

BOX IN →

1 box sb/sth **in, box in** sb/sth: to stop a person or car from moving by putting another car in the way or by staying very close to them ▶ *When I returned to my car, I found I was boxed in by a yellow van.* **get boxed in** ▶ *Williams is in danger of being boxed in by the German defenders.*

2 box sb **in, box in** sb: to prevent someone from doing what they want to do, by limiting them in some way ▶ *Small businesses are boxed in by all sorts of silly rules and regulations.*

BOX UP →

box sth **up, box up** sth: to put things into boxes ▶ *It took us two hours to clean the house and box up the empty bottles.*

BRANCH

BRANCH OFF →

1 branch off: if a road, path etc branches off from another road or path, it separates from it and goes in a different direction. **+ to** ▶ *We took a minor road, which branched off to the left at Wiggen.*

2 branch off: to start talking about something different. **+ into** ▶ *Then the conversation branched off into a discussion about movies.*

BRANCH OUT →

branch out: to start doing something different from what you usually do, especially in business. **+ into** ▶ *a record company that recently branched out into radio*

BRAVE

BRAVE OUT →

brave it out: to stay and face a dangerous or unpleasant situation, rather than trying to avoid it ▶ *A lot of people left Paris when the war broke out, but Elaine decided to brave it out.*

BRAZEN

BRAZEN OUT →

brazen it out: to deliberately behave in a confident way when you know you have done something wrong ▶ *He tried to brazen it out, but in the end was forced to resign.*

BREAK

BREAK AWAY →

1 break away: to stop being part of a group, political party, or country in order to form another one ▶ *In 1920, the majority of socialists broke away to form the Communist party.* **+ from** ▶ *After thirty years of bitter civil war, the southern region broke away from the north.*

> **breakaway** ADJ a breakaway group is one that has separated from a larger group ▶ *The Independent National Party was a breakaway group led by Colonel Johnson.*

2 break away: to manage to get away from someone who is holding you or trying to stop you leaving ▶ *Anna attempted to break away, but he held her tight.*

3 break away: to do something different from what you usually do. **+ from** ▶ *Societies have to break away from the traditions of the past in order to develop.*

BREAK DOWN →

1 break down: if a vehicle or a machine breaks down, it stops working properly ▶ *I*

don't believe it – the photocopier's broken down again!

> **breakdown** N when a vehicle stops working while you are travelling in it ▶ *That's the second breakdown we've had this month.*
> **broken-down** ADJ a broken-down vehicle or machine is old and has stopped working ▶ *There was a broken-down car at the side of road.*

2 break down: to fail because of problems or disagreements ▶ *Negotiations between the two governments broke down last year.*

> **breakdown** N when something fails because there are problems or disagreements ▶ *a breakdown in communication* ▶ *Marriage breakdown accounts for a large number of one-parent families.*

3 break down: to start to cry. **break down in tears** ▶ *"You have to help me," O'Neil said, and he broke down in tears.*

4 break down: to become mentally ill because you cannot deal with all your problems ▶ *When her husband died, she broke down completely.*

> **(nervous) breakdown** N a mental or physical illness caused by being unable to deal with serious problems in your life. **have a breakdown** ▶ *Marty needs to relax more, or she'll end up having a nervous breakdown.*

5 break down sth, **break** sth **down:** to hit something such as a door or wall so hard that it breaks ▶ *Police broke down the door and searched the building.*

6 break down sth, **break** sth **down:** to separate something into smaller parts so that you can deal with it more easily. **+ into** ▶ *The best way to deal with all this information is to break it down into categories.*

B

breakdown N an explanation of the details of something, divided into different parts ▶ *Can you give me a detailed breakdown of how much the whole thing would cost?*

7 break down sth, **break** sth **down**: to change someone's ideas or attitudes ▶ *We aim to break down racial prejudice through education about other cultures.*

breakdown N when an idea or tradition is no longer as strong or popular as it used to be ▶ *the breakdown of traditional attitudes to work*

BREAK FOR →

break for sth: to suddenly run away from someone, especially in order to escape ▶ *Lambert fell as Morton broke for the corner of the field.*

BREAK IN →

1 break in: to get into a building illegally, especially in order to steal something ▶ *Thieves broke in while she was asleep and took all her jewellery.*

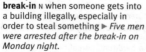

break-in N when someone gets into a building illegally, especially in order to steal something ▶ *Five men were arrested after the break-in on Monday night.*

2 break in: to suddenly say something when someone else is already talking ▶ *"This is all very interesting," James broke in, "but how do I know it's true?"*

3 break sth **in**, **break in** sth: to wear new shoes, boots etc for short periods of time until they become more

comfortable ▶ *I don't think I'll wear these shoes to work until I've broken them in at home first.*

4 break in sth, **break** sth **in**: to train a young horse to behave well and to allow people to ride it ▶ *David had broken the pony in himself.*

BREAK IN ON,
also BREAK IN UPON →

break in on sth/ sb: to interrupt someone ▶ *Lee's voice broke in on the conversation. "They're here," he said.*

BREAK INTO →

1 break into sth: to get into a building or a vehicle illegally by using force, especially in order to steal something ▶ *Someone broke into my car and stole the radio.*

2 break into sth: to suddenly start doing something. **break into a smile/ grin** ▶ *Manion read the letter and his face broke into a smile.* **break into laughter/ applause** ▶ *The curtain came down and the audience broke into loud applause.* **break into a run** ▶ *Realizing that the man was following him, Steve broke into a run.*

3 break into sth: to start to become involved in a new type of activity or business, especially when this is difficult ▶ *Kevin was now keen to break into politics.*

4 break into sth: to use a computer to illegally get or change information that is on someone else's computer ▶ *He was arrested after breaking into computer networks in several states.*

5 break into sth: to start to use money or food that you have been saving ▶ *In order to pay for their daughter's wedding, they had to break into their savings.*

BREAK IN UPON *see* BREAK IN ON
BREAK OFF →

1 break off, **break off** sth, **break** sth

off: if part of something breaks off, or you break it off, it becomes separated from the rest ▶ *Ben broke off a piece of the chocolate and ate it.*

2 break off, break off sth, **break off**: if talks between people, countries etc break off, or someone breaks them off, the talks stop suddenly before they have finished because of a disagreement ▶ *Negotiations towards a new contract broke off again and the strike continued.*

3 break off communication *also* **break off contact etc**: to refuse to communicate with a person or country any more ▶ *Ted threatened to break off all communication with his children.* **break off diplomatic relations** ▶ *The US broke off diplomatic relations with Cuba.*

4 break off sth, **break** sth **off**: if you break off a romantic or sexual relationship with someone, you end it. **break off an engagement** ▶ *Keith became jealous of Angie's other friends, and in the end he broke off their engagement.*

5 break off sth, **break** sth **off**, **break off**: to stop what you are doing, especially so that you can deal with a problem somewhere else ▶ *The prime minister had to break off his holiday and return to the capital to handle the crisis.*

6 break off: to suddenly stop speaking ▶ *"I don't think ...," he broke off and smiled suddenly.*

BREAK OUT →

1 break out: if war, fighting, fire, or disease breaks out, it starts suddenly ▶ *Civil war broke out in 1991.* ▶ *Three prisoners were killed when fighting broke out in the jail.*

    outbreak N when war, fighting, fire, or disease suddenly starts. **+ of** ▶ *a serious outbreak of cholera*

2 break out: to escape from a prison. **+ of** ▶ *Two dangerous robbers had broken out of jail.*

    break-out N an escape from a prison ▶ *There have been a series of break-outs in recent months.*

3 break out: if a noise such as laughter or shouting breaks out, it starts suddenly ▶ *As the crowd grew restless, angry shouting broke out.*

4 break out: to change the way you live or behave, especially so that you have more freedom. **+ of** ▶ *Both Matt and Angela wanted to break out of the traditional male and female roles.*

5 break out in spots/ a rash etc: if your skin breaks out in spots etc, a lot of spots suddenly appear on it ▶ *My arms and legs had broken out in a rash.*

6 break out in a sweat: to suddenly start to sweat (=lose liquid through your skin), because you are very hot, ill, or frightened ▶ *The snake came slowly closer and closer and I broke out in a sweat.*

7 break sth **out, break out** sth: to get something out and prepare to use it ▶ *Break out the cowboy boots and get ready to dance all night!*

BREAK THROUGH →

1 break through sth, **break through**: to force your way through something ▶ *On Friday, workers broke through a police barricade in order to protest outside the minister's office.*

2 break through, break through sth: if the sun breaks through, you can see it again after it has been hidden by clouds ▶ *At that moment the sun*

B

broke through, and the whole field was covered in light.

3 break through sth: if the amount or number of something breaks through a particular level, it becomes higher than that level ▶ *After the election, the level of unemployment broke through the 3 million mark.*

4 break through sth, **break through**: to find a way of dealing with a problem or a situation that limits what you can do ▶ *Women are finally breaking through the barriers that have held them back for so long.*

> **breakthrough** N an important new discovery or development ▶ *a major breakthrough in the fight against cancer*

BREAK UP →

1 break up sth, **break** sth **up**, **break up**: to break, or to make something break, into smaller pieces or parts ▶ *There is a real possibility that the polar ice caps will start breaking up and melting.*

> **break-up** N when something breaks into smaller pieces or parts ▶ *Accident investigators are still not sure what caused the break-up of the plane.*

2a. break up, break up sth, **break** sth **up**: if a marriage or relationship breaks up, or if someone or something breaks it up, it ends ▶ *Simon went to live in London after his marriage broke up.*

> **break-up** N ▶ *It took her years to get over the break-up of her marriage.*

b. break up: if two people who are married or having a relationship break up, their relationship ends ▶ *We'd been together for three years before we broke up.* **+ with** ▶ *Did you know that Pat's broken up with John?*

3 break up sth, **break** sth **up**: to stop a fight or protest ▶ *The fighting was*

eventually broken up by security forces. ▶ *Police used tear gas to break up the demonstration.*

4 break up: if schools, universities, or students break up, their classes end and the holidays begin ▶ *Some schools have already broken up, but we've got another week.*

5 break up, break up sth, **break** sth **up**: to divide or be divided into several separate parts

> **break-up** N when an organization, country etc is divided into several separate parts. **+ of** ▶ *the break-up of the old Empire*

6 break up, break up sth, **break** sth **up**: if a group of people break up, or something breaks them up, they separate and stop living or working together ▶ *The group had recorded ten albums before they decided to break up.*

> **break-up** N when a group of people who live or work together separate ▶ *the break-up of the band*

7 break up sth, **break** sth **up**: to make something such as a journey seem less long and boring, by doing something different in the middle of it ▶ *We stopped off in Cambridge in order to break up the journey.*

8 break it up!: used to tell two or more people to stop fighting ▶ *Break it up, you two, or you'll hurt each other!*

9 break sb **up**: if something breaks you up, it is so funny that you cannot stop laughing at it ▶ *Ethan really broke me up with that story about the alligator.*

BREAK WITH →

1 break with sth/ sb: to stop being part of a group or to stop supporting someone ▶ *Some left-wingers broke with the party leadership over the issue.*

2 break with tradition also **break with**

the past: to stop doing things in the way they were done in the past ▶ *In 1940 Roosevelt broke with tradition and stood for a third term of office.*

BREEZE

BREEZE IN, *also* BREEZE INTO →
breeze in, breeze into sth: to come into a place in a confident, relaxed, and cheerful way ▶ *He just breezed into my office and told me he wanted a job.*

BREEZE THROUGH →
breeze through sth: to succeed at something easily ▶ *At the age of nineteen Sheldon breezed through his final exams.*

BREW

BREW UP →
brew up sth, **brew** sth **up**: to plan something that will cause trouble ▶ *Anti-government newspapers are brewing up mischief wherever they can.*

BRIGHTEN

BRIGHTEN UP →
1 brighten up sth, **brighten** sth **up**: to make a place look more attractive and cheerful ▶ *A warm pink or yellow colour will brighten up a dark room.*

2 brighten up sth, **brighten** sth **up**: to make a situation happier for someone ▶ *It was a real joy to see the children again – you've no idea how it brightened up my day.*

3 brighten up: to suddenly become more cheerful ▶ *She brightened up as soon as she saw us.*

4 brighten up: if the weather brightens up, the sun begins to shine and the sky becomes brighter ▶ *If the weather brightens up, we could walk down to the beach.*

BRIM

BRIM OVER →
brim over: if a container is brimming over, it is so full of something that what it contains flows over the top ▶ *Twelve large sacks were filled with corn until they were brimming over.*

BRIM OVER WITH →
brim over with sth: if someone is brimming over with confidence, happiness, excitement etc, they feel very happy, confident, excited etc ▶ *I started out as a young man brimming over with confidence and ambition.*

BRIM WITH →
1 brim with sth: if someone is brimming with confidence, happiness, excitement etc, they feel very confident, happy, excited etc ▶ *By the end of the day Julia was brimming with happiness.*

2 brim with sth: to be very full of something ▶ *On the table was an enormous silver bowl brimming with strawberries.*

3 be brimming with tears: if someone's eyes are brimming with tears, they are crying, even though they are trying not to show it ▶ *His eyes were brimming with tears as he reached out to embrace her for the last time.*

BRING

BRING ABOUT →
bring about sth, **bring** sth **about**: to make something happen, especially a change or a better situation ▶ *The war brought about huge social and political changes.*

BRING ALONG →
1 bring along sb/sth, **bring** sb/sth **along**: to bring someone or something with you ▶ *The exhibition is open to people of all ages, so bring along your family and friends.*

B

2 bring sb/ sth **along, bring along**
sb/ sth: to train or help a person, team
etc so that they become better ▶ *"Our
plan was to bring this team along
slowly," said the coach.*

BRING AROUND, *also* BRING
ROUND →

1 bring sth/ sb **around/ round, bring
around/ round** sth/ sb: to take
something or someone to someone
else's house ▶ *I'll ask the driver to
bring the car around to your house.*

2 bring sb **around/ round**: to persuade
someone to change their opinion. **+ to**
▶ *Don't worry about Martin, I think I
can bring him round to our way of
thinking.*

3 bring sth **around/ round, bring
around/ round** sth: to move among a
group of people and give them
something ▶ *Waiters brought around
sandwiches and glasses of iced water.*

4 bring sb
around/ round:
to make
someone
become
conscious again
after they have
been
unconscious
▶ *Amy had
fainted, but we
managed to bring her round with
water from the cold tap.*

BRING AROUND TO, *also* BRING
ROUND TO →

bring sth/ sb **around to** sth, **bring** sth/
sb **round to** sth: to gradually change
the subject of a conversation to
something you want to talk about
▶ *It took her a long time to bring him
round to the question of money.*

BRING BACK →

1 bring back sth/ sb, **bring** sth/ sb
back: to bring something or someone

with you when you return from
somewhere. **bring** sb **back** sth ▶ *If
you're going down to the store, would
you bring me back a six-pack of beer?*

2 bring back sth, **bring** sth **back**: to
start using a law, system, or method
again ▶ *They should bring back free
university places.*

3 bring back sth, **bring** sth **back**: to
make something exist again. **+ to** ▶ *It
was hoped that the agreement would
bring peace back to the streets of the
capital.*

4 bring back sth, **bring** sth **back**: to
make someone think of something
that happened in the past. **bring back
memories** ▶ *Hearing that song always
brought back sweet memories.*

5 bring back sb, **bring** sb **back**: to give
someone the job that they had in the
past ▶ *After two bad seasons, the
directors voted to bring back the
former manager.*

6 bring sb **back, bring back** sb: to
make someone come alive again
▶ *Albert is dead and gone, and
nothing can ever bring him back.*

BRING BACK TO →

bring sb **back to earth** *also* **bring** sb
back to reality: to force someone to
think about the real situation they are
in ▶ *Emily was still daydreaming when
a sharp knock at the door brought her
back to reality.*

BRING DOWN →

1 bring down sth, **bring** sth **down**: to
reduce the number, amount, price etc
of something ▶ *Competition between
airlines has brought down fares
dramatically.*

2 bring down sb/ sth, **bring** sb/ sth
down: to remove a ruler or
government from their position of
power ▶ *A defeat on this issue could
bring down the government.*

3 bring down sth, **bring** sth **down**: to make something fall to the ground by shooting at it ▶ *The jet was brought down over British air space.*

4 bring down sth, **bring** sth **down**: to fly a plane down to the ground safely ▶ *The pilot skilfully brought the plane down in a field.*

5 bring sb **down**, **bring down** sb: to make someone fall to the ground ▶ *The goalkeeper brought down Evans on the edge of the penalty area.*

BRING DOWN ON, *also* BRING DOWN UPON →
bring sth **down on/upon** sb, **bring down** sth **on/upon** sb: to make something bad happen to someone ▶ *His behaviour has brought down shame on all his family.*

BRING FORTH →
bring forth sth: to produce something, or to make something happen ▶ *a tragic love affair that brought forth only pain*

BRING FORWARD →
1 bring forward sth, **bring** sth **forward**: to change the time of an event so that it happens earlier than was arranged ▶ *Please note that we have brought forward the date of our next meeting to June 23rd.*

2 bring forward sth, **bring** sth **forward**: to officially suggest a new plan or idea ▶ *She has brought forward a set of proposals for dealing with car crime.*

BRING IN →
1 bring in sth: to earn a particular amount of money ▶ *Paul brings in about £800 a month from his job at the local hospital.*

2 bring in sth, **bring** sth **in**: to introduce and start to use a new law, rule, system etc ▶ *The government is expected to bring in tough new laws on immigration.*

3 bring in sb, **bring** sb **in**: to get someone with special skills or knowledge to help you deal with something. **bring** sb **in to do** sth ▶ *They brought in a team of experts to investigate the causes of the accident.*

4 bring in sth/sb, **bring** sth/sb **in**: to attract new business, trade, customers etc ▶ *The bank's offer of free financial advice has brought in thousands of customers.*

5 bring in sth, **bring** sth **in**: to mention something in a piece of writing or a speech ▶ *Try to bring in a few quotations from the text to illustrate the points you are making.*

BRING INTO →
1 bring sth **into** sth: to add a particular quality to a situation or to someone's life ▶ *Our aim is to bring more fun into children's education.*

2 bring sth **into** sth: to talk about or include something in a discussion ▶ *There is no need to bring a lot of detail into the negotiations at this stage.*

3 bring sb/sth **into** sth: to involve someone or something in a situation ▶ *This is a purely political matter don't try to bring my famil*

BRING OFF →
bring off sth, **bring** in doing some difficult *deals in*

BRING
1 bri pain *su sti*

2

B

BRING ON, *also* **BRING UPON** →
bring sth **on/upon** sb: to make
something bad happen to someone.
bring sth **on yourself** ► *By refusing to
talk to the police he only brought
suspicion on himself.*

BRING OUT →

1 bring out sth, **bring** sth **out**: to
produce a new product, book, CD etc
► *Since it was brought out last
autumn, sales of the new software
have been very slow.*

2 bring out sth, **bring** sth **out**: to make
a quality or taste more noticeable
► *Becoming a father seems to have
brought out the gentle side of his
nature.*

3 bring out the best/worst in sb: to
make someone's best or worst
qualities appear in the way they
behave ► *There's something about
driving a car that brings out the worst
in me.* ► *A crisis very often brings out
the best in people.*

4 bring sb **out**: to make someone
less shy and more confident. **bring**
sb **out of himself/herself** ► *Rick's
teacher has done an excellent job –
she's really brought him out of
~~herself.~~*

~~...~~ IN →

~~...~~ spots/a rash: to cause
~~...~~ r on someone's skin
~~...~~ – they bring

~~...~~OUND

BRING TO →
bring sb **to**: to make someone
conscious again when they have been
unconscious ► *The sound of voices
brought him to, and he found himself
in a room full of strangers.*

BRING TOGETHER →
bring sb **together**, **bring together** sb:
to make people become friends with
each other ► *We aim to bring together
young people of different
backgrounds from all over the world.*
bring sb **closer together** ► *As it
happened, the tragedy of our
daughter's death actually brought us
closer together.*

BRING UP →

1 bring up sb, **bring** sb **up**: to look
after a child until he or she is grown
up ► *After Ben's mother died, he was
brought up by his grandmother.* **be
brought up to do** sth ► *In my day
children were brought up to respect
the law.*

   upbringing N the way that parents
   treat their children and the things
   they teach them while they are
   growing up ► *Mike had a very strict
   upbringing.*

   well brought-up ADJ a child who is
   well brought-up has been taught to
   be polite and to behave well
   ► *a well brought-up little girl*

2 bring up sth, **bring** sth **up**: to
mention a subject or start to talk
about it during a conversation ► *I shall
bring this question up at the next
meeting.*

3 bring sb **up**: to charge someone
with a crime and make them appear
before a court of law. **+ before** ► *Ben
was brought up before the
magistrates, accused of being
drunk and disorderly.*

BRING UPON *see* **BRING ON**

BROADEN

BROADEN OUT →
broaden out sth, **broaden** sth **out**,
broaden out: to include a range of
different subjects ▶ *I'd like to broaden
out the discussion a little.*

BRUSH

BRUSH ASIDE →
brush aside sth/sb, **brush** sth/sb
aside: to refuse to consider something
or someone seriously ▶ *Their request
for more funds was brushed aside.*

BRUSH DOWN →
brush down sb/sth, **brush** sb/sth
down: to remove dirt or dust from your
clothes using a brush or with quick
light movements of your hands. **brush
yourself down** ▶ *He picked himself up
from the ground and brushed himself
down.*

BRUSH OFF →
brush off sth, **brush** sth **off**: to refuse
to consider or discuss something
▶ *The Minister brushed off questions
about her personal finances.*

BRUSH UP (ON) →
brush up (on) sth, **brush** sth **up**: to
quickly practise and improve your
skills or knowledge of something ▶ *I
need to brush up on my Spanish
before we go on holiday.*

BUBBLE

BUBBLE OVER WITH →
**be bubbling over with excitement/
enthusiasm**: to be very excited or
enthusiastic about something ▶ *The
children were bubbling over with
excitement at the thought of visiting
their grandparents.*

BUCK

BUCK UP →
1 buck up, buck up sb, **buck** sb **up**: to
become more cheerful, or to make
someone more cheerful ▶ *Buck up,

Jerry! Things can't be that bad.*
2 buck up sb, **buck** sb **up, buck up**: to
try harder and make more effort
▶ *Sarah needs to buck up a bit or she
could lose her job.* **buck your ideas up**
(=used to tell someone to try harder
to improve what they are doing)
▶ *You'll have to buck your ideas up if
you want to go to university.*

BUCKET

**BUCKET
DOWN →**
bucket down: to
be raining very
hard ▶ *It's been
bucketing down
all afternoon.*

BUCKLE

BUCKLE DOWN →
buckle down: to start working
seriously. + **to** ▶ *The company will be
buckling down to tough negotiations
over the next few months.*

BUCKLE UNDER →
buckle under: to stop trying to do
what you want to do, and do what
someone else wants. + **to** ▶ *The
government has been accused of
buckling under to union pressure.*

BUCKLE UP →
buckle up: to fasten your seatbelt in a
car, plane etc ▶ *Only about 68 percent
of motorists and passengers buckle up
when they're driving.*

BUDDY

BUDDY UP →
1 buddy up: to try to be friends with
someone, especially because you
want them to do something for you.
+ **to** ▶ *Julie's just buddying up to the
boss so she can get promoted.*
2 buddy up: if children buddy up, they
choose a person to be with them
during an activity. + **with** ▶ *Eric

B

buddied up with Stevie for the rest of the trip.

BUDGE

BUDGE UP →
budge up: used to tell someone to move along and make space for someone else ▸ *Budge up boys, make room for your Dad.*

BUDGET

BUDGET FOR →
budget for sth: to carefully plan the way you will spend your money so that you can afford something in particular ▸ *We usually budget for a holiday that will cost about a thousand pounds.*

BUG

BUG OFF →
bug off!: used to tell someone to go away and stop annoying you ▸ *If that's Paul, tell him to bug off!*

BUG OUT →
bug out: if someone's eyes bug out, they are open very wide and look big and round ▸ *Paolo's eyes bugged out in amazement when he heard the whole story.*

BUILD

BUILD AROUND, *also* BUILD ROUND →
build sth **around/round** sth: to base something on information, facts, or ideas, and develop it from there ▸ *The plot is built around the themes of ambition and power.*

BUILD IN →
build in sth, **build** sth **in:** to include a particular idea, quality, attitude etc as part of something else ▸ *All the best speeches have a certain amount of humour built in.*
  built-in/in-built ADJ a built-in quality, feature etc is a permanent feature of someone or something else ▸ *Older*

people tend to have a built-in resistance to change.

BUILD INTO →
build sth **into** sth: to make something a part of a system, arrangement, or agreement ▸ *With the educational reforms, more controls were built into the system.*

BUILD ON, *also* BUILD UPON →
1 build sth **on/upon** sth: to base something that you do on a main idea, principle, aim etc ▸ *All his life he'd wanted to be a doctor; his hopes for the future were built on it.*

2 build on/upon sth: to base further success or progress on something you have already achieved ▸ *The company has had a very good year, and they are hoping to build on that.*

BUILD ROUND *see* BUILD AROUND

BUILD UP →
1 build up: to gradually increase ▸ *The traffic going out of town really builds up after five o'clock.*
  build-up N a gradual increase in something ▸ *a military build-up* ▸ *a build-up of pressure*

2 build up sth, **build** sth **up:** to make something stronger or more effective ▸ *Don't do too much – you need to build up your energy for the match.*
  build up sb's confidence/trust ▸ *She's had a bad experience, and it'll take some time to build up her confidence again.*

3 build up sth, **build** sth **up:** to develop and improve something ▸ *The governor worked hard to build up the state's electronic industry.*

4 build sb/sth **up, build up** sb/sth: to praise someone or something a lot, so that other people expect them to be very good ▸ *It's only an amateur production, so I don't want to build it up too much.*

build-up N when someone praises someone or something a lot, so that other people expect them to be very good ▶ *I thought the group were a bit disappointing, after the terrific build-up they'd had.*

5 build sb **up, build up** sb: to make someone healthier and stronger. **build yourself up** ▶ *You need to go and do some training and build yourself up a bit.*

6 build up a picture of sth *also build up an idea of* sth: to get information that helps you to know and understand more about something ▶ *The police are slowly building up a picture of what happened on that night.*

7 build up your hopes *also build your hopes up*: to hope for something that is not likely to happen ▶ *Don't build your hopes up – a lot of people have applied for the job, and you may not get it.*

BUILD UP TO →
build up to sth: to prepare yourself to do something more difficult than you have done before ▶ *He said he might run for Congress, but that's something he'd have to build up to.*

BUILD UPON *see* BUILD ON

BUM

BUM AROUND, *also* BUM ROUND →
1 bum around/round, bum around/round sth: to travel around without any definite plans ▶ *Greg bummed around South America for a year between school and university.*

2 bum around/about: to spend time doing very little ▶ *I was still bumming around without a job, and had hardly any money at all.*

BUM OFF →
bum sth **off** sb: to get something from someone, by asking them for it and

not paying for it ▶ *He bummed some cigarettes off a group of Swedish students.*

BUM OUT →
bum sb **out**: to make someone feel sad or disappointed ▶ *I don't want to bum you out, but we won't be able to go to the beach this weekend.*

BUM ROUND *see* BUM AROUND

BUMP

BUMP ALONG →
bump along, bump along sth: to continue at the same low level, without making much progress ▶ *The standard of living for the average family has bumped along without showing any significant increase.*

BUMP INTO →
bump into sb: to meet someone that you know by chance ▶ *Guess who I bumped into on holiday – Alex Barrett!*

BUMP OFF →
bump sb **off, bump off** sb: to murder someone ▶ *The rumour was that he had bumped his first wife off to get the insurance money.*

BUMP UP →
bump up sth, **bump** sth **up**: to increase something, usually by a large amount ▶ *We had Mike on our team, which helped to bump up our score.*

BUNCH

BUNCH UP →
1 bunch up: to move closer together and form a close group ▶ *Mr Stephenson stopped suddenly, forcing the rest of them to bunch up behind him.* **be bunched up** ▶ *The sheep were*

B

all bunched up together in a corner of the field.

2 bunch up, bunch up sth, **bunch** sth **up**: to pull material tightly together in folds, or to form tight folds ▶ *The dress was much too big, so she bunched it up with a belt round her waist.*

BUNDLE

BUNDLE OFF →

bundle sb **off, bundle off** sb: to send someone somewhere quickly without asking them if they want to go ▶ *She bundled the kids off to bed and sat down in front of the television.*

BUNDLE UP →

1 bundle up sth, **bundle** sth **up**: to gather or tie a group of things together, especially in order to take them somewhere ▶ *The newspapers were all bundled up, ready to be thrown away.*

2 bundle up sb, **bundle** sb **up, bundle up**: to put warm clothes or blankets on yourself or someone else because it is cold ▶ *My mother bundled me up in the warmest clothes she could find.*

BUNG

BE BUNGED UP →

1 sth is bunged up: to be blocked ▶ *The kitchen sink was bunged up with bits of food.*

2 be bunged up: if someone is bunged up, it is difficult for them to breathe because they have a cold ▶ *I had a headache, and I was so bunged up I decided to stay in bed.*

BUNK

BUNK OFF →

bunk off, bunk off sth: to stay away from school or work without permission ▶ *We often used to bunk off school and go round to my house.*

BUOY

BUOY UP →

1 buoy sb **up, buoy up** sb: to make someone feel more cheerful or confident ▶ *"You look wonderful," Margaret said, in an attempt to buoy Emma up.*

2 buoy up sth, **buoy** sth **up**: to keep something such as profits or prices at a high level ▶ *The pound rose against the dollar, buoyed up by rumours of an increase in interest rates.*

BURN

BURN DOWN →

1 burn down, burn down sth, **burn** sth **down**: to be completely destroyed by fire or to completely destroy something by fire ▶ *The old Palace of Westminster burned down in 1834.* ▶ *Gore had burnt down the house in order to destroy the evidence of his crime.*

2 burn down: if a fire burns down, the flames become smaller and weaker ▶ *Gradually the fire burnt right down, leaving the room in near darkness.*

BURN OFF →

1 burn off sth, **burn** sth **off**: to get rid of something by burning it ▶ *Fires are lit to burn off the remaining forest and make way for agriculture.*

2 burn off sth, **burn** sth **off**: to get rid of unwanted body fat by doing physical exercise

▶ *Regular exercise helps burn off excess fat.*

BURN OUT →

1 burn (yourself) out: to make yourself ill and tired by working too hard, with the result that you cannot continue working ▶ *Promising young*

footballers often burn themselves out before they are twenty.

burned-out also **burnt-out** ADJ tired or ill because you have been working too hard ▶ *I didn't want to become one of those burnt-out writers with nothing left to say.*

burnout N when you are unable to continue working because you have worked too hard ▶ *More and more people suffer from burnout caused by overwork.*

2 be burned out also **be burnt out**: if a vehicle or a building is burned out, the inside of it is destroyed in a fire ▶ *The stolen car was found burnt out near Middlesborough.*

burnt-out also **burned-out** ADJ so badly damaged by fire that only the outside is left ▶ *We passed a burnt-out lorry at the side of the road.*

3 a fire burns (itself) out: if a fire burns out or burns itself out, it stops burning ▶ *She'd fallen asleep in her chair and the fire had burnt out.*

4 burn (itself) out: to gradually becomes less severe and then stop completely ▶ *The doctor said the fever should burn itself out in a few days' time.*

5 burn out: if a piece of electrical equipment burns out, it stops working because it has become too hot ▶ *The electrical system in the car will burn out if you're not careful.*

BURN UP →

1 burn up sth, **burn** sth **up**: to use something up, especially quickly ▶ *The rate at which people burn up energy varies quite a lot between individuals.* ▶ *That girl just burns up money!*

2 burn up, burn up sth, **burn** sth **up**: to be completely destroyed by fire, or to destroy something with fire ▶ *The satellite is expected to burn up in the Earth's atmosphere.*

3 burn sb **up**: to make someone very angry ▶ *It used to burn me up when the kids at school laughed at my name.*

4 burn up sth, **burn** sth **up**: to quickly cover a long distance ▶ *His new car really burns up the miles.*

BURN WITH →

burn with sth: to feel a particular emotion very strongly ▶ *Burning with impatience, Janet waited for the train to finally stop.*

BURST

BURST IN →

burst in: to enter somewhere very suddenly ▶ *Mrs Andrews was just closing the shop when two gunmen burst in.* **burst in on** sb/sth ▶ *A group of protesters burst in on the meeting, which later had to be abandoned.*

BURST INTO →

1 burst into sth: to enter somwhere very suddenly ▶ *She burst into the room, waving a large brown envelope.*

2 burst into sth: to suddenly start doing something, for example crying, laughing, or singing. **burst into tears** (=start crying) ▶ *When I asked her what was wrong, she just burst into tears.* **burst into flames** (=start burning) ▶ *Their car hit a wall and burst into flames.*

BURST OUT →

1 burst out laughing/crying: to suddenly start to laugh or cry ▶ *It was such a funny story – even the newsreader burst out laughing.*

2 burst out: to suddenly say something in an angry or excited way ▶ *"It's all your fault!" she burst out angrily.*

outburst N when someone says something suddenly and angrily ▶ *I'd like to apologise for my outburst at the meeting last night.*

BURST WITH →
be bursting with sth: to have a lot of something, for example energy, confidence, or ideas ▶ *Helen, our teacher, was bursting with ideas and enthusiasm.*

BURY

BURY AWAY →
1 be buried away: if something is buried away somewhere, it is not easy to find, especially because it is hidden by other things ▶ *a lovely old silver teapot buried away at the back of the shop*

2 bury yourself away: to go somewhere quiet where there are not many people. **+ in** ▶ *It's not good for you burying yourself away in that dusty old library day after day.*

BURY IN →
bury yourself in sth: to give all your attention to something, often in order to avoid thinking about something else ▶ *After Sylvie left him, he buried himself in his work and tried to put her out of his mind.*

BUST

BUST OUT →
1 bust out: to escape from a place, especially a prison. **+ of** ▶ *They thought it was impossible for anyone to bust out of Alcatraz.*

2 bust out: to improve your situation or do something different from what you usually do ▶ *Even as a kid Scott couldn't wait to bust out and move to the city.*

BUSTLE

BUSTLE AROUND, also BUSTLE AROUND →
bustle around/about, bustle around/about sth: to move around in a busy way doing something ▶ *She watched him as he bustled about the kitchen.*

BUTT

BUTT IN →
1 butt in: to rudely interrupt a conversation or someone who is speaking ▶ *The interviewer kept butting in while he was trying to answer the questions.*

2 butt in: to get involved in a situation when you are not wanted ▶ *My sister is always butting in, wanting to know exactly what I'm doing.*

BUTT OUT →
butt out!: used to tell someone to keep out of a situation ▶ *This doesn't concern you, so just butt out!*

BUTTER

BUTTER UP →
butter sb **up, butter up** sb: to say nice things to someone or try to please them, so that they will do what you want ▶ *You need his help, so butter him up a bit; get him on your side.*

BUTTON

BUTTON UP →
button up sth, **button** sth **up**: to fasten all the buttons on a coat, shirt etc ▶ *You'd better button up your jacket – it's cold outside.*

BUY

BUY IN →
buy in sth, **buy** sth **in**: to buy a large amount of something, for example because it may be difficult to get at a later time ▶ *People are buying in stocks of food for the winter.*

BUY INTO →
1 buy into sth: to completely accept an idea or belief and allow it to influence

you ▶ *At around fourteen, a lot of boys buy into the idea that they are failures.*

2 buy into sth: to buy part of a business or organization ▶ *American car makers wanted to buy into Japanese firms.*

BUY OFF →
buy off sb, **buy** sb **off**: to give someone money in order to stop them causing trouble or threatening you ▶ *Employers tried to buy off the unions by offering them higher and higher wage settlements.*

BUY OUT →
buy out sb/sth, **buy** sb/sth **out**: to buy someone's share of something that you previously owned together

▶ *After the war, he bought out his brother's interest in the business.*
   buyout N when a group of people join together to buy a company ▶ *The company is threatening to close the mine, but there are rumours of a management buyout.*

BUY UP →
buy up sth, **buy** sth **up**: to quickly buy as much as you can of something ▶ *People are buying up stocks of food in case the storm hits their area.*

BUZZ

BUZZ OFF →
buzz off: used to rudely tell someone to go away because they are annoying you ▶ *Why don't you just buzz off and leave me alone!*

B

Cc

CALL

BE CALLED AWAY →
be called away: to be asked to leave the place where you are in order to deal with something somewhere else ▶ *Peter's been called away to deal with a problem at our Birmingham branch.*

CALL BACK →
call back, call sb back, call back sb: to phone someone again at a later time ▶ *Call me back as soon as you get the test results.*

CALL BY →
call by: to stop and visit someone for a short time ▶ *Dan called by today. He says his mother's not well.*

CALL FOR →
1 call for sth: to publicly demand that something should happen or be done ▶ *Peace campaigners have called for an end to the bombing.*

2 call for sth: to need a particular quality, skill, or course of action ▶ *The situation calls for some tough decisions.*

3 call for sb: to go to someone's house to collect them because you are going somewhere together ▶ *The film starts at 8.00 so I'll call for you at 7.30.*

4 call for sth: to say that something is likely to happen ▶ *The forecast calls for more rain.*

CALL FORTH →
call forth sth, **call** sth **forth**: to make people have a particular feeling or reaction ▶ *What emotion is the author trying to call forth in the reader in this passage?*

CALL IN →
1 call in: to make a short visit to a person or place ▶ *Is it all right if I call in to see you tomorrow after work?*

2 call in: to phone somewhere, especially the place where you work ▶ *Daniel called in to say that he was going to be late.* **call in sick** (=phone to say that you are too ill to go to work) ▶ *On Monday morning she called in sick and said she'd be off all week.*

3 call in sb, **call** sb **in**: to ask someone who has special skills or knowledge to come and help you ▶ *At 6am I called in Dr Minden.* **call in** sb **to do** sth ▶ *Troops were called in to control the demonstration.*

4 call in sth, **call** sth **in**: to ask people who have bought a product to take it back to the shop because there is a problem with it ▶ *The manufacturer has called in the new model because of an electrical fault.*

CALL OFF →
1 call off sth, **call** sth **off**: to stop an event that has been planned, especially because of a problem ▶ *She had seriously considered calling off the wedding two days before her marriage.*

2 call off sth, **call** sth **off**: to stop doing something that you have already started doing ▶ *Rescuers were forced to call off the search beause of bad weather.*

3 call off sth/ sb, **call** sth/ sb **off**: to order an animal or person to stop attacking someone ▶ *Tell your husband to call off those dogs.*

CALL ON →
1 call on sb: to visit someone for a short time ▶ *He stopped in Chicago in order to call on an old friend.*

2 call on sb: to ask someone in a class

or group to answer a question ▶ *Adrian looked down at his paper, but Mrs. Danielson called on him anyway.*

CALL ON, *also* CALL UPON →

1 call on/upon sb **to do** sth: to formally ask someone to do something ▶ *Russia called on the UN to intervene in the situation.*

2 call on/upon sth/sb: to use something or someone in order to achieve what you want ▶ *Our staff are able to call on the latest technology to help them in their work.*

CALL OUT →

1 call out sb/sth, **call** sb/sth **out**: to ask someone such as a doctor or the fire service to come and deal with a problem ▶ *Though my mother was obviously very ill, my father refused to call out a doctor.*

    call-out ADJ a call-out service is one by which someone skilled will come to your home to deal with a problem when you phone them ▶ *a 24-hour call-out service for emergency repairs*

2 call out: to phone a restaurant and order food to be delivered to your home or office. **+ for** ▶ *Let's call out for a pizza tonight.*

3 call out sb, **call** sb **out**: to officially order the members of a trade union to stop working because of a disagreement with their employer ▶ *The union will be calling its members out on strike from midnight tonight.*

CALL OVER →

call over sb, **call** sb **over**: to ask someone to come to the place where you are ▶ *Do you want to ask him about it? Shall I call him over?*

CALL UP →

1 call sb **up, call up** sb, **call up**: to phone someone ▶ *If you have*

computer problems, call up the technician at the helpdesk.*

2 be called up: to be officially ordered to join your country's army, navy, or air force ▶ *When he was 21, Stan was called up for National Service.* **get called up** ▶ *During the war, most men between 19 and 38 got called up.*

3 call up sth, **call** sth **up**: if you call up information on a computer, you ask the computer to show it on the screen ▶ *Rex called up the menu and clicked on "New Message".*

CALL UPON *see* CALL ON

CALM

CALM DOWN →

1 calm down, calm sb **down, calm down** sb: to stop feeling angry, upset, or excited, or to make someone stop feeling like this ▶ *Calm down and tell me what happened.* ▶ *Matt was trying to calm the baby down by singing to her.*

2 calm down: if a situation calms down, people stop fighting, arguing, or behaving angrily ▶ *I'd wait until things calm down before you approach him again.*

3 calm down: if the wind or weather calms down, it stops being windy or stormy ▶ *The fishermen were waiting for the weather to calm down before they went out to sea.*

CAMP

CAMP OUT →

camp out: to sleep outdoors, especially in a tent, or stay in a place where you do not normally stay ► *We used to camp out in my grandma's garden when we were kids.* ► *Dozens of reporters camped out outside the family's country house.*

CAMP UP →

camp it up: to deliberately behave in an extreme way in order to entertain people ► *We all remember our drama teacher camping it up in Hamlet.*

CANCEL

CANCEL OUT →

cancel out sth, **cancel** sth **out**: if one thing cancels out another, it has an opposite effect to it, so that the situation does not change ► *Increases in tuition fees are likely to cancel out tax benefits for college students.*

CAPITALIZE

CAPITALIZE ON →

capitalize on sth: to use something good that you have in order to gain a further advantage ► *Ecuador has capitalized on its natural beauty to attract more tourists.*

CARE

CARE FOR →

1 care for sb: to look after someone because they are too young, old, or ill to look after themselves ► *She cared for her father throughout his long illness.*

   well cared for ADJ if a person or animal is well cared for, people look after them well ► *The animals in the zoo are contented and well cared for.*

2 not care for sb/sth: to not like someone or something ► *I was fond of Uncle Geordie, but I didn't care for his wife.*

3 would you care for sth?: used to politely offer something to someone ► *Would you care for ice with your martini, Madam?*

4 care for sb: to love someone in a romantic way ► *I really love you, Celia. I've never cared for anyone else.*

CARRY

GET CARRIED AWAY →

get carried away: to become so excited that you do something you would not normally do, especially something silly ► *Andrew got a bit carried away and started dancing on the table.*

CARRY FORWARD →

carry forward sth, **carry** sth **forward**: to include an amount of money in a later set of figures or calculations ► *£7000 is carried forward to next month's accounts.*

CARRY OFF →

1 carry it off: to succeed in doing something difficult, especially when it is likely that you could fail ► *The company's plans are extremely ambitious, but director Paul Redstone believes he can carry it off.*

2 carry off sth, **carry** sth **off**: to win a prize ► *My friend carried off the prize for best footballer.*

CARRY ON →

1 carry on: to continue doing something ► *They carried on until all the work was finished.* **carry on doing** sth ► *I waved at him, but he didn't seem to notice and carried on talking.* **+ with** ► *We're going to have to stop now. We can carry on with this in next week's class.*

2 carry on: to continue going somewhere in the same direction ► *Carry on until you get to the traffic lights, then turn left.*

3 carry on: to do the things that you usually do, even though you are in a difficult situation ► *After my wife died, I felt as if I just couldn't carry on.* ► *Despite the fighting all around* *them, people still try to carry on as normal.*

4 carry on sth, **carry** sth **on**: to continue something that someone else has started ▶ *He's hoping his son will carry on the family business.*

5 carry on: to keep talking about something in an annoying way.
+ about ▶ *He's always carrying on about his own problems.*

CARRY OUT →

1 carry sth **out, carry out** sth: to do something that you have organized, planned, or promised ▶ *Police carried out a series of raids on the homes of known drug dealers.* ▶ *The government has promised to carry out an official inquiry into the incident.*

2 carry out instructions/an order: to do something that you have been told to do ▶ *At his trial, he claimed that he had only been carrying out orders.*

CARRY OVER →

1 carry over *also* **be carried over**: to affect or influence another situation.
+ into ▶ *Childhood experiences and feelings are often carried over into adult life.*

2 carry over sth, **carry** sth **over**: to do something or use something at a later time ▶ *Up to five days' holiday can be carried over until the following year.*

CARRY THROUGH →

1 carry through sth, **carry** sth **through**: to complete something successfully ▶ *Educational reforms were proposed, but never carried through.*

2 carry sb **through, carry** sb **through** sth: to help someone deal successfully with a difficult situation ▶ *The course was tough, but Amelia's determination and enthusiasm carried her through.*

CART

CART OFF →
cart off sb, **cart** sb **off**: to take

someone away, especially to prison or hospital ▶ *I collapsed on the pitch, and was carted off on a stretcher.* ▶ *Kirk was arrested and carted off to prison.*

CARVE

CARVE OUT →
carve out sth, **carve** sth **out**: to succeed in achieving or getting something for yourself ▶ *Their aim is to carve out a much bigger share of the UK market.* **carve out a career** ▶ *The former comedian has successfully carved out a career as a serious actor.*

CARVE UP →
carve up sth, **carve** sth **up**: to divide land into smaller parts ▶ *Hitler and Stalin carved up Poland between them.*

CASH

CASH IN →
cash in sth, **cash** sth **in**: to exchange something such as shares for their value in money ▶ *He cashed in all his insurance policies to raise the money for the operation.*

CASH IN ON →
cash in on sth: to make a profit or get an advantage from a bad situation ▶ *Criminals should not be allowed to cash in on their crimes by selling their stories.*

CASH OUT →
1 cash out: to count all the money taken by a shop or business at the end of a day ▶ *It's time to cash out and lock up.*

2 cash out: to sell something valuable and get all the money for it immediately ▶ *Argentine stocks fell as some local investors cashed out.*

CASH UP →
cash up: to count all the money taken by a shop or business at the end of

the day ▸ *Let's cash up and then we can go home.*

CAST

CAST AROUND FOR, *also* CAST ABOUT FOR, CAST ROUND FOR →
cast around/about/round for sth: to try to think of something to do or say ▸ *He cleared his throat, casting about for something appropriate to say.*

CAST ASIDE →
cast aside sb/sth, **cast** sb/sth **aside**: to get rid of or ignore someone or something ▸ *When Henry became King, he cast aside his former friends.* ▸ *Casting aside all thoughts of his own safety, Jimmy plunged into the icy water.*

BE CAST AWAY →
be cast away: to be left on an island where there are no other people, because your ship has sunk ▸ *If you were cast away on a desert island, do you think you'd be able to survive?*

> **castaway** N someone who has been left on an island where there are no other people, because their ship has sunk ▸ *Fishermen discovered the castaway after he had been missing for fifteen years.*

CAST BACK →
cast your mind back: to try to remember something that happened in the past. **+ to** ▸ *Cast your mind back to your first day at school, and try to remember how you felt.*

CAST DOWN →
be cast down: to lose hope or determination because of something bad that has happened ▸ *Churchill was obviously cast down by the news of this latest defeat.*

> **downcast** ADJ sad or upset because something bad has happened ▸ *the sad, downcast faces of disappointed children*

CAST OFF →
1 cast off sth, **cast** sth **off**: to get rid of something because you do not need it, or because it is stopping you from making progress ▸ *It was time to cast off all the old fears and superstitions.*

> **cast-offs** PL N clothes that you do not wear any more and give to someone else ▸ *When I was a kid I always had to wear my older brother's cast-offs.*

2 cast off: to untie the rope that fastens a boat to the shore, and start to sail away ▸ *We cast off from San Diego and set sail for the Philippine Islands.*

CAST OUT →
cast out sb, **cast** sb **out**: to force someone to leave a place, especially home ▸ *He was cast out by his family when they discovered what he'd done.*

> **outcast** N someone who is not accepted by the other people in society ▸ *In these health-conscious times, smokers are often treated like social outcasts.*

CAST ROUND FOR *see* CAST AROUND FOR

CATCH

CATCH ON →
1 catch on: to become popular and fashionable ▸ *A new fitness craze called Body Pump is catching on in the UK.*

2 catch on: to begin to understand or realize something, especially after a long time ▸ *The technique was introduced in America as early as 1956, but the British were slow to catch on.* **+ to** ▸ *Eventually Val caught on to what her husband was doing.*

CATCH OUT →
1 catch sb **out**: to trick someone so that they make a mistake ▸ *He's always asking me really difficult questions, as if he's trying to catch me out.*

2 be caught out: if you are caught out by an unexpected event, you are not ready for it ▶ *Even the most experienced sailor can get caught out by the weather.*

CATCH UP →

1 catch up, catch sb/sth up: to gradually get closer to a moving person or vehicle in front of you ▶ *Richards is still in front, but the other drivers are catching up.* **catch up with** ▶ *The other walkers were catching up with us.*

2 catch up, catch sb up: to reach the same standard as someone else who was better than you ▶ *Ali was by far the most advanced in the class to start with, but the others soon caught up.*

BE/GET CAUGHT UP IN →

1 be/get caught up in sth: to be or get involved in a difficult situation that you did not intend to get involved in ▶ *Most of the injured people were innocent civilians caught up in the fighting.* ▶ *I seemed to have got caught up in some long-standing dispute between them.*

2 be/get caught up in sth: if you are caught up in something, it stops you from moving or making progress ▶ *Sorry I'm late – I got caught up in the traffic.*

CATCH UP ON →

1 catch up on sth: to do something that you did not have time to do earlier ▶ *I needed a couple of days to catch up on my school work.* **catch up on your sleep** ▶ *I spent most of the weekend trying to catch up on my sleep.*

2 catch up on sth: to get the most recent information about something ▶ *He's been away for a month, so it will take him a while to catch up on what's been going on.*

CATCH UP WITH →

1 catch up with sb: if something bad catches up with you, it starts to affect you after a period of time in which it did not ▶ *The player admitted that his long-term knee injury is finally beginning to catch up with him.*

2 catch up with sb: to discover that someone has done something wrong, and punish them for it ▶ *Hughes had avoided paying tax for years before the authorities finally caught up with him.*

3 catch up with sb: to meet someone you know after not seeing them for a period of time ▶ *She's back in the country and keen to catch up with family and friends.* **I'll catch up with you later** (=used to tell someone that you will talk to them later) ▶ *I've got to dash off to a meeting now – I'll catch up with you later.*

4 catch up with sth: to do something that needs to be done, because you did not have time to do it earlier ▶ *Friday is a quiet day, so I usually have chance to catch up with my paperwork.*

5 catch up with sth: to get the most recent information about something ▶ *The event provides an opportunity for members to catch up with each other's news.*

CATER

CATER TO, *also* CATER FOR →

cater to/for sb, **cater to/for** sth: to provide something that a particular type of person wants or needs ▶ *a holiday company that caters for the needs of disabled customers*

CAVE

CAVE IN →
1 cave in,
cave sth in,
cave in sth: if
a roof, ceiling,
or wall caves
in, or if
something
caves it in, it
breaks and
falls down
▶ *The blast caused the roof of the
Grand Hotel to cave in.*

2 cave in: to agree to do something
that you were previously opposed to
▶ *The Transport Department has caved
in to pressure from environmental
groups and abandoned plans for the
new motorway.*

CENTRE

CENTRE AROUND, *also* CENTRE
ROUND →
centre around/round sth, **be centred
around/round** sb/sth: to happen
mainly in a particular place, or to be
mainly about a particular subject or
person ▶ *Village life is centred around
one main street.* ▶ *The story is centred
around a group of single professional
women in New York.*

CENTRE ON, *also* CENTRE UPON →
centre on/upon sb/sth, **be centred
on/upon** sb/sth: to be mainly about a
particular subject or person ▶ *The
story centres on a middle aged actor,
who struggles to save his failing
marriage.*

CENTRE ROUND *see* CENTRE
AROUND

CENTRE UPON *see* CENTRE ON

CHALK

CHALK UP →
chalk up sth, **chalk** sth **up**: to succeed

in winning or achieving something,
especially in sport or business ▶ *The
company chalked up net profits of
£451 million.*

CHALK UP TO →
chalk sth **up to** sth, **chalk up** sth **to**
sth: to think or say that something
happened because of something else
▶ *The instructor couldn't understand
Katz's strange behaviour but chalked
it up to boredom.*

CHANCE

CHANCE UPON, *also* CHANCE ON →
chance upon/on sth, **chance upon/on**
sb: to find something or meet
someone when you are not expecting
to ▶ *I was wandering around a
department store, when I chanced
upon an old school friend.* ▶ *One
evening, he chanced upon an ad for a
guitarist for a local band.*

CHANGE

CHANGE AROUND, *also* CHANGE
ROUND →
change around/round sth, **change** sth
around/round: to move things into
different positions ▶ *When we'd
changed the furniture around, the
room looked quite different.*

CHANGE DOWN →
change down: to put the engine of a
vehicle into a lower gear ▶ *It is
important to change down in plenty of
time to prevent having to brake
sharply.*

CHANGE INTO →
change into sth: to become, or to
make someone or something become,
completely different ▶ *In less than 20
years, Japan had changed into one of
the world's leading economies.* ▶ *All
the old warehouses are being changed
into expensive apartments.*

CHANGE OVER →
change over: to stop doing or using

one system or thing, and to start doing or using a different one. **+ to**
▶ *Wheat was no longer profitable, and many farmers were forced to change over to dairy farming.*

changeover N a change from one way of doing something to another ▶ *The changeover to digital television should be complete by 2006.*

CHANGE ROUND *see* **CHANGE AROUND**

CHANGE UP →
change up: to put the engine of a vehicle into a higher gear. **+ into**
▶ *When you're on the motorway, change up into fifth.*

CHARGE

CHARGE UP →
1 charge up sth, **charge** sth **up, charge up**: if you charge up a battery or a piece of electrical equipment, or it charges up, electricity is put into it and stored ▶ *The shaver can be charged up overnight.*

2 charge up sth: if you charge up a credit card, you use it a lot to buy things ▶ *Karen charged up her Visa card on a shopping trip to Macy's.*

3 be charged up: to feel excited and very eager to do something ▶ *We came out onto the playing field, charged up and determined to win.*

CHARGE WITH →
1 charge sb **with** sth: to state officially that you think someone is guilty of a crime ▶ *Police arrested Reid and charged him with murder.* **charge** sb **with doing** sth ▶ *Ames was charged with spying for the CIA.*

2 be charged with sth: to officially have a particular responsibility or duty ▶ *The Committee is charged with investigating the causes of the accident.*

3 be charged with emotion/anger etc: to be full of emotion or anger etc ▶ *Sabrina spoke with a voice that was charged with emotion.*

CHASE

CHASE AFTER →
1 chase after sth: to use a lot of time and effort trying to get something that you want ▶ *We spent the morning chasing after bargains in the sales.*

2 chase after sb: to try very hard to have a romantic or sexual relationship with someone ▶ *If you keep chasing after guys like that, they're never going to be interested in you.*

CHASE AWAY →
chase sb/sth **away, chase away** sb/sth: to make a person or animal go away by running towards them in a threatening way ▶ *The shopkeeper chased the men away with his gun.*

CHASE DOWN →
chase down sb/sth, **chase** sb/sth **down**: to succeed in finding or catching someone or something ▶ *Police departments should concentrate on chasing down criminals.*

CHASE OFF →
chase off sb/sth, **chase** sb/sth **off**: to make a person or animal go away by running towards them in a threatening way ▶ *We still talk about the time Grandpa chased off a gang of boys with the kitchen broom.*

CHASE UP →
1 chase up sb, **chase** sb **up**: to remind someone to do something they promised to do ▶ *I had to chase Dick up to get the reports I asked for last week.*

2 chase sth **up, chase up** sth: to try to find something or make sure it is dealt with ▶ *Can you chase up that file for me?*

CHAT

CHAT UP →

1 chat up sb, **chat** sb **up**: to talk to someone you feel attracted to and try to start a romantic or sexual relationship with them ▶ *We found Doug in the bar, trying to chat up a waitress.*

2 chat up sb, **chat** sb **up**: to talk with someone in a friendly way, especially when you want them to help you or give you something ▶ *Malone will chat up anyone who walks into his bar.*

CHEAT

CHEAT ON →

cheat on your taxes: to lie about how much money you make in order to pay less tax ▶ *Perkins spent five years in jail for cheating on his taxes.*

CHECK

CHECK IN →

1 check in, check sth **in**: to go to the desk at an airport in order to show your ticket and give them your bags ▶ *Where do we check in for flight 409?* ▶ *How many bags do you want to check in?*

> **check-in** N the place at the airport where you show your ticket and give them your bags ▶ *We rushed over to the check-in and showed the man our tickets.*

2 check in: to go to the desk at a hotel and say that you have arrived ▶ *Bernstein checked in at Miami's most expensive hotel.*

3 check in sth, **check** sth **in**: to return a book, video etc to a library after you have borrowed it ▶ *I need to check my books in by Friday.*

CHECK INTO →

1 check into sth: to go to the desk at a hotel and say that you have arrived ▶ *I got to Burlington and checked into the best hotel.*

2 check into sth: to go and stay in a hospital or medical centre for a while because you need medical help ▶ *Riley checked into the hospital with severe stomach pains.*

CHECK OFF →

a. check off sth, **check** sth **off**: to make a mark next to something on a list to show that you have dealt with it ▶ *Check off each job as you complete it.*

b. check off sth, **check** sth **off**: to make a mark next to an answer on a list of choices or answers, in order to show which one you have chosen ▶ *Look over the list and check off the ten issues that seem most important to you.*

CHECK ON →

1 check on sb/sth: to find out if someone is doing what they are supposed to be doing, or that something is happening the way that you want ▶ *Alice opened the oven door to check on the roast.*

2 check on sb/sth: to make sure that someone or something is safe, or has everything they need ▶ *Adrienne often checks on her elderly neighbours across the street.*

3 check on sth: to try to get more information about something ▶ *I stopped at the camping shop to check on the price of tents.*

CHECK OUT →

1 check out sth/sb, **check** sth/sb **out**: to get more information about something or someone ▶ *After checking out several colleges, Karen decided on Iowa State University.* ▶ *Check us out on our new website!*

2a. check out sth, **check** sth **out**: to make sure that information is true or correct ▶ *You should check out all the facts before you make a decision.*

b. check out: if information checks out, it is shown to be true or correct ▶ *As long as your references check out, we'll give you the job.*

3 check out sb/sth, **check** sb/sth **out**: to look at someone or something because they are interesting, attractive, unusual etc ▶ *I turned around and caught Bill checking me out.*

4 check out: to return your room keys and pay your bill at a hotel before you leave ▶ *What time do we have to check out?*

   checkout N when you prepare to leave a hotel by paying your bill and returning your room keys ▶ *Checkout is at 10am.*

5 check out sth, **check** sth **out**: to borrow or rent something from somewhere ▶ *The library allows you to check out six books at a time.*

6a. check sb **out, check out** sb: to add up prices of a customer's goods in a shop and take payment for them ▶ *I can check you out on cash register 5.*

b. check out: to pay for the things you have bought in a shop after they have been added up ▶ *It's going to take forever to check out! This queue has 10 people in it!*

   checkout N the place in a supermarket where you pay for the goods that you have collected ▶ *We had to wait for ages at the checkout.*

CHECK OVER →

1 check over sth, **check** sth **over**: to examine something to make sure it is correct, acceptable, or working properly ▶ *Mechanics checked over the engine before the plane took off.*

2 check sb **over, check over** sb: to examine someone to make sure they

are healthy ▶ *Dunston was pulled off the football field and checked over by a doctor.*

CHECK THROUGH →

1 check through sth: to examine a collection of things because you are trying to find something ▶ *I've checked through all my drawers, but there's no sign of my red sweater.*

2 check through sth, **check** sth **through**: to examine something to make sure that there are no mistakes in it or no problems with it ▶ *I just want to check through my work before I hand it in to the teacher.*

CHECK UP →

check up, check up sth, **check** sth **up**: to make sure that you have the correct information about something ▶ *I don't know if you need a visa for India – you'd better check up before you buy your ticket.*

   checkup N when a doctor examines you to see if you are healthy ▶ *Doctors recommend a yearly checkup for most adults.*

CHECK UP ON →

1 check up on sb/sth: to try to find out if someone is doing what they should be doing, especially secretly ▶ *Immigration officials checked up on him and found that he was using a stolen passport.*

2 check up on sb: to make sure that someone is still safe and healthy ▶ *"I'll be back in a few minutes to check up on you," promised Dr Finnegan.*

CHEER

CHEER ON →

cheer on sb/sth, **cheer** sb/sth **on**: to shout in order to encourage someone who is taking part in a game, race, or competition ▶ *6,000 fans cheered on their teams in the high school basketball championships.*

C

CHEER UP →

1 cheer up, cheer sb **up, cheer up** sb: to feel happier after you have been feeling sad or upset, or to make someone feel happier ▶ *Cheer up, Jerry. It can't be that bad.* ▶ *Listening to music always cheers me a up a bit.*

2 cheer sth **up, cheer up** sth: to make a place look more attractive and cheerful ▶ *I've brought some flowers – I thought they'd cheer the place up a little.*

CHEW

CHEW ON →

chew on sth: to think about a question, problem, or idea carefully ▶ *Why don't you chew on it over the weekend, and make a decision by Monday?*

CHEW OUT →

chew sb **out, chew out** sb: to talk angrily to someone to show that you disapprove of what they have done ▶ *My boss chewed me out for not getting the report in on time.*

CHEW OVER →

chew over sth, **chew** sth **over**: to think about something carefully for a period of time, or to discuss it in detail ▶ *I can't give you an answer right away – I need some time to chew it over.*

CHEW UP →

chew up sth, **chew** sth **up**: if a machine chews something up, it damages or destroys it ▶ *The printer is chewing the paper up again.*

CHICKEN

CHICKEN OUT →

chicken out: to decide not to do something because you are too frightened ▶ *His opponent chickened out at the last minute and said he didn't want to fight.* **chicken out of doing** sth ▶ *At the last minute I chickened out of going to Africa.*

CHILL

CHILL OUT →

1 chill out: to relax ▶ *"What are you doing?" "Nothing much. Just chilling out."*

2 chill out!: used to tell someone not to worry or not to get annoyed or too excited ▶ *Hey girl, chill out, okay! He's not worth worrying about.*

CHIME

CHIME IN →

chime in: to say something during a conversation ▶ *"It's a great idea," my sister Rose chimed in.*

CHIME IN WITH →

chime in with sth: to be similar to someone else's opinions or feelings ▶ *His political aims chimed in with the national mood at the time.*

CHIP

CHIP AWAY AT →

chip away at sth: to gradually reduce something or make something disappear ▶ *Book sales over the Internet are chipping away at the profits of retail bookstores.*

CHIP IN →

1 chip in: if each person in a group chips in, they all give a small amount of money in order to pay for something together ▶ *If we all chip in, we should be able to get her something really nice.*

2 chip in: to interrupt a conversation in order to say something ▶ *"Chris is also a really good football player," Alex chipped in.*

CHOKE

CHOKE BACK →

choke back tears / anger etc: to force yourself not to cry or show your feelings about something ▶ *He choked back tears as he announced his resignation.*

CHOKE OFF →
choke off sth: to stop a supply of something ▶ *The government is increasing its efforts to choke off the flow of cocaine into the country.*

CHOKE UP →
1 choke up, choke sb **up**: to have difficulty speaking because you are almost crying, or to make someone do this ▶ *This song chokes me up every time I hear it.*
> **choked up** ADJ when you have difficulty speaking because you are almost crying ▶ *Bill wanted to thank the woman, but he was too choked up to speak.*

2 choke up sth, **choke** sth **up**: to block a street or area etc so that people or traffic cannot easily move through it ▶ *Commuter traffic chokes up the main roads during the rush hour.*

CHOOSE
CHOOSE UP →
choose up sth, **choose up**: to divide a group of people into teams, usually to play a game or sport ▶ *We chose up different teams, and started a new game.*

CHOP
CHOP DOWN →
chop down sth, **chop** sth **down**: to make a tree fall to the ground by cutting it with an axe (= a sharp heavy tool) ▶ *The legend says that George Washington chopped down a cherry tree.*

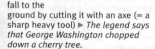

CHOP OFF →
chop off sth, **chop** sth **off**: to remove something using a knife or other sharp tool ▶ *Chop off the ends of the carrots before you peel them.*

CHOP UP →
chop up sth, **chop** sth **up**: to cut something into smaller pieces ▶ *Dad was chopping up wood for the fire.* ▶ *You should chop the onion up into tiny pieces.*

CHOW
CHOW DOWN →
chow down: to eat, especially to eat a lot of food with enjoyment ▶ *It's not the nicest place in town to chow down, but they do serve a good steak dinner.*

CHUCK
CHUCK AWAY →
chuck away sth, **chuck** sth **away**: to get rid of something you no longer need ▶ *We had to chuck a lot of stuff away when we moved.*

CHUCK IN →
chuck in sth, **chuck** sth **in**: to suddenly stop doing something, especially a job or course of study ▶ *She chucked in a perfectly good job and went to live with her boyfriend.*

CHUCK OUT →
chuck out sth, **chuck** sth **out**: to get rid of something you no longer need ▶ *Instead of just chucking out your old clothes, why not give them to charity?*

CHUG
CHUG ALONG →
chug along: to continue slowly and steadily ▶ *Economists expect Japan's economy to keep chugging along.*

CHUM
CHUM AROUND →
chum around: to be friendly with someone or to do things together with someone as a friend. **+ with** ▶ *She chums around with a girl called Carol.*

C

CLAM

CLAM UP →
clam up: to suddenly stop talking or to refuse to say anything about a subject ► *I tried asking him about Eileen, but he just clammed up completely.* **clam up on** sb (=suddenly stop talking to someone about something) ► *Celia wondered why her mother clammed up on her whenever she mentioned her father.*

CLAMP

CLAMP DOWN →
clamp down: to take action to stop someone from doing something or to limit their activities. **+ on** ► *The French government has announced plans to clamp down on illegal protests and road blockades.*

> **clampdown** N when the authorities take action to stop something happening or to limit it. **+ on** ► *calls for a clampdown on gun ownership*

CLAW

CLAW AT →
claw at sth: to tear or pull at something, using your fingers or nails ► *I was woken up by the cat clawing at the bedroom door.*

CLAW BACK →
1 claw back sth, **claw** sth **back:** to gradually get back something that you had lost ► *The former president started to claw back the lead gained by his Communist rival.*

2 claw back sth, **claw** sth **back:** if a government or organization claws back money which it has spent, it finds a way of gradually getting it back ► *Although he cut income tax, the Chancellor was able to claw back the money through hidden charges on investments.*

CLEAN

CLEAN OUT →
1 clean out sth, **clean** sth **out:** to clean the inside of something and throw away anything in it that you do not need ► *I spent Saturday morning cleaning out the fridge and the food cupboards.*

2a. clean sb **out, clean out** sb: if something cleans you out, it costs so much money that you have no more left ► *It was a great holiday, but it really cleaned us out.*

b. clean sb **out:** if someone cleans you out, you have to give them all your money ► *The divorce was very expensive – my wife cleaned me out completely.*

3 clean sth **out, clean out** sth: to steal everything from a place, or all of someone's possessions. **clean the place out** ► *The thieves had completely cleaned the place out.*

CLEAN UP →
1 clean up sth, **clean up** sth, **clean** sth **up:** to make a place or person clean ► *A lot of money needs to be spent on cleaning up our beaches.* **clean yourself up** ► *You'd better clean yourself up before dinner!*

> **clean-up** N when you clean a place thoroughly ► *This kitchen could do with a bit of a clean-up.*

2 clean up sth, **clean** sth **up:** to stop people behaving in an illegal or dishonest way within a particular organization or among a group of people ► *The new governor was determined to clean up the administration.* ► *new laws aimed at cleaning up the financial services industry*

> **clean-up** ADJ concerned with getting rid of dishonest or criminal activities ► *a clean-up campaign to prevent the sale of illegal drugs*

C

3 clean up your act: to start behaving in a more acceptable way ▶ *Lou was really wild as a teenager, but recently he's started to clean up his act.*

4 clean up: to win or earn a very large amount of money ▶ *We really cleaned up at the races today.*

CLEAR

CLEAR AWAY →

1 clear away sth, **clear** sth **away, clear away**: to put away the things that you have been using so that a place is tidy again ▶ *You'd better clear all these toys away before your grandmother gets here.*

2 clear away: to move away from a place ▶ *The protesters slowly cleared away from the building when the police arrived.*

CLEAR OFF →

clear off!: used to tell someone rudely and angrily to go away ▶ *Clear off and don't come back!*

CLEAR OUT →

1 clear out sth, **clear** sth **out**: to make a room, cupboard etc tidy and throw away the things in it you do not need ▶ *While I was clearing out the attic, I found some old photographs of my mother.*

clear-out N when you make a place tidy and throw away the things in it that you do not need ▶ *Look at this mess – it's time we had a big clear-out in here.*

2 clear out: to leave a place or building quickly or suddenly ▶ *By the time the police arrived the men had already cleared out.* **+ of** ▶ *I'll give you two hours to collect your things and*

clear out of here! **clear out!** (=used to tell someone rudely and angrily to leave a place) ▶ *Clear out! I don't want to see you again!*

CLEAR UP →

1 clear up, clear up sth, **clear** sth **up**: to put things back where they are usually kept and make a place clean and tidy again ▶ *Let's clear up as quickly as possible and then we can watch TV.* **clear up after** sb (=make a place clean and tidy after someone else has made it dirty and untidy) ▶ *I'm tired of clearing up after other people all the time!*

2 clear up sth, **clear** sth **up**: to solve a problem or deal with a disagreement or confusing situation ▶ *Talks continued late into the night in an effort to clear up the remaining difficulties.* ▶ *Why don't you phone him and clear up the confusion?*

3 clear up sth, **clear** sth **up**: to find an explanation for something ▶ *Officials have been unable to clear up the mystery of how the ship caught fire.*

4 clear up, clear up sth, **clear** sth **up**: if an illness or infection clears up, or if medicine clears it up, it gets better and disappears ▶ *Keep taking the antibiotics and the infection should clear up within a week.*

5 clear up: if the weather clears up, it stops raining and becomes more pleasant ▶ *The weather forecast said that it would clear up later in the day.*

CLICK

CLICK ON →

click on sth: to make a computer do something by pressing a button on the mouse in order to choose something on the screen ▶ *Once you have entered your data, click on OK.*

C

CLIMB

CLIMB DOWN →

climb down: to admit that you were wrong in an argument, or agree to accept other people's demands ▶ *Neither side in the dispute has been willing to climb down.*

    climbdown N when you admit that you were wrong, or agree to accept other people's demands ▶ *This policy change has been seen as a humiliating climbdown by the government.*

CLING

CLING TO, *also* **CLING ON TO** →

1 cling (on) to the idea/hope etc: to continue to have a particular idea or hope even when it seems unlikely to be true or right ▶ *He was clinging desperately to the hope that his family might be alive.*

2 cling (on) to: to manage to keep something important that you have, but with a lot of difficulty ▶ *The reforms were seen as an attempt by the Communists to cling on to power.*

CLOCK

CLOCK IN, *also* **CLOCK ON** →

clock in/on: to record the time that you arrive at work, especially by putting a special card into a machine ▶ *Workers are expected to clock in when they arrive at the factory.*

CLOCK OUT, *also* **CLOCK OFF** →

clock out/off: to record the time that you leave work, especially by putting a special card into a machine ▶ *She clocks off at 7.15 and goes home to cook her family's supper.*

CLOCK UP →

clock up sth: to reach or achieve a large number or amount of something over a period of time ▶ *The England team clocked up their third successive win.*

CLOG

CLOG UP →

1 clog up,
clog up sth,
clog sth **up**: to become blocked with something, or to block something by filling it ▶ *The coffee machine keeps clogging up.* ▶ *Fallen leaves had clogged up the drains.*

2 clog up the system: to prevent a system from working as well as it should ▶ *All the extra applications for passports have clogged up the system.*

CLOSE

CLOSE DOWN →

1 close down: to stop working as a business or other organization, either for a short time or permanently ▶ *Cafes, shops and offices closed down during the recession.* ▶ *The college has closed down for the summer.*

2 close down sth, **close** sth **down**: to stop a business or an organization operating ▶ *The restaurant was closed down by the Environmental Health Department.*

CLOSE IN →

1 close in: to move closer and closer to someone or something, especially in order to attack or catch them ▶ *The lions were running faster and faster, closing in for the kill.* **+ on** ▶ *I knew that the gang was closing in on me – there was nowhere for me to run.*

2 close in: if bad weather closes in, it starts to get worse ▶ *The fog began to close in and we couldn't see a thing.*

3 close in: if the night closes in, it gradually becomes darker ▶ *It was 8 o'clock, and the night was already starting to close in.*

CLOSE OFF →

close off sth, **close** sth **off**: to block the entrance to an area or road in order to prevent people from going there ▶ *Police closed off the whole road while they dealt with the accident.*

CLOSE ON →

close on sb/sth: to get closer and closer to someone or something ▶ *He ran the length of the field with Steve Hackney closing on him every second.*

CLOSE OUT →

1 close out sth, **close** sth **out**: to sell all of a product cheaply. **+ on** ▶ *Marshall's usually closes out on their summer lines in August.*

2 close out sth: to stop using or having the right to use a bank account ▶ *At the year's end, all temporary accounts are closed out.*

3 close sb **out, close out** sb: to refuse to include someone in a group or an activity ▶ *Swedish companies fear that the EU will close them out of trade agreements.*

CLOSE UP →

1 close up sth, **close** sth **up**: to shut and lock a building and leave it ▶ *She closed up the shop early and went home.*

2 close up: if a shop etc closes up, it ends its business for the day and is locked ▶ *I managed to get to the garage just before it closed up for the night.*

3 close up: if something such as a wound or a hole closes up, the sides join together and it disappears ▶ *It'll take a few weeks for a deep cut like this to close up completely.*

CLOUD

CLOUD OVER →

1 cloud over: if the sky clouds over, it becomes covered with clouds and the sun disappears ▶ *It was starting to cloud over and we decided to go indoors.*

2 sb's **face clouds/eyes cloud over**: if someone's face or eyes cloud over, they suddenly look sad, worried, or angry ▶ *When I mentioned her name, his face suddenly clouded over.*

CLOWN

CLOWN AROUND, *also* CLOWN ABOUT →
clown around/about: to behave in a silly or funny way, especially in order to make people laugh ▶ *She loves clowning around in front of an audience.*

CLUB

CLUB TOGETHER →
club together: if a group of people club together to pay for something, they all give some money and share the cost together ▶ *We all clubbed together to buy her a leaving present.*

CLUE

CLUE IN →
clue sb **in**: to give someone information about something new or something that they need to know. **+ on** ▶ *Mark's already clued me in on what's been happening while I've been away.*

CLUE UP →
be clued up: to know a lot about

something and understand it well ▶ *Ask Margaret, she's pretty clued up about that sort of thing.*

CLUSTER

CLUSTER AROUND, *also* CLUSTER ROUND →

cluster around/round sb/sth: to form a very close group around someone or something ▶ *Everyone was clustering around fires, trying to keep warm.*

CLUTTER

CLUTTER UP →

clutter up sth, **clutter** sth **up**: to fill a room, or cover an area with too many things in an untidy way ▶ *Can't we get rid of these boxes – they've been cluttering up the office for weeks now.*

COAST

COAST ALONG →

coast along: to be fairly successful, but without trying very hard and without making as much progress as you could ▶ *In recent years the team has been content to coast along in the middle of the first division.*

COBBLE

COBBLE TOGETHER →

cobble together sth, **cobble** sth **together**: to make or produce something quickly and often not very well ▶ *We cobbled together some lunch from the food that was left in the fridge.*

COLOUR

COLOUR IN →

colour in sth, **colour** sth **in**: to fill a shape or picture with colour using coloured pencils or paints ▶ *The children were told to colour in the shapes they had drawn.*

COLOUR UP →

colour up: if someone colours up, their face becomes red because they are embarrassed or angry ▶ *He stared at Mary, and she coloured up instantly.*

COMB

COMB THROUGH →

comb through sth: to carefully search through a lot of information or objects in order to find something ▶ *Police spent more than a day combing through every piece of evidence they could find.*

COME

COME ABOUT →

come about: to happen or start to exist ▶ *The discovery of penicillin came about entirely by chance.* ▶ *When did life begin on Earth, and how did it come about?*

COME ACROSS →

1 come across sth/sb: to find something or meet someone by chance ▶ *Jill came across her son's diary while she was tidying his room.*

2 come across sth: to experience a particular type of problem, situation etc ▶ *I expect you'll come across all sorts of difficulties, but it's still worth trying.*

3 come across: to seem to be a particular type of person or thing. **come across as (being)** sth ▶ *He comes across as being rather arrogant.* **come across well/badly** (=make people have a good or bad opinion of you) ▶ *I'm sure she's an excellent politician, but she comes across badly on television.*

4 come across: to be made clear or understood ▶ *What comes across very strongly in her letters is her wonderful sense of humour.*

COME ALONG →

1 come along: to go somewhere with someone ▶ *We're going to watch the football – do you want to come along?*

2 come along: if something new such as a job or an opportunity comes along, it becomes available for you ▸ *This job came along just at the right time.*

3 come along: to arrive or appear somewhere ▸ *The police eventually came along and took the man away.*

4 be coming along: to be making good progress ▸ *The doctor said that Richard was coming along nicely and would be able to go home on Friday.*

5 come along!: used to tell someone to hurry or make more effort ▸ *Come along, girls! We'll be late if we don't go now.*

COME APART →

1 come apart: to fail completely ▸ *The peace agreement seemed to be coming apart.* **come apart at the seams** (=used to emphasize that something is likely to fail completely) ▸ *His whole life seemed to be coming apart at the seams.*

2 come apart: to break or separate into pieces ▸ *Bruce grabbed the book from me and it came apart in his hands.*

COME AROUND, *also* COME ROUND →

1 come around/round: to come to someone's house in order to see them ▸ *Valerie and John said they might come around this evening.*

2 come around/round: to start to agree with or accept something that you did not agree with before ▸ *My mother stopped speaking to me when I first left home, but she's coming round now.*

3 come around/round: to arrive or happen as usual or as expected ▸ *The World Cup will be coming round again soon.* ▸ *The big day for my talk soon came around.*

4 come around/round: to become conscious again, for example after an accident or operation ▸ *"It'll take a couple of hours for him to come around," the doctor said.*

COME AT →

come at sb: to move towards someone in a threatening way ▸ *I was just leaving the club when this guy came at me with a knife.*

COME AWAY →

come away: to break and separate from something else ▸ *Alex pulled at the door handle, but it came away in her hands.*

COME AWAY WITH →

come away with sth: to succeed in winning something, or in getting something that you want ▸ *One of the athletes came away with seven Olympic gold medals.*

COME BACK →

1 come back: to return to a place ▸ *When do you think you'll be coming back to work?*

2 come back: to start to happen or exist again ▸ *As soon as I do any exercise, the pain comes back again.*

3 come back: to become fashionable or popular again ▸ *Apparently, the styles of the 60s and 70s are coming back.* **come back into fashion** ▸ *I never throw away old clothes in case they come back into fashion.*

comeback N when something becomes fashionable again, or a famous person becomes popular again ▸ *Aerosmith's comeback tour was a huge success.* **make a comeback** ▸ *Long boots are expected to make a comeback in the autumn.*

4 come back: if something from the past comes back to you, you remember it ▶ *She looked at the photograph, and suddenly it all came back.*

5 come back: to reply with humour or anger to something someone says ▶ *He always comes back with some kind of wittty reply.*

   comeback N a humorous or angry reply ▶ *I can never think of a good comeback until it's too late.*

COME BEFORE →
come before sb/sth: to be brought to someone with official authority in order to be judged or discussed ▶ *Murphy's case came before Judge Holden at the Crown Court.*

COME BETWEEN →
1 come between sb: to spoil a relationship or friendship ▶ *In the end it was Jed's jealousy and pride that came between us.*

2 come between sb **and** sth: to prevent someone from giving enough attention to something ▶ *He never let anyone come between him and his work.*

COME BY →
1 come by sth: to get something ▶ *I wonder how he came by so much money at his age.*

2 come by: to make a short visit to a place on your way to somewhere else ▶ *Can I come by tonight and get my stuff?*

COME DOWN →
1 come down: to accept a lower price for something than you had asked for ▶ *They're asking £150,000 for the house, but they might come down a bit.*

2 come down: if a building, wall etc comes down, it is destroyed ▶ *The Berlin Wall came down in 1989.*

3 come down: if a plane comes down, it crashes to the ground ▶ *The plane came down in Bilmermeer, and there were no survivors.*

4 come down in favour of sth/sb: to decide to support something or someone, especially officially ▶ *The president is expected to come down in favour of military intervention.* **come down on the side of** sth/sb ▶ *The judge in the case came down on the side of the unions.*

5 come down: to stop feeling the excitement caused by taking an illegal drug ▶ *An addict coming down off heroin is usually in a deeply depressed state.*

COME DOWN ON →
come down on sb: to criticize or punish someone for something ▶ *Your manager will really come down on you if the job isn't finished in time.* **come down on** sb **like a ton of bricks** (=criticize or punish someone very severely) ▶ *He made one tiny mistake and they came down on him like a ton of bricks.*

COME DOWN TO →
1 come down to sth: to be the most important thing to consider. **when it comes down to it** (=this is the most important point) ▶ *When it comes down to it, you have to remember she's only sixteen.*

2 if it comes down to it ...: used to say that if something becomes really necessary, that is what you will have to do ▶ *If it comes down to it, we'll just have to take a later flight.*

COME DOWN WITH →
come down with sth: to get an illness ▶ *Almost everyone in the office came down with flu.*

COME FOR →
come for sb: to arrive in order to take someone somewhere ▶ *The taxi's coming for us at nine.*

COME FORWARD →
come forward: to be willing to do something, especially to give someone information ▶ *People who are bullied at work are often too scared to come forward.*

COME FORWARD WITH →
come forward with sth: to suggest something or to give the money needed for something ▶ *Delors came forward with detailed proposals for a range of reforms.*

COME FROM →
1 come from sth: if you come from a particular place, you were born there or have your home there ▶ *Most of our students come from Europe.*

2 come from sth: to belong to a particular type of family or social class ▶ *The kids at this school come from all kinds of backgrounds.*

3 understand where sb's coming from: to understand why someone thinks the way they do ▶ *I disagree with her all the time – I just don't understand where she's coming from.*

COME IN →
1 come in: used to ask someone to enter the room or building that you are in ▶ *Would you like to come in and have a drink?*

2 come in: if a train, bus, plane, or ship comes in, it arrives at a station, airport, or port ▶ *What time should the train from Boston come in?*
   incoming ADJ travelling towards a place and arriving soon ▶ *incoming flights* ▶ *incoming passengers*

3 come in: to become involved in a plan, activity etc. **+ on** ▶ *Three more top bands have offered to come in on the anti-drugs campaign.* **be where/ how** sb/sth **comes in** (=be what someone or something's part in a plan is) ▶ *We need someone who knows the area, and that's where Mick comes in.*

4 come in: to finish a race, competition etc in a particular position ▶ *The favourite horse only just finished the race, coming in way behind the others.*

5 come in: to start to be used and have an effect ▶ *A new law came in today requiring all bars to close by 2 am.*

6 come in: if a new fashion comes in, it starts to be fashionable ▶ *Bright colours are coming in again for this summer.*

7 come in useful also **come in handy**: to be useful for something ▶ *Keep that box – it might come in handy for something.*

8 the tide comes in: when the tide comes in, the sea moves towards the land ▶ *It's only safe to swim here when the tide's coming in.*
   incoming ADJ an incoming tide is coming towards the land ▶ *The rocks were slowly being covered by the incoming tide.*

COME IN FOR →
come in for criticism/ praise etc: to be criticized, praised etc for something ▶ *In Dr Yates's speech, Samuel Whitbread came in for special praise.*

COME INTO →
1 come into effect also **come into operation**: to begin to be used and have an effect ▶ *The new tax came into operation on April 1st.* ▶ *In 1952, the peace treaty came into effect.*

2 come into being also **come into existence**: to start to exist ▶ *The company came into existence in 1987.*

3 come into sight also **come into view**: if something comes into sight or view, you begin to be able to see it ▶ *We finally reached the top of the hill, and the town came into view.*

4 come into it: to be an important part

C

of a situation ► *You have to consider my feelings too – don't they come into it?*

5 come into office also **come into power**: to start to have a position of power, especially in government ► *When the government came into power, unemployment was 1.25 million.*

6 come into money/land etc: to receive money, land etc from someone, especially someone who has died ► *She came into an enormous sum of money from her grandmother.*

COME OF →

come of sth: to happen as the result of something else ► *Lisa failed her music exam – that's what comes of not practising.*

COME OFF →

1 come off well/badly etc: to be more or less successful or lucky compared to someone else ► *I always came off badly in an argument with her.*

2 come off: to happen as planned or wanted ► *We've been thinking of going to Africa for years, but I don't think it'll ever come off.* ► *Irene was trying to be funny, but the joke didn't quite come off.*

3 come off it!: used to tell someone that you think what they have just said is wrong, dishonest, or stupid ► *"I'm thinking of studying medicine." "Come off it ! You can't even stand the sight of blood!"*

4 come off sth: to stop taking drugs, medicine, or alcohol ► *It can take years to come off heroin.*

COME OFF AS →

come off as sth: to seem to have a particular quality or characteristic ► *Miller sometimes comes off as egotistical and unkind, but he's not really like that at all.*

COME ON →
come on!
a. used to tell someone to come with you or to hurry ► *Come on, Luke, let's go inside.*
b. used to encourage someone to do something ► *"Come on," urged Marie, "You can tell me what's wrong."*
c. used to tell someone that you do not believe what they have just said ► *Oh, come on. She's a lot older than that.*
d. used to comfort someone ► *Come on. Everything's going to be fine.*

1 come on in/over etc: used to tell someone to come in, over etc ► *"Come on in," Miller said, "Make yourself at home."*

2 come on: to start working ► *The front door light will come on automatically when it gets dark.* ► *Why hasn't the heating come on yet?*

3 come on: if a television or radio programme comes on, it begins ► *The news usually comes on after 'Neighbours' doesn't it?*

4 come on: to start to take part in a game, especially instead of another player ► *Arsenal looked stronger after the substitute came on.*

5 come on: to improve or make progress ► *Joe's really come on a lot since he went to his new school.* **how's** sth/sb **coming on?** (=what progress is something or someone making) ► *How's your course coming on?*

6 come on: if an illness or a pain comes on, it starts ► *I think I have a cold coming on.* ► *Nick said he had a headache coming on, so he's gone home.*

COME ON TO →

1 come on to sb: to make it very clear to someone that you are sexually interested in them ► *We'd only just met and she started coming on to me!*

come-on N something that you do or say that is clearly intended to attract someone sexually. **give** sb **the come-on** ▶ *He seems to imagine that every woman he meets is giving him the come-on.*

2 come on to sth: to start talking about something, especially after talking about something else ▶ *I'll come on to that point in more detail later.*

COME OUT →

1 come out: to leave a room, building, or place where you are staying or hiding ▶ *"Come out!" shouted the police officer. "We know you're in there!"* **+ of** ▶ *Donald came out of his office, looking tired and worried.*

2 come out: to go somewhere with someone in order to enjoy yourself socially ▶ *Jack said he couldn't come out tonight because he has an exam tomorrow.*

3 come out: to become available to be bought or to be seen ▶ *People are always waiting for Terry Pratchett's next book to come out.* ▶ *When the movie came out, it was an instant success.*

4 come out: to become known, especially after being kept secret ▶ *I knew that Ruth had problems, but it was several months before the truth came out.* ▶ *The exam results don't come out until the end of August.*

5 come out: used to say how good, bad, successful etc something is. **come out well/badly etc** ▶ *It took him a long time to write the book, but it came out really well.* **come out on top** (=to be better than the others) ▶ *Of all the washing-machines in the survey, this one came out on top.*

6 come out: to be said in a particular way ▶ *I tried to explain how I feel, but it all came out wrong.*

7 come out: if the sun, moon, or stars come out, they appear in the sky after being hidden ▶ *Just as we were about to leave the beach, the sun came out.*

8 come out: if marks or colours come out of something, they disappear or become less strong when they are cleaned ▶ *I don't think this stain will come out, whatever I do.*

9 come out in favour of/against: to publicly support or oppose someone or something ▶ *Over half the party has come out against further reductions in taxation.* **come out in support of** sth/sb ▶ *She has come out in support of the extreme right-wing National Front party.*

10 come out: to tell people that you are gay, after keeping it secret ▶ *We knew Paul was gay for years before he finally decided to come out.*

11 come out: to succeed in getting through an unpleasant experience ▶ *The two girls had been kidnapped and were lucky to come out alive.*

12 come out: if flowers come out, they open ▶ *Roses come out at the end of June.*

13 come out: to lead towards or end at a particular place ▶ *Do you know where this road comes out?*

14 come out: if workers come out, they refuse to work until their employer agrees to their demands ▶ *Other workers came out in support of the miners' strike.* **come out on strike** ▶ *When their pay claims were refused, the teachers came out on strike.*

COME OUT IN →

come out in spots/a rash etc: to develop spots etc on your skin ▶ *I tend to come out in a rash if I eat certain foods.*

COME OUT OF →

1 come out of sth: to result from an

activity, event, or process ▶ *I don't think any good has come out of this war at all.*

2 come out of sth: to stop being in a particular situation or state, especially a bad one ▶ *Various signs suggest that the economy may be coming out of recession.*

3 come out of sth **well/badly etc**: to give someone a good or bad idea about you because of the way you have done or dealt with something ▶ *I've just read a book about him. He doesn't come out of it very well.*

COME OUT WITH →

come out with sth: to say something, especially something wrong, stupid, or annoying ▶ *When I asked for his opinion, he came out with a long list of criticisms.*

COME OVER →

1 come over: to visit you at your house ▶ *Why don't you come over this evening and we'll talk about it then?*

2 come over sb: if a feeling or a change comes over you, you experience it ▶ *She knew he was watching her, and a feeling of panic came over her.* **what has come over** sb? (=used when you are surprised because someone has suddenly started behaving in strange way) ▶ *I don't know what's come over him – he actually said hello to me this morning!*

3 come over: to seem to be a particular type of person or thing, or to have particular qualities. **+ as** ▶ *Mrs Robins came over as a cold strict woman.*

4 come over: to be clearly expressed and easy to notice or understand ▶ *The same message is coming over again and again: we are slowly destroying the planet.*

5 come over: to leave a group, team,

or organization and join one that is competing against it. **+ from** ▶ *Patrice Tardif was one of the three players who came over from the Blues.*

COME ROUND *see* COME AROUND

COME THROUGH →

1 come through: if something comes through, it reaches you and you receive it ▶ *I was in Boston when the news came through.* ▶ *Hank's divorce came through sooner than he had expected.*

2 come through sth: to succeed in getting to the end of a dangerous or difficult situation ▶ *Amazingly, our house came through the storm without much damage.*

3 come through: to provide something that someone needs or has asked for. **+ with** ▶ *The US came through with $1 billion in aid.*

COME TO →

1 come to sth: to reach a particular state or situation – used especially in the following phrases: **come to an end** (=finish) ▶ *My stay in San Francisco was coming to an end.* **come to an agreement** (=agree about something) ▶ *It was several months before we eventually came to an agreement.* **it comes to the point where** (=used to say that you have reached a particular situation) ▶ *It came to the point where we could no longer bear to talk to each other.*

2 come to a decision also **come to a conclusion etc**: to make a decision about something ▶ *All the candidates for the sales job were good, and it took us a long time to come to a decision.*

3 when it comes to sth: used to introduce the subject that you are going to talk about or deal with ▶ *When it comes to relationships, everyone makes mistakes.* ▶ *The* *government has had little success when it comes to education.*

4 come to power: to officially start to rule a country ▶ *The Communists came to power in China in 1949.*

5 come to nothing also **not come to anything**: to develop or not develop into something successful ▶ *It was obvious that their efforts would come to nothing.*

6 come to sth: to start to talk about something or deal with it ▶ *There are reasons for our decision, which I'll come to later.*

7 come to sth: to add up to a particular total ▶ *At the end of the evening the bill came to £50.*

8 come to sb: if a thought or idea comes to you, you think of it ▶ *I've forgotten the name of the restaurant – it'll come to me in a minute.*

9 come to: to become conscious again after an accident or operation ▶ *When I came to, I was lying in a hospital bed.*

COME TOGETHER →

1 come together: to join together with other people, in order to do something. **+ to do** sth ▶ *Several local groups had come together to form the new party.*

2 be coming together: if something is coming together, it is finally starting to be successful ▶ *Linda was just beginning to feel that her life was coming together.*

COME UNDER →

1 come under attack/criticism etc: to be attacked, criticized etc ▶ *Oil tankers and trucks came under air attack on January 29.* ▶ *The government came under strong pressure to negotiate with the hijackers.* **come under fire** (=be criticized) ▶ *TV companies have come under fire for the amount of violence on our screens.*

2 come under scrutiny/review etc: to be examined or considered carefully ▶ *The new policy came under intense scrutiny.*

COME UP →

1 come up: to move towards someone or something until you are next to them ▶ *She came up and put her arms around him.* **+ to** ▶ *A lot of people came up to her and started asking questions.*

2 come up: if an opportunity comes up, it becomes available ▶ *Let me know if you hear of any suitable jobs coming up.* ▶ *If you keep on trying, I'm sure something will come up.*

3 come up: to be mentioned in a conversation ▶ *We'd been going out together for two years before the subject of marriage came up.*

4 come up: if a problem comes up, it suddenly appears ▶ *It's been one of those days when problems keep coming up all the time.* **something's come up** ▶ *I'm afraid I'm going to be late home – something's come up at work.*

5 be coming up: to be going to happen soon ▶ *Your birthday's coming up next month, isn't it?* ▶ *The Annual Folk Festival is coming up on May 3rd.*

6 come up: if the sun or moon comes up, it moves up into the sky where you can see it  ▶ *We got up early to watch the sun come up behind the mountains.*

7 come up: if a plant or seed comes up, it begins to appear above the ground ▶ *If you plant the seeds now they should come up in about ten days' time.*

8 come up: if a number comes up in a

competition, you win something if you have chosen the same number ► *You'll win about sixty pounds if three of your numbers come up.*

9 coming (right) up!: used to tell someone that something they have just ordered will be ready soon ► *"Two Martinis, please." "Coming up, sir!"*

COME UP AGAINST →
come up against sth/sb: to have to deal with a problem or difficult person ► *Women police officers often complain that they come up against a lot of sexism.*

COME UP FOR →
1 come up for sale also **come up for auction**: to become available to buy ► *I'd really love to buy that house, if it ever comes up for sale.*

2 come up for discussion also **come up for debate**: to be formally discussed ► *The issue came up for debate in Parliament three days later.*

3 come up for sth: to reach the time when something should be dealt with or done ► *The case came up for review, and the men were found innocent.* ► *In November, one third of the Senate comes up for re-election.*

COME UP TO →
1 come up to sth: to reach a particular standard. **come up to sb's/sth's standards** ► *Many of Britain's beaches do not come up to EC standards.* **come up to expectations** ► *We loved the island, but the hotel didn't really come up to our expectations.* **come up to scratch** (=be as good as expected or as something should be) ► *Over a third of the schools in the survey didn't come up to scratch.*

2 be coming up to sth: to be nearly a particular time or age ► *It was coming up to two o'clock by the time everyone had left.* ► *My oldest son's just coming up to sixteen.*

COME UP WITH →
1 come up with sth: to think of an idea, plan, or solution ► *A good leader has to be able to identify problems and come up with solutions.*

2 come up with sb/sth: to find a suitable person or thing ► *We've advertised several times, but haven't been able to come up with a suitable candidate.*

COME UPON →
come upon sb/sth: to meet someone or find something by chance or when you do not expect it ► *On the second day we came upon the remains of a Roman villa.*

COME WITHIN →
1 come within seconds/inches etc of doing sth: used to say that someone very nearly does something, or something very nearly happens ► *He came within two percentage points of winning Arizona.* ► *Afterwards I realized I'd come within seconds of death.*

2 come within sight/reach etc: to be close enough to something to see it or reach it, or to be seen or reached. **+ of** ► *As Beatty came within sight of his office, he was surprised to see a small group waiting at the door.* ► *Parts of the city centre were coming within range of heavy artillery.*

COMPOSE

BE COMPOSED OF →
1 be composed of sth: to be made of a particular substance or substances ► *Water is composed of hydrogen and oxygen.* ► *The marble from which the Taj Mahal is built is composed of large crystals.*

2 be composed of sth/sb: to consist of a particular number or type of things, people, organizations, etc

▶ *The Kingdom of Tonga is composed of about 170 islands.*

CONCEIVE

CONCEIVE OF →

1 conceive of sth: to imagine that it is possible for something to happen or exist ▶ *Yuan found it difficult to conceive of life with any other woman but his wife.*

2 conceive of sth/sb: to think of something in a particular way or as being a particular thing. **+ as** ▶ *The Christian God has traditionally been conceived of as masculine.*

CONCENTRATE

CONCENTRATE ON →

concentrate on sth, **concentrate** sth **on** sth: to give more attention to something or do more work on it than anything else ▶ *She left the band in order to concentrate on her solo career.* ▶ *The students here are able to concentrate on the subjects that interest them most.*

CONDEMN

CONDEMN TO →

1 condemn sb **to death/hard labour etc:** to give someone a severe punishment after deciding that they are guilty of a crime ▶ *In 1814, Joseph Guillotin was arrested, tried and condemned to death.*

2 condemn sb/sth **to** sth: to force someone to accept an unpleasant situation or way of life ▶ *The accident condemned her to a lifetime of pain and disability.*

CONFER

CONFER ON, *also* CONFER UPON →

1 confer sth **on/upon** sb, **confer on/upon** sb sth: to make someone have a particular quality or feeling ▶ *Pregnancy seems to confer a feeling of contentment on some women.*

2 confer sth **on/upon** sb: to officially give a title, degree, or honour to someone ▶ *Degrees from Oxford University were first conferred on women in 1920.*

CONFESS

CONFESS TO →

1 confess to sth: to admit that you have done something wrong or illegal ▶ *One of the men broke down and confessed to the murder.*

2 confess to sth: to admit something that you feel embarrassed about ▶ *In the end, Mitchell confessed to not having read my book.*

CONFIDE

CONFIDE IN →

confide in sb: to tell someone something that you have not told other people, because you feel you can trust them ▶ *He had no one to confide in, no one to turn to for advice.*

CONFINE

CONFINE TO →

1 be confined to sth: to affect only one group of people, or to exist in only one place or situation ▶ *Domestic violence is not confined to any one group in society.*

2 be confined to sth: to have to stay somewhere because you are ill or injured ▶ *The prime minister has been confined to a hospital bed for almost seven weeks now.*

3 be confined to sth: to be forced to stay in a place such as a prison ▶ *The prisoners are confined to their cells for almost 23 hours a day.*

4 confine yourself to sth: to only do one thing or only talk about one thing ▶ *There are too many examples to talk about this morning, so I'll confine myself to two.*

CONFRONT

CONFRONT WITH →

1 be confronted with sth: to have a difficult problem or situation that you have to deal with ▶ *Aid workers are now confronted with the task of feeding all the refugees.* ▶ *She was confronted with a seemingly impossible choice.*

2 confront sb **with** sth: to show someone evidence that they have done something wrong or illegal, in order to make them admit it ▶ *When she confronted her husband with the photographs, he suddenly became very quiet.*

CONJURE

CONJURE UP →

1 conjure up sth, **conjure** sth **up**: to make a picture, idea, or memory appear in someone's mind ▶ *The word 'Mediterranean' conjures up images of sunshine, olive trees, and a crystal clear sea.*

2 conjure up sth, **conjure** sth **up**: to produce something quickly and easily ▶ *Grandma went into the kitchen, and within minutes had conjured up a delicious meal.*

CONK

CONK OUT →

1 conk out: if a machine or car conks out, it stops working ▶ *Our car conked out on the way home and we had to walk the rest of the way.*

2 conk out: to fall asleep quickly because you are very tired ▶ *Natalie conked out at around four a.m.*

CONNIVE

CONNIVE AT, *also* **CONNIVE IN** →

connive at/in sth: to allow something illegal or wrong to continue by deliberately not trying to stop it ▶ *The report claims that drugs are freely available in prisons, and that prison staff connive at drug abuse.*

CONSIGN

CONSIGN TO →

1 consign sth/sb **to** sth: to put something or someone somewhere, especially in order to get rid of them ▶ *Natalie read his letter with increasing annoyance, and then consigned it to the wastepaper bin.*

2 consign sb **to** sth: to force someone to accept a bad situation or way of life ▶ *Poor education has consigned them to a life of poverty and crime.*

CONSIST

CONSIST OF →

consist of sth: to include or be made up of a particular group of people or things ▶ *a sauce consisting of minced beef, tomatoes, and onions* ▶ *The team consists of an editor, three full-time journalists, and a photographer.*

CONSORT

CONSORT WITH →

consort with sb: to spend time with someone that other people disapprove of ▶ *They suspected him of consorting with the enemy.*

CONSULT

CONSULT WITH →

consult with sb: to discuss something with someone before you make a decision ▶ *The President consulted with European leaders before taking action.*

CONTEND

CONTEND WITH →

contend with sth: if you have to contend with a problem or a difficult situation you have to deal with it. **have to contend with** sth ▶ *The Prime Minister has to contend with constant criticism from members of his own party.*

CONTENT

CONTENT WITH →

content yourself with sth: to decide to accept something or do something, even though it is not what you really want ▶ *He has refused all interviews, so the media has had to content itself with reporting prepared statements.*

CONTRIBUTE

CONTRIBUTE TO, *also* CONTRIBUTE TOWARDS, CONTRIBUTE TOWARD →

contribute to/towards/toward sth: to be one of the causes of something ▶ *The new drug contributed to a 7% rise in the company's profits this year.*

CONVERGE

CONVERGE ON/UPON →

converge on/upon sth: if a lot of people converge on a place, they come there from different places and form a large crowd ▶ *More than half a million sports fans converged on the capital today for the London Marathon.*

COOK

COOK UP →

cook up sth, **cook** sth **up**: to think of a lie or an excuse ▶ *Rachel cooked up some excuse about her car breaking down.*

COOL

COOL DOWN →

1 cool down, cool sb/sth **down, cool down** sb/sth: to become cooler, or to make someone or something cooler ▶ *We jumped into the swimming pool to cool down.*

2 cool down: to become calm after feeling angry ▶ *Perhaps when they have had time to cool down and think about it, they'll reconsider.*

COOL OFF →

1 cool off: to become cool or cooler ▶ *I took the bread out of the oven, and left it on the table to cool off.*

2 cool off: to become calm after being angry ▶ *Maybe you should go away and cool off before we talk anymore about this.*

3 cool off: if you cool off, or your relationship with someone cools off, you feel less attracted to someone than you did before ▶ *I ended the relationship because I thought Rob was beginning to cool off.*

COOP

BE COOPED UP →

be cooped up: to be in a place which is too small or does not give you enough freedom. **+ in** ▶ *The prisoners are cooped up in their cells for most of the day.* ▶ *It was great to be out in the fresh air after being cooped up in the house all day.*

COP

COP OUT →

cop out: to avoid doing something that you should do or said you would do ▶ *We took a tent with us, but copped out when it started raining and stayed in a hotel.* **+ of** ▶ *He said that he wasn't going to cop out of making tough decisions.*

    cop-out N when someone avoids doing something difficult or something that they should do ▶ *It's an interesting film, but the sentimental ending is a complete cop-out.*

COPY

COPY DOWN →

copy down sth, **copy** sth **down**: to write something that someone has said or written on a piece of paper ▶ *The children were copying down the instructions from the board.*

COPY OUT →

copy out sth, **copy** sth **out**: if you copy out something that has been written, you write it all again on a piece of paper ▶ *I copied out the recipe for her.*

CORDON

CORDON OFF →

cordon off sth, **cordon** sth **off**: to put something around an area to stop people from going into it ▶ *Police have cordoned off the street where the murder took place.*

CORRESPOND

CORRESPOND TO →

correspond to sth: if one thing corresponds to another, it relates to or is similar to the other thing ▶ *The road took us past farmhouses, woods, and a lake, but nothing seemed to correspond to the map.* ▶ *Employees' salaries generally correspond to how long they've worked for the company.*

COTTON

COTTON ON →

cotton on: to start to understand or realize something ▶ *I dropped about six hints before he finally cottoned on.* **+ to** ▶ *At last fashion shops are cottoning on to the fact that not every woman is a standard size.*

COUCH

COUCH IN →

be couched in: to be expressed in a particular type of language ▶ *The letter was long and couched in incomprehensible legal jargon.*

COUGH

COUGH UP →

cough up: to pay money for something, especially when you do not want to ▶ *You owe me £10. Come on, cough up.*

COUNT

COUNT AGAINST →

count against sb: to be likely to make someone less successful at something ▶ *Always dress well for job interviews – an untidy appearance will count against you.*

COUNT AMONG →

count sb/sth **among** sth: to consider that someone or something belongs to a particular group ▶ *I was proud to count myself among his close friends.*

COUNT DOWN →

count down, **count down** sth, **count** sth **down**: to count numbers backwards to zero before an important or special event ▶ *Ok, get ready to count down to midnight – five, four, three, two, one! Happy New Year!*
  countdown N when someone counts backwards to zero before an important event, especially before a space vehicle is sent into the sky ▶ *The countdown has begun at Cape Canaveral.*

COUNT FOR →

count for something: to be considered important or valuable ▶ *It's nice to know that good old-fashioned moral values still count for something.* **not count for much** ▶ *What I say doesn't count for much around here.*

COUNT IN →
count me in!: used to say that you want to take part in an activity that other people are planning ▶ *"Mark, how do you feel about playing volleyball tomorrow?" "Count me in!"*

COUNT OFF →
1 count off sth, **count** sth **off**: to count people or things aloud, especially in order to make sure that they are all there ▶ *Miss Bradshaw stood counting off the children as they got onto the bus.*

2 count off: if a group of people count off, they call out a number when their turn comes to show that they are there ▶ *The soldiers counted off before beginning their training exercises.*

COUNT ON, *also* COUNT UPON →
1 count on/upon sth: to expect something to happen and include it in your plans ▶ *In Spain you can count on sunny, cloudless skies and a warm sea.*

2 can count on/upon sb: if you can count on someone, you know that they will help you or do what you want ▶ *You can count on me. I won't let you down.*

COUNT OUT →
1 count me out!: used to say that you do not want to take part in an activity that other people are planning ▶ *"We're going to the movies." "Count me out," said Jennifer.*

2 count out sth, **count** sth **out**: to count things one by one as you pick them up and put them into a pile ▶ *Joey took out a wad of banknotes and started counting them out on the table.*

3 count sb **out**: to decide that someone is certain to fail ▶ *A lot of people count me out. They keep asking: 'When are you gonna retire?'*

COUNT TOWARDS, *also* COUNT TOWARD →
count towards/toward sth: to be part of and influence the final score, result, or total ▶ *The work that you do over the three years counts toward your final degree.*

COUNT UP →
count up sb/sth, **count** sb/sth **up**: to count the people or things in a group to find out how many of them there are ▶ *The quiz master counts up the scores, and then announces which team is the winner.*

COUNT UPON *see* COUNT ON

COUPLE

COUPLE WITH →
sth **coupled with** sth: used to say that two things together cause something to happen ▶ *Lack of rain coupled with high temperatures cause the crops to fail.*

COVER

COVER OVER →
cover over sth, **cover** sth **over**: to cover the top of something completely with something else ▶ *The planes were covered over with branches so that they could not be seen from the air.*

COVER UP →
1 cover up sth, **cover** sth **up**: to stop people from finding out the truth about a crime or a mistake ▶ *Documents were stolen from the Watergate building, and Nixon tried to cover it up.* **cover up for** sb ▶ *She lied to cover up for her husband, saying that he had been at home with her on the night of the crime.*

cover-up N an attempt to prevent the public from discovering the truth about something ▶ *The government immediately began a massive cover-up, blaming the demonstrators for the violence.*

2 cover up sth/sb, **cover** sth/sb **up**: to cover something or someone with something ▶ We'd better cover up all the furniture while we're doing the decorating.

CRACK

CRACK DOWN →

crack down: if people in authority crack down on an illegal activity, they become much stricter about it. **+ on** ▶ a police campaign to crack down on burglaries ▶ He accused them of failing to crack down on terrorist organizations.

> **crackdown** N when people in authority become much stricter about something in order to prevent it from happening. **+ on** ▶ a crackdown on drug trafficking

CRACK UP →

1 crack up: to become mentally ill and unable to deal with your life or work ▶ Vince worked a 16-hour day and never took time off – eventually he just cracked up under the strain.

2 crack up, crack sb **up**: to suddenly laugh a lot, or to make someone laugh a lot ▶ Everyone in the class cracked up when they saw what was written on the board.

3 sth is not all it's cracked up to be: used to say that something is not as good as people say it is ▶ Being famous is not all it's cracked up to be.

CRAM

CRAM IN, also CRAM INTO →

1 cram in sth, **cram** sth **in**, **cram** sth **into** sth: to push a lot of things into a very small space ▶ Billy tried to see how many chocolates he could cram into his mouth at once.

2 cram in, cram into sth: if a lot of people cram in or cram into a place, they go into it and fill it ▶ We all crammed in and Jill started the car.

3 cram in sth, **cram** sth **in**, **cram** sth **into** sth: to do a lot of activities in a short period of time ▶ You can cram a lot of work into two weeks if you try.

CRANK

CRANK OUT →

crank sth **out, crank out** sth: to produce a lot of something very quickly ▶ He cranks out detective novels at the rate of three a year.

CRANK UP →

crank up sth, **crank** sth **up**: to make the sound of something, especially music, much louder ▶ We cranked up the volume and sang along at the top of our voices.

CRASH

CRASH AROUND, also CRASH ABOUT →

crash around/about: to move around making a lot of noise ▶ Some kind of animal was crashing about in the long grass behind us.

CRASH DOWN →

1 sb's hopes come/world etc comes crashing down: used to say that someone fails to achieve what they want or that something bad happens to them, so that they are very unhappy or disappointed ▶ When Toni left him, his whole world came crashing down.

2 come crashing down/bring sth **crashing down**: to stop working well or being successful, or to make something do this ▶ If the housing market collapsed, it would bring the whole economy crashing down.

CRASH OUT →

crash out: to go to sleep very quickly because you are very tired ▶ I was so *tired last night, I got home and just crashed out on the sofa.*

CRAWL

BE CRAWLING WITH →

1 be crawling with sth: to be covered with insects in a way that is very unpleasant ▶ *I woke up and the sheet was crawling with lice.*

2 be crawling with sb: if a place is crawling with people, it is full of them ▶ *We've got to get out of here – this place is going to be crawling with cops soon.*

CREAM

CREAM OFF →

1 cream off sth, **cream** sth **off**: to unfairly take the profits or the best part of something for yourself ▶ *Most of the profits are creamed off by insider dealers.*

2 cream off sb, **cream** sb **off**: to take the cleverest or most skilful people in a group away from the others, and treat them in a special way ▶ *Academic children were creamed off at the age of eleven and sent to grammar schools.*

CREASE

CREASE UP →

crease up, crease sb **up**: to laugh a lot, or make someone laugh a lot ▶ *Jo could imitate anybody and always made the others crease up.*

CREDIT

CREDIT WITH →

1 credit sb **with** sth: to believe that someone is the cause of something good that happens ▶ *Galileo is credited with changing the face of astronomy.*

2 credit sb **with** sth: to accept that someone has a particular quality ▶ *I wish you'd credit me with a little intelligence!*

CREEP

CREEP IN, *also* **CREEP INTO** →

1 creep in, creep into sth: if a feeling creeps in or into something, you gradually begin to feel or notice it ▶ *Doubt started creeping into her mind. Maybe he was lying?* A note of bitterness crept into his voice.

2 creep in, creep into sth: if something bad creeps in or into something, it appears there even though people have tried to prevent it ▶ *A few spelling mistakes always creep into every book.*

CREEP OUT →

creep sb **out, creep out** sb: to make someone feel nervous and slightly frightened ▶ *The movie has a dark side that may creep out younger kids.*

CREEP OVER →

creep over sb: if an unpleasant feeling creeps over you, you gradually begin to feel it ▶ *A feeling that something was terribly wrong crept over me.*

CREEP TO , *also* **CREEP UP TO** →

creep (up) to sb: to pretend to like someone, especially someone in authority, so that you can get an advantage for yourself ▶ *Nigel makes me sick – he's always creeping up to the lab manager.*

CREEP UP ON →

1 creep up on sb: if a feeling or condition creeps up on you, you experience it gradually, so that you do not notice it at first ▶ *Old age is creeping up on me.* ▶ *Fatigue creeps up on you when you're stressed at work.*

C

2 creep up on sb: if a time or event creeps up on you, it seems to happen sooner than you expected ▶ *The end of term seemed to creep up on us.*

CREEP UP TO *see* CREEP TO

CROP

CROP UP →

1 crop up: if something, especially a problem, crops up, it happens ▶ *Please let me know if anything crops up while I'm away.* ▶ *He's had to go back to the office – apparently something's cropped up.*

2 crop up: if a name or subject crops up, you hear it being talked about or discussed ▶ *Your name kept cropping up in conversation.*

CROSS

CROSS OFF →

cross off sth/sb, **cross** sth/sb **off**, **cross** sth/sb **off** sth: to remove a word or someone's name from a list by drawing a line through it ▶ *Jane said she won't be able to come, so I've crossed her off.*

CROSS OUT →

cross out sth, **cross** sth **out**: to draw a line through something that you have written, usually because it is wrong ▶ *She crossed out the word 'Miss' and wrote 'Dr' instead.*

   crossings-out PL N words that have been crossed out ▶ *His essay was full of crossings-out.*

CROSS OVER →

1 cross over, cross over sth: to go to the other side of something ▶ *Each year thousands of illegal immigrants cross over the border.* ▶ *We crossed over the bridge and followed the path along the bank.*

2 cross over, cross over sth: to walk from one side of a road to the other ▶ *Make sure you look both ways before you cross over.*

3 cross over: to start supporting a person or group that you opposed before ▶ *Churchill used to be a Liberal before he crossed over to the Conservative Party.*

4 cross over: to start doing a different kind of activity from the one you did before ▶ *He crossed over from comedy to serious acting.*

CROWD

CROWD AROUND, *also* CROWD ROUND →

crowd around/round, crowd around/round sb/sth: to form a crowd around someone or something ▶ *Everybody crowded around to have a look at the baby.* ▶ *Hundreds of people crowded round the stage door, waiting for the stars to appear.*

CROWD IN, *also* CROWD INTO →

crowd in, crowd into sth, **crowd** sb **into** sth: to go into a place in large numbers so that it is very full, or to make people do this ▶ *The doors opened, and everyone crowded in.*

CROWD IN ON, *also* CROWD IN UPON →

crowd in on/upon sb: if a lot of thoughts or feelings crowd in on you, you cannot stop thinking about them ▶ *Alvin tried to shut his mind against the fears that kept crowding in on him.*

CROWD INTO *see* CROWD IN

CROWD OUT →

crowd out sth/sb, **crowd** sth/sb **out**: to be so big or successful that another group, company, or organization cannot succeed or exist at the same time ▶ *Bigger software firms are crowding out smaller businesses.*

CROWD ROUND *see* **CROWD AROUND** →

CRUMBLE

CRUMBLE AWAY →

1 crumble away: to gradually break into small pieces and disappear ▶ *The castle walls were slowly crumbling away.*

2 crumble away: to gradually become weak and disappear, especially after being very strong ▶ *The Roman Empire crumbled away over a period of about two centuries.*

CRUSH

CRUSH UP →

crush up: if people crush up, they move very close to each other because there is not much space ▶ *We can fit everyone into my car if you don't mind crushing up.*

CRY

CRY OFF →

cry off, cry off sth: to decide not to do something that you have agreed or arranged to do ▶ *Josh cried off the trip to town, saying he had a headache.*

CRY OUT AGAINST →

cry out against sth: to complain or protest strongly about something ▶ *People have been crying out against the use of chemicals on farm crops for years.*

    outcry N when a lot of people complain or protest strongly about something. **+ against/over** ▶ *There was a public outcry over the decision to raise interest rates again.*

CRY OUT FOR →

be crying out for sth/sb: to need something or someone very urgently ▶ *Small businesses are crying out for skilled workers.* ▶ *Our criminal justice system is crying out for change.*

CUDDLE

CUDDLE UP →

cuddle up: to sit or lie very close to someone and put your arms around them ▶ *Why don't we just cuddle up on the sofa and watch TV?*

CULL

CULL FROM →

cull sth from sth: to choose or collect things from various different places ▶ *a collection of songs culled from five of the group's albums*

CULMINATE

CULMINATE IN →

culminate in sth: if a series of events culminates in something happening, it gradually leads towards it and ends with it ▶ *A series of clashes eventually culminated in a full-scale war.*

CURL

CURL UP →

1 curl up: to lie or sit with your legs and arms bent towards your stomach
▶ *"I like this music," said Rosie, curling up beside Hal on the sofa.* **be curled up** ▶ *Mum was curled up with a book in front of the fire.*

2 curl up: if something flat curls up, its edges start to become curved and point upwards ▶ *The photograph was starting to curl up at the edges.*

CURSE

CURSE OUT →

curse sb out: to shout at someone, saying rude words, because you are angry with them ▶ *He used to curse his workers out for the slightest thing.*

BE CURSED WITH →

be cursed with sth: to have a particular problem or disadvantage ▶ *Rowan was one of those people who seem to be cursed with bad luck.*

CUSS

CUSS OUT →

cuss sb **out, cuss out** sb: to shout at someone, saying rude words, because you are angry with them ▶ *I'm not going to tell you what happened if you keep cussing me out!*

CUT

CUT ACROSS →

1 cut across sth: to go across an area of land instead of going around it, because it is the shortest way ▶ *It only takes ten minutes to get to the village if you cut across the field.*

2 cut across sth: to affect or concern several different groups of people in the same way ▶ *The drug problem cuts across all social classes.*

CUT BACK →

cut back, cut back sth, **cut** sth **back**: to reduce the amount of money that you spend, or the amount of something that you use ▶ *During the recession a lot of businesses had to cut back.* ▶ *Since the children were born, we've had to really cut back our spending.*
   cutback N a reduction in something, especially the amount of money you spend ▶ *2,000 jobs will be lost because of civil service cutbacks.* **+ in** ▶ *a cutback in defence spending*

CUT DOWN →

1 cut down sth, **cut** sth **down, cut down**: to reduce the amount, number, or size of something ▶ *Could you try and cut down the amount of time you spend on the phone?* **+ on** ▶ *If you want to cut down on crime, we need to spend more on law enforcement.*

2 cut down: to eat, drink, or smoke less of something that is bad for you. **+ on** ▶ *You need to cut down on fatty foods if you want to lose weight.*

3 cut down sth, **cut** sth **down**: to remove a tree by cutting it near its base so that it falls to the ground ▶ *Several trees had to be cut down before the building work could start.*

4 cut down sb, **cut** sb **down**: to kill or seriously injure someone with a weapon, especially a gun ▶ *One of the protesters was cut down by a police bullet.*

CUT IN →

1 cut in: to interrupt someone by saying something ▶ *"Actually," Mark cut in, "that's not quite true."*

2 cut in: if a machine cuts in, it starts to operate when it is needed ▶ *The fan will automatically cut in if the engine gets too hot.*

3 cut in: to move in ahead of the people or cars in a queue, when it is not your turn ▶ *A blue sports car cut in right in front of me.*

CUT INTO →

1 cut into sth: to push a knife or a similar tool into something in order to make a cut in it ▶ *She took the knife and solemnly cut into the cake.*

2 cut into sth: to use up a lot of time, money, etc so that you have less of it available ▶ *Simon was working a 70 hour week, which obviously cut into his social life.*

3 cut into sth/sb: if something such as a rope cuts into someone's skin, it is so tight that it cuts the skin ▶ *The ropes began to cut into her flesh as she struggled to get free.*

CUT OFF →

1 cut off sth, **cut** sth **off**: to stop a supply of something from getting to a place ▸ *If there is an earthquake, the electrical supply will be cut off automatically.* ▸ *The president threatened to cut off economic aid to South Africa.*

2 be cut off: to very difficult to get to, for example because of being a long way from anywhere else ▸ *Some villages and farms were cut off by snow for two weeks.*

3 be cut off: to not be able to or allowed to communicate with other people. **+ from** ▸ *Prisoners were left alone for weeks, cut off from all contact.*

4 cut sb **off, cut off** sb: to stop communicating with someone or having a friendly relationship with them ▸ *June came from a religious Protestant family, who cut her off when she married a Catholic.*

5 cut off sb, **cut** sb **off**: to be unable to finish a telephone conversation because the connection is suddenly broken. ▸ *My money ran out and I was cut off.*

6 cut sb **off**: to suddenly drive in front of a moving car in a dangerous way ▸ *When a careless driver cuts you off, get his licence plate number.*

CUT OUT →

1 cut out sth, **cut** sth **out**: to stop eating, drinking, smoking etc something, especially in order to improve your health ▸ *I wish I'd cut out cigarettes years ago.*

2 cut it out! also *cut that out!*: used to tell someone to stop doing something because it is annoying you ▸ *"Cut it out!" Brady yelled as the other guys began throwing his books around the room.*

3 not be cut out for sth: to not have

the qualities that you need for a particular job or activity. **not be cut out to do** sth ▸ *Jim soon realized that he wasn't cut out to be a policeman.*

4 cut out sth, **cut** sth **out**: to remove part of a book, film, speech etc. **+ of** ▸ *A number of scenes had been cut out of the original movie.*

5 cut sb **out**: to stop someone from taking part in something, or from having a share of something. **+ of** ▸ *In a sudden temper, Joss cut me out of the deal.* **cut** sb **out of your will** (=legally say that they will not receive anything from you after you die) ▸ *The old man had threatened many times to cut her out of his will.*

6 cut out sth/sb, **cut** sth/sb **out**: to make part of a process unnecessary ▸ *Internet banking can cut out the need to visit your bank.* **cut out the middleman** (=deal directly with someone, so that you do not have to pay someone else to do it) ▸ *All our goods come straight from the factory, so we can cut out the middleman.*

7 cut out: if an engine or machine cuts out, it suddenly stops working ▸ *Finally the engine cut out altogether.*

8 cut out: to leave suddenly ▸ *Bob cut out right after the movie.*

CUT THROUGH →

1 cut through sth: to go through a place instead of going around it ▸ *It was still light, so we decided to cut through the forest.*

2 cut through sth: to find a way of dealing with something more quickly ▸ *Smith cut through a lot of bureaucracy to get the children out of the country quickly.*

3 cut through sth: if a road, path, or river cuts through an area, it passes through it ▸ *The road cuts through some fantastic scenery.*

C

CUT UP →
1 cut up sth,
cut sth **up**: to
cut something
into small
pieces ▶ *Dan
was in the
garden,
cutting wood
up for the fire.*

2 be cut up: to be very upset about
something that has happened.
+ about ▶ *When Frederick's father
died last year, he was really cut up
about it.*
3 cut up: if a class of students cuts
up, the students behave badly ▶ *By
3:00 on Friday, even the best class
cuts up.*

Dd

DABBLE

DABBLE IN →
dabble in sth: to get involved in something that interests you, but not in a very serious way ▶ *He became a wealthy man, bought a big house and dabbled in politics.*

DAM

DAM UP →
dam up sth, **dam** sth **up**: to stop the water from flowing away in a river, stream etc, especially by building a wall across it ▶ *The river has been dammed up to form a series of lakes.*

DAMP/DAMPEN

DAMP DOWN, *also* DAMPEN DOWN →
damp/dampen down sth, **damp/dampen** sth **down**: to try to prevent something from increasing further ▶ *Tax increases were a way of temporarily damping down consumer spending.*

DASH

DASH OFF →
1 dash off: to leave or go somewhere very quickly ▶ *He dashed off before I had a chance to thank him.*

2 dash off sth, **dash** sth **off**: to write or draw something very quickly ▶ *Lilly dashed off a note and left it on the table.*

DATE

DATE BACK →
date back: to have existed since a particular time in the past ▶ *a tradition which dates back well over a thousand years.* **+ to** ▶ *Parts of the castle date back to the fifteenth century.*

DAWN

DAWN ON, *also* DAWN UPON →
dawn on/upon sb: if something dawns on you, you begin to realize it ▶ *It suddenly dawned on Steve that she was talking to the headmistress herself.* ▶ *The size of the task in front of us was slowly dawning on me.*

DEAL

DEAL IN →
1 deal in sth: to buy and sell a particular type of thing ▶ *My father used to deal in stamps, medals and coins.* ▶ *Penalties for dealing in illegal drugs are strict.*

2 deal in sth: to have particular aims, methods, or interests ▶ *Kirov dealt in getting results and it didn't matter how he got them.*

3 deal sb **in**: to give someone cards so that they can play in a game ▶ *Shall I deal you in, Mick?*

4 deal me in: used to say that you want to be included in something ▶ *If you can find a way of making money from it, deal me in!*

DEAL OUT →
1 deal out sth, **deal** sth **out**: to give playing cards to each of the players in a game ▶ *The girl opposite Karl began dealing out the cards.*

D

2 deal out sth, **deal** sth **out**: to punish someone in a particular way ▶ *The punishments dealt out to the rioters were extremely harsh.*

DEAL WITH →

1 deal with sth: to take action to solve a problem or make sure that something is done properly ▶ *Who is dealing with the accommodation arrangements for the conference?* ▶ *We're still trying to deal with all the replies we had to our advertisement.*

2 deal with sth: to be about a particular subject ▶ *His books all deal with the events leading up to the war.*

3 deal with sb/sth: to do business with or discuss something important with someone ▶ *We've dealt with that particular company for many years.*

4 deal with sb: to meet or talk to someone as part of your work ▶ *As a lawyer, I deal with hundreds of people every year.*

5 deal with sth: to succeed in facing a difficult situation ▶ *Simon's still struggling to deal with his divorce.*

6 deal with sb: to punish someone in a particular way ▶ *Suspected terrorists are severely dealt with by the courts.*

DEBAR

DEBAR FROM →

debar sb **from**: to officially prevent someone from taking part in something ▶ *Terrorist groups were debarred from participation in the talks.*

DECIDE

DECIDE AGAINST →

decide against sth/sb: to decide not to do or choose something or someone ▶ *Many engineering students eventually decide against a career in engineering.* ▶ *The committee decided against me, and appointed a much younger man.*

DECIDE ON, *also* DECIDE UPON →

decide on/upon sth/sb: to choose something or someone after thinking about it ▶ *Have you decided on a date for your wedding yet?*

DECK

DECK OUT →

1 deck out sb, **deck** sb **out**: to put on special clothes for a particular occasion. **+ in** ▶ *Everyone was decked out in their best Sunday clothes.*

2 deck out sth, **deck** sth **out**: to decorate something with flags, flowers, bright colours etc. **+ with** ▶ *All the ships were decked out with flags and coloured lights.*

DECLARE

DECLARE AGAINST →

declare against sb/sth: to state publicly that you do not agree with or support someone or something ▶ *Austria and Russia were ready to take action, but Serbia declared against it.*

DEDICATE

DEDICATE TO →

1 dedicate sth **to** sb: to say that a book, film, song etc has been written or made in order to express love or respect for a particular person ▶ *This book is dedicated to my children, Jamie, Laurie and Jo.*

2 dedicate sth **to** sb: to give a building a particular person's name in order to show respect for them ▶ *The church is dedicated to St Nicholas and dates from 1125.*

3 dedicate yourself to (doing) sth *also* *dedicate your life to (doing)* sth: to give a lot of your time and effort to something or someone ▶ *When Rosie became ill, he dedicated himself to caring for her.*

4 be dedicated to sth: to be intended

for one particular purpose ▶ *The research centre is dedicated to space biology.*

DEFER

DEFER TO →
defer to sb/sth: to accept what someone else decides, even if you disagree with it ▶ *My father deferred to my mother on all the important matters.*

DEGENERATE

DEGENERATE INTO →
degenerate into sth: to become more and more confused, violent, unpleasant etc ▶ *The march quickly degenerated into violence.*

DELIGHT

DELIGHT IN →
delight in sth: to get a lot of pleasure from something, often something that other people disapprove of. **delight in doing** sth ▶ *He was an unpleasant boy who delighted in teasing younger children.*

DELIVER

DELIVER ON →
deliver on a promise/agreement etc: to do something that you promised or agreed to do ▶ *Ministers have failed to deliver on promises made at the last election.*

DELIVER UP, *also* DELIVER OVER →
deliver up/over sth/sb, **deliver** sth/sb **up/over**: to give something or someone to a person in authority ▶ *All relevant documents must be delivered up to the court.*

DELVE

DELVE INTO →
delve into sth: to try to find more detailed information about something ▶ *I spent some time delving into the history of the area.*

DEPART

DEPART FROM →
depart from sth: to do something in a way that is different from the usual or expected way ▶ *In the 1970s, a lot of schools departed from traditional educational practices.*

DEPEND

DEPEND ON, *also* DEPEND UPON →
1 depend on/upon sth/sb: to need something or someone's help in order to be able to do something ▶ *I bought a bike so I didn't have to depend on my car all the time.* **+ for** ▶ *Most of these birds depend upon insects for food.*
2 depend on/upon sth/sb: to be influenced or changed according to something else that happens ▶ *The park closes between 5 and 7 pm, depending on the time of year.* **it depends on** sth ▶ *I'm not sure what time we'll arrive. It depends on the traffic.*
3 can depend on sb/sth: to be able to trust someone and feel confident that they will help you or do what you want ▶ *You can depend on Jane – she's always ready to help.*

DEPRIVE

DEPRIVE OF →
deprive sb/sth **of** sth: to prevent someone or something from having something that they need or want ▶ *A lot of these children have been deprived of a normal home life.* ▶ *A large section of the population was deprived of the right to vote.*

DERIVE

DERIVE FROM →
1 derive sth **from** sth: to get satisfaction, pleasure, or an advantage from something ▶ *It's a demanding job, but he derives a lot of satisfaction from it.*

D

2 derive from *also* **be derived from**: to develop or come from something else ▶ *A lot of the words in English are derived from Latin.*

DESCEND

DESCEND FROM →

be descended from sb: to be related to someone who lived in the past ▶ *My mother claims she's descended from Abraham Lincoln.*

DESCEND INTO →

descend into sth: to gradually become more and more confused, violent, disorganized etc ▶ *There is a danger that the country will descend into further violence and poverty.*

DESCEND ON, *also* DESCEND UPON →

descend on/upon sb/sth: to visit a person or place, often without being invited ▶ *The whole family usually descends on me at Christmas.* ▶ *Thousands of football fans descended on the town.*

DESCEND TO →

descend to sth: to behave in an immoral, dishonest, or unacceptable way, when you do not usually behave like this ▶ *We were so hungry we even descended to taking animal feed from farm sheds.*

DESCEND UPON *see* DESCEND ON

DESPAIR

DESPAIR OF →

1 despair of sth: to feel that there is no hope that something will ever happen or improve ▶ *I really despair of public transport in this country!*
despair of doing sth ▶ *Months passed, and I began to despair of ever seeing her again.*

2 despair of sb: to feel that there is no hope that someone will ever be successful or do what you think they should do ▶ *"You're not even trying at*

school!" my father said. "I despair of you!"

DETRACT

DETRACT FROM →

detract from sth: to make something seem less good or valuable ▶ *The other team certainly played badly, but we shouldn't let that detract from our victory.*

DEVIATE

DEVIATE FROM →

deviate from sth: to do something differently from the way that was planned or the way in which it is usually done ▶ *The Chancellor did not deviate from the original text of his speech.*

DEVOLVE

DEVOLVE ON, *also* DEVOLVE UPON →

devolve sth **on/upon** sb, **devolve on/upon** sb: if power or responsibility devolves on a person, group, or organization, or you devolve it on them, it is given to them ▶ *With the collapse of central government, power devolved on the regional leaders.*

DEVOTE

DEVOTE TO →

1 devote sth **to** sth: to put a lot of time and work into something ▶ *He worked nights in order to have more time to devote to his music.* **devote yourself to (doing)** sth ▶ *For twenty years Sutchbury devoted himself to the Socialist cause.*

2 devote sth **to** sth: to give money, space, or attention to a particular activity or subject ▶ *Every US newspaper devotes a lot of space to weather forecasts.*

3 be devoted to sb/sth: to love someone a lot, and give a lot of your time to them ▶ *Mr Summerfield was* *described as a shy man, who was devoted to his family.*

DIAL

DIAL IN, *also* **DIAL INTO** →
dial in, dial into sth: to connect one computer to others by using a modem ▶ *People working at home can dial in over a modem, and get access to their files.*

dial-in ADJ a dial-in service, system etc connects one computer to others by using a modem ▶ *Comcast plans to set up a dial-in service.*

DIAL OUT →
dial out: to phone someone who is not in the same building as you ▶ *If you want to dial out, press nine and then dial the number.*

DIDDLE

DIDDLE AROUND →
diddle around: to waste time and not try hard to succeed ▶ *Samuel mostly diddled around in college, getting by with the lowest pass grades.*

DIDDLE WITH →
1 diddle with sth: to play with something by making small movements with your hands ▶ *Ruth was sitting in an easy chair, diddling with a small flag.*

2 diddle with sth: to make small changes to something which are intended to improve it but do not ▶ *The President and Congress keep diddling with the national debt.*

DIE

DIE AWAY →
die away: to gradually become weaker and then stop ▶ *The sound of footsteps eventually died away.*

DIE BACK →
die back: if a plant dies back, its leaves and flowers die, but its roots are still alive ▶ *Cold weather causes the plants to die back, but they will usually return in the spring.*

DIE DOWN →
die down: if something such as noise, excitement, or fighting dies down, it gradually gets less until it stops completely ▶ *Forester looked around the room, waiting for the laughter to die down.*

BE DYING FOR →
be dying for sth: to want or need something very much ▶ *I'm dying for a cup of tea.*

DIE OFF →
die off: if a group of people or animals die off, they die over a period of time until none of them are left ▶ *Most of the older generation had died off, and the young people had moved to the towns.*

DIE OUT →
1 die out: to gradually decrease in numbers and then stop existing ▶ *Many wild plants and animals are in danger of dying out.*

2 die out: if a custom, tradition, or skill dies out, people stop doing it or using it ▶ *During this century, a lot of the old country crafts have died out.*

DIG

DIG IN →
1 dig your heels in also **dig in your heels:** to refuse to do something in spite of other people's efforts to persuade you ▶ *When we tried to argue about the price, he dug his heels in.*

2 dig in: if soldiers dig in, they dig deep holes that they can go into for protection ▶ *The German army was dug in along a ten-mile front.*

3 dig in sth, **dig** sth **in:** to push something sharp into a surface or into part of someone's body ▶ *She reached for his hand and dug in her long nails.*

4 dig in!: used to tell people to start eating their food ▶ *Dig in! There's plenty for everyone.*

DIG INTO →

1 dig into sth: to put your hand into something such as a pocket or bag in order to try to find something ▶ *Mrs Bennet dug into her purse and handed the girl a few coins.*

2 dig into sth: to use part of a supply of something, especially money, that you had intended to keep ▶ *We've had to dig into our savings to pay off the debt.*

3 dig into sth: to try to find out more information about something ▶ *As detectives dug deeper into her secret life, they discovered some surprising facts.*

4 dig into sth, **dig** sth **into** sth: to press or be pressed painfully against part of someone's body ▶ *The straps of my rucksack were digging into my shoulder.*

5 dig into sth: to start eating food ▶ *He sat down at the table and dug into a plate of steaming pasta.*

DIG OUT →

1 dig out sth, **dig** sth **out**: to search for and find something that you have not seen for a long time ▶ *Dig out your old dancing shoes and join in the fun.*

2 dig out sth, **dig** sth **out**: to look for and find information, especially information that is difficult to find ▶ *I took the opportunity to dig out a few facts and figures about the island.*

DIG OUT OF →

dig sth **out of trouble** also **dig** sth **out of a mess etc**: to succeed in helping an organization, country etc which is failing or in a bad situation ▶ *They decided that he was just the right man to dig the company out of trouble.*

DIG OVER →

dig over sth, **dig** sth **over**: to dig a piece of ground and break up the soil, before planting things in it ▶ *Dig over the flowerbeds and remove any weeds.*

DIG UP →

1 dig up sth, **dig** sth **up**: to dig holes in the ground ▶ *Can you believe it – they're digging up the road again!*

2 dig up sth, **dig** sth **up**: to dig and remove something from the ground ▶ *Ancient Roman treasure has been dug up in a field in Suffolk.*

3 dig up sth, **dig** sth **up**: to discover hidden or forgotten information by searching carefully

▶ *When you become famous, the press dig up everything they can about your past.* **dig up (the) dirt on** sb (=try to discover something bad or illegal that someone has done in the past) ▶ *They searched through confidential files to dig up dirt on the new candidate.*

4 dig up sth, **dig** sth **up**: to search for and find something that you have not seen for a long time ▶ *I know I've got the book somewhere at home – I'll see if I can dig it up for you*

DIN

DIN INTO →

din sth **into** sb: to make someone learn or believe something by repeating it to them many times ▶ *Respect for our elders was dinned into us at school.*

DINE

DINE OFF, also DINE ON →

dine off/on sth: to eat a particular kind of food for dinner, especially expensive food ▶ *We dined on lobster and strawberries at the Ritz Hotel.*

DINE OUT →

dine out: to eat dinner in a restaurant ▶ *Dine out in style in this grand Victorian mansion.*

DINE OUT ON →

dine out on sth: to often tell a story about something special that happened to you, in order to impress people ▶ *Bessie once met the Dalai Lama and has dined out on it ever since.*

DINK

DINK AROUND →

dink around: to waste time, especially by doing small, unimportant jobs slowly ▶ *Quit dinking around and get to work!*

DIP

DIP INTO →

1 dip into sth: to use part of an amount of money that you had intended to keep ▶ *She's had to dip into her savings to pay the medical bills.*

2 dip into sth: to read short parts of a book, magazine etc, without reading the whole thing ▶ *It's the kind of book you can dip into now and again.*

DISABUSE

DISABUSE OF →

disabuse sb **of** sth: to persuade someone that something they believe is untrue ▶ *My tutor soon disabused me of the idea that I could make it as a writer.*

DISAGREE

DISAGREE WITH →

disagree with sb: if something, especially a type of food, disagrees with you, it makes you feel ill ▶ *I never eat seafood – it disagrees with me.*

DISAPPROVE

DISAPPROVE OF →

disapprove of sth/sb: to think that something or someone is bad, wrong, or unsuitable ▶ *Sophie's parents disapproved of her new boyfriend.*

DISASSOCIATE *see* DISSOCIATE

DISH

DISH OUT →

1 dish out sth, **dish** sth **out**: to give something to each person in a group ▶ *They want me to dish out presents at the kids' Christmas party.*

2 dish out sth, **dish** sth **out**: to serve food to people by putting it onto their plates ▶ *Jo, would you dish out the ice cream?*

3 dish out sth, **dish** sth **out**: to give people advice or criticism without thinking about it carefully enough ▶ *These lawyers make a fortune dishing out expensive advice to clients.*

DISH UP →

1 dish up sth, **dish** sth **up**, **dish up**: to put food onto plates so that it is ready to eat ▶ *Can you dish up the vegetables? They're on the sideboard.*

2 dish up sth, **dish** sth **up**: to produce something for someone without much care of effort ▶ *Throughout the summer, TV channels have been dishing up a diet of old movies.*

DISPENSE

DISPENSE WITH →

dispense with sth/sb: to stop using

D

something or someone that you would normally use, especially because you no longer need them ▶ *Some companies have dispensed with middle managers altogether.*

DISPOSE

DISPOSE OF →

1 dispose of sth: to get rid of something, especially something that is difficult to get rid of ▶ *He had disposed of his victim's body by burying it in the woods.*

2 dispose of sth: to sell something that is worth a lot of money ▶ *The government wanted to dispose of its shares in the state rail network.*

3 dispose of sb: to defeat an opponent ▶ *Having disposed of Rovers, United went on to beat Rangers in the final.*

4 dispose of sb: to kill someone or arrange for them to be killed ▶ *The secret police disposed of all anti-government agitators.*

DISSOCIATE

DISSOCIATE FROM →

dissociate yourself from sb/sth: to show that you do not agree with or approve of someone, so that you avoid being criticized for something they do ▶ *The organisers of the protest were quick to dissociate themselves from the violence that followed.*

DISSOLVE

DISSOLVE INTO →

dissolve into tears/laughter: to lose control of yourself and start to cry or laugh ▶ *She suddenly dissolved into floods of tears.*

DISTANCE

DISTANCE YOURSELF FROM →

distance yourself from sb/sth: to say that you are not involved with

someone or something ▶ *The Prime Minister was careful to distance himself from the MP's outspoken remarks.*

DIVE

DIVE IN →

dive in: to start doing something very eagerly ▶ *Think carefully about what sort of computer you want, before diving in and buying one.*

DIVE INTO →

1 dive into sth: to start doing an activity very eagerly ▶ *Williams dived into the election campaign with tremendous enthusiasm.*

2 dive into sth: to go into a place very quickly and suddenly ▶ *I dived into the nearest shop when I saw him approach.*

DIVEST

DIVEST OF →

1 divest yourself of sth: to get rid of something that you own ▶ *The Corporation has already divested itself of properties worth over £3 million.*

2 divest sb **of** sth: to take away someone's power, wealth, or rights ▶ *On 8 March 1198, the Cologne assembly divested King Philip of his title.*

DIVIDE

DIVIDE BY →

divide sth **by** sth: to calculate how many times a smaller number fits into a larger one ▶ *Divide 21 by 3.*

DIVIDE OFF →

divide off sth, **divide** sth **off**: to separate part of a room or area from the rest of it ▶ *A wooden fence divides off the western side of the garden.*

DIVIDE UP →

1 divide up sth, **divide** sth **up**, **divide up**: to separate something,  or become separated, into smaller parts or groups ▶ *Divide up the time you spend on each question equally.* **+ into** ▶ *The frog's egg divides up into two separate cells.*

2 divide up sth, **divide** sth **up**: to separate something into parts and share them between two or more people. **+ between/ among** ▶ *The money is to be divided up equally between her two sons.*

DIVORCE

DIVORCE FROM →

1 be divorced from sth: to be completely separated from something ▶ *With our air-conditioned lifestyles, we have become completely divorced from the natural world.*

2 divorce sth **from** sth: to separate two ideas, subjects, or things completely ▶ *Gandhi asserted that it was impossible to divorce morality from religion.*

DIVVY

DIVVY UP →

divvy up sth, **divvy** sth **up**: to divide something and share it among two or more people or groups ▶ *When we've finished collecting, we'll divvy up the profits between us.*

DO

DO ABOUT →

do sth **about** sth: to do something in order to solve a problem or improve a bad situation ▶ *I really don't know*

what to do about my weight – it just keeps going up and up. **do something/nothing etc about** sth ▶ *It's time they did something about the traffic in London.*

DO AWAY WITH →

1 do away with sth: to get rid of something or stop using something ▶ *The government has done away with free eyes tests for everyone.*

2 do away with sb: to murder someone ▶ *My father joked that perhaps Ben's wife had done away with him.*

DO DOWN →

do sb **down**: to criticize someone unfairly. **do yourself down** (=criticize yourself because you lack confidence) ▶ *Don't do yourself down! You look lovely.*

DO FOR →

be done for: to be in serious trouble ▶ *If we get caught, we're done for.*

DO IN →

1 do sb **in**: to make someone extremely tired ▶ *All that running around has completely done me in.* **be done in** ▶ *I'm going to bed – I'm done in.*

2 do sb **in**: to murder someone or attack them so that they are badly hurt ▶ *I reckon her husband did her in.*

DO OUT →

do out sth, **do** sth **out**: to make a room look nice by decorating it ▶ *The kitchen's been done out really nicely.*

DO OUT OF →

do sb **out of** sth: to cheat someone by not giving them money that they are owed ▶ *The way I see it, they've done me out of three weeks' wages.*

DO OVER →

1 be done over: if someone's house is done over, thieves get into it and steal things from it ▶ *Did you know Mark's flat has been done over again?*

D

D

2 do sb over: to attack and injure someone ▶ *If you don't pay up, he'll send his mates round to do you over.*

3 do over sth, do sth over: to decorate a room or house to make it more attractive ▶ *We really should do the bathroom over – it's looking very shabby.*

DO UP →

1 do up sth, do sth up: to fasten clothes, shoes etc ▶ *"I'm cold." "Well why don't you do up your coat?"*

2 do up sth, do sth up: to repair or decorate an old car or building ▶ *They bought an old house which they're doing up themselves.*

3 do yourself up: to put on nice clothes, and make yourself look attractive ▶ *Sue spent hours doing herself up for her date.*

DO WITH →

1 have something to do with sth *also* **be something to do with** sth: to be connected with something in some way ▶ *I don't know much about his job, but I think it's something to do with banking.* ▶ *I know she's been married before, but what's that got to do with it?*

2 it's got nothing to do with you *also* **what's it got to do with you?**: used to tell someone that they should not ask about something because it is private ▶ *Yes, I have a boyfriend – but what's it got to do with you?*

3 could do with sb/ sth: to need or want someone or something ▶ *I could do with a drink.* ▶ *I could have done with some help this morning.*

4 what do you do with yourself?: used to ask someone what they spend their time doing ▶ *What are you going to do with yourself this weekend?*

5 what has sb **done with** sth?: used to ask where someone has put

something ▶ *What have you done with the paper?*

6 what is sb **doing with** sth?: used to ask why someone has something when it does not belong to them ▶ *What are you doing with my diary?*

7 what shall we do with sth/ sb?: used to ask what arrangements should be made for something or someone ▶ *What shall we do with the kids while you're working?*

DO WITHOUT →

1 do without, do without sb/ sth: to manage without someone or something ▶ *I can't afford a car, so I guess I'll just have to do without.*

2 I can/ could do without sth: used to say that something is annoying you or is causing problems for you ▶ *I could do without all this hassle at the moment.*

DOLE

DOLE OUT →

dole out sth, **dole** sth **out**: to give someone something, especially large amounts of money ▶ *The federal government doles out $58 billion in student grants every year.*

DOLL

DOLL UP →

doll yourself up: to put on nice clothes and make yourself look attractive ▶ *The girls were in the bathroom, dolling themselves up.*

DOOM

DOOM TO →

be doomed to failure/ disaster etc: to be certain to fail, be destroyed etc ▶ *Many marriages are doomed to failure from the start.*

DOPE

BE DOPED UP →

be doped up: to be under the

influence of drugs ▶ *He was so doped up he didn't even know what day it was.*

DOSE

DOSE UP →

dose sb **up**: to give someone a lot of medicine to make them sleep or feel better. **+ with** ▶ *The nurse dosed him up with aspirin and sent him to bed.*

DOSS

DOSS ABOUT, *also* DOSS AROUND →

doss about/around: to spend your time relaxing and doing nothing ▶ *We just dossed around all day on Saturday.*

DOSS DOWN →

doss down: to sleep somewhere such as the floor because there is no bed available ▶ *Harry has been dossing down on a friend's floor for the past two weeks.*

DOT

BE DOTTED ABOUT, *also* BE DOTTED AROUND →

be dotted about/around: if things are dotted around an area, they are in different parts of it ▶ *Aside from a few houses dotted about the hillside, the area was deserted.*

DOT WITH →

1 be dotted with sth: to have several things in different parts of an area ▶ *Pike Street is dotted with cozy cafes and unique shops.*

2 dot sth **with** sth: to put a small amount of something in several places on a surface ▶ *Dot the vegetables with butter and add salt.*

DOTE

DOTE ON, *also* DOTE UPON →

dote on/upon sb: to love someone very much ▶ *Leonard Stein was a hard-*

working man who doted on his wife and children.

DOUBLE

DOUBLE AS →

double as sth: to have a second use, job, or purpose ▶ *The living room doubles as a guest bedroom.* ▶ *Many years ago, the old church also doubled as the town hall.*

DOUBLE BACK →

double back: to turn around and go back in the direction you have just come from ▶ *The driver doubled back and headed for Howard Bay.*

DOUBLE OVER →

double over: to suddenly bend your body forward, for example because you are in a lot of pain or laughing a lot ▶ *Nathan doubled over in pain and was rushed to the hospital.*

DOUBLE UP →

1 double up: to suddenly bend your body forward, for example because you are in a lot of pain or laughing a lot ▶ *Emilio doubled up, clutching his stomach.*

2 double up: to share something with another person ▶ *I don't have enough books for everyone, so some of you may have to double up.* **+ with** ▶ *Sean has to double up with Janey whenever we need to use his bedroom for guests.*

DOUBLE UP AS →

double up as sth: to have a second use, job, or purpose ▶ *Can this sofa double up as a bed?*

DOVETAIL

DOVETAIL WITH →

dovetail with sth, **dovetail** sth **with** sth: to fit together or be able to be done together easily ▶ *Her working hours dovetailed perfectly with her family responsibilities.*

D

DOZE

DOZE OFF →
doze off: to fall asleep, usually for a short time, when you did not intend to ► *I'm sorry, I must have dozed off for a minute.*

DRAFT

DRAFT IN →
be drafted in: to be asked or ordered to work in a place where you do not normally work ► *Extra staff were drafted in to deal with the Christmas rush.*

DRAG

DRAG AWAY →
drag sb away: to make someone stop doing something that they are extremely interested in ► *Nothing can drag Jim away from his sports programmes on TV.*

DRAG DOWN →
1 drag sb down, drag down sb: to make someone feel unhappy, weak and tired ► *All the stress at work is really dragging her down.*

2 drag sth down, drag down sth: to make the price, level, or quality of something go down ► *The threat of job cuts is dragging down workers' performance.*

3 drag down sb/sth, drag sb/sth down: to put someone or something else in the same bad situation that you are in ► *A recession in Germany could drag down the rest of Europe.*

4 drag sb down, drag down sb: to make another person start behaving as badly as you behave ► *I'm afraid some of the kids at school are dragging our daughter down.*

DRAG IN, *also* **DRAG INTO** →
1 drag sb into sth, drag sb in, drag in sb: to get someone involved in a situation that they do not want to be involved in ► *Western leaders fear that other countries will be dragged into the war.*

2 drag sb/sth in, drag sb/sth into sth: to mention someone or something in a discussion or argument, even though they are not connected with the situation ► *Don't drag my past into this – it has nothing to do with it.*

DRAG OFF →
drag sb off: to take someone away somewhere, using force. **+ to** ► *The protestors were dragged off to the nearest police station.*

DRAG ON →
drag on: to continue for far too long ► *An expensive court battle could drag on for years.*

DRAG OUT →
1 drag out sth, drag sth out, drag out: to last longer than is usual or necessary, or to make someone do this ► *Neither of them wanted to drag out the divorce for longer than they had to.*

2 drag sth out: if you drag information out of someone, you make them tell it to you, even though they do not want to. **+ of** ► *Police finally dragged a confession out of him.*

DRAG UP →
drag sb/sth up: to mention someone or something unpleasant or embarrassing that happened in the past ► *We all know she had a breakdown. There's no need to drag it up again.*

DRAIN

DRAIN OFF →
drain off sth, drain sth off: to remove the liquid from something by letting it

flow away ▶ *After cooking the meat, drain off the excess fat from the pan.*

DRAW

DRAW BACK →

draw back: to move backwards from something, especially because you are nervous or shocked ▶ *Dexter drew back in horror when he saw the body.*

DRAW IN →

1 the days draw in *also* **the nights draw in**: if the days or nights are drawing in, it gets dark earlier in the evening ▶ *In October the nights start drawing in.*

2 draw in a breath: to breathe in very deeply ▶ *He drew in a sharp breath as he saw the gun, and tried to remain calm.*

DRAW IN, *also* **DRAW INTO →**

1 draw sb in, draw sb into sth: to involve someone in a situation that they do not want to be involved in ▶ *As his roommates continued to argue, Yuri found himself being drawn in.*

2 draw sb in, draw sb into sth: to make someone notice or become interested in something ▶ *Your eye is drawn into the picture by the figure in the foreground.*

3 draw in, draw into sth: if a train draws in, it arrives at a station and stops ▶ *The train drew into the station five minutes late.*

DRAW OFF →

draw off sth, **draw** sth **off**: to remove liquid from somewhere, especially by using a pipe or a tube ▶ *Farmers draw off water from the river and use it for their crops.*

DRAW ON →

draw on: if a period of time draws on, it passes slowly or comes towards its end ▶ *Night drew on, and still there was no sign of Warren.*

DRAW ON, *also* **DRAW UPON →**

1 draw on/upon sth: to use part of a supply of something, especially money you have saved ▶ *The state drew on emergency funds to help victims of the tornado.*

2 draw on/upon sth: to use knowledge, information, or your personal experiences to help you do something ▶ *Writers often draw on their own experience to create stories and characters.*

DRAW OUT →

1 draw sb **out**: to make a shy or nervous person feel more comfortable and willing to talk ▶ *Margaret had a way of drawing me out, even in a big crowd of people.*

2 draw out: if the days draw out, it stays light until later in the evening ▶ *The summer days drew out, and life took on a slower pace.*

DRAW UP →

1 draw up sth, **draw** sth **up**: to prepare a contract, agreement, list, or plan ▶ *I'll have my lawyer draw up a contract for you to look over.* ▶ *We drew up a list of everyone we thought might be willing to help.*

2 draw up: if a vehicle draws up, it arrives somewhere and stops ▶ *A man in a hatchback drew up beside her.*

3 draw up a chair: to bring a chair closer to something or someone so that you can sit near them ▶ *Miller shyly drew up a chair and joined the men at the poker table.*

4 draw yourself up (to your full height): to stand up very straight, especially in a way that shows you are annoyed or determined ▶ *Polly drew herself up to her full height and said "This is outrageous!"*

DRAW UPON *see* **DRAW ON**

DREAM

DREAM OF →

sb **wouldn't dream of (doing)** sth: used to say that someone would never do something because they think it is wrong or stupid ▸ *Stan wouldn't dream of asking his parents for money.* ▸ *You know I didn't mean to hurt you – I wouldn't dream of it.*

DREAM ON →

dream on!: used to say that you think that what someone is hoping for will not happen ▸ *So you think you're going to win the lottery? Dream on, honey!*

DREAM UP →

dream up sth, **dream** sth **up**: to think of a plan or idea, especially one that seems unusual or silly ▸ *Whoever dreamed up this idea should have their head examined.*

DREDGE

DREDGE UP →

1 dredge up sth, **dredge** sth **up**: to talk about something that happened a long time ago, especially something embarrassing or annoying ▸ *The newspapers are always dredging up stories about what movie stars did before they became famous.*

2 dredge up sth, **dredge** sth **up**: to remember something with great difficulty ▸ *Robertson tried to dredge up an image of her in his mind.*

3 dredge up sth, **dredge** sth **up**: to make yourself feel something, such as interest or sympathy, when this is not easy ▸ *Vologsky managed to dredge up some sympathy for the old man.*

DRESS

DRESS DOWN →

dress down: to wear clothes that are more informal than you usually wear ▸ *Employees are allowed to dress down on Fridays.*

DRESS UP →

1 dress up: to put on formal clothes or your best clothes ▸ *Do you have to dress up for work?* **get dressed up** ▸ *I love to get dressed up and go out to a concert or the theatre.*

2 dress up, dress up sb, **dress** sb **up**: to put on special clothes for fun, especially so that you look like someone else. **+ in** ▸ *Little girls often like dressing up in grown-ups' clothes.* **+ as** ▸ *At Christmas, my mother used to dress me up as an elf.*

3 dress up sth, **dress** sth **up**: to make something sound more interesting, attractive, or acceptable than it really is ▸ *The government has tried to dress up its policies and make them sound more environmentally friendly.*

DRIFT

DRIFT APART →

drift apart: if people drift apart, their relationship gradually ends ▸ *As we grew older, we started to drift apart.*

DRIFT OFF →

1 drift off: to gradually fall asleep ▸ *It was 2 am when I finally drifted off to sleep.*

2 drift off: to walk slowly to another place or area ▸ *We drifted off down the road, not in any hurry to return to work.*

3 drift off: to stop listening or paying

attention to someone or something ▶ *I tried to concentrate on what he was saying, but I kept drifting off.*

DRILL

DRILL INTO →

drill sth **into** sb: to tell someone something again and again until they know it very well ▶ *My parents have drilled the importance of education into me since I was a small child.*

DRINK

DRINK IN →

drink in sth, **drink** sth **in**: if you drink in something that you see, read, or hear, you give it all your attention and enjoy it very much ▶ *Don't rush through Paris – take time to drink everything in.*

DRINK TO →

1 drink to sb/ sth: to wish someone or something success, good luck, or good health by holding up your glass before drinking ▶ *Let's drink to the New Year!* ▶ *Guests drank to the bride and groom.*

2 I'll drink to that!: used to say that you like or agree with what someone has said ▶ *"If things don't change soon, I'm going to quit my job." "I'll drink to that!"*

DRINK UP →

drink up sth, **drink** sth **up**, **drink up**: to drink all of something ▶ *Drink up – the bar will be closing soon.*

DRIP

DRIP WITH →

1 be dripping with blood/ sweat etc: to be covered with so much blood, sweat etc that it is falling off your body ▶ *I tried to move but I couldn't – my right arm was dripping with blood.*

2 be dripping with sth: to have a lot of a particular quality ▶ *"How fascinating," she said, her voice dripping with sarcasm.* **be dripping**

with money (=be very rich) ▶ *They were absolutely dripping with money.*

DRIVE

DRIVE AT →

what sb **is driving at:** what someone is really trying to say, when they are not saying it directly ▶ *"Morton, what are you driving at?" "I think we're in trouble, Mahoney, big trouble."*

DRIVE AWAY →

1 drive away sb, **drive** sb **away:** to behave in a way that makes someone leave you ▶ *His heavy drinking eventually drove Beth away.*

2 drive sb **away, drive** sb **away:** to make people stop coming to a place ▶ *Reports about drug-related crime in the area are driving tourists away.*

3 drive away sth, **drive** sth **away:** to make someone stop feeling or thinking something, especially something negative ▶ *The look in the little girl's eyes drove away all his doubts. "OK, I'll help you," he said.*

DRIVE DOWN →

drive down sth, **drive** sth **down:** to force prices or costs to a lower level ▶ *Cheap imported steel would drive down the price of steel in the US.*

DRIVE OFF →

1 drive off: to leave in a car ▶ *She drove off into the night.*

2 drive off sb, **drive** sb **off:** to force someone who is attacking or threatening you to stop and go away ▶ *They keep dogs in the yard to drive off intruders.*

DRIVE ON →
drive on: to continue travelling in a vehicle, without stopping or after stopping for a short time ▶ *Maxwell drove on, in spite of the thickening fog.*

DRIVE OUT →
drive out sb/sth, **drive** sb/sth **out**: to force someone or something to leave a place. **+ of** ▶ *Huge rent increases are driving many small businesses out of the area.*

DRIVE UP →
drive up sth, **drive** sth **up**: to force prices or costs to increase very quickly ▶ *Wealthy city people looking for second homes are driving up house prices in country areas.*

DRONE

DRONE ON →
drone on: to speak for a long time in a very boring way. **+ about** ▶ *She droned on and on about how sad her life was.*

DROOL

DROOL OVER →
drool over sb/sth: to look at someone or something in an excited and often silly way that shows you think they are very attractive ▶ *The girls lay on the beach, drooling over a couple of young men playing volleyball.*

DROP

DROP AWAY →
drop away: if land drops away, it slopes down very steeply ▶ *To her left, the ground dropped away to the river below.*

DROP BACK →
drop back: to let other people go ahead of you so that you are in a position nearer the back of a group ▶ *Jones was in the lead, but now he's dropped back to fourth place.*

DROP BEHIND →
drop behind: to move more slowly than the other person or people you are with, so that they move ahead of you ▶ *Gareth walked much too fast for her, and got annoyed whenever she dropped behind.*

DROP BY →
drop by: to make a short informal visit to someone you know well ▶ *If you're in the area again just drop by and say hello.*

DROP IN, *also* DROP INTO →
1 drop in, **drop into** sth: to make a short visit to someone or go into an office, shop, bar etc for a short time. **drop in on** sb ▶ *I think I'll drop in on Jill on my way home.* **+ at** ▶ *For more information, call this number or drop in at your local welfare office.*

> **drop-in centre** N a place where people can go to get advice and information, without having to make an arrangement before ▶ *a drop-in centre for the unemployed*

2 drop in sth, **drop** sth **in**, **drop** sth **into** sth: to deliver something to a person or place ▶ *I'll drop it into the office while I'm in town.*

3 drop sb **in it**: to cause trouble for someone, especially by saying something that makes someone else angry with them ▶ *I'm sorry if I dropped you in it, but she asked me why you weren't here.*

DROP OFF →
1 drop off sb/sth, **drop** sb/sth **off**: to take someone or something to a place by car ▶ *I'm going past the station. I can drop you off if you like.*

2 drop off: to begin to sleep ▶ *A third of all drivers said they had been in danger of dropping off while driving.*

3 drop off: if the amount or number of something drops off, it becomes less ▶ *The movie attracted large audiences* *at first, but then the numbers rapidly dropped off.*

DROP OUT →

1 drop out: to leave school, college, or university before you have finished your course ▶ *Too many students are getting into drugs and dropping out.*

    drop-out N someone who leaves school, college, or university without finishing their course ▶ *a high school drop-out*

2 drop out: to refuse to take part in ordinary society, especially by not getting a job ▶ *In the 60s my mother dropped out, and went to live in a commune.*

    drop-out N someone who refuses to take part in ordinary society because they do not agree with its social customs, moral standards etc ▶ *the place was full of hippies and drop-outs*

3 drop out: to not take part in an activity, or to leave it before it has finished ▶ *The next meeting is just before Christmas, so we're expecting a lot of people to drop out.*

DROP ROUND →

1 drop round: to make a short informal visit to someone who lives near you ▶ *Her grandchildren drop round and see her from time to time.*

2 drop sth round: to deliver something to someone who lives near you ▶ *I've got a present for you – I'll try and drop it round this weekend.*

DROWN

DROWN IN →

be drowning in sth: to have more of something than you can deal with ▶ *I'm drowning in work at the moment. Can I call you back next week?*

DROWN IN, *also* **DROWN WITH** →

drown sth **in/with** sth: to cover a dish with too much of another liquid food

▶ *The fish was drowned in a bland, lumpy sauce.*

DROWN OUT →

drown out sth, **drown** sth **out**: if one noise drowns out another noise, it stops that noise from being heard ▶ *John started to speak, but his voice was drowned out by the traffic.*

DROWN WITH *see* **DROWN IN**

DRUG

BE DRUGGED UP →

be drugged up: to have been given a lot of drugs by a doctor, or have taken a lot of drugs ▶ *He was still drugged up after the operation.* **be drugged up to the eyeballs** (=given a lot of drugs) ▶ *It's no fun lying in a hospital bed, drugged up to the eyeballs.*

DRUM

DRUM INTO →

drum sth **into** sb: to tell someone something and repeat it many times, so that they will understand how important it is ▶ *Our coach drummed into us the importance of working together as a team.*

DRUM OUT OF →

drum sb **out of** sth: to force someone to leave an organization because they have done something wrong ▶ *Jack was caught stealing and was drummed out of the army.*

DRUM UP →

drum up sth: to get people's support for something, or increase their interest in something ▶ *She was in town last week, trying to drum up support for her camapign.*

DRY

DRY OFF →

dry off, dry off sth, **dry** sth **off**: to become dry or make something dry ▶ *We left our wet clothes to dry off in the sun.*

DRY OUT →

1 dry out, dry out sth, **dry** sth **out**: to become or to make something completely dry on the inside and the outside ► *Put your coat near the fire or it won't dry out properly.*

2 dry out: to stop drinking alcohol after you have regularly been drinking far too much ► *a well-known TV actor who spent eight weeks in a clinic, trying to dry out*

DRY UP →

1 dry up: if a river or lake dries up, the water in it disappears ► *Most of the rivers in the area have dried up in the drought.*

> **dried-up** ADJ a dried-up river or lake is one that no longer has any water in it ► *We walked along the dried-up river bed.*

2 dry up, dry up sth, **dry** sth **up**: if something dries up, or something dries it up, it loses the liquid that was in it ► *Have you got a pen I can borrow? This one's dried up.*

3 dry up: if a supply of something dries up, it comes to an end and there is no more available ► *Work on the tunnel stopped when the money dried up.*

4 dry up, dry up sth, **dry** sth **up**: to dry plates, cups, dishes etc with a cloth after they have been washed ► *Would you mind drying up the breakfast things?*

5 dry up: to forget or not be able to think of what you should say next, especially when you are speaking in public ► *I was terrified that I would forget all my lines and dry up.*

DUCK

DUCK OUT →

duck out: to avoid doing something that you should do or have promised to do. **+ of** ► *Parents who do not* discipline their children are ducking out of their responsibilities. ► *I've got a meeting at three o'clock but I'll try to duck out of it.*

DUKE

DUKE OUT →

duke it out: if two people or two groups duke it out, they fight or compete against each other.
+ with ► *She rolled up her sleeves as if getting ready to duke it out with him.*

DUMB

DUMB DOWN →

dumb down sth, **dumb** sth **down**: to produce television programmes, educational courses etc that avoid serious or difficult subjects or make them too simple ► *TV news has already been dumbed down to the point where it is almost pure entertainment.*

> **dumbing-down** N when things are dumbed down. **+ of** ► *There's too much dumbing-down of serious issues.*

> **dumbed-down** ADJ made too simple, and avoiding the need for serious thinking ► *Hollywood has produced a series of dumbed-down versions of literary classics.*

DUMP

DUMP ON →

1 dump sth **on** sb, **dump on** sb: to give someone work to do or a problem to deal with when you should deal with it yourself ► *I'm fed up with listening to your problems – why don't you go and dump on someone else?* ► *My boss is always dumping all the boring jobs on me.*

2 dump on sb: to criticize someone strongly and often unfairly ► *If you dump on your employees, don't expect morale to be high.*

DUST

DUST DOWN, *also* **DUST OFF** →

1 dust down/ off sth, **dust** sth **down/ off**: to remove dirt or dust from something, using your hands, a brush etc ▶ *He got up off the ground and dusted down his trousers.* **dust yourself down/ off** ▶ *She got to her feet and dusted herself off.*

2 dust yourself down: to make an effort to deal with a difficult experience and continue with your life ▶ *It was a painful divorce, but the only option was to dust myself down and get things back to normal.*

DWELL

DWELL ON, *also* **DWELL UPON** →

dwell on/upon sth: to think or talk for too long about something bad that has happened ▶ *It doesn't do any good to dwell on the past – try to be more positive.*

DWINDLE

DWINDLE AWAY →

dwindle away: to gradually become smaller and smaller, weaker and weaker etc ▶ *Maria looked at Fran lying in the hospital bed, her hope dwindling away.* **+ to** ▶ *Their business had collapsed and their savings had dwindled away to nothing.*

D

Ee

EASE

EASE OFF, *also* **EASE UP** →

1 ease off/up: to gradually become less painful, difficult, or unpleasant ▶ *I think the rain is beginning to ease off.* ▶ *The pain in my shoulder was easing up a little.*

2 ease off/up: to treat someone less severely or criticize them less than before. **+ on** ▶ *Ease off on Roger, will you – he's doing all right.*

3 ease off/up: to work less hard or do something with less energy than before ▶ *Dan should ease up or he'll have a nervous breakdown.*

EASE OUT →

ease out sb, **ease** sb **out:** to gradually force someone to leave their job or position of authority. **+ of** ▶ *He was eased out of his job as presidential adviser after fierce criticism from the press.*

EASE UP *See* **EASE OFF**

EAT

EAT AWAY →

1 eat sth **away, eat away** sth: to gradually reduce something by taking parts of it away ▶ *New housing estates are gradually eating away our countryside and woodlands.*

2 eat away sth, **eat** sth **away:** to gradually destroy something, especially through chemical action ▶ *The floor of the car had been eaten away by rust.*

EAT AWAY AT →

1 eat away at sb: to make you feel very worried over a long period of time ▶ *The memory of her mistake has never stopped eating away at her.*

2 eat away at sth: to gradually destroy something by continuously damaging it ▶ *It was discovered that air pollutants were eating away at the carvings.*

EAT IN →

1 eat in: to eat a meal at home instead of going to a restaurant ▶ *I'm too tired to go out – let's eat in instead.*

2 eat in: to eat inside a restaurant instead of taking your food somewhere else to eat ▶ *"Two burgers and two coffees, please." "To eat in or take away?"*

EAT INTO →

eat into sth: to use or take away part of something such as money or time ▶ *Jet lag can eat into precious holiday time.*

EAT OUT →

eat out: to eat a meal in a restaurant, instead of at home ▶ *People today eat out far more often than they used to.*

EAT UP →

1 eat up sth, **eat** sth **up, eat up:** to eat all of something ▶ *Joey ate up all the casserole, and then started hungrily on his dessert.* **eat up!** (=used to tell a child to eat all of his or her food) ▶ *Come on, Kaylee, eat up!*

2 eat up sth, **eat** sth **up:** to use all or almost all of something ▶ *The job ate up most of his time, including weekends and holidays.*

3 eat up sb, **eat** sb **up:** to make you feel extremely upset, angry, worried etc ▶ *It just eats me up to see the way those kids are treated by their teachers.*

4 eat sth **up, eat up** sth: to be excited about something and enjoy it very much ▶ *Vicky uses games to teach* *little kids how to get fit, and the kids eat it up.*

EBB

EBB AWAY →

ebb away: to gradually become weaker and then disappear completely ▶ *The team had almost won, but their strength was ebbing away by the minute.*

EDIT

EDIT OUT →

edit out sth, **edit** sth **out**: to remove part of a film, programme, book etc before it is shown or printed ▶ *Most of the violent scenes had to be edited out before the film could be shown on TV.*

EGG

EGG ON →

egg sb **on**, **egg on** sb: to encourage someone to do something, especially something that is not sensible or safe ▶ *The two men, egged on by an excited crowd, started to fight.*

EKE

EKE OUT →

1 eke out sth, **eke** sth **out**: to make money, food, supplies etc last as long as possible by using them carefully ▶ *Most single parents have to eke out very small incomes as well as they can.*

2 eke out a living *also* **eke out an existence**: to get just enough food or money to live ▶ *A few families still try to eke out an existence on the barren land.*

3 eke out a win *also* **eke out a victory**: to win by only a few points or votes ▶ *Hopes of the team eking out a victory are quickly fading.*

ELBOW

ELBOW OUT →

elbow out sb/sth, **elbow** sb/sth **out**: to force someone or something out of a job or high position ▶ *They seem all set to elbow the champions out of their position.*

EMANATE

EMANATE FROM →

emanate from sth/sb: to come from a particular place or person ▶ *Delicious smells were emanating from the kitchen.*

EMBARK

EMBARK ON, *also* EMBARK UPON →

embark on/upon sth: to start doing something, especially something new or difficult ▶ *In the 1950s, the country embarked on a major programme of social reform.*

EMBROIDER

EMBROIDER ON →

embroider on sth: to add details to an account of something, in order to make it seem more impressive ▶ *Don't believe everything he tells you – he's got a habit of embroidering on most of his wartime experiences.*

EMBROIL

BE EMBROILED IN →

be embroiled in sth: to be deeply involved in an argument, war, or other unpleasant situation ▶ *They found themselves embroiled in a long and bitter legal battle.*

EMPTY

EMPTY OUT →

1 empty out sth, **empty** sth **out**: to remove everything from inside a container ▶ *I emptied out the shopping bags and put everything*

E

away. ▶ *Jo emptied out the contents of the cash box onto the table.*
2 empty out: if a place empties out, all the people in it leave ▶ *The club usually empties out about two in the morning.*

ENCASE
ENCASE IN →
encase sth **in** sth: to cover or enclose something with something else ▶ *The statue was transported back to Britain and encased in glass to protect it.*

ENCROACH
ENCROACH ON, *also* ENCROACH UPON →
1 encroach on/upon sth: to gradually take away someone's rights, freedom, or authority ▶ *Civil Liberty groups are worried that the new laws will encroach upon freedom of speech.*
2 encroach on/upon sth: to reduce the amount of time that someone has available to do something ▶ *Most people try to prevent their work from encroaching on their private lives.*
3 encroach on/upon sth: to gradually cover more and more land ▶ *Everywhere we look, new housing developments are encroaching on our countryside.*

END
END IN →
end in sth: to have a particular result, or to finish in a particular way ▶ *In Britain, two out of three marriages end in divorce.* **end in tears** (=end with people feeling unhappy, annoyed etc) ▶ *Stop quarrelling you two! You know it'll all end in tears.*

END UP →
1 end up: to be in a situation that you did not intend or want to be in. **end up**

in court/prison etc ▶ *Tom got into a fight and ended up in court.* **+ with** ▶ *You'll end up with pneumonia if you're not careful.*
2 end up doing sth: to do something that you did not intend to do at first ▶ *He came for a couple of days and ended up staying a month!*
3 end up: to arrive in a place without planning or wanting to go there ▶ *They ended up in a bar near the docks.*

ENDEAR
ENDEAR TO →
endear sb **to** sb: to do something to make people like or approve of you ▶ *If you're keen to learn, you're bound to endear yourself to your teachers.*

ENDOW
ENDOW WITH →
be endowed with sth: to naturally have a particular ability, quality, or feature, especially a good one ▶ *Healy was a good public speaker and endowed with extraordinary energy.*
be well/richly endowed with sth (=have a lot of it) ▶ *The island is well endowed with mineral deposits.*

ENGAGE
ENGAGE IN →
1 be engaged in sth: to be involved in something, especially something that continues for a long time ▶ *Officials are engaged in a debate with the company over the safety of its newest aircraft.*
2 engage in sth: to take part in a particular activity ▶ *Women were actively discouraged from engaging in political life.*
3 engage sb **in conversation**: to start a conversation with someone ▶ *She tried to engage Anthony in conversation, but he didn't respond.*

ENGROSS

BE ENGROSSED IN →
be engrossed in sth: to be very interested or involved in something, so that you do not notice what is happening around you ▶ *Rourke was so engrossed in conversation with the girl that he didn't even see me come in.*

ENLARGE

ENLARGE ON, *also* **ENLARGE UPON** →
enlarge on/upon sth: to give more details or information about something that you have already mentioned ▶ *I sat patiently, waiting for Tom to enlarge on his last remark.*

ENQUIRE *see* INQUIRE

ENTER

ENTER INTO →
1 enter into an agreement/contract etc: to make an official agreement, contract etc to do something ▶ *The two software giants entered into an agreement to develop new products and markets.*

2 enter into sth: to start to become involved in something ▶ *At the time I didn't feel ready to enter into a new relationship.*

3 enter into sth: to be an important part of a situation or be something that you consider when you are making a decision ▶ *Of course, other factors entered into the decision-making process.* **enter into it** ▶ *If we are choosing a new employee, age doesn't enter into it.*

ENTER ON, *also* **ENTER UPON** →
enter on/upon sth: to begin something, especially something that will continue for a long time ▶ *The economy is entering upon a period of sustained growth.*

ENTITLE

BE ENTITLED TO →
be entitled to sth: to have the right to have or do something ▶ *All children under sixteen are entitled to free medical treatment.* **entitle** sb **to** sth ▶ *Three of these tokens entitle you to free entry to the Castle.*

ENURE *see* INURE

ERODE

ERODE AWAY →
1 be eroded away *also* **erode away**: if rock or soil is eroded away or erodes away, water or the wind gradually removes its surface or breaks it into pieces ▶ *Parts of the cliff are in danger of eroding away.*

2 be eroded away *also* **erode away**: if someone's power, confidence, freedom etc is eroded away or erodes away, it is gradually destroyed ▶ *When John left me, I felt that all my self-respect had been eroded away.*

EVEN

EVEN OUT →
a. even out: to become more equal after seeming unequal ▶ *Some people seem to get all the luck – but it usually evens out in the end.*

b. even out sth, **even** sth **out**: to make something become more equal, by sharing it more equally ▶ *We want to try to even out the work load a little.*

EVEN UP →
even up sth, **even** sth **up**: to make a situation more equal or fair, especially in a game or competition ▶ *Mike came in and joined our team, which helped to even things up a little.*

EXPAND

EXPAND ON, *also* **EXPAND UPON** →
expand on/upon sth: to give more details about something that you have

E

already said or written ▶ *I'd like to expand on that point in a minute, if I may.*

EXPECT

EXPECT OF →

expect sth **of** sb/sth: to think that someone or something should do something or behave in a particular way ▶ *When I first joined the company, I wasn't sure what was expected of me.* **expect a lot/more of** sb ▶ *She seems to expect an awful lot of her staff.* ▶ *Middle-class parents expect more of their children and push them harder at school.*

EXPLAIN

EXPLAIN AWAY →

explain away sth, **explain** sth **away**: to give reasons for something bad, to make people think it is not your fault or not serious ▶ *The unemployment figures were not easy to explain away.* **+ as** ▶ *Dad's illness could no longer be explained away as the flu.*

EYE

EYE UP →

eye up sb, **eye** sb **up**: to look at someone in a way that shows you think they are sexually attractive ▶ *That guy at the bar keeps eyeing you up, Kelly.*

Ff

FACE

FACE DOWN →

face down sb/sth, **face** sb/sth **down**: to deal with someone or something in a strong and confident way ▸ *Lyman says he faced down a roaring lion when he was on safari.*

FACE OFF →

face off: to fight, argue, or compete against someone ▸ *The two candidates will face off in the second election on November 16.*

    face-off N when two people or groups fight or compete against each other ▸ *There was a 24-hour face-off between demonstrators and the police in Central Square.*

FACE UP TO →

face up to sth: to accept that an unpleasant fact is true or that a difficult situation exists ▸ *It won't be easy to find another job; you'd better face up to it.* **face up to the fact (that)** ▸ *It's often difficult to face up to the fact that you are no longer young.*

BE FACED WITH →

be faced with sth: to have to deal with a difficult problem or situation ▸ *The police were faced with a seemingly impossible task.* ▸ *The business was doing badly, and we were faced with mounting debts.*

FADE

FADE AWAY →

1 fade away: to gradually become less loud or clear, and then disappear

▸ *She listened to Zach's footsteps fading away down the staircase.* **+ into** ▸ *Dave's figure faded away into the darkness.*

2 fade away: to gradually become less strong or likely, and then disappear completely ▸ *Hopes of a peace settlement were beginning to fade away.*

3 fade away: to gradually become weaker, and then die ▸ *Mum never really recovered after the operation – she just faded away.*

FADE IN →

fade in, **fade in** sth, **fade** sth **in**: if recorded sound or a picture in a film, television programme etc fades in, or is faded in, it gradually becomes louder or clearer
▸ *Romantic music slowly fades in, as the lovers walk hand in hand into the sunset.*

FADE OUT →

1 fade out: to gradually disappear or stop happening ▸ *The marches and the protests faded out and people went back to their normal lives.*

2 fade out, **fade out** sth, **fade** sth **out**: if recorded sound or a picture in a film, television programme etc fades out, or you fade it out, it becomes less loud or clear and gradually disappears
▸ *The DJ faded out one record and put on another.*

FAKE

FAKE OUT →

fake sb **out**, **fake out** sb: to deceive someone by making them think you are planning to do something when you are really planning to do something else ▸ *Sherrard faked out Jesperson, moved past him, and scored the winning goal.*

FALL

**FALL
ABOUT →**

fall about: to laugh a lot about something, especially without being able to stop

▶ *The situation was so ridiculous that we all just fell about.* **fall about laughing** ▶ *All the kids fell about laughing as soon as the teacher left the room.*

FALL APART →

1 be falling apart: to be in very bad condition, and need repairing ▶ *I'm not going in your car – it's falling apart!*

2 fall apart: if something falls apart, it breaks into pieces, especially because it is old or badly made ▶ *I'd only had the shoes a couple of months before they fell apart.*

3 fall apart: if an organization, system, relationship etc falls apart, it stops working successfully ▶ *No-one realized that her marriage was falling apart.* ▶ *By the end of 1934, the Party was falling apart.*

4 fall apart: to have serious emotional problems, so that you cannot think or behave normally ▶ *She's so tense about her job – if she goes on like this, she'll fall apart.*

5 sb's world falls apart also **sb's life falls apart**: if someone's world or life falls apart, something very bad happens that changes their life and makes them extremely unhappy ▶ *When Jim's wife left him, his world just fell apart.*

FALL AWAY →

1 fall away: to break off from something ▶ *The flower's petals fell away and fluttered to the ground.*
+ from ▶ *Several large rocks had fallen away from the cliff into the sea.*

2 fall away: if land, a road etc falls away, it slopes down, especially suddenly and steeply ▶ *Sarah ran forward and then stopped as the ground fell away before her.*

3 fall away: if a feeling or something that has a bad effect on you falls away, you stop feeling it or being affected by it ▶ *As soon as I found out the truth, all my worries fell away.*

4 fall away: to decrease in amount or value ▶ *Our profits have fallen away sharply during the last two years.*

FALL BACK →

1 fall back: to move backwards and away from someone or something ▶ *As she ran forward, the rest of the crowd fell back.*

2 fall back: if soldiers fall back, they move back away from the enemy in order to avoid fighting ▶ *The general immediately ordered his men to fall back.*

3 fall back: to move more slowly than another person, car etc, with the result that you are behind them ▶ *As soon as we were in sight of the lorry, we fell back in order not to be seen.*

FALL BACK ON, *also* **FALL BACK UPON →**

fall back on/upon sth: to have to use or do something because other things have failed or been used up ▶ *If this doesn't work, we'll just have to fall back on our original plan.* ▶ *Do you have any savings to fall back on?*

FALL BEHIND →

1 fall behind, fall behind sb: to gradually get behind other people you are with, because you are moving more slowly than them ▶ *The little boy had fallen behind his mother and was crying.*

2 fall behind, fall behind sb/sth: to not make as much progress or achieve the same standard as someone or something else ▶ *Children from poor families are more likely to fall behind at school.*

3 fall behind, fall behind sth: to not do something by the time you have agreed to do it, especially by not paying money that you should pay regularly. **+ with** ▶ *After losing his job, Darren fell behind with his mortgage payments.*

4 fall behind sth: to fail to increase at the same rate as something else ▶ *Over the last few years, our salaries have fallen behind inflation.*

FALL DOWN →

1 fall down: to fall onto the ground from an upright position ▶ *She slipped on the ice, fell down and broke her leg.* ▶ *During the night, several trees had fallen down.*

2 be falling down: if a building is falling down, it is in very bad condition and needs repairing ▶ *There were very few hospitals, and the ones that did exist were falling down.*

3 fall down: to not be good enough or not be successful for a particular reason ▶ *"What if someone doesn't keep up with the payments?" "That's when the whole system falls down."*
   downfall N when someone loses their position of power or stops being successful. **+ of** ▶ *the downfall of the old regime* **be sb's downfall** ▶ *In the end, his pride was his downfall.*

FALL FOR →

1 fall for sth: to be tricked into believing something that is not true

▶ *You didn't think I'd fall for that old excuse, did you?* ▶ *Politicians seem to think that we'll fall for any old rubbish.*

2 fall for sb: to suddenly feel sexually or romantically attracted to someone ▶ *It's the story of a middle-aged teacher who falls for one of his students.*

3 fall for sth: to like something very much as soon as you see it ▶ *Mark fell for the old house immediately.*

FALL IN →

1 fall in: if a roof or ceiling falls in, it falls to the ground because it is old or damaged ▶ *The windows were all broken and the roof had fallen in.*

2 fall in: to start walking or forming lines behind or next to other people, ▶ *The soldiers fell in, one behind the other.*

FALL IN WITH →

1 fall in with sb: to become friends with a particular group of people ▶ *She fell in with quite a wild set at college.*

2 fall in with sth: to accept what someone else suggests, and not try to change it or disagree with it ▶ *I'm quite happy to fall in with whatever you decide.*

FALL INTO →

1 fall into sth: to start to be in a bad condition or in a bad situation – used in the following phrases: **fall into disrepair/disuse etc** ▶ *The cathedral fell into disrepair over the next fifty years.*

2 fall into sth: to start doing something or being involved in something – used especially in the following phrases: **fall into conversation/a discussion** (=start talking) ▶ *I fell into conversation with the man sitting beside me.* **fall into the habit of doing** sth ▶ *He had fallen into the habit of walking home across*

F

the fields. **fall into a deep sleep**
▶ *I fell into a deep sleep as soon as I lay down.*

3 fall into a category/ group etc: to belong to a particular group of things or people ▶ *Our customers have always fallen into several distinct categories.*

4 fall into sth: to be divided into two or more different parts ▶ *The evening's discussion falls into three parts.*

FALL OFF →

1 fall off: if something falls off, it becomes separated from the thing that it is joined to ▶ *I picked up the suitcase and the handle fell off.*

2 fall off: if the amount, rate, or standard of something falls off, it decreases or becomes lower ▶ *The standard of acting seemed to fall off in the second half of the play.*

    fall-off also **falling-off** N when the amount, rate, or standard of something decreases or becomes lower. **+ in** ▶ *Some clubs have had to close due to a fall-off in attendance.* ▶ *a falling-off in demand*

FALL ON →

fall on sth: if a date falls on a particular day of the week, it happens on that day ▶ *Christmas fell on a Saturday that year.*

FALL ON, *also* **FALL UPON** →

1 fall on/upon sb: if a duty or job falls on someone, they are responsible for dealing with it ▶ *When her mother died, responsibility for the family fell upon Sheila.* **it falls on** sb **to do** sth ▶ *Jane was off sick, so it fell on me to organize the whole thing.*

2 fall on/upon sb: to suddenly attack someone ▶ *Some of the older boys fell on him, and broke his glasses.*

FALL OUT →

1 fall out: to have an argument with someone and stop being friendly with them. **+ with** ▶ *She left the club after she fell out with the manager.* **+ over** ▶ *Apparently the two men fell out over money.*

    falling-out N an argument or serious disagreement ▶ *There were reports that some members of the team had had a falling-out.*

2 fall out: if your hair or a tooth falls out, it becomes loose and separates from your body ▶ *My Dad's hair fell out when he was only thirty.*

3 fall out: if soldiers fall out, they stop standing in a line and move away to different places ▶ *The soldiers were ordered to fall out and return to base.*

FALL OVER →

1 fall over: to fall to the ground, or to fall down from an upright position ▶ *That pile of books will fall over if you put any more on top.*

2 fall over sth: to hit your foot against something by mistake, and fall to the ground ▶ *I fell over an empty box that someone had left outside the door.*

3 be falling over yourself to do sth: to be very eager to do something ▶ *The manager was falling over herself to help us.*

FALL THROUGH →

fall through: if an agreement, plan etc falls through, something prevents it from happening or being completed ▶ *My holiday plans have fallen through, so I don't know where I'll go this year.*

FALL TO →

1 fall to sb: if a duty or job falls to someone, they become responsible for dealing with it ▶ *No one else wanted to do it, so the job fell to me.* **it fell to** sb **to do** sth ▶ *It fell to me to give her the bad news.*

2 fall to sth: to suddenly start doing something ▶ *Everyone fell to work, and they didn't stop till midnight.*

FALL UNDER →

1 fall under sb's control/influence etc: to become controlled or influenced by a particular group, country, or person ▶ *Large areas of the country had fallen under enemy control.*

2 fall under sb/sth's **spell**: to become very attracted by someone or something ▶ *The first time I went to Paris, I fell under its spell.*

3 fall under a category/heading etc: to be included in a particular group or description of things ▶ *The new job falls under the heading of Sales and Marketing.*

FALL UPON *see* **FALL ON**

FAN

FAN OUT →

fan out: if a group of people or things fans out, they move forward and away

from each other so that they gradually spread over a wide area ▶ *He ordered his men to fan out and search every inch of the field.*

FARM

FARM OUT →

1 farm out sb, **farm** sb **out**: to arrange for someone to be looked after by someone else, because you are too busy to look after them yourself ▶ *My parents were both working, so I ended up being farmed out to a childminder.*

2 farm out sth, **farm** sth **out**: to arrange for work to be done by another company or by someone

outside your company ▶ *Most of the editing is farmed out to freelancers these days.*

FASTEN

FASTEN ON, *also* **FASTEN UPON** →

fasten on/upon sth: to give particular attention to something ▶ *The press was quick to fasten on the dangers of genetically modified foods.*

FASTEN ONTO →

fasten onto sb: to follow someone and stay with them, especially when they do not want you to ▶ *She immediately fastened onto the best-looking man at the party.*

FASTEN UP →

fasten up sth, **fasten** sth **up**, **fasten up**: to join together two sides of something such as a coat, shirt, bag etc so it is closed, or to become joined in this way ▶ *Fasten up your coat – it's freezing outside.* ▶ *My fingers were so numb I couldn't fasten my shirt.*

FASTEN UPON *see* **FASTEN ON**

FATHOM

FATHOM OUT →

fathom out sth/sb, **fathom** sth/sb **out**: to understand something or someone after thinking about them carefully, especially when their behaviour seems strange or confusing ▶ *I sometimes find it difficult to fathom out the workings of Emma's mind.*

FATTEN

FATTEN UP →

fatten up sth/sb, **fatten** sth/sb **up**: to make an animal fatter by giving it a lot of food. Also used humorously about people. ▶ *The turkeys are being fattened up for Christmas.* ▶ *Keith always looks so thin – he needs fattening up a bit.*

F

FAVOUR

FAVOUR WITH →
favour sb **with** sth: to give someone a look or a reply, or do something special for them ▶ *He favoured Lucy with a broad grin, then went back to his work.*

FAWN

FAWN ON, *also* **FAWN OVER** →
fawn on/over sb: to praise someone and be friendly to them, especially in a way that is not sincere ▶ *Political candidates are always fawning over wealthy businessmen, hoping for campaign donations.*

FEAR

FEAR FOR →
fear for sb/sth: to feel worried that someone or something might be in danger or in trouble ▶ *Calaway assured him that he has no reason to fear for his job.* **fear for** sb's **life/safety** ▶ *Fearing for his life, Williams left the country.*

FEAST

FEAST ON, *also* **FEAST UPON** →
feast on/upon sth: to eat a lot of a particular food with enjoyment ▶ *They feasted on smoked salmon and champagne.*

FEED

FEED BACK →
feed back, feed back sth: to give someone your opinion about something, especially so it can be improved. **+ to** ▶ *Consumers are able to feed back to the company about its products.* **+ with** ▶ *I am grateful to all those who fed back with their comments and suggestions.*

    feedback N advice, criticism etc about how good or useful something is ▶ *We've received some negative feedback from customers on the new software.*

FEED IN, *also* **FEED INTO** →
feed sth **in, feed in** sth, **feed** sth **in**: to put something into a machine, especially information ▶ *Data about weather conditions is fed into a computer so that forecasts can be made.*

FEED INTO →
feed into sth: if a river or road feeds into a bigger river or road, it joins it ▶ *The River Derwent and the River Ouse both feed into the Humber.*

FEED OFF →
1 feed off sth: if an animal feeds off something, it gets food from it ▶ *Minute organisms feed off household dust.*

2 feed off sth: to use something in order to continue to exist or to get an advantage for yourself ▶ *Some people accused him of feeding off his father's reputation as a writer.*

FEED ON →
1 feed on sth: if an animal feeds on a particular food, it usually eats that food ▶ *Owls feed on mice and other small animals.*

2 feed sth/sb **on** sth: to regularly give an animal or person a particular kind of food to eat ▶ *The cattle are fed on barley and grass.*

3 feed on sth: to use something in order to become stronger or more successful, especially people's fears or worries ▶ *The Fascists were able to feed on people's fears about the country's economic situation.*

FEED UP →
1 feed sb **up**: to give someone a lot of food, especially to make them healthy and not too thin

▶ *A lot of models these days look as if they need feeding up.*

2 be fed up: to be bored, annoyed, or unhappy ▶ *You look fed up. What's the matter?* **+ with** ▶ *She got fed up with being treated like some kind of servant.*

FEEL

FEEL AROUND FOR →
feel around for sth, **feel around** sth **for** sth: to use your hands to search for something you cannot see ▶ *I felt around in my pocket for some loose change.*

FEEL FOR →
1 feel for sb: to feel sympathy for someone because they are in a difficult, sad, or unpleasant situation ▶ *She felt for Karen, but she had a family of her own to look after.*

2 feel for sth: to use your hands to search for something you cannot see ▶ *Suzanne entered the dark room and felt for the light switch.*

FEEL UP TO →
feel up to sth: to feel well or energetic enough to do something ▶ *Can we go for a run another time? I don't really feel up to it today.* **feel up to doing** sth ▶ *Are you sure you feel up to going into work?*

FENCE

FENCE IN →
1 fence in sth, **fence** sth **in**: to surround an area or building with a fence ▶ *The prison compound was fenced in with barbed wire.*

2 fence in sth, **fence** sth **in**: to keep animals in an area surrounded by a fence ▶ *Jimmy is planning to fence in his chickens to protect them from foxes.*

3 fence in sb, **fence** sb **in**: to make someone feel that they cannot leave a place or do what they want ▶ *Mothers with young children often feel fenced in at home.*

FENCE OFF →
fence off sth, **fence** sth **off**: to separate one area from another with a fence ▶ *The owner has fenced off the woodland to stop people getting in.* **+ from** ▶ *The resort was fenced off from the rest of the island.*

FEND

FEND FOR →
fend for yourself: to take care of yourself without help from other people ▶ *Towards the end of his life he could no longer fend for himself.*

FEND OFF →
1 fend off sb/sth, **fend** sb/sth **off**: to stop someone or something who is trying to attack or harm you ▶ *He managed to fend off his attackers until the police arrived.*

2 fend off sth, **fend** sth **off**: to avoid having to deal directly with something difficult or annoying ▶ *Ashley tried to fend off any awkward questions about his business affairs.*

FERRET

FERRET OUT →
ferret out sth, **ferret** sth **out**: to succeed in finding something that is difficult to find, especially a piece of information ▶ *She had a way of ferreting out people's secrets.*

FESS

FESS UP →
fess up: to tell people about something wrong you have done, especially something that is not serious ▶ *Come on, fess up! Who ate the last cookie?*

FETCH

FETCH UP →
fetch up: to arrive somewhere without

expecting to or intending to ▶ *He spent some time in Europe and eventually fetched up in Naples.*

FIDDLE

FIDDLE AROUND, *also* **FIDDLE ABOUT →**

1 fiddle around/about: to make small changes to something in order to try to repair it or make it work better ▶ *Derek fiddled around for half an hour, trying to get the TV to work.* **+ with** ▶ *The government should stop fiddling around with the education system.*

2 fiddle around/about: to waste time doing silly or unimportant things ▶ *I'm fed up with fiddling around here all day. Can we go?*

FIGHT

FIGHT BACK →

1 fight back: to take action to defend yourself when someone attacks you or causes problems for you ▶ *Finn was wounded several times but he continued to fight back.* ▶ *People who are discriminated against often lack the confidence to fight back.*

   fight-back N when a person, team, organization etc defends themselves against an attacker or opponent ▶ *In the second half, United staged a fight-back.*

2 fight back sth: to force yourself with difficulty not to do something you very much want to do ▶ *I had to fight back a growing desire to hit him.* **fight back tears** (=manage not to cry) ▶ *Fighting back his tears, he waved goodbye to her from the station platform.*

FIGHT DOWN →

fight down sth, **fight** sth **down**: to force yourself not to do something that you very much want to do, or force yourself not to be affected by your feelings ▶ *Janice fought down the*

impulse to scream. ▶ *He leaned against the door, fighting down a wave of nausea.*

FIGHT OFF →

1 fight off sb/sth, **fight** sb/sth **off**: to use violence to make someone who is attacking you go away ▶ *The man tried to strangle her, but she managed to fight him off.*

2 fight off sth, **fight** sth **off**: to get rid of or try to get rid of an illness or an unpleasant feeling ▶ *Vitamin C helps your body to fight off colds.*

3 fight sb/sth **off**, **fight off** sb/sth: to prevent an opponent from defeating you ▶ *So far, he has succeeded in fighting off every challenge to his leadership.*

FIGHT OUT →

fight it out: to fight or argue until one person, team etc wins ▶ *John and Margot are prepared to fight the matter out in court.* **fight it out among yourselves** (=used to say that you do not want to be involved in someone else's argument) ▶ *Let them fight it out among themselves – it's none of our business.*

FIGURE

FIGURE ON →

figure on sth: to expect that something will happen in a particular way, and include it in your plans ▶ *Ken figured on about 100 people coming to the party.* **figure on doing** sth ▶ *Figure on spending £70 to £90 for a ticket to Paris.*

FIGURE OUT →

figure out sth/sb, **figure** sth/sb **out**: to understand something or someone, or find the answer to a question, problem etc, after thinking carefully ▶ *I've know Zack for years but I still can't figure him out.* ▶ *I'm trying to figure out a way* *of paying him back the money I owe him.*

FILE

FILE AWAY →

1 file away sth, **file** sth **away**: to keep papers with information on them in a particular place so that they are easy to find ▶ *Should we file away these receipts or throw them out?*

2 file away sth, **file** sth **away**: to carefully remember information so that you can use it later ▶ *Every little mistake gets filed away in the back of her mind.*

FILE FOR →

file for sth: to officially ask for legal permission to do something. **file for divorce/bankruptcy** ▶ *After 10 years of marriage, the couple have decided to file for divorce.*

FILL

FILL IN →

1 fill in sth, **fill** sth **in**: to write all the necessary information in the empty spaces on a document ▶ *Make sure that you fill in your name, address, and daytime telephone number.*

2 fill in sth, **fill** sth **in**: to put a substance in a hole or crack in order to make a surface smooth ▶ *You'll need to fill in all the cracks before you paint the walls.*

3 fill sb **in**, **fill in** sb: to tell someone about things that have happened recently or tell them something that they need to know. **+ on** ▶ *Talk to Jenny – she can fill you in on the details.* ▶ *Dad calls us every Sunday to fill us in on all the family news.*

4 fill in: to do someone's job while they are ill or not at work ▶ *Who's going to fill in when Helen's on maternity leave?* **+ for** ▶ *Quinn is filling in for the newspaper's regular reporter.*

5 fill in time: to do something while you are waiting for something to happen so that you do not get bored ▶ *We've got some time to fill in before the show – let's have a look around town.*

6 fill in sth, **fill** sth **in**: to paint or colour the space inside a shape ▶ *She drew a picture of a bird and used crayons to fill it in.*

FILL OUT →

1 fill out sth, **fill** sth **out**: to write all the necessary information in the empty spaces in a document ▶ *If you want to join the library, you'll need to fill out an application form.*

2 fill out: if your body fills out, it becomes fatter or bigger ▶ *By age 12, her body had already started to fill out.*

FILL UP →

1a. fill up sth, **fill** sth **up**: to make a container full by putting liquid or other things in it ▶ *Can I fill up your glass?* ▶ *We brought two big baskets for the apples, and quickly filled them up.*
b. fill up, **fill up** sth, **fill** sth **up**: to put petrol in a car so that the tank is full ▶ *They stopped to fill up at the next petrol station.*
  fill-up N when you put enough petrol in your vehicle to fill the tank ▶ *We're offering a free carwash with every fill-up.*

2 fill up: to become full ▶ *The pubs fill up quickly on Saturday nights.* **+ with** ▶ *The stadium was already starting to fill up with eager fans.*

3 fill up sth: to use a period of time for

a particular activity or purpose ▶ *The manager expects us to fill up every minute of the day with work.*

FILTER

FILTER IN →

filter in: to slowly drive your car into a line of traffic that is already moving ▶ *We had to slow down as more traffic filtered in.*

FILTER OUT →

1 filter out sth, **filter** sth **out**: to remove a harmful or unwanted substance from a liquid or gas to stop it affecting someone or something ▶ *Workers have to wear masks to filter out all the dust in the air.* ▶ *a sun cream which filters out harmful UV rays*

2 filter out sth/sb, **filter** sth/sb **out**: to prevent something or someone that you do not want from being successful or having an effect ▶ *The interviews are intended to filter out unsuitable candidates.*

FILTER THROUGH →

filter through: if news or information about something filters through, people start to hear about it ▶ *Reports began to filter through of mass executions.*

FIND

FIND AGAINST →

find against sb: to officially decide that someone is guilty of a crime or does not have a legal right to something ▶ *If the judge finds against him, he'll spend the rest of his life in jail.*

FIND FOR →

find for sb: to officially decide that someone is not guilty of a crime or has a legal right to something ▶ *Judge Hayes found for the defendant and ordered that he should be released immediately.*

FIND OUT →

1 find out, find out sth, **find** sth **out**: to get information about something ▶ *I don't know who wrote the song, but I'll try and find out.* ▶ *Teachers should encourage kids to find things out for themselves.* **+ what/where etc** ▶ *Dad was really mad at me when he found out where I'd been.* **+ if** ▶ *Find out if there's anyone here who speaks English.* **+ about** ▶ *You'll be in trouble if anybody finds out about this.*

2 find sb **out**: to discover that someone has done something wrong ▶ *Billie knew she would find him out if he tried to lie to her.*

FINISH

FINISH OFF →

1 finish off sth, **finish** sth **off**: to complete the last part of something that you are doing ▶ *Don't disturb him, he's just finishing off his homework.*

2 finish off sth, **finish** sth **off**: to eat, drink, or use the last part of something ▶ *Ally and I sat outside, finishing off our meal.*

3 finish off, finish off sth, **finish** sth **off**: to end an event, programme, meal etc in a particular way ▶ *We finished off the evening by opening a bottle of champagne.* **+ with** ▶ *Let's finish off with a roundup of the news.*

4 finish sb **off, finish off** sb: to make someone feel very tired, weak, or unhappy ▶ *That last job's finished me off for the day! I'm going home.*

5 finish sb/sth **off, finish off** sb/sth: to kill a person or animal when they are already wounded or weak ▶ *Two of the hunters clubbed the seals to finish them off.*

6 finish off sb/sth, **finish** sb/sth **off**: to defeat a person or team that you are competing against ▶ *They were a* *team we should have easily beaten, but we couldn't quite finish them off.*

FINISH UP →

1 finish up: to arrive or end at a particular place, after going to other places first ▶ *I took a long holiday in Italy and finished up in Rome.*

2 finish up: to get into a particular state or situation as the result of something you have done ▶ *One of the guys tried to bribe a police officer and finished up in jail.*

3 finish up doing sth: to do something at the end of a process, especially without planning to ▶ *I often start off thinking of one story, and finish up writing something completely different.*

4 finish up sth, **finish** sth **up**: to eat or drink all of something ▶ *Come on! Finish up your drinks. We have to go now.*

5 finish sth **up, finish up** sth, **finish up**: to complete the final part of something ▶ *Moore is finishing up his first season with the 49ers.*

FINISH WITH →

1 be finished with sth *also* **have finished with** sth: to have stopped using or needing something ▶ *Have you finished with the newspaper yet?* ▶ *I usually give my old clothes away when I'm finished with them.*

2 be finished with sb *also* **have finished with** sb: to have finished talking to someone, or dealing with them, especially when you are angry with them ▶ *Don't go, Anna. I haven't finished with you yet!*

3 finish with sb: to end a romantic or sexual relationship with someone ▶ *Did you know that Mike's finished with Theresa?*

FINK

FINK ON →

fink on sb: to tell the police or someone in authority that someone else has done something wrong ▶ *Rita finked on me for taking long lunches at work.*

FIRE

FIRE AWAY →

fire away!: used to tell someone that you are ready for them to begin asking you questions ▶ *"Do you mind if I ask you something, Woody?" "Fire away."*

FIRE OFF →

1 fire off sth, **fire** sth **off**: to fire a bullet, bomb etc into the air ▶ *The terrorists fired off several shots over the crowd.*

2 fire off sth, **fire** sth **off**: to send an angry letter or message to someone ▶ *I fired off another furious e-mail to the editor.*

FIRE UP →

1 fire up sb, **fire** sb **up**: to make someone become very excited, interested, or angry ▶ *By the time we went into the contest we were fired up with enthusiasm.*

2 fire up sth, **fire** sth **up**: to make something start to burn ▶ *Millions of Americans are preparing to fire up their barbecues this weekend.*

3 fire up sth, **fire** sth **up**: to make an engine, computer etc start to work ▶ *He fired up the engines and prepared to lift off.*

FIRM

FIRM UP →

1 firm up sth, **firm** sth **up**: to make the details of arrangements, ideas etc more definite and exact ▶ *I'll call you nearer the time of the trip to firm things up.*

2 firm up sth, **firm** sth **up**: to make

F

your muscles stronger and get rid of fat by exercising ▶ *These exercises are good for firming up your stomach.*

3 firm up sth, **firm** sth **up**: to make your position of power stronger or safer ▶ *The party was keen to firm up its support before the coming election.*

FISH

FISH FOR →
fish for sth: to try to get information or praise from someone by asking them for it in an indirect way ▶ *Jed was fishing for information about whether my sister had a boyfriend.* **fish for compliments** (=try to get someone to say something nice about you) ▶ *I'm not fishing for compliments, but do you think this dress suits me?*

FISH OUT →
1 fish out sth/sb, **fish** sth/sb **out**: to pull something or someone out of water ▶ *I couldn't swim, so Dad had to jump in and fish me out.* **+ of** ▶ *Police fished her body out of the East River a week later.*

2 fish out sth, **fish** sth **out**: to take something out of a bag, pocket etc after searching for it with your hand ▶ *Phil put his hand in his pocket and fished out a few coins.*

FIT

FIT IN →
1 fit in: to be happy with a group of people because you have the same interests and attitudes ▶ *As soon as we moved to this area, we felt that we fitted in.* **+ with** ▶ *Ben doesn't seem to fit in with the other children at school.*

2 fit in sth/sb, **fit** sth/sb **in**: to succeed in finding time to do something or see someone ▶ *The doctor said that he can fit me in at 4.30.*

3 fit in: to arrange what you do in a way that is convenient for someone else ▶ *In a large family like ours, everyone has to learn to fit in.* **+ with** ▶ *What's best for you? I'll try and fit in with your schedule.*

4 fit in: if activities or arrangements fit in, they can take place between other arrangements without causing any problems. **+ with** ▶ *The dates you've suggested fit in neatly with my own plans.*

5 fit in: to seem suitable in a particular place, or with other things ▶ *The new houses that they're building in the village really don't fit in.* **+ with** ▶ *I'm looking for a sofa that will fit in with the room's general style.*

6 where sb **fits in** also **how** sb **fits in**: used to ask or say what part someone has in a plan or situation ▶ *It sounds like a great idea, but how do I fit in?* ▶ *We'll need someone who speaks Russian, and that's where Sam fits in.*

FIT IN WITH →
1 fit in with sth: to be suitable for or work successfully with another system, idea, or method ▶ *These ideas fit in well with traditional views of language learning.*

2 fit in with sth: if something fits in with a particular idea, statement etc, it says the same thing or has the same effect ▶ *Sonny's behaviour did not fit in with what I knew of him.*

FIT INTO →
1 fit into sth: to become a suitable part of a plan, situation, or system ▶ *His policies did not easily fit into the Marxist way of thinking.* **where** sth **fits into** sth also **how** sth **fits into** sth

(=used to ask or say what part someone or something has in a plan, situation etc) ▶ *We need to consider how this software will fit into our training programme.*

2 fit into sth: to be the right kind of person to be in a particular group or situation and feel happy in it ▶ *The people living opposite us didn't seem to fit into our small community at all.*

3 fit into sth: to seem to be of a particular type or belong in a particular group. **fit into a category/ pattern etc** ▶ *His problems don't seem to fit into any of the usual categories.* ▶ *George didn't fit into any recognizable social type.*

FIT OUT →

fit out sb/sth, **fit** sb/sth **out**: to provide someone or something with equipment, furniture, clothes etc ▶ *The money we raise will be used for fitting out a new laboratory.*

FIT UP →

1 fit up sb/sth, **fit** sb/sth **up**: to provide someone or something with the equipment, furniture, clothes etc they need ▶ *Anne and John spent their holiday fitting up their first home.*

2 fit up sb, **fit** sb **up**: to deliberately make someone seem guilty of a crime, although they are not ▶ *It was obvious that they had been fitted up and were innocent.*

FIT WITH →

fit with sth: to say the same thing or have the same effect as another statement, idea etc ▶ *The research shows that girls study harder than boys, and this certainly fits with our experience.*

FIX

FIX ON →

fix on sth/sb: to decide on a particular thing, date, or person ▶ *They've finally fixed on October 16th for their wedding.* ▶ *We talked about the money for a long time before we fixed on a figure.*

FIX UP →

1 fix up sth, **fix** sth **up**: to arrange something such as a meeting or date ▶ *Can we fix up a time when we can meet?* **fix up to do** sth ▶ *Sorry, I've already fixed up to go on holiday that week.*

2 fix up sb, **fix** sb **up**: to provide someone with something that they need ▶ *If you need anything, come and see me. I'll fix you up.* **+ with** ▶ *When he came out of prison, they fixed him up with a job in a factory.*

3 fix sth **up**, **fix up** sth: to work on something such as a building or room in order to repair it or improve it ▶ *We spent months fixing up the old flat and make it reasonably comfortable.*

4 fix sb **up**, **fix up** sb: to provide a suitable partner for someone to meet in a romantic way. **+ with** ▶ *I've been trying to fix my sister up with some nice guy for years.*

5 fix up sth, **fix** sth **up**: to make something quickly using whatever is available ▶ *We fixed up a table, using some old boxes.*

6 fix yourself up: to make yourself look attractive, especially before a special event ▶ *Zoe spent two hours fixing herself up for the Christmas party.*

FIZZLE

FIZZLE OUT →

fizzle out: to gradually end or disappear, often in a disappointing way ▶ *The rebellion fizzled out after a couple of weeks.*

FLAG

FLAG

DOWN →
flag down
sth, **flag** sth
down: to
make a
vehicle stop
by waving at
its driver ▶ *I*

went outside and flagged down a taxi.

FLAG UP →
flag up sth, **flag** sth **up**: to bring
people's attention to a particular idea,
subject etc ▶ *The conference aims to
flag up concerns about the local
environment.*

FLAKE

FLAKE OFF →
flake off, **flake off** sth: to break away
from a surface in small, very thin pieces
▶ *The walls were damp, and some of
the white paint was flaking off.*

FLAKE OUT →
1 flake out: to suddenly fall asleep
because you are very tired ▶ *He was
so exhausted that he flaked out on the
sofa.*

2 flake out: to forget to do something
that you promised to do ▶ *Paula
flaked out and didn't get the tickets
for the play tonight.*

FLARE

FLARE OUT →
flare out: to say something suddenly
in an angry way. **+ at** ▶ *Rothschild
flared out at Julia when she
questioned him.*

FLARE UP →
1 flare up: if something such as
violence, an argument, or anger flares
up, it suddenly starts ▶ *Violence has
flared up again in the capital city.*
▶ *Anger flared up inside her.*

2 flare up: to suddenly get very angry
with someone ▶ *Helen flared up.
"Look what you've done!" she
shouted.*

3 flare up: to get an illness, pain etc
again after it had gone away or got
better ▶ *The pain in my legs tends to
flare up when the weather's damp.*

   flare-up N when an illness, pain etc
   that you had before suddenly comes
   back or gets worse ▶ *A flare-up of
   her arthritis had kept her in bed.*

4 flare up: to suddenly begin to burn
brightly ▶ *Daniel lit a match and it
flared up in the dark.*

FLASH

FLASH AROUND, *also* FLASH
ABOUT →
1 flash your money around/ about: to
spend a lot of money in a way that is
very noticeable ▶ *Eddie's always
enjoyed flashing his money around.*

2 flash sth **around/ about**: to
show people that you have something
valuable ▶ *If you have jewellery with
you, don't go flashing it around.*

FLASH BACK TO →
flash back to sb/ sth: to suddenly
think of someone or something in the
past ▶ *His mind flashed back forty
years to what his father had once told
him.*

   flashback N **1** a sudden memory of
   something in the past, often
   something unpleasant. **+ to**
   ▶ *Rachel, 25, still has vivid
   flashbacks to the day when she was
   attacked.*
   2 a scene in a film. play, or book,
   that shows something that
   happened in the past ▶ *In a series of
   flashbacks we follow the sisters
   through their teenage years.*

FLASH ON →
flash on sth: to suddenly remember

something or have a new idea ▶ *It was then that I flashed on the idea of spending Easter in Hawaii.*

FLATTEN

FLATTEN OUT →

1 flatten out, flatten out sth, **flatten** sth **out**: to become, or make something become, flat or flatter ▶ *East of Richmond, the countryside begins to flatten out.* ▶ *I opened the map and flattened it out on my knee.*

2 flatten out: if the rate or number of something flattens out, it stops increasing ▶ *House prices have started to flatten out after years of steady growth.*

FLESH

FLESH OUT →

flesh out sth, **flesh** sth **out**: to add more details to a piece of writing, a speech etc ▶ *Scott fleshes out the original story with details from his own imagination.*

FLICK

FLICK OFF →

flick off sth, **flick** sth **off**: to quickly make an electric light, machine etc stop working by pressing a switch ▶ *Flicking off the downstairs lights, she went upstairs.*

FLICK ON →

flick on sth, **flick** sth **on**: to quickly make an electric light, machine etc start working by pressing a switch ▶ *I flicked on the TV and took a can of beer from the fridge.*

FLICK THROUGH →

flick through sth: to quickly look at the pages of a book, magazine etc ▶ *Jilly was lying on the sofa, flicking through a magazine.*

FLINCH

FLINCH FROM →

flinch from sth: to avoid doing something because you do not like it or are afraid of it ▶ *He was a great leader who never flinched from his duty.* **not flinch from doing** sth ▶ *Ruth knew that she must not flinch from telling him the truth.*

FLING

FLING INTO →

fling yourself into sth: to suddenly begin to take part in an activity with a lot of determination or enthusiasm ▶ *When the war ended, Party workers flung themselves into the campaign for free elections.*

FLIP

FLIP FOR →

flip for sb: to suddenly begin to like someone very much ▶ *Ben has really flipped for Laura, hasn't he?*

FLIP OUT →

flip out: to become very excited, very angry, or completely crazy ▶ *My boyfriend flipped out when he saw me with another guy.*

FLIP OVER →

1 flip over, flip over sth, **flip** sth **over**: to quickly turn over, or to make something do this ▶ *The car went out of control and flipped over onto its roof.*

2 flip over sth, **flip over**: to change to another television channel. **+ to** ▶ *It is OK if I flip over to the news?*

FLIP

THROUGH →

flip through sth: to quickly look at the pages of a book, magazine etc ▶ *Alex was flipping through his address book.*

FLIRT

FLIRT WITH →

1 flirt with sth: to consider doing something, or to be interested in something, but not very seriously ▶ *In the 30s he flirted briefly with fascism.* **flirt with the idea of** ▶ *One or two of them were flirting with the idea of joining a rock band.*

2 flirt with danger/death etc: to do something that involves taking unnecessary risks ▶ *The driver knew he was flirting with death in every race.*

FLOAT

FLOAT AROUND, *also* FLOAT ABOUT →

1 be floating around/about: if an idea or story is floating around, a lot of people are talking about it ▶ *There are a lot of rumours floating about, but nobody really knows what's going to happen.*

2 be floating around/about (sth): used to say that you know something is somewhere near you, even though you are not sure exactly where ▶ *That book is definitely floating around the house somewhere.*

FLOOD

FLOOD BACK →

sth **comes flooding back**: if something comes flooding back, you suddenly remember it ▶ *As soon as she was alone, all her fears came flooding back.* **it all comes flooding back** ▶ *Every time I hear that song, it all comes flooding back.*

FLOOD IN, *also* FLOOD INTO →

flood in, flood into sth: to arrive somewhere in very large numbers ▶ *Letters of thanks have been flooding in from viewers.*

FLOOD OUT →

1 be flooded out: to be forced to leave your home because of floods ▶ *Hundreds of Londoners were flooded out after the worst rain for twenty years.*

2 flood out: to leave a place in very large numbers. **+ of** ▶ *200,000 people were reported to be flooding out of the country.*

FLOOD WITH →

1 flood sth **with** sth: to send a large number of letters, complaints, phone calls etc into an organization ▶ *Campaigners flooded the Governor's office with angry letters of protest.* **be flooded with calls/complaints etc** ▶ *The telephone lines were flooded with calls from people wanting to help.*

2 flood sth **with** sth: to provide such large amounts of something in a place that it causes a problem ▶ *A plot to flood Britain with the drug Ecstasy has been smashed by the police.*

FLOP

FLOP DOWN →

flop down: to suddenly sit or lie down somewhere, especially because you are tired. **+ in/on etc** ▶ *"I'm exhausted," said Max, flopping down in a battered armchair.*

FLOUNDER

FLOUNDER AROUND, *also* FLOUNDER ABOUT →

1 flounder around/about: to move unsteadily and with difficulty, especially in water, mud etc ▶ *Men were floundering about in the water, splashing and yelling.*

2 flounder around/about: to try hard and with difficulty to think of what to say or what to do ▶ *I floundered around, trying to think of the right word.*

FLOW

FLOW FROM →

flow from sth: to be the result of a particular situation, event, plan etc ▶ *Patients are already enjoying the benefits flowing from this new technology.*

FLOW OVER →

flow over sb: if a feeling flows over you, you suddenly feel it strongly ▶ *A wave of sadness flowed over her.*

FLUNK

FLUNK OUT →

flunk out: to be forced to leave school or college because your work is not good enough ▶ *If Jacob doesn't study more, he's going to flunk out for sure.*
+ of ▶ *Mulroney flunked out of law school at 25.*

FLUSH

FLUSH OUT →

1 flush sb/sth **out, flush out** sb/sth: to force a person or an animal to come out of the place where they are hiding ▶ *Armed police flushed the rebels out without firing a shot.*

2 flush out sth, **flush** sth **out**: to clean something thoroughly by forcing a large amount of water or other liquid through it ▶ *The radiators had to be taken outside and flushed out with a hose.*

FLY

FLY AROUND, also FLY ABOUT →
fly around/about, fly around/about sth: if rumours, stories, or accusations etc are flying around, people are talking about them a lot in an excited way ▶ *Rumours were flying around that the band was about to split up.*

FLY AT →

fly at sb: to suddenly rush towards someone because you are very angry with them ▶ *The old man flew at her in a rage.*

FLY BY →

fly by: if time flies by, it seems to pass very quickly ▶ *They started talking about old times, and the evening just flew by.*

FLY IN →

1 fly in: to arrive somewhere by plane **+ from** ▶ *Her sister flew in from New York to be at the wedding.*

2 fly sth/sb **in**: to bring something or someone to a place by plane ▶ *Cocaine is flown in from across the border.*

FLY INTO →

fly into a rage/panic: to suddenly become extremely angry or frightened ▶ *Whenever his girlfriend talked to other men, Joe would fly into a rage.*

FLY OUT →

1 fly out: to go somewhere by plane ▶ *We didn't fly out until 11:30 last night.*

2 fly sth/sb **out**: to send something or someone to another place by plane ▶ *As soon as the trouble began, all the women and children were flown out.*

FOB

FOB OFF →

1 fob off sb, **fob** sb **off**: to stop someone complaining or asking questions by giving them explanations, excuses etc that are not true. **fob** sb **off with** sth ▶ *Alan tried to fob her off with some story about losing his telephone number.*

2 fob off sb, **fob** sb **off**: to make someone accept something that is not as good as what they really want. **fob** sb **off with** sth ▶ *Don't let them fob you off with some cheap imitation.*

F

FOB OFF ON, *also* **FOB OFF ONTO** →
fob sth **off on/onto** sb, **fob off** sth **on/onto** sb: to persuade someone to do or have something that you do not want ▶ *She always tries to fob the worst jobs off onto me.*

FOCUS

FOCUS ON, *also* **FOCUS UPON** →
focus on/upon sth/sb, **focus** sth **on/upon**: to give a lot of attention to a particular thing or person instead of others ▶ *At that time all her energy was focused on her career.* **focus on doing** sth ▶ *Recent research has focussed on studying the background to the disease.*

FOG

BE FOGGED IN →
be fogged in: if a place or the people there are fogged in, the place is surrounded by low clouds so that it is impossible to see much or travel around ▶ *"We're completely fogged in," said Lisa Howard, a spokeswoman for O'Hare Airport.*

FOG UP →
fog up, fog up sth, **fog** sth **up**: if glass fogs up, or something fogs it up, very small drops of water cover it so that it is difficult to see through it ▶ *The cold, wet air fogged up her glasses as soon as she stepped outside.*

FOIST

FOIST (OFF) ON, *also* **FOIST (OFF) UPON** →
foist sth **(off) on/upon** sb: to force someone to accept or deal with something that they do not want ▶ *I wish he wouldn't keep trying to foist his problems off on other people.*

FOLD

FOLD AWAY →
1 fold sth **away, fold away** sth: to fold something into a small, neat, and

usually flat shape ▶ *Can you fold away the chairs and put them in the shed?*
2 fold away: if furniture or equipment folds away, it can be folded and made smaller ▶ *The good thing about this bed is that it folds away.*

FOLD IN, *also* **FOLD INTO** →
fold in sth, **fold** sth **in, fold** sth **into** sth: to gently mix a food into a mixture when you are cooking ▶ *Beat the egg whites and fold them into the batter.*

FOLD UP →
1 fold up sth, **fold** sth **up**: to fold something into a small, usually flat shape ▶ *She reached for the map and folded it up neatly.*
2 fold up: if something such as furniture or equipment folds up, it can be folded and made smaller ▶ *The table folds up for easy storage when you're not using it.*
3 fold up: if a business folds up, it closes permanently because it has not been successful ▶ *Experts predict that over 8,000 new businesses could fold up.*

FOLLOW

FOLLOW ON →
1 follow on: to happen after or as a result of something else. **+ from** ▶ *The discussion groups are intended to follow on from this morning's lecture.*
   follow-on N something that happens after or as the result of something else ▶ *The new coursebook is a follow-on of an earlier one.*
2 follow on: to go somewhere at a later time than someone else ▶ *The two climbers set off alone – the rest were expected to follow on later.*

FOLLOW THROUGH →
1 follow sth **through, follow through** sth, **follow** sth **up**: to do what needs to be done in order to make something happen successfully

► Peter has a lot of great ideas, but he never seems to follow them through.

2 follow sth through, follow through sth: to consider all the things that are connected with an idea, suggestion etc and what might result from it *► If you follow that idea through, you'll see it ends up being quite illogical.*

FOLLOW THROUGH ON →

1 follow through on sth: to do what you have promised, planned, threatened etc to do. **follow through on a promise/threat etc** *► Officials waited to see whether the terrorists would follow through on their promise to release the hostages.*

2 follow through on sth: to deal with something such as instructions or complaints after you have received them *► The report found that managers rarely followed through on complaints from women in the company.*

FOLLOW UP →

1 follow up sth, follow sth up: to find out more information about something, and take action if necessary *► The police received a tip about the robbery, but they never followed it up.*

2 follow up sth, follow sth up: to do something soon after you have done something else, especially in order to make sure it is successful *► The treatment is usually followed up by a series of check-ups at the local hospital.*

follow-up N something that is done after something else *► The talks were a follow-up to the first meeting in London.*

follow-up ADJ done after and resulting from something else *► They had a follow-up session to find out how much progress had been made.*

FOOL

FOOL AROUND, *also* FOOL ABOUT →

1 fool around/about: to behave in a silly way for fun *► We used to fool around a lot in class. ► Stop fooling about, will you! I'm trying to work!*

2 fool around/about: to use something in a careless and often dangerous way. **+ with** *► The fire was started by some children who were fooling about with matches.*

3 fool around, fool around sth: to go around a place, especially in a car, on a bicycle etc *► She fools around on a bicycle in her jeans.*

4 fool around: to waste time doing unnecessary things, or do something much too slowly *► We have to get to the supermarket by five and he's just fooling around!*

FOOL WITH →

fool with sth: to touch, play with, or keep changing something *► He's upstairs fooling with his computer.*

FORCE

FORCE BACK →

force back sth, force sth back: to try hard not to show your feelings, especially when you are upset. **force back tears** *► Forcing back her tears, she waved goodbye from the taxi window.*

FORCE DOWN →

1 force down sth, force sth down: to make yourself eat or drink something with difficulty *► I didn't want to be rude, so I forced down the meal and smiled at my hosts.*

2 force down sth, force sth down: to force a plane to land *► Officials forced down about 20 planes carrying illegal drugs.*

FORCE ON, *also* FORCE UPON →

force sth on/upon sb: to make someone accept or do something, even though they do not want to ▶ *Nancy always tries to force her religious views on everyone else.*

FORGE

FORGE AHEAD →

forge ahead: to make a lot of progress and become more and more successful ▶ *The on-line shopping industry continues to forge ahead.* **+ with** ▶ *The president said he will forge ahead with the economic reforms.*

FORK

FORK OUT →

fork out sth: to spend a lot of money on something ▶ *We had to fork out £900 to fix our car.*

FORK OVER →

fork sth over, fork over sth: to give someone something, especially money, even though you do not want to ▶ *Taxpayers have forked over £1.1 billion in interest payments.*

FOUL

FOUL UP →

1 foul up sth, foul sth up, foul up: to do something badly or fail at something ▶ *I really fouled up the final exam – there's no way I'll pass the course now.*

    foul-up N when someone does something badly or fails at something ▶ *The new minister puts the blame firmly on foul-ups made by the previous government.*

2 foul up sth, foul sth up: to completely spoil something such as a plan, a situation, or a relationship ▶ *I hope I haven't fouled up all your plans.*

3 foul up sth, foul sth up: to cause an engine, machine, or system to stop working properly ▶ *Problems with the software fouled up the whole computer system.*

    foul-up N when an engine, machine, or system stops working properly ▶ *delays caused by air traffic control foul-ups*

FOUND

FOUNDED ON, *also* FOUNDED UPON →

be founded on/upon: to be based on something, especially a particular idea or belief ▶ *Any relationship has to be founded on some degree of trust.*

FREAK

FREAK OUT →

1 freak out, freak sb out, freak out sb: to suddenly feel very shocked, worried, or frightened, or to make someone feel like this ▶ *My parents freaked out when I quit school.* ▶ *When I first saw the film it really freaked me out.*

2 freak out: to suddenly start behaving in a strange and uncontrolled way ▶ *The poor woman freaked out completely, banging her head against the wall and screaming.*

FREE

FREE UP →

1 free up sth, free sth up: to make something that is being used for one thing, for example time or money, available to be used for something else ▶ *The budget cuts will free up £2 billion, which can be used for other projects.*

2 free up sth, free sth up: to make a system work more easily and effectively by getting rid of things that prevent this from happening ▶ *We aim to free up the economy by getting rid of unnecessary rules and regulations.*

FREEZE

FREEZE OUT →

freeze sb out, freeze out sb: to make it impossible for someone to take part in something, for example by ignoring them or causing problems for them ▶ *I feel like Gary is trying to freeze me out of his life.* ▶ *Many people feel that they have been frozen out of the housing market by rocketing prices.*

FREEZE

FREEZE OVER →
freeze over: to become covered with ice ▶ *The lake freezes over for much of the winter.*

FREEZE UP →
1 freeze up: to become blocked with ice and impossible to use ▶ *We left the heating on in the house to stop the pipes from freezing up.*

2 freeze up: to be unable to move, speak, or do anything because you are very nervous or frightened ▶ *He freezes up whenever the teacher asks him a question.*

3 freeze up: if a machine, engine, etc freezes up, its parts stop moving and it cannot be used ▶ *Inspectors believe the train's brakes froze up, causing a wheel to skip off the tracks.*

FRESHEN

FRESHEN UP →
1 freshen up: to quickly wash yourself or make yourself look more tidy so that you feel cleaner and more comfortable ▶ *I'd like to freshen up back at the hotel room before dinner.*

2 freshen up sth, **freshen** sth **up:** to make something look cleaner, brighter, and more attractive ▶ *Use flowers from the garden to freshen up your house.*

FRIGHTEN

FRIGHTEN AWAY, *also* **FRIGHTEN OFF →**
1 frighten away sb/sth, **frighten** sb/sth **away, frighten off** sb/sth, **frighten** sb/sth **off:** to make a person or animal go away by doing something that makes them afraid ▶ *The boys threw stones into the bushes to frighten off the bears.* ▶ *Reeves said he only fired the pistol to frighten the man away.*

2 frighten away sb/sth, **frighten** sb/sth **away, frighten off** sb/sth, **frighten** sb/sth **off:** to make someone decide not to do something they might have done, by making them feel worried or nervous ▶ *The war has hurt the economy and has frightened away many potential investors who were interested in the region.*

FRITTER

FRITTER AWAY →
fritter away sth, **fritter** sth **away:** to carelessly waste money or time on unimportant things, especially in small amounts over a long period of time ▶ *His wife frittered away all their savings on fancy clothes and trips into town.* ▶ *Kitty felt she was frittering her life away.*

FRONT

FRONT FOR →
front for sb/sth: to be the person or organization used for hiding a secret or illegal activity ▶ *The FBI suspected that he was fronting for a gang of drug smugglers.*

FRONT ON, *also* **FRONT ONTO →**
front on/onto sth: if a building or town fronts on something, it faces it ▶ *My childhood home was a huge Victorian house that fronted onto a park.*

F

FROST

FROST OVER, *also* **FROST UP** →
frost over/up: to become covered in
frost ▶ *When we woke up, the room
was freezing and the windows had
frosted over.*

FROWN

FROWN ON, *also* **FROWN UPON** →
frown on/upon sb/sth: to disapprove
of someone or something ▶ *In those
days divorce was still frowned on.*
▶ *Strict dieting is frowned upon by
most medical authorities.*

FRY

FRY UP →
fry up sth, **fry** sth **up**: to quickly fry
food ▶ *Do you want me to fry up some
eggs?*

    fry-up N a meal made of fried eggs,
    sausages etc ▶ *He has a really
    unhealthy diet – all he ever eats is
    fry-ups.*

FUMBLE

FUMBLE AROUND, *also* **FUMBLE
ABOUT** →
fumble around/about: to move your
hands around in order to find
something or do something, but with
difficulty, for example because you
cannot see or you are nervous
▶ *Frank fumbled around in the
darkness, unable to find the light
switch.* **+ with** ▶ *John awkwardly
fumbled around with the papers on
his desk.*

FUNCTION

FUNCTION AS →
function as sth: to have a particular
use or purpose ▶ *In the daytime the
dining room functions as an office.*

FUR

FUR UP →
fur up: if the inside of a pipe or kettle
furs up, it becomes covered with a
hard grey substance which is formed
by chemicals in the water ▶ *There's a
lot of chalk in the water, and the kettle
tends to get all furred up.*

FURNISH

FURNISH WITH →
furnish sb/sth **with** sth: to provide
something that is needed or wanted
▶ *He should be able to furnish you
with the information you need.*

FUSS

FUSS AT →
fuss at sb: to tell someone
continuously that you do not like
something about them ▶ *The girls'
mother fussed at them, saying their
clothes were sloppy and their hair was
too long.*

FUSS OVER →
fuss over sb/sth: to give someone or
something a lot of attention,
especially in a way that is unnecessary
or annoying ▶ *My aunts and uncles
always fuss over me when I stay at
their house.* ▶ *Karen spent an hour
fussing over her hair.*

F

Gg

GABBLE

GABBLE ON, *also* GABBLE AWAY →

gabble on/away: to talk quickly for a long time in a way that is boring or difficult to understand ▶ *She spent the whole journey gabbling on about her last holiday.*

GAD

GAD ABOUT, *also* GAD AROUND →

gad about/around: to go to many different places to enjoy yourself, especially when you should be doing something else ▶ *I'm stuck at home with the kids while he's gadding about with his friends!*

GAIN

GAIN ON →

1 gain on sb/sth: to gradually get closer to a person, car etc when you are chasing them ▶ *Max turned and saw that the police car was gaining on them.*

2 gain on sth/sb: to gradually improve compared to something or someone else ▶ *In the 1980s women's wages started seriously gaining on men's for the first time.*

GALLIVANT

GALLIVANT ABOUT, *also* GALLIVANT AROUND →

gallivant about/around, gallivant around sth: to spend time going to different places to enjoy yourself ▶ *Bob's wife spent six months gallivanting around Europe while he was in hospital.*

GALLOP

GALLOP THROUGH →

gallop through sth: to do something or say something very quickly in order to finish it as soon as possible ▶ *The priest galloped through the service as fast as he could.*

GALVANIZE

GALVANIZE INTO →

galvanize sb **into** sth: to make someone suddenly realize that they must start doing something. **galvanize** sb **into action** ▶ *The urgency of his voice galvanized the staff into action.*

GAMBLE

GAMBLE AWAY →

gamble sth **away, gamble away** sth: to lose lots of money or possessions by playing card games, trying to win money at races etc and not winning ▶ *He gambled away his entire fortune on the horses.*

GAMBLE ON →

gamble on sth: to make your plans according to what you hope will happen, even though this is not certain ▶ *They were gambling on reaching the summit before the snow started falling again.*

GANG

GANG TOGETHER →

gang together: to join together in a group, especially to oppose someone ▶ *The smaller supermarkets are ganging together to beat the bigger ones at their own game.*

GANG UP →

gang up: to join together in a group to attack or oppose someone. **+ on** ▶ *She felt we were all ganging up on her.* **+ against** ▶ *His rivals ganged up against him and forced him to give up the Party leadership.*

G

G

GAS

GAS UP →

gas up, gas sth up, gas up sth: to put petrol into a car or other vehicle ▶ *We'd better gas up before we get on the freeway.*

GATHER

GATHER AROUND, *also* GATHER ROUND →

gather around sb/sth, **gather round** sb/sth, **gather around/round**: to come together and form a group around someone or something ▶ *A small crowd of admirers gathered around her after the concert.*

GATHER IN →

gather in sth, **gather sth in**: to collect a group of things together and store them somewhere, especially farm crops ▶ *The farmers were out in the fields, gathering in the harvest.*

GATHER ROUND *see* GATHER AROUND →

GATHER UP →

1 gather sth up, gather up sth: to collect things from different places in order to take or put them somewhere ▶ *She gathered up her things and quietly left the office.*

2 gather sth up, gather up sth: to pull cloth together, especially in folds ▶ *Jenny gathered up the curtain material and stitched it together.*

GEAR

GEAR TO, *also* GEAR TOWARD, GEAR TOWARDS →

be geared to sth/sb, **be geared towards** sth/sb: to be designed in a way that is suitable for a particular purpose, situation, or type of person ▶ *All of our holidays are geared to maximum fun.* ▶ *a fitness programme which is geared towards the needs of older people*

GEAR UP →

gear up: to prepare for something that is going to happen soon. **+ for** ▶ *The whole region is starting to gear up for the tourist season.* **gear yourself up** ▶ *They have been gearing themselves up for the launch of their new computer.*

GEN

GEN UP →

1 be genned up: to know a lot about a particular subject ▶ *Why don't you ask Sue? She's pretty genned up about that sort of thing.*

2 gen up: to find out all the information you can about something. **+ on** ▶ *It's a good idea to gen up on the company before you go to an interview.*

GET

GET ABOUT →

1a. get about: to be able to move around and get to places without much difficulty ▶ *My grandfather's eighty now, and he doesn't get about much.* ▶ *Phil had broken his leg, but could still get about on crutches.*
b. get about: to travel around a city or area ▶ *Bicycles are still the best way of getting about in Cambridge.*

2 get about: if news or information gets about, a lot of people hear about it ▶ *"Who told you that!" "Well, you know how things get about in a small town."* **word gets about** (=when a lot of people hear about something) ▶ *Word had got about that the company was in trouble.*

3 get about: to travel to a lot of different places ▶ *Tommy certainly gets about – last month he was in Japan, and now they've sent him to Singapore.*

GET ABOVE →

get above yourself: to think that you

are more important than you really are ▶ *That guy's getting above himself – he's only been in the job a few weeks and he thinks he runs the place.*

GET ACROSS →

a. get sth **across, get across** sth: to succeed in making someone understand an idea or message. **get a point/message across** ▶ *Animal rights activists held a demonstration outside the store to get their point across.*

b. get across: if an idea or message gets across, someone succeeds in making people understand it ▶ *The message about safe sex isn't getting across to many young people.*

GET AFTER →

1 get after sb/sth: to chase someone or something ▶ *You'd better get after your dog! He's in the garden next door again.*

2 get after sb: to tell someone to do something and remind them again and again ▶ *Paul's mother always gets after him for leaving the kitchen in a mess.*

GET AHEAD →

get ahead: to make good progress in your job ▶ *Work hard and you'll get ahead – it's as simple as that.*

GET ALONG →

1 get along: to deal with a job or situation, especially when you make good progress with it ▶ *John's getting along really well in his job – his boss thinks he's wonderful.* **how is** sb **getting along?** (=used to ask how someone is dealing with a new job or situation) ▶ *How's your daughter getting along at university?* **+ with** ▶ *"How are you getting along with the painting?" "Fine – it's almost done."*

2 get along: if two or more people get along, they have a friendly relationship. **+ with** ▶ *Rachel doesn't get along*

with her dad at all. **get along well (together)** ▶ *"How's your new roommate?" "Great – we get along really well together."* **be easy/difficult to get along with** ▶ *I've always found him a bit difficult to get along with.* **get along like a house on fire** (=get along very well) ▶ *It was clear that he and Simone were getting along like a house on fire.*

3 I must be getting along: used to tell someone that you must leave, because you have things to do ▶ *Well, I must be getting along – the kids'll be home from school soon.*

GET AROUND →

1a. get around, get around sth: to travel around a city or area ▶ *One of the best ways to get around Amsterdam is by boat.*

b. get around: to be able to move around places without much difficulty ▶ *Even though she's over 90, she still gets around pretty well.*

2 get around sth: if you get around a problem, you find a way of dealing with it, especially by avoiding it ▶ *There's no way your mother can stay here – we'll just have to get around it somehow.* ▶ *Experienced shoplifters often find ways to get around security systems.*

3 get around sth: to find a legal way of doing something that a law or rule was intended to prevent ▶ *Most companies are looking for ways to get around the tax laws.*

4 get around: if news or information gets around, a lot of people hear about it ▶ *The rumours are already starting to get around.* **word gets around** (=many people hear about something) ▶ *Word must have got around that the band was staying there, and by evening the hotel was surrounded by reporters.*

G

5 get around sb: to gently persuade someone to do what you want by being friendly to them ▶ *"Won't your dad mind?" "Don't worry – I know how to get around him."*

6 get around: to travel to a lot of different places ▶ *Steve's just come back from Hong Kong – he certainly gets around.*

7 there's no getting around sth: used when you are mentioning an unpleasant fact that cannot be changed or ignored ▶ *He didn't love his wife anymore. There was no getting around it.*

GET AROUND TO →

get around to sth: to finally do something that you have been intending to do for some time ▶ *I kept meaning to write to him, but I just never got around to it.* **get around to doing** sth ▶ *One day I'll get around to fixing that tap.*

GET AT →

1 what sb **is getting at**: what someone really means, when they are not saying it directly ▶ *I see what you're getting at, but I think you're wrong.* **what are you getting at?** ▶ *What are you getting at? Are you trying to suggest that I knew something about it?*

2 get at sth: to succeed in reaching or getting something ▶ *The book you want is up there. You'll have to stand on a chair to get at it .* ▶ *software that enables you to get at the information you need more quickly*

3 get at the truth also **get at the facts**: to discover the truth about a situation ▶ *The film is about a government investigator determined to get at the truth when his friend disappears.*

4 get at sb/sth: to reach someone or something and attack or harm them ▶ *An angry crowd surrounded the van in an attempt to get at the prisoner.*

5 get at sb: to criticize someone in an unfair and annoying way ▶ *Rob feels as if he's being got at all the time.*

6 get at sb: to threaten the people who decide whether someone is guilty in a court of law, in order to influence their decision ▶ *At least eight members of the jury had been got at.*

GET AWAY →

1 get away: to succeed in leaving a place or a person, especially when this is difficult ▶ *She just wouldn't stop talking – I couldn't get away.* **+ from** ▶ *People come to the national park to get away from city noise and traffic.*

2 get away: to escape from someone who is chasing you ▶ *The two men got away in a blue pickup truck.* **+ with** ▶ *Thieves got away with a million dollars' worth of jewellery.*

> **getaway** N if you make a getaway, you escape after doing something illegal ▶ *He made his getaway in a waiting taxi.*
>
> **getaway** ADJ a getaway vehicle is used by thieves to escape after they have stolen something ▶ *Smith's girlfriend had driven the getaway car.*

3 get away: to take a holiday away from the place where you normally live ▶ *Are you going to be able to get away this summer?* **get away from it all** (=have a relaxing holiday) ▶ *an island paradise, the perfect place to get away from it all*

> **getaway** N a relaxing holiday ▶ *Valentine's Day is the perfect time for a romantic getaway.*

4 get away!: used to say that you are

very surprised by something or do not believe it ► *"Simon asked me to marry him." "Get away!"*

GET AWAY FROM →

1 get away from sth: to start doing or thinking about something in a new or different way ► *We need to get away from the old idea that the doctor knows everything.*

2 get away from sth: to begin to talk about other things, rather than the subject you should be discussing ► *I think we are getting away from the main issue.*

3 there's no getting away from sth also **you can't get away from** sth: used when talking about an unpleasant fact that cannot be ignored ► *If you want to lose weight, you have to give up alcohol – you can't get away from it.*

GET AWAY WITH →

1 get away with sth: to not be noticed or punished when you have done something wrong. **get away with it** ► *The boy was being incredibly rude, and his mother just let him get away with it!* **get away with doing** sth ► *I don't know how they manage to get away with paying such low wages.* **get away with** sth ► *They were identical twins, and so cute they could get away with anything.* **get away with murder** (=do something serious and not be punished for it) ► *These are people with money and influence, so they can get away with murder.*

2 get away with sth: to be able to do something that it is not the best thing to do, but that is acceptable ► *I think we can get away with one coat of paint on the ceiling.*

GET BACK →

1 get back: to return to a place after going somewhere else ► *We'll probably get back at about nine.* ► *I'm*

tired. *We got back really late last night.*

2 get sth **back:** to have something given back to you ► *Did you get your books back from your sister?* **get your money back** (=when a shop or company returns money that you paid for something) ► *If they cancel the show, will we get our money back?*

3 get sb **back:** to do something to harm or embarrass someone, in order to punish them for harming or embarrassing you ► *His wife got him back by selling his Rolls Royce for £100.* **+ for** ► *I'll get you back for this!*

4 get sb **back:** to persuade someone to start having a relationship with you again ► *"Do you think she's trying to get him back?" asked Melissa, anxiously.*

5 get back!: used to tell someone to move away from something or someone ► *Get back, he's got a gun!*

GET BACK AT →

get back at sb: to do something to hurt or harm someone, in order to punish them for hurting or harming you ► *Then she started dating my ex-boyfriend, just to get back at me.* **+ for** ► *The court heard how the man had kidnapped his boss to get back at her for firing him.*

GET BACK INTO →

get back into sth: to start doing a job or activity again after not doing it for a period of time ► *The children were growing up, and I decided I wanted to get back into nursing.* ► *I hadn't done any exercise for a long time, so it took me a while to get back into it.*

GET BACK TO →

1 get back to sth: to start doing something again after stopping doing it for a period of time ► *I found it really hard getting back to studying after my vacation.* **get back to sleep** ► *Judy* *woke up in the middle of the night and couldn't get back to sleep.*

2 get back to sb: to talk to someone again at a later time, especially by telephone ▶ *I'll get back to you about the job within the next few days.*

3 get back to sth: to start talking about something after not talking about it for a period of time ▶ *As usual, we got back to the subject of money.*

GET BACK TOGETHER →

get back together: if people who are married or who used to have a relationship get back together, they start having a relationship again ▶ *Do you think Eleanor and Mark will get back together?*

GET BACK WITH →

get back with sb: to start having a relationship with someone again, after spending a period of time apart ▶ *I don't think there's much chance of me getting back with him after all this time.*

GET BEHIND →

1 get behind: if you get behind with a regular payment such as rent, you have not paid it when you should have. **+ with** ▶ *The couple are six months behind with their mortgage repayments.* **+ on** ▶ *Werner started to get behind on his rent after he lost his job.*

2 get behind: if you get behind with your work, you have not done as much as you should have ▶ *I'm worried that if I stay off sick I'll get behind.* **get behind with your work** ▶ *Lauren was getting behind with her work, but there was no one to turn to.*

3 get behind sb/ sth: to support or encourage someone or something ▶ *The England fans were great. They really got behind us.*

GET BY →

1 get by: to have or know just enough of something to deal with a situation, but not enough to make it easy ▶ *"Can you speak French?" "I know enough to get by."* **+ on** ▶ *He routinely works 14-hour days, getting by on four or five hours of sleep a night.*

2 get by: to have enough money to buy the things you need to live, but no more ▶ *He only earns just enough to get by.* **get by on £200 etc** ▶ *"I have families in my district trying to get by on £4.25 an hour," Green said.*

3 get by: to pass something that was preventing you from continuing ▶ *Cars pulled into the side of the road to let the ambulance get by.*

GET DOWN →

1 get down: to move so that your body is in a position close to the ground ▶ *Two*

men burst in with guns: "Everyone get down! Get down on the floor!" **get down on your hands and knees** (=kneel with your hands on the floor) ▶ *Every morning my grandmother would get down on her hands and knees and wash the kitchen floor.* **get down on your knees** (=kneel, especially to pray) ▶ *For the first time in his life, he got down on his knees and prayed.*

2 get sth **down**: to succeed in reducing the amount or number of something ▶ *40 members of staff were made redundant in an attempt to get costs down.* **+ to** ▶ *The government has got inflation down to 4%.*

3 get sb **down**: if a situation gets you down, it makes you feel increasingly unhappy and tired ▶ *I'd been* unemployed since I left college, and it was really getting me down. **let** sb/sth **get you down** ▶ *She refused to let her illness get her down.*

4 get sth **down**: to write something quickly, especially so that you do not forget it ▶ *Let me get your number down before I forget it.* **get** sth **down on paper** (=write something instead of just thinking or saying it) ▶ *You should get all your ideas down on paper before you start.*

5 get sth **down**: to succeed in swallowing food or drink, especially when this is difficult ▶ *My throat was still sore and I couldn't get anything down.*

GET DOWN ON →

get down on sb: to criticize someone continuously over a period of time ▶ *The press should stop getting down on our troops.*

GET DOWN TO →

get down to sth: to finally make a serious effort to start doing something ▶ *After Christmas I'm going to get down to some serious jobhunting.* ▶ *By the time we got down to work, it was already 10.30.* **get down to doing** sth ▶ *I must get down to writing that letter.* **get down to business** (=start dealing with the most important things) ▶ *There's a lot to get through today, so let's get down to business.*

GET IN →

1 get in: to go into something such as a car or small boat ▶ *Eric held the boat steady while the children got in.*

2 get in: to be allowed to enter a place ▶ *There's a new club opened in town, but you have to be 21 to get in.*

3 get in: to succeed in entering a place ▶ *How did you get in? I thought the door was locked.*

4 get in: to arrive at your home or at

work ▶ *Listen, I'll ask Mike to call you when he gets in.*

5 get in: if a train, ship, or plane gets in at a particular time, it arrives at that time ▶ *What time does your train get in?* **+ to** ▶ *We get in to Dallas around noon.*

6 get sb **in**: to arrange for someone to come to your home, office etc to do a job ▶ *The washing machine isn't working – we'd better get someone in to fix it.*

7 get sth **in, get in** sth: to find the time to do something even though you have other things to do ▶ *I want to get a couple of hours' work in before I go out.* ▶ *We need to get some more practice in before the performance.*

8 get sth **in**: to give or send something to someone before a particular time or date ▶ *Please get your assignments in by Thursday.* ▶ *Did you get that application form in?*

9 get in: if a politician or political party gets in, they are elected ▶ *The Democrats got in with a huge majority.*

10 get sth **in**: to go outside and gather things together, and put them in a place where they will not be spoiled by the weather ▶ *Can you help me get the washing in?*

11 get in: to succeed in getting a place at a university, college etc ▶ *Students who don't have at least a B grade don't have a chance of getting in.*

12 get sth **in**: to buy a supply of something you need and bring it home ▶ *We need to get some food in – I'll go to the supermarket on my way home.*

13 get sb **in**: if a shop, theatre etc gets people in, it attracts them in ▶ *We're putting on a special promotion to try and get people in.*

G

14 get in first: to say something before the person that you are competing or arguing with is able to say anything ▶ *She started to speak, but he got in first. "Where the blazes have you been?".*

GET IN ON →

get in on sth: to start doing something that other people are planning, because you think you will get an advantage ▶ *Retailers are all rushing to get in on the Internet shopping boom.* **get in on the act** (=get in on something that seems to be successful) ▶ *They started offering cut-price flights, and now other airlines are getting in on the act.*

GET INTO →

1 get into sth, **get** sb **into** sth: to become involved in, or get someone involved in, an unpleasant or difficult situation ▶ *These are dangerous men! Have you any idea what you are getting into?* **get (yourself) into trouble/a mess** ▶ *These kids get into all sorts of trouble while their parents are at work.* **get** sb **into trouble/a mess** ▶ *They got us into this mess – it's up to them to get us out of it.*

2 get into a fight/argument etc: to become involved in a fight or argument ▶ *Ryan got into a shouting match with the coach, and then stormed out of the club.*

3 get into sth: to start to do something regularly. **get into the habit of doing** sth ▶ *Get into the habit of taking regular exercise.* **get into a routine** (=start doing things regularly, at the same time every day or week) ▶ *The work seemed overwhelming at first, but I soon got into a routine.*

4 get into sth: to be accepted as a student by a college or university ▶ *My father was sure he would get into Oxford without any trouble.*

5 get into sth: to be accepted as a member of a sports team ▶ *I practised every day, determined to get into the school football team.*

6 get into sth: to succeed in getting a particular job or working in a particular area ▶ *She wanted to get into environmental law.* ▶ *TV can be a very difficult business to get into.*

7 get into a state/panic etc: to become upset, anxious, frightened etc ▶ *David got into a terrible state over his exams.* ▶ *When the children didn't arrive, she got into a panic and phoned the police.*

8 get into sth: to become interested in a book, film, piece of music etc, so that you want to read, see, or hear more ▶ *I tried to read "Moby Dick" when I was at college, but I just couldn't get into it.*

9 get into sth: to start talking about a particular subject ▶ *Before we get into a debate about funding, I'd just like to make a few announcements.*

10 what's got into sb?: used to show that you are surprised because someone is behaving in a very strange way ▶ *"This is crazy!" he said. "What's the hell's got into you?"*

11 can't get into: if you cannot get into clothes, they are too small for you ▶ *It's a lovely dress but I'm too fat to get into it now.*

12 get into power also **get into government**: to start having political control of a country ▶ *I'm leaving the country if that party gets into power again.*

13 get into groups/threes etc: to form

G

small groups so that you can work together with other people ► *Could you get into groups of about four, and come up with some possible solutions.*

GET IN WITH →

get in with sb: to become friendly with someone, especially to get an advantage for yourself ► *She had married a rich man, and then used his money to get in with the city's social elite.* **get in with the wrong crowd** (=become friendly with people who influence you to behave badly) ► *Shanie wasn't a bad kid – she just got in with the wrong crowd.*

GET OFF →

1 get off sth, **get off**: if you get off a bus, plane, large boat, train etc, you leave it ► *They saw Edwin getting off the ferry and raced to meet him.* ► *This is where I get off – I'll call you!*

2 get off, get off sth: to leave your place of work when you have finished work for that day ► *I get off early on Friday, so maybe we could go for a drink or something?*

3a. get off: to leave the place where you are or start a journey ► *What time do you want to get off in the morning?* **+ to** ► *Right, I'll get off to the shops and get her the stuff that she wants.*

b. get sb **off**: to help someone, especially a child, so that they are ready to leave a place. **+ to** ► *I'll come round after I get the kids off to school.*

4a. get off: to not be punished for a crime or something you have done wrong ► *If he gets off, it's because he has a smart lawyer.* **get off with a fine/2 months etc** (=get a punishment that is less severe than you deserve) ► *If she's very lucky, she may get off with a fine.* **get off lightly** (=get a punishment that is less severe than you deserve) ► *You got off lightly. You could have been sent to prison.*

b. get sb **off**: if a lawyer gets a criminal off, he or she succeeds in persuading the court that the criminal should not be punished ► *I know a man who killed his wife. His lawyer got him off on a plea of temporary insanity.*

5 get off sth, **get** sb **off** sth: to stop being dependent on something that you used to do or have regularly, or to make someone else do this ► *I wanted to get off drugs, but my family wouldn't support me.* ► *government plans to get people off welfare and into work*

6 get off the phone: to stop using the telephone ► *I'm waiting for Jill to get off the phone, so I can call Harry.*

7 get off!, get off sth!: used to tell someone to stop touching you or stop touching something ► *Get off those chocolates – they're mine!*

8 get sth **off**: to send a letter, package etc by mail ► *I have to get this application off today.* **+ to** ► *I'll get that confirmation letter off to you as quickly as possible.*

9 get off sth, **get** sb **off** sth: to stop talking about a subject and talk about something else, or to make someone else do this ► *Can we get off politics and talk about something else for a change?* ► *Try to get him off the subject of work.*

10a. get off: to succeed in going to sleep, especially when this is difficult. **get off to sleep** ► *When she finally got off to sleep, she was tortured by dreadful nightmares.*

b. get sb **off**: to succeed in making a baby go to sleep ► *Duncan's upstairs trying to get the baby off.*

11 get off sth: to succeed in doing something ► *They failed to get off a single goal.*

G

12 where does sb **get off doing** sth?: used when you think someone has done something to you that they have no right to do ▶ *Where does he get off telling me how to live my life?*

13 tell sb **where to get off**: to speak angrily to someone because what they have done, said, or asked is unreasonable or rude ▶ *Morris asked me to work late again." "I hope you told him where to get off."*

GET OFF ON →

get off on sth: if you get off on something, it gives you a feeling of pleasure and excitement ▶ *This guy enjoys scaring people – he gets off on that kind of thing.*

GET ON →

1 get on: if two or more people get on, they have a friendly relationship. **+ with** ▶ *"How do you get on with Julie?" "Oh, fine."* **get on well (together)** ▶ *Janet's a lovely person. We've always got on well together.* **be easy/difficult to get on with** ▶ *I've always found him a bit difficult to get on with.* **not get on** ▶ *Those two really don't get on, do they?*

2 get on sth, **get on**: to go onto a bus, train, boat, plane etc ▶ *I got on the train at Glasgow and immediately fell asleep.*

3 get on: to deal with a job or situation, especially when you do it successfully and make progress ▶ *Martin's getting on very well in his new job.* **how is** sb **getting on?** (=used to ask how someone is dealing with a new job or situation) ▶ *How's your daughter getting on in New York?* **+ with** ▶ *How are you getting on with your research project?*

4 how did you get on?: used to ask someone about the result of their visit, examination etc ▶ *"How did you get on at the interview?" "All right, I think."*

5 get on, get on with sth: to continue doing something that you were doing before ▶ *I'd like to stop and chat, but I really must get on.* **+ with** ▶ *Get on with your work!* ▶ *We should let the government get on with the business of running the country.* **get on with it!** (=used to tell someone to work faster) ▶ *Come on, get on with it! We haven't got all day!*

6 get on: to be successful in your job so that you can progress to a more important job ▶ *That new guy's very keen – you can see he really wants to get on.* **+ in** ▶ *If you want to get on in politics, you have to take every opportunity that comes your way.*

7 be getting on: if someone is getting on, they are getting old ▶ *We're both getting on now, and we can't travel about like we used to.*

8 get on the phone also **get on the telephone**: to start talking to someone on the telephone. **+ to** ▶ *He got on the phone to the company and told them we were cancelling our order.*

9 it's getting on also **time's getting on**: used to say that it is getting late ▶ *We'd better get started – time's getting on.*

GET ON AT →

get on at sb: to keep criticizing someone ▶ *My mother's always getting at me – she says my room's a disgrace.*

GET ON FOR →

be getting on for 90/ £500 etc: to be almost a particular age, time, number, or price ▶ *Her grandad must be getting on for eighty.* ▶ *I should be going home – it must be getting on for midnight.*

GET ONTO, also GET ON TO →

1 get onto sth: to begin to talk about a particular subject, after you have been talking about something else ▶ *I don't* know how we got on to this, but we were just talking about funerals. ▶ As usual we got onto the subject of money.

2 get onto sb: to phone or write to a person or organization ▶ *"Did you get on to the electrician?" "Yes, he's coming tomorrow."*

3 get onto sb: to find out about someone who is doing something wrong or illegal ▶ *The police got onto Robertson just as he was planning to leave the country.*

4 get onto sth: to be elected as a member of a committee, political organization etc ▶ *Her political career began when she got onto the local council in 1979.*

5 get onto sth: to succeed in being accepted on a course etc ▶ *It's an excellent programme, but it's really difficult to get onto it.*

6 get onto sth: to start dealing with a problem in an effective and determined way ▶ *Our new solicitor got onto the case and won us £2,000 compensation.*

GET OUT →

1 get out: to get out of a car, train, small boat etc ▶ *We all got out and helped to push the car.* **+ of** ▶ *I got out of the taxi and paid the driver.*

2a. get out: to manage to escape from a place ▶ *How did the dog manage to get out?* **+ of** ▶ *Nobody's managed to get out of the jail in over 50 years.* **get out alive** ▶ *We were lucky to get out alive. The whole building was on fire.*

b. get sb **out:** to help someone to escape from a place ▶ *There were two people trapped in the house, but firefighters managed to get them out.*

3 get sth **out:** to take something out of a bag, cupboard, container etc ▶ *I got my phrase book out and looked up the*

word for "passport". **+ of** ▶ *Kelly got a bottle of pills out of her handbag.*

4 get out!: used to rudely or angrily order someone to leave a room or a building

▶ *Get out! I'm trying to do my homework.* **+ of** ▶ *Miriam was shaking with anger: "Get out of this house now!"*

5 get out: to manage to leave an unpleasant situation ▶ *After nearly five years in the Navy, he decided he had to get out.* **+ of** ▶ *I've got to get out of this relationship or I'll go crazy.*

6 get out: to go to different places in order to meet people ▶ *You need to get out more and build up some kind of social life.* ▶ *It's difficult to get out when you've got young children.*

7 get out: if news or information gets out, people hear about it, even though it is supposed to be secret ▶ *If this gets out, I'll probably lose my job.* **word gets out** (=people hear a secret) ▶ *Word got out that the band would be arriving in London that evening.*

8 get sth **out:** to succeed in saying something when this is very difficult ▶ *She was so upset she couldn't get the words out at first.*

9 get sth **out:** to succeed in producing something, so that it is available for people to buy ▶ *We have to get the album out in time for Christmas.*

10 get sth **out:** to remove dirt from cloth. **+ of** ▶ *I couldn't get that stain out of your blue dress.*

GET OUT OF →

1 get out of sth: to avoid doing something that you have promised to do or are supposed to do ▶ *I've got a meeting at 2.00, but I'll see if I can get*

G

out of it. **get out of doing** sth ▶ He's not really ill – he's just trying to get out of going to school.

2 get sth **out of** sb: to force or persuade someone to tell you or give you something ▶ The police finally managed to get the information out of him after 8 hours of questioning. ▶ We are trying to get more money out of the government to help fund the project.

3 get sth **out of** sth: to get enjoyment from doing something, or to think that it was useful ▶ The more work you put into something, the more you get out of it. **get pleasure/satisfaction out of** sth ▶ I get a lot of satisfaction out of what I do for a living.

4 get out of sth: to stop a habit, or to stop doing an activity that you did regularly. **get out of the habit of doing** sth ▶ My mother just can't get out of the habit of telling me what to do.

GET OVER →

1 get over sth/sb: to begin to feel better after a shock or bad experience. **get over** sth ▶ It's been a terrible shock, losing her job like this – she needs time to get over it. **get over** sb (=stop feeling upset about a relationship that has ended) ▶ It's been over a year since you split up – it's about time you got over him.

2 get over sth: to get well again after an illness ▶ He's still trying to get over that bout of flu he had.

3 get over sth: to succeed in controlling feelings of fear or nervousness ▶ If you can just get over your nerves, you should pass your driving test easily.

4 get sth **over**, **get over** sth: to succeed in communicating ideas so that other people understand them. **get a point/message etc over** ▶ Anti-smoking campaigners are using a series of commercials to get their message over to the public. **get over to** sb **that** ▶ We're trying to get over to people that they must drive more slowly in built-up areas.

5 get over sth: to successfully deal with a problem or difficulty ▶ We got over the problem of worker fatigue by insisting on regular breaks throughout the day.

6 can't get over sth: used to say that you are very surprised or shocked by something ▶ I can't get over the way you look – you've lost so much weight!

7 get sth **over**: to do and finish something unpleasant that you have to do ▶ The bridegroom looked as if he just wanted to get the whole thing over as quickly as possible.

GET OVER WITH →

get sth **over with**: to do and finish something unpleasant or difficult that you have to do ▶ I just want to get these exams over with. **get** sth **over and done with** (=get something over with) ▶ It's going to be hard to tell her the news, but the sooner we get it over and done with the better.

GET ROUND →

1 get round sth: if you get round a problem, you find a way of dealing with it, especially by avoiding it ▶ We're having a problem with one of the machines, but we'll get round it somehow.

2 get round sth: to find a legal way of doing something that a law or rule was intended to prevent ▶ Arms manufacturers found ways of getting round the ban on trade.

3 get round: if news or information gets round, a lot of people hear about it ▶ News soon got round that Nick was back in town. **word gets round** (=many people hear something) ▶ Word soon got round that they were selling off their stock at bargain prices.

4 get round sb: to gently persuade someone to do what you want by being friendly to them ► *Freddie knows exactly how to get round his mum.*

5 there's no getting round sth: used when talking about an unpleasant fact that cannot be changed or ignored ► *There's no getting round the fact that racism remains a problem in many of our institutions.*

6 get round to sth: to finally do something that you have been intending to do for a long time ► *I always meant to learn to drive, but somehow I never got round to it.* **get round to doing** sth ► *When the office finally got round to answering my letter, it was too late.*

GET THROUGH →

1 get through sth, **get** sb **through** sth: to deal with a difficult experience or period of your life and come to the end of it, or to help someone to do this ► *It's going to be hard to get through the next couple of days.* ► *It was his determination and sense of humour that got him through the crisis.*

2 get through: to succeed in talking to someone on the telephone ► *Dave's been trying to call them all day, but he just couldn't get through.* **+ to** ► *When I finally got through to the helpline, they put me in a queuing system for half an hour.*

3 get through sth: to finish something that you are doing ► *I've got some work left to do, but I should get through it fairly quickly.*

4a. get through sth: to pass a test or examination, or successfully complete a course ► *If you can get through the initial exams, you shouldn't have too many problems after that.*

b. get sb/sth **through** sth: to do what is necessary to help someone or something pass a test or examination ► *A good school does more than just get its students through their exams.*

5a. get through, get through sth: if a new law or plan gets through, it becomes officially accepted by a parliament, committee etc ► *The Council meets on Wednesday, and we're hoping that these proposals will get through.*

b. get sth **through, get** sth **through** sth: if a government, president etc gets a new law or plan through, it becomes officially accepted ► *The government had intended to get the bill through before Christmas.*

6 get through, get sth **through**: to succeed in reaching a place in spite of difficulties, or succeed in sending something there ► *The Red Cross parcels were not getting through, and refugees were beginning to starve.* ► *Our priority is to get vital supplies through as quickly as possible.*

7 get through sth: to spend a lot of money, or use a lot of something such as food or drink ► *She gets through at least £200 every weekend.*

GET THROUGH TO →

1 get through to sb: to succeed in making someone understand something, especially when this is difficult ► *What do you have to do to get through to these stupid people!* **get it through to** sb **that** ► *You must try to get it through to him that you're not happy.*

2 get through to sth: to succeed in reaching the next stage of a competition ► *The contestant that gets through to the final round has a chance to win £50,000.*

GET TO →

1 get to sth: to arrive at a place or

G

reach a particular stage in a process, story etc ▶ "What time did you get to the hotel?" "About 3 o'clock." ▶ We'd just got to the bit in the play where Macbeth sees Banquo's ghost.

2 get to sb: to make someone feel more and more annoyed or upset ▶ She's always complaining – it's really beginning to get to me.

3 where has sb/ sth **got to?**: used to ask where someone or something is ▶ Where's my bag got to? It was here on the table a minute ago.

4 get to doing sth: to start doing something, especially without intending to ▶ I got to thinking perhaps I ought to try a different kind of job.

GET TOGETHER →

1 get together: to meet for a social occasion, or in order to discuss something ▶ We must get together for a drink sometime. ▶ I've got a meeting at 3.00, but we can get together and talk about it after that. **+ with** ▶ When are we getting together with Terry and Pat? Next Saturday?

> **get-together** n a party or informal social occasion ▶ We're having a get-together on Saturday, if you'd like to come.

2 get sth **together**: to collect several things and put them in one place ▶ Hang on a minute – I just need to get my things together.

3 get sb **together**: to arrange for people to meet in order to do something ▶ Why don't we get everyone together and go bowling or something?

4 get together, get it together: if two people get together or get it together, they start a romantic or sexual relationship ▶ I always thought those two should get together – they've got a lot in common. **+ with** ▶ When did she first get it together with Michael?

5 get sth **together, get together** sth: to organize or prepare something ▶ He's going to be hungry – maybe I'd better get a meal together.

6 get yourself together: to begin to be in control of your life and emotions ▶ Amanda was still trying to get herself together when another crisis devastated her life.

7 get it together also **get your act together**: to begin to be in control of a situation, and do things in an organized and confident way ▶ If she can just get it together, she should win this race. ▶ Come on, Doyle, get your act together, or we'll never solve this case.

8 get sth **together**: to succeed in getting enough money for a particular purpose ▶ Money's really tight at the moment. Some months I can barely get the rent together.

GET UP →

1a. get up: to wake up and get out of your bed, especially in the morning ▶ What time  do you have to get up tomorrow? ▶ I hate getting up in the morning, especially in winter.

b. get sb **up**: to make someone wake up and get out of bed, especially in the morning ▶ Can you get the kids up? They're going to be late for school.

2 get up: to stand up after you have been sitting or lying down ▶ Sherman got up and went over to the window. ▶ I just got up and left the room. I was absolutely furious.

3 get up sth, **get** sth **up**: to organize something, especially something that involves asking other people to help or take part ▶ She's getting up a *collection for Sue's birthday.* ▶ *One of the teachers tried to get up a football team, but the kids weren't interested.*

4 get up: if a wind or storm gets up, it starts and gets stronger ▶ *The wind got up during the night, and blew their tent away.*

5 get yourself up: to dress in unusual clothes, especially clothes that make you look like someone else. **+ in/as** ▶ *Margaret and Mitzi had got themselves up in 1920s dresses.* **be got up as/like** ▶ *He was got up as Count Dracula, complete with fangs and a long black cloak.*

6 get sth **up, get up** sth: to improve your knowledge of something ▶ *If you're going to Mexico this summer, you'd better get your Spanish up.*

GET UP TO →

get up to sth: to do something, especially something slightly bad ▶ *God knows what they get up to while their parents are away.*

GINGER

GINGER UP →

ginger sth **up, ginger up** sth: to make something more exciting by adding new or unusual things ▶ *The director tried to ginger things up by adding some dramatic special effects.*

GIVE

GIVE AWAY →

1 give away sth, **give** sth **away:** to give something that you do not want or need to someone ▶ *I've given most of my university course books away.* **+ to** ▶ *Before leaving America she gave away her furniture to her family and friends.*

2 give away sth, **give** sth **away:** to give a product to people without asking them to pay, especially in order to attract more customers ▶ *They're*

giving away free glasses with every bottle of wine.

giveaway N something that a company or shop gives to people without asking for payment ▶ *There are usually a lot of giveaways on offer at Christmas.*

giveaway ADJ given free by a company in order to advertise its products ▶ *giveaway diaries*
giveaway prices prices that are very low ▶ *The shop was selling off all its old stock at giveaway prices.*

3 give away sth, **give** sth **away:** to give something as a prize in a competition ▶ *We have baseball caps to give away in this week's show .*

4 give away sth, **give** sth **away:** to let someone know about something that should be a secret, especially by mistake ▶ *I don't want to give away the ending. You'll have to see the movie for yourself.* **give the game away** (=make someone realize something that other people wanted to keep a secret) ▶ *She gave the game away by mentioning that she'd spoken to him the day before.*

giveaway N something that makes it easy for you to guess a fact that people are trying to keep secret ▶ *The lipstick on his collar was a bit of a giveaway.*

5 give sb **away:** to accidentally show other people how you really feel when you are trying to hide this ▶ *Karen was trying to look cool, but her face gave her away immediately.* **give yourself away** ▶ *Most shoplifters give themselves away by constantly looking round for cameras.*

6 give sb **away:** to tell the police or soldiers where someone who is hiding from them is or who they are ▶ *Someone in her family gave her away to the local police.*

G

7 give away sth, **give** sth **away**: to let your opponents have an advantage or allow them to win ▶ *Arsenal gave away two goals in the first five minutes of the game.*

GIVE BACK →

1 give back sth, **give** sth **back**: to give something back to the person who owns it or who gave it to you ▶ *If the engagement is cancelled, do I have to give back the ring?* **+ to** ▶ *The government is giving back nine million pounds to the City Council.* **give** sb **back** sth ▶ *Give him back his hat!* **give sb** sth **back** ▶ *Hey! Give me my book back!*

2 give sth **back**, **give back** sth: to make it possible for someone to have a particular quality, ability, or right that they used to have in the past. **+ to** ▶ *The protesters are calling for the government to give power back to the people.* **give** sb **back** sth ▶ *A little warm food and rest will give you back some strength.* **give** sb sth **back** ▶ *The doctors are hoping the operation will give Murphy his sight back.*

GIVE IN →

1 give in: to finally agree to something you were unwilling to agree to before ▶ *In the end he gave in and paid her the full price for the painting.* **+ to** ▶ *The government has so far refused to give in to the terrorists' demands.*

2 give in: to accept that you have been defeated and stop competing or fighting ▶ *The French team refused to give in, and scored three goals in the second half.*

3 give in sth, **give** sth **in**: to give something such as an official letter or a piece of written work to someone in a position of authority ▶ *The next day Davies gave in his resignation.* ▶ *I'm supposed to give in this essay tomorrow morning.*

GIVE IN TO →

give in to sth: if you give in to a feeling that you want to do something, you allow yourself to do it, especially after trying not to ▶ *In the end he gave in to temptation and lit up his first cigarette of the day.*

GIVE OFF →

1 give off sth, **give** sth **off**: to produce something such as a smell, heat, light, energy, gas etc ▶ *The flowers gave off a powerful sweet scent.* ▶ *the enormous amount of energy which is given off by nuclear reactions*

2 give off sth: to seem to have a particular quality from the way you look or behave ▶ *Felicity gave off an impression of intelligence and efficiency.*

GIVE ONTO →

give onto sth: if a door, window, room, garden etc gives onto a place, it leads to that place ▶ *Our apartment gave onto a balcony that overlooked the sea.*

GIVE OUT →

1 give out sth, **give** sth **out**: to give something to a lot of people ▶ *Protesters were giving out leaflets in front of the embassy.* ▶ *"Are there any more plates?" "No. I've given them all out."*

2 give out sth, **give** sth **out**: to tell people information, especially publicly or officially ▶ *You should be careful about giving out your credit card details over the Internet.* ▶ *The Foundation gives out free advice on pregnancy and contraception.*

3 give out: to stop working properly, for example because of being old or damaged ▶ *She shouted so much that in the end her voice gave out.* ▶ *The light's starting to go very faint. I think the batteries have given out.*

4 give out: if a supply of something

gives out, there is no more left because it has all been used ► *How much longer before the fuel gives out?* ► *Her patience finally gave out and she started yelling.*

5 give out sth, **give** sth **out**: to produce something such as a smell, heat, light etc ► *Oil stoves don't always give out a lot of heat.*

6 give out: to seem to have a particular quality from the way you look or behave ► *The speaker gave out an air of confidence and calm authority.*

7 give out a message also **give out a signal**: to make people have a particular idea about something by what you say and do ► *I believe we're giving out the wrong message to children about drugs.*

GIVE OVER →

give over!: used to tell someone rudely to be quiet ► *Give over you two! I can't hear the television.*

GIVE OVER TO →

1 be given over to sth: to be used only for a particular purpose or activity ► *Tuesday afternoons were usually given over to sports and leisure activities.*

2 give yourself over to sth also **give your life over to** sth: to spend all your time and energy doing something or thinking about something ► *She had given her whole life over to caring for Jane.*

3 give sth/sb **over to** sb: to allow another person, organization etc to have control of something or someone ► *He gave the boy over to the care of the local authority.* ► *Control over the country's finances was given over to parliament.*

GIVE UP →

1 give up sth, **give** sth **up**: to stop doing something that you used to do

regularly ► *She gave up her job at the nursing home and moved to London.* **give up doing** sth ► *I had to give up playing football after the accident.*

2 give up sth, **give** sth **up**, **give up**: to stop smoking, drinking etc because you think it is bad or unhealthy ► *He gave up alcohol over three years ago.* ► *"Cigarette?" "No thanks, I'm trying to give up."* **give up doing** sth ► *Vanessa's been feeling much better since she gave up smoking.*

3 give up, **give up** sth: to stop trying to do something, especially because it is too difficult ► *They searched for the ball for a while, but eventually gave up and went home.* **give up doing** sth ► *After about ten minutes I gave up trying to explain it to her.* **I give up** (=used to say that you cannot guess the answer to a question or joke) ► *"How much do you think this suit cost?" "I don't know. £200, £500 ... £1000? Oh, I give up!"*

4 give up sth: to let someone else have something that is yours, especially when you do not really want to ► *Lack of money forced him to give up his London apartment.*

5 give yourself up: to allow the police or enemy soldiers to make you a prisoner when they

have been trying to catch you ► *The General sent a message to the rebels, urging them to give themselves up.* **+ to** ► *Two of the escaped prisoners have given themselves up to the police.*

6 give up sth, **give** sth **up**: to use some of your time to help other

people or to help something succeed.
+ to do sth ▶ *We should like to thank the mayor for giving up his valuable time to support our campaign.*

7 give up hope: to stop hoping that something good will happen or that things will get better ▶ *Just when they had almost given up hope, Jenny became pregnant.* **give up hope of doing** sth ▶ *When the factory closed, most of the workers gave up hope of ever getting another job.*

8 give up sb, **give** sb **up:** to give your child to someone else so that the child legally becomes part of that person's family. **give sb up for adoption** ▶ *I refused to give up my baby for adoption – he was mine.*

9 give sb **up for dead:** to begin to believe that someone is dead and stop looking for them ▶ *Three Americans who had been given up for dead were found alive yesterday.*

GIVE UP ON →

1 give up on sth: to stop trying to make something happen or succeed ▶ *Never give up on your dreams – the things you really want to do.* **give up on doing** sth ▶ *By 4 am I'd given up on trying to sleep.*

2 give up on sb: to stop hoping that someone will improve or do what you want them to ▶ *He'd been in a coma for six months, and the doctors had almost given up on him.*

GIVE UP TO →

1 give yourself up to sth: to allow a strong feeling of pleasure, desire etc to completely fill your mind ▶ *He gave himself up to the irresistible delights of the big city .*

2 be given up to sth: if a period of time is given up to an activity, all of it is used for that activity ▶ *The afternoons were given up to sport and recreation.*

GLANCE

GLANCE OFF →

glance off sth, **glance off:** to hit something at an angle and then move away in another direction ▶ *Light from the setting sun glanced off the metal buildings.* ▶ *A bullet struck the side of their car and glanced off.*

GLAZE

GLAZE OVER →

glaze over: if someone's eyes glaze over, they start to look bored or tired ▶ *Whenever anyone tried to explain the statistics to Mr Vernon, his eyes would start to glaze over.*

GLOM

GLOM ONTO →

1 glom onto sth: if one thing gloms onto another, the first thing fastens itself firmly to the second ▶ *Researchers found that the antibodies glom onto the virus and destroy it.*

2 glom onto sb: to try to spend time with someone and become friends with them, especially when they do not want you to do this ▶ *Lisa glommed onto Rita and her friends and followed them wherever they went.*

GLORY

GLORY IN →

glory in sth: to enjoy something very much and feel proud of it, especially something that other people disapprove of ▶ *Her brother was not ashamed of his violent behaviour. On the contrary, he gloried in it.*

GLOSS

GLOSS OVER →

gloss over sth, **gloss** sth **over:** to deliberately avoid talking about unpleasant facts, or to say as little as possible about them ▶ *There were*

G

problems in our relationship that couldn't be glossed over. ▶ a skilful speech that had glossed over all the embarrassing details

GLOW

GLOW WITH →

glow with pleasure/pride etc: to look very happy because you are pleased, proud etc ▶ Parker glowed with pleasure at the thought of all the money he was going to make.

GLUE

BE GLUED TO →

be glued to the television/ screen etc: to be watching the television etc with all your attention for a long time ▶ Those kids are glued to the TV all day.

GNAW

GNAW AT →

gnaw at sb/sth: to make someone feel continuously worried, frightened, or uncomfortable ▶ Feelings of guilt gnawed at him. ▶ The problem had been gnawing at his mind for months.

GNAW AWAY →

gnaw away sth, gnaw sth away: to gradually destroy something ▶ The disease steadily gnaws away the body's defences.

GO

GO ABOUT →

1 go about sth: to start to do or deal with something in a particular way ▶ Growing herbs is not difficult, providing you go about it in the right way. **how do you go about doing sth?** (=what is the best way to do something?) ▶ How do I go about

finding out about the different courses available?

2 go about your business/work etc: to continue doing your activities or your job in the usual way ▶ Even after last night's air attack, the people of the town are going about their business as usual.

3 go about doing sth: to do something a lot, especially something that annoys other people ▶ You shouldn't go about spreading malicious gossip.

4 go about: to dress or behave in a particular way. **+ in** ▶ In the days that followed, Liza went about in a daze. ▶ You can't go about in shorts and sandals at the office.

5 go about sth, go about: to move or travel around a place ▶ She went about the room, putting everything back in its place.

6 go about, go about sth: if a story or piece of information is going about, a lot of people are talking about it ▶ That story's been going about for weeks now, and it's absolute rubbish! **+ that** ▶ Rumours have been going about that the couple are planning to get married.

7 go about: if an illness is going about, a lot of people are getting it ▶ At least three people are away with flu – there's a lot of it going about at the moment.

GO ABOUT WITH, also GO ABOUT TOGETHER →

go about with sb, go about together: to spend a lot of time with someone because you are friends or are having a relationship with them ▶ Didn't you and Frank use to go about together when you were at university?

GO AFTER →

1 go after sb/sth: to follow or chase someone, in order to catch them, attack them, or talk to them ▶ She

G

*looked so upset. Do you think I should
go after her?*

2 go after sth: to try to get something,
especially a job or a particular type of
business ▶ *I've decided to go after
that job in Ohio.* ▶ *Tobacco companies
are going after teenage smokers in a
big way.*

GO AGAINST →

1 go against sth: if something goes
against an idea, principle, or rule, it
seems very different from it, or breaks
that rule ▶ *Her parents didn't want her
to get a divorce. It went against their
religious beliefs.* **it goes against the
grain** (=used to say that something is
very different from what you would
normally do) ▶ *It goes against the
grain to tell a complete stranger
everything about your private life.*

2 go against sth/sb: to not do what
someone has asked or advised you to
do, or to do something different to it.
go against sb's advice/wishes etc
▶ *He went against his doctor's advice
and went back to work the following
week.* **go against** sb ▶ *She never
expected her mother to go against her
father like that.*

3 go against sb: if a court case,
decision, vote etc goes against you,
you lose or you do not get the result
that you want ▶ *Our lawyer had
warned us that the case might go
against us.* **things go against you**
(=used to say that events happen in a
way that is bad for you) ▶ *By the end
of the 1980s, things started to go
against us, and we lost a lot of
money.*

GO AHEAD →

1 go ahead: to do something that you
have been planning or preparing to
do. **+ with** ▶ *Last night railway
workers looked likely to go ahead with
their strike.* **go ahead and do** sth ▶ *In*

*the end, the newspaper went ahead
and published the story.*

the go-ahead N if someone gives
you the go-ahead to do something,
they give you official permission to
start doing it ▶ *The movie was given
the go-ahead and production
started in May.*

2 go ahead: to take place, especially
in spite of problems or opposition
▶ *The match went ahead, despite the
terrible weather conditions.* ▶ *Mr
Connelly went into hospital, but was
told that his operation could not go
ahead.*

3 go ahead!: a. used to give someone
permission to do something ▶ *"Do you
mind if I smoke?" "No, go ahead."*
b. used to encourage someone to start
doing something ▶ *Go ahead, Matt,
we're all dying to hear your story.*
c. used to tell someone in a
threatening way that you do not care if
they do something ▶ *"If you don't get
off my land, I'll take you to court." "Go
ahead."*

4 go ahead: to go somewhere before
or in front of other people you are with
▶ *I'll go ahead in my car, because I
know the way.*

GO ALONG →

1 go along: to go to a place or an
event ▶ *They're having a party at
Patrick's house. Do you feel like going
along?*

2 do sth **as you go along**: to do
something at the same time as you are
doing something else, especially
because you have not planned or
prepared it properly ▶ *I'm sure she
was making her speech up as she
went along.* ▶ *You can't just make the
rules of the game as you go along!*

3 be going along: to progress in a
particular way ▶ *They've been going
out together for six months, and*

everything seems to be going along quite nicely.

GO ALONG WITH →

go along with sth/sb: to accept someone's idea or suggestion, especially because it might upset someone or cause trouble if you do not ▶ *I wasn't very keen on the idea, but I went along with it just to keep everyone happy.*

GO AROUND, *also* **GO ROUND** →

1 go around/round: to go to see someone for a short time, especially at the place where they live ▶ *I think I'll go round and see Jim on my way home tonight.* **+ to** ▶ *Marie went around to Bella's place, to try and persuade her to come to the party.*

2 go around/round sth: to move or travel around a place ▶ *I spent the morning going around the city taking photographs.*

3 go around/round sth, **go around/round**: to go to a number of different places of the same type, one after the other ▶ *Mrs Taylor went around the shops, ordering what she thought was necessary.* **+ to** ▶ *We went round to all the clubs, but Des wasn't in any of them.*

4 go around/round doing sth: to say or do something a lot, especially something annoying ▶ *You can't go around accusing people of things like that.*

5 go around/round: to dress or behave in a particular way, especially regularly ▶ *I can't see anything without my glasses – I might as well go around with my eyes shut.*

6 go around/round, go around/round sth: if a story or piece of information is going around, a lot of people are talking about it ▶ *I don't usually pay any attention to the gossip going around at work.* **+ that** ▶ *There's been*

a rumour going round that they're planning to close the factory.

7 enough/plenty etc to go around: if there is enough food, drink, work etc to go around, there is enough for everyone to have some ▶ *Do you think we've got enough pizza to go round?* ▶ *Builders are really having a hard time these days – there just isn't enough work to go around.*

8 go around/round, go around/round sth: if an illness is going around, a lot of people are getting it ▶ *A particularly unpleasant virus was going around the school.*

GO AROUND WITH, *also* **GO AROUND TOGETHER, GO ROUND TOGETHER** →

go around/round with sb, **go around/round together**: to spend a lot of time with someone, for example because you are friends or are having a romantic relationship with them ▶ *There was a gang of about six of us who went round together all the time.*

GO AT →

1 go at sth: to start to do something or deal with it in a particular way, especially in a determined or energetic way. **go at it** ▶ *The women went at it with tremendous enthusiasm.*

2 go at sb: to start to fight, attack, or argue with someone ▶ *Sophie went at him with a kitchen knife.*

GO AWAY →

1 go away: to leave a place or a person ▶ *Go away and let me get some sleep!* ▶ *He pushed the letter under the door and went away.*

2 go away: to leave your home in order to spend some time somewhere else ▶ *We're going away to France for a week.* ▶ *Dad often had to go away on business.*

3 go away: if a problem, pain, or

something unpleasant goes away, it disappears ▶ *After about an hour, the pain started to go away.* sth **goes away by itself** (=it disappears without anyone doing anything) ▶ *Traffic problems won't just go away by themselves – it's up to us to take action.*

GO BACK →

1 go back: to return to a place where you have been before, or to the place where you were until recently ▶ *They left Africa in 1962, and they never went back.* **+ to** ▶ *We went back to the hotel for dinner.*

2 go back: if something goes back to a time in the past, it started to exist then. **+ to** ▶ *Parts of the castle here go back to the twelfth century.* sth **goes back a long way** (=it started a long time ago and has existed for a long time) ▶ *They're a very old family – their name goes back a long way.*

3 go back, go back sth: to consider or discuss things that happened at a time in the past ▶ *Let's go back a few million years and look at the time of the dinosaurs.* **+ to** ▶ *To understand many emotional problems, you often have to go back to the patient's childhood.*

4 you can't go back also **there's no going back**: used to say that you cannot change your situation back to how it used to be ▶ *If we sell the house, there's no going back.*

5 go back: if schools or students go back, the schools open and the students start studying again after the holidays ▶ *When do the schools go back?* **+ to** ▶ *The kids go back to school in the first week of September.* —see GO BACK TO

6 go back: to be returned to the place where something was bought or borrowed from ▶ *Don't forget the car*

has to go back tomorrow – we only hired it for a week.

7 go back: to start working again after a strike ▶ *The miners say they won't go back unless they get more money.*

8 go back a long way: if two people go back a long way, they have known each other for a long time ▶ *Annie and Richard go back a long way – at least fifteen years.*

9 the clocks go back: when the clocks go back in the autumn, the time officially changes so that it is one hour earlier than it was before ▶ *The clocks go back some time in October, don't they?*

GO BACK ON →

1 go back on sth: to not do what you have promised, agreed, or said you would do ▶ *He said he won't lend us any money, and I can't see him going back on his decision.* **go back on your word** (=not do what you have promised or agreed to do) ▶ *"You can trust me," said Professor Higgins. "I never go back on my word."*

2 go back on sth: to change what you said before, or say that you never said it ▶ *One of the witnesses has gone back on her original story.*

GO BACK OVER →

go back over sth: to examine, consider, or repeat something again ▶ *Would you mind going back over the rules for me again?*

GO BACK TO →

1 go back to sth: to start to do something again that you were doing before, or used to do in the past. **go**

ack to work/school etc ▶ *After the peration, it was six weeks before I ould go back to work.* **go back to leep/bed** ▶ *I tried to go back to leep, but I couldn't stop thinking.* **o back to doing** sth ▶ *I'd hate to go ack to living abroad now.*

go back to sth: to return to a ituation or state that used to exist efore ▶ *It will be a long time before hings start to go back to normal after he war.* ▶ *Can't we just go back to eing friends?*

go back to sb: to start to have a elationship with someone again after had ended ▶ *He'll never go back to is girlfriend now.*

go back to sth: to start talking about r considering something again ▶ *Can ve just go back to Alan's point for a ninute?*

GO BEFORE →

have gone before: to have happened r existed before ▶ *Industrialization reated a form of society that was different from any that had gone before.* **what has gone before** ▶ *In many ways this program improves on what has gone before.*

go before sb: to be considered by someone in authority, so that they can nake an official decision ▶ *The proposal will go before the Planning Committee at their next meeting.*

GO BEYOND →

go beyond sth: to be much better, more serious, more advanced etc than something else ▶ *The book's success went beyond anything we had expected.* ▶ *She didn't just feel unhappy – it went beyond that.*

GO BY →

1 go by: if time goes by, it passes ▶ *Twenty years had gone by since I last saw him.* ▶ *As time went by, our fears for her safety increased.*

bygone ADJ used to describe a period of time as one that existed a long time ago ▶ *Their way of life is a reminder of a bygone age.*

2 go by: to move past you, especially when you are not moving ▶ *I sat down at an open-air cafe, and watched the people going by.*

3 go by sth: to stop at a place for a short time, usually to get something ▶ *On the way home I went by Jason's to pick up my jacket.*

4 go by sth: to use a particular thing when you are making a judgement or deciding what you should do ▶ *You can't go by that old map. It's completely out of date.* **if** sth's **anything to go by** (=used when saying that something is likely to be true, because something else is true) ▶ *It should be a great movie, if Kubrick's other work is anything to go by.*

5 go by sth: to obey the rules of something ▶ *There was one point in the game when he certainly wasn't going by the rules.* **go by the book** (=be very careful to obey all the rules exactly) ▶ *There is a fixed procedure for making a complaint, and we prefer it if you go by the book.*

6 let sth **go by**: to deliberately ignore or not react badly to someone's remarks or behaviour ▶ *"I'll let it go by this time," the teacher said, "but I don't want it to happen again."*

GO DOWN →

1 go down sth: to move along a street, passage etc in order to get somewhere ▶ *I went down the corridor and knocked on the staffroom door.*

2 go down, go down sth: to go to a particular place near where you live, or the one that you usually go to. **+ to** ▶ *The kids have gone down to the river.* **go down the shops/pub etc**

▶ *My dad always used to go down the pub after Sunday dinner.*

3 go down: to visit or travel to a place, especially somewhere that is further south or in the country ▶ *At weekends, Wright used to go down and stay with his father in Mississippi.* **+ to** ▶ *Three days a week Kate went down to Camberwell to teach.*

4 go down: to reach as far as a particular point or place. **+ to** ▶ *The road doesn't go down to the beach – we'll have to walk from here.*

5 go down: if a price or the level of something goes down, it gets lower ▶ *The price of fruit tends to go down in the summer.* **+ to** ▶ *When I came out of hospital, my weight had gone down to eight stone.*

6 go down: if the standard or quality of something goes down, it becomes worse ▶ *The standard of the food in the canteen has gone down a lot recently.* **things have gone down** ▶ *Things have really gone down at the school since the old head teacher left.*

7 go down: if a computer goes down, or the telephone lines go down, they stop working because of a fault ▶ *Make sure you save your work regularly, just in case the computers go down.* ▶ *The lines had gone down in the storm, and we were cut off for days.*

8 go down well/badly etc: to get a good, bad etc reaction from people ▶ *The band's given several performances so far, and they all went down really well.* ▶ *I could see at once that my comments had gone down badly.*

9 go down well *also* **go down nicely etc**: if food or drink goes down well, nicely etc you enjoy eating or drinking it ▶ *A long cold drink would go down very nicely, thank you.*

10 go down: when the sun goes down at the end of the day, it gradually gets lower in the sky until it disappears ▶ *The sun was going down in the West.*

11 go down: to fall to the ground, especially because of an accident or injury ▶ *The leading horse went down at the last jump.*

12 go down on your knees *also* **go down on all fours**: to get into a kneeling position, or in a position with your hands and knees on the floor ▶ *Did he go down on his knees when he asked you to marry him?* ▶ *I quickly went down on all fours and started to crawl towards the door.*

13 go down: if a ship or boat goes down, it sinks ▶ *Then our small boat began to go down and we found ourselves in the river.*

14 go down: if a plane goes down, it crashes to the ground ▶ *The aircraft went down somewhere over the Atlantic.*

15 the lights go down: if lights go down in a theatre, cinema etc, they are turned off or made less bright so that the show can begin ▶ *The lights went down as the orchestra started to play.*

16 go down: to lose a game against another team or player. **+ to/against** ▶ *United went down 2-0 against Rovers.*

17 go down: to move down to a lower group of teams or players who play against each other. **+ to** ▶ *At the end of the season, five clubs went down to the second division.*

18 go down:
if a tyre, balloon etc goes down, the air goes out of it ▶ *It looks as if the front tyre has gone down.*

19 go down: if a swelling on your body goes down, it disappears ▶ *If you rest your leg, the swelling should go down soon.*

20 go down: to be sent to prison ▶ *It was a horrible crime and the boys involved deserved to go down.* **go down for life/10 years etc** ▶ *If they ever catch the murderer, he'll go down for life.*

21 go down: to happen ▶ *I'll never understand exactly what went down that night.*

22 what's going down?: used as a greeting when you meet someone ▶ *Hey, Bob! What's going down?*

GO DOWN AS →

go down as sth: to be remembered or recorded as being a particular thing or type of person ▶ *He's sure to go down as one of the greatest ever basketball players.* **go down in history as** sth ▶ *She'll go down in history as one of our most courageous war heroes.*

GO DOWN WITH →

go down with sth: to get an illness, especially one that is not very serious ▶ *Several people at work have gone down with flu.*

GO FOR →

1 go for sth: to try to get, win, or achieve something ▶ *What sort of job are you going for, Tim?* **go for it!** (=used to encourage someone to try to do or get something) ▶ *It sounds like a good deal! Go for it!* **sb really goes for it** (=used to say that someone tries as hard as they can to get something) ▶ *If she sees a chance for promotion, she really goes for it.*

2 go for sth: to choose a particular thing because you think it is better or more suitable ▶ *I'd go for the black dress if I were you.*

3 go for sth/sb: to like a particular

type of thing or person ▶ *I don't normally go for bright colours.*

4 go for sth: to be sold or available to buy for a particular price ▶ *How much did the painting go for in the end?*

5 go for sb: to attack someone physically or criticize them very severely ▶ *Ben lifted his arm and for a second I thought he was going to go for me.* ▶ *She always used to go for him in meetings.*

6 that goes for sb/sth also **the same goes for** sb/sth : used to say that the same thing is also true about someone or something else ▶ *I've always hated living in cities. Fortunately the same goes for my husband.*

7 have a lot going for you: to have a lot of advantages or good qualities ▶ *We've always thought that the Austrian skiing resorts have a lot going for them.* **have everything going for you** ▶ *She had everything going for her, and then she had that terrible accident.*

8 go for sth: to be used for a particular purpose ▶ *£54 million went for the resettlement of refugees.*

9 go for your gun/knife etc: to move your hand quickly towards your gun, knife etc, in order to use it ▶ *The police officer thought he was going for his gun, and shot him through the chest.*

GO FORWARD →

1 go forward: to start to happen or to make progress ▶ *The project can only go forward if we are able to get further financial support.*

2 go forward: if someone or something's name goes forward for a job, prize etc, their name is officially suggested for it ▶ *Six names went forward for the position of chairman.*

G

3 go forward: to compete in the next stage of a competition after winning the previous stage. **+ to** ▸ *The winner of the competition will go forward to the national final.*

4 the clocks go forward: when the clocks go forward in the spring, the time officially changes so that it is one hour later than it was before ▸ *The clocks go forward this Saturday.*

GO FORWARD TO →

go forward to sth: to be taken to a group of people in authority in order to be considered or officially decided ▸ *Our recommendations went forward to the Finance Committee.* ▸ *The case then went forward to the European Court of Human Rights.*

GO FORWARD WITH →

go forward with sth: to start to do something that you have planned ▸ *Are you sure you want to go forward with these charges?*

GO IN →

1 go in: to enter a building or room ▸ *It's starting to rain. Do you want to go in?*

2 go in: to go to the place where you work ▸ *Ed went in early every day last week.* **+ to** ▸ *Can I take the car if you're not going in to work tomorrow?*

3 go in: to go and stay in hospital in order to receive treatment ▸ *He's got to go in to have an operation on his eye.* **+ for** ▸ *The actress reportedly went in for cosmetic surgery last week.*

4 go in: to enter a dangerous building, area, or country in order to try and deal with the problems there ▸ *OK men. We're going in!*

5 go in sth, **go in**: to fit inside a container, space, hole etc ▸ *There must be something wrong with this cassette; it won't go in.*

6 go in, go in sth: to join a company or organization ▸ *Bob went in at quite a low level, but he was quickly promoted.*

7 go in:
if the sun or moon goes in, it disappears behind clouds ▸ *The sun had gone in and it was starting to get cold.*

8 go in: if a piece of information goes in, you understand it and remember it ▸ *I tried to concentrate on what he was saying, but it just wasn't going in.*

GO IN FOR →

1 go in for sth: to do, use, have etc a particular type of thing, because you like it, or because it seems a good idea ▸ *In our family we don't go in much for formal meals.* ▸ *Men don't usually go in for displays of emotion.*

2 go in for sth: to take part in a competition or examination ▸ *I decided I'd go in for the Young Entertainer of the Year contest.* ▸ *There are several exams you can go in for if you want to improve your qualifications.*

GO INTO →

1 go into work/ hospital etc: to go to work, hospital etc ▸ *You don't look well enough to go into work today.*

2 go into sth: to go to the centre of the town that you live in or near ▸ *I thought I'd go into Cambridge this afternoon.* **go into town** ▸ *Could you give me a lift if you're going into town?*

3 go into sth: to fit inside a container, space, hole etc ▸ *Which hole does this screw go into?*

4 go into sth: to join a company, organization, or profession ▸ *At sixteen he left school and went into the family business.*

5 go into sth: to talk about something, especially in a detailed way ▶ *It's a difficult subject and there isn't time to go into it here.*

6 go into sth: to find out more about something, by getting all the necessary information ▶ *Before you make any further plans, you'd better go into the cost of all this.*

7 go into sth: to start to be in a particular state or situation, especially a bad one ▶ *Her son went into a coma and never came out of it.* **go into debt** ▶ *We had to go into debt in order to pay for our daughter's wedding.*

8 go into sth: to start behaving in a particular way. **go into a mood/temper** ▶ *She's gone into one of her moods and is refusing to talk to anyone.* **go into a panic** ▶ *The crowd went into a panic, and started to run for the exits.*

9 go into sth: if a lot of time, money, effort etc goes into doing something, it is used in order to do it ▶ *Years of research went into the book.* **go into doing** sth ▶ *Huge amounts of money have gone into developing new cancer drugs.*

10 go into sth: to be used in something you are making ▶ *Some quite expensive ingredients go into this recipe.*

11 go into sth: to take part in a competition, election, or exam ▶ *The US team is extremely confident as it goes into Thursday's game.*

12 go into sth: to accidentally hit something such as a wall, tree, car etc ▶ *I didn't see the red lights and I went into the back of a BMW.*

13 go into sth: if a number goes into a second number, the second number can be divided exactly by the first ▶ *Seven doesn't go into thirty-two.*

GO OFF →

1 go off: to leave the place where you are and go somewhere else. **+ to** ▶ *All the men had gone off to the war.* **+ to do** sth ▶ *Dad went off to watch the baseball game.*

2 go off sb/sth: to stop liking someone or something that you used to like ▶ *Pete went off me after he met another girl on holiday.* ▶ *I used to enjoy tennis, but I've gone off it a bit now.*

3 go off: if food or drink goes off, it is not good to eat or drink any more because it is no longer fresh ▶ *Milk usually goes off after a few days.*

4 go off: if a bomb goes off, it explodes ▶ *A bomb went off in East London last night, killing two people.*

5 go off: if a light, machine etc goes off, it stops working ▶ *Suddenly all the lights went off.*

6 go off: if a gun goes off, it fires ▶ *I heard a gun go off in the distance.*

7 go off: if an alarm goes off, it makes a sudden loud noise ▶ *I set my alarm clock to go off at six.*

8 go off well *also* **go off smoothly**: to happen successfully in the way that you had planned ▶ *Rosie was very nervous, but all the arrangements went off really smoothly.*

9 go off: to suddenly start talking or thinking about something completely different ▶ *Ian suddenly went off into a description of his childhood.*

10 go off: to become worse in standard or quality ▶ *It used to be a lovely hotel, but it's gone off a bit in recent years.*

11 go off: to talk to or shout at someone very angrily. **+ on** ▶ *Melissa really went off on Rich as soon as he got home.*

G

GO OFF WITH →

1 go off with sb: to leave your husband, wife, boyfriend etc in order to have a relationship with someone else ► *Ken went off with a woman half his age.*

2 go off with sth: to take something away from somewhere without permission, or to steal something ► *I think someone went off with my coat by mistake.* ► *He went off with thousands of pounds worth of jewellery.*

GO ON →

1 go on: to continue to happen or exist ► *The party went on until four in the morning.* **+ for** ► *The talks are expected to go on for several weeks.* **go on and on** (=continue for a very long time) ► *The meeting went on and on, until we were practically falling asleep.*

> **ongoing** ADJ used to emphasize that something continues to happen and does not stop ► *Learning is an ongoing process – it doesn't stop when you leave school.*

2 go on: to continue doing something without stopping or changing ► *If you go on like this, you'll end up in hospital.* **go on doing** sth ► *Philip completely ignored what I said and went on eating.* ► *It could go on raining like this all day.*

3 go on: if something is going on, it is happening, especially something strange, unusual, or confusing ► *It was obvious that something very suspicious was going on.* **what's going on** ► *There seems to be a lot of noise – what's going on in there?*

> **goings-on** PL N events or activities that seem strange or that you disapprove of ► *There've been some strange goings-on in the house next door.*

4 go on: to do or achieve something, after you have finished doing something else. **+ to do** sth ► *He went on to win an Olympic Gold medal in the 400 metres.* **+ to** ► *In 1980 fewer than 30% of girls went on to higher education.*

5 go on: to continue talking about something ► *"There's only one other possibility," Jed went on.* **+ with** ► *After a short pause, Maria went on with her story.*

6 go on: to talk too much in a boring way. sb **does go on** ► *Pam's a really nice person but she does go on a bit!* **go on and on** ► *The speaker went on and on until several people left the hall.*

7 go on: to keep complaining about something ► *I wish you'd stop going on, Mum!* **+ about** ► *He's always going on about how much work he's got to do.*

8 go on: to continue travelling towards a particular place or in a particular direction ► *They stopped at a cafe and had a meal before going on again.*

9 go on: to go somewhere before the other people you are with ► *Bill and the girls went on in the car and the rest of us followed on foot.* **go on ahead** ► *Why don't you go on ahead – we'll catch up with you later.*

10 go on: to continue for a particular distance, especially a long one, or over a particular area ► *In front of us, the desert went on as far as the eye could see.*

11 go on!: used to encourage someone to do something ► *Go on, James, tell us what happened!*

12 go on (then): used to tell someone that you will agree to something that you had refused to agree to before ► *"Don't you think I could borrow the car, just for once?" "Oh, go on then."*

G

13 go on sth: to base your opinion on the information that is available ▶ *I can only go on the information that I've got in this report.*

14 go on sth: to spend money or time on something ▶ *A large proportion of my salary goes on our mortgage.* **go on doing** sth ▶ *The money we raised went on rebuilding the church tower.*

15 go on: if a light, machine, or piece of equipment goes on, it starts working ▶ *The inside light goes on automatically when you open the door.*

16 as time/the day etc goes on: used to describe what happens while time passes ▶ *As time went on, we no longer seemed to have much in common.*

17 go on sth: to start taking a type of medical drug ▶ *I don't want to go on sleeping pills, if I can possibly avoid it.*

GO ON WITH →

have enough to go on with: to have enough of something, so that you do not need any more at the moment ▶ *Have you got enough money to be going on with?*

GO OUT →

1 go out: to leave a building, room etc in order to go somewhere else ▶ *Maria got up and went out.* ▶ *Do you want to go out into the garden?*

2 go out: to leave your house in order to meet people, enjoy yourself etc ▶ *Let's go out and celebrate!* **+ for** ▶ *Do you want to go out for a pizza tonight?* **+ to do** sth ▶ *Will's just gone out to play football with the other boys.*

3 go out: to travel to another country, especially one that is far away ▶ *My sister lives in Toronto and we're all going out there in the summer.* **+ to** ▶ *Louise has gone out to Australia to try and find a job for the summer.*

4 goes out: if a light goes out, it stops shining ▶ *I sat and watched all the lights go out one by one.*

5 go out: to stop burning ▶ *By now, the barbecue had gone out and it was starting to rain.*

6 go out: if news or an official message goes out, it is announced or sent ▶ *The news went out that Mandela was about to be released.* **+ to** ▶ *Invitations to the conference went out to twenty-five countries.*

7 go out: to stop being fashionable, or stop being usual ▶ *People used to wear white leather boots – but they went out years ago.* **go out of fashion** ▶ *Computer games can quickly go out of fashion.*

8 go out and do sth: to do something difficult in a determined way ▶ *"I want you to go out there and win," said the coach.*

9 go out: if money goes out, it is spent ▶ *Everything's so expensive – my money goes out almost as soon as I get it.*

  outgoings PL N the money that you have to spend regularly each month or year ▶ *If your outgoings are high, it's difficult to save money as well.*

10 go out: to be broadcast on television or radio ▶ *The interview will go out live at 7 o'clock on Wednesday evening.*

11 the tide goes out: if the tide goes out, the sea moves away from the land ▶ *It can be dangerous to swim here when the tide's going out.*

12 go out: to lose a game against another player or team, so that you cannot continue in a sports competition ▶ *She went out in the quarter finals at Wimbledon.*

GO OUT OF →

go out of sth/sb: if the excitement,

G

energy etc goes out of something or someone, they no longer have it ▶ *All the fun and excitement had gone out of her life.*

GO OUT TO →
your sympathy goes out to sb *also* **your heart etc goes out to** sb: used to say that you feel a lot of sympathy for someone because they are in a very sad or difficult situation ▶ *Our sympathy goes out to all the families affected by this tragedy.*

GO OUT TOGETHER, *also* GO OUT WITH →
go out together, go out with sb: to have a romantic or sexual relationship with someone, but not be married to or live with them ▶ *I only went out with Pete a couple of times – he wasn't really my type!*

GO OVER →
1 go over: to visit someone who lives near you for a short time ▶ *Debbie's out of hospital – I think I might go over and see her this evening.* **+ to** ▶ *I'm going over to Steve's for dinner.*

2 go over: to visit a place that is across the sea. **+ to** ▶ *We're going over to Ireland to see Jenny's family.*

3 go over sth: to examine or discuss something carefully and in detail ▶ *The President was in his study, going over his speech for the following day.*

4 go over sth: to explain something to someone to make sure that they have understood it ▶ *Our boss went over what we had to do when the visitors arrived.*

5 go over sth: to keep thinking about something that has happened, especially something bad or annoying ▶ *Neil kept going over what had happened, trying to work out how it had all gone wrong.* **go over** sth **in your mind** ▶ *She went over it again and again in her mind. Why had Robert been so unfriendly?*

6 go over sth: to clean something thoroughly ▶ *Simon went over the carpet with the vacuum cleaner.*
  going-over N **give** sth **a going-over** to clean something ▶ *I need to give the house a good going-over before Mum comes to stay.*

7 go over sth: to search a place very carefully ▶ *I've gone over every inch of the house, but I can't find my ring anywhere.* **go over** sth **with a fine-tooth comb** (=search a place extremely carefully) ▶ *The police went over the area with a fine-tooth comb.*

GO OVER TO →
1 go over to sth: to change to a different system or a different way of doing things ▶ *We used to have gas heaters, but now we've gone over to solar power.*

2 go over to sth: to leave a group or organization and join the one that is opposing them ▶ *If the army went over to the rebels, the government would collapse.*

GO OVERBOARD →
go overboard: to do something too much, or react in an extreme way ▶ *"It's one of the best films I've ever seen." "There's no need to go overboard – it wasn't that good."* **+ on/with** ▶ *People seem to be going overboard on health and fitness these days.*

GO ROUND *see* GO AROUND

GO ROUND TOGETHER *see* GO AROUND WITH

GO ROUND WITH *see* GO AROUND WITH

GO THROUGH →

1 go through sth: to experience something, especially a difficult or unusual situation ► *We've been through a tough time lately, but hopefully things will start to improve.* ► *The company is going through a period of great change.* sb **went through a lot** (=a lot of bad things happened to them) ► *She went through a lot when she was young – her mother died when she was only 6 years old.*

2 go through sth: to carefully examine all of a group of things in order to try to find something ► *Dave went through his pockets again, but he still couldn't find the address.*

3 go through sth: to carefully read or discuss something, to check that it is correct and acceptable ► *Could you just go through this file and mark anything that seems wrong?*

4 go through sth: to talk about all of the details of something to someone, in order to make sure that they understand it ► *Do you want to go through the main points again?*

5 go through sth: to practise something such as a song or dance ► *Let's go through the song again from the beginning.*

6 go through sth: to be tested, checked, or officially examined ► *Every car goes through a series of safety checks before it leaves the factory.* ► *You have to go through a lengthy process before being allowed to adopt a child.*

7 go through: to be officially accepted or approved ► *Your application for a loan has gone through.* ► *Donna plans to remarry as soon as her divorce goes through.*

8 go through sth: to use all or a lot of something in a short time ► *We went through all of our money in the first week of our holiday.*

9 go through sb/sth: to ask a particular person, department etc to deal with something because they are officially responsible for it ► *All requests for new books must go through the headteacher.*

10 go through: to take part in the next part of a competition, because you have won the part before it. **+ to** ► *United went through to the FA Cup final for the first time in 11 years.*

11 go through sb's **mind** *also* *go through* sb's **head**: if something goes through your mind or head, you think about it ► *The same questions kept going through my mind again and again.*

GO THROUGH WITH →

go through with sth: to do something you had promised or planned to do, even though it is difficult ► *Giving evidence in court was terrifying, but I'm glad that I went through with it.* **can't go through with it** ► *Jenny was going to make an official complaint, but decided that she couldn't go through with it.*

GO TO →

1 go to sb: if money or a prize goes to someone, they are given it ► *All the money raised will go to local charities.*

2 go to a lot of trouble/expense etc: to try very hard or spend a lot of money in order to do something ► *Parents often go to a lot of expense in order to make sure their children get a good education.*

3 go to it: used to tell or encourage someone to do something ► *"The kitchen really needs to be cleaned." "Yeah, go to it."*

GO TOGETHER →

1 go together: if two things go together, they look, taste, or sound

G

good together ▶ *Do these trousers and this jacket go together?* ▶ *Tina's voice and Rhys' songwriting style go together perfectly.* **go well together** ▶ *Tomatoes and pasta go very well together.*

2 go together: if two things go together, they often exist together or are connected ▶ *The problems of poor housing and bad health often go together.* ▶ *Traditionally, Christmas and snow have always gone together.*

GO TOWARDS, *also* GO TOWARD →
go towards/toward sth: to be used to help pay for something ▶ *My parents gave me £300 to go toward a new computer.*

GO UNDER →
1 go under: if a company or business goes under, it has to close because it does not make enough money to continue ▶ *Many restaurants go under in their first year.*

2 go under, go under sth: to become unconscious because you have been given an anaesthetic (=a drug used by doctors to make you unconscious) while you are having medical treatment ▶ *It will take you about ten seconds to go under.*

3 go under:
to sink below
the surface of
the water
▶ *We
watched from
the lifeboat
as the great ship finally went under.*

GO UP →
1 go up: if a price or the level of something goes up, it increases ▶ *The rate of violent crime among young people is still going up.* ▶ *House prices in this area are going up and up.*

2 go up: to go to a town or city from a smaller place, or to somewhere further north ▶ *I'd like to go up to London to do some Christmas shopping.*

3 go up: to go towards someone or something, for example until you are near enough to talk to them ▶ *The boys went up and asked her for her autograph.* **+ to** ▶ *Dylan went up to the microphone and started singing.*

4 go up: if new buildings go up, they are built ▶ *New high-rise apartment buildings are going up all around the town.*

5 go up: to explode or start burning strongly ▶ *A lit cigarette fell on the sofa, and within minutes the whole room had gone up.* **go up in flames** ▶ *The car rolled down the bank, and went up in flames.*

6 go up: if a shout, cry etc, goes up, the people in a place start to shout etc ▶ *A groan went up as Miss Hirsch reminded the class about their vocabulary test.*

7 go up: to move to a higher group of sports teams and players who play together ▶ *United will go up to the first division next season.*

GO UP AGAINST →
go up against sb: to compete against someone, especially in sport, business, or in a court of law ▶ *It's very difficult for an ordinary person to go up against a big company that can afford top lawyers.*

GO UP TO →
go up to sb/sth: to reach as far as a particular place, time, amount etc ▶ *Our garden goes up to these bushes – the rest belongs to the neighbours.* ▶ *The financial year only goes up to April.*

GO WITH →
1 go with sth: if one thing goes with another, they look, taste, or sound good together ▶ *Do you think these*

hoes go with this dress? **go well with** th ► *This wine should go well with meat dishes and cheese.*

go with sth: to be a usual part of something ► *She talked about the pressure that often goes with being famous.* sth **goes with the territory** =used to say that something is a usual part of a job or situation) ► *Young doctors have to work extremely long hours, but that just goes with the territory.*

go with sth: to be provided with something else ► *The house goes with the job.* ► *a blue silk evening dress that has a matching bag to go with it*

go with sth: to accept someone's idea or suggestion and decide to use it ► *"What do you think of Jo's idea?" "I think we should go with it."*

GO WITHOUT →
go without, go without sth: to not have something that you usually have ► *We can't really afford a holiday this year, so we'll just have to go without.*

GOAD
GOAD INTO →
goad sb **into** sth: to deliberately make someone react in an angry way or in a way they did not intend ► *Alexei refused to be goaded into an argument.*

GOBBLE
GOBBLE DOWN →
gobble down sth, **gobble** sth **down**: to eat something very quickly and eagerly ► *Joseph gobbled down his lunch and rushed back to work.*

GOBBLE UP →
1 gobble up sth, **gobble** sth **up**: to use or take a lot of something such as land or money ► *Developers were gobbling up hundreds of acres of land to build houses.*

2 gobble up sth, **gobble** sth **up**: to eat all of something very quickly and eagerly ► *I thought I'd made too many sandwiches, but everyone just gobbled them up.*

GOOF
GOOF AROUND →
goof around, goof around sth: to spend time doing something in a silly or not very serious way ► *We weren't really playing basketball. We were mostly just goofing around.*

GOOF OFF →
goof off: to spend time doing silly things and having fun, when you should be working ► *In high school I goofed off most of the time.*

GOOF UP →
goof up, goof sth **up, goof up** sth: to make a silly mistake or do something badly ► *If I try to say it in Spanish, I'll goof it up.* **+ on** ► *The good news was that she didn't goof up on the test.*

GORGE
GORGE ON →
1 gorge (yourself) on sth: to eat large amounts or too much of something ► *As a boy, he used to gorge on chocolate and candy.*

2 gorge yourself on sth: to have or do something that you enjoy so much that it has a bad effect on you ► *When I first left home I gorged myself on an endless round of late-night parties.*

GOUGE
GOUGE OUT →
gouge out sth, **gouge** sth **out**: to remove something or dig it out,

G

especially in a very violent way using something sharp ► *The attacker hit Robert with a bottle and attempted to gouge out his eyes.*

GRAB

GRAB AT →
1 grab at sb/sth: to quickly try to catch or hold someone or something ► *We both grabbed at the bird, but it flew up into the trees.*

2 grab at sth: to take an opportunity very eagerly ► *Seline grabbed at every chance to go out in the evening.*

GRAFT

GRAFT ON, *also* GRAFT ONTO →
graft sth **on/onto** sth: to add a new idea, method, system etc to one that already exists ► *Several ancient practices were grafted onto the new religion.*

GRAPPLE

GRAPPLE WITH →
grapple with sth: to try to deal with or understand a difficult problem, subject etc ► *Some of the students are having difficulty in grappling with the mysteries of electronics.*

GRASP

GRASP AT →
1 grasp at sth: to quickly try to catch or hold someone or something ► *His foot slipped and he grasped onto a piece of jutting wood.*

2 grasp at sth: to try to use any opportunity or idea that might help you in a difficult situation ► *Leonore grasped at the chance to prove herself as a member of the team.*

3 be grasping at straws: to be willing to try anything that might help you in a hopeless situation, even though it is very unlikely to be successful ► *"We may be able to appeal," the lawyer said. He was grasping at straws.*

GRASS

GRASS ON →
grass on sb: to tell people in authority about something illegal or bad that someone has done ► *Some of the men had been beaten up for grassing on other prisoners.*

GRASS OVER →
grass sth **over, grass over** sth: to plant grass over an area of land ► *Eventually, the flower beds were flattened and grassed over.*

GRASS UP →
grass sb **up, grass up** sb: to tell people in authority about something illegal or bad that someone has done ► *When my mum found out about the drugs, she grassed me up to the police*

GRATE

GRATE ON →
grate on sb/sth: to annoy someone, especially after continuing for a long time ► *I know I shouldn't say so, but his accent really grates on me.* **grate on sb's nerves** ► *The sound of Anna crunching her toast was grating on his nerves.*

GRAVITATE

GRAVITATE TO, *also* GRAVITATE TOWARDS, GRAVITATE TOWARD →
gravitate to sth/sb, **gravitate towards** sth/sb: to be attracted to something or someone and therefore move towards them or become interested in them ► *Tourists naturally gravitate to the city's older section.* ► *As students in the early 1960s, we gravitated towards politics.*

GRIND

GRIND AWAY →
grind away: to work very hard for a long period of time ► *I've been grinding away for eight hours now, and I'm getting nowhere.*

GRIND DOWN →
grind down sb/sth, **grind** sb/sth
down: to gradually make someone
lose their confidence, hope, or energy
► *A lot of the women have been
ground down by illness and poverty.*

GRIND ON →
grind on: to continue for a long time in
a slow and boring way ► *The trial
ground on all through the long hot
summer.*

GRIND OUT →
grind out sth, **grind** sth **out**: to keep
producing the same type of thing,
without ever producing anything
different or interesting ► *In nine months
she ground out five romantic novels.*

GRIND UP →
grind up sth, **grind** sth **up**: to make
something solid into a powder, by
crushing it ► *Local people grind up the
leaves and use them to make tea.*

GROAN

GROAN WITH →
be groaning with sth: to be covered or
filled with a very large amount of
something ► *We sat down at a table
groaning with food.* ► *The shelves
were groaning with ancient books.*

GROPE

GROPE FOR →
grope for sth: to try hard to find a way
of saying or doing something, often
without success ► *"It was incredible,"
Martin said, groping for words to
describe the scene.*

GROSS

GROSS OUT →
gross sb **out**, **gross out** sb: if you
or something grosses you out, they
are so unpleasant that they almost
make you feel ill ► *The thought of
eating insects grosses many western
people out.*

GROUND

BE GROUNDED IN →
be grounded in sth: to have a
thorough basic knowledge of
something. **be well grounded in** sth
► *In those days, he said, students
were well grounded in spelling.*

BE GROUNDED IN, *also* **BE
GROUNDED ON →**
be grounded in/on sth: to be based
on something ► *All these beliefs and
attitudes are grounded in experience.*

GROW

GROW APART →
grow apart: if two people grow apart,
they gradually stop having a close
relationship with each other ► *Sadly,
after eight years of marriage, they just
grew apart.*

GROW AWAY FROM →
grow away from sb: to gradually feel
less close to someone, because you
have changed as you have got older
► *All children grow away from their
parents eventually.*

GROW INTO →
1 grow into
sth: if children
grow into
clothes, they
become big
enough for the
clothes to fit
them ► *The coat
looks big on him
now; but he'll
soon grow into it.*

2 grow into sth: to gradually learn how
to deal with a new job or situation
confidently ► *I was very nervous when
I first started acting, but I soon grew
into it.*

GROW ON →
grow on sb: if someone or something
grows on you, you gradually come to

like them ► *I didn't like my new boss at first, but now she's grown on me.*

GROW OUT OF →

1 grow out of sth: to stop doing something or get less interested in something as you get older ► *As a teenager my son was very shy, but luckily he's grown out of it.*

2 grow out of sth: if children grow out of clothes, they become too big to wear them ► *Kids grow out of shoes within three to six months.*

3 grow out of sth: to develop as the result of something ► *The Labour Party grew out of the Trade Union movement.*

GROW UP →

1 grow up: to change from being a child into an adult ► *The kids have all grown up now, so we want to move to a smaller house.*

grown-up N an adult – used especially by or to children ► *All grown-ups seem to do is to sit around talking and smoking.*

grown-up ADJ if someone's children are grown-up, they have become adults ► *She's got three grown-up children.*

2 grow up: if you grow up in a place, you live there during the time when you are a child ► *Phillips grew up in Southern California.*

3 grow up doing sth: to spend a lot of time doing something when you are a child ► *I grew up listening to this kind of music.*

4 grow up: to start to behave in a more sensible, adult way ► *Gabrielle's grown up a lot since she started her new school.* ► *I wish you'd stop fooling around and grow up!*

5 grow up: if something grows up, it begins to exist and then gradually becomes bigger or more important

► *The town grew up around the magnificent 13th century castle.*

GROW UP ON →

grow up on sth: to experience or do something a lot during the time when you are a child, so that it has a strong influence in your life ► *This generation has grown up on TV. They can't imagine life without it.*

GRUB

GRUB ABOUT, *also* **GRUB AROUND** →

1 grub about/ around: to search for something by digging or moving things with your hands ► *Jasper had got down on the floor and was grubbing about under the carpet.*

2 grub about/ around: to try to find something that is difficult to find.

+ for ► *We were desperately grubbing around for a solution.*

GUARD

GUARD AGAINST →

1 guard against sth: to provide protection against something ► *Fibre in the diet is thought to guard against heart disease.*

2 guard against sth: to be careful to avoid doing, feeling etc something, because it could be dangerous or harmful ► *It's vital to guard against getting overtired when you're driving long distances.*

GUESS

GUESS AT →

guess at sth: to give an answer or opinion about something which you realize may not be correct, because you do not have all the information you need ► *The police can only guess at the scale of the problem.*

GULP

GULP DOWN →

gulp down sth, **gulp** sth **down**: to

swallow large amounts of drink or food very quickly ▶ *She ordered a glass of wine, gulped it down and rushed off.*

GUM

GUM UP →

1 gum up sth, **gum** sth **up**: to prevent something from happening or working properly ▶ *Lack of communication between the departments can quicky gum up the system.* **gum up the works** (=prevent a machine or system from working properly) ▶ *Dust gets in between the keys and gums up the works.*

2 be gummed up: if your eyes are gummed up, it is difficult to open them because they feel sticky ▶ *If your baby's eyes are gummed up, gently clean them with cotton wool and water.*

GUN

GUN DOWN →

gun sb **down, gun down** sb: to shoot someone and kill or badly injure them ▶ *The journalist was gunned down in the driveway of his San Francisco home.*

BE GUNNING FOR →

be gunning for sth: to be trying to achieve or win something ▶ *United were gunning for their third straight win.*

G

Hh

HACK

HACK

INTO →

hack into sth: to use a computer to secretly get into someone else's

computer system ► *A student used a simple desktop machine to hack into computers around the world.*

HACK OFF →

be hacked off: to feel very annoyed with someone or about something ► *I'm really hacked off at work at the moment.* **+ with/about** ► *Fans are hacked off with the team's poor performance in recent games.*

HAIL

HAIL AS →

hail sb/sth **as** sth: to publicly describe someone or something as being very good or special in a particular way ► *Haydn was hailed as a genius only at the end of his life.* ► *Car safety campaigners hailed the new seatbelt law as a great victory.*

HAIL FROM →

hail from sth: to come from a particular place or type of family ► *Joan hails from Newcastle, and her hobbies are reading and listening to music.*

HAM

HAM UP →

ham it up: to behave or perform in a silly or funny way, or with a lot of false emotion ► *Crowds flocked to the theatre to see him ham it up as Malvolio.*

HAMMER

HAMMER AT →

hammer at sth: to keep talking about a particular subject because you think it is important ► *The senator continued to hammer at the issues of crime, welfare, and taxes.*

HAMMER AWAY →

1 hammer away: to hit something hard continuously, especially making a loud noise ► *I could hear the workmen hammering away downstairs.*

2 hammer away: to work hard at something for a long time. **+ at** ► *He hammered away at the article all night.*

3 hammer away: to keep talking about something a lot in order to persuade people to agree with you etc ► *"Keep hammering away," David said. "They'l see what we mean in the end."*

HAMMER IN, *also* **HAMMER INTO →**

hammer sth **in, hammer** sth **into** sb: t(repeat something again and again so that people completely understand or learn it ► *Principles of right and wrong have been hammered into us since childhood.* ► *Just telling them once won't work. You've got to hammer it in.*

HAMMER OUT →

hammer out sth, **hammer** sth **out**: to manage to get an agreement with another person, country, organization etc after a lot of discussion ► *The two sides met to try to hammer out a peace agreement.* ► *It took a further four months to hammer out the detail of the treaty.*

HAND

HAND AROUND, *also* **HAND ROUND →**

hand around/round sth, **hand** sth **around/round**: to give something to each person in a group ► *I'm handing* round a summary of last week's lecture. ▶ Sally put the chicken soup into bowls and handed them around.

HAND BACK →

1 hand back sth, **hand** sth **back**: to give something back to someone after they have given it to you ▶ She handed back the money and told him she didn't want it. **+ to** ▶ The customs officer looked at his passport and handed it back to him.

2 hand back sth, **hand** sth **back**: to give something back to the person, organization, country etc that owns it, or that used to own it ▶ The occupied islands were handed back to the national government at the end of the war.

HAND DOWN →

1 hand down sth, **hand** sth **down**: to give or teach something to someone so that they will have it or know about it after you have died. **+ from** ▶ ancient stories handed down from father to son. **+ to** ▶ The ring had been handed down to her from her grandmother.

2 hand down a decision/sentence etc: to announce an official decision, especially about the punishment that someone should receive ▶ Sentences of up to 16 years in prison were handed down to the people responsible for the attack.

HAND IN →

1 hand in sth, **hand** sth **in**: to give something to someone in authority so that they can have it or deal with it ▶ I left my bag on the train, but luckily someone handed it in. ▶ All foreign residents have been ordered to hand in their passports.

2 hand in sth, **hand** sth **in**: to give written work to a teacher so that he or she can check it ▶ All essays must be handed in by Friday.

3 hand in your resignation also **hand in your notice**: to officially tell your employer that you are leaving your job ▶ She's threatening to hand in her notice if they don't give her a pay rise.

HAND ON →

1 hand on sth, **hand** sth **on**: to give or teach something to someone so that they will have it or know about it after you have died. **+ from** ▶ The house was handed on from one generation of the family to the next.

2 hand on sth, **hand** sth **on**: to give something to someone else so that they can deal with it, look at it, or use it ▶ He handed the letter on to his lawyers. ▶ Your employer will hand on your details to the tax office.

HAND OUT →

1 hand out sth, **hand** sth **out**: to give something to each of the people in a group or to people who  are passing you ▶ At the end of the class, I'll hand out the application forms. ▶ Students were standing outside the station handing out anti-war leaflets.

    handout N a piece of paper given to people who are attending a lesson, meeting etc, with information on it about the subject being discussed ▶ As usual, Mr Collier started the lesson by passing round several handouts.

2 hand out sth, **hand** sth **out**: to give something, especially money or food, to people who need it ▶ The organization hands out around £50,000 a year to young people with special educational needs.

H

handout N money, food etc that is given to someone who needs it ▶ *A £700,000 government handout will help pay for vital repairs to the school buildings.*

3 hand out sth, **hand** sth **out**: to give advice, information, criticism etc to someone ▶ *She's always handing out unwanted advice about people's personal lives.*

4 hand out sth, **hand** sth **out**: to officially give someone a punishment ▶ *Harsher punishments are being handed out to drunk drivers.*

HAND OVER →

1 hand over sth, **hand** sth **over**: to give something to someone, especially after they have asked for it ▶ *The robbers ordered him to hand over all his money.*

2 hand over sth, **hand** sth **over**: to give control or responsibility for something to another person, country, organization etc. **+ to** ▶ *She officially handed over all her duties to her deputy.*

handover N when control or responsibility for something is given to another person, country, organization etc ▶ *the handover of Hong Kong to China in 1997.*

HAND OVER TO →

hand over to sb: to let another person speak in a discussion, news report etc after you have finished talking ▶ *Now I'd like to hand over to Dave to tell his side of the story.*

HAND ROUND *see* HAND AROUND

HANG

HANG ABOUT →

1 hang about, hang about sth: to spend time somewhere not doing anything, for example because you are waiting for someone ▶ *Daisy hung about until Drew and the team came*

back to the bus. **keep** sb **hanging about** (=make someone have to wait somewhere for a long time) ▶ *They kept us hanging about at the airport for nearly 5 hours.*

2 hang about: to be slow to start doing something, or to move slowly ▶ *The boss wants it done by this afternoon, so you'd better not hang about.*

3a. hang about!: used when you suddenly think of something that you want to say or ask ▶ *Hang about! Where did she get all the money from.*

b. used to tell someone to stop and wait for you ▶ *Hang about! Can I come too?*

HANG ABOUT TOGETHER, *also* HANG ABOUT WITH →

hang about together, hang about with sb: to spend a lot of time with someone and be friendly with them ▶ *We used to hang about together when we were young.* ▶ *Jim tends to hand around with older people.*

HANG AROUND, *also* HANG ROUND →

1 hang around/round: to be slow to start doing something, or to move slowly ▶ *There are only a few tickets left, so you'd better not hang around*

2 hang around/round, hang around/round sth: to spend time somewhere not doing anything, for example because you are waiting for someone ▶ *A crowd of photographers had begun hanging around outside the courtroom.*

3 hang around/round, hang around/round sb: to spend a lot of time with someone, especially when they do now want you to be with them ▶ *When you're famous you get all kinds of people hanging round you..*

4 hang around/round, hang around/round sth: if something is hanging around, it is not being used or has not been dealt with ▶ *I'm sure I've got an old pair of walking boots hanging around somewhere.*

HANG AROUND TOGETHER, *also* **HANG AROUND WITH, HANG ROUND TOGETHER, HANG ROUND WITH →** **hang around/round together, hang around/round with** sb: to spend a lot of time with someone and be friendly with them ▶ *They used to hang around together a lot when they were at college.*

HANG BACK →
1 hang back: to not move forward, for example because you are nervous or shy ▶ *Ruth hung back for fear of being seen.*

2 hang back: to not do something or delay doing something, for example because you are worried about what will happen. **+ from doing** sth ▶ *People are hanging back from demanding full independence, because they feel uncertain about the future.*

HANG IN →
hang in there: to keep trying even when you seem unlikely to succeed or the situation is difficult ▶ *Just hang in there – things soon get better.*

HANG ON →
1 hang on: to wait for something or someone for a short time ▶ *I suppose I could hang on here till she comes back.* **hang on a minute/second** ▶ *Hang on a minute! We're just coming!*

2 hang on!: used when you suddenly think of something that you want to say ▶ *Hang on! Why don't we go tomorrow instead? The roads will be much less busy.* **hang on a minute/second** ▶ *Now hang on a minute! I thought you said that you didn't need any more money!*

3 hang on sth: to depend on the result of something ▶ *Everything hangs on the next game. If England lose, they're out of the World Cup.*

4 hang on: to hold something tightly, for example so that you do not fall ▶ *The boy tried to get away, but she hung on and refused to let go.* **hang on for dear life** (=hang on very tightly, especially because you are very worried that you will fall) ▶ *The boat was going up and down, and we were all hanging on for dear life.*

5 hang on sb's **every word:** to listen very carefully and eagerly to what someone is saying ▶ *The children were hanging on his every word, waiting to find out what happened next.*

6 hang on: to continue doing what you have been doing until now, especially when this is difficult ▶ *Everyone is wondering if the President can hang on for another year.*

7 hang sth **on** sb: to blame something on someone, often in an unfair way ▶ *It's your own fault he won't talk to you – don't hang it on me!*

HANG ON TO, *also* **HANG ONTO →**
1 hang on to/onto sth: to succeed in keeping something, even though there is a danger that you will lose it ▶ *The Republicans managed to hang on to their majority in the Senate.*

2 hang on to/onto sth: to hold something tightly, for example so that you do not fall or you do not lose it ▶ *The little girl hung on to her mother's arm.* ▶ *The driver hung onto the steering wheel and somehow managed to bring the truck to a halt.*

3 hang on to/onto sth: to keep something and not sell it, give it to someone, or get rid of it ▶ *It's a beautiful painting. You should hang on to it.* ▶ *She had hung onto his letters for all these years.*

H

HANG OUT →

1 hang out: if something is hanging out, part of it is not inside the place where it should be ► *Your shirt's hanging out!* (=it is not in your trousers)

2 hang out sth, **hang** sth **out**: to hang clothes somewhere outside in order to dry them ► *Mrs Drake was hanging out the washing in the garden.*

3 hang out: to spend a lot of time somewhere or with someone ► *The cafe was a place where students and musicians hung out.* **+ with** ► *I was hanging out with some friends and having a good time.*

hangout N a place where a particular type of person often goes ► *The bar was a well-known hangout for off-duty police officers.*

HANG OVER →

1 hang over sb/sth: if something unpleasant hangs over you, it seems likely to happen ► *In 1962 the threat of nuclear war hung over the whole world.*

2 hang over sth: if doubts hang over something, people do not feel sure that it will happen or be successful ► *A big question mark still hangs over the future of the company.*

HANG ROUND *see* **HANG AROUND**

HANG ROUND TOGETHER *see* **HANG AROUND TOGETHER**

HANG ROUND WITH *see* **HANG AROUND TOGETHER**

HANG TOGETHER →

1 hang together: to be well-organized, with all the separate parts connected in a sensible way ► *I didn't think that the book really hung together.*

2 hang together: if people hang together, they stay together and help each other to achieve something ► *We hung together and came back to win the game.*

HANG UP →

1 hang up,
hang up sth:
to end a
telephone
conversation
by putting
the
telephone
down ► *She
said "I'll be there in a minute" and
hung up.* **+ on** ► *Listen, I'm really
sorry. Don't hang up on me!*

2 hang up sth, **hang** sth **up**: to hang things such as clothes on a hook or other object ► *Marlow hung up his coat and went through into his office.*

3 be hung up on/about sth: to be very worried about or interested in something and spend too much time thinking about it ► *Like most teenagers I was hung up about my weight.* **get hung up on/about** sth ► *Why do men get so hung up on the size of their car's engine?*

hang-up N something you feel unreasonably worried or embarrassed about it ► *All parents want their children to grow up happy and free from hang-ups.*

4 hang sb/sth **up, hang up** sb/sth: to delay someone or something ► *The traffic in the city hung us up a little.*

5 hang it up: to stop doing a particular activity or type of work ► *Fred went into the boss's office and announced: "I'm hanging it up."*

6 be hung up on sb: to be very attracted to someone and not be able to change your feelings about them ► *She's hung up on some guy she met at the gym.*

HANG WITH →

hang with sb: to spend lot of time somewhere or with someone, relaxing and enjoying yourself ► *He used to* *hang with his brother's friends because no-one his age lived in the neighbourhood.*

HANKER

HANKER AFTER, *also* HANKER FOR →

hanker after/for sth: to want something very much, especially something that it is difficult for you to get ▶ *Now and then I really hanker after big home-cooked meals.*

HAPPEN

HAPPEN ALONG, *also* HAPPEN BY →

1 happen along/by: to arrive or be passing somewhere by chance ▶ *Fortunately a policeman on patrol happened by.*

2 happen along/by: to find a place or thing by chance ▶ *We happened by a picnic site just off the road.*

HAPPEN ON, *also* HAPPEN UPON →

happen on sth/sb, **happen upon** sth/sb: to find something or meet someone when you do not expect it ▶ *Once or twice I happened on her on the way to college.*

HAPPEN TO →

1 happen to sb/sth: if something happens to someone or something, they are affected by it without planning to be ▶ *You'll never believe what happened to me on the way home.* ▶ *Something's happened to the washing machine – it's not working!*

2 what/whatever happened to sb: used to ask where someone is and what they are doing, after you have not seen them for a long time ▶ *Whatever happened to that nice girl you were going out with?*

HAPPEN UPON *see* HAPPEN ON

HARDEN

BE HARDENED TO →

be hardened to sth: to have become

so familiar with something unpleasant that you do not feel upset by it any more ▶ *The first time she saw an operation she nearly fainted, but now she's hardened to it.*

HARK

HARK AT →

hark at him/you etc: used when someone has just said something unreasonable, especially because they have criticized you for doing something that they do themselves ▶ *Hark at her, telling me I shouldn't drink so much, when she's in the pub most evenings!*

HARK BACK TO →

1 hark back to sth: to remember or keep talking about a time or event in the past ▶ *They are always harking back to the good old days before the war.*

2 hark back to sth: to be similar to something that existed or was fashionable in the past ▶ *The newest shoe styles hark back to the seventies.*

HARP

HARP ON →

harp on about sth *also* **harp on** sth: to talk about something so much that it is boring or annoying ▶ *He's always harping on about how much money he earns.*

HASH

HASH OUT →

hash out sth, **hash** sth **out**: to discuss the details of a plan, idea etc with someone ▶ *As we hashed out the deal, people on the trading floor began to grow curious.*

HASH OVER →

hash sth **over**, **hash over** sth: to talk about something in detail for a long time ▶ *Officials met to hash over the future of public TV.*

H

HASH UP →
hash sth **up, hash up** sth: to do something very badly ▶ *She was so nervous at the interview that she completely hashed it up.*

HAUL

HAUL BEFORE →
be hauled before sth/sb *also **be hauled in front of** sth/sb*: to be forced to appear in a court of law or to see someone in authority, so that they can decide what will happen to you ▶ *He was hauled up in front of the headmaster and asked to explain his behaviour.*

HAUL IN →
1 haul sb **in**: if the police haul someone in, they take that person to the police station to answer questions about something. **+ for** ▶ *Labourers were continually being hauled in for petty crime and drunkenness.*

2 haul in sth, **haul** sth **in**: to pull something heavy towards you using a rope ▶ *The fishermen were hauling in their nets and getting ready to go home.*

HAUL OFF →
haul sb **off**: to take someone away somewhere, using force ▶ *A big male nurse came up and hauled Tom off.* **+ to** ▶ *I was handcuffed and hauled off to the County jail.*

HAUL UP →
be hauled up: to be forced to appear in a court of law or to see someone in authority, so that they can decide what will happen to you. **+ for** ▶ *Her grandfather was hauled up for tax evasion.*

HAVE

HAVE AGAINST →
have sth **against** sb/sth: to dislike someone or something for a particular reason ▶ *I can't see what you have against Alex's friends.* **have nothing against** sb/sth (=used to say that there is nothing you dislike about someone or something) ▶ *Potter had nothing against the monarchy, in principle.*

HAVE AROUND,
also HAVE ROUND →
have sb **around/round, have** sb **around/round** sb/sth: to have someone near you or available to help you if necessary ▶ *It's a help to have your family around when you've got a new baby.*

HAVE AT →
1 have at it: used to encourage someone to do or try something ▶ *"If that's what you want, have at it," said Marvin.*

2 have at it: to fight or attack someone ▶ *The brothers both looked ready to have at it, but something held them back.*

HAVE BACK →
1 have sth **back**: to have something that you had before because someone has given it back to you ▶ *I don't need the book anymore – you can have it back if you like.*

2 have sb **back**: to agree to start to have a romantic relationship with someone again after you have separated from them ▶ *Do you think he'd have her back after all she's done?*

HAVE DOWN AS →
have sb **down as**: to think that someone or something has a particular character, especially when you later find out that you were wrong

▶ *I didn't have her down as the motherly type.* ▶ *Until then, we all had him down as a bit of a wimp.*

HAVE IN →

have sb **in**: to get builders, workers etc to come to your house to do a job for you ▶ *We've already had an architect in to look at the plans.*

HAVE ON →

1 have sth **on, have on** sth: to be wearing something ▶ *Everyone in the room had a dark suit on except me.* ▶ *She had on a red skirt and high heels.* **have nothing on** also **not have anything on** ▶ *Don't come in! I don't have anything on!*

2 have sth **on**: if you have the radio, television, light etc on, you use it and it is working ▶ *Are we allowed to have the TV on?*

3 be having sb **on**: to pretend to someone that something is true when it is not, as a joke ▶ *When he told me he was a nuclear physicist, I thought he was having me on.*

4 have sth **on you**: to have something in your pockets, bag etc ▶ *Do you have any money on you? I've left mine in the car.*

5 have sth **on**: to have an arrangement to do something ▶ *Let's meet up next week – I don't think I've got anything on.* **have a lot on** (=be very busy) ▶ *Jo seems to have a lot on at the moment.*

6 have something on sb: to have information about someone that shows they have been involved with something bad or illegal ▶ *I think the police must have something on him.* **have nothing on** sb also **not have anything on** sb ▶ *"He's not on our records," the detective said, "We've got nothing on him."*

HAVE OUT →

1 have sth **out**: to have something such as a tooth or a part of your body

removed in a medical operation ▶ *She was rushed to hospital to have her appendix out.*

2 have it out with sb: to try to end a disagreement or a difficult situation by talking to the person you are angry with ▶ *Joe's really upset. He's going to see Mum and have it out with her right now.*

HAVE OVER, *also* **HAVE ROUND** →

have sb **over/round**: to invite someone to come to your house for a meal, drink etc ▶ *We had some people round at the weekend.* ▶ *Is it all right if I have a few friends over this evening?*

HAVE ROUND *see* **HAVE AROUND, HAVE OVER**

HAVE UP →

be had up, be had up for sth: to be taken to court because the police think you committed a crime ▶ *Sarah was had up for theft when she was only 14.*

HAWK

HAWK AROUND, *also* **HAWK ABOUT, HAWK ROUND** →

hawk sth **around/about/round, hawk** sth **around/about/round** sth: to try to sell something by offering it to a lot of different people ▶ *Apparently she's hawking her story around to the newspapers for a six-figure sum.*

HEAD

HEAD FOR →

1 head for sth: to travel towards a place ▶ *The ships were heading for Cuba.* ▶ *We climbed on our horses, and headed for the hills.* **be headed for** sth (=be travelling towards a place) ▶ *The men said they were headed for the next town.*

2 be heading for sth *also* **be headed for** sth: if someone or something is heading for a particular situation, it

H

seems likely that it will happen in the future ▶ *The company seems to be heading for financial collapse.* ▶ *The country was heading for a period of political uncertainty.*

HEAD INTO →
head into sth: to start to experience or deal with something that is completely new ▶ *As we head into the new millennium, we will see considerable changes.*

HEAD OFF →
1 head off: to go somewhere in order to do something ▶ *The film ends with Parker heading off to join the army in Germany.*

2 head off sth, **head** sth **off**: to prevent something unpleasant from happening ▶ *Talks continued throughout the night in the hope of heading off the strike.*

3 head off sth, **head** sth **off**: to try to make someone or something change direction, by blocking their way ▶ *A policeman held out his arms to head them off.*

HEAD OUT →
head out: to leave in order to go somewhere or do something ▶ *He found a taxi and headed out to Dean's house.*

HEAD UP →
head up sth, **head** sth **up**: to lead an organization, team, or project ▶ *We'd like to head up the next research project.*

HEAL

HEAL UP, *also* HEAL OVER →
heal up/over: if a wound or injury heals up, the damaged part of the body returns to a healthy normal condition ▶ *Apply a little antiseptic and the cut will probably heal up by itself.*

HEAP

HEAP ON, *also* HEAP UPON →
heap sth **on** sb/sth, **heap** sth **upon** sb/sth: if you heap praise, blame etc on someone or something, you praise or blame them a lot ▶ *Their political opponents heaped scorn on this suggestion.*

HEAP UP →
heap sth **up**, **heap up** sth: to put a lot of things on top of each other in a pile ▶ *Mr Rocke looked at all the papers heaped up in his in-tray.*

HEAP UPON *see* HEAP ON

HEAR

HEAR ABOUT →
hear about sth/sb: to get news or information about something or someone ▶ *We were both in London when we heard about the accident.*
be sorry to hear about sb (=used to express sadness when someone is ill or has died etc) ▶ *I was so sorry to hear about your mother, Lisa.*

HEAR FROM →
1 hear from sb: to get a letter or a telephone call from someone ▶ *I haven't heard from Maria in a while.*

2 hear from sb, **hear** sth **from** sb: to receive information from someone about something ▶ *The police would like to hear from anyone who was in the area when the robbery took place.*

HEAR OF →
1 have heard of sb/sth: to have heard the name of a person, place etc before, so that you recognize it ▶ *Everybody's heard of Winston*

Churchill. ➤ *"You know Piers Morrison?" "No, I've never heard of him."*

2 hear of sth: to get news or information about something ➤ *You sometimes hear of people having very strange experiences when they are close to death.*

3 be heard of: to have been seen in a place so that people know you are still alive ➤ *He disappeared into the icy wastes, and was never heard of again.*

4 won't/ wouldn't hear of sth: to refuse to allow something, or refuse an offer ➤ *My mother wanted to be a doctor but her father wouldn't hear of it.*

HEAR OUT →

hear sb **out**: to listen to what someone wants to say, without trying to interrupt them ➤ *Hear me out first, Jane, and then you can say what you think.*

HEAT

HEAT THROUGH →

heat through sth, **heat** sth **through**, **heat through**: if you heat food through or if it heats through, you make it hot ➤ *The rice may be prepared in advance and heated through later.*

HEAT UP →

1 heat up, **heat up** sth, **heat** sth **up**: to become hotter, or to make something hotter ➤ *I'll heat up some of last night's stew for you, if you want.* ➤ *Because of environmental pollution, the Earth's climate is slowly heating up.*

2 heat up: to become more serious or exciting, because people start to argue, fight, compete harder etc ➤ *The company is experiencing some difficulty as competition heats up.* ➤ *Although the election is still a year away, the political scene is already heating up.*

HEAVE

HEAVE TO →

heave to: if a ship or boat heaves to, it stops ➤ *About two miles from the coast, the ship hove to.*

HEDGE

HEDGE AROUND, *also* HEDGE ABOUT →

be hedged around/ about: to be limited or controlled by a lot of complicated rules, laws, or conditions. **+ with** ➤ *Nowadays employment is hedged around with legislation.*

HEDGE IN →

be hedged in: to be closely surrounded or enclosed by something ➤ *The cathedral is in the town centre, hedged in by other buildings.*

HELP

HELP ALONG →

1 help sth/ sb **along**: to make it easier for something to happen or for someone to succeed ➤ *His career was helped along by his manager, who was a personal friend.*

2 help sb **along**: to help someone to walk when they are injured or ill, by holding their arm ➤ *He took the old lady's arm and helped her along.*

HELP OFF WITH →

help sb **off with** sth: to help someone to take off their coat, shoes etc ➤ *Can I help you off with your coat?*

HELP ON WITH →

help sb **on with** sth: to help someone to put on their coat, shoes etc ➤ *Do you want me to help you on with those boots?*

HELP OUT →

help out, help sb **out, help out** sb: to help someone, especially by doing some work for them or giving them money ➤ *As a teenager he had helped out at his family's garage.* ➤ *When I*

H

was unemployed, my mother helped me out. **+ with** ▶ *The Ministry of Agriculture have offered to help out with the extra costs.*

HELP TO →

1 help yourself to sth: **a.** to take and use something, especially food and drink, whenever you want it ▶ *Help yourself to whatever's in the fridge.* **b.** to put food on your plate yourself, or pour a drink into your own glass ▶ *Help yourselves to the vegetables.*

2 help sb to sth: to put food on someone else's plate for them, or pour a drink into their glass ▶ *Shall I help you to some rice?*

HELP UP →

help sb up: to help someone to stand up after they have fallen over ▶ *Peter put out his hand to help her up.*

HEM

HEM IN →

1 be hemmed in: to be closely surrounded or enclosed with something ▶ *The park was hemmed in with tall trees.*

2 be hemmed in: to feel you are being prevented from having the freedom to do what you want ▶ *If employees feel hemmed in, they become frustrated and angry.*

HERD

HERD TOGETHER →

herd together sb/sth, **herd** sb/sth **together**, **herd together**: to gather people or animals together into a group, or to gather together in a group ▶ *The prisoners were herded together into the courtyard.*

HERD UP →

herd up sb/sth, **herd** sb/sth **up**: to gather people or animals together into a group ▶ *The rest of the group were herded up and taken back to the hotel.*

HEW

HEW OUT →

hew sth **out, hew out** sth: to make something by cutting it out of something hard, for example rock or wood ▶ *The caves are man-made, hewn out of the rock by hand.*

HEW TO →

hew to sth: to strongly believe in or follow particular ideas, rules, or principles ▶ *As a politician, he hewed to a moderate course that didn't upset the majority.*

HIDE

HIDE AWAY →

1 hide sth/sb **away, hide away** sth/sb: to put something or someone in a place where other people will not find them ▶ *He knew his grandparents had plenty of money hidden away.* ▶ *The baby girl was taken and hidden away in the country.*

2 hide (yourself) away: to go somewhere where you can be alone or cannot be found ▶ *Writers often hide themselves away for months at a time.* ▶ *Wild animals tend to hide away when they are ill or injured.*

hideaway N a secret place where you can go when you want to be alone ▶ *He has a secluded hideaway in a remote area of Scotland.*

3 be hidden away: to be built or placed in a very quiet peaceful area ▶ *Hidden away in the countryside is Britain's most luxurious health resort.*

HIDE BEHIND →

1 hide behind sth: to deliberately behave in a way that gives people a false idea of what you are really like or what you really think ▶ *Jeremy tends to hide behind a mask of extreme politeness.*

2 hide sth **behind** sth: to not show what you are really feeling or thinking, because your appearance or behaviour hides it ▶ *Paula quickly hid her embarrassment behind a bright smile.*

HIDE OUT →

hide out: to go or stay somewhere secret, especially in order to escape from someone ▶ *The terrorists are thought to be hiding out somewhere in London.*

hideout N a place where someone goes when they do not want to be found ▶ *The suspects were tracked down to their hideout in the mountains.*

HIKE

HIKE UP →

1 hike sth **up, hike up** sth: to pull up a piece of clothing you are wearing so that it is higher up your body than before ▶ *She hiked up her skirt and waded into the river.*

2 hike up sth: to increase a price or other sum of money suddenly and by a large amount ▶ *The Central Bank hiked up interest rates in early December.*

HINGE

HINGE ON, *also* HINGE UPON →

1 hinge on/upon sth: if one thing hinges on another, its future or success depends on it ▶ *A student's job prospects can completely hinge on his performance in these exams.*

2 hinge on/upon sth: to be the most basic part of something, upon which everything else depends ▶ *The whole plot of the movie hinges on what happens in the first scene.*

HINT

HINT AT →

hint at sth: to suggest that something is true or likely without saying it directly ▶ *In his speech the president hinted at the possibility of further tax*

cuts. **+ what/why etc** ▶ *Sometimes my mother hinted at why she'd left my father, but that was all.*

HIRE

HIRE OUT →

hire out sth/sb, **hire** sth/sb **out**: to allow someone to use a building, a piece of equipment, or someone's services in return for money ▶ *Tony plans to hire the house out for weddings and film work.*

HIT

HIT BACK →

hit back: to criticize or attack a person or group, especially publicly, because they have criticized or attacked you. ▶ *The multi-millionaire has already hit back by threatening to take the newspaper to court.* **+ at** ▶ *Police last night hit back at claims that they had mishandled the arrest.*

HIT OFF →

hit it off: if two or more people hit it off, they like each other as soon as they meet each other ▶ *I met Frank at a conference and we hit it off straight away.* **+ with** ▶ *I didn't really hit it off with the office manager.*

HIT ON, *also* HIT UPON →

1 hit on/upon sth: to think of an idea or plan, especially one that is successful ▶ *They tried various methods before hitting on the right one.*

2 hit on/upon sth: to discover the true facts about a situation, the real reason for something etc ▶ *You've hit on precisely the thing that's worrying me most.*

HIT ON →

hit on sb: to talk to someone in a way that shows you think they are sexually attractive ▶ *This weird guy hit on every woman on our floor in the first week of college.*

H

HIT OUT →

hit out: to criticize something or someone strongly because you disapprove of them or in order to defend yourself. **+ at** ▸ *The industry hit out yesterday at the increase in business taxes.* ▸ *When he's upset he tends to hit out at those closest to him.*

HIT UP →

hit sb **up**: to ask someone to give you something, especially money. **+ for** ▸ *Why don't you hit Marty up for a loan and go shopping?*

HIT UPON *see* HIT ON

HITCH

HITCH UP →

hitch up sth, **hitch** sth **up**: to pull up a piece of clothing, so that it is higher up your body than before ▸ *She quickly hitched up her tights.*

HIVE

HIVE OFF →

hive sth **off, hive off** sth: to separate one or more parts, people, or things from all the rest ▸ *They want to hive off the publishing sector of the company and sell it to the highest bidder.*

HOARD

HOARD AWAY →

hoard away sth, **hoard** sth **away**: to secretly keep large quantities of something hidden somewhere ▸ *The old man had been hoarding his money away for years.*

HOARD UP →

hoard up sth, **hoard** sth **up**: to collect and save large amounts of food,

money etc, so that you will have it later if you need it ▸ *People are hoarding supplies of food in case there's another bad winter.*

HOLD

HOLD AGAINST →

hold sth **against** sb: to feel angry, upset etc with someone because of something they have done ▸ *Lack of experience won't be held against you – we offer full training.* **hold it against** sb ▸ *"I know I've been a bit silly," said Claudia "but please don't hold it against me."*

HOLD BACK →

1 hold back sth/sb, **hold** sth/sb **back**: to prevent something or someone from moving forward or getting near something ▸ *Police did their best to hold back hundreds of screaming fans.*

2 hold sb/sth **back, hold back** sb/sth: to prevent someone or something from making progress ▸ *Many students are held back at school by poor reading skills.* ▸ *the male-dominated society which has held women back for so long*

3 hold back sth, **hold** sth **back, hold back**: to stop yourself from showing how you feel, especially with difficulty. **hold back tears** ▸ *Struggling to hold back her tears, Justine watched him get onto the plane.* **hold back laughter** ▸ *In the end she couldn't hold back the laughter any longer.*

4 hold back, hold sb **back**: to not do or say something you had intended to do or say ▸ *The president's instinct was to send in troops, but he decided to hold back.* **something holds** sb **back** ▸ *She was tempted to tell him everything, but something held her back.*

5 hold sth **back, hold back** sth: to keep something secret ▸ *You're sure* *you're telling me everything – you're not holding anything back?*

6 hold back sth, **hold** sth **back**: to keep the money you had intended to give to someone, for example so that they are more likely to do what you want ▶ *Congress had threatened to hold back $5 million in aid until a peace agreement is signed.*

HOLD DOWN →

1 hold sb/sth **down**, **hold down** sb/sth: to make someone or something stay in the same place and stop

them from moving ▶ *It took four policemen to hold him down.* ▶ *The roof consisted of sheets of corrugated iron, held down with stones.*

2 hold down sth, **hold** sth **down**: to prevent the level of something from increasing, especially prices, wages etc ▶ *Colleges must hold down tuition fees to attract more students.*

3 hold down a job: to succeed in keeping a job for a fairly long period of time ▶ *He's never held down a job for longer than a few weeks.*

4 hold down sb, **hold** sb **down**: to keep people under strict control or limit their freedom ▶ *a race of people held down for centuries by invaders and conquerors*

5 hold down the noise also **hold it down**: used to tell someone to be quieter or stop talking ▶ *Hey, could you hold it down in there please?*

HOLD FORTH →

hold forth: to talk or give your opinion about something for a long time, especially in a way that is boring and

annoying ▶ *Edward was holding forth in the corner of the bar.*

HOLD OFF →

1 hold off, **hold off** sth: to delay doing something ▶ *If you need a computer but have been holding off because of the expense, now is the time to buy.* **hold off (on) doing** sth ▶ *We've decided to hold off making an announcement until next week.*

2 hold off sb, **hold** sb **off**: to prevent someone from being successful when they are trying to attack you, defeat you, or cause you problems ▶ *They managed to hold off their attackers until the police arrived.* ▶ *The company is in deep trouble – they need to raise £15 million to hold off their creditors.*

3 hold off: if rain or snow holds off, it does not start falling, although it looks as if it will soon ▶ *I hope the rain holds off until we get home.*

HOLD ON →

1 hold on: to hold something tightly, especially to stop yourself from falling or from losing what you are holding ▶ *The dog wouldn't let go of the stick – it just held on and snarled.* **hold on tight** ▶ *Nancy got onto the back of the bike and held on tight.* **hold on for dear life** (=hold something very tightly because you are afraid) ▶ *Jake clung to the branch, holding on for dear life.*

2 hold on: to wait for a short time – used especially to tell someone to wait. **hold on a minute/second etc** ▶ *Hold on a moment – I'm just coming.* sb **can't hold on much longer** ▶ *I'm afraid I can't hold on much longer, I've got a taxi waiting.*

3 hold on!: used when you want someone to stop what they are saying and listen to you ▶ *Hold on – what are you talking about?* **hold on a minute/**

H

second ▶ *Now hold on a minute! That's my money, not yours.*

4 hold on: to succeed in preventing someone from defeating you, even though this is difficult ▶ *The town's defenders were able to hold on for several weeks.*

5 hold on: to manage to continue to exist or to do something ▶ *The company managed to hold on, in spite of the recession.*

6 hold on: if someone who is very ill holds on, they succeed in staying alive with great difficulty ▶ *You could see that Ed was just barely holding on.*

HOLD ONTO, *also* HOLD ON TO →

1 hold onto/on to sth: to hold something tightly, especially to stop yourself from falling or losing what you are holding ▶ *She held on to the counter to steady herself.*

2 hold onto/on to sth: to keep something, and not give it to someone else, throw it away etc ▶ *Hold onto the receipt in case you need to take the dress back to the shop.* **hold onto** sth **for** sb (=look after something for someone) ▶ *I've got nowhere to put this table. Could you hold on to it for me for a while?*

3 hold onto/on to sth: to succeed in keeping something, when there is a danger that you will lose it ▶ *Although rebel forces have captured the city, they won't be able to hold on to it for long.*

4 hold onto/on to sth: to continue to have a hope or belief, even though you feel less sure about it than you did ▶ *I hold on to the philosophy that most people are basically good.*

HOLD OUT →

1 hold out sth, **hold** sth **out**: to stretch your hand forwards in order to give or show someone what you are holding ▶ *"Have you seen this?" Casey said, holding out a piece of paper.* **hold out**

your hand *also* **hold your hand out** (=stretch forward your hand) ▶ *She came towards me, holding out her hand. "Welcome to New York!"*

2 hold out: if a supply of something holds out, there is enough for you to use, but only for a limited period of time ▶ *I'll stay as long as the money holds out.* ▶ *It hasn't rained for weeks – do you think the water will hold out?*

3 hold out: to try to prevent change or prevent yourself from being forced to do something ▶ *The Council wants to buy the land, but the owners are holding out and refusing to sell.* **hold out against** sth/sb ▶ *Republicans are determined to hold out against proposals to increase welfare spending.*

> **holdout** N a person, country etc that refuses to accept change or does not agree with something ▶ *He is one of the few holdouts against abolishing capital punishment.*

4 hold out: to continue to defend yourself against an enemy attack without being defeated ▶ *The rebels held out for as long as they could.* **hold out against** sth/sb ▶ *Their troops held out against a massive bombardment by enemy warplanes.*

5 hold out the possibility/prospect of sth: to suggest that something good might happen in the future ▶ *The government held out the possibility of another cut in interest rates.*

HOLD OUT FOR →

hold out for sth: to refuse to accept anything less than what you have asked for ▶ *Personally, I'm holding out for £30 an hour.* ▶ *It's clear that the company was trying to hold out for a higher price.*

HOLD OUT ON →

hold out on sb: to refuse to give someone information that they need

▶ *I'm sure they know what happened, but they're holding out on me.*

HOLD OVER →

1 hold sth **over** sb: to use information about someone or your power over them to make them do what you want ▶ *My brother held that secret over me for thirty years.*

2 hold sth **over, hold over** sth: to delay something until a later time ▶ *The race has been held over until next week.*

3 be held over: if a film, concert etc is held over, it is shown for longer than planned because it is very popular ▶ *Come see "Pulp Fiction", held over for another week.*

> **holdover** N something or someone that existed or was used in the past and still exists or is used now ▶ *The idea of a permanent job is a holdover from yesterday's world.*

HOLD TO →

1 hold sb **to** sth: to make someone do what they have promised or agreed to do ▶ *"Next time, I'll buy you a drink." "I'll hold you to that!"*

2 hold sb **to a draw etc**: to prevent the opposing team or player from getting more points or goals than you ▶ *United were held to a 2-2 draw by Rangers.*

3 hold to sth: to refuse to change your beliefs, ideas, principles etc ▶ *We must hold to principles of fairness and treat everyone equally.*

HOLD TOGETHER →

1 hold sb/sth **together, hold together** sb/sth: to make people, countries etc stay together and not separate ▶ *The only thing that held their marriage together was the children.*

2 hold together: if people, countries etc hold together, they stay together and do not separate ▶ *The big question is, can the Alliance hold together till the end of the war?*

3 hold sth **together, hold together** sth: to prevent something from breaking into separate parts ▶ *The shed was held together by a few old rusty nails.*

4 hold together: to stay in one piece instead of breaking into separate parts ▶ *If the pastry mixture doesn't hold together, add some more water.*

5 hold together: if a story, plan, explanation etc holds together, it is good and you find it easy to understand, believe, or agree with ▶ *I don't think his argument holds together.*

HOLD UP →

1 hold up sth, **hold** sth **up**: to raise your hand or arm, or something that you have in your hand ▶ *One child at the back of the class held up her hand.* ▶ *The crowd held up posters demanding his release from prison.*

2 hold sth/sb **up, hold up** sth/sb: to delay something or someone ▶ *Protesters held up work on the new road for weeks.* ▶ *The concert should have started at 8, but a series of problems held things up.* **get held up** ▶ *Sorry we're late – we got held up in the traffic.*

> **hold-up** N an unexpected delay ▶ *A crash this morning is causing big hold-ups on the M25.*

3 hold up sth, **hold** sth **up**: to support something and stop it from falling down ▶ *This mirror's only being held up by one tiny hook.*

4 hold up sth/sb: to stop a vehicle or go into a bank, shop etc with a weapon and demand money from people ▶ *Stealing money by computer is far easier than holding* *up a bank.* **hold** sb **up at gunpoint/ knifepoint** ▶ *He was charged with holding up a cab driver at gunpoint.*

hold-up N when someone stops a vehicle or goes into a bank, shop etc with a gun and demands money ▶ *A man was shot dead in a hold-up at a bank yesterday.*

5 hold up: to continue to be healthy, successful, or at a high level, especially in a difficult situation ▶ *Is she holding up under all the pressure?* ▶ *Sales held up well in the fourth quarter of the year.*

6 hold up: if a machine, piece of equipment, or system holds up, it continues to work and does not break ▶ *It will be interesting to see how well the new computer system holds up.*

7 hold up: to still seem good or right after being checked or tested ▶ *She did not believe the man's evidence would hold up in court.* ▶ *If these findings hold up, scientists will have to develop a completely new theory.*

HOLD UP AS →

hold sb/sth **up as** sth, **hold up** sb/sth **as** sth: to use someone or something as an example, especially an example that other people should copy ▶ *He's only a footballer – he shouldn't be held up as a role model for our kids.*

HOLD WITH →

not hold with sth: to not approve of something ▶ *I don't hold with all this Internet dating.* **hold with doing** sth ▶ *She didn't hold with smacking children in any circumstances.*

HOLE

HOLE UP →

hole up also **be holed up**: to be or to go and stay somewhere quiet and away from other people ▶ *She was holed up a hotel on Fifth Avenue.*

▶ *The kids hole up in their rooms with their computer games all day long.*

HOLLOW

HOLLOW OUT →

hollow sth **out, hollow out** sth: to make a hole or empty space in something by removing the inside part ▶ *Cut the top off of a large pineapple and carefully hollow out the fruit.*

hollowed-out ADJ having a hole or space in the middle, made by removing the inside part ▶ *a hollowed-out log*

HOME

HOME IN ON →

1 home in on sth: to move directly towards something in order to attack and destroy it ▶ *Modern missiles can home in on their targets with incredible accuracy.*

2 home in on sth: to direct your attention or efforts towards a particular subject or problem ▶ *He immediately homed in on the weak point in her argument.*

HOOK

HOOK INTO →

1 hook into sth: to become connected to a system such as the Internet or a telephone system ▶ *New telecom companies will be allowed to hook into the national phone system.*

2 hook sb **into** sth: to persuade someone to do what you want in a skilful way, even though they may not want to do it ▶ *The TV companies persuade you to watch a steady stream of programmes, one hooking you into the next.*

HOOK UP →

1 hook up sth/sb, **hook** sth/sb **up**: to connect something or someone to a piece of equipment, an electronic system, or an electricity supply ▶ *The* *air conditioning isn't hooked up yet, and it's incredibly hot in here!* **+ to** ▶ *a device for hooking up users to the Internet*

hook-up N a temporary connection between two pieces of equipment, for example computers ▶ *Walford was speaking to a reporter via a satellite hookup.*

2 hook up: to start a romantic or sexual relationship with someone ▶ *So, did you and Dan finally hook up?* **+ with** ▶ *Guess what – Jessie hooked up with Paul last night!*

3 hook up: to meet someone in order to do something together socially. **+ with** ▶ *Matt and I went out for a drink and hooked up with Janet later on.*

4 hook up: to agree to work with another person or organization for a particular purpose. **+ with** ▶ *The Beatles hooked up with another band for a tour of the US.*

HORN

HORN IN →

horn in: to interrupt or try to take part in an activity when you are not wanted ▶ *Pardon my rudeness for horning in where I have no business.* **+ on** ▶ *the guy who horned in on my date*

HOSE

HOSE DOWN →

hose down sth/sb, **hose** sth/sb **down:** to wash something or someone using a hose ▶ *Take Louis' car out on the forecourt and hose it down.*

HOT

HOT UP →

1 hot up: to become more exciting or dangerous, with a lot more activity ▶ *The election campaign is already hotting up.*

2 hot up: to become hotter ▶ *As the climate hots up, the polar ice caps will start to melt.*

HOUND

HOUND OUT →

hound out sb, **hound** sb **out:** to force someone to leave a place or job by making the situation very unpleasant for them ▶ *She didn't resign; she was hounded out by her colleagues.* **+ of** ▶ *a man who was hounded out of one country after another*

HOWL

HOWL DOWN →

howl down sb, **howl** sb **down:** to prevent a speaker from being heard by shouting loudly and angrily ▶ *At a public meeting today union officials were howled down by angry strikers.*

HUDDLE

HUDDLE UP →
be huddled up: to sit or lie with your arms and legs folded close to your body because you are cold or frightened ▶ *She sat huddled up in a corner, pale and shivering.*

HUDDLE UP, *also* HUDDLE TOGETHER →

huddle up/together: to stand or sit very close together with other people ▶ *They sheltered in a doorway and huddled up close for warmth.* **be huddled up/together** ▶ *They spent Christmas huddled together in a church hall after their homes were flooded.*

H

HUM

HUM WITH →
hum with sth: if a place is humming with activity, it is very busy ▶ *By 8 o'clock the streets are usually humming with life.*

HUNGER

HUNGER AFTER, *also* **HUNGER FOR** →
hunger after/for sth: to want something very much ▶ *a nation hungering for change*

HUNKER

HUNKER DOWN →
1 hunker down: to bend your knees so that you are sitting on your heels very close to the ground ▶ *We hunkered down around the campfire.*

2 hunker down: to make yourself comfortable in a safe place, especially for a long time ▶ *I think I'll just hunker down in my room this evening.* **be hunkered down** ▶ *You were hunkered down so cosy I didn't like to disturb you.*

3 hunker down: to prepare yourself for a difficult situation ▶ *Negotiators hunkered down for a weekend of non-stop talks.*

HUNT

HUNT DOWN →
hunt down sb, **hunt** sb **down**: to search for a person or animal by chasing them until you catch them ▶ *Runaway slaves were hunted down like wild beasts.* ▶ *The sole purpose of his voyage was to hunt down the Great White Whale.*

HUNT OUT →
1 hunt out sb/sth, **hunt** sb/sth **out**: to search for and find someone or something in order to kill or destroy them ▶ *A squadron of aircraft was* ordered to hunt out every last enemy submarine.

2 hunt out sth, **hunt** sth **out**: to search for and find something that you need or want ▶ *I must try and hunt out my old riding boots.*

HURRY

HURRY ALONG →
1 hurry sth/sb **along**: to make something happen more quickly, or to make someone do something more quickly ▶ *Everyone was getting impatient, so I thought I'd try and hurry things along.* ▶ *Can you hurry the kids along a bit – they're going to be late for school.*

2 hurry along: to go somewhere quickly ▶ *People hurried along, their heads bent against the wind.*

HURRY ON →
1 hurry on: to continue walking or going somewhere more quickly than before ▶ *Patrick called after her, but she hurried on, almost running.* **hurry on ahead** (=go somewhere quickly without waiting for other people) ▶ *Ellis hurried on ahead to get the tickets.*

2 hurry on: to quickly continue talking, often changing the subject ▶ *Lisa hurried on before he could interrupt her.* **+ to** ▶ *The chairman dealt briefly with the first item and then hurried on to Item Two.*

HURRY UP →
1 hurry up: to do something more quickly ▶ *You'd better hurry up and get dressed if you want to come with me.* ▶ *I wish they'd hurry up and fix the TV.* **hurry up!** (=used to tell someone to come or go somewhere quickly) ▶ *Hurry up, or you'll get no dinner.*

2 hurry sth/sb **up**, **hurry up** sth/sb: to make something happen more quickly, or make someone do something more quickly ▶ *I'm sorry the job's taking so long – I'll try to hurry things up a bit.*

HUSH

HUSH UP →

hush sth **up, hush up** sth: to prevent other people from knowing about something immoral or shocking ▶ *Gran wanted it all hushed up, but everyone knew her son's death was suicide.*

HYPE

HYPE UP →

1 hype up sth/sb, **hype** sth/sb **up**: to make something or someone seem more important or better than they really are, so that people will expect them to be very good ▶ *a show that was hyped up as the big sensation of the television season*

hyped-up ADJ a hyped-up event, film, team etc has been made to seem more important or better than it really is, especially by being advertised a lot ▶ *another hyped-up dinosaur movie*

2 be hyped up: to be very excited or anxious about something ▶ *Now she's all hyped up and dying to see him.*

get hyped up ▶ *Before a big game the players get hyped up, restless and agitated.*

H

Ii

ICE

ICE OVER →

ice over: to become covered with ice ▶ *The lake had iced over by the next morning.* **be iced over** (=be covered with ice) ▶ *In some places the road was iced over.*

ICE UP →

ice up: if something such as a window or a machine ices up, it becomes covered or blocked with ice ▶ *My*

windscreen was icing up and I could hardly see the car in front. ▶ *The aircraft plunged to earth after its engines iced up at 35,000 feet.*

IDENTIFY

IDENTIFY WITH →

1 identify with sb/sth: to feel able to understand someone, especially because they seem similar to you in some way ▶ *Young readers can easily identify with Helen, the main character in the story.*

2 be identified with sth: to be considered by many people to have a close connection with someone or something ▶ *Fats Waller's name came to be identified with a unique style of jazz.*

3 identify (yourself) with sb/sth: to consider yourself to be part of a group that has a particular set of beliefs ▶ *politicians who wanted to identify*

themselves with the democracy movement

IDLE

IDLE AWAY →

idle away sth, **idle** sth **away**: to spend time in a relaxed way, doing nothing ▶ *Natasha would sit idling away the long summer days by the river.*

IMBUE

IMBUE WITH →

imbue sth/sb **with** sth: to fill something or someone with a particular quality or feeling ▶ *All his poetry is imbued with a sense of spirituality.* ▶ *They are a people deeply imbued with national pride.*

IMMERSE

IMMERSE IN →

1 be immersed in sth: to be completely involved in an activity or in thinking about something ▶ *Some people are so immersed in their careers that they almost forget about their families.*

2 immerse yourself in sth: to take part in something and become completely involved in it ▶ *After his wife's death, he immersed himself in his work.*

IMPACT

IMPACT ON →

impact on sth/sb: to have an important and noticeable effect on something or someone ▶ *How do you expect the rising price of oil to impact on European economies?*

IMPINGE

IMPINGE ON, *also* IMPINGE UPON →

impinge on/upon sb/sth: to affect someone or something, especially in a way that limits their freedom ▶ *new police powers that may impinge on the rights of protesters*

IMPOSE

IMPOSE ON, *also* **IMPOSE UPON** →

1 impose a tax/ban etc on sth/sb: to officially order that something must be taxed, that someone should be banned etc ▶ *The government considered imposing a tax on books.* ▶ *Parliament imposed a ban on all strikes among public sector workers.*

2 impose sth **on/upon** sb: to make someone have the same ideas or beliefs as you, by influencing them strongly ▶ *teachers who try to impose their own moral values on their students*

3 impose on sb: to expect or ask someone to do something for you that they might consider unreasonable ▶ *We could ask them to let us stay the night, but I don't want to impose on them.*

IMPRESS

IMPRESS ON, *also* **IMPRESS UPON** →

impress sth **on/upon** sb: to make someone understand clearly that something is very important ▶ *He was very careful to impress upon his officers the need for absolute secrecy.* **+ that** ▶ *It had always been impressed on Alice that she must tell the truth.*

IMPROVE

IMPROVE ON, *also* **IMPROVE UPON** →

improve on/upon sth: to do something better than before or to make it better than before ▶ *She has scored 165 points, and I don't think anyone will improve on that.* ▶ *Advances in radiotherapy will enable us to improve on existing cancer treatments.*

INDULGE

INDULGE IN →

indulge in sth: to let yourself do or have something that you enjoy ▶ *A new diet book claims you can indulge in any foods and still lose weight.* ▶ *They stopped off in Fort William to indulge in some leisurely shopping.*

INFLICT

INFLICT ON, *also* **INFLICT UPON** →

1 inflict sth **on/upon** sb: to talk about your opinions and not accept that other people might disagree with them ▶ *He shouldn't try to inflict his beliefs on everyone else.*

2 inflict sb **on/upon** sb: to make you have to spend time with someone you would rather not be with ▶ *I wish she wouldn't insist on inflicting her family on us every Christmas!*

3 inflict yourself on sb: to visit or spend time with someone when they do not want you to be with them ▶ *"Sorry to inflict myself on you again." "Don't be silly. Come in and have a drink."*

INFORM

INFORM ON, *also* **INFORM AGAINST** →

inform on/against sb: to tell people in authority about something dishonest or illegal that someone has done ▶ *They were arrested in 1996 when a member of their gang informed on them.*

INFRINGE

INFRINGE ON, *also* **INFRINGE UPON** →

infringe on/upon sth: to limit someone's freedom or take their rights away from them ▶ *Some students believe the new law infringes upon their freedom of expression.*

INFUSE

INFUSE WITH →

infuse sth **with** sth: to fill something with a particular feeling or quality, especially a good one ▶ *Jan infuses all her classes with an air of energy and enthusiasm.*

INJECT

INJECT INTO →

inject sth **into** sth: to add a good quality such as excitement or enthusiasm to something ▶ *Better communication between management and workers has injected new optimism into the workforce.* ▶ *It is hoped that the building of the leisure centre will inject new life into the town.*

INQUIRE

INQUIRE AFTER, *also* ENQUIRE AFTER →

inquire after sb/ sth: to ask how someone is or what they have been doing ▶ *Mr. Collins inquired politely after Joe.*

INQUIRE INTO, *also* ENQUIRE INTO →

inquire into sth: to officially look for more information about something in order to decide if, why, or how it happened ▶ *The Football League appointed a commission to inquire into alleged illegal payments by the club.*

INQUIRE OF, *also* ENQUIRE OF →

inquire of sb: to ask someone a question about something ▶ *"Have you any family?" she inquired of Mr Oaks.*

INSINUATE

INSINUATE →

insinuate yourself into sth: to gradually gain someone's trust, by pretending to be friendly and sincere ▶ *She delights in insinuating herself into other people's lives, then turning those lives upside down.*

INSIST

INSIST ON, *also* INSIST UPON →

1 insist on/ upon sth: to demand something and refuse to accept or do anything else ▶ *She insisted on absolute obedience at all times.* **insist on doing** sth ▶ *Guy insisted on paying for the meal, so I offered to cook him dinner some time.*

2 insist on/ upon sth: to behave in a particular way, especially in a way that annoys other people, and refuse to behave any differently. **insist on doing** sth ▶ *He insisted on bringing his dog everywhere with him.*

INSURE

INSURE AGAINST, *also* ENSURE AGAINST →

insure against sth: to do something to reduce the risk of something bad happening to you ▶ *Police powers should be increased, to insure against further violence in the streets.*

INTEREST

INTEREST IN →

1 interest sb **in** sth: to try to persuade someone to do something, often to buy something ▶ *The salesman was trying to interest him in one of the more expensive models.*

2 can/ could I interest you in sth?: used to try to persuade someone to buy or accept something ▶ *Can I interest you in one of our new discount phone cards?*

INTERFERE

INTERFERE WITH →

1 interfere with sth: to prevent someone from doing something properly, or to prevent something from making progress ▶ *Students should*

ot work so many hours that the job
nterferes with school work. ► *He
*efused to let his illness interfere with
is duties as President.*

interfere with sth: to deliberately
*amage something so that it does not
vork properly* ► *Police say the thieves
*managed to interfere with the bank's
larm system.

NTERSPERSE

*E INTERSPERSED WITH →
e interspersed with sth: to include
omething in various places or at
arious times ► *Tomorrow there will be
unny periods interspersed with
ccasional showers.*

NURE

*E INURED TO, also BE ENURED
*O →
e inured/enured to sth: to have
ecome so used to something
unpleasant that you are no longer
upset by it ► *Have we become so
*nured to suffering that we don't think
o help people in need?

NVALID

*E INVALIDED OUT →
be invalided out: to be officially
allowed to leave a job, especially in
he army, navy etc, because of injury
or illness ► *Her father joined the Irish
Guards, but was invalided out in 1917.

NVEST

*NVEST IN →
invest in sth: to buy something that
you think will become more valuable
over time so you can sell it for a profit
► *Jones had made a small fortune by
investing in new Internet companies.

2 invest in sth: to buy something
because it is very useful and it will be
worth the money you spend ► *It's
sensible to invest in a good pair of
running shoes.*

3 invest sth **in** sth/sb, **invest in**
sth/sb: to spend a lot of time, effort,
money etc trying to make something
or someone successful ► *Robin's
father had invested so much in her
musical career that she didn't want to
disappoint him.*

4 invest sth **in** sb: to give someone
the official authority to do something
► *the constitutional power invested in
Congress to declare war*

INVEST WITH →
invest sb **with** sth: to give someone
official authority to do something
► *The Court is invested with the power
to decide constitutional cases.*

INVITE

INVITE ALONG →
invite sb **along, invite along** sb: to ask
someone to come with you when you
are going somewhere ► *We're all
going to see a film tonight – why don't
you invite Tom along?* **+ with** ► *They
invited me along to the beach with
them.*

INVITE AROUND *see* INVITE ROUND

INVITE BACK →
invite sb **back**: to ask someone to
come to your home after you have
been out somewhere together ► *Annie
invited Sheila back for coffee after the
meeting.*

INVITE IN →
invite sb **in**:
to ask
someone to
come into
your home,
room, office,
etc ► *Ken
invited her in
to see his new house.*

INVITE OUT →
invite sb **out**: to ask someone to go to
a film, restaurant, concert etc with

you. **invite** sb **out to dinner/the cinema etc** ▶ *I've been invited out to dinner, but I don't feel like going.* **+ for** ▶ *Ben met Joan at a party, and invited her out for a drink.*

INVITE OVER →

invite sb **over**: to ask someone to come to where you live, for example to have a meal or drink ▶ *John and Susan have invited me over for Sunday lunch.* ▶ *You should invite her over some time.*

INVITE ROUND, *also* INVITE AROUND →

invite sb **round/around**: to ask someone to come to where you live, for example to have a meal or drink

▶ *I often invite people round for Friday evening drinks.*

IRON

IRON OUT →

iron out sth, **iron** sth **out**: if you iron out small problems, you deal with them ▶ *The managers meet once a month to iron out any problems.*

ITCH

ITCH FOR →

itch for sth: to want something very much and be very impatient to do it ▶ *She could tell he was itching for a fight.* ▶ *He says he's itching to get back into Formula One racing.*

Jj

JABBER

JABBER AWAY →
jabber away: to talk quickly and continuously in an annoying way ▶ *I could hear Mike in the kitchen, jabbering away to the cook.*

JACK

JACK AROUND →
jack sb around: to deliberately make things difficult for someone and waste their time ▶ *The realtors kept jacking us around so we found another agency to sell the house.*

JACK IN →
jack sth in, jack in sth: to stop doing a job or other regular activity ▶ *If I still don't like the job after another month, I'm jacking it in.*

JACK UP →
1 jack up sth, jack sth up: to increase prices, rates etc suddenly and by a large amount ▶ *All the hotels jack up their prices for the festival week.*

2 jack sth up, jack up sth: to lift a vehicle off the ground using a piece of equipment that you put under the vehicle to support it ▶ *He jacked the car up and removed the damaged wheel.*

JAM

JAM ON →
jam on the brakes: to suddenly put your foot hard on the brake in order to stop your car ▶ *Panicking, she jammed*

on the brakes and the car turned in a half circle.

JAM UP →
1a. jam sth up, jam up sth: if a lot of people or vehicles jam up a place, they block it so that it is difficult to move ▶ *So many people were rushing to get out at once, they jammed up the exits.*
b. jam up: if a place jams up, there are so many people or vehicles there that it becomes blocked and no one can move ▶ *A stretch of road will always jam up quickly after an accident.*

2a. jam up sth, jam sth up: to prevent a machine from working properly by getting stuck in a part of it ▶ *The paper keeps getting trapped and jamming up the printer.*
b. jam up: if a part of a machine jams up, it no longer works properly because something is preventing it from moving ▶ *Her gun suddenly jammed up and wouldn't fire.*

3 be jammed up against sth: to be too close to something or in an uncomfortable position against it ▶ *a tiny room with a single bed jammed up against the fireplace*

JAR

JAR ON →
jar on sb: to make someone feel annoyed or uncomfortable ▶ *She had a hard unpleasant laugh, which really jarred on me.* **jar on the nerves/ears** ▶ *The same old music blared out, jarring on everyone's nerves.*

JAZZ

JAZZ UP →
jazz up sth, jazz sth up: to improve something that is old or boring by adding new or interesting things to it ▶ *plain rice jazzed up with mushrooms and sun-dried tomatoes* ▶ *If your Web*

site looks a bit boring, you could jazz it up by adding a few graphics.
jazzed-up ADJ made more exciting and interesting ▸ *jazzed-up cuisine*

JERK

JERK AROUND →
jerk sb **around, jerk around with** sth/ sb: to treat someone badly by deliberately making things difficult for them ▸ *I got tired of being jerked around by everyone in the department, so I quit.*

JET

JET OFF →
jet off: to travel somewhere by plane for a holiday, for your work etc ▸ *She has a very glamorous lifestyle – she's always jetting off to somewhere or other.*

JIBE

JIBE WITH →
jibe with sth: if one statement, opinion, report etc jibes with another, the information in them is similar ▸ *The survey's results jibe with what bankers and economists are saying.*

JOCKEY

JOCKEY FOR →
jockey for position/ power: to compete with other people to try to get into the best position or situation, or to get control ▸ *Photographers jockeyed for position outside the courtroom.* ▸ *As the president's health declined, potential rivals began jockeying for power.*

JOCKEY INTO →
jockey sth **into** sth: to move something large into a particular place

or position ▸ *Space controllers jockeyed the satellite into a 62-mile-high orbit.*

JOG

JOG ALONG →
jog along: to continue steadily in the same way as usual, without anything exciting or unusual happening ▸ *United have been jogging along in the middle of the league tables all season.*

JOIN

JOIN IN →
join in, join in sth: to start doing or becoming involved in something with other people ▸ *When we get to the chorus, I want everybody to join in.* ▸ *Politely, he joined in the laughter.*

JOIN UP →
1 join up: to become a member of the army, navy, or air force ▸ *Young men and women were urged to join up and serve their country.*
2 join up sth, **join** sth **up**: to connect or fasten things together ▸ *You have to join up the dots to make a picture.*
3 join up: if two things join up they come together and connect with each other ▸ *There are two paths around the lake and they join up by the bridge.*
4 join up: to work with other people or go somewhere with them in order to do something ▸ *We joined up to make a quiz team.* **+ with** ▸ *The SS Brilliant will join up with the other ships and head west.*

JOLLY

JOLLY ALONG →
jolly sb/ sth **along**: to make someone feel more cheerful, by talking to them in a friendly and encouraging way ▸ *She tried to jolly him along and get him to join in with the others.*

JOT

JOT DOWN →

jot sth down, jot down sth: to quickly write something on a piece of paper ▸ *Jot down your suggestions on a piece of paper and give them to me.*

JUGGLE

JUGGLE ABOUT WITH *see* JUGGLE WITH

JUGGLE AROUND WITH *see* JUGGLE WITH

JUGGLE WITH →

juggle sth with sth, juggle with sth: to try to do or deal with more than one job or situation at the same time ▸ *Grace was juggling a full-time job with looking after three young children.*

JUGGLE WITH, *also* **JUGGLE ABOUT WITH, JUGGLE AROUND WITH →**

juggle with sth, juggle about with sth, juggle around with sth: to arrange sets of numbers, information, amounts etc in various ways, changing them if necessary in order to get the result you want ▸ *My accountant juggles with the figures, and then tells me how much tax I have to pay.*

JUICE

JUICE UP →

juice up sth, juice sth up: to make something more interesting or exciting ▸ *He became known for his skill at juicing up old tunes for the dance floor.*

JUMBLE

JUMBLE UP →

jumble sth up, jumble up sth: to mix things together so that they are no longer arranged neatly or in order ▸ *All the papers on my desk were jumbled up and I couldn't find a thing.*

JUMP

JUMP AT →

jump at sth: to eagerly accept an opportunity to do something ▸ *If I was offered the job, of course I'd jump at it.*
jump at the chance ▸ *Most people would jump at the chance to meet their childhood hero.*

JUMP IN →

jump in: to interrupt someone or suddenly start talking when other people are having a conversation ▸ *He was going to say more, but she jumped in. "You can't be serious!"*

JUMP ON →

jump on sb/sth: to unfairly criticize or punish someone as soon as they do anything slightly wrong ▸ *Mum's being so mean these days – every time I say something she jumps on me.*

JUMP OUT AT →

jump out at sb: if something jumps out at you, you notice it quickly ▸ *As I read it through again, several mistakes jumped out at me.*

JUMP UP →

jump up: to stand up very suddenly ▸ *When she heard Clarissa scream, she jumped up and ran outside.*

JUT

JUT OUT →

jut out: to come out further than the rest of something, or beyond the edge of something. **+ into/from/of** ▸ *Cape Finisterre juts out into the Atlantic Ocean.* ▸ *A piece of metal jutting out from the loaded vehicle caught him on the head.*

JUT UP →

jut up: to come up above the surface of something, or to point upwards ▸ *The paving was wrecked, with pieces of stone jutting up at odd angles.*

J

Kk

KEEL

KEEL OVER →

keel over: to fall over sideways, especially because you feel weak or unsteady ▶ *He looked as if he was ready to keel over from exhaustion.*

KEEP

KEEP AFTER →

keep after sb: to ask someone again and again to do something until they do it ▶ *Tony's children and relatives kept after him to stop drinking.*

KEEP AT →

1 keep at sth: to continue to do something, although it is difficult or hard work ▶ *How long do you think you'll keep at this job?* **keep at it** ▶ *I know the training is hard, but keep at it.*

2 keep sb **at it**: to make someone continue to work hard and not let them stop ▶ *You'll have to keep him at his piano practice or he'll never pass the exam.*

KEEP AWAY →

1 keep away: to not go near a person, place, or animal ▶ *You'd better keep away, I don't want you to get my cold.* **+ from** ▶ *If I were you I'd keep away from that area at night.*

2 keep sb/sth **away, keep away** sb/sth: to prevent someone or something from going near a person or place ▶ *Rub the liquid onto your skin to keep mosquitoes away.* **+ from** ▶ *Dad kept us away from school for a week.*

3 keep away sth, **keep** sth **away**: to prevent an illness from infecting someone ▶ *Vitamin C is supposed to keep away colds.*

KEEP BACK →

1 keep back: to not stand near something or not move towards it ▶ *Keep well back, please. This could be dangerous.* **+ from** ▶ *Police were telling people to keep back from the side of the road.*

2 keep back sb/sth, **keep** sb/sth **back**: to prevent someone or something from moving forward ▶ *The organizers have put up barriers to keep back the crowds.* ▶ *He tied a scarf around his head to keep his hair back.*

3 keep sth **back, keep back** sth: to keep part of something instead of using it all immediately, so that you have it to use later ▶ *I managed to keep back a couple of cases of beer, just for our own use.*

4 keep sth **back**: to deliberately not tell someone all that you know about something ▶ *I've honestly no idea what happened – do you think I'd keep anything back if I knew?* **+ from** ▶ *Ellie was sure he was keeping something back from her.*

5 keep back sth, **keep** sth **back**: if you keep back your tears or your feelings, you do not cry or show your feelings ▶ *I tried to explain, trying hard to keep back the tears.* ▶ *He was unable to keep back his anger any longer.*

6 keep sb **back**: to make someone stay after a class ▶ *After the first lesson the teacher kept me back for a little chat.*

7 keep sb **back**: to make someone stay at the same level, and not let them progress to a higher level ▶ *Mick was kept back a year at college after he failed all his exams.*

KEEP DOWN →

1 keep sth **down, keep down** sth: to prevent the size, cost, or quantity of something from increasing ▶ *No sugar*

hanks – I'm trying to keep my weight own. **keep prices/costs down** ▶ *The hop keeps prices down by buying ocal produce.*

keep sth down, keep down sth: used o ask someone to make less noise. **eep your voice down** ▶ *Keep your oice down! She'll hear you!* **keep it own** ▶ *Can you ask the kids to keep it own, I'm trying to work.*

keep down also **keep your head own:** to stay close to the ground in rder to hide ▶ *Joey told me to keep own and stay quiet so the guard vouldn't spot us.*

keep sb down, keep sb down: to eep people under strict control or mit their freedom in an unfair way *Women have been kept down for far oo long.* ▶ *an oppressive society in vhich people from ethnic minorities vere kept down*

EEP FROM →

keep sb/sth from sth: to prevent omeone from doing something or omething from happening. **keep sb rom doing sth** ▶ *He complained that e had been kept from seeing his hildren by his ex-wife.* **keep sb from th** ▶ *I hope I haven't kept you from our work.* **keep sth from doing sth** ▶ *Stand the plant in a bowl of water to eep the soil from getting dry.*

keep (yourself) from doing sth: to revent yourself from doing omething, with difficulty ▶ *I looked uickly away to keep from laughing.*

keep sth from sb: to deliberately not ell someone about something ▶ *The overnment has tried to keep this nformation from the public.* ▶ *I felt hat he was keeping something from ne.*

EEP IN →

keep sb in: to make someone stay in place, especially as a punishment

▶ *The children behaved so badly that the teacher kept them in at lunchtime.*

2 keep sb in: to make someone stay in a hospital because they are too ill to go home ▶ *They kept me in overnight just for observation.*

KEEP IN WITH →

keep in with sb: to try to remain friendly with someone ▶ *Young people often do silly things because they want to keep in with their friends.*

KEEP OFF →

1 keep off sth: to not go onto an area of land ▶ *The children had been told to keep off the beach.* ▶ *There was a sign saying 'Keep off the grass.'*

2 keep sb/sth off sth: to prevent someone or something from going onto an area of land, a road etc ▶ *Please could you keep your dog off the flower beds.* ▶ *Rain kept both teams off the pitch for long periods.*

3 keep sth off sth/sb, keep sth off, keep off sth: to prevent something from touching or harming something or someone ▶ *Jinny was wearing a hood to keep off the rain.* ▶ *How are we going to keep these wasps off the food?*

4 keep your hands off sb/sth: to not touch or go too close to someone or something ▶ *"Keep your hands off me!" Linda shouted at Don.*

5 keep off sth: to not eat, drink, or take something that is bad for you ▶ *If you want to lose weight, you should keep off fatty foods.*

6 keep sb off sth: to stop someone from eating, drinking, or taking something that is bad for them ▶ *The programme is aimed at keeping teenagers off drugs.*

7 keep off sth: to avoid talking about a particular subject, especially because it might upset someone ▶ *I think we*

K

*ought to keep off the subject of
personal relationships.*

8 keep sth **off, keep off** sth: if you
keep weight off, you do not get
heavier again after you have lost
weight ▶ *It's usually easier to lose
weight than to keep it off.*

9 keep off: if bad weather keeps off, it
does not begin, although it looks as if
it might begin soon ▶ *The rain kept off
until we boarded our coach at 6.15.*

KEEP ON →

1 keep on: to continue to do
something or go somewhere. **keep on
doing** sth ▶ *She kept on walking until
she came to a phone box.* ▶ *The album
has made over £30m already, and
people keep on buying it.* **keep on
with** sth ▶ *If it continues to rain, the
players won't be able to keep on with
the game.*

2 keep on doing sth: to do something
a lot of times ▶ *I don't like to keep on
borrowing money from the bank.*
▶ *He's a brilliant player – he just keeps
on scoring goals.*

3 keep on: to continue to talk about
something in an annoying or boring
way. **+ about** ▶ *I wish my parents
wouldn't keep on about my exams all
the time.* **keep on and on** ▶ *I know
what you think, so there's no need to
keep on and on about it.*

4 keep sb **on, keep on** sb: to continue
to employ someone ▶ *The company
have kept on a staff of thirty, out of an
original 900.*

KEEP ON AT →

keep on at sb: to tell someone
something or ask them something a
lot of times, especially in an annoying
way ▶ *If I didn't keep on at the
children, they'd never get their
homework done.* ▶ *Please don't keep
on at me. I'd tell you if I knew.*

KEEP OUT →

1 keep out: to not go into a place or
building ▶ *Danger: Keep out!* ▶ *They
boarded up the windows and put up
'Keep Out' notices.* **+ of** ▶ *Please keep
out of my office when I'm not there.*

2 keep sb/sth **out, keep out** sb/sth:
to prevent someone or something
from coming into a place ▶ *Barricades
were put up to keep out the
protestors.* **+ of** ▶ *I try to keep other
people out of the kitchen when I'm
cooking.*

KEEP OUT OF →

1 keep sb/sth **out of** sth: to prevent
someone or something from getting
involved in a situation ▶ *Anna had
tried hard to keep John out of her life.*
▶ *They somehow managed to keep
their country out of the war.*

2 keep out of sth: to not get involved
in a situation ▶ *"What's the matter?" I
asked. "You keep out of this," Charlie
replied sharply.*

KEEP TO →

1 keep to sth: to stay in one particular
area or place ▶ *Tourists are advised to
keep to the well-lit areas of the town.*
▶ *Keep to the main road and you can't
go far wrong.*

2 keep to sth: to do what has been
stated in an agreement, plan, or law
▶ *There would be fewer accidents if
people kept to the speed limits.*

3 keep sth **to** sth: to limit something
to a particular number or amount
▶ *Your stories should be kept to no
more than 500 words.* **keep** sth **to a
minimum** ▶ *Hospital waiting times
must be kept to a minimum.*

4 keep sth **to yourself**: to not tell
anyone about something ▶ *What I'm
going to tell you now is a secret. Can
you keep it to yourself?*

5 keep yourself to yourself also **keep**

to yourself: to prefer to be alone rather than with other people ▶ *Neighbours described him as a quiet man who kept himself to himself.*

6 keep to sth: to continue to talk about one particular subject, instead of starting to talk about others ▶ *Please try and keep to the subject under discussion.* **keep to the point** ▶ *He's a hopeless speaker. He can't keep to the point.*

KEEP UP →

1 keep up sth, **keep** sth **up**: to continue doing something ▶ *The doctor advised me to keep up the treatment for two weeks.* ▶ *Any exercise is good for you, but ideally you should keep it up regularly.* **keep up the good work** (=continue to work hard and well) ▶ *Well done, people! Keep up the good work.* **keep it up** (=continue to work hard and well) ▶ *He had been revising for nearly five weeks and felt he couldn't keep it up for much longer.*

2 keep up: if something keeps up, it continues without stopping or changing ▶ *Everyone was wondering how long the rain could keep up.*

3 keep up: to go as quickly as someone else ▶ *Maggie had a stone in her shoe, and was finding it hard to keep up.* **+ with** ▶ *She had to walk fast to keep up with him.*

4 keep up: to manage to do as much or as well as other people ▶ *Teachers should offer advice to children in hospital on how to keep up at school.* **+ with** ▶ *Older employees often find it difficult to keep up with their younger colleagues.*

5 keep up: to keep changing the way in which you do something because the situation you are in keeps changing ▶ *Fashions change so quickly nowadays that you need a lot*

of money to keep up. **+ with** ▶ *Many smaller firms have been unable to keep up with the pace of change.* **keep up with demand** (=supply as much of something as is wanted) ▶ *It's difficult to produce computer games fast enough to keep up with demand.*

6 keep up: to know about and understand the most recent facts of a situation or subject ▶ *Technology changes all the time. It's almost impossible to keep up.* **+ with** ▶ *We encourage all our employees to keep up with new developments.*

7 keep up sth, **keep** sth **up**: to make something continue at its present level or amount ▶ *The hostages sang songs and swapped stories to keep their spirits up.*

8 keep up: to increase at the same speed as something else. **+ with** ▶ *Salaries have not kept up with inflation in the last few years.*

9 keep up sth, **keep** sth **up**: to continue to practise something that you learned so that you do not forget it ▶ *Greg used to play the piano, but I'm afraid he hasn't kept it up.*

10 keep sth **up, keep up** sth: to look after a building and pay for any work that needs to be done, so that it stays in good condition ▶ *In the end the family didn't have enough money to keep the old house up.*

upkeep N the process and cost of looking after a building ▶ *On a house this size, the upkeep is enormous.*

11 keep sb **up, keep up** sb: to prevent someone from going to bed at the usual time ▶ *The noise from the party next door kept everyone up.*

KEEP UP WITH →

keep up with sb: to write to, phone, or meet a friend regularly, so that you do not forget each other ▶ *I've kept up with several of my old schoolfriends.*

KEY

KEY IN →
key sth in,
key in sth: to
type
information
into a
computer ▶ *If*
you key your
message in first, I'll show you how to
send it.

KEY UP →
be keyed up: to be very nervous or
excited about something ▶ *He soon*
arrived, all keyed up at the thought of
seeing Rosie again.

KICK

KICK ABOUT *see* **KICK AROUND**

KICK AGAINST, *also* **KICK OUT**
AGAINST →
kick (out) against sb/sth: to go
against what someone in authority
wants, because you feel they are
trying to control you too much ▶ *It's*
the story of a young girl growing up
and kicking against society.

KICK AROUND, *also* **KICK ABOUT** →
1 kick around/about sth, **kick** sth
around/about: to discuss an idea with
a group of people in an informal way
▶ *The idea of a business merger has*
been kicked around for some time
now.

2 be kicking around/about (sth): if
something is kicking around a place, it
is somewhere in that place but you do
not know exactly where ▶ *That book*
was kicking around the house for
ages, but now it's disappeared!

3 kick sb **around/about**: to treat
someone badly, especially by
expecting them to do whatever you
tell them to do ▶ *Some of the staff*
definitely feel that they get kicked
around too much.

KICK BACK →
1 kick back: to relax ▶ *Stewart decided*
to kick back and enjoy himself that
afternoon.

2 kick back sth, **kick** sth **back**: to
pay someone part of the money
you earned from a deal because
they helped you to make the
deal ▶ *The travel agencies kicked*
back part of their commission to
companies who signed contracts
with them.

  kickback N money that you pay to
  someone because they have helped
  you get more, usually from a secret
  or illegal deal ▶ *Roth has been*
  charged with collecting more than
  £224,000 in kickbacks.

KICK DOWN →
kick sth **down, kick down** sth: to break
a door or other structure by kicking it
violently ▶ *He threatened to kick down*
the door if she didn't open it straight
away.

KICK IN →
1 kick in sth, **kick** sth **in**: to break open
a door, window etc by kicking it very
hard ▶ *Firemen kicked in a window*
and managed to get the children out
of the house.

2 kick in: to start to have an effect or
start to work ▶ *For some people it can*
take several hours before the effects
of the drug kick in.

3 kick in sth, **kick in**: to join with
others in giving money or help ▶ *He*
doesn't really kick in and do his share
of the housework.

KICK OFF →
1 kick off, kick off sth, **kick** sth **off**: if
an event kicks off or you kick it off, it
starts ▶ *The conference is scheduled*
to kick off at noon. **+ with** ▶ *The band*
kicked off the night's music with an
old Bill Hayley number.

K

2a. kick off: if a game of football kicks off, it starts ▶ *The game kicked off an hour late after heavy rain.*

kick-off N the time when a game of football starts ▶ *United were the better team right from the kick-off.*

b. kick off: if a team or its players kick off, they start to play a game. **+ against** ▶ *England will kick off against France at 2 o'clock this afternoon.*

KICK OUT →

kick sb/sth **out, kick out** sb/sth: to force someone or something to leave a place, organization, or position of power ▶ *The landlord kicked me out of my room because I couldn't pay the rent.* **+ of** ▶ *Amy was kicked out of university for failing her exams.*

KICK OUT AGAINST *See* KICK AGAINST

KICK OVER →

kick over: if an engine kicks over, it starts working ▶ *It won't kick over, so I guess we'll have to tow the car to the garage.*

KICK UP →

1 kick up a fuss also **kick up a stink**: to complain a lot about something ▶ *Local residents are kicking up a fuss about the noise from the airport.*

2 kick up a storm: to cause a lot of trouble or discussion about something ▶ *If the government goes ahead with the new tax, it will kick up a political storm.*

3 kick up sth, **kick** sth **up**: to increase something, usually a price ▶ *When the landlord kicked up his rent, Mallory packed his bags and left.*

KID

KID AROUND →

kid around: to make jokes or behave in a silly way ▶ *Don't pay any attention to him. He's just kidding around.*

KILL

KILL OFF →

1 kill off sth/sb, **kill** sth/sb **off**: to kill things or people in large numbers ▶ *Disease killed off over half the population.*

2 kill off sth, **kill** sth **off**: to destroy or get rid of something completely and finally ▶ *The show was so unpopular that the producers decided to kill it off.*

KIP

KIP DOWN →

kip down: to sleep somewhere, especially somewhere where you do not usually sleep ▶ *The party didn't finish till three, so I kipped down at Jane's house.* **+ on** ▶ *You have the bed, I'll kip down on the sofa.*

KISS

KISS AWAY →

kiss away sth, **kiss** sth **away**: to kiss someone to try to make them feel better ▶ *Harry held her tightly, kissing away her tears.*

KISS OFF →

1 kiss off!: used to tell someone to go away or stop saying rude things ▶ *Kiss off, Joe! If you can't say anything nice, then just shut up!*

2 kiss off sth, **kiss** sth **off**: to decide that something is not worth the time, effort, money etc that is involved ▶ *Perhaps you can try talking to your wife, instead of just kissing off the relationship.*

KISS UP TO →

kiss up to sb: to try to please someone, especially in order to get

K

them to do something for you ▶ *Dan is perfectly capable of getting a promotion without kissing up to the boss.*

KIT

KIT OUT →

kit sb/sth **out, kit out** sb/sth: to provide someone or something with the clothes or equipment they need. **+ with** ▶ *First you will be kitted out with a safety helmet and a lamp.* ▶ *The London studio is lavishly kitted out with six cameras.*

BE KITTED OUT, *also* BE KITTED UP →

be kitted out/up in sth: to be dressed in clothes of a particular type ▶ *The children were kitted out in matching ski suits.*

KNEEL

KNEEL DOWN →
kneel down: to move into a position in which your knees are on the ground

▶ *She knelt down and put her arms around the child.*

KNIT

KNIT TOGETHER →
1 knit together sth/sb, **knit** sth/sb **together:** if two or more people are knit together by something, they are united by it ▶ *Communities are knit together by laws, religion, and custom.*

2 knit together: if people or things knit together well, they fit together or work together well ▶ *The lads in the team have knitted together extremely well.*

3 knit together: if broken bones knit together, they join and grow together

again ▶ *I had to rest my leg for a month, to give the bones a chance to knit together.*

KNOCK

KNOCK ABOUT WITH *see* KNOCK AROUND WITH

KNOCK AROUND, *also* KNOCK ABOUT →
1 knock sb **around/about:** to hit or kick someone several times ▶ *Her husband was a big man who used to knock her around.* **get knocked about** ▶ *I get the feeling some of the kids are getting knocked about at home.*

2 knock around/about sth, **knock around/about:** to spend time somewhere, without doing anything very serious or important ▶ *I didn't want to leave the city now. I'd spent enough time knocking about in the country.*

3 be knocking around/about: if something is knocking around, it is in a particular place, but it has been forgotten about, or not used for a long time ▶ *I used an old tennis racket that I found knocking around in the attic.*

4 knock sth **around/about:** to kick or hit a ball around, especially in a not very serious way ▶ *The boys were knocking a ball around on the grass.*

5 knock around/about sth: to spend time travelling around a place, doing whatever you want to do or doing very little ▶ *Sarah had knocked around the world a bit and seen a lot of places.*

KNOCK AROUND WITH, *also* KNOCK ABOUT WITH →
knock around/about with sb: to spend a lot of your free time with someone ▶ *On Saturdays I knock around with my friends from school.*

KNOCK BACK →
1 knock back sth, **knock** sth **back:** to drink something, especially alcohol,

uickly or in large amounts ► *She poured herself a glass of whisky and knocked it back.*

knock sb back: to shock or surprise someone ► *When my Dad went off with another woman, it knocked the whole family back.*

KNOCK DOWN →

1 knock sb down, knock down sb: if a vehicle knocks someone down, it hits them so that they fall to the ground and may be injured or killed ► *As Tracey was getting out of her car, a motorcycle nearly knocked her down.*

2 knock down sth, knock sth down: to deliberately destroy and remove a building or a part of a building ► *A lot of the older houses were knocked down to make space for new ones.*

3 knock sth down, knock down sth: to reduce the price of something. **+ to** ► *The agents recommended knocking the price down to £150,000.* **+ from** ► *He's knocked down the painting from £200 to £170.*

knockdown ADJ a knockdown price is very cheap ► *In the end the land was sold at a knockdown price.*

4 knock sb down: to persuade someone to reduce the price of something they are selling you. **+ to** ► *She wanted £2,000 for the car, but I knocked her down to £1,800.*

5 knock down sth, knock sth down: to argue that an idea, suggestion etc is not right, or not worth considering ► *His argument was completely illogical, and easily knocked down.*

KNOCK OFF →

1 knock off sth, knock sth off: to reduce a price by a particular amount ► *I'll knock £100 off your loan if you repay it by the end of the month.*

2 knock it off!: used to tell someone to stop doing something that is annoying you ► *Knock it off, Liz!*

There's no reason to drive like an idiot!

3 knock off sth, knock sth off: to reduce a total by a particular amount ► *I'd like to knock a minute off my running time.*

4 knock off sb/sth, knock sb/sth off: to defeat a person or a team in a race, game etc ► *The Bulls had knocked off The Rockets in the first round.*

5 knock off: to stop working because it is time to go home ► *All the factory workers knock off at 3 p.m. on Fridays.* ► *I'm going to knock off early today.*

6 knock off sb, knock sb off: to murder someone ► *They say he knocked off his wife for the insurance money.*

7 knock sth off, knock off sth: to steal something ► *Who would want to knock off these old bicycles?*

KNOCK OUT →

1 knock sb out, knock out sb: to make someone become unconscious

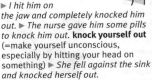

► *I hit him on the jaw and completely knocked him out.* ► *The nurse gave him some pills to knock him out.* **knock yourself out** (=make yourself unconscious, especially by hitting your head on something) ► *She fell against the sink and knocked herself out.*

2 knock sb/sth out, knock out sb/sth: to defeat a person or a team in a competition so that they can no longer take part ► *England had been knocked out of the World Cup.*

knockout N a competition in which only the people or teams that win one part play in the next part ► *a semi-final knockout* ► *a knockout competition*

K

3 knock sb **out**: if something knocks you out, you are surprised by how good it is ▶ *When I first saw the movie, it really knocked me out.*

knockout ADJ extremely good ▶ *another knockout performance by United*

be a knockout V PHRASE if someone or something is a knockout, they are extremely good or attractive ▶ *She was a real knockout in that dress.*

4 knock sth **out, knock out** sth: to stop the flow of electricity to an area ▶ *High winds have knocked out power in many parts of North Chicago.*

5 knock sb **out**: to make someone extremely tired or sleepy ▶ *It had been a hard day, and I was completely knocked out by the time I got home.*

KNOCK OUT OF →

knock sth **out of** sb: to stop someone behaving in a particular way by being very strict or unkind ▶ *Leonard was always trouble. His Dad tried to knock it out of him but it made no difference.*

KNOCK OVER →

1 knock sth/ sb **over, knock over** sth/ sb: to hit or push something or someone with the result that

they fall down ▶ *At that moment Sally jumped up, knocking over her glass of wine.*

2 knock sb **over, knock over** sb: to hit someone with a car while you are driving ▶ *An eighty-two-year-old woman was knocked over outside her home on Sunday.*

KNOCK TOGETHER →

1 knock sth **together, knock together** sth: to make something quickly and without much effort, especially using things that you find or have by chance ▶ *They'd got sheets of plastic and bits of wood and knocked them together into a shelter.*

2 knock sth **together, knock together** sth: to make two rooms or buildings into one room or building, by removing the wall that separates them ▶ *Two or three little rooms were knocked together to make one big spacious kitchen.*

KNOCK UP →

1 knock up sth, **knock** sth **up, knock up** sth: to make something, quickly and without much effort, especially using things that you have or find by chance ▶ *She was the sort of girl who could knock up wonderful dinners in fifteen minutes.*

2 knock sb **up, knock up** sb: to wake someone by knocking on the door of their room or house ▶ *We had to be knocked up at three in the morning to catch the plane home.*

3 knock up sth, **knock** sth **up**: to succeed in winning a particular number of points in a game ▶ *He's knocked up 25 goals in ten games.*

KNOW

KNOW OF →

1 know of sth/ sb: to have heard or read about something or someone ▶ *I know of a woman who went to prison for five years for stealing a few pounds.* ▶ *Did Mr Macarron have any enemies that you know of?*

2 little/ nothing is known of sth/ sb: used to say that there is little or no information about something or someone ▶ *Little is known of Shakespeare's early years.*

KNUCKLE

KNUCKLE DOWN →
knuckle down: to start to work or study more seriously than you have been doing ▶ *The manager called on his players to knuckle down after a series of disappointing results.* **+ to** ▶ *The holiday was over and it was time to knuckle down to work.*

KNUCKLE UNDER →
knuckle under: to agree to do what someone is trying to force you to do ▶ *She's wrong if she thinks we're just going to knuckle under without fighting back.*

KOWTOW

KOWTOW TO →
kowtow to sb/sth: to do whatever someone in authority wants you to do ▶ *The days when people used to automatically kowtow to their employer are gone.*

K

PHRASAL VERB ACTIVATOR

This special section contains 8 different topic areas, in which groups of phrasal verbs that are similar in meaning are shown together. For example, around the topic area **LIKE/DISLIKE**, you will find various phrasal verbs meaning liking someone, and also various phrasal verbs meaning not liking. Once you have found the group of phrasal verbs you are interested in, you can then check in the main part of the dictionary to find out exactly what each phrasal verb means.

to like someone or something
▶ take to
▶ fall for
▶ go for
▶ go in for
▶ see sth in sb

to start to like someone or something
▶ warm to
▶ warm up to
▶ grow on
▶ come around/round to

to like someone or something very much
▶ rave about/rave over
▶ revel in
▶ be sold on

LIKE/DISLIKE

not to like someone or something
▶ not care for
▶ have sth against
▶ react against
▶ take against

to stop liking someone or something
▶ go off
▶ turn against
▶ tire of

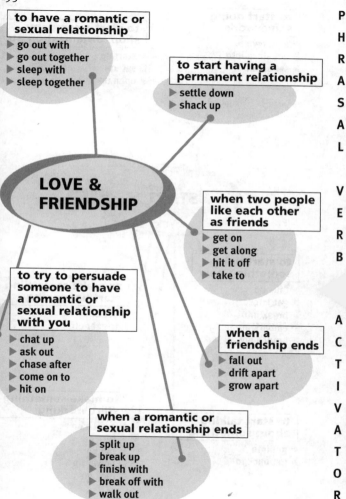

to have a romantic or sexual relationship
- go out with
- go out together
- sleep with
- sleep together

to start having a permanent relationship
- settle down
- shack up

LOVE & FRIENDSHIP

when two people like each other as friends
- get on
- get along
- hit it off
- take to

to try to persuade someone to have a romantic or sexual relationship with you
- chat up
- ask out
- chase after
- come on to
- hit on

when a friendship ends
- fall out
- drift apart
- grow apart

when a romantic or sexual relationship ends
- split up
- break up
- finish with
- break off with
- walk out

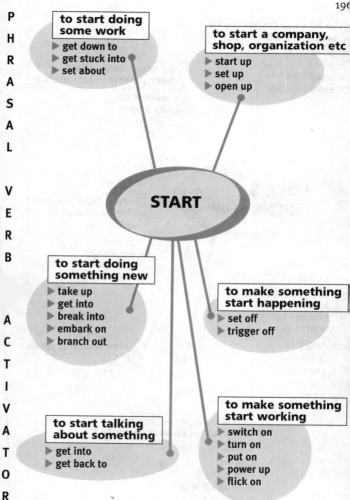

PHRASAL VERB ACTIVATOR

START

to start doing some work
- get down to
- get stuck into
- set about

to start a company, shop, organization etc
- start up
- set up
- open up

to start doing something new
- take up
- get into
- break into
- embark on
- branch out

to make something start happening
- set off
- trigger off

to start talking about something
- get into
- get back to

to make something start working
- switch on
- turn on
- put on
- power up
- flick on

to stop doing something
- give up
- pack up
- chuck in
- pack in
- jack in

to make a machine, light etc stop working
- switch off
- turn off
- turn out
- put off
- flick off
- shut down

STOP

to stop annoying someone
- pack it in!
- knock it off!
- back off!
- leave off!
- cut it out!

a machine stops working
- break down
- conk out
- cut out
- shut down
- go out

to stop talking
- shut up
- clam up
- dry up
- break off

PHRASAL VERB ACTIVATOR

198

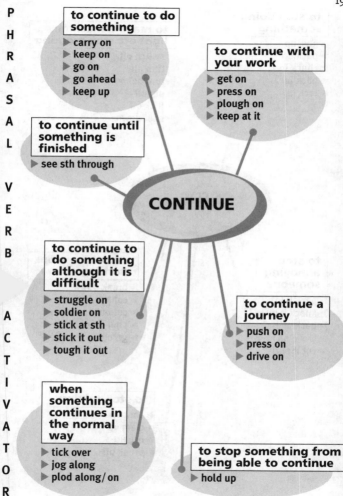

P H R A S A L   V E R B   A C T I V A T O R

to leave the place where you are
- go away
- go off
- rush off
- dash off
- take off
- run away
- run off
- be called away

to leave at the start of a journey
- set off
- head off
- drive off
- take off

to leave because you are angry
- walk out

to leave quietly
- slope off

LEAVE

to leave for a short time
- pop out
- step out

to leave your home
- move out

to make someone leave
- kick sb out
- throw sb out
- chase sb away
- frighten sb away

to leave your job or school
- pack it in
- jack it in
- drop out
- hand in your resignation/ notice

ways of telling someone to leave because they are annoying you
- go away
- get out
- clear off

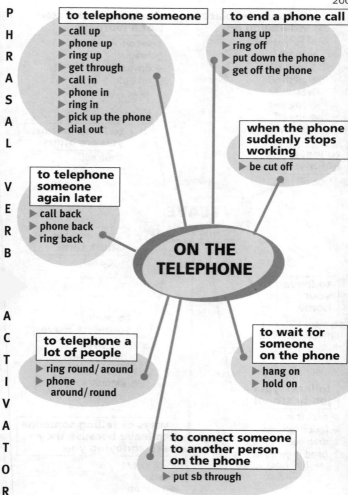

PHRASAL VERB ACTIVATOR

to telephone someone
► call up
► phone up
► ring up
► get through
► call in
► phone in
► ring in
► pick up the phone
► dial out

to end a phone call
► hang up
► ring off
► put down the phone
► get off the phone

when the phone suddenly stops working
► be cut off

to telephone someone again later
► call back
► phone back
► ring back

ON THE TELEPHONE

to telephone a lot of people
► ring round/around
► phone around/round

to wait for someone on the phone
► hang on
► hold on

to connect someone to another person on the phone
► put sb through

to make something start working
▶ switch on
▶ turn on
▶ put on
▶ start up
▶ plug in
▶ set off
▶ power up

when something starts working
▶ come on
▶ go on
▶ warm up

to make something louder
▶ turn up
▶ crank up

TV/RADIO/ LIGHTS/MACHINES

to make something stop working
▶ switch off
▶ turn off
▶ shut off
▶ put out
▶ turn out the light

to make something quieter
▶ turn down

when something stops working
▶ break down
▶ go off
▶ give out
▶ conk out
▶ jam up
▶ pack up
▶ play up
▶ cut out

LI

LABOUR

LABOUR UNDER →

1 labour under a misapprehension also **labour under an illusion etc**: to believe something that is not true, especially with the result that you make bad decisions ▶ *The whole country was labouring under the dangerous illusion that they were the strongest nation on earth.*

2 labour under sth: to be badly affected by something which makes it difficult for you to progress or be successful ▶ *Many poorer families labour under a massive burden of deprivation and debt.*

LACE

LACE UP →

lace up sth, **lace** sth **up**: to fasten shoes, boots, or other clothes by tying the laces ▶ *She sat down and laced up her shoes.*

LACE WITH →

1 lace sth **with** sth: to secretly put alcohol or a drug into someone's food or drink ▶ *Staff found food in the kitchens that had been laced with poison.*

2 be laced with sth: if something is laced with a particular quality, it contains some of it all the way through ▶ *Leigh's play is heavily laced with irony.*

LADLE

LADLE OUT →

1 ladle out sth, **ladle** sth **out**: to serve soup or other food into dishes using a big spoon ▶ *Alice began ladling out the stew.*

2 ladle out sth, **ladle** sth **out**: to give

people a lot of something, especially information, advice, or praise ▶ *Schools are constantly ladling out advice on drugs and sex to young people.*

LAG

LAG BEHIND →

1 lag behind, lag behind sb/sth: to make less progress or be less successful than someone or something else ▶ *In the past, girls lagged behind boys in maths and science.*

2 lag behind, lag behind sb/sth: to move more slowly than the other people or things in a group, so that you are a long distance behind them ▶ *She noticed that Beth was lagging behind, and stopped to wait for her.*

LAND

LAND IN →

land (sb) in trouble/jail etc: to get into a bad situation, or put someone in a bad situation ▶ *I hope I haven't landed you in trouble with the boss.* ▶ *Her husband had a violent temper, which often landed him in court.*

land sb in it (=cause a lot of trouble for someone, especially by telling a person in authority about something wrong they have done) ▶ *You've really landed me in it this time! I wish you'd kept quiet!*

LAND UP →

land up: to finally arrive in a place or situation after a long time, especially when this was not intended ▶ *She got on the wrong train and landed up somewhere just outside Newcastle.* ▶ *The letter eventually landed up on his desk a few days later.*

LAND WITH →

land sb with sth: to make someone do or deal with something, especially something they do not want to do ▶ *Penny was always being landed with the job of looking after the kids at weekends.* **land yourself with** sth (=get into situation in which you have to deal with something, or have to pay a lot of money) ▶ *I'd do what they say if I were you. You don't want to land yourself with a huge fine.*

LAP

LAP UP →

1 lap up sth, **lap** sth **up**: to enjoy something such as praise or attention and accept it eagerly ▶ *Ian was clearly lapping up all the attention from his new group of fans.*

2 lap up sth, **lap** sth **up**: if an animal laps up milk, water etc, it drinks the milk, water etc ▶ *The cat was lapping up the milk.*

LAPSE

LAPSE INTO →

1 lapse into silence/unconsciousness etc: to become silent or unconscious etc ▶ *Laura lapsed into a frosty silence, staring blindly out through the window.*

2 lapse into sth: to change into a much worse state or condition ▶ *The economy continued to lapse into decline.*

3 lapse into sth: to start behaving or speaking in a way that you used to speak or behave in the past but are now trying not to ▶ *Now and again she lapsed into her native Glasgow accent.* ▶ *Joe managed to give up the drinking, but soon lapsed back into his old ways.*

LARK

LARK ABOUT, *also* **LARK AROUND** → **lark about/around**: to have fun by behaving in a silly way ▶ *The kids took little interest in their lessons, and spent most of the time larking about.*

LASH

LASH DOWN →

lash down: if the rain lashes down, a lot of rain falls and there is often a lot of wind ▶ *The rain was lashing down and the wind was howling through the trees.*

LASH OUT →

1 lash out: to suddenly speak angrily to someone or suddenly criticize someone very strongly. **+ at/against** ▶ *She lashed out in fury at her colleagues, accusing them of sexism.*

2 lash out: to suddenly try to hit or attack someone. **+ with** ▶ *Brendan lashed out with his fist and caught the thief on the jaw.* **+ at** ▶ *He lashed out at the policeman, but missed.*

LAST

LAST OUT →

1 last out sth, **last out**: to continue living or continue working properly ▶ *His father wasn't expected to last out the night.* ▶ *She wasn't sure if her voice would last out until the end of the concert.*

2 last out sth, **last out**: to continue what you are doing until the job, journey, or experience is finished, even though it is difficult ▶ *At times I thought I would never last out the trial.* ▶ *"Do you want me to stop the car?" "No I think I can last out till we get home."*

3 last out, last out sth: if supplies of something last out, there is enough for a particular period of time ▶ *Is there enough fuel to last out until the next delivery?*

L

LATCH

LATCH ON, *also* **LATCH ONTO** →
latch on, latch onto sth: to understand what someone means or realize that something is happening ▶ *By the time I'd latched onto what was happening, the thieves were already halfway down the street.*

LATCH ON TO, *also* **LATCH ONTO** →
1 latch on to/onto sth: to decide that something is very good or useful and start using it ▶ *People are starting to latch onto the idea of shopping on the Internet.*

2 latch on to/onto sth, **latch on to/onto** sb: to pay a lot of attention to something or someone because you think they are important or interesting ▶ *The press are always quick to latch onto any story involving the Royal family.*

3 latch on to/onto sb, **latch yourself on to/onto** sb: to spend time with someone and talk with them, especially when they do not want you with them ▶ *A young man had latched onto her earlier on in the evening.*

LAUGH

LAUGH AT →
1 laugh at sth: to think that an idea, suggestion etc is silly and should not be considered seriously ▶ *People used to laugh at the idea of interplanetary travel.*

2 laugh at sb: to make jokes about someone and make unkind remarks about them ▶ *The other kids used to laugh at him and call him names.*

3 laugh at sth: to seem not to care about something that other people think is serious ▶ *Young offenders often just laugh at warnings from the police.*

LAUGH OFF →
laugh sth **off, laugh off** sth: to pretend that you are not worried about a problem or criticism by laughing and making jokes about it ▶ *He laughed off suggestions that the club was planning to sack him.*

LAUNCH

LAUNCH INTO →
launch into sth: to suddenly start talking about something, especially with a lot of enthusiasm or force ▶ *He then launched into a blistering attack on his critics.*

LAUNCH OUT →
launch out: to start doing something new, especially something that involves risk ▶ *He left his father's firm and launched out in business on his own.*

LAVISH

LAVISH ON, *also* **LAVISH UPON** →
lavish sth **on/upon** sb, **lavish** sth **on/upon** sth: to give someone or something a lot of praise, attention, presents etc ▶ *When the series was first shown, the media lavished praise on its creator.*

LAY

LAY ABOUT →
lay about sb: to attack someone by hitting them violently ▶ *His attackers began laying about him with sticks.*

LAY ASIDE →
1 lay aside sth, **lay** sth **aside**: to stop doing something or stop thinking about something, especially so that you are able to make progress ▶ *The two communities will have to lay aside their differences and learn to live in peace with each other.*

2 lay aside sth, **lay** sth **aside**: to keep something, especially money, and not use it now, so that you can use it in the future ▶ *They laid aside a small amount of money each month.*

L

LAY BEFORE →

lay sth **before** sb/sth: to give something to a parliament, court, committee etc to officially consider ▶ *Legislation was laid before Parliament last spring, banning the sale of handguns.*

LAY DOWN →

1 lay down sth, **lay** sth **down**: to officially establish a rule or way of doing something, or say officially what someone should do ▶ *The Geneva Convention lays down conditions for the treatment of prisoners of war.*
+ that ▶ *The Sex Discrimination Act lays down that men and women should receive equal pay for equal work.*

2 lay down your weapons also **lay down your arms**: to stop fighting, or agree to give up your weapons ▶ *Many of the soldiers had already begun to lay down their arms before the final peace treaty was signed.*

3 lay down the law: to tell someone very firmly what they should or should not do ▶ *Her husband tried to lay down the law about what friends she went out with.*

4 lay down sth, **lay** sth **down**: to establish something that will develop in the future ▶ *The foundations of future health are laid down in childhood.*

5 lay down sth, **lay** sth **down**: to store wine for several years so that it will improve ▶ *a wide range of fine wines which are suitable for laying down*

6 lay down a challenge: to ask someone if they will try to compete with you, defeat you, or do something difficult ▶ *Following the challenge laid down by President Kennedy, the first Americans finally landed on the moon in 1969.*

lay down your life: to give up your life in order to help other people ▶ *a*

memorial to the soldiers who laid down their lives in the First World War

LAY IN →

lay in sth, **lay** sth **in**: to obtain and store a supply of something so that you can use it in the future ▶ *The villagers have begun laying in supplies of food and firewood for the winter.*

LAY INTO →

1 lay into sb/sth: to criticize someone or something very strongly, especially in a way that seems unfair ▶ *When I got home my wife started laying into me because I'd forgotten it was our wedding anniversary.*

2 lay into sb: to attack someone and hit or kick them ▶ *The rock star laid into the photographer with his fists and grabbed his camera.*

LAY OFF →

1 lay off sb, **lay** sb **off**: to stop employing a worker because there is not enough work for him or her to do ▶ *Thousands of workers were laid off during the recession of the late 1980s.*
lay-offs PL N when a company stops employing workers because there is not enough work for them to do ▶ *There are expected to be lay-offs at the factory because of the fall in demand.*

2 lay off sth: to stop doing or having something, especially in order to rest or because it may have a bad effect on your health ▶ *His doctors have told him to lay off the drugs and the all-night partying.*

3 lay off sb: to stop annoying, upsetting, or criticizing someone ▶ *Listen, just lay off her, will you? She doesn't need you telling her what to do.*

LAY ON →

1 lay on sth: to provide something for someone, for example food or

L

entertainment ▶ *The organizers had laid on a huge meal for everyone who took part in the race.* ▶ *Special buses were laid on to take the fans to the airport.*

2 lay it on (thick): a. to describe or complain about something in a way that makes it seem much more serious than it really is ▶ *Whenever Claire's ill she always really lays it on thick and makes out she's about to die.*

b. to praise someone too much in a way that seems insincere ▶ *He kept saying what a wonderful boss she was, and really laying it on.*

3 lay sth **on** sb: to tell someone something that they did not know before and that is unpleasant or annoying ▶ *I hate to lay this on you, but it looks like you owe £400 in taxes this year.*

4 lay sth **on** sb: to give someone something such as a responsibility, job, or problem that is difficult to deal with ▶ *I'm sorry to lay this on you, but we need someone to give a talk to the board next week.*

LAY ON, *also* **LAY UPON** →
lay stress on/upon sth *also* **lay emphasis on/upon** sth: to treat something as being particularly important or necessary ▶ *Great emphasis is laid on trying to help students develop practical skills.*

LAY OUT →
1 lay sth **out, lay** sth **out:** to put or arrange something on a surface ▶ *Ashi laid out her clothes on the bed.* ▶ *The plates were already laid out for the evening meal.*

2 lay out sth, **lay** sth **out:** to plan the way something such as a garden, newpaper etc is designed ▶ *The palace gardens are laid out in the same style as the ones at Versailles.*

layout N the way something is arranged or designed, for example a town, garden, or a page in a book, magazine etc ▶ *a change from the traditional newspaper layout* ▶ *The layout of the office makes it possible for the boss to watch us all while we are working.*

3 lay out sth, **lay** sth **out:** to explain your plans or reasons for doing something clearly and in detail ▶ *The Director General laid out his plans for the future of the BBC.*

4 lay out sth, **lay** sth **out:** to spend money on something, especially a large amount of money ▶ *I've already had to lay out £500 on course fees.*

outlay N the amount of money that you have to spend in order to buy something or start doing something ▶ *She wasn't hoping to make a huge profit, she just wanted to get back her initial outlay.*

5 lay out: to lie in the sun ▶ *We laid out by the pool all afternoon.*

6 lay sb **out:** to hit someone so hard that they become unconscious ▶ *She swung her umbrella at him, and practically laid him out.*

7 lay out sth/sb, **lay** sth/sb **out:** to prepare a dead body so that it can be buried ▶ *Evita Peron's body was laid out in a glass-topped coffin.*

LAY UP →
1 be laid up: to have to stay in bed because you are ill or injured ▶ *Both his legs were broken and* *he was laid up for nine months.* **+ with** ▶ *Chas isn't coming in to work today – he's laid up in bed with flu.*

2 be laid up: to be stored somewhere while not in use ▶ *All the fishing boats were laid up for the winter.*

3 lay up: to hide or stay somewhere without doing anything for a period of time ▶ *The men laid up all the following day, expecting to be attacked at any moment.*

4 lay up problems (for yourself) *also* **lay up trouble for yourself**: to do something that will cause problems for yourself in the future ▶ *I really think that anyone who goes out with a married man is just laying up trouble for themselves.*

5 lay up sth, lay sth up: to collect and store a supply of something so that you can use it in the future ▶ *The villagers were already laying up firewood for the winter.*

LAY UPON *see* LAY ON

LAZE

LAZE AROUND, *also* LAZE ABOUT →
laze around/about: to spend time relaxing and not doing very much ▶ *We spent the day lazing around on the beach.* ▶ *My eldest son just lazes about at home all day.*

LEAD

LEAD ASTRAY →
1 lead sb astray: to encourage someone to do bad things that they would not normally do ▶ *The boy's mother is convinced that her son was led astray by his friends.*

2 lead sb astray: to make someone believe something that is not true, with the result that they make the wrong decision ▶ *Don't be led astray by promises of free insurance or free drinks in holiday brochures.* ▶ *Officials may have led people astray by telling them that it was safe to eat beef.*

LEAD INTO →
lead into sth: to follow naturally from something else ▶ *A slow clarinet melody leads into the finale of this great symphony.*

LEAD OFF →
1 lead off, lead off sth: to begin a discussion or event by saying or doing something ▶ *A jazz band led off with a series of old numbers.* ▶ *She always used to lead her classes off with a short spelling test.*

2 lead off: if one room, road, path etc leads off another, you can get to the first one directly from the second ▶ *a narrow road leading off the High Street*

LEAD ON →
1 lead sb on: to deceive someone by telling them things that are not true, especially by making them believe that you are sexually attracted to them ▶ *The defendant claimed that the girl led him on and also told him she was 18.*

2 lead sb on: to encourage someone to do something that they should not do ▶ *Many young kids start smoking at school, led on by their friends.*

LEAD ON TO, *also* LEAD ONTO →
lead on to/onto sth: to make something develop or make it likely that someone will do something at a later time ▶ *an advanced course of study that leads on to university* ▶ *I took a job as a secretary, hoping that this would lead onto better things.*

LEAD TO →
lead to sth: to make something happen, especially at a later time ▶ *the events which led to the downfall of the government* ▶ *The bank has offered a reward for information leading to the arrest of the robbers.*

L

LEAD UP TO →

1 lead up to sth: to come before an important event, and often help to make it happen ▶ *a discussion of the events leading up to the Second World War*

lead-up N the period of time before an important event. **the lead-up to** ▶ *A record number of stores are opening on Sundays in the lead-up to Christmas.*

2 lead up to sth: to gradually introduce a particular subject into a conversation or speech ▶ *I could see that he was leading up to a request for more money.*

LEAF

LEAF THROUGH →
leaf through sth: to turn the pages of a book or magazine quickly, looking at it without reading it carefully ▶ *He began to leaf through a magazine while he waited.*

LEAK

LEAK OUT →
leak out: if secret information leaks out, people find out about it and it becomes publicly known ▶ *News of the couple's marriage problems began to leak out to the press.*

LEAN

LEAN ON →

1 lean on sb: to depend on someone for support and encouragement ▶ *Friendship is important – you need someone you can trust and lean on.*

2 lean on sb: to try to persuade someone to do something by using influence or threats. **lean on sb to do** sth ▶ *A group of senators has been leaning on their leaders to cut welfare.*

LEAN TOWARDS, also **LEAN TOWARD** →

lean towards/toward sth: to tend to support a particular opinion or decision. **lean towards/toward doing** sth ▶ *The prime minister was leaning towards running for re-election.* ▶ *Their eldest daughter seems to be leaning towards a career in computing.*

LEAP

LEAP AT →
leap at sth: to eagerly accept the opportunity to do something ▶ *If I got the opportunity to go to the Wimbledon finals, I'd leap at it.* **leap at the chance/opportunity** ▶ *When her boss asked if she'd like to go to the conference, she leaped at the chance.*

LEAP IN →
leap in: to suddenly start doing or saying something, especially without thinking carefully ▶ *Alan immediately leapt in and started shouting at everyone.*

LEAP ON, also **LEAP UPON** →

1 leap on/upon sb: to suddenly jump towards someone and attack them violently ▶ *The bigger boys leapt on him as he came out of school.* ▶ *computer games with monsters waiting to leap on you at every corner*

2 leap on/upon sth: to immediately show a lot of interest in something or eagerly accept a suggestion ▶ *The newspapers always leap on any story to do with soap opera stars.*

LEAP OUT AT →
1 leap out at sb: to suddenly move forward and attack or frighten someone ▶ *She walked quickly down the dark street, terrified that someone would leap out at her.*

2 leap out at sb: if something leaps out at you, you notice it quickly especially because it is important, impressive, or unusual ► *I looked through some magazines hoping that some interesting ideas would leap out at me.*

LEAP UPON *see* **LEAP ON**

LEAVE

LEAVE ASIDE →

leave aside sth, **leave** sth **aside**: to not consider or talk about a particular subject immediately, so that you can consider something else first ► *Let's leave aside the question of cost – which computer would be the best one?* **leaving aside** sth / **leaving** sth **aside** (=not including something) ► *Leaving aside mortgage interest rates, prices rose only two percent last year.*

LEAVE BEHIND →

1 leave sth / sb **behind**: to not take something or someone with you when you leave somewhere ► *I think I left my credit card behind at the restaurant.* ► *Whenever we go out, her little sister always refuses to be left behind.*

2 leave behind sth, **leave** sth **behind** you: to have caused a particular situation to exist that continues after you have left ► *The hurricane swept through the islands, leaving behind a trail of destruction.* ► *The previous government left a huge budget deficit behind them.*

3 leave sth **behind**, **leave** sth **behind** you: to be no longer affected by a bad situation, feeling, or system ► *I felt very bitter after the divorce, but I've left all that behind me now.*

4 leave sb / sth **behind**, **leave behind** sb / sth: if you leave behind your family or possessions when you die, they remain after you have died ► *The murdered hostage leaves behind a wife and two sons.*

5 leave sb **behind**, **leave behind** sb: to make progress much more quickly than someone else ► *a new contestant in the games who has left the other competitors way behind.* **be/get left behind** ► *I don't want to miss any of the classes or I'll get left behind.*

6 leave sth **behind**, **leave behind** sth: to remain or be the result of a process after the process has finished ► *The water evaporates, leaving the crystals behind.*

LEAVE OFF →

1 leave off sth, **leave off**: to stop doing something. **leave off doing** sth ► *He left off shouting at the boy and suddenly became quiet.* **start where** sb / sth **leaves off** also **begin where** sb / sth **leaves off** (=start from the point where someone or something stopped before) ► *Her second novel begins where her first one left off.* ► *The computer saves the game so you can start again where you left off.*

2 leave off!: used to tell someone to stop doing something, especially when they are annoying you ► *Leave off, Alex – you're hurting me!*

LEAVE OUT →

1 leave out sb / sth, **leave** sth / sb **out**: to not include someone or something ► *You've left out a zero from this phone number.* ► *Right at the end of the exam, I realized I'd left out something important.* **+ of** ► *Fans were shocked that he had been left out of the team.*

2 feel left out: to feel as if you are not accepted or welcome in a group of

people ▶ *Everyone seemed to know each other at the club and I felt really left out.*

3 leave it out!: used to tell someone that you do not believe what they have just said ▶ *Oh, leave it out, Mick – I've heard it all before!*

BE LEFT OVER →

1 be left over: if something such as money or food is left over, you still have some after you have used or eaten as much as you need ▶ *After we've paid the bills there's never any money left over.* **+ from** ▶ *Dan made a sandwich with some cold chicken left over from lunch.*

> **leftovers** PL N food that has not been eaten at the end of a meal ▶ *He was fed on scraps and leftovers.*
> **leftover** ADJ leftover food is food that has not been eaten at the end of a meal ▶ *Here are some great recipes for using leftover turkey.*

2 be left over: if something is left over, it remains after the situation that caused it no longer exists. **+ from** ▶ *a huge puddle left over from that morning's storm* ▶ *He keeps his hair very short – a habit left over from his days in the army.*

> **leftover** N something that remains from an earlier time ▶ *The restaurant's name – The Old Mill – is a leftover from the days when flour was produced here.*

LEAVE TO →

1 leave sb to sth: to go away and let someone continue what they are doing ▶ *I'll leave you to your meal and call again at a more convenient time.*
leave sb to it ▶ *"I'll be finished in an hour." "Right. I'll leave you to it – see you later."*

2 leave sth **to** sb: to give something to someone after you die ▶ *She left the house to her only son.*

LEAVE TO, *also* LEAVE UP TO →

leave sth **to** sb, **leave** sth **up to** sb: to let someone decide something or be responsible for something ▶ *"What colour shall we paint this room?" "I'll leave that up to you."* **leave it (up) to sb (to do sth)** ▶ *Don't worry about the computer; leave it to me, I'll get it fixed.* ▶ *Most patients will leave it up to the doctor to decide what's best.*

LEND

LEND OUT →

lend out sth, **lend** sth **out**: to let someone borrow or use something for a period of time ▶ *Many libraries have CDs that they can lend out.*

LEND TO →

lend itself to sth: to be suitable to be used for a particular purpose or treated in a particular way ▶ *It's an old house, and it doesn't lend itself to a very modern style of decoration.*

LET

LET DOWN →

1 let sb **down, let down** sb: to not do something that someone is depending on you to do ▶ *Joey promised he'd phone today, but he's let me down again.* ▶ *The education system is letting down our children.* **be let down (by sb)** ▶ *People are often let down by the politicians they elected to power.*
let the side down (=not do what the other people in your family, team, group etc expect you do do) ▶ *Many women feel they are letting the side down by giving up work to look after their children.*

> **letdown** N something that is disappointing because it is not as exciting, interesting, or successful as you expected ▶ *The wedding ceremony itself was a bit of a letdown.*

2 let down sth/ sb, **let** sth/ sb **down**:

o make something or someone less successful than they should be, by not achieving a high enough standard ▶ *It's quite a good film, but it's let down by the ending.* **let yourself down** ▶ *I always feel I let myself down by wasting so much time at school.*

let sth down, let down sth: to deliberately allow all the air to come out of something such as a tyre ▶ *When he came back to his bike, some idiot had let his tyres down.*

LET IN →

let sb in, let in sb: to allow someone to enter a room or building, especially by opening the door ▶ *"Let me in!" she screamed, banging at the door.* ▶ *They won't let you into the club if you're wearing jeans.* **let yourself in** ▶ *I've got a key, so I can let myself in.*

let in sth, let sth in: to allow air, light, water etc to enter a place ▶ *Then the door opened, letting in a cold damp gust of wind.* ▶ *I pulled back the curtains to let in as much light as possible.*

LET IN FOR →

let yourself in for sth: to become involved in something that may be difficult or cause problems ▶ *She's decided to marry him? She doesn't know what she's letting herself in for!*

LET IN ON →

let sb in on sth: to tell someone a secret, or about something that only a few people know ▶ *Could someone please let me in on the joke – what's so funny?*

LET INTO →

let sb into sth: to allow someone to enter a place ▶ *Officials refused to let him into the country.* ▶ *Youths attacked a woman after she let them into her house yesterday.* **let yourself into sth** (=open the door to a room or building with a key and go in) ▶ *She*

let herself into the apartment and had a good look around.

2 let sb into a secret: to tell someone something that is secret or private ▶ *I'll let you into a secret – Julie's expecting a baby!*

LET OFF →

1 let sb off, let off sb: to not punish someone when they have done something wrong ▶ *"I'm sorry, I'm late!" "I'll let you off this time."* **+ with** ▶ *Kids who are caught stealing are often just let off with a warning.* **let sb off lightly** (=give someone a punishment that is less serious than they deserve) ▶ *Next time I won't be letting you off so lightly.*

2 let sb off sth, let sb off, let off sb: to allow someone not to do something that they are supposed to do or usually do ▶ *As you've all worked so hard, I'll let you off your homework tonight.* ▶ *The company was let off a debt of over a million dollars.*

3 let off sth, let sth off: to make something such as a bomb explode, or to fire a gun ▶ *Terrorists let off a massive bomb in the city centre.* ▶ *What time do they start letting off the fireworks?*

4 let sb off: to stop a car, bus etc in order to allow someone to get out ▶ *Ask the bus driver to let you off by the post office.*

5 let off sth, let sth off: to produce heat, gas, sound etc ▶ *It's only a small radiator, so it doesn't let off much heat.*

LET ON →

let on: to tell someone about something such as a secret or your true feelings ▶ *Perhaps Anna's death upset him more than he let on.* **+ about** ▶ *Lizzy made Kate promise not to let on about the money.*

L

LET OUT →

1a. let sb **out, let out** sb: to allow someone to leave somewhere ▶ *Stop the car and let me out!*

+ of ▶ *He was recently let out of prison after serving 10 years for murder.*

b. let sb **out, let out** sb: to open or unlock a door so that someone can leave ▶ *Hayley went downstairs to let the cat out.* **let yourself out** ▶ *Don't get up – I'll let myself out.*

2 let out sth: to make a particular sound ▶ *Eugene let out a long loud laugh when he heard what had happened.* ▶ *As soon as he had gone, they all let out a deep sigh of relief.*

3 let out sth, **let** sth **out**: to express or get rid of strong feelings that you have not been showing ▶ *Sometimes it's good to cry and just let it all out.*

4 let sth **out, let out** sth: to allow air, water etc to escape or flow out of something ▶ *The kitchen door was open, letting out all the warmth from the room.* **let out a breath** (=breathe air out of your lungs) ▶ *"Take a deep breath," the doctor said, "and then let it out slowly."*

5 let sth **out, let out** sth: to tell people something that was intended to be a secret ▶ *George was the only person who could have let this information out.* ▶ *Who let out that it's my birthday today?*

6 let out sth, **let** sth **out**: to allow someone to rent a house, apartment etc that you own ▶ *We could let out a room to make a bit of extra cash.*
+ to ▶ *They let their house out to students during term time.*

7 let sb **out of a contract/agreement**: to allow someone not to have to do what they have legally or officially agreed to do ▶ *She was let out of her radio contract in order to pursue film and TV roles.*

LET THROUGH →

let sb/sth **through, let through** sb/sth
let sb/sth **through** sth: to allow someone or something to pass through and get somewhere ▶ *The security guard refused to let me through the gate.* ▶ *There were thick velvet curtains that didn't let any light through.*

LET UP →

1 let up: if bad weather or an unpleasant situation lets up, it stops or becomes less serious than before ▶ *I'll drive you into town as soon as the snow lets up.* ▶ *The economic crisis showed no sign of letting up.*
let-up N a pause in bad weather or an improvement in an unpleasant situation. **+ in** ▶ *Many houses were flooded and still there was no let-up in the rain.*

2 let up: to stop doing something or to do it less than before ▶ *Little kids ask questions all the time. They won't let up.* **+ in/on** ▶ *A police spokesman said that they would not let up in their campaign against drugs.*
let-up N when you stop doing something that you have been doing or you do it less than before. **+ in** ▶ *The government wants no let-up in the war against the rebels.*

LEVEL

LEVEL AT, *also* LEVEL AGAINST →

level sth **at/against** sb: to publicly criticize someone or say that they have done something wrong ▶ *A number of criticisms were levelled at the book.* ▶ *Accusations of racism and corruption have been levelled against the police.*

L

LEVEL OFF, *also* **LEVEL OUT →**

1 level off/out: to stop increasing or decreasing and stay at the same level ► *Car sales levelled out in September after several months of growth.* **+ at** ► *The world population could level off at around 8.5 billion by the middle of the next century.*

2 level sth **off/out, level off/out** sth: to make the surface of something flat and smooth ► *You should level off the soil with a rake before sowing the seeds.*

LEVEL WITH →

level with sb: to tell someone the truth about a situation, when you have not been completely honest about it before ► *I decided to level with Charlie, but I made him swear not to tell anyone else.*

LIE

LIE AROUND, *also* **LIE ABOUT →**

1 be lying around/about (sth): if something is lying around, someone has left it carelessly in a place where it should not be ► *Have you seen my watch lying around anywhere?* ► *It's not a good idea to leave so much money lying about the house.*

2 lie around/about: to spend your time being lazy and doing very little, especially lying down ► *My fifteen-year-old son just lies around all day, watching videos.*

LIE AHEAD →

lie ahead: to be likely to happen or likely to be the situation in the future ► *A long hard struggle lies ahead before we can arrive at a settlement.* **+ of** ► *I felt very anxious about what lay ahead of me.* **+ for** ► *A great future lies ahead for this talented young woman.*

LIE BACK →

lie back: to move your body backwards from a sitting position until you are lying down or almost lying down ► *I lay back, closed my eyes, and listened to the music.*

LIE BEFORE →

lie before sb: if something lies before you, you will have to deal with it or experience it in the future ► *A major challenge lies before us.* ► *In the past most women accepted without question the life that lay before them.*

LIE BEHIND →

lie behind sth: to be the reason or explanation for something, especially when this is not clear or not generally known ► *Anna never discussed what lay behind the break-up of her marriage.* ► *These statistics are interesting but we need to find out what lies behind them.*

LIE DOWN →

lie down: to move into a position in which your body is flat, usually in order to sleep or rest ► *He went straight upstairs and lay down on his bed.* **be lying down** (=be in a position in which your body is flat on a surface) ► *Jane was lying down on the floor, doing some exercises.*

   lie-down N a short rest on a bed ► *You don't look very well. Why don't you go and have a lie-down?*

LIE IN →

1 lie in: to stay in bed in the morning later than usual ► *Don't wake me up tomorrow morning. I'm going to lie in.*

   lie-in N if you have a lie-in, you stay in bed in the morning for longer than usual ► *On Sunday mornings we usually have a lie-in.*

2 lie in sth: if a particular quality lies in something, the quality exists in it or as a result of it ► *The charm of the painting lies in its simplicity.*

LIE UP →

lie up: to hide somewhere in order to

hide from people who are looking for you ▶ *Our men lay up in the woods during the day, expecting to be attacked at any moment.*

LIE WITH →

lie with sb: to be someone's fault, decision, responsibility etc ▶ *The fault lies with the school for not informing the parents that there was a problem.* ▶ *Responsibility for the environment lies with us all.*

LIFT

LIFT OFF →

lift off: if a space vehicle or plane lifts off, it leaves the ground in order to start a journey ▶ *The space shuttle will lift off on Sunday at 6.30 am.* ▶ *The plane lifted off and began to climb steeply.*

  lift-off N when a space vehicle leaves the ground in order to travel into space ▶ *They decided they would attempt a lift-off, in spite of the bad weather.*

LIGHT

LIGHT ON, *also* **LIGHT UPON** →

light on/upon sth: to suddenly notice or find something, by chance ▶ *Then my eye lit on that morning's newspaper.*

LIGHT UP →

1 light up sth, **light** sth **up**: to make something bright with light or to shine light on something ▶ *There was a storm that lit up the night sky all over Colorado.* ▶ *In the centre of the town the main streets were all lit up for Christmas.*

2 light up, light up sth, **light** sth **up**: if your face or eyes light up, or a smile lights up your face, you suddenly look very pleased, happy, or excited ▶ *Steve's eyes lit up as he described his new project.* **+ with** ▶ *Bella's face lit up with pleasure at the thought of a holiday.*

3 light up, light up sth: to light a cigarette, pipe etc and begin to smoke it ▶ *She took a cigarette from the pack and lit up.*

4 light up: if something lights up, it begins to shine brightly, because lights inside it start working ▶ *If anybody tries to enter the building at night, the whole place lights up.* ▶ *The computer screen lit up and Jonathon typed in a code.*

5 light up sth: to make a place seem happier or more interesting and attractive ▶ *A smile from Jimmy always seemed to light up the world.* **light up** sb's **life** (=make someone's life happier and more interesting) ▶ *Just the thought of her lit up his life.*

LIGHT UPON *see* **LIGHT ON**

LIGHTEN

LIGHTEN UP →

1 lighten up sth, **lighten** sth **up**, **lighten up**: to make something look lighter or to become lighter ▶ *Outside the sky was just beginning to lighten up.*

2 lighten sth **up, lighten up** sth: to make something less serious and more enjoyable ▶ *The film script was too depressing so we've tried to lighten it up a little.*

3 lighten up: to behave in a less serious way and be more relaxed ▶ *Dad's so tense all the time. I wish he'd lighten up a little.*

LIKEN

LIKEN TO →

liken sth/sb **to** sth/sb: to describe

something or someone as similar to another thing or person ► *The newspapers likened the new hospital to a five-star hotel.*

LIMBER

LIMBER UP →

limber up: to do gentle exercises in order to stretch your muscles and prepare your body for physical activity. **+ for** ► *The athletes were already limbering up for the race.*

LINE

LINE UP →

1 line up, line sb up, line up sb: to stand in a line or to make people stand in a line ► *The children were asked to line up according to their height.* ► *The rebels had lined the captives up and threatened to shoot them.*

> **line-up** N a row of people that the police bring together so that someone can try to recognize which one of them carried out a crime ► *The victim later identified Thomas from a police line-up.*

2 line sth up, line up sth: to arrange things in a row ► *I stared at the dentist's instruments lined up in front of me.*

3 line sth/sb up, line up sth/sb: to arrange for something to happen or for someone to take part in something ► *The organizers had lined up a team of experts to discuss their views.* ► *We have some great comedy acts lined up for you this evening.*

> **line-up** N the group of people who have been chosen to take part in a particular event, programme, team etc ► *There are a few changes to the England line-up for next week's game.*

4 line up: if a lot of people, organizations etc line up to do

something, they are all very eager to do it ► *She's a brilliant lawyer. People line up to hire her.* ► *People are lining up to buy these new luxury apartments.*

5 line up sth, line sth up: to make something straight or in the right position in relation to something else ► *Make sure you have lined up the text on the page before you print it out.*

LINE UP AGAINST →

line up against sb/sth: if people line up against someone or something, they all oppose that person or thing ► *Democrats quickly lined up against the tax cuts.* ► *My brothers all lined up against me in the argument.*

LINGER

LINGER ON →

1 linger on: to continue to exist, especially for longer than was expected ► *In some places, the old way of life still lingers on.* ► *The disease only lingers on in very poor areas.* **the memory lingers on** ► *The war might be over, but the memory lingers on.*

2 linger on, linger on sth: to stay somewhere for a long time or longer than expected ► *It was past twelve o'clock, but some of the guests were still lingering on.* **sb's gaze lingers on** sb/sth also *sb's eyes linger on* sb/sth (=someone continues to look at someone or something for a long time) ► *"Is that really true?" he asked, his eyes lingering on her face.*

LINGER OVER →

linger over sth: to take a long time doing something, usually in order to enjoy it ► *There was still one couple in the restaurant, lingering over their coffee.*

L

L

LINK

LINK UP →

1 link up: to join with another person or organization in order to do something together ▶ *The two parties linked up to form the Social Democratic Party.* **+ with** ▶ *They linked up with an American band for the charity concert.*

link-up N when two or more companies, organizations etc join together ▶ *Shares in the company rose sharply as news of the link-up got out.*

2 link up sth/sb, **link** sth/sb **up**: to connect two or more places, people, or things ▶ *Millions of people around the world are now linked up by the Internet.* ▶ *The Channel Tunnel linked up Britain and France for the first time.* **+ to** ▶ *The company's alarm system is linked up to a twenty-four hour security service.*

link-up N a connection between two or more computers or electronic systems ▶ *Each room has its own colour TV and video link-up.*

LISTEN

LISTEN IN →

listen in: to secretly listen to someone's private conversation, especially on the telephone ▶ *Peter had*

picked up the other phone and was listening in when I got the news. **+ on** ▶ *Are you sure no-one's listening in on this conversation?*

LISTEN FOR →

listen for sth: to listen carefully so that you will hear a sound that you are expecting or hoping to hear ▶ *I lay awake for a while, listening for the sound of his steps on the stairs.*

LISTEN OUT FOR →

listen out for sth: to listen carefully in order to hear something that you are expecting or hoping to hear ▶ *Farmers are being urged to listen out for flood warnings.*

LITTER

BE LITTERED WITH →

1 be littered with sth: to be covered with a lot of something in an untidy way ▶ *The floor was littered with cigarette ends and empty cans.*

2 be littered with sth: to contain a lot of something, especially mistakes or examples of something bad ▶ *Even at university, students' essays are often littered with spelling mistakes.*

LIVE

LIVE BY →

live by sth: to follow carefully particular rules or beliefs ▶ *He refuses to live by anyone else's rules.* ▶ *Clare lives by the philosophy that you can do anything if you are determined enough.*

LIVE DOWN →

live sth **down**, **live down** sth: to make people forget about something silly or embarrassing that you have done ▶ *I don't think he'll ever live this down!* ▶ *What if the people at work found out about it? How could I ever live it down*

LIVE FOR →

live for sth/sb: to feel that someone or something is the most important thing in your life ▶ *Throughout the football season, I lived for Saturdays.*
have something/everything to live for (=have something, everything etc that makes life seem good and worth living) ▶ *She seemed to have everything to live for.*

LIVE IN →

live in: to live at the place where you work ▶ *The bar staff all live in.*

live-in ADJ a live-in worker lives at the place where they work ► *a live-in nanny*

LIVE OFF →

live off sth: to get money or produce from something and use it in order to live ► *Will your investments give enough interest for you to live off?* **live off the land** (=live by growing or catching your own food) ► *Most of the people on the island live off the land.*

live off sb: to get the money that you need to live from someone else ► *She can't go on living off her parents forever.*

live off sth: to only eat a particular kind of food ► *Many teenagers tend to live off junk food.*

LIVE ON →

live on sth: to have a particular amount of money available to buy the things you need to live ► *At that time we were living on £50 a week.* **not have/make enough to live on** (=not have or earn enough money to buy the things you need) ► *A lot of artists can't make enough to live on.*

live on sth: to only eat a particular kind of food ► *Most of the population live on a diet of rice.*

live on: to continue to exist or live, especially for a long time or for longer than expected ► *Great music lives on, long after the composer is dead.* ► *Many of the old traditions still live on.*

LIVE OUT →

live out your life also **live out your days etc**: to live for the rest of your life in a particular place or situation. **+ in** ► *Too many old people live out their days in poverty.*

live out sth: to do or experience something that you have always wanted to do ► *The money they won made it possible for them to live out their dreams.*

3 live out: to not live in the place where you study or work ► *A lot of second-year students decide to live out and share a house.*

LIVE THROUGH →

live through sth: to experience a difficult situation or event, often one that continues for a long time ► *My grandfather lived through two World Wars.* ► *We've lived through some very hard times together.*

LIVE TOGETHER →

live together: if two people live together, they share a house and have a sexual relationship, but they are not married ► *We lived together for several years before we decided to get married.*

LIVE UP →

live it up: to spend time doing exciting and enjoyable things ► *My brother always liked living it up at expensive hotels and night clubs.*

LIVE UP TO →

live up to sth: to be as good as people expect or hope ► *All holiday resorts claim you'll have a wonderful time – but I've found one that really lives up to its promises.* **live up to expectations** ► *I'm afraid your progress with the company has not lived up to expectations.*

LIVE WITH →

1 live with sb: to share a house and have a sexual relationship with someone, without being married ► *Frank asked her to come and live with him, but she wasn't sure.*

2 live with sth: to accept something unpleasant as part of your life,

L

because there is nothing you can do to change it ► *I don't think I can live with these constant arguments.*

LIVEN

LIVEN UP →

1a. liven up sth, **liven** sth **up**: to make something become more interesting or exciting ► *You could always liven up the room with some colourful curtains and cushions.* ► *Miller was great to have at parties. He quickly livened things up.*
b. liven up: to become more interesting and exciting ► *The game didn't liven up until midway through the second half.*

2a. liven sb **up, liven up** sb: to make someone more cheerful and full of energy ► *He could do with a couple of drinks to liven him up!*
b. liven up: to become more cheerful and full of energy ► *When the guests started arriving, he seemed to liven up.*

LOAD

LOAD DOWN →

1 be loaded down with sth: to be carrying or holding a lot of things or people ► *We were all loaded down with luggage, so we took a taxi to the airport.* ► *A truck loaded down with refugees was fleeing from the fighting.*
2 load sb **down, load down** sb: to give someone a lot of work, duties etc, especially more than they can deal with. **+ with** ► *Everyone in the department is loaded down with work at the moment.*

LOAD UP →

load up sth, **load** sth **up, load up**: to put a lot of things into a vehicle or onto an animal before you start a journey ► *Dad loaded up the car the night before we left, so that we could leave early the next day.* **+ with**

► *Everyone on the expedition had to load up with enough food and water for two weeks.*

LOAD UP ON, *also* LOAD UP WITH →
load up on/with sth: to get or buy a lot of something ► *She always loads up on vitamin pills before she goes on holiday.*

LOAF

LOAF AROUND, *also* LOAF ABOUT →
loaf around/about (sth): to spend your time being lazy or doing nothing ► *Gary could only find a part-time job. The rest of the time he just loafed around.*

LOAN

LOAN OUT →
loan sth/sb **out, loan out** sth/sb: to lend something or someone to someone else for a period of time ► *Some of the paintings were loaned out to the museum by private collectors.*

LOCK

LOCK AWAY →

1 lock sth **away, lock away** sth: to put something in a safe place and lock the door, so that no-one else can get or take it ► *The police are advising people to lock their cars away at night.* ► *The pills were safely locked away in the school secretary's cupboard.*
2 lock sb **away, lock away** sb: to put someone in prison or in a hospital for people who are mentally ill ► *That brother of yours is crazy. He should be locked away.*
3 lock yourself away: to go somewhere in order to be quiet or get away from other people ► *He used to lock himself away in the garden shed in order to do his writing.* **be locked away** ► *She's been locked away in her office all afternoon.*

L

lock sth **away, lock away** sth: to keep information, feelings etc secret or hidden from people ► *I was happy to keep the events of that night locked away in my head.*

LOCK IN →
lock sb **in, lock in** sb: to prevent someone from leaving a room or building by locking the door ► *The guard locked*

him, then sat down outside the door. **be locked in** (=be unable to get out of a room or building because you cannot open the door) ► *Help! I'm locked in!*

BE LOCKED IN, *also* BE LOCKED INTO →
be locked in/into sth: to be involved in an argument, fight etc with someone, especially one that it is difficult to get out of ► *The couple, now divorced, are locked in a long battle over their children.* **get locked into** sth, *also* **become locked into** sth: ► *Neither side wants to get locked into a long civil war.*

LOCK IN ON, *also* LOCK ONTO →
lock in on sth, **lock onto** sth: if a missile locks in on the object it is aimed at, it finds its position and moves straight towards it ► *The pilot reported that the missile had locked in on its target.*

LOCK OUT →
1 lock sb **out, lock out** sb: to deliberately prevent someone from entering a place by locking the door ► *The court heard that Simms had beaten his wife and locked her out.*

lock yourself out: to leave your keys inside a building, room, car etc by mistake, with the result that you cannot get back inside ► *Oh no! I've locked myself out of my room!* ► *We always leave a spare key next door, in case we lock ourselves out.*

3 lock sb **out, lock out** sb: to prevent workers from entering their place of work in order to make them do what their employers want ► *Car workers returned to the factory only to find they had been locked out.*

   lockout N when employers prevent workers from coming to work until the workers agree to what the employers want ► *When the miners went on strike, management responded with a lockout.*

LOCK UP →
1 lock sth **up, lock up** sth, **lock up**: to lock all the doors and windows of a building or a car so that no-one can get in ► *The house was all locked up and there was no sign of anyone.* ► *Did you remember to turn off the lights and lock up?*

2 lock sb **up, lock up** sb: to put or keep someone in prison, or in a hospital for people who are mentally ill ► *People who abuse children should be locked up for life.*

   lockup N a prison, especially a small one ► *There were already five guys inside the police lockup that night.*

3 lock sth **up, lock up** sth: to put something in a safe place and lock the door ► *The silver was always locked up when it wasn't in use.*

LOG

LOG IN, *also* LOG ON, LOG INTO, LOG ONTO →
log in/on, log into/onto sth: to do the things that are necessary to start using a computer system ► *Someone else had logged in under my name and used my password.* ► *When I*

L

*logged onto my computer I found
dozens of e-mails waiting for me.*
log onto the Internet ▶ *These days
children can log onto the Internet and
find out information about anything
they want.*

log-in, log-on N a name or special
word needed to start using a
computer system ▶ *Normally the
person's log-in is not known to
anyone else.*

LOG OFF, *also* LOG OUT →
log off, log out, log off sth: to finish
using a computer system by typing in
a special word or instruction ▶ *Make
sure you save your work before you
log off.* ▶ *I logged out and switched
off my machine.*

LOG ON *see* LOG IN

LOG ONTO *see* LOG IN

LOLL

LOLL ABOUT, *also* LOLL AROUND →
loll around/about, loll around/about
sth: to sit or lie somewhere in a very
lazy or relaxed way, doing very little
▶ *Her husband spends the evenings
lolling around on the sofa watching
TV.*

LONG

LONG FOR →
long for sth/sb: to want something or
someone very much ▶ *After 20 years
of marriage she was longing for a little
more excitement.* ▶ *The couple had
always longed for a child.*

LOOK

LOOK AFTER →
1 look after sb: to spend time with
someone and make sure that they are
safe and have the things they need
▶ *Her husband looks after the children
while she's at work.* ▶ *The doctors
there are very good, and I'm sure
you'll be well looked after.*

2 look after sth: to keep something in
good condition or make sure that it is
safe ▶ *Who is responsible for looking
after the gardens?* ▶ *Can you look afte
my bags while I go up to the bar?*

3 look after sth: to be responsible for
dealing with something over a period
of time ▶ *Hugh looks after the
financial side of the business.*

4 look after yourself: used when you
are saying goodbye to someone in a
friendly way ▶ *"See you, Tony." "Yeah,
you look after yourself!"*

5 be able to look after yourself: to no
need anyone else to keep you safe or
to help you ▶ *Don't worry about Jo –
she's perfectly capable of looking afte
herself.*

LOOK AHEAD →
look ahead: to think about what will
happen in the future ▶ *It's important
to look ahead and think about what
you really want to do in your career.*

look ahead N if you have a look
ahead, you think or talk about
something that will happen in the
future ▶ *And finally, a quick look
ahead to what's on Channel 4 this
weekend.*

LOOK AROUND, *also* LOOK
ROUND →
**1 look around/round, look around/
round** sth: to walk around a place
looking at the various things there
▶ *They spent the morning looking
around the old part of the city.*

look around *also* **look round** N wher
someone walks around a place,
looking at the various things there
▶ *Do you mind if I have a quick look
around, just to make sure that
everything's OK?*

2 look around/round: to try to find
something by looking in different
places, asking people etc ▶ *She spent
several months looking around, trying*

to find a better job. **+ for** ► *Tom began to look around for a place to live.*

LOOK AT →

1 look at sth: to examine something carefully, especially to find out what is wrong with it or to find out more about it ► *He took the car to his nearest garage so that a mechanic could look at it.*

2 look at sth: to study and consider something, especially in order to decide what to do about it ► *The company is currently looking at ways in which it can improve its image.*

3 look at sth: to read something, especially quickly and not very carefully ► *Have you had time to look at your e-mail this morning?* ► *Mo asked him to look at the report for her before she sent it out.*

4 look at sth: to consider something in a particular way ► *You'll look at things differently when you get to my age.* ► *The way I look at it, I might be poor, but at least I'm doing what I want to do.*

5 look at sb/sth!: used when you are mentioning someone or something as an example to prove what you have just said ► *You don't have to be young to be a rock star. Look at the bands from the sixties.*

6 not look at sb/sth: to not want to accept an offer because it is too low, or not be interested in someone or something because they are not the right type ► *I don't think they'd look at anything under £200,000 for the house.* **not look twice at** sb/sth (=not be even slightly interested in something or someone) ► *I'm old enough to be her father. She wouldn't look twice at me.*

LOOK AWAY →

look away: to turn your eyes away from someone or something so that

you are not looking at them ► *When the old man asked her for money she just looked away.* **+ from** ► *Shirley looked away from the road in front of her for a second, and the car skidded.*

LOOK BACK →

1 look back: to think about or remember a situation that happened in the past ► *Looking back, I wish I hadn't said some of those things.* **+ on** ► *I look back on my childhood with a great deal of happiness.* **+ to** ► *In his latest novel, he looks back to the early 1970s.*

2 sb hasn't looked back (since): used to say that someone has continued to be successful since a particular time ► *He won his first Wimbledon title when he was 20, and hasn't looked back since.*

LOOK DOWN ON →

1 look down on sb: to think you are better than someone else ► *Adam always felt that we looked down on him*

because he hadn't been to university.

2 look down on sth: to think that something is not very good ► *Romantic novels are generally looked down on by serious literary scholars.*

LOOK FOR →

1 look for sb/sth: to try to find someone or something ► *He said he was looking for a place to stay for a few weeks.* ► *Scientists believe they have found the answer they've been looking for.* **the police are looking for** sb (=they are trying find someone who may have been involved in a crime)

L

▶ *The police are looking for a man in his early twenties.*

2 be looking for sb: to be trying to find a particular kind of person for a job ▶ *I'm sorry, but we're looking for someone with more experience.*

LOOK FORWARD TO →
look forward to sth: to be excited and happy about something good that is going to happen ▶ *It had been a long day, and he was looking forward to a hot shower when he got home.* **look forward to doing** sth ▶ *I'm really looking forward to seeing my family again.*

LOOK IN →
look in: to visit someone for a short time, usually when you are going somewhere else. **+ on** ▶ *I thought I'd look in on Michael on my way home.*

LOOK INTO →
1 look into sth: to try to find out the facts about something such as a crime, a problem, or an accident ▶ *Police authorities say they will look into the matter.*

2 look into sth: to find out more about something by getting all the necessary information ▶ *It sounds like an interesting idea for a holiday – I'll definitely look into it.*

LOOK ON, also LOOK UPON →
look on: to watch something while it is happening but not take part in it or try to stop it ▶ *Reporters looked on in horror as the man was dragged away and beaten to death.*

  onlooker N someone who watches something while it happens, without being involved in it ▶ *A crowd of curious onlookers had gathered around the building.*

LOOK ON, also LOOK UPON →
look on/upon sb/sth: to consider someone or something in a particular way. **+ as** ▶ *We've always looked on*

Jack as one of the family. ▶ *Instead of being pleased, he appeared to look on the offer as an insult.* **+ with** ▶ *There are places where a video camera is looked upon with great suspicion.*

LOOK OUT →
look out!: use this to warn someone that they are in danger and that they must do something to avoid it ▶ *Look out! There's a train coming!* ▶ *"Look out!" yelled Willie. "He's got a gun!"*

  lookout N **1** someone whose duty is to watch carefully for signs of danger ▶ *One of the lookouts saw a column of tanks approaching in the distance.*
  2 a high place where people can watch for signs of danger ▶ *a mountain lookout*

LOOK OUT FOR →
1 look out for sb/sth: to look carefully and pay close attention in order to try to see someone or something ▶ *We kept looking out for him, but there was no sign at all.*

  lookout N **be on the lookout for** sb/sth: to watch a place or situation continuously in order to find something you want or to be ready for any problems or chances ▶ *Police were on the lookout for anyone behaving suspiciously.* ▶ *We're always on the lookout for new business opportunities.*

2 look out for sb: to do what is best for someone or protect them ▶ *We were a close group of friends, and we all looked out for each other.* **look out for yourself** ▶ *No one else is going to help you get to the top. You have to look out for yourself.*

LOOK OVER →
look sb/sth **over, look over** sb/sth: to quickly examine someone or something, to see if there is anything wrong with them or to see what they

are like ▶ *Jarrell held the gun up to his eyes and looked it over carefully.* ▶ *The girl looked him over coldly and laughed. "A writer! That's the funniest thing I've heard all week."*

LOOK ROUND *See* **LOOK AROUND**

LOOK THROUGH →

1 look through sth: to look for something among a pile of paper, in a drawer, in someone's pockets etc ▶ *FBI agents are looking through her apartment for fingerprints.* ▶ *We looked through Bob's drawer to see if there were any clues.*

2 look through sth: to read something quickly ▶ *Can you look through the report and tell me what you think of it?*

3 look through sb: to look at someone and seem not to notice them or pretend not to recognize them. **look straight through** sb *also* **look right through** sb ▶ *I waved to her in the street, but she just looked straight through me.*

LOOK TO →

1 look to sb/sth: to depend on someone or something to provide you with help, advice etc. **+ for** ▶ *People are already looking to the Internet for all of their shopping needs.* ▶ *Artists like Gaugin looked to the East for their inspiration.* **look to** sb **to do** sth ▶ *I always looked to my older brother to protect me.*

2 look to sth: to pay attention to something so that it affects what you do ▶ *We need to stop thinking about the past and start looking to the future.*

LOOK UP →

1 look up sth, **look** sth **up**: to try to find information about something in a book, in a list, in computer records etc ▶ *If you don't know what the word means, look it up in a dictionary.* ▶ *She looked up his number in the phone book.*

2 look sb **up, look up** sb: to visit someone, when you are visiting the area where they live ▶ *If you're ever in Atlanta, look me up.*

3 look up: if a situation is looking up, it is improving ▶ *The Cuban economy is looking up.* **things are looking up** (=the situation is improving) ▶ *They had a lot of problems last year, but now things are looking up.*

LOOK UP TO →

look up to sb: to admire or respect someone a lot, for example because they are older or more experienced than you ▶ *The player I used to look up to when I was younger was Don Bradman.* ▶ *Children will usually look up to their older brothers and sisters.*

LOOK UPON *See* **LOOK ON**

LOOM

LOOM AHEAD →

loom ahead: if an unpleasant or worrying situation looms ahead, it is going to happen soon ▶ *With economic difficulties looming ahead, people are cutting down on their spending.*

LOOM UP →

loom up: to suddenly appear as a large unclear shape ▶ *The city's skyscrapers loom up out of the mist.* ▶ *A huge truck loomed up in front of them.*

LOOSE

LOOSE OFF →

loose off sth, **loose** sth **off**: to fire bullets, bombs etc ▶ *The soldiers loosed off a few rounds of ammunition over the heads of the crowd.*

LOOSE ON, *also* **LOOSE UPON** →

loose sth **on** sb/sth, **loose** sth **upon** sb/sth: to allow something very dangerous to harm people or destroy something ▶ *Although no one realised it at the time, a deadly disease had been loosed on the public.*

L

LOOSEN

LOOSEN UP →

1 loosen up: to become more relaxed ► *After a couple of drinks she began to loosen up a little.* ► *"Come on honey, loosen up!" his wife said to him.*

2 loosen up sth, **loosen** sth **up**, **loosen up**: to make your muscles more relaxed, usually by doing exercises, for example before playing a sport ► *The players were loosening up before the game*

LOP

LOP OFF →

1 lop off sth, **lop** sth **off**: to quickly cut off a part of something such as a branch of a tree ► *He picked up the axe and began lopping off branches from a nearby tree.*

2 lop off sth, **lop** sth **off**: to reduce something by a large amount ► *£10 billion has been lopped off the defence budget.*

LORD

LORD OVER →

lord it over sb: to behave in a way that shows you think you are better than someone else ► *She seemed to enjoy lording it over the other members of her team.*

LOSE

LOSE IN →

1 be lost in sth: to be thinking about something so much that you do not pay attention to what is happening

around you ► *Kerry was sitting in her armchair, lost in a book.* ► *a dreamy child who was lost in his own little world* **lost in thought** ► *I walked slowly back to my office, lost in thought.*

2 lose yourself in sth: to become so involved in what you are doing that you do not think about anything else ► *When Warren left her, she tried to lose herself in her work.*

LOSE OUT →

lose out: to not get an advantage that someone else has ► *Single people could lose out financially under the new tax system.* **lose out to** sb (=another person, organization etc succeeds in getting something instead of you) ► *US firms are losing out to foreign competitors because of the high value of the dollar.* **+ on** ► *The company has lost out on an oil bonanza worth at least $1 billion.*

LOUNGE

LOUNGE AROUND, *also* LOUNGE ABOUT →

lounge around/ about, lounge around/ about sth: to spend time doing very little in a relaxed and lazy way ► *They spent most of the first week lounging around the hotel pool.*

LOUSE

LOUSE UP →

louse sth **up, louse up** sth: to do something very badly, especially by making a lot of careless mistakes ► *Don't give the job to John, he'll only louse it up.* ► *"How did you do in your test?" "I really loused it up."*

LUCK

LUCK INTO →

luck into sth: to get something you want without expecting to get it ► *Reed lucked into a simple TV role that led to his successful acting career.*

L

LUCK OUT →
luck out: to be very lucky ▶ *"I lucked out," said the driver after the accident. "I could have been killed."*

LULL

LULL INTO →
lull sb **into** sth: to deceive someone and make them feel safe or confident, so that they are completely surprised when you attack them or when something bad happens to them.
lull sb **into a false sense of security** ▶ *They lulled their opponents into a false sense of security, and then scored three goals in the last 15 minutes.* **lull** sb **into doing** sth ▶ *The police managed to lull the gang into believing that no one knew about their activities.*

LUMBER

LUMBER WITH →
be lumbered with sb/sth: to have to deal with someone or something that is difficult, annoying, expensive etc ▶ *I'm sorry you got lumbered with the bill.* ▶ *She's just so boring – I don't like the idea of being lumbered with her all evening.*

LUMP

LUMP TOGETHER →
lump sb/sth **together**: to consider two or more different people or things as a single type or group ▶ *They were all lumped together as troublemakers and kept under close watch by the police.* ▶ *A great many plants are lumped together under the label of herbs.*

LUNGE

LUNGE AT →
lunge at sb/sth: to suddenly jump towards a person or animal in order to attack them ▶ *The man lunged at her with a knife.*

LUST

LUST AFTER →
1 lust after sb: to feel very attracted to someone ▶ *Apparently Jane had been secretly lusting after Chris for years.*
2 lust after sth: to want something very much, especially something that is very expensive or difficult to get ▶ *A lot of guys spend their lives lusting after Porsches and Jaguars.*

LUXURIATE

LUXURIATE IN →
luxuriate in sth: to spend time enjoying something very much and getting a lot of pleasure from it ▶ *She imagined herself at home luxuriating in a nice hot bath.*

L

Mm

MAGIC

MAGIC AWAY →
magic sth **away, magic away** sth: to make something bad

disappear quickly and without any effort ▸ *The government was facing a serious problem which couldn't be magicked away.*

MAJOR

MAJOR IN →
major in sth: to study something as your main subject at a college or university ▸ *She decided to major in biology.*

MAKE

MAKE AWAY WITH →
make away with sth: to steal something and escape with it ▸ *Thieves made away with thousands of dollars worth of jewellery.*

MAKE FOR →
1 make for sth: to move towards something ▸ *At last the film finished and we got up and made for the exit.*

2 be made for each other: if two people are made for each other, they each seem to be the perfect person for the other to have a happy relationship with ▸ *I'd like to see Seb and Carrie get married. They're made for each other.*

3 make for sth: to help to cause a particular effect or situation, or to produce a particular result ▸ *The game was played in heavy rain, which*

made for very dangerous conditions. ▸ *With restaurants open late into the night, it all makes for a festive atmosphere.*

MAKE INTO →
1 make sth **into** sth: to change something in order to use it in a different way or for a different purpose ▸ *Sagan's best-selling book is being made into a movie.* ▸ *an ordinary-looking sofa that can be made into a bed*

2 make sb **into** sth: to change someone so that they become a different sort of person or have a different position in society ▸ *The film made her into a star overnight.* ▸ *Russell's experiences in court had made him into a bitter man.*

MAKE OF →
what do you make of sth/ sb?: used to ask what someone thinks about something or someone ▸ *"What do you make of this?" Martin said, pointing to a small article in that morning's paper.* **not know what to make of** sth/ sb (=not know how to understand or react towards something or someone) ▸ *Hudson didn't like children, and never really knew what to make of his stepson.*

MAKE OFF →
make off: to leave quickly, especially in order to escape ▸ *Detectives believe that the gunmen made off in the direction of the park.*

MAKE OFF WITH →
make off with sth: to steal something and escape with it ▸ *They made off with over £6m of gold bullion.*

MAKE OUT →
1 make out sth, **make** sth **out**: to be able to hear or see something, but with difficulty ▸ *In the semi-darkness, Delaney could just make out the Russian's face.* **not be able to make**

sth **out** (=not be able to see or hear something clearly) ▶ *He could hear voices in the kitchen below, but couldn't make out what was being said.*

2 make out sth, **make** sth **out**: to be just able to understand something ▶ *Nobody could make out exactly what Murphy was trying to say.* ▶ *I can't make out why she did that, can you?* **from what** sb **can make out ...** (=according to what someone understands about a situation) ▶ *From what I can make out, the girl ran straight into the road without stopping to look.*

3 make sth/ sb **out to be** sth: to describe something or someone, usually wrongly, as a particular type of thing or person ▶ *He was a good man, but the press made him out to be weak and unimportant.*

4 make out (that): to try to make people believe that something is true when it is not ▶ *Don't you make out I'm a liar, Eric, or I'll knock you down!*

5 make out a cheque/ bill etc: to write the necessary information on a cheque, bill etc ▶ *We sat down to wait while the receptionist made out our bill.*

6 can't make sb **out**: to not be able to understand what kind of person someone is, or why they behave as they do ▶ *Dorothy's always so quiet, I've never been able to make her out at all.*

7 how did you make out?: used to ask if someone was successful ▶ *How did you make out in the race yesterday?*

MAKE OVER →

make over sth, **make** sth **over**: to officially give money or property to someone else. **+ to** ▶ *When Rose reached sixty, she made over the farm to her son.*

MAKE TOWARDS →

make towards sth: to start moving towards something ▶ *Bert gently picked up the frightened child and made towards the house.*

MAKE UP →

1 make up sth: if a number of parts or members make up something, they combine together to form it ▶ *Women made up over 40% of the workforce.* ▶ *the countries that make up the United Nations.* **be made up of** ▶ *Indonesia is made up of over 13,000 islands.*

make-up N the things or people that something consists of ▶ *There have been a lot of changes to the make-up of the team.*

2 make up your mind also **make your mind up**: to make a definite decision or choice ▶ *I wish he'd hurry up and make up his mind.* ▶ *In the autumn of 1945 he made up his mind to quit school.* **+ what/ which etc** ▶ *The doctors couldn't make up their minds what to do.* **+ (that)** ▶ *He had already made up his mind that he wanted to marry her.* sb's **mind is made up** (=they have decided to do something and are determined to do it) ▶ *From the moment she saw her first ballet her mind was made up. She wanted to be a dancer.*

3 make up sth, **make** sth **up**: to think of a lie, excuse, or story that is not true in order to deceive someone ▶ *He accused the press of harassing his sister and making up stories about her.* ▶ *I bet he's making it all up.*

made-up ADJ not true and intended to deceive someone ▶ *She gave them some made-up story about how she needed the money for an operation.*

4 make up sth, **make** sth **up**: to think of something new using your

M

imagination ▶ *The soldiers used to make up rude songs about him.* ▶ *She made up a story about a magic carpet.* **make it up as you go along** (=decide how to do something while you are doing it instead of planning it before) ▶ *We didn't have any experience when we started the company, so we just made it up as we went along.*

5 make up sth, **make** sth **up**: to prepare or arrange something so that it is ready to be used ▶ *My wife's made up a bed for you in the spare room.* ▶ *Shall I make up some sandwiches?*

6 make (it) up: if two people who have had an argument make up, they agree to become friends again. **+ with** ▶ *Father and son didn't make up with each other for another 15 years.* **kiss and make up** (=become friendly again with someone after an argument) ▶ *I wish someone could persuade those two to kiss and make up.*

7 make up sth, **make** sth **up**: if you make up time that you have taken off work, you spend that time working later ▶ *I'm going home early – I'll make up the time tomorrow.*

8 make up sth: to add to an amount or number, so that you have as much or as many as you need ▶ *We need two more players to make up the team.*

9 make up sb, **make** sb **up**: to put coloured creams, powders etc onto someone's face to change the way they look ▶ *She had been made up to look like an old woman.*

> **make-up** N coloured creams, powders etc that people put on their face to change or improve their appearance ▶ *She paused before applying her make-up and stared at the mirror.*

10 make up sth, **make** sth **up**: to make a dress, suit etc by cutting and sewing cloth ▶ *We have these suits made up for us in London.*

MAKE UP FOR →

1 make up for sth: if a good situation makes up for a bad one, it makes you forget the bad situation and feel happy again ▶ *Last night's victory made up for all the problems we've had in previous games.* **more than make up for** sth (=be so good that it makes the bad situation seem unimportant) ▶ *She was exhausted, but the sheer pleasure of having reached the summit more than made up for it.*

2 make up for sth: to do something good for someone after doing something bad to them, so that they forgive you ▶ *Can I buy you lunch to make up for being late?* ▶ *Mike forgot his wife's birthday so he took her to Paris to make up for it.*

3 make up for sth: to have so much of a good quality that it is not important that you do not have enough of another quality ▶ *Perhaps Sue lacked skill, but she certainly made up for that with her enthusiasm.*

4 make up for lost time: a. to do something at a later time, because something prevented you from doing it when you should have ▶ *I was ill last week, so I had to work all weekend to make up for lost time.*

b. to become involved in an activity very eagerly, because you wish you had discovered it earlier in your life ▶ *She didn't start dancing until she was 40, so now she feels she's trying to make up for lost time.*

MAKE UP TO →

make it up to sb: to do something good for someone after disappointing them or treating them badly ▶ *I'm sorry I haven't seen you much lately, but I'll make it up to you, I promise.*

M

MAP

MAP OUT →

map out sth, **map** sth **out**: to plan something carefully or to explain carefully what your plans are
▶ *Felicity's future had been mapped out for her by wealthy and adoring parents.* ▶ *The Chancellor mapped out Britain's road to economic recovery.*

MARCH

MARCH ON →

march on sth: to walk to a particular place in a large group in order to attack it or to protest about something
▶ *He gathered his troops and prepared to march on the capital.*
● *Demonstrators marched on the government in Washington.*

MARK

MARK AS →

mark sb/sth **as** sth: to think that someone or something is a particular type of person or thing ▶ *When she first saw Patrick she had marked him as a bully.*

MARK DOWN →

1 mark sth **down**, **mark down** sth: to reduce the price of something ▶ *The store was having its final sale on Friday, with everything marked down by 20%.*

   markdown N a reduction in the price of something ▶ *We are offering a 30% markdown on selected products.*

2 mark down sth, **mark** sth **down**: to write something down, especially in order to keep a record ▶ *As part of the diet, I had to mark down everything I ate each day.*

3 mark sb/sth **down**, **mark down** sb/sth: if teachers mark a student or their work down, they give the student a lower score ▶ *Miss Perkovich*

marked me down three points for beginning a sentence with 'but'.

MARK DOWN AS →

mark sb/sth **down as** sth: to consider someone or something to be a particular type of person or thing
▶ *From the very start, Andrew had been marked down as a very exciting player.*

MARK OFF →

1 mark off sth, **mark** sth **off**: to separate an area of ground or show where its border is ▶ *The Voskresenye gates mark off the north side of Red Square.*

2 mark sth/sb **off**, **mark off** sth/sb: to make something or someone different from other things or people of a similar type. **+ from** ▶ *Each of the city's districts has its own distinct character that marks it off from its neighbour.*

3 mark sth **off**, **mark off** sth: to put a mark beside or through something that is written on a list, to show that it has been dealt with ▶ *He marked off the names of people he could rely on for support.*

MARK OUT →

1 mark sb/sth **out**, **mark out** sb/sth: to make someone or something seem clearly different from or better than other people or things ▶ *Philippe still had that athletic look that had marked him out so long ago.* **+ as** ▶ *Her considerable experience of international law marked her out as exceptional.*

2 mark out sth, **mark** sth **out**: to separate a particular area from the

M

area around it, by drawing lines or using other signs ▶ *The area marked out here is intended as a viewing platform.*

3 be marked out: if someone is marked out for something, they have special qualities and abilities which make them likely to achieve it. **+ for** ▶ *Right from the beginning, he seemed to have been marked out for a career in baseball.*

MARK UP →

1 mark up sth, **mark** sth **up**: to increase the price of something to more than you paid for it ▶ *It annoys farmers to see how much their produce has been marked up by the time it reaches the shops.*

> **mark-up** N an increase in the price of something ▶ *The mark-up is between producer and supermarket is between 160% and 170%.*

2 mark sth **up**, **mark up** sth: to put a mark beside something that is written on a list, to show that you have dealt with it or chosen it ▶ *It was Lawrie's job to collect the rents and mark them up in a book.*

3 mark up sth, **mark** sth **up**: to write any necessary instructions for changes on a piece of writing or music ▶ *Text must be checked and marked up for corrections.*

MARRY

MARRY INTO →

marry into sth: to marry someone from a particular family or social group, especially a rich or important one, and become part of it ▶ *Douglas Robinson married into the Roosevelt family of Oyster Bay.*

MARRY OFF →

marry off sb, **marry** sb **off**: to arrange for someone to get married to someone you have chosen. **+ to** ▶ *The*

Duke's daughter, Anne, was married off to Charles VIII of France.

MARVEL

MARVEL AT →

marvel at sth: to be very surprised and impressed by something ▶ *Those who watch the programme marvel at the speed of Carole's brain.* ▶ *Visitors never cease to marvel at the beauty of the Taj Mahal.*

MASH

MASH UP →

mash sth **up**, **mash up** sth: to crush food until it is soft and smooth ▶ *He was busy mashing up vegetables for the baby's lunch.*

MASQUERADE

MASQUERADE AS →

masquerade as sth/sb: to pretend or appear to be something or someone different ▶ *By masquerading as poisonous insects, these flies avoid attacks from birds.* ▶ *We had a cup of hot brown stuff which masqueraded as coffee.*

MATCH

MATCH AGAINST →

1 match sb/sth **against** sb/sth: to make two people, teams etc compete against each other ▶ *The two men were matched against each other in Game 3 of the League Championship.*

2 match sth **against** sth: to compare one thing with another in order to see whether they are the same ▶ *No fingerprints were found in the car which could be matched against the ones in the flat.*

MATCH UP →

1 match up: if two things match up, they are similar or suitable for each other in some way. **+ with** ▶ *What other people say does not always match up with our own experience.*

+ against ▶ *It's important to select employees who match up against a particular job profile.*

2 match sb/sth **up, match up** sb/sth: to bring together two people or things that seem to be suitable for each other. **+ with** ▶ *She only invited me to dinner to try and match me up with her brother.*

3 match up: to be of a good enough standard ▶ *It was fashionable to be incredibly thin, and my figure just didn't match up.*

4 match up: to play at a similar standard as another person or team in a game or competition. **+ against/with** ▶ *The Raiders didn't match up well against the Chiefs.*

MATCH UP TO →

match up to sth/sb: to be as good, interesting etc as something or someone else ▶ *I'd already read the book, and the film matched up to it in every way.* **match up to your expectations/ideals etc** (=be as good as you expected, hoped etc) ▶ *I was really disappointed by Hollywood. It didn't match up to my expectations at all.*

MAUL

MAUL ABOUT, *also* MAUL AROUND →

maul sth/sb **around/about:** to pull something or someone from one position to another in a rough or violent way ▶ *Some of the women complained that they had been mauled about by customs officials.*

MAX

MAX OUT →

1 max out: to have too much of something and not want any more. **+ on** ▶ *Today's audiences have maxed out on violent movies and are demanding family-oriented films.*

2 max out: to put as much time, effort, money etc as possible into doing something ▶ *Jordan has been maxing out in every game and keeping up a fast pace.*

    maxed-out ADJ if a system, process, method etc is maxed-out, it is being used to the highest degree possible ▶ *We need to take care of the city's maxed-out sewage system by finding ways to conserve water.*

3 max out your credit card: to spend the highest amount that your credit card will allow ▶ *College students often max out their credit cards and spend years repaying the debt.*

MEASURE

MEASURE AGAINST →

measure sb/sth **against** sb/sth: to judge someone or something by comparing them with someone or something else ▶ *It is now possible to measure each child's progress against fixed standards.* **measure yourself against** sb/sth ▶ *If all musicians measured themselves against Mozart, they would get very depressed.*

MEASURE OFF →

measure sth **off, measure off** sth: to measure a length of something, especially cloth, and cut it off from a larger piece. ▶ *The assistant measured off two metres of green silk.*

MEASURE OUT →

measure out sth, **measure** sth **out:** to weigh or measure a particular amount of something ▶ *I showed the children how to measure out and mix the ingredients.*

MEASURE UP →

1 measure up: to be of a good enough standard. **+ to** ▶ *Some of the college's courses do not measure up to the required standard.* **how does** sb/sth **measure up** (=used when asking what someone or something is like and

M

whether they are good enough)
▶ *What happens to teachers who don't measure up?* ▶ *How does your new house measure up?*

2 measure up, measure sth up, measure up sth: to measure the exact size of something ▶ *In most cases, when you buy new carpets the firm will measure up for you.*

3 measure sb **up, measure up** sb: to look at someone carefully in order to decide what your opinion of them is ▶ *The two men shook hands and silently measured each other up.*

MEASURE UP AGAINST →
measure sb/sth **up against** sb/sth: to compare someone or something with another person or thing, in order to find which is better, bigger etc ▶ *How does the company's performance measure up against the best in the world?*

MEASURE UP TO →
measure up to sb/sth: to be as good as someone or something else, when you compare them ▶ *According to our research, girls still do not measure up to boys in science subjects.*

MEET

MEET UP →
1 meet up: to meet someone, especially because you have arranged to ▶ *If you'd like to meet up for a drink sometime, give me a call.* **+ with** ▶ *We met up with the rest of the group in Frankfurt.*

2 meet up: if two or more things meet up, they join or come together at a particular place ▶ *A number of paths run down through the woods and meet up at the bottom.* **+ with** ▶ *She was wearing a tiny white T-shirt that didn't meet up with her jeans.*

MEET WITH →
1 meet with sb: to have a meeting with someone in order to discuss or

arrange something ▶ *He will meet with his advisers on Thursday to decide on his next course of action.*

2 meet with sth also **be met with** sth: to cause a particular reaction from someone ▶ *The architect's design did not meet with their approval.* ▶ *News of the merger has been met with great excitement in the city.*

3 meet with sth: if someone or something meets with success, failure, problems etc, they experience success, failure, problems etc ▶ *The company's efforts to expand met with some success.*

MELLOW

MELLOW OUT →
mellow out, mellow sb **out**: to become relaxed and calm, or to make someone become relaxed and calm ▶ *I just like to go home and mellow out in front of the TV after work.*

MELT

MELT AWAY →
1 melt away: to gradually disappear ▶ *Justine saw her hopes of promotion slowly melt away.* **+ into** ▶ *The high rocky cliffs melted away into long stretches of silvery beach.*

2 melt away: if people melt away, they gradually move away from someone or somewhere ▶ *By the time the police appeared, most of the crowd had melted away.* **+ into** ▶ *He looked back briefly, but Coleman had already melted away into the darkness.*

3 melt away, melt away sth, **melt** sth **away**: to melt or to make something melt completely until it has disappeared ▶ *The next day it was a surprise to*

wake up and find that the snow had melted away.

MELT DOWN →

melt sth **down**, **melt down** sth: to heat something made of metal until it becomes a liquid, especially so that it can be made into something else ► *The beautiful copper engravings had been melted down to make a tea-kettle.*

MELT INTO →

1 melt into sth: to disappear or change and be replaced by something else ► *She watched the hope in his face melt into disappointment.* ► *The crowd's cheers melted into gasps of admiration and approval.*

2 melt into sth: if people melt into a crowd, a wood etc, they move into it until they are part of it and cannot be seen. ► *Lesley said goodbye and watched him melt into the crowds.*

MERGE

MERGE IN →

merge in: if two or more things merge in, they are so similar in style, colour, appearance etc that you do not notice much difference between them.
+ with ► *I chose very pale curtains that would merge in with the walls.*

MERGE INTO →

merge into sth: to gradually disappear or seem to disappear and become part of something else ► *Autumn slowly merged into winter.* ► *As night fell, their figures merged into the landscape.*

MESS

MESS ABOUT *see* MESS AROUND

MESS ABOUT WITH *see* MESS AROUND WITH

MESS AROUND, *also* MESS ABOUT →

1 mess around/about: to behave in a silly way, when you should be working or doing something else ► *Stop messing about you two!* ► *I used to mess about a lot in class when I was at school.*

2 mess around/about: to spend your time enjoying yourself and relaxing or playing ► *She spends most of her weekends messing around at the beach.*

3 mess sb **around/about**: to treat someone badly, for example by not doing what you have agreed to do ► *Linda's upset because some guy's been messing her around.* ► *I still haven't had my money from the insurance company – they've really messed me around.*

MESS AROUND WITH, *also* MESS ABOUT WITH →

1 mess around/about with sth: to try to change something in order to try to improve it, especially when it would be better if you did not ► *I came home to find Mike messing around with the television.* ► *It's a lovely song – I just wish people wouldn't mess around with it.*

2 mess around with sb: to treat someone badly, for example by not being completely honest with them ► *Cranberg told his attorneys to quit messing around with him.*

MESS UP →

1 mess up sth, **mess** sth **up**: to spoil something important ► *If you make a mistake like that it can easily mess up a whole day's work.* ► *I'm sorry if I messed up all your plans.* **mess things up** (=spoil someone's plans) ► *If we can't get our passports in time it'll really mess things up for the holiday.*

2 mess sth **up**, **mess up** sth: to make something dirty or untidy ► *Don't come in here with those muddy boots.*

M

You'll mess up the carpet. **be messed up** ▶ *Her hair was all messed up.*

3 mess up, mess sth **up**: to make a mistake or do something badly ▶ *"How did the exam go?" "Terrible. I think I really messed it up."* **mess up big time** (=make a bad mistake) ▶ *When political figures mess up big time like this, they always make the same excuse.*

4 mess sb **up, mess up** sb: to upset someone badly or to make them have emotional or mental problems ▶ *She had a lot of problems when she was young, which really messed her up in later years.*

> **messed-up** ADJ having serious emotional or mental problems ▶ *a messed-up adolescent*

MESS WITH →

1 mess with sth/sb: to get involved with something or someone that may cause problems or be dangerous ▶ *She always told her kids never to mess with drugs.*

2 mess with sb: to annoy or cause trouble for someone, especially someone dangerous ▶ *"If you mess with me, Deacon," he said in a low voice, "I'll rip your head off."*

3 mess with sth: to try to change or improve something that does not look right or is not working well ▶ *I wish you'd stop messing with the TV, I'm trying to watch this programme.*

METE

METE OUT →

mete sth **out, mete out** sth: to give someone a punishment or type of treatment, especially one that is severe or unfair ▶ *Severe penalties are meted out to anyone who dares to oppose the military government.*

MILITATE

MILITATE AGAINST →

militate against sth/sb: to make it difficult or unlikely for something to happen or for someone to be successful ▶ *long working hours that militate against family life*

MILL

MILL AROUND, *also* **MILL ABOUT** →

mill around/about, mill around/about sth: if a lot of people mill around, they all move around within a place or area ▶ *The guests were milling about the courtyard, with glasses of champagne in their hands.*

MIND

MIND OUT →

mind out!: a. used to warn someone that they need to be careful ▶ *Mind out! The handle's very hot!*
b. used to ask someone to move so that you can get past them ▶ *Mind out! I need to get something out of the oven.*

MINISTER

MINISTER TO →

minister to sb/sth: to look after someone who is ill or needs help ▶ *The organization operates about eighty centres ministering to the needs of the homeless.*

MINOR

MINOR IN →

minor in sth: to study a second subject at a college or university that is less important for your degree than your main subject ▶ *Business students often minor in a foreign language.*

MISS

MISS OUT →

1 miss sth/sb **out, miss out** sth/sb: to not include something or someone, especially accidentally ▶ *Read through*

M

the form again to make sure you haven't missed anything out.

2 miss out: to not get the chance to do or have something that you would enjoy or that would be good for you, ▶ *Many women who have spent their lives raising children do feel they've missed out.* **+ on** ▶ *I didn't want to go away at Christmas and miss out on all the fun at home.*

MIST

MIST OVER →

mist over: if your eyes mist over, they fill with tears ▶ *Kathleen felt her eyes misting over as she told her story.*

MIST OVER, *also* MIST UP →

mist over/up, mist sth over/up: if something made of glass mists over or is misted over, it becomes covered with very small drops of water ▶ *Without running the engine running, the inside of the car was beginning to mist up.*

MIX

MIX IN →

1 mix in sth, **mix sth in**: to add one substance to another and combine them ▶ *When the rice is cooked, gently mix in all the other ingredients.*

2 mixed in: combined with something else. **+ with** ▶ *The movie has lots of action and adventure, mixed in with some comedy.*

MIX UP →

1 mix sb/sth **up, mix up** sb/sth: to make the mistake of thinking that someone or something is another person or thing ▶ *The hospital has been accused of mixing up two newborn babies.* **get** sb/sth **mixed up** (=mix up two people or things) ▶ *The interviewer was terrible – he kept getting the names of his guests mixed up.* **+ with** ▶ *"You've got me mixed up with some other guy," Marty said nervously.*

mix-up N a mistake that happens when people understand the details of a situation differently and often wrongly. **+ over** ▶ *I think there's been a bit of a mix-up over who was providing the food.*

2 get mixed up: to become confused about something ▶ *I could see that the old man was getting more and more mixed up.*

    mixed-up ADJ confused, especially because you have emotional problems ▶ *Frankie was a lonely and mixed-up teenager*

3 mix sb **up, mix up** sb: to make someone feel confused ▶ *Coaches can mix up a player during a game by yelling at him.*

4 mix sth **up, mix up** sth: to change the order of a group of things, with the result that they are not arranged in the right order ▶ *I've sorted all my clothes into piles, so please don't mix them up.* **+ with** ▶ *His money and private letters were all mixed up with the newspapers on his desk.*

5 mix sth **up, mix up** sth: to put different substances together and combine them ▶ *Mix the ingredients up into a paste.*

6 be/get mixed up in sth: to be or become involved in something illegal or unpleasant ▶ *He got mixed up in some shady dealing when he first worked for the company.*

7 be/get mixed up with sb: to be or become involved with a person or group that has a bad influence on you ▶ *Mum and Dad were worried that I was getting mixed up with the wrong crowd.*

8 mix it up: a. to argue or fight angrily with someone ▶ *He was arrested on Tuesday after mixing it up with a police officer.*
b. to talk and spend time socially with

M

other people ► *The youngest coach in the league isn't afraid to mix it up with the veterans.*

MIX WITH →

mix it with sb: to get involved in a fight with someone ► *He was sent off for mixing it with the referee.*

MOCK

MOCK UP →

mock sth **up, mock up** sth: to make a simple copy of something that is going to be made, in order to show people what the real thing will be like ► *I showed them a sample I had mocked up of the kind of book they could make.*

   mock-up N a simple copy of something that shows how it will look or how it will work ► *The architect produced a miniature three-dimensional mock-up of the building.*

MODEL

MODEL ON, *also* MODEL UPON →

1 model sth **on/upon** sth: to base a design or structure on something ► *The architecture of the building was modelled on the Doge's Palace in Venice.*

2 model yourself on sb: to copy another person's behaviour, style etc, because you admire them ► *a young boxer who modelled himself on Joe Frazier*

MONKEY

MONKEY ABOUT *see* MONKEY AROUND

MONKEY ABOUT WITH *see* MONKEY AROUND WITH

MONKEY AROUND, *also* MONKEY ABOUT →

monkey around/about: to behave in a silly or annoying way ► *Tell the kids to stop monkeying around and go to sleep.*

MONKEY AROUND WITH, *also*
MONKEY ABOUT WITH →

monkey around/about with sth: to touch or use something that is not yours or change something that does not need to be changed ► *I think all criminals know what to expect if they monkey about with other people's cars.*

MOOCH

MOOCH AROUND, *also* MOOCH ABOUT →

mooch around/about, mooch around/about sth: to spend your time doing very little and often feeling bored or lazy ► *I spent most of the day mooching around the town centre, looking in shop windows.*

MOON

MOON AROUND, *also* MOON ABOUT →

moon around/about, moon around/about sth: to spend your time doing very little, especially because you feel sad or because you are thinking about someone ► *I just mooned about the house all the time my wife was in hospital.*

MOON OVER →

moon over sb: to spend all your time thinking about someone that you are in love with ► *I wish Alice would get on with her life, instead of just mooning over Lester.*

MOP

MOP UP →

1 mop up sth,
mop sth **up,**
mop up: to
remove
liquid
from a
surface,
using a cloth
or something similar ► *A waitress*

rushed forward to mop up the spilt beer.

2 mop up, mop up sth, **mop** sth **up**: to deal with the water, dirt etc that has been caused by a flood ▶ *Britain was mopping up yesterday after one month's rain fell overnight.*

> **mopping up operation** N a mopping up operation involves dealing with the water, dirt etc caused by a flood or a fire ▶ *Mopping-up operations began as the floods receded.*

3 mop up sth, **mop up, mop up**: to easily succeed in getting or winning something, especially when you are competing against others ▶ *John Liley mopped up all the points in the Pilkington Cup semi-final.*

4 mop up sth, **mop** sth **up, mop up**: to deal with a problem so that it no longer exists ▶ *The president's first year in office was mainly spent mopping up after the previous administration.*

MOPE

MOPE AROUND, *also* MOPE ABOUT →

mope around/about, mope around/about sth: to spend your time doing very little, feeling unhappy and thinking about your problems ▶ *Since he left his job, he's done nothing except mope about and complain.*

MORPH

MORPH INTO →

morph into sth: to change into another person or thing by magic or by changing images on a screen ▶ *In the movie, Johnson's character had the power to morph into animals.*

MOULDER

MOULDER AWAY →

1 moulder away: to decay slowly as the result of not being used or needed

▶ *While people in some countries are starving, food supplies all over Europe are mouldering away.*

2 moulder away: to grow old and waste your life because you never do anything new or exciting ▶ *I don't want to moulder away in the same old job for years and years.*

MOUNT

MOUNT UP →

mount up: to increase and become very large ▶ *The costs can quickly mount up when you buy your own home.* ▶ *A lack of qualified engineers is causing long delays to mount up.*

MOUTH

MOUTH OFF →

mouth off: to give your opinion about something in a loud and annoying way ▶ *He's going to get himself in trouble if he keeps mouthing off like that.*
+ about/at ▶ *Nobody likes it when a player mouths off about an opponent.*

MOVE

MOVE AHEAD →

1 move ahead: to make progress with something that you have planned ▶ *Scientists can only move ahead if they get the approval of their colleagues.* **+ with** ▶ *The committee is moving ahead with plans to build a new stadium.*

2 move ahead: if a plan or process moves ahead, it begins to happen or make progress ▶ *The proposals for electoral reform are now moving ahead.*

3 move ahead: to make faster progress than someone or something else. **+ of** ▶ *At that point the Republicans were moving ahead of the Democrats in the polls.*

MOVE ALONG →

1 move along: to develop well and

M

make good progress ▶ *The story moves along so well it's hard to put the book down.*

2 move sth **along, move along** sth: to help something to develop well and make good progress ▶ *The movie is full of lively dialogue that helps to move the action along.* **move things along** (=make something develop or progress more quickly than before) ▶ *We're bringing in some temporary workers to help move things along.*

3 move along, move sb **along**: to move away from a place or ask someone to move away from a place ▶ *A policeman was at the stage door, trying to move the crowd along.* ▶ *Move along, folks, move along there, please.*

MOVE AWAY →

move away: to leave the place where you live and go to live in a different area ▶ *When Anna was nine the family moved away.* **+ from** ▶ *I moved away from home to work in another town a year ago.*

MOVE AWAY FROM →

move away from sth: to stop having a particular idea, method, habit etc and to begin to have a different one ▶ *As our eating habits change, we are moving away from a diet of milk, cream, and cheese.*

MOVE IN →

1 move in: to begin living in a new house or flat ▶ *My parents helped us to buy furniture and carpets when we first moved in.*

2 move in: if one person moves in with another or two people move in together, they decide to live together and share a house or flat. **+ with** ▶ *To save on expenses, Susan moved in with her mother.* **+ together** ▶ *Stephen and I had been seeing each other for a*

year when he suggested that we should move in together.

3 move in: to go towards something or someone, often in order to attack them. **+ on** ▶ *Police moved in on the protesters, but still the crowds increased.*

4 move in: to start to influence or control a situation, often in an unfair way ▶ *At that point the big multinationals moved in and started pushing up the prices.* **+ on** ▶ *I decide to keep my idea a secret, so that other people couldn't move in on it.*

MOVE INTO →

1 move into sth: to begin living in a new house, flat, or area ▶ *Jim was no longer living with his first wife, and had moved into a flat in Chelsea.*

2 move into sth: to start to become involved in a particular area of activity or business ▶ *The former financial boss is now moving into computers.*

3 move into sth: to go somewhere in order to deal with a particular situation ▶ *Volunteer workers moved into the area to set up a water supply.*

4 move into sth: to enter a new period of time ▶ *The ambulance strike was moving into its eighth week.*

MOVE OFF →

move off: to leave a place in order to go somewhere ▶ *They picked up their rucksacks and got ready to move off.* **+ towards/ into** etc ▶ *Kate excused herself and moved off towards the exit.*

MOVE ON →

1 move on: to leave a place after staying there for some time, in order to continue a journey or go somewhere new ▶ *"Every five years I have to move on," Enrico said. "I just can't settle in one town."* **+ to** ▶ *The exhibition then moved on to other cities on the eastern coast.*

M

move on: to stop thinking about something that you have been thinking about for some time, and begin thinking about or doing something new or different ▶ *You have to learn from your mistakes and then move on.* **+ to** ▶ *It's time to leave the theory behind, and move on to the practical side of the subject.*

move on: to leave your job in order to do a new and better one ▶ *I've been doing this job for five years now, so I think it's time to move on.*

move on: to become more modern or more advanced ▶ *Has the legal profession moved on from those days? Perhaps not a great deal.*

move sb on, move on sb: if the police or someone in authority moves you on, they order you to leave a particular place ▶ *It's no good just moving homeless people on – where are they supposed to go?*

MOVE OUT →

move out: to stop living in a particular house, flat, or area ▶ *We moved out about seven years ago.* **+ of** ▶ *He moved out of London to the countryside, in order to concentrate on his writing.*

move out: to leave ▶ *Okay, kids, we've got to move out by 3:00 sharp.*

move out: if a vehicle moves out, it moves away from the side of the road in order to pass the traffic or pass another vehicle ▶ *Always look in the mirror before moving out.* **+ into** ▶ *I*

watched him move out into the traffic heading back towards Boston.

4 move sb **out, move out** sb: to arrange for someone to leave or make them leave ▶ *As the crisis continued, British diplomats were being moved out of the area.*

MOVE OUT OF →

move out of sth: to stop being involved in a particular business, especially in order to become involved in a different one ▶ *A lot of farmers are moving out of dairying, and growing crops instead.*

MOVE OVER →

1 move over: used to ask someone to change their position or seat so that there is space for you ▶ *He walked round to the driver's side. "Move over," he said, "I'll drive."*

2 move over: to start a new job after leaving one of a similar type or level. **+ to** ▶ *She's now moving over to the international sales side of the business.*

3 move over: to leave your job so that someone else can have it ▶ *My career is very important to me and I don't intend to move over for anyone.*

4 move over: to start using a different system or method. **+ to** ▶ *Most companies have moved over to computer-aided design systems.*

MOVE TOWARDS →

move towards sth: to make it more likely that you will do or achieve something ▶ *Europe is moving steadily towards political and monetary union.*

MOVE UP →

1 move up: used to ask someone to move so that there is more space for someone else ▶ *Could you move up a bit – there's just room for Alec if you do.*

2 move up: to get a better job or position, or go to a higher class or

M

level. **+ into/to** ▸ *Many of the workers were able to move up into better paid and more skilled jobs.* ▸ *By 1995, James too had moved up to the senior school.* **move up the ladder** (=get a better job or position in society) ▸ *If I want to move up the ladder, I'll have to get a job somewhere else.*

3 move sb **up, move up** sb: to give someone a better job or position or move them to a higher class or level. **+ into/to** ▸ *Soon after that, Matilda was moved up into the top class.*

MOW

MOW DOWN →

1 mow down sb/sth, **mow** sb/sth **down**: to kill someone by firing a lot of bullets at them ▸ *The men were mown down as soon as they emerged from their trenches.*

2 mow sb **down, mow down** sb: to kill or seriously injure someone by driving into them in a vehicle ▸ *The elderly couple were mown down yards from their home.*

MUCK

MUCK ABOUT, *also* MUCK AROUND →

1 muck about/around: to behave in a silly way when you should be behaving sensibly ▸ *Stop mucking about, Ben, and come and sit here!*

2 muck about/around: to have fun by doing whatever you want to do, rather than doing anything organized ▸ *We spent most of our time mucking around on the beach.*

MUCK ABOUT WITH, *also* MUCK AROUND WITH →

muck about/around with sth: to touch something that is not yours, or to change something that does not need to be changed ▸ *I wish you wouldn't muck about with the things in my room.* ▸ *They're always*

mucking about with the bus timetables!

MUCK IN →

muck in: to share whatever work needs doing in order to help get it done ▸ *The members of a family should share the domestic duties and muck in together.*

MUCK OUT →

muck out, muck out sth, **muck** sth **out**: to clean the place where a horse or a farm animal lives ▸ *We weren't allowed to go home till we'd mucked out the stables.*

MUCK UP →

1 muck up sth, **muck** sth **up**: to spoil something ▸ *Mark not turning up really mucked up our plans.*

2 muck up sth, **muck** sth **up**: to do something very badly ▸ *Lisa aimed the gun carefully, anxious not to muck up her second shot.*

3 muck up sth, **muck** sth **up**: to make something dirty or untidy ▸ *Take those boots off or you'll muck up my clean floor.*

MUDDLE

MUDDLE ALONG, *also* MUDDLE ON →

muddle along/on: to live, work, or do something in a confused and not very successful way ▸ *Students are often left to muddle along on their own.*

MUDDLE THROUGH →

muddle through, muddle through sth: to succeed in doing or dealing with something, but often in a disorganized or confused way ▸ *Most people don't really know how to manage their money properly, and just muddle through.*

MUDDLE UP →

1 muddle up sth/sb, **muddle** sth/sb **up**: to make the mistake of thinking that something or someone is another

M

thing or person ▶ *Is his girlfriend Joanne or Joanna? I keep muddling them up.* **get** sth/sb **muddled up** ▶ *It's easy to get the twins muddled up.* **get muddled up** ▶ *Sorry, I got a bit muddled up over the dates.*

muddle sth **up, muddle up** sth: to put something in the wrong order or to spoil the order that things are in ▶ *If you had a proper filing system, you wouldn't get all your papers muddled up.*

MUFFLE
MUFFLE UP →
muffle sb **up, muffle up** sb: to dress yourself in a lot of thick clothes in order to keep warm ▶ *Everyone was muffled up in coats and hats and gloves.*

MUG
MUG UP →
mug up sth, **mug** sth **up**: to try to learn as much as you can about a subject in a short time. **+ about** ▶ *Bob wants to mug up about Greece before we go there.* **+ on** ▶ *I'll have to mug up on my history notes before tomorrow's test.*

MULL
MULL OVER →
mull over sth, **mull** sth **over**: to think about something carefully and for a long time. **mull it over** ▶ *You don't have to make a decision now – take a few days to mull it over.*

MUSCLE
MUSCLE IN →
muscle in, muscle into sth: to use your power or influence to get involved in something that people do not want you involved in ▶ *They are worried that the big banks will muscle in and start taking away their business.* **muscle in on** sth ▶ *He accused them of muscling in on his territory.*

MUSCLE OUT →
muscle out sb, **muscle** sb **out**: to use your power and influence to force someone to leave a job or an area of business ▶ *Big banks can afford to cut fees to muscle out their competitors.*

MUSS
MUSS UP →
muss up sth, **muss** sth **up**: to make something untidy, especially hair or clothing ▶ *She smiled sweetly, mussing up his hair as she knelt beside him.*

MUSTER
MUSTER UP →
muster up sth, **muster** sth **up**: to find enough strength, courage, enthusiasm etc to do something, especially something difficult ▶ *I don't think I can muster up the energy even to go out for a walk today.*

N

Nn

NAIL

NAIL DOWN →

1 nail down sth/sb, **nail** sth/sb **down**: to make something definite, especially by getting other people to agree about the details ▶ *So far, we have been unable to nail down a date for the talks.* **nail** sb **down to** sth (=make someone give you a definite decision or statement) ▶ *Before they start the work, nail them down to a price.*

2 nail down sth, **nail** sth **down**: to understand or describe something correctly or exactly ▶ *It's taken me a long time to nail down the cause of the problem.*

NAIL UP →

nail up sth, **nail** sth **up**: to fasten a door, window etc with nails, in order to prevent it from being opened ▶ *The door of the shed had been nailed up.*

NAME

NAME AFTER, *also* NAME FOR →

name sb/sth **after** sb/sth, **name** sb/sth **for** sb/sth: to give someone or something the same name as another person, thing, or place ▶ *My daughter was named after her grandmother.* ▶ *The street is named for Nelson Mandela.*

NARROW

NARROW DOWN →

narrow down sth, **narrow** sth **down**: to reduce the number of things you can consider or choose from, by getting rid of those that are not suitable ▶ *There aren't many cars within your price range, so that narrows down your choice considerably.* **+ to** ▶ *Police*

have narrowed the list of suspects down to one.

NIBBLE

NIBBLE AT →

nibble at sth: to eat something taking very small bites ▶ *Emma nibbled at a piece of toast in thoughtful silence.*

NIBBLE AWAY AT →

nibble away at sth: to gradually reduce a large amount by taking smaller amounts from it ▶ *All these expenses are nibbling away at our savings.*

NOD

NOD OFF →

nod off: to begin to sleep when you do not intend to ▶ *Old Tom had nodded off in front of the television.* ▶ *I missed the end of her lecture – I think I must have nodded off.*

NOSE

NOSE AROUND, *also* NOSE ABOUT →

nose around/about, nose around/about sth: to look around a place trying to find out things about people in a way that annoys them ▶ *I found him nosing about in my office, looking at the papers on my desk.* ▶ *We don't want the police nosing around the place.*

NOSE OUT →

nose out sth, **nose** sth **out**: to discover information that someone else does not want you to discover ▶ *It didn't take him long to nose out where the money was hidden.*

NOTCH

NOTCH UP →

notch up sth, **notch** sth **up**: to achieve something such as a win in a game or a number of years in a job ► *The Astros have notched up another amazing victory.* ► *She's notched up 15 years as the principal of the college.*

NOTE

NOTE DOWN →

note down sth, **note** sth **down**: to quickly write down information ► *Note down the dates and times of your exams.* ► *I checked all the phone numbers and noted them down in my diary.*

NUMBER

NUMBER AMONG →

number sb/sth **among** sth, **number among**: to include someone or something among a particular group, or to be included in such a group ► *He numbers among the best of our young writers.* ► *a beautiful woman who numbered Zola among her admirers*

NUZZLE

NUZZLE UP AGAINST, *also* NUZZLE UP TO →

nuzzle up against/to sb: to gently press your nose or head against someone in a way that shows you like them ► *David's dog came and nuzzled up against me.*

Oo

OBJECT

OBJECT TO →

1 object to sth/sb: to dislike and disapprove of something or someone ▶ *Most of the students strongly object to the new rules.* **object to** sb **doing** sth ▶ *I don't object to people smoking in the privacy of their own homes.*

2 object to sth: to say formally and officially that you oppose something or disapprove of it ▶ *Opposition politicians immediately objected to the proposals.*

OCCUR

OCCUR TO →

occur to sb: if an idea or a thought occurs to you, it comes into your mind ▶ *It all seemed so simple – she wondered why the idea hadn't occurred to her before.* **+ that** ▶ *It suddenly occurred to him that maybe his daughter was lying.* **occur to** sb **to do** sth ▶ *I suppose it never occurred to you to phone the police?*

OFFEND

OFFEND AGAINST →

offend against sth: to do something that is wrong according to an accepted rule or principle ▶ *behaviour that offends against standards of common decency*

OFFER

OFFER UP →

1 offer up a prayer/sacrifice etc: to pray to or give something to a god ▶ *Thomas knelt and offered up a silent prayer of thanksgiving.*

2 offer up sth, **offer** sth **up:** to show or suggest something to someone for them to consider, judge, or enjoy ▶ *an occasion when young artists offer up their work for the critics to review*

OPEN

OPEN INTO →

open into sth: to lead directly to another place ▶ *The hallway opened into a large well-lit room.* ▶ *At the bottom of the stairs was a door opening into the cellar.*

OPEN OFF →

open off sth: if a room or area opens off another room or area, you can enter one directly from the other ▶ *The breakfast room opened off the kitchen.*

OPEN ONTO, also OPEN ON TO →

open onto sth: if a room, door, or window opens onto a place, you can enter or look out at that place directly from it ▶ *The windows of our flat opened onto the market square.*

OPEN OUT →

1 open out: if a road, path, valley etc opens out, it becomes wider or reaches a wide space ▶ *Beyond Villeneuve the valley begins to open out.* **+ into** ▶ *The drive opened out into a large paved courtyard.*

2 open out: if a room opens out onto another place, the two areas are connected by doors or windows. **+ onto** ▶ *The hotel lounge opens out onto a wide, covered terrace.*

3 open out sth, **open** sth **out:** to unfold something and spread it into a wide shape ▶ *Opening out the map, he traced the line of the river with his finger.*

open out: if something that is folded or closed opens out, it can be unfolded and spread into a wide shape ► *The film was speeded up so that you could see the flowers opening out in a few seconds.*

open out sth, open out: to begin to include a wider variety of things in a discussion, book, programme etc ► *I think we should open out the discussion a bit and think more about general policies.*

OPEN UP →

open up, open up sth, open sth up: if a new shop, business etc opens up or is opened up, someone starts it ► *Expensive restaurants and night clubs were opening up all over the city.*

open up, open up sth, open sth up: if opportunities open up, or a new situation opens them up, they become available or possible ► *A whole new life was opening up before her.* ► *A move to New York would open up all kinds of exciting possibilities.*

open up sth, open sth up, open up: to make it easier for people to travel to a country or area or to do business there ► *They saw the new railroad as a means of opening up the far west of Canada.* **+ to** ► *The country has only recently opened up to Western tourists.*

open up sth, open sth up: to open something that is closed, locked, or covered ► *He opened up his briefcase and took out a photograph.*

open up sth, open sth up: to unfold something and spread it into a wide shape ► *I opened up the map to try to find Milwaukee Avenue.*

open up sth, open sth up: to open the door of a building so that people can enter ► *Open up! This is the police!* ► *The janitor was the only person authorized to lock and open up the building.*

7 open up sth, open sth up: to start a discussion or argument about a subject ► *Recent events have opened up a public debate about the future of the Royal Family.*

8 open up: to start shooting, especially with a large gun ► *As our troops moved forward, the enemy opened up with machine guns.*

9 open up: to stop being shy and say what you really think ► *Once she knew she could trust me, Melissa started to open up.*

10 open up a lead/gap: to increase the number of points or the distance by which you are winning ► *Minutes later the Australians scored again and opened up a 12 point lead.*

11 open up, open up sth, open sth up: if a hole, crack etc opens up, or if something opens it up, it appears and becomes wider ► *An earthquake struck the city and a 20 metre-deep crack opened up in the main square.*

12 open sb/sth up, open sb/sth up: to do a medical operation on a person or animal's body, by cutting it open ► *The doctors said they'll have to open him up and remove the damaged tissue.*

OPPOSE

BE OPPOSED TO →

1 be opposed to sth: to disagree with something and try to stop it happening ► *Many Americans were opposed to the war in Vietnam.*

2 be opposed to sth: if two ideas or opinions are opposed to each other, they are completely different from each other ► *The principles of capitalism and environmentalism are directly opposed to each other.*

OPT

OPT FOR →

opt for sth: to choose one thing or action instead of another ► *an* *engineering graduate who finally opted for a career in teaching.*

OPT IN, *also* OPT INTO →

opt in, opt into sth: to decide to join a group or take part in a system ▶ *a referendum on whether to opt into the single European currency*

OPT OUT →

1 opt out: to decide not to join a group or take part in a system ▶ *The company has a pension plan, but employees are given the right to opt out.*

2 opt out: to avoid doing a job or accepting a duty. **+ of** ▶ *You can't simply opt out of all responsibility for the child.*

ORDER

ORDER AROUND, *also* ORDER ABOUT →

order sb **around/about**: to keep telling someone what to do in an annoying way ▶ *You've no right to order the children around like that.*

ORDER IN →

1 order in sth, **order** sth **in**: to order food that is ready to eat to be delivered to your home or office ▶ *Gloria ordered in sandwiches from the deli.*

2 order sb **in, order in** sb: to order soldiers or police to go into a place to deal with trouble ▶ *Special police units were ordered in from outside the city.*

ORDER OUT →

order out: to order food that is ready to eat to be delivered to your home or office ▶ *Let's order out tonight.* **+ for** ▶ *We ordered out for pizza and bought a bottle of Chianti.*

OWN

OWN TO →

own to sth: to admit that something is true even though you are ashamed of it ▶ *I'll own to being a coward, but I am not a traitor.*

OWN UP →

own up: to admit that you have done something wrong, especially something that is not serious ▶ *Unless the guilty person owns up, the whole class will be punished.* **own up to (doing)** sth ▶ *No one ever owned up to breaking the window.*

Pp

PACK

PACK AWAY →

pack sth **away**, **pack away** sth: to put something back in its box, case etc after you have finished using it ▶ *It's time to take down the Christmas decorations and pack them away.*

pack away sth, **pack** sth **away**: to eat a large amount of food ▶ *Billy can really pack it away.*

PACK IN →

pack in sth, **pack** sth **in**: to stop doing something, especially a job that you find unpleasant or annoying ▶ *He packed in his job and went travelling in Australia.* **pack it (all) in** ▶ *At times I feel like packing it all in.*

pack it in!: used to tell someone to stop doing something that is annoying you ▶ *"Susan just punched me!" "Well pack it in, both of you!"*

pack sb **in**: to tell a boyfriend or girlfriend that you want to end the relationship ▶ *He's always letting her down – I think she should pack him in.*

pack sth **in**, **pack in** sth: to do a lot of different things or visit a lot of different places in a short period of time ▶ *You can pack in a lot of sightseeing in seven days if you try.*

pack sb **in**, **pack in** sb: if a film, play etc packs people in, large numbers of people come to watch it ▶ *The latest blockbuster has packed in audiences across the country.*

PACK INTO →

pack sth **into** sth: to do a lot of different things or visit a lot of different places in a short period of time ▶ *We managed to pack a lot into our two days in Paris.*

PACK OFF →

pack off sb, **pack** sb **off**: to send someone to a place without asking them if they want to go ▶ *As soon as the children were old enough, they were packed off to boarding school.*

BE PACKED OUT →

be packed out: to be very crowded ▶ *Most of the bars in Soho are packed out on a Friday night.* **+ with** ▶ *Stratford is packed out with tourists in the summer.*

PACK UP →

1 pack up, **pack up** sth, **pack** sth **up**: to put your things into bags, boxes etc, so that you can move them to another place ▶ *She packed up her few belongings and left.*

2 pack up: to finish working or finish what you are doing at the end of a day ▶ *I think it's about time we packed up and went home.*

3 pack up: if a machine packs up it stops working ▶ *The washing machine's packed up again!*

PAD

PAD OUT →

pad out sth, **pad** sth **out**: to make a piece of writing, speech or story longer by adding unnecessary words ▶ *Concentrate on the important points – don't pad your essay out with waffle.*

PAGE

PAGE DOWN →

page down: to press a button on your computer so that you can see the next page of writing ▶ *Page down after you've finished each block of text.*

PAGE THROUGH →

page through sth: to turn the pages of a book, magazine etc, but not read it carefully ▶ *Kathy paged through an old magazine while she was waiting.*

PAGE UP →

page up: to press a button on your computer so that you can see the previous page of writing ▶ *Can you page up, please? I'd like to look at the introduction.*

PAINT

PAINT IN →

paint in sth, **paint** sth **in**: to fill a space in a picture or add more details to it, using paint ▶ *The figures on the side were painted in at a later date.*

PAINT OUT →

paint out sth, **paint** sth **out**: to hide something that has been drawn or painted by covering it with paint ▶ *Volunteers spent two hours picking up litter and painting out graffiti.*

PAIR

PAIR OFF →

1 pair off: if two people in a group pair off, they start to have a romantic or sexual relationship with each other ▶ *Everyone else at the party had paired off, and I was left on my own.*

2 pair sb **off**: to try to get two people to start a romantic relationship with each other. **+ with** ▶ *My mother's always trying to pair me off with "nice" young men.*

3 pair off, **pair off** sb, **pair** sb **off**: if people in a group pair off or you pair them off, each person gets together with one other person to do a particular job or activity ▶ *Could you all pair off and have a go at exercise 5?*

PAIR UP →

1 pair up: to get together with another person to do something ▶ *Johnson*

and *Valenzuela paired up to write 'Memphis Time'.*

2 pair sb **up**, **pair up** sb: if you pair people up in a group, you make them do something together in groups of two. **+ with** ▶ *The teacher pairs up students who are doing well in her class with those who are having trouble.*

PAL

PAL AROUND →

pal around: to go to places and do things with someone as a friend ▶ *They palled around New York while making their latest movie.* **+ with** ▶ *We can pal around with my brother when he's not at work.*

PAL UP →

pal up: to become friends with someone for a short time ▶ *She quickly palled up with some other girls she met in the hotel.*

PALM

PALM OFF →

palm sb **off**, **palm off** sb: to give someone an explanation or excuse that is not true. **+ with** ▶ *Her husband tried to palm her off with excuses about working late.*

PALM OFF ON →

palm sth **off on** sb, **palm off** sth **on** sb: to get rid of something by giving or selling it to someone else, without telling them about its faults ▶ *I've managed to palm that early morning class off on Mary – she's desperate for work.*

PALM OFF AS →

palm sth **off as** sth, **palm off** sth **as** sth: to make people believe that something is better or more valuable that it really is, especially so that they will pay more for it ▶ *Some jewellers may try to palm off worthless bits of glass as diamonds.*

PAN

PAN OUT →
pan out: to happen or develop in a successful way ▶ *If this trip doesn't pan out, I might go to Thailand instead.*

pan out: the way something pans out is the way it develops or the way in which it happens ▶ *Let's see how the first round of talks pans out before we start thinking further ahead.*

PANDER

PANDER TO →
pander to sb/sth: to do or provide what someone else wants in order to get an advantage for yourself ▶ *Even the quality newspapers pander to people's interest in the private lives of soap stars.*

PAPER

PAPER OVER →
paper over sth: to try to hide the fact that there is a problem because you do not want people to know about it ▶ *The two parties tried to paper over their differences and form a government together.*

PARCEL

PARCEL OUT →
parcel out sth, **parcel** sth **out**: to divide or share something among several people ▶ *Much of the best land in the country was parcelled out among rich landowners.*

PARCEL

UP →
parcel up sth, **parcel** sth **up**: to wrap something with paper, string etc so that you can send it somewhere ▶ *She asked for*

the books to be parcelled up and sent to her.

PARE

PARE BACK →
pare back sth, **pare** sth **back**: to reduce something, especially in order to save money ▶ *In many universities, arts courses have been pared back.*

PARE DOWN →
pare down sth, **pare** sth **down**: to reduce the size of something, by getting rid of what you do not need ▶ *It is likely the company will continue to pare down its workforce over the next few years.*

PART

BE PARTED FROM →
be parted from sb/sth: to be separated from someone or something ▶ *My parents were hardly ever parted from each other in thirty years of marriage.* ▶ *She refused to be parted from her favourite doll, even for a minute.*

PART WITH →
part with sth/sb: to give or sell something to someone else, when you do not really want to ▶ *She took the gun from Jack, who parted with it reluctantly.*

PARTAKE

PARTAKE IN →
partake in sth: to take part in an activity or event ▶ *At least 200 kids were there, ready to partake in the annual Giants baseball camp.*

PARTAKE OF →
1 partake of sth: to eat or drink something, especially something that is offered to you ▶ *There are several excellent restaurants nearby, where you can partake of a selection of local delicacies.*

2 partake of sth: to take part in an

activity or event ▶ *Organized children's activities will keep the kids happy while you partake of exercise classes.*

PARTITION

PARTITION OFF →

partition off sth, **partition** sth **off**: to separate one area from another area using a thin wall, glass, furniture etc ▶ *The foreman's office was partitioned off from the rest of the factory floor.*

PARTNER

PARTNER UP, *also* PARTNER OFF →

partner up/off, partner sb **up/off**: to join with someone in order to do something together, or to make someone do this ▶ *Sam and I partnered up for our club's tennis tournament.* **+ with** ▶ *Joey partnered off with Dana, and we began the game.*

PASS

PASS AROUND, *also* PASS ROUND →

1 pass around/round sth, **pass** sth **around/round**: to give something to one person in a group for them to give to the next person, until everyone has had it ▶ *Write your name on this list then pass it round.*

2 pass sth **around/round, pass around/round** sth: to offer something to each person in a group ▶ *Carla brought some cakes in and passed them around.*

PASS AS →

1 pass as sb: to make other people think that you are someone that you are not. **sb could pass as** sb ▶ *With my hair cut short I could have passed as a boy.*

2 pass as sth: if one thing passes as another, it is called or considered to be the second thing even though it is not ▶ *chocolate-covered cereal bars*

that pass as healthy snacks. **what passes as** (=what is called or considered) ▶ *The houses had no bathrooms, and what passed as running water came through garden hoses.*

PASS AWAY →

1 pass away: to die ▶ *He had been ill for some time, and passed away peacefully on 12 April.*

2 pass away: to slowly disappear or stop existing ▶ *We pray that this threat of war may quickly pass away.*

3 pass away: when a period of time passes away, it finishes ▶ *Day after day passed away, but still we heard nothing from Kendall.*

4 pass away sth, **pass** sth **away**: if you pass a period of time away, you spend time doing something so that you are not bored ▶ *The old men sit outside cafes, and play cards to pass the time away.*

PASS BETWEEN →

1 pass between sb: if a look passes between two people, they look at each other quickly in a way that shows they are thinking the same thing ▶ *A look of disgust passed between Jim and his wife.* ▶ *He saw a quick glance pass between Joanna and Helen, and wondered if they knew his secret.*

2 pass between sb: if something passes between people, they talk to each other ▶ *Hardly a word passed between them for the rest of the journey.*

PASS BY →

1 pass by, pass by sb/sth: to go past someone or something without stopping ▶ *The express train passed by with a deafening noise.* ▶ *Our dog barks at anyone who passes by the house.*

passer-by N someone who is walking past when something such as a crime or accident happens ▶ *The fire was reported by a passer-by who saw flames coming from the building.*

2 pass sb by: if an event passes you by, it happens without your noticing it much or being affected by it ▶ *My mother lived in a remote village, and all the excitement of the 1960s passed her by.*

3 pass sb by: if an opportunity passes you by, you do not take it when it is available. **let a chance pass you by** also **let an opportunity pass you by** ▶ *He'll never forgive himself for letting the opportunity of a lifetime pass him by.* **life passes you by** also **the world passes you by** (=you fail to get any advantage from the opportunities that life offers) ▶ *Life can easily pass you by if you don't reach out and grab it.*

4 pass by, pass by sth: to go near a place on the way to another place, especially by chance ▶ *Come in and see us if you happen to be passing by.*

PASS DOWN →

pass down sth, **pass** sth **down**: to give or teach something to people who are younger than you or live after you ▶ *traditions which have been passed down through the generations.* **+ to** ▶ *She passed down to her children and grandchildren a love of reading.*

PASS FOR →

1 could pass for sb: to make other people think you are a type of person that you are not. sb **could pass as** sb ▶ *The Mitchell brothers could easily pass for twins.*

2 pass for sth: if one thing passes for another, it is called or considered the second thing even though it is not ▶ *some of the rubbish that passes for music in the pop charts these days*

PASS OFF →

pass off peacefully / well: if an event passes off peacefully or well, it is peaceful or a success ▶ *Today's demonstration passed off peacefully, as 50,000 people gathered in Hyde Park.*

PASS OFF AS →

1 pass sth **off as** sth: to make people believe that something is better or more valuable then it really is ▶ *The forger painted in various styles and passed them off as originals.*

2 pass yourself off as sb: to make people think that you are someone that you are not ▶ *He survived the war by passing himself off as a loyalist soldier.*

3 pass off sth, **pass** sth **off**: to ignore something or pretend it is not very serious, because you do not want it to hurt you. **+ as** ▶ *Laughing lightly, Claire passed the remark off as a joke.* ▶ *He passed off his boss's comments as insignificant, but inside he was furious.*

PASS ON →

1 pass sth **on, pass on** sth: to tell someone something that someone else has told you ▶ *If I get any news, I'll pass it on.* **+ to** ▶ *He had been passing secrets on to enemy states while working at the Pentagon.*

2 pass sth **on, pass on** sth: to give something, especially a disease or special quality, to your children, so that they are born with it. **+ to** ▶ *Older mothers have a higher risk of passing genetic disorders on to their children.* ▶ *He seems to have passed on his footballing ability to his son.*

3 pass sth **on, pass on** sth: to give something such as property to someone younger than you after your death. **+ to** ▶ *Paul bought the farm hoping that one day he could pass it on to his son.*

4 pass on sth, **pass** sth **on**: to teach a

P

skill, knowledge, tradition etc to someone younger than you ▶ *The old stories were passed on throughout the generations.*

5 pass sth **on, pass on** sth: to give an illness or disease to someone else ▶ *The virus cannot be passed on to another person through normal social contact.*

6 pass on: to die ▶ *Marty passed on before his grandchildren were born.*

7 pass sth **on, pass on** sth: to give something to someone else, after you have had it or finished with it ▶ *Take some sandwiches and pass the rest on.*

PASS ON TO →

1 pass sth **on to** sb, **pass on** sth **to** sb: to make your prices higher or lower according to how much they cost you ▶ *Supermarkets usually pass on the high cost of transporting goods to their customers.*

2 pass sb **on to** sb, **pass on** sb **to** sb: to suggest to someone that they should speak to another person, because you think that person will be able to help them ▶ *I'll pass you on to our customer services department.*

3 pass on to sth: to start talking about a new subject ▶ *We haven't got much time, so let's pass on to item two on the agenda.*

PASS OUT →

1 pass out:
to become unconscious ▶ *Kevin drank so much vodka that he passed out on the stairs.*

2 pass out sth, **pass** sth **out**: to give something to each person in a group

▶ *Jose put on a Santa hat and passed out presents to the children.*

PASS OVER →

1 pass over sth: to deliberately not discuss a particular subject or deal with a particular problem ▶ *Many school textbooks pass over upsetting details about the war.* ▶ *Less serious crimes are passed over, as police concentrate on major drugs dealers.*

2 pass sb **over, pass over** sb: to not consider someone for a job and give it to someone else, especially unfairly ▶ *She claims that she was passed over in favour of a man who was less experienced.*

PASS ROUND *see* PASS AROUND

PASS TO →

pass to sb: if something passes to you, you become the owner of it or responsible for it ▶ *If you die without making a will, your property will usually pass to your spouse and children.*

PASS UP →

pass up sth, **pass** sth **up**: to not take an opportunity when it becomes available ▶ *They're offering me a fantastic salary, so I'd be crazy to pass it up.* **pass up a chance (to do** sth) *also* **pass up an opportunity (to do** sth)* ▶ *William couldn't pass up the opportunity to work in Hollywood.*

PAT

PAT DOWN →

pat sb **down, pat down** sb: to search someone, especially in order to check if they are carrying a dangerous weapon, illegal drugs etc ▶ *A security guard was patting him down at the airport when he found a pack of cocaine.*

PATCH

PATCH TOGETHER →

patch together sth, **patch** sth

together: to make or arrange something quickly and carelessly from several different parts or ideas ▶ *A new plan was quickly patched together.*

PATCH UP →

1 patch up sth, **patch** sth **up**: to stop arguing with someone and agree to be friendly with them again ▶ *Mindy wanted to patch up her marriage after a year of separation.* **patch things up** ▶ *They seem very happy now they've patched things up.* **patch up your differences** ▶ *Aragon agreed to meet with Campbell to try to patch up their differences.*

2 patch up sth, **patch** sth **up**: to repair something by adding a piece of material to it ▶ *We can patch these curtains up and make them look almost new.*

3 patch up sth, **patch** sth **up**: to give quick and basic medical treatment to someone who is hurt ▶ *Liam fell and hurt his knee, and was sent to the school nurse to patch it up.*

PAVE

PAVE OVER →

pave over sth: to cover a path, road etc with a hard level surface ▶ *Two years ago this area was paved over to make an extra airport runway.*

PAW

PAW AT →

paw at sth: if an animal paws at something, it touches or rubs it again and again with its paws ▶ *Buster kept pawing at my legs and trying to jump up on my lap.*

PAY

PAY BACK →

1 pay sb/sth **back, pay back** sb/sth, **pay** sb **back** sth: to give someone the money that you owe them ▶ *I have ten*

years to pay back my student loans. ▶ *Did I pay you back that £5?*

2 pay sb **back**: to do something unpleasant to someone because they have done something unpleasant to you. **+ for** ▶ *She vowed to find her daughter's killer and pay him back for what he did.*

PAY FOR →

pay for sth: to suffer or be punished for something you have done ▶ *We must make criminals pay for their crimes.*

PAY IN, *also* PAY INTO →

pay sth **in, pay in** sth, **pay** sth **into** sth: to put money in your bank account or a savings plan ▶ *Did you remember to pay that cheque in?* ▶ *I paid £250 into my savings account.*

PAY OFF →

1 pay off sth, **pay** sth **off**: to pay all the money you owe someone ▶ *He is working overtime to pay off his debts.* ▶ *Two years after the accident, the Thompsons have finally paid off their son's hospital bills.*

2 pay off: if something that you do pays off, it is successful or worth doing ▶ *The band's hard work finally paid off when their single shot to number one.* ▶ *They took a hell of a risk, but it really paid off in the end.*

    payoff N an advantage or good result you get from something you do ▶ *Expensive, long-term projects need to have an adequate pay-off.*

3 pay sb **off, pay off** sb: to give someone money so they will not tell other people about something ▶ *City leaders have been accused of paying off people who want to file complaints.*

    payoff N a payment that you make to someone secretly or illegally in order to stop them from causing you any trouble ▶ *Our main witness is* refusing to talk – the gang must have threatened her, or given her a payoff.

4 pay sb off, pay off sb: to stop employing a worker after paying them the wages that you owe them ▶ *Although the engineering firm paid off 90 workers, 700 other jobs have been saved.*

payoff N a payment that you make to someone when you make them leave their job ▶ *He received an incredible £15 million payoff after he was forced to resign.*

PAY OUT →

1 pay out sth, pay sth out: to pay money to someone because they are owed it, or have earned it, or won it ▶ *£6 million of prize money is paid out every week.* ▶ *I'm still waiting for the insurance company to pay out.*

payout N a sum of money paid to someone because they are owed it, or have earned it, or won it ▶ *They won a £500,000 payout from the hospital where their son died.*

2 pay out, pay out sth: to spend a lot of money on something, especially when you do not want to ▶ *I'm sick of paying out all this money on rent.* ▶ *Why pay out £300 for a dress, when you're never going to wear it again?*

PAY OVER →

pay over sth, pay sth over: to make an official payment of money to someone. **+ to** ▶ *Clancy's share of the inheritance was paid over to him.*

PAY UP →

pay up: to pay money that you owe, especially when you do not want to ▶ *My credit card's been stolen – will I have to pay up if someone*

uses it? ▶ *You've lost the case, so now you'll just have to pay up.*

paid-up ADJ a paid-up member is someone who has paid the money necessary to join a club, political party etc ▶ *a paid-up member of the Labour Party*

PEAL

PEAL OUT →

peal out: to make a loud sound which can be heard a long way away – use this about bells ringing ▶ *The bells pealed out all over the Palace of Westminster.*

PECK

PECK AT →

1 peck at sth: if a bird pecks at something, it tries to eat it with its beak ▶ *Two geese were pecking at some grain in the farmyard.*

2 peck at sth: to eat only a small part of your meal, because you are not very hungry ▶ *She pecked at her food for a few minutes and then pushed her plate away.*

PEEL

PEEL OFF →

1 peel off sth, peel sth off: to take off clothes, especially when they are wet or tight ▶ *She peeled off her wet clothes, and jumped into a hot shower.*

2 peel off, peel off sth: to come away from a surface in small pieces ▶ *Paint was peeling off the faded white walls.*

3 peel off sth, peel off sth: to remove the outside layer or something flat from the surface of something ▶ *He peeled off the label to reveal another address underneath.*

4 peel off sth, peel sth off: to take some money from a thick pile of paper money that you are holding ▶ *The man peeled off two bank notes from the*

...oll in his pocket.

PEG

PEG AWAY →

peg away: to work hard for a long time at something difficult. **+ at** ▶ *The South African team kept pegging away at Australia, and managed to get them all out for 230 runs.*

PEG OUT →

1 peg out sth, peg sth out: to fasten clothes or sheets to a line outside, so that they can dry ▶ *Can you help me peg these sheets out?*

2 peg out sth, peg sth out: to fasten something to the ground using small metal or wooden sticks ▶ *Place the tent on the ground and peg out the four corners.*

3 peg out sth: to die – used especially humorously ▶ *I thought I was going to peg out in the heat.*

PELT

PELT DOWN →

it's pelting down: used to say that it is raining very heavily ▶ *It's been pelting down all morning.*

PEN

PEN IN →

1 feel penned in: to feel that you are too limited by the situation that you are in ▶ *Anna was fed up with her life in England. She felt bored and penned in.*

2 pen in sth/sb, pen sth/sb in: to shut animals or people in an enclosed area so that they cannot escape ▶ *The sheep were penned in for the night.*

PEN UP →

pen up sth/sb, pen sb/sth up: to shut animals or people in an enclosed area so that they cannot escape ▶ *He kept his victims penned up in his garage.*

PENCIL

PENCIL IN →

pencil sb/sth in, pencil in sb/sth: to make an arrangement that is not definite and which may be changed later ▶ *He has a meeting pencilled in with the Prime Minister in May.* **+ for** ▶ *I'll pencil you in for next Tuesday morning at 10 o'clock.*

PENSION

PENSION OFF →

pension sb off, pension off sb: to arrange for someone to stop working and receive money from your company, because they are old, ill, or no longer needed ▶ *The Defence Ministry pensioned off 750 officers including 10 generals.*

PEP

PEP UP →

1 pep up sth, pep sth up: to make something more exciting, interesting, or effective ▶ *Adding a little chilli powder helps pep up the flavour.* ▶ *TV scriptwriters have tried to pep up the series by introducing some new characters.*

2 pep up sb, pep sb up: to give someone more energy and make them feel less tired ▶ *Some aromatherapy oils help you relax, and others pep you up.*

PEPPER

PEPPER WITH →

1 pepper sth with sth: to include a lot of a particular type of words or phrases in a book, speech etc ▶ *The script is peppered with four-letter words and slang.* **pepper sth with sth** (=use a lot of a particular type of language in a book, speech etc) ▶ *He peppered his speeches with nationalistic slogans.*

2 be peppered with sth: if something

P

is peppered with smaller things, there are a lot of the smaller things all over it ▶ *He had thick black hair, peppered with grey.*

PERK

PERK UP →

1 perk up, perk sb **up, perk up** sb: to become, or make someone become, more cheerful, interested, or energetic ▶ *Their faces seemed to perk up a little when she mentioned the subject of money.* ▶ *I like to start the day with a cup of coffee. It helps to perk me up.*

2 perk up, perk up sth, **perk** sth **up**: to improve and become more interesting or exciting, or to make something do this ▶ *The housing market is starting to perk up, and prices have been rising steadily.*

PERMIT

PERMIT OF →

permit of sth: to make it possible for something to happen ▶ *His financial situation did not permit of marriage to a woman of Lady Sarah's rank.*

PERTAIN

PERTAIN TO →

pertain to sth: to be directly connected with a particular subject, event, or person ▶ *Five of the charges pertained to the torture and murder of political prisoners.*

PETER

PETER OUT →

1 peter out: if something peters out, there is gradually less and less of it until it stops completely ▶ *The rain will peter out later on in the day.* ▶ *Our conversation began to peter out and I struggled to think of something to say.*

2 peter out: if a path or road peters out, it gradually becomes narrower and less

clear, until it ends completely ▶ *As they went further into the forest, the path gradually petered out.*

PHASE

PHASE IN →

phase in sth, **phase** sth **in**: to gradually introduce something such as a new system or product ▶ *The new taxes will be phased in over a three-year period.*

PHASE OUT →

phase out sth, **phase** sth **out**: to gradually stop using something such as a system or product ▶ *The old trains will gradually be phased out over the next 18 months.*

PHONE

PHONE AROUND, *also* PHONE ROUND →

phone around/round, phone sb **around/round**: to telephone several people, companies etc especially in order to find out about something ▶ *Why don't you phone around and see if you can get a better price somewhere else?*

PHONE BACK →

phone back, phone sb **back, phone back** sb: to telephone someone for a second time or after they have telephoned you ▶ *The woman said she'd phone back straight away.* ▶ *To my surprise, he phoned me back a few days later, and offered me the job.*

PHONE FOR →

phone for sth, **phone** sb **for** sth: to

telephone someone and ask them to provide you with something or send you something ▶ *She phoned for a taxi, which arrived 20 minutes later.* ▶ *Group bookings available, phone for details.*

PHONE IN →

1 phone in: to telephone a television or radio company in order to give your opinion, join in a discussion etc ▶ *Hundreds of viewers phoned in to complain.*

> **phone-in (programme)** N a radio or television programme in which people telephone the programme to give their opinions, or ask or answer questions ▶ *She hosts a radio phone-in programme.*

2 phone in: to telephone an organization in order to report or ask about something ▶ *Someone phoned in to the hospital to report the accident.* ▶ *An anonymous caller phoned in claiming to have seen one of the suspects.* **phone in sick** (=telephone your company to say that you are ill and cannot come to work) ▶ *I felt awful, so I phoned in sick and went straight to bed.*

PHONE ROUND *see* **PHONE AROUND**

PHONE THROUGH →

phone through sth, **phone** sth **through, phone through**: to telephone someone to give them a message or order, or to give or ask for information ▶ *Phone through your order, and it will be delivered the next day.*

PHONE UP →

phone up sb, **phone** sb **up, phone up**: to telephone someone and speak to them ▶ *I kept phoning her up, asking to see her and the children.* ▶ *Jonathan has just phoned up to say that he'll be late.*

PICK

PICK AT →

1 pick at sth: to eat only small amounts of food without showing much interest in it ▶ *Chantal was picking at the salad without much enthusiasm.*

2 pick at sth: to scratch or pull something gently again and again ▶ *Wayne sat picking at an old scab on his knee.*

3 pick at sb: to keep criticizing someone or complaining about things that they do ▶ *My two boys pick at each other all day about stupid little things.*

PICK OFF →

1 pick off sb, **pick** sb **off**: to shoot and kill people or animals one after the other ▶ *The British soldiers wore red tunics, which made it easy for the enemy to pick them off.*

2 pick off sb, **pick** sb **off**: to choose and take the best people or things from a group ▶ *The big clubs are able to pick off rising young stars early in their career.*

PICK ON →

1 pick on sb: to treat one person in a group badly in a way that seems very unfair ▶ *She was a shy, quiet girl who was always being picked on by the other kids.* ▶ *He says that this particular teacher is always picking on him.*

2 pick on sb/sth: to choose one person or thing when you could easily have chosen someone or something else ▶ *My son's first word was "dada", but for some reason my daughter picked on "toaster".*

PICK OUT →

1 pick out sth/sb, **pick** sth/sb **out**: to choose one particular thing or person from a group ▶ *Sophie naturally*

P

picked out the most expensive ring in the whole shop. ▶ *The judges picked her work out as the best in the show.*

2 pick out sb/sth, **pick** sb/sth **out**: to recognize a person or thing from a group ▶ *He was asked to pick out the man who attacked him.*

3 pick out sb/sth, **pick** sb/sth **out**: to succeed in seeing someone or something, even though this is difficult ▶ *I could just pick out a little boat some way from the shore.*

4 pick out, pick sth **out**: to play a tune on a musical instrument, especially slowly or with difficulty ▶ *Sinead was picking out an old Beatles song on her guitar.*

PICK OVER →

1 pick over sth: to examine a group of things carefully in order to choose the ones you want ▶ *People were picking over piles of clothes on the market stalls.* ▶ *The seabirds picked over the debris that washed up on the shore.*

2 pick over sth: to examine or discuss something very carefully and in detail ▶ *She hated the idea of her personal life being picked over by the media.*

PICK THROUGH →

pick through sth: to search through things in order to find something ▶ *Rescue workers are picking through the ruins, looking for survivors.*

PICK UP →

1 pick up sth/sb, **pick** sth/sb **up**: to lift something or someone up, especially with your hands ▶ *Maurin picked up the gun and put it in her pocket.* ▶ *The little girl's mother laughed and bent down to pick her up.* **pick up the phone** (=lift up the phone so that you can use it) ▶ *The phone rang, and he picked it up.*

2 pick up sb/sth, **pick** sb/sth **up**: to collect someone from a place where they are waiting for you ▶ *I went to*

pick Korey up from the airport. ▶ *The boys were eventually picked up by a rescue boat.*

pick-up N when you go somewhere to collect something or someone ▶ *Drug dealers used the place for pick-ups of heroin and cocaine.*

3 pick up sb, **pick** sb **up**: to stop your car so that someone can get in and travel with you ▶ *We stopped to pick up a couple of hitchhikers.*

4 pick up sth, **pick** sth **up**: to get or buy something, especially something that you find by chance ▶ *Did you manage to pick up any bargains in the sales?* ▶ *Arnold had picked up the painting in the sixties for just a few pounds.*

5 pick up sth, **pick** sth **up**: to get or win something such as a prize or votes in an election ▶ *Last year the movie picked up six Academy Awards.*

6 pick sth **up, pick up** sth: to learn how to do something by watching or listening to other people, or by trying to do it yourself ▶ *While I was in Tokyo I picked up quite a bit of Japanese.* ▶ *The system's easy to use. You'll soon pick it up.*

7 pick sth **up, pick up** sth: to learn about something such as a useful piece of information, an interesting idea, or a story about someone ▶ *I went to see Lucy, hoping to pick up some juicy gossip.* **pick up a tip** (=a useful piece of information) ▶ *Here's a useful tip I picked up the other day.*

8 pick sth **up, pick up** sth: to get an infectious disease ▶ *Kids can pick up all sorts of illnesses when they first start school.*

9 pick up sth, **pick** sth **up**: if you pick up a way of speaking or behaving, you start to do it because other people are doing it ▶ *She seems to quickly pick up the local accent wherever she goes.*

10 pick up sth, **pick** sth **up**: to earn a particular amount of money for your work, especially a surprisingly large amount ▶ *Top city lawyers can pick up well over £100,000 a year.*

11 pick sb **up, pick up** sb: to start to talk to someone you do not know, with the intention of having sex with them ▶ *Gary went home with some girl he picked up in a bar.*

12 pick up: to start to improve after having problems ▶ *In recent months the economy has started to pick up again.* ▶ *Don't worry, I'm sure things will soon pick up.*

   pick-up N a time when trade, business, or the economic situation improves ▶ *There's been a pick-up in sales over the last quarter.*

13 pick up, pick up sth, **pick** sth **up**: to start doing something again from the point where you or someone else stopped before ▶ *His new detective thriller picks up at the point where the previous one ended.* **pick up where** sb/sth **left off** ▶ *After half-time the team picked up again where they'd left off, and won the match easily.*

14 pick up sb, **pick** sb **up**: if the police pick up someone, they stop them and take them somewhere to ask them questions ▶ *Police officers were waiting to pick him up for questioning when he arrived at the airport.*

15 pick up sth, **pick** sth **up**: to receive a radio signal, a television signal etc ▶ *The Titanic's distress signal was picked up by other ships in the area.*

16 pick up sth, **pick** sth **up**: to notice a smell or signs that show that someone or something is there or has been there ▶ *The dog picked up the missing child's scent, and followed the trail to some bushes.*

17 pick up sth, **pick** sth **up**: to notice a mistake or something that seems odd about something ▶ *Don't worry about spelling mistakes – the spell-checker should pick them up.*

18 pick yourself up: to get up off the ground and stand after you have fallen down ▶ *Curtis picked himself up and looked around for his wallet.*

19 pick up the bill also **pick up the tab**: to pay a bill for someone ▶ *The government will have to pick up the bill for all the damage.* ▶ *We went out for a meal in a fancy restaurant, and she picked up the tab.*

20 pick up speed also **pick up steam**: to start to move more quickly ▶ *The car picked up speed and shot off into the distance.*

21 pick up sth: to make a place tidy ▶ *You can't go out until you pick up your room.*

22 the wind picks up: if the wind picks up, it starts to get stronger ▶ *That evening the wind picked up and storm clouds gathered.*

PICK UP AFTER →

pick up after sb: to put things back in the right place and make everything neat and tidy after someone has made it untidy ▶ *All I seem to do is wash, clean, and pick up after the children.*

PICK UP ON →

1 pick up on sth: to notice something, especially something that other people do not notice ▶ *Children tend to pick up on any strain between their parents.*

2 pick up on sth: to notice something and realize that it is important ▶ *The press were quick to pick up on the story.*

3 pick up on sth: if you pick up on something that was mentioned earlier, you say more about it ▶ *To pick up on an earlier theme, there are two main traditions in the history of Western art.*

P

4 pick sb **up on** sth: to tell someone that they have made a mistake or done something that you disapprove of ▶ *Glyn took his remark as an insult, and immediately picked him up on it.* ▶ *She asked me to pick her up on any mistakes in her English.*

PICK UP WITH →
pick up with sb: to start meeting someone again and start doing things together as friends ▶ *Amelia was looking forward to picking up with her old friends when she got back home.*

PIECE

PIECE OUT →
piece out sth, **piece** sth **out**: to gradually find out about and understand the facts of a situation ▶ *It took me several days to piece out what had happened to the money.*

PIECE TOGETHER →
piece together sth, **piece** sth **together**: to put together all the information that you have about a situation in order to try to understand what happened ▶ *Accident investigators are still trying to piece together the events that led up to the crash.*

PIG

PIG OUT →
pig out: to eat a lot of food, especially more than you need or more than is sensible.
+ on ▶ *It just isn't possible to pig out on a lot of junk food and still stay slim.*

PILE

PILE IN →
pile in: if a group of people pile in, they all enter a place or vehicle, quickly and not in an organized way ▶ *We were sitting at the bar when a group of tourists suddenly piled in.*

PILE INTO →
pile into sth: if a group of people pile into a place or vehicle, they all enter it, quickly and not in an organized way ▶ *Bunny, Martin and the four girls piled into the taxi.*

PILE ON →
1 pile on sth, **pile** sth **on**, **pile** sth **on** sth: to give or do more and more of something in order to achieve the result that you want ▶ *She's a good writer, but she's boring when she piles on endless details about her childhood.* ▶ *The Scots piled on the pressure and achieved a comfortable win.*

2 pile it on: to talk about something a lot in a way that makes a situation seem much worse than it really is ▶ *Nobody pays any attention when I do something right, but they certainly pile it on when I make a mistake.*

3 pile on the agony: to make a situation even more difficult for someone than it already is ▶ *Hodges scored yet again, piling on the agony for United who were already 3-0 down.*

4 pile on weight: to become much fatter and heavier ▶ *Most people pile on some extra weight at Christmas.*

PILE OUT →
pile out: if a group of people pile out, they all leave a vehicle or a place quickly and not in an organized way ▶ *All the people on the coach piled out.* **+ of** ▶ *An alarm went off and everyone began piling out of their rooms in their pyjamas.*

PILE UP →
1 pile up: to gradually form a large pile or mass ▶ *Dorcas stared at the snow piling up against the walls outside.*

2 pile sth **up**, **pile up** sth: to put a lot of things on top of each other so that they form a pile ▶ *Helen carefully piled up the logs in front of the stove.*

3 pile up: if work, debts, problems etc pile up, they increase to a level that is too much for you to deal with ▶ *The business was in serious trouble, and its debts were rapidly piling up.* ▶ *Traffic going out of town is really starting to pile up by five o'clock.*

4 pile up sth, **pile** sth **up**: to make the number or amount of something increase in a way that causes problems ▶ *The company has piled up losses of over £20 million.*

5 pile up: if a lot of vehicles pile up, they crash into each other ▶ *It's been a bad week for traffic accidents, with twenty-one cars piling up on the M23.*

   pile-up N a road accident in which a lot of vehicles crash into each other ▶ *Several people were injured in a 12-vehicle pile-up on the M25.*

PIN

PIN DOWN →

1 pin down sth, **pin** sth **down**: to understand or explain exactly what something is or what it is like ▶ *Bobby heard a voice that sounded familiar, but he couldn't quite pin it down.*

2 pin sb **down**, **pin down** sb: to make someone give you exact details or make a definite decision about something ▶ *I never know where Bernard is these days – it's impossible to pin him down.* **+ to** ▶ *They've been promising to meet us for ages, but I can't pin them down to a date.*

3 pin sb **down**, **pin down** sb: to hold someone down so that they cannot move ▶ *He had the child pinned down on the grass.*

PIN ON, *also* PIN UPON →

1 pin sth **on/upon** sb: to say that

something is a particular person's fault ▶ *Don't try to pin the blame on me.* ▶ *The president was trying to pin the economic problems on the previous administration.*

2 pin sth **on/upon** sb: to say that someone is guilty of a crime ▶ *"I don't know anything about a burglary," the boy said. "You can't pin it on me."*

3 pin your hopes on sb/sth: to hope very much that something will happen successfully or someone will help you, because your plans depend on it ▶ *Harry needed someone to do him a favour, and was pinning his hopes on Guy.*

PIN UP →

pin sth **up**, **pin up** sth: to fasten a picture, note, photograph etc to a wall

▶ *A photograph of her son was pinned up by her desk.*

   pin-up N a photograph of an attractive famous person that people stick on their walls, or a person who appears in one of these photographs ▶ *America's favourite pin-up girl*

PIN UPON *see* PIN ON

PINE

PINE AWAY →

pine away: to become more and more unhappy, usually because you cannot be with someone that you love ▶ *The dog simply pined away and died after his mistress abandoned him.*

PINE FOR →

1 pine for sb: to feel unhappy because you miss someone very much ▶ *It's been ten years since Ralph left, but she still pines for him.*

2 pine for sth: to wish that you could have a particular thing, especially something that you used to have ▶ *A lot of doctors pine for the old days, when they had more authority.*

PIPE

PIPE DOWN →

pipe down: used to tell someone to talk more quietly, or to stop complaining ▶ *"Everybody pipe down," said Uncle Alfred. "There's no need to get so excited."*

PIPE UP →

pipe up: to suddenly say something, especially when people are not expecting it ▶ *"Definitely not," piped up Mum, who I'd thought was asleep until then.*

PIT

PIT AGAINST →

pit sb/sth **against** sb/sth: to make someone or something fight or compete against another person or thing ▶ *The girls plan to pit their talents against the boys in the end-of-term competition.*

PITCH

PITCH FOR →

pitch for sth: to try to get something that others are competing for too ▶ *Already a giant telecommunications empire, the corporation is now pitching for Internet access businesses.*

PITCH IN →

1 pitch in: to help other people to do work that needs to be done ▶ *Everyone pitched in, working day and night to get the new club ready on time.* **+ with** ▶ *After the floods, volunteers pitched in with trucks to help the three thousand residents.*

2 pitch in: to help someone that you know by giving them money ▶ *Eventually, when Mary needed a*

car, all her family and friends pitched in.

3 pitch in: to give your opinion during a discussion between a lot of people. **+ with** ▶ *When Simon had given his presentation, the chairman asked everyone to pitch in with their views.*

PITCH INTO →

1 pitch into sth: to start doing some work that needs to be done, in a willing and cheerful way ▶ *More than 20,000 young people throughout Britain pitched into an annual countryside clean-up yesterday.*

2 pitch into sb: to suddenly attack or strongly criticize someone ▶ *The man at the bar suddenly pitched into a group of teenagers standing nearby.*

PITCH UP →

pitch up: to arrive somewhere ▶ *Bill hasn't pitched up yet, has he?*

PIVOT

PIVOT ON →

pivot on sth: to depend or be based on something in order to be possible or successful ▶ *"Concentrate," said Fielding, "the entire plan pivots on this decision."*

PLAGUE

PLAGUE WITH →

1 be plagued with: if you are plagued with a lot of unpleasant or annoying things, these things keep happening to or affecting you ▶ *Frederick was plagued with one illness after another throughout his childhood.*

2 plague sb **with** sth: to annoy someone by continuously asking questions or making difficult demands ▶ *She was immediately surrounded by a crowd of reporters, plaguing her with questions.*

PLAN

PLAN AHEAD →
plan ahead: to make decisions and plans about what you will do in the future ▶ *Students who don't plan ahead may have difficulty in completing all their work in time.*

PLAN FOR →
plan for sth: to make plans that include thinking about a particular situation or event ▶ *I hadn't planned for the expense of studying in London.* ▶ *His problems were now behind him, and it was time to start planning for the future.*

PLAN ON →
1 plan on doing sth: to intend to do something ▶ *David had always saved money because he planned on retiring early.*

2 not plan on (doing) sth: to not expect something to happen ▶ *Kate looked at her watch and groaned – she hadn't planned on this sort of delay.* ▶ *I'm not planning on staying out very late.*

3 plan on sb **doing** sth: to intend or expect that someone will do something ▶ *Molly's father had never planned on her going to college.*

PLAN OUT →
plan out sth, **plan** sth **out**: to decide in detail what you are going to do, and how and when you will do it ▶ *I'm not one of those people who can just begin writing – I have to plan it all out before I start.*

PLANT

PLANT OUT →
plant sth **out**, **plant out** sth: to plant young plants outside in the ground ▶ *Tomatoes that have been grown indoors can be planted out in May or early June.*

PLANT UP →
plant up sth, **plant** sth **up**: to plant flowers, plants, vegetables etc in a container ▶ *Many gardeners plant up colourful tubs, window boxes, and baskets for the summer.*

PLAY

PLAY ABOUT *see* **PLAY AROUND**

PLAY ABOUT WITH *see* **PLAY AROUND WITH**

PLAY ALONG →
play along: to pretend to agree with someone or to do what they want, in order to get some advantage ▶ *Hugh realized that the only way to get more information was to play along.* **+ with** ▶ *I was surprised when she introduced me as her uncle, but I played along with it.*

PLAY AROUND, *also* PLAY ABOUT →
play around/about: to behave in a silly way or do something in a way that is not serious ▶ *In this business you can't play around – you have to be in control all the time.* ▶ *We didn't mean to hurt him. We were just playing around.*

PLAY AROUND WITH, *also* PLAY ABOUT WITH →
1 play around/about with sth: to think about or try different ideas or different ways of doing something ▶ *I like to play around with different recipes and ingredients.*

2 play around/about with sth: to change something when it is not safe or sensible to do this ▶ *I don't think you should play about with a young girl's future like that.*

PLAY AT →
1 what's sb **playing at?**: used to ask what someone is doing or why they are doing it, because you are very annoyed by it ▶ *What the hell do you think you're playing at, going out at this time of night?*

P

2 play at sb/sth: to pretend to be a particular type of person or to do a particular thing, usually as a game ▶ *Little girls often play at doctors and nurses.* **play at doing** sth ▶ *two little old ladies who were playing at being detectives*

3 play at sth: to do a job or activity for only part of the time, and without being very serious about it ▶ *If you're serious about politics, you can't just play at it – it's your whole life.*

PLAY BACK →

1 play back sth, **play** sth **back**: to listen to or watch something that has recently been recorded ▶ *When he got home he played back the messages on his answering machine.*

2 play back, play back sth, **play** sth **back**: if a machine plays back sound or pictures, it produces them when you operate it ▶ *Most video machines can record and play back at three different speeds.*

PLAY DOWN →

1 play down sth, **play** sth **down**: to try to make people believe that something is less important or serious than it really is ▶ *The government has been trying to play down the scandal.* ▶ *State department officials sought to play down the significance of the visit.*

2 play down sth, **play** sth **down**: to try to make people believe that something is not likely to happen ▶ *Senior management has repeatedly played down the possibility of further redundancies.*

3 play down sth, **play** sth **down**: to try to make an emotion that you are feeling less noticeable to other people ▶ *"I expect he'll be late," Cathy said, playing down her excitement.*

PLAY OFF →

1 play off: to play the last game in a sports competition, in order to decide who is the winner ▶ *At the end of the season, the top two teams will play of at Twickenham.*

   play-off N a game between people o teams in order to decide the winner of an important competition ▶ *Leeds fans will be able to watch their team's European Cup play-off against Stuttgart on Friday.*

2 play off sth: to deliberately use a fact, idea, or emotion in order to get what you want ▶ *This TV show plays off irrational fears that many people in our society have.*

3 play off each other: if two or more people or things play off each other, each makes the other's good qualities more noticeable ▶ *During the interview the two brothers played off each other very effectively.*

PLAY OFF AGAINST →

play sb/sth **off against** sb/sth, **play off** sb/sth **against** sb/sth: to encourage one person or group to compete or argue with another, in order to gain an advantage ▶ *The seller's intention is to play one buyer off against another.* ▶ *Children will often play off each parent against the other.*

PLAY ON →

1 play on: to continue playing in a game or sport after an interruption ▶ *Simpkins played on, despite an early injury.* ▶ *The referee signalled to play on.*

2 play on: to continue playing music in spite of an interruption ▶ *The conductor suddenly walked out, but the orchestra played on.*

PLAY ON, *also* PLAY UPON →

1 play on/upon sth: to deliberately use a fact, idea, or emotion in order to do or get what you want ▶ *Advertising achieves its aim by playing on our weaknesses and emotions.*

play on sth: to use your position, influence, or strong qualities in order to do or get what you want ▶ *Some people said that she had played on her connections in order to get the job.*

play on sb's **mind**: if something plays on your mind, you cannot stop thinking about it, and it worries or upsets you ▶ *It wasn't your fault – you mustn't let it play on your mind.*

play on sth: if light plays on a surface or an object, it falls on it and moves backwards and forwards across it ▶ *Daniel watched the sunlight playing on the roofs of the fishing village.*

PLAY OUT →

1. be played out: if an event is played out, especially an exciting or important one, it takes place ▶ *The final scenes of their marriage were played out in a villa in St Tropez.*

2. play (itself) out: if an event plays out or plays itself out, it happens and finally ends with a particular result ▶ *I don't know if he'll win again. We'll just have to see how the election plays out.*

3. play out sth, **play** sth **out**: if people play out their feelings, dreams etc, they express them by pretending that a particular situation is really happening ▶ *In a novel the writer is able to play out his own strange fantasies.*

PLAY THROUGH →

play sth **through**, **play through** sth: to play a piece of music from the beginning to the end ▶ *Could we play that through again from the beginning please?*

PLAY UP →

1. play up sth, **play** sth **up**: to emphasize something in order to attract people's attention to it or to make it seem important ▶ *When applying for a job, it's a good idea to play up your strong points in the opening paragraph.*

2 play up, play sb **up**: if a part of your body plays up or plays you up, it causes you pain or trouble ▶ *Bertie had given up alcohol because his heart was playing up.*

3 play up: if a machine, an electrical system etc plays up, it is not working as well as it should ▶ *Sorry I didn't get back to you sooner – my email's been playing up.*

4 play up, play sb **up**, **play up** sb: to behave badly – used especially about children who are deliberately behaving badly towards an adult ▶ *Some of the boys in our class really played up – especially when a teacher was new.*

PLAY UP TO →

1 play up to sb: to try to make someone like you by behaving in a way you think will please them ▶ *Angie always played up to men – she enjoyed seeing how they reacted to her.*

2 play up to an image/a stereotype: to behave in a way that people expect you to behave ▶ *He plays up to his tough guy image in his latest movie.*

PLAY UPON *see* PLAY ON

PLAY WITH →

1 play with sth: to keep touching something, or moving it from one position to another ▶ *Charlene was walking up and down and playing with her hair.* ▶ *All the time we were talking, he was playing with the money in his pocket.*

2 play with sth: to try using different types of something, or try different ways of doing something ▶ *Cooking Asian dishes is a marvellous way of playing with different flavours.*

P

3 play with sth: to consider an idea or a possibility, but not very seriously. **play with the idea of doing** sth ▶ *When I left university, I played with the idea of teaching for a while.*

4 play with sb/sth: to treat someone in a way that is not sincere or fair ▶ *I hope you're not playing with Jane's feelings – she's such a nice person.*

5 play with sth: if you play with words or ideas, you use them in a clever and unusual way ▶ *He has a way of playing with words that makes his readers laugh out loud.*

6 have time/money etc to play with: to have time, money etc that is still available to be used ▶ *Don't panic – we've got plenty of time to play with!* ▶ *We'd spent all our money on the house, so there wasn't much left to play with.*

7 be playing with fire: to be doing or dealing with something that is very difficult or dangerous ▶ *In dealing directly with terrorist organizations, the government is really playing with fire.*

PLOD

PLOD ALONG, *also* PLOD ON →
1 plod along/on: to continue walking or working in a slow but determined way ▶ *We plodded along with the rain spitting in our faces.* **+ with** ▶ *The police are still plodding on with their investigation, despite the lack of any new evidence.*

2 plod along/on: to make progress very slowly ▶ *His speech plodded on for what seemed like hours.*

PLONK

PLONK DOWN →
1 plonk sth/sb **down, plonk down** sth/sb: to put something or someone down without being careful with them ▶ *Marge plonked her shopping bags down on the table.*

2 plonk down, plonk yourself down: to sit down quickly and heavily, especially when you need to relax ▶ *I plonked down on the sofa and began thinking about what had happened.* **plonk yourself down** ▶ *Just then a group of soldiers came in and plonked themselves down.*

PLOT

PLOT OUT →
plot out sth, **plot** sth **out**: to plan or show the details of something or how it is expected to happen ▶ *a graph that plots out predicted economic growth*

PLOUGH

PLOUGH AHEAD →
plough ahead: to continue doing something, or making progress when it is difficult ▶ *I could hardly hear her voice on the end of the line, but decided to plough ahead anyway.* **+ with** ▶ *The government will plough ahead with national tests this year, despite protests from teachers.*

PLOUGH BACK →
plough sth **back, plough back** sth: to spend the money that you have earned from a business on improving the business. **+ into** ▶ *Profits were ploughed back into investment in staff and technology.*

PLOUGH IN, *also* POUGH INTO →
1 plough sth **into** sth, **plough in** sth: to spend or provide large amounts of money in order to help something develop or be successful ▶ *The big drug companies have already ploughed billions of dollars into AIDS research.*

2 plough in sth, **plough** sth **in, plough** sth **into** sth: to dig crops or another substance into the land in order to improve it ▶ *Waste from animals is a valuable fertilizer – all you have to do is plough it into the soil.*

PLOUGH INTO →

plough into sth: if a vehicle ploughs into something, it crashes into it with a lot of force because its driver cannot control it ► *A runaway lorry ploughed into a wall but the driver escaped unharmed.*

PLOUGH ON →

plough on: to continue doing something or going somewhere even though it is difficult or boring. **+ with** ► *It was late, but I knew I'd have to plough on with the work until it was done.* **plough on regardless** (=continue doing something, even though there are difficulties) ► *Stephen didn't seem to be listening to anything I said, and just ploughed on regardless.*

PLOUGH THROUGH →

plough through sth: to read, write, or deal with all of something, when there is a lot to do and it takes a long time ► *All we used to do in English was to plough through dozens of grammar exercises.* ► *It took me over four hours to plough through the report.*

plough through sth: to slowly eat all of something, especially when there is a lot of it and you are not enjoying it ► *Jamie was sitting in the canteen, ploughing through a huge salad.*

plough through sth: to move through something that is blocking your way ► *They spent most of the walk ploughing through waist-high nettles.*

plough through sth: if a vehicle ploughs through something, it hits it and continues moving through it because the driver is not in control ► *The car ploughed through the traffic barrier and ended up on the wrong side of the road.*

PLOUGH UP →

1 plough up sth, **plough** sth **up**: to break up the surface of land using a machine called a plough, in order to prepare it for planting crops ► *At the end of the year the fields are ploughed up and fertilized, ready for the spring.*

2 plough up sth, **plough** sth **up**: to spoil the surface of an area of ground by driving or riding over it, so that it becomes very muddy and uneven ► *The mountain paths are constantly being ploughed up by tourists in off-road vehicles.*

PLUG

PLUG AWAY →

plug away: to keep working hard in order to try to do something ► *They kept plugging away until they found a solution to the problem.* **+ at** ► *I'm sure if you keep plugging away at it, your English will improve.*

PLUG IN →

plug sth **in**, **plug in** sth: to connect a piece of electrical equipment to the main supply of electricity or to another piece of electrical equipment ► *Marion filled the kettle and plugged it in.* ► *I checked the phone cord and made sure it was plugged in correctly.*

PLUG INTO →

1 plug sth **into** sth: to connect a piece of electrical equipment to another piece of electrical equipment or to a supply of electricity ► *Plug the microphone into your videocassette recorder.*

2 plug into sth: if a piece of electrical equipment plugs into another piece of electrical equipment or into a supply of electricity, it can be connected to it ▶ *The printer plugs into a socket at the back of your computer.*

3 plug into sth: to connect your computer to an information system ▶ *Encourage your kids to plug into educational websites.* **be plugged into** sth (=have a computer that is connected to an information system) ▶ *Almost all the students are plugged into the Internet.*

PLUG UP →
plug up sth, **plug** sth **up**: to fill or block a small hole by putting something in it ▶ *With his ears plugged up, Albert could sleep undisturbed.* ▶ *He used mud and straw to plug up the holes in the roof.*

PLUMB

PLUMB IN →
plumb in sth, **plumb** sth **in**: to connect a bath, toilet, washing machine etc to the water supply ▶ *We have got a dishwasher, but it isn't plumbed in yet.*

PLUMP

PLUMP DOWN →
1 plump (yourself) down: to sit down suddenly and heavily ▶ *Jack staggered in and plumped down exhausted onto a chair.*

2 plump down sth, **plump** sth **down**: to put something down suddenly and carelessly ▶ *Plumping down her bag on the table between us, Mrs Horrocks leaned forward and stared at me.*

PLUMP FOR →
plump for sth/sb: to choose a particular thing or person, especially after not being able to decide ▶ *In the end we plumped for an evening out at the bowling alley.*

PLUMP UP →
1 plump up sth, **plump** sth **up**: to make a cushion, pillow etc rounder and softer by shaking and pressing it ▶ *Lydia heaved herself up in bed while the nurse plumped up her pillows.*

2 plump up: to swell or become fatter ▶ *Raisins plump up during cooking whereas sultanas fall apart.*

PLUNGE

PLUNGE IN →
plunge in: to start talking or doing something quickly and confidently, without thinking about it first ▶ *You should have let her explain her problems before plunging in with a lot of advice.*

PLUNGE INTO →
1 plunge sth **into** sth: to push something firmly and deeply into something else ▶ *Plunge the asparagus into boiling water.* ▶ *Jill plunged her hands deep into her pockets.*

2 plunge sth/sb **into** sth, **plunge into** sth: to suddenly cause someone to be in a bad situation or state, or to suddenly get into a bad situation or state ▶ *The latest massacre has plunged the country into a new cycle of violence.*

3 plunge sth/sb **into darkness**: to suddenly make a place dark so that the people in it have no light ▶ *There was a loud bang and the whole building was plunged into darkness.*

PLY

PLY WITH →

ply sb **with** sth: to keep giving someone large quantities of food or drink ▶ *He would ply his victims with drink and then rob them.*

ply sb **with questions**: to ask someone a lot of questions ▶ *The three girls were plying Rupert with questions about himself, his life, and his work.*

POINT

POINT OUT →

point out sth/sb, **point** sth/sb **out**: to show something or someone to another person, for example by saying where they are ▶ *We drove along Market Street and she pointed out the house where she was born.* **+ to** ▶ *I'll point him out to you if I see him.*

point out sth, **point** sth **out**: to tell someone something that they need to realize ▶ *As I've already pointed out, it takes a long time to learn a foreign language.* **+ that** ▶ *It is worth pointing out that one in ten children still leave school unable to read or write.*

POINT TO →

point to sth: to mention a fact that you think is important because you think it proves something ▶ *The Prime Minister pointed to economic growth as evidence that the government's policies were working.*

POINT TO, also POINT TOWARDS →

point to/towards sth: to show that something is likely to be true or is likely to happen ▶ *All the evidence pointed to drugs gangs being involved in the murders.*

POINT UP →

point up sth, **point** sth **up**: to make a particular fact, problem etc clearer and more noticeable, so that people pay attention to it ▶ *The latest rail tragedy points up the need for more investment in our railway system.*

POKE

POKE ABOUT *see* **POKE AROUND**

POKE ALONG →

poke along: to move very slowly ▶ *The car in front of me poked along at 20 miles an hour.*

POKE AROUND, also POKE ABOUT →

1 poke around/about, poke around/about sth: to look around a place in order to see exactly what is there or to find something you want ▶ *I was poking around in the attic looking for an old photo album.* ▶ *Andrew used to poke around the Internet to see what was new online.*

2 poke around/about: to try to find out things about someone else in a way that annoys them ▶ *I don't like it when journalists start poking around, digging up my past.*

POKE INTO →

poke into sth: to try to find out things about someone else, in a way that annoys them ▶ *Wouldn't you resent it if you found a stranger was poking into your personal affairs?*

POLISH

POLISH OFF →

polish off sth, **polish** sth **off**: to finish food, drink, or work, quickly and easily ▶ *When I got home, Mrs Marsh had polished off half the biscuits in the tin.*

POLISH UP →

1 polish up sth, **polish** sth **up**: to improve your knowledge of something, or something that you do, by working at it ▶ *I started going to evening classes to polish up my French.*

2 polish up sth, **polish** sth **up**: to rub an object with a piece of cloth in order to make it shine ▶ *Put a clean shirt on and polish up those shoes.*

3 polish up your image: to make an effort to improve the way you seem to other people ▶ *The government was trying to polish up its image after a year of bad publicity.*

POP

POP IN →

pop in: to go into a friend's house, an office, a shop etc for a short time ▶ *She sometimes used to pop in for a cup of tea and a chat on her way home.*

POP OFF →

pop off: to die – use this when you do not want to say 'die' because it sounds too serious ▶ *I'm only sixty, you know – I'm not going to pop off yet!*

POP ON →

pop sth **on, pop on** sth: to quickly put on a piece of clothing ▶ *Just pop this jacket on and we'll see if it fits.*

POP OUT →

pop out: to go out of a room or building quickly, suddenly, or for a short time ▶ *"Where's Colin?" "He's just popped out for a moment."*

POP ROUND →

pop round: to go to someone's house for a short time ▶ *Ben said he might pop round one evening next week.*

POP UP →

pop up: to appear suddenly in an unexpected way or in unexpected places ▶ *New Italian restaurants are popping up all over the city.* ▶ *a face that keeps popping up on our television screens*

PORE

PORE OVER →

pore over sth: to read or study something very carefully for a long time ▶ *We pore over the local newspaper every week, hoping to find an affordable apartment.*

PORTION

PORTION OUT →

portion out sth, **portion** sth **out**: to divide something into separate parts and give the parts to different people **+ among** ▶ *After he died, the land was portioned out among his grandchildren.*

POSSESS

BE POSSESSED OF →

be possessed of sth: to have a particular quality or ability ▶ *They knew of only one man who was possessed of such knowledge.*

POST

POST OFF →

post off sth, **post** sth **off**: to send something such as a letter or package to someone ▶ *I finally wrote the letter and posted it off.*

POST UP →

post sth **up, post up** sth: to put a sign or announcement on a wall so that a lot of people can read it ▶ *Exam results will be posted up on my office door by 5:00 Friday.*

POTTER

POTTER ABOUT, *also* **POTTER AROUND →**

potter about/around, potter about/around sth: to do small jobs in the house, garden etc in a relaxed way ▶ *We spent the morning pottering about in the garden.*

POUNCE

POUNCE ON, *also* **POUNCE UPON** →

pounce on/upon sth: to criticize someone's mistakes or ideas very quickly and eagerly ▶ *Teachers are quick to pounce on students' grammatical errors.* ▶ *Any mistakes were immediately pounced on by the press.*

pounce on/upon sth: to eagerly take an opportunity as soon as it becomes available ▶ *When they offered McNab the chance to become manager, he pounced on it.*

POUND

POUND OUT →

pound out: a. if music is pounding out, it is playing very loudly ▶ *Heavy metal music was pounding out in my son's bedroom.*

b. if you pound out music, you play it very loudly on instruments ▶ *I turned on the TV to see a boy band pounding out one of their numbers.*

pound out sth, **pound** sth **out**: to write something very quickly, especially on a computer or typewriter ▶ *He was pounding out the final chapter of his latest thriller on his old typewriter.*

pound out hits/wins: to succeed in achieving a winning score in a game of sport, by competing very hard ▶ *In the second game, the Waves pounded out 14 hits against the Broncos.*

POUR

POUR AWAY →

pour away sth, **pour** sth **away**: to get rid of a liquid by pouring it out of its container ▶ *The wine was so bad I just poured it away.* ▶ *Farmers have no choice but to pour away the contaminated milk.*

POUR

DOWN →

pour down: if the rain pours down, it rains very hard ▶ *Rain poured down on Northern California last Friday,*

decreasing the threat of forest fires. **it's pouring down** ▶ *It's been pouring down all morning.* **it's pouring down rain** ▶ *When I looked out my window, it was pouring down rain.*

downpour N when a lot of rain falls quickly in a short period of time ▶ *A heavy downpour delayed the firework display.*

POUR IN, *also* **POUR INTO** →

a. pour in, pour into sth: if letters, phone calls, complaints etc pour in, a lot are received in a short period of time ▶ *Letters of complaint poured in after the programme was shown.*

b. pour in, pour into sth: if people pour in or pour into a place, a lot of them arrive at the same time ▶ *Fans poured into the streets of Miami to celebrate the occasion.*

POUR INTO →

pour sth **into** sth: to provide a lot of money for something over a period of time in order to make it successful ▶ *They've poured thousands of pounds into the business over the years, but they still haven't made a profit.*

POUR OFF →

pour off sth, **pour** sth **off**: to remove some liquid from a larger quantity of liquid by pouring it ▶ *Pour off the juices from the turkey and use them to make gravy.*

P

POUR ON, *also* **POUR UPON** →
pour scorn on sb/sth *also* **pour scorn upon** sb/sth: to say that something or someone is stupid and not worth considering ▶ *Her father was quick to pour scorn on her suggestions.*

POUR OUT →
1 pour sth **out, pour out** sth: if you pour out your thoughts or feelings you tell someone all about them ▶ *She came to see me that night and poured out all her troubles.* **pour out your heart** *also* **pour out your soul** (=tell someone all about your most secret feelings) ▶ *Jill spent the whole evening pouring out her soul about her affair with Ben.*
   outpouring N when people show very strong feelings of sadness ▶ *an outpouring of grief*

2 pour out sth, **pour** sth **out**: to fill someone's glass, cup etc with a drink ▶ *Mandy was pouring out tea and passing around sandwiches.*

3 pour out: if a lot of people pour out from somewhere, they all leave at the same time. **+ of** ▶ *The fire alarm sounded, and everyone poured out of the building.*

POUR UPON *see* **POUR ON**

POWER
POWER UP →
power up, power up sth, **power** sth **up**: to start working and become ready to use, or to make a machine or computer start working ▶ *It'll just take a few minutes to power up.*
▶ *Technicians are attempting to power up the computers after the network failure.*

PREDISPOSE
BE PREDISPOSED TO, *also* **BE PREDISPOSED TOWARDS** →
be predisposed to/towards sth: to be more likely to have a particular illness

or problem ▶ *Children of drug users are often predisposed to addiction.*

PRESIDE
PRESIDE OVER →
1 preside over sth: to be in charge of a formal meeting or ceremony, or a large company or organization ▶ *Who's presiding over the Oscar ceremonies this year?*

2 preside over sth: to be the person who is in charge when an important event happens ▶ *The last Prime Minister presided over a massive increase in unemployment.*

PRESS
PRESS AHEAD →
press ahead: to continue doing something in a determined way, especially when it is difficult ▶ *We will press ahead to complete the building as soon as possible.* **+ with** ▶ *A spokeswoman said the government would press ahead with reforms, despite growing opposition.*

PRESS FOR →
1 press for sth, **press** sb **for** sth: to keep trying to persuade the government or someone in authority to do something or give you something ▶ *The engineering unions have been pressing for a 35 hour working week.*

2 be pressed for time/money etc: to not have enough time, money etc, with the result that it is difficult for you to do something ▶ *If you are pressed for time in the mornings, try setting the alarm 30 minutes earlier.* ▶ *I'd love to go out for a meal, but I'm a little pressed for cash right now.*

PRESS FORWARD →
press forward: to continue doing something in a determined way, especially even though it is difficult. **+ with** ▶ *France and Germany decided*

to press forward with plans for economic and monetary union.

PRESS ON →

1 press on: to continue doing something in a determined way, even though it is difficult. **+ with** ▶ *He was keen to press on with modernizing the party.* ▶ *After university, she pressed on with her ambition to become a journalist.*

2 press on: to continue with your journey, even though it is very difficult ▶ *The soldiers pressed on, hoping to reach camp before nightfall.*

PRESS ON, *also* PRESS UPON →
press sth on/upon sb: to offer something to someone in a very forceful way, so that it is very difficult for them to refuse it ▶ *Nick kept pressing drinks on me all night.*

PRESUME
PRESUME ON, *also* PRESUME UPON →
presume on/upon sth: to use someone's kindness, trust, or friendship etc in a way that seems wrong ▶ *She did not want to presume on her friendship with Eve by expecting her to lend her the money.*

PRETEND
PRETEND TO →
pretend to sth: to claim that you have a particular quality, especially when this is not true ▶ *Archer could not pretend to anything like the young actor's romantic good looks.*

PRETTY
PRETTY UP →
pretty sth/sb **up, pretty up** sth/sb: to try to make something look more attractive or acceptable to people ▶ *I tried to pretty the place up a bit with a few vases of flowers.*

PREVAIL
PREVAIL ON, *also* PREVAIL UPON →
prevail on/upon sb: to succeed in persuading someone to do something, especially when they do not want to ▶ *Weir, who had been prevailed upon to play the piano, went red with embarrassment.*

PREY
PREY ON, *also* PREY UPON →
1 prey on/upon sth: if an animal preys on another animal, it kills it and uses it for food ▶ *Owls fly low and prey on insects, mice, and other small animals.*

2 prey on/upon sb: to attack, hurt, or get money dishonestly from a particular group of people who are easy to hurt or trick ▶ *Gangs of thieves have been preying on foreign tourists at the city's central train station.* **prey on** sb's **fears** (=use people's fears to get advantages for yourself) ▶ *He accused environmental groups of preying on people's fears about food safety.*

3 prey on your mind/conscience: if something preys on your mind, you worry about it a lot and you cannot stop thinking about it. ▶ *The accident has been preying on my mind all week.* ▶ *Tim's words were beginning to prey on her mind.*

PRIDE
PRIDE YOURSELF ON, *also* PRIDE YOURSELF UPON →
pride yourself on/upon sth: to be proud of something that you do well,

or of a good quality that you have ▶ *The company prides itself on its friendly family atmosphere.* **pride yourself on doing** sth ▶ *Thomas always prided himself on being able to speak three languages fluently.*

PRINT

PRINT OFF →

print off sth, **print** sth **off**: to produce a printed copy of something ▶ *They had already printed off thousands of copies of the book before it was banned.*

PRINT OUT →

print out sth, **print** sth **out**: to produce a printed copy of something, especially from a computer ▶ *I usually print out all my e-mail messages so that I can keep a paper copy of them.*

> **printout** N a piece of paper with printed information on it, produced by a computer ▶ *The travel agent gave us a printout of our flight details.*

PRISE

PRISE OUT OF →

prise sth **out of** sb: to succeed in getting something from someone with difficulty, especially information that they do not want to tell you ▶ *In the end I managed to prise the girl's name out of him.*

PROCEED

PROCEED AGAINST →

proceed against sb: to begin a legal case against someone in a court of law ▶ *There has never been enough evidence to proceed against him.*

PROCEED FROM →

proceed from sth: to be based on a particular idea or belief, or to be originally caused by something ▶ *Their problems proceed from a lack of understanding of each other's needs.* ▶ *diseases that proceed from poverty*

PROCEED WITH →

proceed with sth: to start doing something that you have already planned or arranged to do ▶ *He said the government would proceed with plans to increase the number of seats in the Legislative Assembly.* ▶ *a Supreme Court decision not to proceed with corruption charges*

PROFIT

PROFIT FROM, *also* PROFIT BY →

profit from/by sth: to use a situation to get advantages for yourself ▶ *Offenders should not be able to profit from their crime by selling their story to the press.* ▶ *The country was able to profit from its central geographical position.*

PRONOUNCE

PRONOUNCE ON, *also* PRONOUNCE UPON →

pronounce on/upon sth: to give an opinion or judgment about something especially publicly or officially ▶ *Politicians love to pronounce on the importance of the family.* ▶ *He himself did not feel best qualified to pronounce on such matters.*

PROP

PROP UP →

1 prop up sth, **prop** sth **up**: to keep something in a particular position by putting something against it or under it ▶ *Ralph propped his feet up on the couch.* ▶ *She propped up the table with an old wooden box.*

2 prop yourself up: to support yourself by leaning on something ▶ *She had propped herself up with pillows so that she could read in bed.*

3 prop up sth, **prop** sth **up**: to help a government, business etc that is failing by giving it financial or military support ▶ *The brothers took out a loan to prop up the failing family business.*

PROVIDE

PROVIDE AGAINST →
provide against sth: to make plans in order to prevent or deal with a bad situation that might happen ▶ *Health insurance provides against loss of income due to sickness.*

PROVIDE FOR →
1 provide for sb: to give someone the things they need, such as money, food, clothes etc ▶ *My mother had to provide for her children on a very small salary.*

2 provide for sth: to make plans in order to deal with something that might happen in the future ▶ *We provided for a 2% increase in inflation when we calculated the original cost.*

3 provide for sth: if a law or rule provides for something, it makes that thing possible ▶ *a law that provides for the protection of court witnesses*

PRUNE

PRUNE BACK →
1 prune back sth, **prune** sth **back**: to cut some of the branches of a tree or bush to make it grow better ▶ *To encourage growth, prune back your rose bushes by about a third.*

2 prune back sth, **prune** sth **back**: to reduce something or to get rid of the unnecessary parts of something ▶ *Airlines announced they intended to prune back weekday flights from London to Glasgow.*

PRY

PRY OUT →
pry sth **out**: to make someone give you information that they do not want to tell you. **+ of** ▶ *At first he wouldn't*

tell me where he'd been, but in the end I finally managed to pry it out of him.*

PSYCH

PSYCH OUT →
psych sb **out**, **psych out** sb: to behave in a way that is intended to make someone, especially an opponent, feel nervous ▶ *Kelly's just trying to psych me out by not answering.*

PSYCH UP →
1 psych sb **up**: to make someone become excited and confident about something. **psych yourself up** ▶ *What do top athletes do to psych themselves up before a race?* **+ for** ▶ *He tried to psych me up for the interview, asking practice questions and checking my appearance.*

2 be psyched up: to be very excited and mentally prepared for an event or activity ▶ *The children were really psyched up for the holidays.*

PUFF

PUFF AWAY →
puff away: to smoke a cigarette, pipe etc ▶ *Nate just puffed away calmly on his pipe.*

PUFF OUT →
puff out sth, **puff** sth **out**: to make something become bigger by filling it with air ▶ *He puffed out his chest proudly as the audience applauded.* ▶ *A gentle breeze puffed out the curtains.*

PUFF UP →
1 puff up, **puff up** sth, **puff** sth **up**: to become bigger by filling with air, or to make something do this ▶ *Birds puff up their feathers to stay warm.* ▶ *The biscuits will puff up while in the oven, and then flatten out again as they cool.*

2 puff up:
if your eye, face, ankle etc puffs up, it swells because it is injured or infected
► *Judging by how your ankle has puffed up, I think it might be broken.* ► *Sylvia's finger really puffed up where the bee stung her.*

PULL

PULL AHEAD →

1 pull ahead: to succeed in getting in front of or doing better than someone you are competing against
► *Then, with just four minutes left to play, Stanford began pulling ahead.*

2 pull ahead: to become more successful than other people, places, organizations etc ► *The industrial north performed badly, while the south-east was clearly pulling ahead.*
+ of ► *They managed to pull ahead of their rivals in the soft drinks business.*

3 pull ahead: to go past a vehicle that is travelling beside or in front of yours.
+ of ► *Chrissie stepped on the accelerator and pulled ahead of the lorry again.*

PULL APART →

1 pull sth/sb **apart, pull apart** sth/sb: to make people argue or fight with each other, so that a relationship ends, or a family group, country etc becomes divided ► *We mustn't let this criticism pull the team apart.*
► *The community was pulled apart by violence, drug abuse, and poverty.*

2 pull sth **apart:** to destroy something completely by breaking it or tearing it into pieces
► *The crowd went wild*

and proceeded to pull the place apart.

3 pull apart sth, **pull** sth **apart:** to criticize every part of an idea, piece of work, organization etc very severely
► *Every single one of our proposals was pulled apart.*

4 pull sb/sth **apart, pull apart** sb/sth: to separate people or animals when they are fighting ► *The referee intervened to pull the pair apart.*

5 pull sb **apart:** to make someone feel very upset and confused ► *The conflicting demands of career and family were pulling her apart.*

PULL AT →

1 pull at sth: to pull something towards you, especially something that is heavy or difficult to move
► *Gordon pulled at the gate, and it swung open.*

2 pull at sb's sleeve/arm etc: to pull someone's clothes or arm several times to try and attract their attention
► *She pulled at her mother's sleeve saying, "Come on, hurry up."*

3 pull at sb/sth: if something pulls at you or your emotions, it affects your feelings strongly ► *Two opposite feelings pulled at her – one of delight and the other of guilt.*

PULL AWAY →

1 pull away: if a vehicle pulls away, it starts moving away from the place where it has stopped ► *Matt jumped onto the bus just as it was pulling away.* **+ from** ► *I watched as a black* *saloon car pulled away from the kerb behind us.*

2 pull away: to suddenly move your body away from someone who is holding or touching you. **+ from** ▶ *"You're hurting me," Lily said, pulling away from him.*

3 pull away: to succeed in getting more points than another person or team in a game ▶ *The US team began to pull away a little in the second half.*

4 pull away: to avoid becoming involved in something. **+ from** ▶ *This gave the government one last chance to pull away from disaster.*

PULL BACK →

1 pull back sth, **pull** sth **back:** to succeed in scoring a goal or winning points when you are losing in a game ▶ *Liverpool managed to pull one goal back in the final minutes of the match.*

2 pull back: to decide not to do or become involved in something ▶ *Share prices fell, as foreign investors pulled back after several days of gains.*

pullback N when a person, company etc decides not to continue doing something ▶ *There have been fears of a major pullback in bank lending.*

3 pull sth **back, pull back** sth: to help a company, organization etc to get out of a difficult situation. **+ from** ▶ *It won't be easy for the new leader to pull the party back from its present position.*

4 pull back: to suddenly move your body away from someone who is holding or touching you. **+ from** ▶ *She gave a cry, and pulled back from him.*

PULL DOWN →

1 pull sth **down, pull down** sth: to deliberately destroy a building or other structure, for example because it is not safe ▶ *That's where the mill used to be – they pulled it down to make space for new development.*

2 pull down sth: to earn a particular amount of money in your job ▶ *TV weather readers are pulling down $1 million annually.*

3 pull down sth, **pull** sth **down:** to make something fall to a lower level or standard than it was before ▶ *Estate agents say that the recession is really pulling down house prices.*

PULL IN →

1 pull in: to drive to the side of the road or to a place where you can stop your car ▶ *I'm going to pull in at the next garage – I want to check the tyres.* ▶ *Would you mind pulling in over there?*

2 pull in: if a train, bus etc pulls in, it arrives at the railway or bus station ▶ *We ran onto the platform just as the train was pulling in.*

3 pull in sb, **pull** sb **in:** to attract people in large numbers ▶ *The bank advertised heavily to pull in thousands of new investors.* **pull in the crowds etc** ▶ *Opera and ballet are just not pulling in the crowds like they used to do.*

PULL INTO →

1 pull into sth: if a train, bus, ship etc pulls into a place, it arrives there ▶ *By the time the train pulled into King's Cross Station the next day, we were all exhausted.*

2 pull into sth: to drive your car to a place where it can stop ▶ *At lunchtime we pulled into a roadside picnic area.*

3 pull sb/sth **into** sth: to involve a person, country etc in a particular situation or activity, especially a bad one ▶ *It was only a matter of time before America was pulled into the conflict.*

PULL OFF →

1 pull sth **off, pull off** sth: to succeed in doing or achieving something difficult ▸ *She is confident that she will be able to pull off a deal.*

2 pull off sth, **pull off**: if a vehicle pulls off a road, it leaves the road ▸ *I pulled off the road, put my seat back and fell asleep.*

3 pull off: if a vehicle pulls off, it starts moving away from the place where it has stopped ▸ *It wasn't very long before the train pulled off and we were on our way.*

PULL ON →

pull on sth: to put clothes on ▸ *Shelley hastily pulled on a pair of jeans and a thin cotton sweatshirt.*

PULL OUT →

1 pull out: to drive your car away from the side of a road ▸ *Mike got into the car and pulled out onto the highway.*

2 pull out: to drive your car towards the middle of the road, in order to pass someone in front ▸ *Always look in your side mirror before pulling out.* ▸ *A lorry suddenly pulled out in front of him.*

3 pull out: if a train pulls out, it starts to leave the station. **+ of** ▸ *The train began to pull out of the station.*

4 pull out, pull sb/sth **out, pull out** sb/sth: **a.** to stop doing or being involved in something ▸ *The British runner had to pull out with a knee injury.* **+ of** ▸ *The company is pulling out of the US hotel market after eight years.*

b. to remove someone or something from a situation that they have been involved in ▸ *As the crisis deepened, both the US and Britain decided to pull out their embassy staff.*

5 pull out: a. if a country's army pulls out of a place where it has been fighting, it leaves it ▸ *The rebel leader said that if the troops did not pull out, the hostages would be shot.*

b. pull out sth/sb, **pull** sth/sb **out**: to make an army leave a place that it has been fighting in or controlling ▸ *By the end of May the Russian government had decided to pull out its troops.*

pull-out N when an army leaves a place where it has been fighting ▸ *Following the pull-out of western forces from the region, a peace plan was put forward.*

6 pull out, pull sth **out**: to manage to get out of a difficult economic situation. **+ of** ▸ *The economy has been struggling to pull out of the recession.*

7 pull out sth: to separate particular facts or ideas from others that you do not need ▸ *I'd like you to read through the report and pull out any points that you want us to look at.*

PULL OVER →

1 pull over: to drive to the side of a road and slow down or stop ▸ *I pulled over to let the ambulance pass.*

2 pull sb/sth **over, pull over** sb/sth: if the police pull a vehicle over, they make the driver move to the side of the road and stop ▸ *He was pulled over for speeding.*

PULL ROUND →

1 pull round: to gradually get better after an illness, or to become conscious after you have been unconscious ▸ *It was several weeks before George began to pull round after his operation.*

2 pull round sth, **pull** sth **round**: to gradually make a business, organization etc begin to be more successful after it has been failing ▸ *It took the new boss three years to pull the firm round and make it profitable.*

PULL THROUGH →

1 pull through, pull sb **through**: to succeed in staying alive and gradually get better after you have been seriously ill or injured ▶ *Both the boys have serious injuries, but we're confident that they'll pull through.*

2 pull through, pull through sth, pull sb through, pull sb through sth: to succeed in dealing with a difficult time or situation in your life, or to help someone do this ▶ *One way or another the President will probably pull through.* ▶ *I was in a pretty bad way, but my husband helped pull me through.*

PULL TOGETHER →

1 pull yourself together: to control your feelings and behave calmly after you have been very upset or angry ▶ *Nina made an effort to pull herself together, and wiped away her tears.*

2 pull together: to work together with other people in order to achieve an aim that you share ▶ *I want everyone in the department to pull together as a team.*

3 pull sth together, pull together sth: to bring together various ideas, facts etc so that you can study them and compare them ▶ *The report pulled together the results of various surveys carried out since 1986.*

4 pull sth together, pull together sth: to improve something by making all the people or groups that are involved in it work together more effectively ▶ *We aim to pull together all the aid agencies that are working in the area.*

PULL UP →

1 pull up: if a vehicle pulls up somewhere, it stops ▶ *A line of limousines drove slowly past and pulled up to the gates.* ▶ *We pulled up outside the theatre.*

2 pull up a chair: to get a chair and move it so that you can sit near someone or something ▶ *Pull up a chair – we can go through this report together.*

3 pull sth **up, pull up** sth: to remove plants and their roots from the ground ▶ *I spent the afternoon in the garden pulling up weeds.*

4 pull sb **up:** to tell someone that they have done something wrong, or that they must try to improve in some way ▶ *Quite a lot of the better restaurants will pull you up if you're not wearing a tie.* **+ on** ▶ *All of his teachers have tried pulling him up on his behaviour, but he doesn't listen.*

5 pull your socks up: to improve in your work, behaviour etc, because it is not good enough ▶ *He'll have to pull his socks up if he wants to pass his exams.*

6 pull sb **up short** also **pull** sb **up sharp:** to make someone suddenly realize they have made a mistake or are wrong about something ▶ *The question pulled Rosy up short, freezing the smile on her lips.*

PUMP

PUMP IN →

pump sth **in, pump in** sth: to provide a lot of money in order to make a particular plan, place, or organization successful ▶ *Eventually the government will see the need to pump in more money to get good teachers.*

PUMP INTO →

pump sth **into** sth: to put a lot of money into a particular plan, place, or organization to make it successful ▶ *Pumping money into the Health Service is not the only way to make it more efficient.*

PUMP OUT →

1 pump sth **out, pump out** sth: to force a liquid or gas to flow out of a place by using a pump. **+ of** ▶ *This engine was originally used for pumping water out of the mines.*

2 pump out: to flow out of a place

quickly, continuously, and in large amounts. **+ of** ▶ *Blood was pumping out of a deep wound in his side.*

3 pump out sth, **pump** sth **out**: to produce something continuously in large amounts, especially something bad ▶ *Every year the city's industries and vehicles pump out five million tonnes of pollutants.*

PUMP UP →

1 pump up sth, **pump** sth **up**: to fill something with air, for example a tyre, using a pump ▶ *I had to pump up the tyres on my bike before I could leave.*

2 pump sth **up**, **pump up** sth: to force liquid to come up from under the ground to the surface, using a pump ▶ *Salt water is pumped up from deep below the ground.*

3 pump sb **up**, **pump up** sb: to make someone feel very confident or excited about something ▶ *Jody's parents have always pumped her up with their enthusiastic support.*

pumped-up ADJ very confident or excited, especially in an annoying way ▶ *Everybody disliked the pumped-up ways of the college boys who came into town at the weekend.*

4 pump up sth, **pump** sth **up**: to increase the amount or number of something ▶ *At least the government haven't pumped up taxes yet.*

5 pump up sth, **pump** sth **up**: to make something improve ▶ *Economists assumed that the central banks could pump up the economy.*

6 pump up: to lift weights so that you become stronger ▶ *If you want to pump up, you'll need to go to the gym regularly.*

pumped up ADJ having a lot of muscles because you lift weights ▶ *Linda Hamilton plays the pumped up heroine in 'Terminator 2'.*

PUNCH

PUNCH UP →

punch up sth, **punch** sth **up**: to make something more interesting or exciting ▶ *They'd tried to punch up the movie with some exotic music, but it was still boring.*

PUSH

PUSH ABOUT *see* PUSH AROUND

PUSH AHEAD →

push ahead: to continue doing something, even though there are problems ▶ *I'd like you all to push ahead and get the job done as soon as possible.*

PUSH AROUND, *also* PUSH ABOUT →

push sb **around/about**: to tell someone what to do in a rude way ▶ *Why do you always let other people push you around?*

PUSH ASIDE →

push sth **aside**, **push aside** sth: to decide not to think about something, for example because it is unpleasant ▶ *For a moment Denny felt guilty – but quickly pushed it aside.*

PUSH BACK →

1 push sth **back**, **push back** sth: to deliberately delay an event, date, project etc that has already been arranged ▶ *The start date for the talks has now been pushed back to the end of the month.*

2 push back sth, **push** sth **back**: to force a crowd or army to move backwards from their present position ▶ *Police pushed the crowd back from the gates of the palace.*

3 push back the boundaries of sth *also* **push back the frontiers of** sth: to discover or do something that had not been known or done before ▶ *Over the past decade, we have pushed back the frontiers of space exploration.*

P

PUSH FOR →

push for sth: to try to persuade people that something should happen or be done ▶ *Parents are pushing for a nursery school place for every child.*

PUSH FORWARD →

1 push forward, push forward sth, **push** sth **forward**: to continue doing or planning something in a determined way. **+ with** ▶ *The two leaders will attempt to push forward with the peace process.*

2 push forward sth, **push** sth **forward**: to try to make people think about or accept a particular idea ▶ *He was still trying to push forward the idea of a coalition government.*

3 push forward: if an army pushes forward, it moves further in a particular direction ▶ *The western armies were pushing forward rapidly as planned.*

4 push forward the boundaries of sth also **push forward the frontiers of** sth: to make more things acceptable or possible than before ▶ *researchers who are pushing forward the boundaries of scientific knowledge*

PUSH IN →

push in: to force yourself in front of

other people who are already waiting in a queue ▶ *We were just about to get on the bus when someone else pushed in.*

PUSH INTO →

push sb **into** sth: to force someone to do something that they do not really want to do ▶ *At the time I didn't want to stay at school, but I'm glad my parents pushed me into it now.*

PUSH OFF →

1 push off!: used to rudely tell someone to go away ▶ *"Push off," she shouted. "How dare you come here?"* ▶ *I told him to push off and he hit me.*

2 push off: to leave a place ▶ *It's time I pushed off home – they'll be wondering where I am.*

PUSH ON →

1 push on: to continue travelling somewhere instead of stopping ▶ *Finding the roads almost traffic-free, I decided to push on towards the west coast.*

2 push on: to continue doing something in a determined way ▶ *Charlie was a great leader – he could motivate everybody to push on.* **with** ▶ *The president decided to push on with his re-election campaign, despite his heart problems.*

PUSH OUT →

push sb **out, push out** sb: to force someone out of their job or position ▶ *Many children feel they have been pushed out when a new baby arrives in the family.*

PUSH OVER →

push sb/sth **over, push over** sb/sth: to make someone or something fall to the ground by pushing them ▶ *One of the older boys pushed him over and sat on him.* ▶ *Maggie jumped up quickly, pushing her chair over by mistake.*

pushover N something that is easy to do or a person who is easy to persuade ▶ *Because Tom's quiet and polite, people tend to think he's a pushover.*

PUSH THROUGH →

push through sth, **push** sth **through**: to succeed in getting a plan, law etc officially accepted ▶ *Reagan pushed* through the greatest increase in defence spending in US history.

PUSH TO →
push the door/window to: to close or nearly close a door or window by pushing it ▶ *Marcus climbed out of the window and pushed it to.*

PUSH TOWARDS, *also* **PUSH TOWARD** →
1 push sb towards/toward sth: to strongly influence or encourage someone to achieve something ▶ *Officials met on Tuesday in an effort to push negotiators towards a settlement.*

2 push towards/toward sth: to try hard to do or achieve something ▶ *The country has been pushing towards independence for nearly ten years.*

PUSH UP →
push sth up, push up sth: to make the price, rate, amount etc of something increase ▶ *House sales are starting to push up prices.*

PUT

PUT ABOUT →
put sth about, put about sth: to tell people that something is true so that a lot of people believe it, even if it is not true ▶ *Rumours were put about that the company was planning to close the factory.* **put it about that** ▶ *Tammy's been putting it about that I'm trying to get her job, which is rubbish.*

PUT ACROSS →
1 put across sth, put sth across: to explain your ideas, opinions etc clearly ▶ *The Democrats ran a series of TV commercials, in an effort to put their message across.*

2 put yourself across: to make someone understand you and realize what sort of person you are ▶ *He's a brilliant artist, but he doesn't put himself across very well in interviews.*

PUT AROUND, *also* **PUT ROUND** →
put around/round sth, put sth around/round: to tell people that something is true so that a lot of people believe it ▶ *I know it's not true, but that's the story they've been putting around in the press.*

PUT ASIDE →
1 put aside sth, put sth aside: to stop thinking or worrying about something, so that you can think about or achieve something else ▶ *Ken put aside his own personal ambitions in order to help his wife with her career.* **put aside your differences** ▶ *She urged the people to put aside their differences and work together for peace.*

2 put aside sth, put sth aside: to save money, especially regularly ▶ *Her parents used to put aside a little money each month for her college fees.*

3 put aside sth, put sth aside: to keep something so that you can use it later ▶ *Drain the rice and put it aside to cool.*

PUT AT →
put sth at sth: to calculate or guess an amount, number, age etc, without being very exact ▶ *The cost of this year's show has been put at over £350,000.*

PUT AWAY →
1 put away sth, put sth away: to put something in the place where it is usually kept when it is not being used ▶ *The girl stopped writing and put away her notebook.* ▶ *"Put that gun away, you idiot," said Baker.*

2 put sb away: to put someone in prison or a hospital for people who are mentally ill ▶ *If the police get to him, he'll be put away for life.*

3 put away sth, put sth away: to get rid of thoughts, feelings, or attitudes that you had before ▶ *She decided to* *put away such childish thoughts and get on with her work.*

4 put away sth, **put** sth **away**: to save money, especially regularly ► *They'd been putting away a little money each week to pay for their wedding.*

5 put away sth, **put** sth **away**: to eat or drink a lot of something, especially a surprisingly large amount ► *The girl sitting next to me on the plane must have put away half a bottle of vodka during the flight.*

PUT BACK →

1 put sth **back**, **put back** sth: to put something in the place where it was before ► *He put the watch back in his waistcoat pocket and rose to his feet.* ► *Can you put the milk back in the fridge?*

2 put back sth, **put** sth **back**: to arrange for something to happen at a later time than was planned ► *The meeting's been put back to 3 o'clock.* ► *The prison authorities have put back his release date till next December.*

3 put back sth, **put** sth **back**: to delay something so that it happens at a later time ► *a series of strikes that could put back the opening of the new bridge by two or three months*

4 put sth **back**, **put back** sth: to make someone or something be something that they used to have before ► *Read this. It'll put the smile back on your face!* ► *The band says their mission is to put the soul back into rock'n'roll.*

5 put back sth, **put** sth **back**: to change a clock or watch so that it shows an earlier time ► *The clocks get put back this weekend.*

6 put back sth, **put** sth **back**: to drink a lot of alcohol quickly. **put it back** ► *He must have drunk ten pints. He can certainly put it back.*

PUT BEFORE →

1 put sth/sb **before** sth/sb: to pay more attention to one thing or person than another ► *Some airlines are putting profits before passenger safety.* ► *Most employers expect their workers to put their job before their family life.*

2 put sth **before** sb/sth: to give something to a committee, parliament etc, so that they can officially discusss or examine it ► *A report into the accident will be put before the Civil Aviation Authority.*

PUT BEHIND →

1 put sth **behind** sb: to try to forget about an unpleasant experience and not let it affect you in the future ► *His first wife committed suicide in 1961, and he was really never able to put this behind him.*

2 put sth **behind** sth: to support something by giving money or by working to make it a success ► *American companies put millions of dollars behind the bid to host the games.*

PUT BY →

put by sth, **put** sth **by**: to save money so that you can use it later for a particular purpose ► *Luckily I had some money put by in case of emergencies.*

PUT DOWN →

1 put down sth, **put** sth **down**: to stop holding, carrying, or using something and put it somewhere ► *Stanley put down his newspaper and glared at her.* ► *What are you doing with that knife? Put it down!*

2 put down the phone also **put the phone down**: to put the receiver back onto the telephone after you have finished your conversation ▶ *"I can't talk now," she said and put the phone down.*

3 put sb down: to criticize someone in an unkind way ▶ *Her ex-husband was always putting her down in front of her friends.* ▶ *I'm fed up with being put down and made to feel stupid.*

putdown N an unkind remark or criticism ▶ *The comment was clearly intended as a putdown.*

4 put yourself down: to tell other people that you are not very successful, do not have good qualities etc, when in fact this is not true ▶ *Of course you're a good teacher. You shouldn't put yourself down all the time.*

5 I couldn't put it down also **it's impossible to put down**: used to say that a book is so exciting or interesting that you do not want to stop reading it ▶ *It's one of the best novels I've ever read. I just couldn't put it down.*

6 put down a rebellion/riot etc: to use force to stop a violent attempt to change the government or a protest ▶ *In 1745 the Prince led his army into England, but the rebellion was soon put down.*

7 put sth down, put down sth: to kill an animal without causing it any pain, because it is old or ill ▶ *The horse had to be put down after breaking a leg yesterday.*

8 put sth down, put down sth: to write something on paper instead of just thinking about it ▶ *"Have you got the phone fixed yet?" "No. I'll put it down on my list of things to do."* **put sth down on paper** ▶ *It often helps to put your thoughts down on paper.*

9 put down sth, put sth down: to pay part of the total cost or value of something when you arrange to buy it or rent it. **put down a deposit** (=a deposit is the part of the total cost or value of something that you put down) ▶ *They put down a £10,000 deposit on the house when they bought it.*

10 put down sth, put sth down: to put a carpet or other covering onto the floor or the ground ▶ *They're having a wooden floor put down in the bedroom.*

11 put sb down, put down sb: to stop a car, bus etc at a particular place and let someone get out there ▶ *They asked the driver to put them down at the station.*

12 put sb down: to put a baby in a bed so that it can sleep ▶ *Harry seems a lot quieter now. I think I'll put him down for a nap.*

PUT DOWN AS →

put sb/sth down as sth: to decide that someone or something is a particular type of person or thing, often when they are not ▶ *When she first met him, she immediately put him down as a boring middle-aged businessman.*

PUT DOWN FOR →

put sb down for sth: to write someone's name on a list so that they can take part in an activity, join a school etc ▶ *His parents have put him down for the best school in the area.*

PUT DOWN TO →

1 put sth down to sth: to think that something, especially a problem or a bad situation, is caused by something else ▶ *I didn't feel too good the next morning, but I put it down to what I'd eaten the night before.*

2 put sth down to experience: to try to forget about something unsuccessful or embarrassing, or try to learn something useful from it ▶ *There'll be* *other girlfriends. It's just one of those things you have to put down to experience.*

PUT FORWARD →

1 put forward sth, **put** sth **forward**: to suggest something for other people to consider and discuss ▶ *A number of theories were put forward at the time about the possible causes of his death.*

2 put sb **forward, put forward** sb: to say officially that you think someone should be considered for a job, allowed to join an organization etc.
+ for ▶ *The names of four possible candidates have been put forward for the post.*

3 put sth **forward, put forward** sth: to arrange for something to happen at an earlier time than was planned ▶ *The meeting has been put forward to tomorrow. I hope you can still come.*

4 put sth **forward**: to change a watch or clock so that it shows a later time ▶ *We have to put the clocks forward one hour this weekend.*

PUT IN →

1 put in sth, **put** sth **in**: to officially make a request, order, claim, or offer ▶ *I've put in a request for a transfer.* ▶ *Buyers have until next Monday to put in their bids.*

2 put in sth, **put** sth **in**: to connect a new piece of equipment to an electricity supply, water supply etc ▶ *They've had a new central heating system put in.*

PUT IN FOR →

put in for sth: to make an official request to be allowed to do or have something ▶ *Her husband's decided to put in for early retirement.* ▶ *Why don't you put in for a pay rise?*

PUT IN, *also* PUT INTO →

1 put in sth, **put** sth **in**, **put** sth **into** sth: to use effort, work, or time in

order to try to do something ▶ *She's puts all her emotional energy into her job.* ▶ *The whole team put in a tremendous amount of effort.*

2 put in sth, **put** sth **in**, **put** sth **into** sth: to provide money so that people can do something, or buy shares in a company so that you can make a profit ▶ *More money needs to be put into cancer research.* ▶ *Remember, when putting your money into the stock market, that prices can go down as well as up.*

3 put sb **in/into** sth: to make someone go to a prison, a hospital etc ▶ *Opposition leaders are being arrested and put in prison.* ▶ *They decided to put their grandmother into a nursing home.*

PUT OFF →

1 put off sth, **put** sth **off**: to delay doing something until later, especially something you do not want to do ▶ *Why don't you talk to him about it? You can't keep putting it off forever.*
put off doing sth ▶ *I'd put off going to the dentist for as long as I could.*

2 put sb **off, put** sth **off** sb: to stop someone from liking another person or thing or stop them from being interested in it ▶ *Don't be put off by the name. It's actually a very pretty plant.* ▶ *My last boyfriend put me off men for life.* **put** sb **off doing** sth ▶ *A lot of people are put off travelling by rail because of high fares.*

   off-putting ADJ likely to make you dislike someone or something ▶ *There was something rather off-putting about his manner.*

3 put off sth, **put** sth **off**: to make a light stop working by pressing a switch ▶ *Don't forget to put the lights off when you leave.*

4 put sb **off**: to delay meeting someone, talking to someone, paying someone etc ▶ *Every time she asked for her money back they kept putting her off with some excuse or other.*

5 put sb off, put sb off sth: to make it difficult for someone to pay attention to what they are doing ▶ *Stop giggling! You're putting me off!* ▶ *He complained that the photographers were putting him off his game.*

> **off-putting** ADJ making it difficult for you to pay attention to what you are doing ▶ *It's a bit off-putting having someone following you around all the time.*

PUT ON →

1 put on sth, put sth on: to put clothes on your body ▶ *She put on her coat and went outside.* ▶ *I liked the shoes, and when I put them on they fitted perfectly.*

2 put on sth, put sth on: to put make-up, cream etc on your skin ▶ *She sat down in front of the mirror and began to put on her make-up.*

3 put on sth, put sth on: to make a light or a piece of equipment start working ▶ *Can you put the lights back on? I can't see what I'm doing.* ▶ *She put on the kettle for her morning cup of coffee.*

4 put on sth, put sth on: to put a CD, tape, or record in a machine and make it start playing ▶ *Perry went over to the stereo and put on some jazz.*

5 put on sth, put sth on: to arrange for a performance, show, competition etc to take place ▶ *They often put on exhibitions of work by local artists.*

6 put sb on sth: to give someone a particular type of medicine or medical treatment ▶ *I went to the hospital about my asthma, and they've put me on steroids.*

7 put sb on a diet: to tell someone to eat only certain types of food because they are unhealthy or too fat ▶ *His wife says he's overweight, and keeps threatening to put him on a diet.*

8 put on weight/ 2 kilos etc: to become fatter and heavier ▶ *Can it be possible that I've put on eight pounds in three weeks?*

9 put the blame/responsibility on sb/sth: to say that someone should be blamed or should be considered responsible for something ▶ *That girl was going to try to put the blame on him, he could tell.*

10 put a restriction/ban etc on sth: to make a rule that controls or stops something ▶ *New restrictions are to be put on tobacco advertising.* ▶ *Japan, Norway, and the other countries agreed to put a ban on commercial whaling.*

11 put on sth: to deliberately behave or speak in a way that is different from usual or different from how you really feel ▶ *Whenever she's on the phone she always puts on a posh voice.* **put on a brave face** (=try not to show that you are worried or upset) ▶ *She continued to put on a brave face, despite reports of serious problems with her marriage.*

12 be putting it on: to pretend to be ill, upset, injured etc, especially in order to make other people feel sorry for you ▶ *Of course he's not sick. He's just putting it on.*

13 be putting sb **on**: if someone is putting you on, they are not telling the truth ▶ *You scored three goals? You're putting me on!*

14 put on a show also *put on a display*: to show what you are able to do or what power you have ▶ *Allied troops put on a devastating show of force.* **put on an impressive/poor etc performance** ▶ *The French team will have to put on an impressive performance if they are to win today.*

15 put on sth, **put** sth **on**: to provide something for people to use, eat, drink etc ▶ *Special buses are being put on to take fans to and from the concert.*

16 put emphasis on sth also *put stress on* sth: to say that you think that something is particularly important ▶ *Parents are not putting enough emphasis on healthy eating.*

17 put sth **on** sth: to risk an amount of money on the result of a race, game etc ▶ *I never put money on horses, I always lose.*

18 put sth **on** sth: to increase the cost or price of something by a particular amount ▶ *There are rumours that the government plans to put 10p on the price of fuel.*

19 put sth **on, put on** sth: to start cooking something ▶ *I put your supper on an hour ago. It should be ready by now.*

PUT ONTO, also **PUT ON TO →** **put** sb **onto/on to** sb/sth: to tell someone about an interesting or useful place, product, person etc ▶ *It's a great restaurant. I think it was Wendi who first put me onto it.*

PUT OUT →
1 put out sth, **put** sth **out**: to make a light stop working by pressing or

turning a switch ▶ *Don't forget to put the lights out before you leave the building.*

2 put out sth, **put** sth **out**: to make a fire, cigarette, or candle stop burning ▶ *Please stay in your seats and put out your cigarettes.*

3 put sb **out**: to cause extra work or trouble for someone, especially by asking them to help you ▶ *Thanks for letting me use your car. I hope I'm not putting you out.*

4 put yourself out: to use a lot of effort or time in order to help someone, when this is not convenient for you ▶ *He felt he had already put himself out by agreeing to see Dougal at such short notice.*

5 put out sth, **put** sth **out**: to produce an official statement, warning, or request ▶ *A lot of the information that is put out on the Internet is not totally accurate.* ▶ *He later put out a TV appeal for his wife to come home.*

6 put out sth, **put** sth **out**: to produce a record, book, or other product and make it available for people to buy ▶ *The band put out a string of hit records in the early sixties.*

7 put out sth, **put** sth **out**: to broadcast a programme on the television or the radio ▶ *Shows that contain a lot of sex or bad language are usually put out after 9 o'clock.*

8 put out sth, **put** sth **out**: to move your hand, arm, foot etc forward ▶ *When he put out his hand to shake hands with her, she just ignored him.*

9 put your tongue out also *put out your tongue*: to push your tongue out of your mouth, especially as a rude sign to someone ▶ *The little boy put his tongue out and ran away.*

10 be put out: to feel annoyed, upset, or offended by something ▶ *We were a* *little put out at not being invited to the wedding.*

11 put out sth, **put** sth **out:** to put something somewhere for people to use, eat, look at etc ▶ *I'll put out the knives and forks on the table.*

12 put out sth, **put** sth **out:** to take something outside your house and leave it there ▶ *Eric was just about to put out the washing when the rain started.*

13 put out sth, **put** sth **out:** to injure part of your body by stretching or twisting it too much ▶ *Catherine put her back out trying to carry a box of books up the stairs.*

14 put out sth, **put** sth **out:** if a plant or tree puts out leaves, flowers etc, it starts to grow them ▶ *The roses have already started to put out new buds.*

15 put sb **out:** to make someone unconscious before a medical operation ▶ *One patient claimed that they hadn't put him out properly before his operation.*

PUT OUT OF →

put sb **out of** sth: to stop someone from being able to do something, or continue taking part in something ▶ *He had a knee injury, which threatened to put him out of the World Cup.* **put** sb **out of business** (=make someone be unable to continue their business) ▶ *Local fishermen say the new fishing quotas will put them out of business.*

PUT OUT TO →

put sth **out to** sb/ sth: if work is put out to a particular company, it is offered to them ▶ *Existing waste disposal operations will be put out to private companies.*

PUT OVER →

1 put over sth, **put** sth **over:** to succeed in making other people understand your ideas, opinions etc ▶ *The champion is the ideal man to put this message over to young athletes.*

2 put one over (on) sb: to trick someone by making them believe something that is not true ▶ *She realized that the salesman was trying to put one over on her, and said she wasn't interested.*

PUT PAST →

I wouldn't put it past sb: used to say that you would not be surprised if someone did something bad or unusual ▶ *"Do you think Harry took the money?" "I wouldn't put it past him."*

PUT ROUND *see* PUT AROUND

PUT THROUGH →

1 put sb **through:** to connect someone to the person they want to speak to on the telephone ▶ *One moment, caller, I'm just putting you through.* **+ to** ▶ *She was put through to the manager's personal assistant.*

2 put through a call *also* **put a call through:** to make a telephone call to someone ▶ *Someone had put a call through to the embassy, warning them about the attack.*

3 put sb **through** sth: to make someone do something difficult or experience something unpleasant. **put** sb **through it** ▶ *He says his last wife really put him through it, and he never wants to get married again.* **put** sb **through hell** ▶ *I must have put my mother through hell when I was a teenager.*

4 put through sth, **put** sth **through, put** sth **through** sth: to formally agree to a new law or plan ▶ *The UN Security Council put through a resolution calling for an immediate ceasefire.*

5 put sb **through college/ university etc:** to pay for someone to study at a college or university ▶ *Mick had a* huge car loan and three kids to put through college.

6 put sth through sth: to make something go through a process or system, in order to change it or test it ▶ *Every car is put through a series of safety checks before it leaves the factory.*

PUT TO →

1 put sth to sb: to ask someone a question, especially officially or publicly ▶ *When the same question was put to his deputy, we got a completely different answer.*

2 put sth to sb: to ask someone to officially consider a plan, suggestion etc ▶ *"I'll put your suggestion to the committee,"* she said. **put sth to the vote** (=ask people to vote about something in order to make a decision about it) ▶ *The issue of capital punishment is to be put to the vote yet again.*

3 put it to sb that: to suggest to someone that something is true, especially in a court of law ▶ *I put it to you that you murdered your husband for his money.*

4 put an end to sth *also* **put a stop to sth:** to stop something from continuing to happen ▶ *It's about time we put an end to all this nonsense.*

5 put sb to a lot of trouble/expense etc: to make someone have to use a lot of effort, money etc ▶ *I hope I haven't put you to too much trouble.*

6 put your name to sth *also* **put your signature to sth:** to sign your name at the end of an official document, letter etc, saying that you agree with it ▶ *They refused to put their names to the agreement and were fired on the spot.*

PUT TOGETHER →

1 put together sth, put sth together: to produce something by getting a group of things together and organizing them ▶ *The Rolling Stones have recently put together an album of their greatest hits.* ▶ *With a little effort, you can put together a meal that's light, refreshing, and also very healthy.*

2 put together sth, put sth together: to produce something such as a plan or an agreement by collecting ideas, information, or suggestions ▶ *A group of local people put together a rescue plan to try to save the theatre.*

3 put together sth, put sth together: to make something by joining all the pieces together ▶ *There should be some instructions that show you how to put it all together.*

4 put together sth, put sth together: to form a group or team ▶ *He put his first band together while he was still at college.*

5 put sth together: to think about several pieces of information or parts of a situation together, for example so that you can understand something better ▶ *When you put it all together, it sounds like he must be guilty.* ▶ *Paul needed to be somewhere quiet where he could put his thoughts together.*

6 than the rest put together *also* **than the others put together:** used to emphasize that something or someone is much better, cleverer, bigger etc than something or someone else ▶ *Josie's sure to do well. She's smarter than all the others put together.*

PUT TOWARDS, *also* PUT TOWARD →

put sth towards/toward sth: to use some money in order to pay part of the cost of something ▶ *She says that if she wins, she's going to put the money towards a trip to Italy.*

PUT UP →

1 put up sth, **put** sth **up**: to build something such as a building, wall, or a statue ▶ *After the war huge apartment buildings were put up around Paris.* **put up a tent** ▶ *At 25,000 feet they decided to put up their tent and wait for the dawn.*

2 put up sth, **put** sth **up**: to increase something, for example prices, taxes, or rents ▶ *The government should put up taxes on things that damage the environment.*

3 put up sth, **put** sth **up**: to put a sign, notice, picture etc on a wall or other place so that it can be seen ▶ *The owner had put up signs everywhere saying 'Private Property, Keep Out'.*

4 put up sth, **put** sth **up**: to attach a shelf, cupboard etc to a wall ▶ *We've had some new cupboards put up in our kitchen.*

5 put sth **up**, **put up** sth: to open something such as an umbrella or put something such as a hood over your head ▶ *Some people in the crowd had started putting up their umbrellas.* ▶ *He put his hood up so that his face was partly hidden.*

6 put up sth, **put** sth **up**: to provide the money that is needed to pay for something ▶ *It's a great idea, but who's going to put up the money?* **+ for** ▶ *Twentieth Century Fox is putting up the money for the movie.*

7 put up a fight also **put up a struggle etc**: to try to fight or compete with someone, or try to stop something from happening ▶ *England put up a great fight, but in the end the better team won.* ▶ *He didn't put up much of a struggle when he was arrested.*

8 put sth **up for sale/auction**: to make something available for people to buy, especially a house, land, business, or a valuable object ▶ *When my father died, the house and all its contents were put up for auction.* ▶ *The business was losing money and they decided to put it up for sale.*

9 put sb **up**: to provide someone with a place to stay, usually for a short time ▶ *Some friends have offered to put us up for the night.*

10 put up sth, **put** sth **up**: to suggest an idea, argument, or reason for something ▶ *Leith put up several arguments, but she had an answer for every one of them.*

11 put up sb, **put** sb **up**: to choose someone to represent your party at an election ▶ *The Alliance Party put up substantially fewer candidates at the last election.*

PUT UP TO →

put sb **up to** sth: to encourage someone to do something stupid or dangerous ▶ *"Did Candy put you up t[o] this?" Rory demanded.* ▶ *He's normal[ly] such a well-behaved child. Someone must have put him up to it.*

PUT UP WITH →

put up with sth/sb: to accept an unpleasant situation or someone's annoying behaviour without complaining ▶ *The police have to put up with a lot of abuse.* ▶ *I'm surprise[d] that she's put up with him for all thes[e] years.*

PUT UPON →

1 feel put upon: to feel that you are being treated unfairly, for example because you are asked to do more work than someone else ▶ *It's often the most productive staff who feel most put upon.*

2 put emphasis upon sth also **put stress upon** sth: to say that you thin[k]

that something is particularly
important ▶ *Particular stress was put
upon the study of languages such as
Latin.*

3 put an interpretation/value upon
sth: to consider that something has a
particular meaning or value ▶ *Dawkins
puts a different interpretation upon
the word "selfish" from the usual
meaning.*

4 put limitations upon sb/sth: to
make rules that control or limit
someone or something ▶ *the
limitations that are put upon us by our
genes*

PUZZLE

PUZZLE OUT →
puzzle out sth, **puzzle** sth **out**: to try
to understand a confusing situation or
solve a difficult problem by thinking
about it carefully ▶ *He stared at his
old neighbour trying to puzzle out why
she looked so different.*

PUZZLE OVER →
puzzle over sth: to try hard to
understand something that seems
difficult or confusing ▶ *Mark puzzled
over the words, but they meant
nothing to him.*

P

Qq

QUARREL

QUARREL WITH →

quarrel with sth: to disagree with an idea or opinion ▶ *Not many people would quarrel with the idea of more choice and more personal freedom.*

QUEUE

QUEUE UP →

1 queue up:
to form or join a line of people waiting to do something or go somewhere ▶ *The four of us queued up outside the stadium for over two hours.*

2 be queuing up to do sth: if people are queuing up to do something, they all want to do it very much ▶ *The school is the best in the area, and parents are queuing up to send their children there.*

QUIET

QUIET DOWN →

quiet down, quiet sb **down**: to become calmer and less active or noisy, or to make someone do this ▶ *Quiet down and get ready for bed!* ▶ *Lee bounced the child on his knee to quiet her down.*

QUIETEN

QUIETEN DOWN →

1 quieten down, quieten sb **down**: if someone quietens down, or if you quieten them down, they become quieter and calmer ▶ *I spent the first half of the lesson trying to quieten the kids down.*

2 quieten down: to become quieter, calmer, and less busy ▶ *Things tend to quieten down after the Christmas rush is over.* ▶ *The fighting in our immediate area seems to have quietened down*

QUIT

QUIT OF →

be quit of sth: to get rid of something or someone that was causing you problems ▶ *She was tired of his selfish demands, and determined to be quit of him.*

QUIT ON →

quit on sb: to stop helping or working with someone, when they need you ▶ *So you're going to quit on me? I thought i could rely on you!*

quit on sb: if a machine or vehicle quits on you, it stops working while you are using it ▶ *Then his computer simply quit on him and he went crazy.*

Rr

RABBIT

RABBIT ON →

rabbit on: to talk continuously for a long time in a boring or annoying way ▶ *I'm not going to stand around here listening to you rabbiting on.* **+ about** ▶ *I had to listen to Tony rabbiting on for hours about his work.*

RACK

RACK UP →

rack up sth, **rack** sth **up**: to achieve a large total of something ▶ *They racked up a £7.4 billion trade surplus during 1995.*

RAG

RAG ON →

rag on sb: to criticize someone or keep telling them that they should do something ▶ *Quit ragging on me! I'll do it in a minute.*

rag on sb: to make jokes about someone and laugh at them in order to embarrass them ▶ *Everybody's ragging on Steve about his new girlfriend.*

RAGE

RAGE AGAINST, *also* RAGE AT →

rage against sth, **rage at** sth/sb: to feel extremely angry about something and to express this strongly ▶ *Roosevelt believed passionately in equality, and raged against social injustice.* ▶ *"You never gave a damn about us" her son raged at her.*

RAILROAD

RAILROAD INTO →

railroad sb **into** sth: to persuade someone to do something without giving them time to think about it ▶ *She hesitated, unwilling to be railroaded into a decision.*

RAILROAD THROUGH →

railroad through sth, **railroad** sth **through**: to force a parliament to vote on something very quickly, so that people do not have much time to think about it ▶ *The government is hoping to avoid awkward questions by trying to railroad the bill through.*

RAIN

RAIN DOWN →

rain down, **rain down** sth, **rain** sth **down**: to fall in large quantities, or make something fall in large quantities ▶ *Falling debris rained down as firefighters fought the flames.* **+ on** *also* **+ upon** ▶ *I put my arms over my head as pieces of glass started to rain down on me.*

BE RAINED OFF, *also* BE RAINED OUT →

be rained off/out: if an event is rained off or rained out, it cannot take place or has to stop because there is too much rain ▶ *Last night's match against Manchester United was rained off.* ▶ *We had tickets to the Blue Jays game but it was rained out.*

RAKE

RAKE IN →

rake in sth: to earn a large amount of money ▶ *The report said that the nation's top lawyers raked in some £860 million in one year.* **be raking it in** ▶ *Everyone assumes that if you're on TV, you must be raking it in.*

RAKE OFF →

rake off sth, **rake** sth **off**: to get part of the profits of a business or organization dishonestly ▶ *He ran a cancer charity, and was believed to have raked off much of the cash for himself.*

R

RAKE OVER →

rake over sth: to talk or think about something unpleasant again and again, when it would be better to forget it ▶ *"There's no point in raking over the past," my mother always said.*

RAKE UP →

1 rake up sth, **rake** sth **up**: to talk about something unpleasant from the past that people do not want you to mention ▶ *They don't seem to realize how painful it is for her to have all this raked up again.*

2 rake sth **up, rake up** sth: to collect things together for a particular purpose, when this is difficult to do ▶ *Between them they only managed to rake up £50.*

RALLY

RALLY AROUND, *also* **RALLY ROUND** →

rally around/round, rally around/round sb: if a group of people rally around, they all work to try to help and support someone ▶ *Her friends all rallied round when her father died.* ▶ *The cabinet publicly rallied around the Prime Minister, but in private began to think about replacing her.*

RAMBLE

RAMBLE ON →

ramble on: to talk or write for a long time in a boring and confused way ▶ *She rambled on, but Stacey wasn't listening.* **+ about** ▶ *Sarah glanced at the clock – he had been rambling on about himself for over an hour.*

RANGE

BE RANGED AGAINST →

be ranged against sb/sth: to oppose someone or something and be ready to fight against them ▶ *By now there were over seven European states ranged against them.*

RANK

RANK AMONG →

rank among sth/sb, **be ranked among** sth/sb: to be one of the best of a particular type ▶ *The Lebanon produces some red wines that rank among the world's finest.*

RAP

RAP OUT →

rap out sth, **rap** sth **out**: to give an order or say something quickly, suddenly, and in a way that sounds angry ▶ *The ambassador rapped out an order and four servants hurried across the room.*

RAT

RAT ON →

1 rat on sb: to be disloyal to someone by telling a person in authority about something that they have done wrong ▶ *I never ratted on Albert. I wouldn't rat on a friend.*

2 rat on sth: to not do something that you have promised to do for someone ▶ *The government was accused of ratting on its promises.*

RATION

RATION OUT →

ration out sth, **ration** sth **out**: to divide something among a group of people so that each person gets a small amount ▶ *Their short supplies of food and water had to be carefully rationed out.*

RATTLE

RATTLE AROUND →

rattle around: to live in a building that is much bigger than you need it to be so that you do not feel comfortable. **+ in** ▶ *This house is much too big for us now the kids have left – we're just rattling around in it.*

RATTLE OFF →
rattle off sth, **rattle** sth **off**: to say something quickly without stopping, especially a list or something that you have learned ▶ She rattled off a list of all the best hotels and restaurants in town.

RATTLE ON →
rattle on: to talk quickly and for a long time in a boring way ▶ I stifled a yawn, but Elsie didn't notice and just rattled on.

RATTLE THROUGH →
rattle through sth: to speak or do something very quickly because you want to finish as quickly as possible ▶ She rattled through her speech as if she couldn't wait to leave.

RAVE

RAVE ABOUT, also **RAVE OVER** →
rave about/over sb/sth: to talk in an excited way about how much you admire or like someone or something ▶ The critics are raving about the latest performance of Macbeth.

REACH

REACH OUT FOR →
1 reach out for sth: to try to achieve a better situation, for example peace, love, or happiness ▶ We were never satisfied – we were always reaching out for new experiences and highs.

2 reach out for help also **reach out for assistance etc**: to ask someone for help ▶ Many of these people need protection, and we urge them to reach out for help.

REACH OUT TO →
1 reach out to sb: to offer help, comfort, or support to someone ▶ We must reach out to the many children who have no-one to turn to.

2 reach out to sb: to try and communicate your ideas to people that you have not succeeded in communicating with in the past ▶ How does your party plan to reach out to poorer voters?

3 reach out to sb: to ask for help, comfort, or support ▶ She reached out to him as a last source of help.

REACT

REACT AGAINST →
react against sth: to show that you dislike or disagree with someone's rules or ideas by deliberately doing the opposite ▶ It's normal for teenagers to react against their parents' beliefs. ▶ Feminists were reacting against traditional ideas of a woman's role in society.

READ

READ BACK →
read sth **back, read back** sth: to read something that you have written, to check that it satisfactory ▶ When I read back my story, I was quite pleased with it. **+ to** ▶ He would dictate a letter to Dinah and then get her to read it back to him.

READ INTO →
read sth **into** sth: to think that something has a meaning or importance that it may not really have ▶ Robert wondered if she was reading more into his comments than he actually meant. **read too much into** sth ▶ Only 15 % of the population voted in last week's election, so don't read too much into the result.

READ OUT →
read sth **out, read out** sth: to say the words you are reading to other people ▶ He opened the envelope and read out the name of the winner. **+ to** ▶ Sarah left a message – I'll read it out to you. **read** sth **out loud** ▶ I read the letter out loud to my wife.

READ OVER →
read over sth, **read** sth **over**: to read

something carefully in order to check details or find mistakes ▶ *Read the contract over carefully before you sign it.*

READ THROUGH →

read through sth, **read** sth **through**: to read something from beginning to end, especially in order to check details or find mistakes ▶ *Always read through what you have written before you leave the exam room.*

READ UP →

read up sth, **read** sth **up**, **read up**: to read about a particular subject, because you want to know more about it ▶ *Barry spent his first day in the job reading up all the relevant facts and figures.* **+ about** *also* **read up on** ▶ *I'll have to read up on the new tax laws before that meeting tomorrow.*

REAR

REAR UP →

rear up: if a horse or similar animal rears up, it suddenly rises upright on its back legs ▶ *Ralph's horse reared up, throwing him to the ground.*

REASON

REASON OUT →

reason sth **out**, **reason out** sth: to think carefully about a problem in order to understand it or decide how to solve it ▶ *Before attempting to fix the program, the engineer has to reason out why it went wrong in the first place.*

REASON WITH →

reason with sb: to talk calmly and sensibly to someone who you think is behaving in an unreasonable way ▶ *I* tried to reason with her, but she locked herself in the bathroom, crying.

REBOUND

REBOUND ON, *also* REBOUND UPON →

rebound on/upon sb: if an action rebounds on someone, it has a harmful effect on them even though it was intended to affect someone else ▶ *Strikers were warned that any further industrial action would rebound upon themselves and their communities.*

RECKON

RECKON ON →

reckon on sth: to expect something to happen and include it in your plans ▶ *We hadn't reckoned on the heavy holiday traffic on the way home.* **reckon on doing** sth ▶ *You can reckon on paying over a thousand pounds for a good computer.* **reckon on** sb **doing** sth ▶ *They didn't reckon on anyone objecting to their scheme.*

RECKON WITH →

1 reckon with sth: to realize that you must be prepared to deal with a particular problem ▶ *The new Republic had to reckon with at least three hostile nations on its borders.*

2 sb/sth **to be reckoned with**: someone or something that must be respected as a serious competitor, opponent, or danger ▶ *I think we showed them that we're a football team to be reckoned with.* **a force to be reckoned with** ▶ *The old aristocracy, however weakened, was still a force to be reckoned with.*

RECKON WITHOUT →

reckon without sth/sb: to make plans without realizing that a particular thing or person may cause you problems ▶ *Watson decided to swim to the island, but had reckoned without the strong currents.*

RECONCILE

RECONCILE TO →

reconcile yourself to sth: to accept something and realize that there is nothing you can do to change it ▶ *Over the years she had reconciled herself to the fact that she would probably never marry.* **be/become reconciled to** sth ▶ *The islanders had never become reconciled to British rule.*

REDUCE

REDUCE TO →

1 reduce sb **to tears/silence etc**: to make someone very upset, quiet etc ▶ *As a manager he was a complete bully, often reducing staff to tears.* **reduce** sb **to a nervous wreck** (=make someone feel extremely frightened) ▶ *The thought of going to the dentist reduces him to a nervous wreck!*

2 reduce sb/sth **to** sth: to cause someone or something to be in a much worse situation or position ▶ *A disastrous business venture had reduced him to near ruin.* ▶ *a once-famous musician reduced to poverty*

3 be reduced to (doing) sth: to have to do something unpleasant, boring, embarrassing etc because you have no choice ▶ *She lost her job as manager and was reduced to doing barwork.* ▶ *Many unemployed people were reduced to begging on the streets.*

4 reduce sth **to** sth: to damage or destroy something so that there is almost nothing left ▶ *The fire spread rapidly, reducing the factory to a pile of twisted metal.* **reduce** sth **to ashes/rubble** ▶ *Much of the city centre was reduced to rubble by the bombing.*

REEK

REEK OF →

1 reek of sth: to smell strongly of something unpleasant ▶ *The bedroom was filthy and reeked of cigarettes.*

2 reek of sth: to seem to have a lot of a particular unpleasant quality ▶ *Their government reeked of corruption.*

REEL

REEL IN →

1 reel in sth, **reel** sth **in**: to pull something on a fishing line or rope towards you by winding the line around a circular piece of equipment ▶ *Luke felt a tug on the line and reeled in a beautiful salmon.*

2 reel in sth/sb, **reel** sth/sb **in**: to attract a large number of people or things ▶ *The programme reels in more than 13 million viewers a show.*

REEL OFF →

reel off sth, **reel** sth **off**: to say something quickly and easily, especially a list ▶ *The waitress reeled off a choice of dishes in rapid Italian.*

REFER

REFER TO →

1 refer to sb/sth: to mention or speak about someone or something, often indirectly ▶ *Although she didn't say his name, everyone knew who she was referring to.* **refer to** sb/sth **as** sth (=call them by a particular name) ▶ *The computer screen is referred to as the monitor.*

2 refer to sth: to read or look at a book, note, map etc in order to get information ▶ *Refer to the course textbook if you need further information on this subject.* ▶ *Without referring to my notes, I can't remember exactly what she said.*

R

3 refer to sth/sb: to describe or relate to a particular person or thing ▶ *The blue line on the graph refers to sales.* ▶ *The table on page three refers to rainfall in the region.*

4 refer sb/sth **to** sb: to send a person or problem to someone with the special skills or knowledge needed to deal with that particular situation or problem ▶ *Your family doctor will refer you to a specialist at the eye hospital.* ▶ *The case has been referred to a higher court.*

REFLECT

REFLECT ON, *also* REFLECT UPON →

1 reflect on/upon sth: to spend time thinking carefully about something ▶ *New Year's Day is a time to reflect on the past year and plan ahead.* ▶ *Reflecting on what he had said, she found herself close to tears.*

2 reflect on/upon sb/sth: to influence other people's opinion about someone or something, especially in a bad way ▶ *Anna felt ashamed, realizing that her father's rudeness would reflect upon her.*

REFRAIN

REFRAIN FROM →

refrain from sth: to not do something, even though you would like to ▶ *Doctors advised him to refrain from all sports for at least three months.* **refrain from doing** sth ▶ *Please refrain from smoking in the restaurant.*

REGALE

REGALE WITH →

regale sb **with** sth: to tell someone stories about things in order to entertain or impress them ▶ *In the bar she met a man called Patrick, who began regaling her with tales of the old days.*

REIN

REIN IN, *also* REIN BACK →

1 rein in/back sth, **rein** sth **in/back**: to control something in order to stop it increasing, especially the amount of money you spend ▶ *the failure of the government to rein in public spending* ▶ *Unless the company reins back its expenditure, jobs will have to go.*

2 rein in/back sb, **rein** sb **in/back**: to try to control the behaviour of a group of people ▶ *After the attempted coup, the government realized it would have to rein in the military.*

REJOICE

REJOICE IN →

rejoice in sth: to be very pleased about something, or to enjoy something very much ▶ *The hostages were busy rejoicing in their new-found freedom.* ▶ *a spiteful man who rejoices in the humiliation of others*

RELATE

RELATE TO →

1 relate to sth/sb *also* **be related to** sth/sb : to be about or connected with a particular subject or person ▶ *The document explains the policy relating to discipline in the school.* ▶ *I still can't understand how all this relates to me.*

2 relate to sth: to be able to understand someone else's situation or feelings, especially because you have been in a similar situation yourself ▶ *She said she felt really angry when he died – I can relate to that.* ▶ *My biggest problem with the film was that I couldn't relate to any of the characters.*

RELIEVE

RELIEVE OF →

1 relieve sb **of** sth: to help someone by taking a problem, responsibility etc, away from them ▶ *They have established a fund to pay her expenses, thereby relieving her of all financial worries.*

2 relieve sb **of** sth: to take away from someone something that they are holding or carrying ▶ *Carl jumped up to relieve Paula of her shopping bag.*

3 relieve sb **of their post** also **relieve** sb **of their duties etc**: to officially take away someone's job from them, especially because they have done something wrong ▶ *The board has decided to relieve you of your duties as head teacher.*

4 relieve sb **of** sth: to steal something from someone – used humorously ▶ *This part of town is full of crooks who'll be happy to relieve you of your wallet!*

RELY

RELY ON, *also* RELY UPON →

1 rely on/upon sth/sb: to need something or someone in order to exist or do something successfully ▶ *The charity relies on public donations in order to continue with its work.* ▶ *She relies completely on public transport.* **+ for** ▶ *Early sailors had to rely on the stars for navigation at night.*

2 rely on/upon sb/sth: to trust someone or something to do what you expect or need. **can rely on** sb ▶ *"You will get the job finished by Friday, won't you?" "You can rely on me."* **+ to do** sth ▶ *The alarm clock isn't working properly, so don't rely on it to wake you up.* **rely on** sth/sb **doing** sth ▶ *You can't rely on your parents lending you the money.*

REMEMBER

REMEMBER TO →

remember me to sb: used to ask someone to say hello for you to another person ▶ *As I left, Carl said, "Remember me to Susan."*

REMIND

REMIND OF →

1 remind sb **of** sth/sb: to think that someone or something is similar to someone or something else ▶ *Cathy reminds me of myself when I was that age.* ▶ *Her voice reminds me a lot of Joni Mitchell.*

2 remind sb **of** sth/sb: to make you remember someone or something ▶ *The smell of boiled cabbage always reminds me of school.* ▶ *The song reminded her of her youth.*

RENDER

RENDER INTO →

render sth **into English/Greek etc**: to translate a piece of language into English, Greek etc ▶ *The ancient manuscripts were rendered into Latin.*

RENDER UP →

render up sth, **render** sth **up**: to give something to someone, especially when you are forced to ▶ *There were severe penalties for anyone who failed to render up their taxes.*

RENEGE

RENEGE ON, *also* RENEGE UPON →

renege on/upon sth: to not do something that you have promised or agreed to do ▶ *Union leaders have accused the company of reneging on its part of the deal.*

RENT

RENT OUT →

rent out sth, **rent** sth **out**: to allow someone to use a room, building, or area of land in return for regular payment ▶ *He sold the business, rented out his house, and set off on a trip around the world.* **+ to** ▶ *There's a separate flat upstairs, which they rent out to students.*

R

REPAIR

REPAIR TO →
repair to sth: to go to a place, especially in order to relax ▶ *Shall we repair to the smoking room, gentlemen?*

REPORT

REPORT BACK →
report back: to give someone information about something that they asked you to find out about ▶ *I was asked to listen in on their conversation and report back later.* **+ to** ▶ *We'd like you to report back to the class when you come back.* **+ on** ▶ *The commission will report back on its findings some time later this year.*

REPORT TO →
report to sb: if you report to someone at work, they are your manager and are in charge of you ▶ *"Who do you report to?" "Paula Davies. She's head of the sales department."*

RESIDE

RESIDE IN →
reside in sth: to exist in something or be caused by something ▶ *Much of the book's value resides in its humour and simplicity.*

RESIDE WITH, *also* RESIDE IN →
reside with/in sb: if power or responsibility resides with or in someone, they have that power or responsibility ▶ *Real political power resided with the army.* ▶ *Ultimate control resides with the company's share-holders.*

RESIGN

RESIGN TO →
resign yourself to sth *also* **be resigned to** sth: to realize that you must accept a difficult or unpleasant situation because you cannot change it ▶ *I'd resigned myself to the fact that*

my political career was over. **resign yourself to doing** sth *also* **be resigned to doing** sth ▶ *She says she's now resigned to living on her own.*

RESONATE

RESONATE WITH →
resonate with sb: if an idea or plan resonates with a particular group of people, they approve of it and strongly support it ▶ *The President's emphasis on job creation clearly resonated with voters.*

RESORT

RESORT TO →
resort to sth: to use a particular method in order to try to achieve something, because other methods have failed ▶ *The government says it is willing to resort to force if necessary in order to get the hostages released.* **resort to doing** sth ▶ *During the coldest winters, people would resort to chopping up and burning their furniture to keep warm.*

RESOUND

RESOUND WITH, *also* RESOUND TO →
resound with/to sth: to be filled with a loud sound ▶ *On summer evenings, the canyon resounds with the cries of frogs and birds.*

REST

REST ON, *also* REST UPON →
1 rest on/upon sth: to depend on something in order to succeed ▶ *Success in business ultimately rests on good judgment and luck.*

2 rest on/upon sth: to be based on a particular idea or set of facts ▶ *The case against my client rests entirely on uncertain evidence.*

3 sb's eyes rest on/upon sth: if your eyes rest on something, you look at it for a period of time after looking at other things ▶ *He stopped abruptly, his eyes narrowing as they rested on her face.*

REST UP →
rest up: to relax and not do anything for a period of time ▶ *We'll rest up here for the night and drive on in the morning.*

REST UPON *see* **REST ON**

REST WITH →
rest with sb: if a decision or duty rests with someone, they are responsible for it ▶ *The final decision about the case rests with the court.*
▶ *Responsibility for a child's behaviour should rest with the family.*

RESULT
RESULT IN →
result in sth: to be the cause of something ▶ *The factory will close at the end of the month, resulting in 5000 job losses.* ▶ *a tragic accident that resulted in the death of three children*

RETURN
RETURN TO →
1 return to sth: to continue doing an activity, job etc again, after you had stopped ▶ *Ian finally gave up trying to entertain the children and returned to his newspaper.*

2 return to sth: to talk again about something that was mentioned before ▶ *Let's return to the subject of your previous employment.*

REV
REV UP →
1 rev up, rev up sth, **rev** sth **up:** if an engine revs up or you rev it up, you

make it work a lot faster by pressing the control down hard ▶ *The police car revved up and raced off into the night.*

2 rev up sth, **rev** sth **up:** to improve something, for example by making it more exciting ▶ *He revved up his game and came back to win 6-3.*
  revved-up ADJ made better, more interesting, exciting etc ▶ *Their new revved-up camera also records dates and titles on the film.*

REVEL
REVEL IN →
revel in sth: to enjoy something very much, especially praise, attention etc ▶ *The champion ran around the track, revelling in the applause from his fans.* ▶ *The singer seems to be revelling in his new-found fame.*

REVENGE
REVENGE YOURSELF ON, *also* **BE REVENGED ON** →
revenge yourself on sb *also* **be revenged on** sb: to punish a person who has harmed or upset you or someone you love ▶ *He swore to be revenged on those who had killed his brother.*

REVERT
REVERT TO →
1 revert to sth: to start doing or using something again ▶ *After the divorce, she reverted to using her own family name.*

2 revert to sth: to change back to a previous state or condition ▶ *The land soon reverted to its natural state.*

3 revert to sb: if land or a building reverts to someone, it becomes their property again after belonging to someone else ▶ *After the war, control of the estate reverted to the Earl of Norfolk.*

REVOLVE

REVOLVE AROUND, *also* **REVOLVE ROUND** →

1 revolve around/round sth/sb: to be mainly about a particular subject or person ▶ *The story revolves around Poole's relationship with a married woman.* ▶ *a conversation that revolved around the latest political scandal*

2 revolve around/round sth: if something revolves around a particular thing, that thing is more important than anything else ▶ *His entire life revolves around music.*

3 think the world revolves around you: to think that you are more important than anyone or anything else ▶ *She thinks the world revolves around herself and her children.*

RID

RID OF →

1 rid sth/sb **of** sth/sb: to remove someone or something that is bad, harmful, or causes problems ▶ *The mayor offered a reward to anyone who could rid the town of rats.* ▶ *a vaccination programme that finally succeeded in ridding the world of smallpox.* **rid yourself of** ▶ *She couldn't rid herself of her feelings of inadequacy and failure.*

2 be rid of sth/sb: to no longer have something or someone that was causing you problems ▶ *When the teacher finally resigned, the school was glad to be rid of him.* **be well rid of** sth/sb (=be lucky to be rid of something or someone) ▶ *She was lazy and incompetent – we're well rid of her.*

RIDDLE

BE RIDDLED WITH →

be riddled with sth: to be full of something bad, unpleasant, or

harmful ▶ *He died eight months later, his body riddled with cancer.* ▶ *There were allegations that the police force was riddled with corruption.*

RIDE

RIDE ON →

ride on sth: if something important rides on the result of something else, it depends on it ▶ *It's really stressful when you know that your whole future may be riding on one exam.*

RIDE OUT →

ride out sth, **ride** sth **out**: to manage to get to the end of a difficult situation without being badly harmed by it ▶ *The Government is determined to ride out the present crisis.* **ride out the storm** ▶ *Despite the scandal, I don't think he'll resign – my guess is he'll ride out the storm.*

RIDE UP →

ride up: if a piece of clothing, especially a skirt, rides up, it gradually moves upwards ▶ *She reached forward to pull down her skirt, which had ridden up over her thighs.*

RIFLE

RIFLE THROUGH →

rifle through sth: to search quickly through a cupboard, drawer, papers etc, in order to find something ▶ *She rifled through her wardrobe, looking for a suitable dress.*

RIG

RIG OUT →

rig sb **out**, **rig out** sb: to dress someone in special or unusual clothes ▶ *They rigged young Billy out in a blue sailor suit.*

RIG UP →
rig up sth, **rig** sth **up**: to quickly make a temporary piece of equipment from objects that you find around you ▸ *One of the boys had rigged up a sort of tent by draping a large plastic sheet over a pole.*

RING

RING AROUND *see* **RING ROUND**

RING BACK →
ring back, **ring** sb **back**: to phone someone for a second time, or to phone someone who phoned you when you were not available ▸ *Can I give Jane a message, or will you ring back later?* ▸ *Mr. Harrison's busy right now, but I'll ask him to ring you back.*

RING IN →
ring in: to telephone the place where you work or where you are expected ▸ *Joan rang in to say she was sick.*

RING OFF →
ring off: to end a phone call ▸ *Don't ring off. I've something else to tell you.* ▸ *I have to ring off now – there's someone at the door.*

RING OUT →
ring out: if the sound of a bell, a voice, gunshot etc rings out, you can hear it loudly and clearly ▸ *Shots rang out and at least 20 demonstrators fell to the ground.* ▸ *church bells ringing out over the sunlit streets*

RING ROUND, *also* **RING AROUND** →
ring round/around, **ring round/around** sth/sb: to phone several people or places in order to arrange or find out something ▸ *I'm just ringing round to remind everybody about the meeting next Friday.* ▸ *I rang around all the hotels in town, but they were all full.*

RING UP →
1 ring sb **up**, **ring up** sb, **ring up**: to phone someone ▸ *He rang me up that*

same evening and asked me out for a drink. ▸ *Someone rang up while you were out.*

2 ring up sth: if a company, especially a shop, rings up a profit, it makes that profit ▸ *They're expected to ring up another 28% rise in profits.*

3 ring up sth: to spend a large amount of money ▸ *He rang up a bill of about £1000 before catching his flight home.*

RINSE

RINSE OUT →
1 rinse sth **out**, **rinse out** sth: to wash a piece of clothing or cloth quickly in clean water ▸ *I rinsed out a few things and put them on the radiator to dry.*

2 rinse sth **out**, **rinse out** sth: to quickly wash the inside of something, usually using only water ▸ *Would you rinse out a couple of mugs while I make the coffee.*

RIP

RIP INTO →
1 rip into sth: if a storm, an explosion, or bullets rip into something, they hit it violently and cause a lot of damage ▸ *Tornadoes ripped into the southern part of the country last night.*

2 rip into sb: to talk to someone angrily and criticize them very strongly ▸ *What's wrong with old Moreton? He ripped into me just now for being two minutes late.*

RIP OFF →
1 rip sb **off**, **rip off** sb: to cheat someone by making them pay much more than the usual price for something ▸ *A lot of the taxi drivers here will try and rip you off if they think you're a tourist.*

　　rip-off N when something is much too expensive, making you feel you are being cheated ▸ *£2.50 for a cup of coffee ! It's a complete rip-off!*

2 rip off sth, **rip** sth **off**: to quickly

remove a piece of clothing by pulling it off in a careless or violent way ▶ *Ripping off his tie and jacket, he dived into the river.*

3 rip off sth, **rip** sth **off**: to steal someone else's idea by copying something that they have made or invented ▶ *Their songs are being ripped off and copied by bands in other countries.*

4 rip off sth, **rip** sth **off**: to steal other people's money or possessions ▶ *He was caught ripping off money from church funds.*

RIP THROUGH →
rip through sth: to go through something very quickly and violently, causing a lot of damage ▶ *A hail of bullets ripped through the side of the general's car.*

RIP UP →
1 rip up sth, **rip** sth **up**: to tear something quickly and violently into small pieces ▶ *She ripped up Tom's*

photograph and threw it on the fire.

2 rip up sth: to pull up something that is fixed to the floor or the ground ▶ *Vandals had chopped down trees and ripped up fences.*

RISE

RISE ABOVE →
1 rise above sth: to not let a bad situation affect or influence you ▶ *He had the ability to rise above the petty differences of party politics.*

2 rise above sth: to be much better than the standard that someone or something else achieves ▶ *Evans is the one player capable of rising above*

the pretty poor performance of his team.

RISE AGAINST →
rise against sb/sth: to start to fight against your ruler or government ▶ *The people were urged to rise against their colonial rulers.*

RISE UP →
1 rise up: if a mountain, cliff, wall etc rises up, it appears as a very tall shape ▶ *Sheer cliffs rose up around them on all sides.* ▶ *steep forested banks rising up from the waters of the lake*

2 rise up: to go upwards ▶ *The birds suddenly rose up into the air and flew away.* ▶ *Smoke was rising up from the chimney.*

3 rise up: if a feeling or thought rises up in you, you suddenly have that feeling or thought ▶ *I could feel the anger rising up inside me.*

4 rise up: to start to fight against your ruler or government ▶ *One day the people will rise up and overthrow this tyrant.* **+ against** ▶ *The peasants rose up in armed rebellion against King Richard.*

> **uprising** N an attempt by a group of people to defeat their rulers or government ▶ *the popular uprising against President Ceaucescu*

5 rise up: to stand after you have been sitting, kneeling, or lying down ▶ *The young organist stopped playing and rose up from his seat.*

ROB

ROB OF →
rob sb/sth **of** sth: to take away an important quality, ability, right etc from someone or something ▶ *Wilson's early failures had completely robbed him of his confidence.*

ROLL

ROLL AROUND, also ROLL ABOUT →

roll around/about: to laugh at something so much that your body moves around ► *Harry's jokes had us all rolling about helplessly.* **roll around/about with laughter** ► *The two boys were rolling around with laughter at the memory of what had happened.*

ROLL AROUND, also ROLL ROUND →

roll around/round: to come or happen again as expected ► *By the time the evening rolled around, we felt it was time to go home.*

ROLL AWAY →

roll away: if countryside rolls away, you can see for a long distance over it ► *The grassy plains roll away in all directions as far as the eye can see.*

ROLL BACK →

1 roll back sth, **roll** sth **back:** to reduce the power or influence of a system, government etc ► *reforms aimed at rolling back state control of the economy*

2 roll sth **back, roll back** sth: to reduce the cost of something ► *The Senate voted to roll back fuel tax by 5 cents a gallon.*

ROLL BY →

years/months roll by: if years or months roll by, time passes, especially quickly ► *As the years rolled by, we saw less and less of our wealthy cousins.*

ROLL DOWN →

roll down sth, **roll** sth **down:** to open a car window by making the glass move down. **roll down the window** ► *Dad, will you roll down your window a little?*

ROLL IN →

1 roll in: if money, letters etc roll in, large amounts of them arrive ► *Letters from fans keep rolling in.* **come rolling in** ► *Sales of the new drug were massive and the profits came rolling in.*

2 roll in: if clouds, storms, mist etc roll in, they move into an area ► *A blanket of fog rolled in from the sea.*

3 be rolling in money also **be rolling in it:** to be very rich ► *Her new husband's absolutely rolling in it.*

ROLL IN, also ROLL INTO →

roll in, roll into sth: to arrive somewhere, usually late ► *It was after midnight when we finally rolled in.* ► *You can't just roll into the office two hours late.*

ROLL ON →

1 roll on: if a period of time or a process rolls on, it continues to pass or happen ► *The long ceremony rolled on towards its climax.*

2 roll on Friday/summer etc!: used to say that you want a more enjoyable time such as Friday or summer to come soon ► *I've had enough of work this week – roll on the weekend!*

ROLL OUT →

1 roll out sth, **roll** sth **out:** to make a food mixture flat and thin before you cook it, by rolling a tube-shaped object over it ► *Roll out the pastry thinly on a lightly floured surface.*

2 roll out sth, **roll** sth **out:** to unfold something that has been folded into a round shape ► *We rolled out our sleeping bags inside the tent.*

3 roll out sth, **roll** sth **out:** to make a new product available for people to buy or use ► *It's some time since they rolled out their latest computer processor.*

R

ROLL OVER →

1a. roll over: to turn your body when you are lying down, so that you are lying on the other side of your body ▶ *She rolled over and went back to sleep.*

b. roll sb over: to turn someone's body when they are lying down so that they are lying on the other side of their body ▶ *Magee knelt beside the dying man and rolled him over onto his back.*

2 roll over sth, roll sth over: to officially arrange to pay a debt later than you are usually supposed to ▶ *The government has approved a law that rolls over the tax debt until the following year.*

3 roll over: to allow someone to force you to do something without making any effort to stop them ▶ *You're not going to roll over and let them close down the business, are you?*

ROLL UP →

1 roll up sth, roll sth up: to turn the ends of your sleeves or trousers over several times in order to make them shorter. **roll up your sleeves/trousers** ▶ *The boatmen rolled up their trouser legs and waded ashore.*

2 roll up sth, roll sth up: to make something made of paper, cloth etc into the shape of a tube or ball ▶ *Just roll up the carpet and take it downstairs.* ▶ *She paused to roll up the magazines and push them into her bag.*

> **rolled-up** ADJ rolled-up paper, cloth etc has been folded over and made into the shape of a tube ▶ *Bertie was busy swatting flies with a rolled-up newspaper.*

3 roll up sth, roll sth up: to wrap something in paper, cloth, bread etc that forms a tube shape around it. **+ in** ▶ *chicken pieces rolled up in corn tortillas*

4 roll up: if an animal rolls up, it curls its body into the shape of a ball with its tail close to its head ▶ *When threatened, a hedgehog will roll up into a tight ball.*

5 roll up: to arrive somewhere, especially in large numbers or in a vehicle ▶ *Thousands rolled up to watch the race.*

6 roll up sth, roll sth up: to close a car window by making the glass move up. **roll up the window** ▶ *I rolled up my window – it was getting cold.*

ROMP

ROMP THROUGH →

romp through sth: to succeed in doing something quickly and easily ▶ *He romped through every game and won the first set 6-0.*

ROOF

ROOF IN, *also* ROOF OVER →

roof in/over sth, **roof sth in/over**: to cover an open space by building a roof over it ▶ *The old swimming pool had been roofed over with glass panels.*

ROOM

ROOM WITH →

room with sb: to share the room that you live in with someone ▶ *You remember Maria – I roomed with her at college.*

ROOT

ROOT FOR →

1 root for sb: to give support or encouragement to someone ▶ *Good luck – we'll all be rooting for you!*

2 root for sb: to support a sports team

or player by shouting and cheering
▶ *We were all rooting for Green Bay to win the Championship Game.*

BE ROOTED IN →
be rooted in sth: to have developed from something and be strongly influenced by it ▶ *political policies that are rooted in Marxist theory*

ROOT OUT →
1 root out sth/ sb, **root** sth/ sb **out**: to find out where a particular kind of problem exists and get rid of it ▶ *The new Chief Officer promised to root out corruption in the city's police force.* ▶ *a campaign to root out racism and sexism in the music industry*

2 root out sth, **root** sth **out**: to find something by searching for it ▶ *I've got a sleeping bag somewhere – I'll root it out for you next time you come.*

ROOT UP →
root sth **up, root up** sth: to dig or pull a plant and its roots out of the ground ▶ *I'll just root up these weeds.*

ROPE

ROPE IN, *also* **ROPE INTO** →
rope sb **in, rope in** sb, **rope** sb **into** sth: to persuade someone to help you do something, especially when they do not want to. **get roped in** ▶ *Whenever they need someone to look after the kids, I get roped in.* **rope** sb **into doing** sth ▶ *Have they roped you into selling tickets?* **rope** sb **in to do** sth ▶ *We've roped Dad in to help with the entertainment.*

ROPE OFF →
rope off sth, **rope** sth **off**: to put ropes around an area, to stop people from going into it ▶ *Police roped off the area where the body was found.*

ROT

ROT AWAY →
rot away: to decay and disappear through a gradual natural process

▶ *Out in the rain-soaked fields, the potato crop was gradually rotting away.*

ROT DOWN →
rot down: if leaves, plants etc rot down, they decay by a gradual natural process and become soil ▶ *Cover the weeds with black plastic so that they rot down.*

ROUGH

ROUGH OUT →
rough out sth, **rough** sth **out**: to draw or write something without including all the exact details ▶ *I sat down at my desk and began to rough out a report.*

ROUGH UP →
rough up sb, **rough** sb **up**: to attack someone and hurt them by hitting them ▶ *It wasn't worth the risk of being arrested and getting roughed up by the police.*

ROUND

ROUND DOWN →
round down sth, **round** sth **down**: to reduce an exact number to the nearest whole number, or to the nearest 10, 100 etc below it. **+ to** ▶ *Please do not include pence. Round down your calculations to the nearest pound.*

ROUND OFF →
1 round off sth, **round** sth **off**: to be a pleasant and suitable way of ending an event, or to do something as a pleasant and suitable way of ending it ▶ *Fresh strawberries will round the meal off nicely.* **+ with** ▶ *We rounded off the evening with carols around the Christmas tree.*

2 round off sth, **round** sth **off, round off**: to change an exact number to the nearest whole number ▶ *Peter's net income after taxes was £3,159 (rounding off to the nearest pound).*

ROUND ON, *also* **ROUND UPON** →
round on/upon sb: to suddenly attack

R

someone when they do not expect it, either physically or by speaking angrily to them ▶ *Sibyl rounded on him, knife in hand, and he moved back out of her reach.*

ROUND UP →

1 round sb/sth **up, round up** sb/sth: to find and gather a group of people or animals together ▶ *See if you can round up a few friends to help you.* ▶ *They rounded up the ponies and drove them into the corral.*

2 round up sb, **round** sb **up**: to search for and find a particular group of people and force them to go to prison ▶ *Police quickly rounded up dozens of suspected terrorists and threw them in jail.*

3 round up sth, **round** sth **up**: to increase an exact number to the nearest higher whole number, or the nearest 10, 100 etc above it ▶ *The total came to £299.50, so I rounded it up to £300.*

ROUND UPON *see* ROUND ON

RUB

RUB ALONG →
rub along: if two people rub along, they live or work together in a fairly friendly way ▶ *Me and my workmates rub along OK most of the time.*

RUB DOWN →
rub down sb/sth, **rub** sb/sth **down**: to dry a person or animal by rubbing them with a towel ▶ *He was rubbing down his horse in the stable yard.*

RUB IN →
1 rub it in: to deliberately remind

someone about something that they want to forget ▶ *"Just remember that while you're unemployed, I have to pay for everything." "All right, there's no need to rub it in."*

2 rub sth **in, rub** sth **into** sth: to put a cream or oil onto someone's skin, hair etc and rub it in order to make it go into their skin, hair etc ▶ *Always keep hand cream available in the kitchen and rub it in frequently.*

RUB OFF →
1a. rub off sth, **rub** sth **off, rub** sth **off** sth: to remove something from a surface by rubbing it ▶ *Mr Owen took one look at the drawing on the blackboard, and rubbed it off.*

b. rub off: to come off the surface of something because of being rubbed ▶ *She noticed that the necklace was a forgery when the gold colouring began to rub off.*

2 rub off: if someone else's quality, feeling, or habit rubs off on you, you start to have it too ▶ *We hoped that some of Procter's fighting spirit would rub off and inspire the others.* **rub off on** sb ▶ *The teacher's enthusiasm had clearly rubbed off on the children.*

RUB OUT →
rub out sth, **rub** sth **out**: to remove writing or pictures from paper by rubbing it with a piece of rubber, or remove writing or pictures from a board by rubbing it with a cloth ▶ *Do it in pencil first then you can rub it out.*

RUCK

RUCK UP →
ruck up, ruck up sth, **ruck** sth **up**: if a piece of cloth or clothing rucks up or if you ruck it up, it gets pulled upwards and forms folds in an untidy way ▶ *Flora had bent forward, rucking up her skirt.* **be rucked up** ▶ *Your shirt's all rucked up at the back.*

RUFFLE

RUFFLE UP →

ruffle up sth, **ruffle** sth **up**: to make a smooth surface uneven ▶ *She ruffled up his hair affectionately.* ▶ *Birds ruffle up their feathers to keep warm.*

RULE

RULE OUT →

1 rule out sth, **rule** sth **out**: to decide that something is not possible or suitable ▶ *The police have ruled out murder, saying the girl probably committed suicide.* ▶ *Job losses cannot be ruled out.*

2 rule out sth, **rule** sth **out**: to make it impossible for something to happen ▶ *The severe weather ruled out any attempts to reach the survivors by helicopter.*

RUN

RUN ACROSS →

run across sb/sth: to meet someone or find something by chance ▶ *He ran across his old friend as he was coming out of a restaurant.* ▶ *I ran across an advertisement in the paper, which said they were looking for English teachers for Japan.*

RUN AFTER →

1 run after sb/sth: to chase someone or something ▶ *My father ran after the thieves, but they got away.* ▶ *She began to run after him, calling his name.*

2 run after sb: to keep trying to persuade someone to have a romantic or sexual relationship with you ▶ *When we were at college she was always running after some man or other.*

RUN ALONG →

run along!: used to tell a child to go away ▶ *Run along now children! It's time you were in bed!*

RUN AROUND, *also* RUN ROUND →

run around/round: to be very busy doing a lot of different things, and rushing from one place to another. **run around/round doing** sth ▶ *I've been running around all morning trying to get everything ready for Cathy's birthday.*

RUN AROUND AFTER, *also* RUN ROUND AFTER →

run around/round after sb: to be busy doing a lot of small jobs for someone, especially when that person could easily do them himself or herself ▶ *His last wife got fed up with running around after him all the time.*

RUN AROUND WITH →

run around with sb: to spend a lot of time with someone and be friendly with them ▶ *Tony used to run around with a gang of students from the art college.*

RUN AWAY →

1 run away: to leave somewhere by running, especially in order to escape ▶ *When the police arrived, one man ran away and the other made his escape in a car.*

2 run away: to leave the place where you live, especially without telling anyone, because you are unhappy there ▶ *When she was young she wanted to run away and join the circus.* **run away from home** ▶ *Darren ran away from home five times in two years.*

runaway N someone who has secretly run away from their home ▶ *Many homeless people start out as teenage runaways from broken homes.*

3 run away: to try to avoid dealing with a problem. **+ from** ▶ *He shouldn't keep running away from his responsibilities.* ▶ *You can't run away from these things forever.*

R

R

RUN AWAY WITH →

1 run away with sb: to secretly leave your wife, husband etc, in order to go and live with someone else ▶ *Derek abandoned his wife and ran away to Italy with a singer.*

2 run away with sth: to win something easily such as a competition, game, or prize ▶ *They ran away with the championship, scoring nearly twice as many points as their nearest rival.*

3 let your imagination/emotions etc run away with you: to become very excited, upset, or worried, because you think that something may have happened, even though this seems very unlikely ▶ *You mustn't let your imagination run away with you. I'm sure your son's perfectly OK.*

4 run away with the idea also **run away with the impression**: to wrongly think that something is true ▶ *I don't want people running away with the idea that this is going to be easy.*

RUN BY →

1 run sth **by** sb **again**: to say something to someone again, in order to make sure they have understood it ▶ *Sorry, I was thinking about something else. Can you run that one by me again?*

2 run sth **by** sb: to tell someone about something such as a plan or idea, for example in order to find out what they think of it ▶ *It sounds like a good idea, but we'd better run it by Michael first.*

RUN DOWN →

1 run down sb, **run** sb **down**: to drive into someone and hurt or kill them ▶ *I almost got run down by a bus as I was crossing the road.*

2 run sb/sth **down**, **run down** sb/sth: to criticize someone or something, especially unfairly ▶ *Never run down your previous employer at an interview. It will always reflect badly*

on you. **run yourself down** ▶ *As a nation we're always running ourselves down.*

3 be run down: to feel tired and unhealthy because you have been working too hard, not getting enough sleep etc ▶ *Is Sue all right? She looked rather run down when I last saw her.*

4 run down sth, **run** sth **down**: to gradually reduce the amount of work that a company or other organization does, in order to prepare for closing it ▶ *The local hospital was being run down and no longer took emergency cases.*

5 run down sth, **run** sth **down**: to let something such as a company or economy get into very bad condition ▶ *They accused the previous government of deliberately running down manufacturing industry.*

6 run down, run down sth, **run** sth **down**: if supplies of something run down, or are run down, they gradually all get used ▶ *Supplies of gas from the North Sea will proably start to run down within the next 20 years.*

7 run down sth: to quickly look at or read aloud a list of things or people ▶ *Do you want me to run down the list of possible candidates?*

> **rundown** N a short report or explanation in which you mention the most important information ▶ *a brief rundown of the main decisions that had been made*

RUN FOR →

1 run for sth: to try to be elected to a particular position ▶ *Burns wants to run for governor at the next election.* **run for office** (=try to be elected to an important political position) ▶ *She has made no secret of her wish to run for office.*

2 run for it: to run as quickly as you

...an, especially in order to escape ▸ *I think he's seen us. We'd better run for* ...

RUN INTO →

run into sb: to meet someone you know by chance ▸ *While I was in Paris I ran into an old school-friend who I hadn't seen in years.*

run into sth: to suddenly experience problems, difficulties etc and have to deal with them ▸ *The company had run into serious financial difficulties during the recession.* ▸ *Plans to build the airport have run into strong opposition from local residents.*

run into hundreds / thousands etc: to reach a total of several hundreds, thousands etc ▸ *The cost of repairing the damage is expected to run into millions of dollars.*

run into sth: to accidentally drive into something such as a car or a wall ▸ *Someone had run into the back of the bus.*

run into sth: if one thing runs into another, for example another word, colour, or quality, it joins it and mixes with it ▸ *The words seemed to run into each other, and I couldn't catch what she was saying.*

RUN OFF →

run off: to leave somewhere by running, for example to avoid being caught ▸ *The robbers ran off down a nearby street.*

run off: to suddenly leave someone or leave the place where you live, without telling anyone ▸ *His wife ran off and left him.* ▸ *The popular story is that Arthur was so heartbroken that he ran off to Africa.*

run off sth, **run** sth **off**: to quickly print several copies of something ▸ *Nowadays you can run off your invitations on a laser printer for virtually nothing.*

4 run off sth, **run** sth **off** sth: to work by using power from a particular power supply ▸ *It's designed to run off batteries or mains electricity.*

RUN OFF WITH →

1 run off with sb: to secretly go away with someone and have a romantic or sexual relationship with them ▸ *His wife ran off with someone she met at work, and left Joe with two kids to bring up.*

2 run off with sth: to steal something and take it away ▸ *Her employers thought she had run off with the contents of the safe.*

RUN ON →

1 run on sth, **run** sth **on** sth: to operate, or operate something, using a particular kind of computer or computer system ▸ *The software will run on any PC.* ▸ *Can you run it on Windows 98?*

2 run on: to continue happening for longer than was expected ▸ *The meeting ran on until after 6 o'clock.*

3 run on sth, **run** sth **on** sth: to use a particular kind of fuel or power supply, or make something do this ▸ *Every new car that is sold in the UK must be able to run on unleaded fuel.*

4 run on: to talk for a long time, especially when other people are not interested. **+ about** ▸ *My dad will run on for hours about golf if you give him the chance.*

RUN OUT →

1 run out: if you run out of something, you have no more of it left because you have used all of it ▸ *"Is there any more cat food?" "No. We've run out."*

run out of sth ▶ *He'd better hurry up. We're running out of time.* ▶ *They never seemed to run out of things to say to each other.*

2 run out of: if something runs out, there is no more of it left ▶ *Their adventure lasted until the money ran out.* ▶ *My husband tries to be sympathetic, but I can tell his patience is running out.*

3 run out: if ticket or an official document runs out, it reaches the end of the time when it is officially allowed to be used or have an effect ▶ *His contract with the club is due to run out in December.* ▶ *My passport won't run out for at least another year.*

4 run out of steam also **run out of gas**: to no longer feel eager or energetic enough to do something ▶ *She always starts playing brilliantly, but runs out of steam after the first few sets.*

RUN OUT OF →

1 run out of sth —see RUN OUT 1

2 run sb out of sth: to force someone to leave a town or area ▶ *They burnt his house down and ran him out of the district.* **run sb out of town** ▶ *Her father threatened to run him out of town if he so much as went near the girl.*

RUN OUT ON →

run out on sb: to suddenly leave your wife, husband, friends etc ▶ *Joey's wife had run out on him 13 years earlier.*

RUN OVER →

1 run over sb/sth, **run** sb/sth **over**: to drive over someone or something, especially with the result that they are injured or killed ▶ *Barthes was run over by a laundry van as he was crossing a busy Paris street.* ▶ *Lee was really upset when her cat got run over.*

2 run over sth: to quickly explain something to someone ▶ *I'll just run over how the burglar alarm works.*

3 run over sth: to quickly read or repeat something in order to remember it or to check that it is correct ▶ *Sean ran over his notes one last time, then made his way to the exam hall.*

4 run over also **run over time**: if something runs over or runs over time, it continues past the time when it was planned to end ▶ *We should be through by eight, but the session might run over.* **+ into** ▶ *The tunnel project ran over into the following year.*

5 run sth **over in your mind** also **your mind runs over** sth: to think about something such as a series of events, possibilities etc ▶ *She let her mind run over the events of the previous day.*

RUN ROUND see RUN AROUND

RUN ROUND AFTER see RUN AROUND AFTER

RUN THROUGH →

1 run through sth: if an idea, quality, feeling etc runs through something, it is present in all of it ▶ *This sense of sadness and loss runs through many of Housman's poems.*

2 run through sb: if a feeling runs through you, you suddenly feel it very strongly ▶ *He felt a thrill of excitement run through him at the mention of her name.*

3 run through sb's mind: if something runs through your mind, you think about it or imagine it ▶ *The thought ran through my mind that the other man was probably as frightened as I was.*

4 run through sth: to think about or imagine something from beginning to end ▶ *Helen ran through the scene in her mind again and again.*

5 run through sth: to quickly read or look at something, especially in order to check or find something ▶ *She ran through the names in the notebook to see if there were any that she recognized.*

6 run through sth: to quickly talk about or explain something from beginning to end ▶ *Can you run through your movements on the night of the murder?*

7 run through sth: to quickly do a series of things, especially in order to practise them ▶ *I think we'll start by running through the opening dance routine.*

    run-through N when you do a series of things, especially in order to practise them ▶ *They did a complete run-through of the whole play, and it went off perfectly.*

8 run sth **through** sth: to ask a computer to check something, change it, do calculations with it etc ▶ *The police run this information through a special database.*

9 run sb **through**: to push a sharp weapon through someone's body. **+ with** ▶ *He rushed forward and ran him through with a bayonet.*

RUN TO →

1 run to sth: to reach a particular number or amount, especially a large one ▶ *The report runs to several hundred pages.* ▶ *Dinner for two should run to around £50.*

2 can/will run to sth: to have enough money to be able to pay for something ▶ *We couldn't quite run to vintage champagne, so we chose a decent bottle of wine instead.*

3 run to sb: to go to someone and expect them to help or protect you ▶ *Natalie had run to her new lover, only to be turned away.* **come running to** sb (=expect someone to help and protect you when you should be able to deal with a problem yourself)

▶ *Whenever there's the slightest problem he always comes running to me.*

RUN UP →

1 run up: to suddenly run to where someone or something is ▶ *A man with a gun ran up and shot him dead.* **+ to** ▶ *Anne ran furiously up to Mrs Lynde. "I hate you!" she shouted.*

2 run up debts/a bill etc: to borrow or have to pay a lot of money for something ▶ *While she was at college she ran up a huge phone bill.*

3 run up sth: to succeed in achieving something ▶ *The Sonics ran up 64 victories this year.*

4 run up sth, **run** sth **up**: if you run up a flag, you raise it on a pole, usually by pulling a rope ▶ *The school ran up the South African flag in honour of Mandela's visit.*

5 run up sth, **run** sth **up**: to quickly make something, especially a piece of clothing using a sewing machine ▶ *If I give her the material, she can easily run up the dress for me at home.*

RUN UP AGAINST →

run up against sth/sb: to have to deal with unexpected problems, a difficult opponent etc ▶ *The developers have run up against strong opposition from the local community.*

RUSH

RUSH AROUND, *also* RUSH ABOUT →

rush around/about, rush around/ about sth: to move around quickly and busily doing a lot of things ▶ *I've been rushing around all day trying to get ready for my holiday.*

RUSH IN, *also* RUSH INTO →

rush in, rush into sth, **rush** sb **into** sth: to do something quickly, especially without thinking about it carefully enough, or to make someone do this

► *The President insisted that he would not be rushed into a decision.* **rush into doing** sth ► *The couple explained that they didn't want to rush into having children.* **rush into things** (=rush into something) ► *We haven't talked about marriage yet. We don't want to rush into things.*

RUSH OFF →
rush off: to leave very suddenly or quickly ► *There's no need to rush off just yet, we've got plenty of time.* ► *Sorry to rush off like this. I promise I'll be free tomorrow.*

RUSH OUT →
rush out sth, **rush** sth **out**: to produce a new product very quickly, especially because a lot of people want to buy it ► *A special video of the series was rushed out in time for Christmas.*

RUSH THROUGH →
rush through sth, **rush** sth **through**: to pass a law or deal with official

business as quickly as possible ► *The government rushed through the Public Order Act in response to the rioting.*

RUST

RUST AWAY →
rust away: to be damaged and gradually destroyed by rust ► *He had an old Cadillac which was quietly rusting away in his garage.*

RUST UP →
rust up: if something rusts up, so much rust forms on it that it does not work ► *The house had metal windows that had completely rusted up.* **be rusted up** ► *The car radiator was all rusted up and kept overheating.*

RUSTLE

RUSTLE UP →
rustle up sth, **rustle** sth **up**: to find or make something quickly ► *Mel went downstairs to rustle up some breakfast.*

Ss

SADDLE

SADDLE UP →

saddle up, saddle up sth, **saddle sth up**: to put a saddle on a horse's back ▶ *We saddled up and set off back to the farm.*

SADDLE WITH →

saddle sb with sth: to give someone a job, responsibility, or problem that they do not want ▶ *I've been saddled with the job of organizing the kids' party.* **saddle yourself with** ▶ *Students are saddling themselves with enormous debts to pay their living expenses.*

SAFEGUARD

SAFEGUARD AGAINST →

safeguard against sth: to do something to prevent something bad from happening ▶ *information about how to safeguard against illness when travelling in tropical countries*

SAIL

SAIL THROUGH →

sail through, sail through sth: to pass a test or deal with a difficult experience very easily ▶ *Some women sail through pregnancy without any problems at all.*

SALT

SALT AWAY →

salt away sth, **salt sth away**: to save money for the future, especially money that you have got dishonestly ▶ *Drug traffickers are salting away their funds and then coming out of prison to a life of luxury.*

SANDWICH

BE SANDWICHED BETWEEN →

be sandwiched between sth: to be in a small space between two much larger people or things ▶ *The car was sandwiched between two huge trucks.*

SAVE

SAVE ON →

1 save on sth: to spend less money on something than you did before ▶ *If I cycled to work I could save on petrol.* ▶ *We moved to a smaller apartment to save on rent.*

2 save on sth: to reduce the amount of work that you have to do ▶ *Let's use paper plates – it'll save on the washing up.*

SAVE UP →

save up, save up sth, **save sth up**: to keep money so that you can use it in the future, especially when you add more money every week, month etc ▶ *If you want to buy a car, you'll have to start saving up now.* ▶ *We've saved up £2000 so far.* **+ for** ▶ *I'm saving up for a holiday.*

SAW

SAW UP →

saw up sth, **saw sth up**: to cut something into many pieces using a saw ▶ *I sawed up the fallen tree for firewood.*

SAY

SAY FOR →

1 it says a lot for sb/sth: to show that someone or something has a lot of good qualities ▶ *It says a lot for Darren that he gives up his Saturdays to coach the kids' football team.*

2 not say much for sth: to show that something is not of a high standard or

S

quality ► *These results don't say much for the quality of the teaching.*

SCALE

SCALE DOWN, *also* **SCALE BACK** →

1 scale down/back sth, **scale** sth **down/back**: to make something such as an organization or activity smaller, or spend less money on something ► *Several countries have scaled down their plans for expanding nuclear power.* ► *The whole industry is scaling back.*

scaled-down *also* ***scaled-back*** ADJ reduced or made smaller ► *The planning committee eventually agreed on a scaled-down version of the project.*

2 scale down sth, **scale** sth **down**: to reduce the size of something such as a drawing or a model ► *The design will have to be scaled down before we can publish it.*

scaled-down ADJ reduced to a smaller size ► *a scaled-down model of the statue*

SCALE UP →

1 scale up sth, **scale** sth **up**: to make something such as an organization bigger, or do more of an activity than before ► *The company is scaling up production of mobile phones.*

2 scale up sth, **scale** sth **up**: to increase the size of something such as a drawing or a model ► *Does the software allow graphics to be scaled up and down?*

SCAN

SCAN IN →

scan in sth, **scan** sth **in**: to copy images from paper onto a computer screen ► *You can put in five or ten pages of text and scan them in automatically.*

SCARE

SCARE AWAY, *also* **SCARE OFF** →

1 scare away/off sb, **scare** sb **away/off**: to make a person or animal go away by  frightening them ► *Her sister came home unexpectedly and scared the intruder off.*

2 scare away/off sb, **scare** sb **away/off**: to stop someone from doing something they intended to do, by making them feel worried or nervous ► *The mayor blames the media for exaggerating the city's crime problem and scaring tourists away.* ► *Rising prices are scaring off many potential customers.*

SCHLEP

SCHLEP AROUND →

schlep around, schlep around sth: to spend time relaxing and not doing much ► *I spent the next couple of days just schlepping around the house.*

SCHOOL

BE SCHOOLED IN →

be schooled in sth: to have been thoroughly taught something ► *He had been carefully schooled in the duties of the monarchy.*

SCOOP

SCOOP OUT →

scoop out sth, **scoop** sth **out**: to remove the inside part of something using your hand, or a spoon ► *Cut the melon in half and scoop out the seeds.*

SCOOP UP →

scoop up sth, **scoop** sth **up**: to put your hands under something and lift it up with a quick movement ▶ *His mother scooped him up in her arms and cuddled him.*

SCOPE

SCOPE OUT →

scope out sth/sb, **scope** sth/sb **out**: to look at something or someone to see what they are like ▶ *At our high school dances, we used to scope out the prettiest girls first thing.*

SCORE

SCORE OFF →

score off sb: to try to make someone seem stupid and make yourself seem clever ▶ *I never liked Professor Lyle – he was always trying to score off his students.*

SCOUT

SCOUT AROUND, *also* SCOUT ABOUT, SCOUT ROUND →

scout around/about/round: to look for something in a particular area ▶ *We haven't got much food in. I'll scout around in the village and see what I can find.* **+ for** ▶ *I put up the tent and then went scouting round for firewood.*

SCOUT OUT →

scout out sth: to examine an area in order to get information about it, especially in a military situation ▶ *They had sent in advance troops to scout out the dangers.*

SCOUT ROUND *see* SCOUT AROUND

SCRABBLE

SCRABBLE AROUND, *also* SCRABBLE ABOUT, SCRABBLE ROUND →

1 scrabble around/about/round: to try to find something by making quick movements with your fingers ▶ *She scrabbled around for a piece of paper to write on.*

2 scrabble around/about/round: to try to find a way of getting something that you need urgently. **+ for** ▶ *They found themselves scrabbling around for alternative sources of income.*

SCRAMBLE

SCRAMBLE FOR →

scramble for sth: to struggle or compete with other people to get or reach something ▶ *People scrambled for the exits as flames tore through the building.*

SCRAPE

SCRAPE BY →

scrape by: to just about manage to do something such as pass an exam, or have just enough money to pay for things ▶ *Somehow she scrapes by on just £120 a week.* ▶ *Bob barely scraped by in college.*

SCRAPE IN, *also* SCRAPE INTO →

scrape in, scrape into sth: to only just succeed in winning something or getting a particular job or position ▶ *The Socialist candidate scraped in with a majority of only 80 votes.*

SCRAPE THROUGH →

scrape through, scrape through sth: to only just succeed in passing an examination or course, or winning a game, competition etc. **+ to** ▶ *Johnson just manged to scrape through to the finals, winning 12 points to 11.*

SCRAPE TOGETHER, *also* SCRAPE UP →

scrape together/up sth, **scrape** sth **together/up**: to manage to get enough money for something, even though this is difficult ▶ *The brothers eventually scraped together enough money to buy the farm.*

SCRATCH

SCRATCH AROUND, *also* SCRATCH ABOUT, SCRATCH ROUND →

scratch around/about/round: to try

S

hard and often with difficulty to find money, food, or something else you need. **+ for** ▶ *I spent the next couple of months scratching around for a room to rent.*

SCREEN

SCREEN OFF →
screen off sth, **screen** sth **off**: to separate one part of a room, garden etc from the rest of it with

a curtain or something similar ▶ *An area at the far end of the hall had been screened off as a waiting-room.*

SCREEN OUT →
1 screen out sb, **screen** sb **out**: to make sure that people you do not want do not succeed in getting a job in an organization ▶ *strict procedures to sceen out job applicants with criminal records*

2 screen out sth, **screen** sth **out**: to prevent harmful or unwanted light, gas, sound etc from entering somewhere or affecting something ▶ *a face cream that screens out harmful UV rays from the sun*

SCREW

SCREW AROUND →
1 screw around: to waste time doing silly or annoying things ▶ *The guys in the back of the class always used to screw around and learn nothing.*
2 screw sb **around**: to cause problems for someone, for example by changing your mind a lot or stopping them doing something ▶ *The immigration office really screwed us around, and it was three months before we got our visas.*

SCREW AROUND WITH →
screw around with sth: to make unnecessary and annoying changes to something ▶ *He spent the afternoon screwing around with my computer.*

SCREW OUT OF →
screw sth **out of** sb: to force someone to give you money or information ▶ *landlords who screw all the money they can out of their tenants*

SCREW OVER →
screw sb **over, screw over** sb: to deceive someone, especially to get money from them, or to cause someone a lot of problems ▶ *No wonder workers feel sore when their own managers are screwing them over.*

SCREW UP →
1 screw sb **up**: to make someone feel unhappy, anxious, and confused for a long period of time ▶ *I used to do a lot of drugs, and they really screwed me up.*

  screwed-up ADJ ▶ *a screwed-up rich kid* ▶ *The guy's really screwed-up.*

2 screw up, screw up sth, **screw** sth **up**: to make a mistake or to spoil something ▶ *Somebody screwed up, and the email got copied to the wrong people.* ▶ *Don't ask Charlie to do it – he always screws things up.*

3 screw up sth, **screw** sth **up**: to twist and crush a piece of paper with your hands ▶ *Kim screwed up the letter and threw it in the bin.*

SCRIBBLE

SCRIBBLE DOWN →
scribble down sth, **scribble** sth **down**: to write something quickly ▶ *I scribbled down his phone number and promised to call.*

SCRIMP

SCRIMP ON →
scrimp on sth: to spend less money than you should do on something

▶ *There's no point in scrimping on essentials like heating.*

SCRUNCH
SCRUNCH UP →
1 scrunch up sth, **scrunch** sth **up**: to twist or crush something into a small shape ▶ *I scrunched up the report I was writing and started over.*

2 scrunch up: if people scrunch up, they sit or stand very close to each other to make more room for other people ▶ *Scrunch up, please! More people are waiting to get on the bus.*

SEAL
SEAL OFF →
seal off sth, **seal** sth **off**: to stop people from entering an area or building, for example because it is dangerous ▶ *The whole area has been sealed off following the discovery of an unexploded bomb.*

SEARCH
SEARCH FOR →
1 search for sb/sth, **search** sth **for** sb/sth: to look hard for something in a particular place ▶ *Firefighters are still searching the building for anyone left alive.*

2 search for sth, **search** sth **for** sth: to try to find a solution to a problem or an explanation for something ▶ *The money will be used to search for a cure for cancer.*

SEARCH THROUGH →
search through sth: to look at or in several things in order to find something in particular ▶ *Police patrolled the airport, searching through journalists' bags.*

SECTION
SECTION OFF →
section off sth, **section** sth **off**: to separate part of an area or building from the rest ▶ *Part of the field was* sectioned off to be used as a children's play area.

SEE
SEE ABOUT →
1 see about sth: to arrange to deal with or find out about something ▶ *I'm too tired to phone them now – I'll see about it in the morning.*

2 I'll/we'll have to see about that: used to tell someone that you do not know if something will be possible ▶ *"Dad, can I go to the ball game?" "We'll have to see about that."*

3 we'll see about that: used to say that you intend to stop someone from doing something that they are planning to do ▶ *You're thinking of leaving school, are you? Well, we'll see about that!*

SEE IN →
1 see sth **in** sb: to notice something good or attractive about someone that makes you like them ▶ *He saw in her a rare mixture of intelligence and good humour.*

2 I don't know what sb **sees in** sb/sth: used to say that you do not understand why someone likes someone or something ▶ *He treats her so badly. I just don't know what she sees in him.*

3 see sb **in, see in** *also* **see** sb **into** sth: to show a visitor the way into a building, office etc ▶ *The receptionist will see you in.*

SEE OFF →
1 see sb **off**: to go to an airport, train station etc to say goodbye to someone who is leaving ▶ *My best*

S

friend Judy came to the airport to see me off.

2 see sb **off, see** sb **off** sth: to chase someone away ▶ *Grandpa saw the hunters off our property.*

SEE OUT →

1 see sb **out**: to show a visitor the way out of a place ▶ *Hang on a second – I'll see you out.* **I'll see myself out** (=used to tell someone they do not have to come to the door with you) ▶ *It's OK, don't get up. I'll see myself out.*

2 see sth **out**: to continue to do something until it finishes, even if this is difficult ▶ *My job is terrible, but I'm going to see it out until the end of the year.*

SEE THROUGH →

1 see through sth/sb: to realize that someone is trying to influence or deceive you ▶ *Eventually I saw through her lies and ended the relationship.*

2 see sth **through**: to continue to do something until it finishes, even if this is difficult ▶ *It's not going to be easy, but I'm determined to see it through.*

3 see sb **through, see** sb **through** sth: to help someone during a difficult time in their life ▶ *The whole thing was a nightmare, but my friends helped see me through.*

4 see sb **through, see** sb **through** sth: if food or money sees you through, you have enough of it for a particular period of time ▶ *Can I borrow £30? That should be enough to see me through until payday.*

SEE TO →

1 see to sth: to deal with something or make sure it happens ▶ *"These papers need filing." "Don't worry, I'll see to it."* ▶ *Our uncle took care of us and saw to our education.*

2 have sth **seen to, get** sth **seen to**: to have a wound or injury treated by a nurse or doctor ▶ *That looks like a nasty cut – you should get it seen to.*

SEEK

SEEK OUT →

seek out sth/sb, **seek** sth/sb **out**: to try to find someone or something ▶ *The charity is aiming to seek out sponsors among local firms.*

SEEP

SEEP AWAY →

seep away: to gradually disappear ▶ *Two years later, the president watched as his power and authority seeped away.*

SEIZE

SEIZE ON, *also* SEIZE UPON →

seize on/upon sth: to be very interested in an idea, opportunity, or what someone says because you can use it to get an advantage for yourself ▶ *Opposition leaders seized on the opportunity to portray the Prime Minister as indecisive.* ▶ *The press seized on the story, and exaggerated ▶ out of all proportion.*

SEIZE UP →

1 seize up: if an engine or part of a machine seizes up, its moving parts stop working properly ▶ *"The engine's seized up," the mechanic said. "When did you last put oil in it?"*

2 seize up: if a part of your body seizes up, if becomes very stiff and painful ▶ *His legs started seizing up in the last 10 metres of the race.*

SEIZE UPON *see* SEIZE ON →

SELL

SELL OFF →

1 sell off sth, **sell** sth **off**: to sell something cheaply because you no longer want or need it ▶ *We sold off most of Grandma's things after she died.*

2 sell off sth, **sell** sth **off**: to sell all or part of an industry or company ▶ *The UK sold off most of its nationalized industries in the 1980s.*

SELL ON →

be sold on sth/sb: to be enthusiastic about something or someone, especially a new idea or plan ▶ *I was never particularly sold on the new set-up at work.*

SELL OUT →

1 sell out: to have no more of something left to sell, because they have all been bought. **+ of** ▶ *Most music stores have already sold out of his new album.* **be sold out** (=a shop has sold out of something) ▶ *"Do you have any croissants left?" "Sorry, they're sold out."*

2 sell out: to do something that is against your beliefs, principles, or promises in order to get power, money etc ▶ *Union members have accused their leaders of selling out to the management.*

    sell-out N when you do something that is against your beliefs or principles because you want more money, power etc ▶ *Some authors think writing romantic novels is a sell-out.*

3 sell out: to sell your business or your share of a business ▶ *After four years, Glenn sold out to his sister, who continued to operate the restaurant alone.*

SELL UP →

sell up, **sell up** sth, **sell** sth **up**: to sell your house or business so that you can go somewhere else or do something else ▶ *Rosa wanted Mum to sell up and go and live with her in Rome.*

SEND

SEND AWAY →

1 send away: to send a letter to a company or organization asking them to send something to you. **+ for** ▶ *She sent away for information after reading a newspaper article about voluntary teaching overseas.*

2 send sb **away**, **send away** sb: to tell someone to leave a place, or to arrange for them to go somewhere ▶ *She was sent away to boarding school at the age of seven.*

SEND BACK →

send sth **back**, **send back** sth: to return something to the company or shop where it came from ▶ *I think I'll send the sweater back. It just doesn't look right.*

SEND DOWN →

1 send sb **down**: to put someone in prison ▶ *He was found guilty of armed robbery and sent down for six years.*

2 be sent down: to be made to leave a university because of bad behaviour ▶ *My brother was sent down from Oxford for smoking dope.*

SEND FOR →

1 send for sb: to ask someone to come to you by sending them a message ▶ *Elise's mother became worried about her cough and sent for the doctor.* **send for help** ▶ *Quick – someone please send for help!*

2 send for sth: to ask or order that something be brought or sent to you ▶ *I'll send for the rest of my furniture when I get there.*

SEND IN →

1 send in sth, **send** sth **in**: to send something to a place where it can be dealt with ▶ *Send in your payment by the 5th of June or your insurance policy will be cancelled.*

S

2 send in sb, **send** sb **in**: to send soldiers, police etc somewhere to deal with a dangerous situation ▶ *Police were sent in to break up fights between rival football fans.*

3 send sb **in, send in** sb: to ask or tell someone to enter a room ▶ *"Kelly is waiting, Mr Nelson." "Send her in."*

SEND OFF →

1 send off sth, **send** sth **off**: to send something somewhere by mail ▶ *Have you sent off that application form yet?*

2 send off: to send a letter to a company or organization asking them to send something to you. **+ for** ▶ *Laura sent off for their latest catalogue.*

3 send sb **off, send off** sb: to tell someone to leave a place, or to arrange for them to go somewhere ▶ *His father sent him off at the age of 10 to live with friends in Moscow.*

   send-off N when people gather together to say goodbye to someone ▶ *It's a shame she's leaving, but we'll give her a good send-off.*

4 be sent off: if a sports player is sent off, they are forced to leave the field  because they have broken the rules ▶ *United had their captain sent off and four other players were booked.*

   sending-off N when a sports player is forced to leave the field because they have broken the rules ▶ *This is his third sending-off this season.*

SEND OUT →

1 send sb/sth **out, send out** sb/sth: to make something or someone go from one place to various other places ▶ *Sussman had sent out teams of reporters to interview demonstrators.*

2 send out sth, **send** sth **out**: to broadcast a message or produce sound or light ▶ *The ship sent out a distress call when its engine room caught fire.* ▶ *The lighthouse sends out a powerful beam that can be seen miles out to sea.*

3 send out a message also **send out a signal etc**: to make people have a particular idea about something by what you say or do ▶ *We don't want to send out the wrong message and make people think we support the use of drugs.*

SEND OUT FOR →

send out for sth: to telephone a restaurant and ask them to bring food to your home or work ▶ *Could we send out for a pizza? I'm too tired to cook tonight.*

SEND UP →

send up sb/sth, **send** sb/sth **up**: to copy someone or something in a funny way ▶ *The director seems to spend most of the film sending up James Bond.*

   send-up N a book, film etc that copies something in a funny way ▶ *a hilarious send-up of the King Arthur story*

SEPARATE

SEPARATE OFF →

1 separate off sth, **separate** sth **off**: to separate part of something from the rest of it ▶ *The kitchen area is separated off by a wooden partition.*

2 separate off sb/sth, **separate** sb/sth **off**: to remove someone or something from a group of people or things. **+ from** ▶ *Infected cattle have to be separated off from the rest of the herd.*

SEPARATE OUT →

1 separate out sb/sth, **separate** sb/sth **out**: to divide a group of people or things into smaller groups ► *New York householders are required by law to separate out different types of waste for recycling.*

2 separate out sth, **separate** sth **out**: to remove something from other things ► *The machine cuts the crop and separates out the grain.*

SERVE

SERVE AS →

serve as sth: to be used instead of something when nothing more suitable is available ► *There was an upturned box in the middle of the room that served as a table.*

SERVE ON →

1 serve on sth: to be a member of an official committee, council etc ► *She serves on the board of the Women's Economic Development Council.*

2 serve sth **on** sb: to officially give or send someone a written order to appear in a court of law ► *Court orders had already been served on six debtors.*

SERVE OUT →

1 serve out sth, **serve** sth **out**: to continue doing something, until the end of a fixed period of time ► *Many people believed that Roosevelt was too ill to serve out his term as President.*

2 serve out sth, **serve** sth **out**: to put food onto plates so that people can eat it ► *We sat round the table chatting, as Pat served out the stew.*

SERVE UP →

1 serve up sth, **serve** sth **up**: to put food onto plates so that people can eat it ► *Do you want me to serve up the vegetables?*

2 serve up sth: to provide something as entertainment ► *a new TV channel serving up 24-hour sports coverage*

SET

SET ABOUT →

1 set about sth: to start doing something ► *We then set about the task of decorating the interior of the offices.* **set about doing** sth ► *When the war was over, they set about trying to rebuild their lives.*

2 set about sb: to attack someone by hitting or kicking them ► *Two men leaped out of the shadows and set about him with baseball bats.*

SET AGAINST →

1 set sth **against** sth: to compare the advantages and disadvantages of a situation ► *The recent increase in output has to be set against increased labour costs.*

2 set sth **against** sth: to compare two amounts, numbers, periods etc ► *The £6 million grant seems less impressive when set against the £800 million the government has to spend.*

3 be set against sth: if a film, play, story etc is set against a particular place or period of history, the story takes place in that place or during that period. **be set against the background of** sth *also* **be set against the backdrop of** sth ► *Many of her novels are set against the background of the American Civil War.*

4 set against sth, **set** sth **against** sth: to be in front of a particular background, especially in a way that is attractive ► *red and orange autumn leaves, set against a clear blue sky*

5 set sb **against** sb: to make someone start a fight or quarrel with another person ► *The bitter civil war had set brother against brother.*

6 be (dead) set against sth: to be strongly opposed to something

▶ *What made you change your mind? Last night, you were dead set against the idea.*

SET AHEAD →

set sth **ahead**: to change your clock or watch so that it shows a later time ▶ *Don't forget to set your clocks ahead tonight.*

SET APART →

1 set sb/sth **apart, set apart** sth/sb: to make someone or something seem different and often better than other people or things ▶ *It is humans' ability to use language that sets them apart from other animals.*

2 set apart sth, **set** sth **apart**: to keep something for a particular purpose ▶ *I try to set apart half an hour each day to sit and relax.* **+ for** ▶ *This part of the house was set apart for guests to stay in.*

SET ASIDE →

1 set aside sth, **set** sth **aside**: to keep something, especially time or money, for a particular purpose. **+ for** ▶ *Try to set aside at least an hour each day for learning new vocabulary.* ▶ *You should have set aside some cash to pay household expenses.*

2 set aside sth, **set** sth **aside**: to decide that you will not be influenced by a particular feeling, belief, or principle, because something else is more important ▶ *Louis knew that he must set all thoughts of revenge aside.*

3 set aside sth, **set** sth **aside**: to officially state that a previous legal decision no longer has any effect ▶ *Mr Justice Rock allowed the appeal and set aside the order of the Divisional Court.*

SET BACK →

1 set back sth, **set** sth **back**: to delay the progress or development of something ▶ *The revolution set back*

the modernization of the country by many years.

setback N something that delays the progress or development of something ▶ *The peace talks have suffered a series of setbacks.*

2 be set back: if a building is set back, it is some distance from the road ▶ *The museum is a cool sandstone building, set back among trees.*

3 set sb **back**: to cost someone a lot of money ▶ *That's a nice coat – I bet that set you back a bit.* **set** sb **back £100 etc** ▶ *Many of these wines will set you back £15–£20.*

4 set sth **back**: to change your clock or watch so that it shows an earlier time ▶ *When should we set the clocks back?*

SET DOWN →

1 set sth **down, set down** sth: to put down something that you have been holding ▶ *The waiter brought over two bowls of noodles and set them down on the table.*

2 set down sth, **set** sth **down**: to state officially how something should be done ▶ *Please read carefully the conditions set down in the credit agreement.*

3 set down sth, **set** sth **down**: to write down your thoughts or feelings ▶ *Encourage your students to set down their ideas on paper.*

SET IN →

set in: if the rain, the winter, or a difficult period sets in, it begins and seems likely to continue ▶ *When the worldwide economic recession set in, many poorer nations faced bankruptcy.*

SET OFF →

1 set off: to start to go somewhere ▶ *I wanted to set off early to avoid the traffic.* **+ for** ▶ *Merl kissed her husband goodbye and set off for work.*

2 set off sth, **set** sth **off**: to make a bomb or something else explode ▶ *A bunch of kids were messing around in the street and setting off fireworks.*

3 set off sth, **set** sth **off**: to make something such as an alarm system start operating, especially accidentally ▶ *Put that cigarette out you idiot – you'll set the smoke detector off.*

4 set off sth, **set** sth **off**: to make something start happening, or make people start doing something ▶ *The earthquake set off landslides, which destroyed several villages.*
▶ *Government plans to make divorce easier have set off a national debate.*

5 set sb **off**: to make someone start crying, laughing, or talking about something that they often talk about ▶ *Don't mention anything about weddings – you'll only set her off again.*

SET ON →

1 set sb/sth **on** sb: to make people or animals attack someone ▶ *The farmer threatened to set his dogs on us if we didn't get off his land.*

2 *see* SET UPON

SET OUT →

1 set out: to start a journey, especially a long journey. **+ for** ▶ *In late 1941, he set out for China.* **set out on a journey/**

drive etc ▶ *The next morning they set out on the long drive to Lake Tahoe.*

2 set out to do sth: to start doing something in order to get a particular result ▶ *I've achieved what I set out to achieve – I'm ready for a new challenge now.* ▶ *salesmen who deliberately set out to defraud customers*

    outset N the beginning of something.
    from/at the outset ▶ *It was clear from the outset that there were going to be problems.*

3 set out sth, **set** sth **out**: to explain ideas, facts, or opinions in a clearly organized way ▶ *The guidelines are set out in paragraph two.*

4 set out sth, **set** sth **out**: to arrange a group of things so that they can be used or seen easily ▶ *In the market square, traders had set out displays of items for sale.*

SET OUT ON →

set out on sth: to start something, especially something difficult, important, or new ▶ *The government set out on a programme of economic and social reform.*

SET UP →

1 set up sth, **set** sth **up** to start a business or organization ▶ *The Race Relations Board was originally set up in 1965.* **set (yourself) up** (=start your own business) ▶ *He borrowed £5000 and set himself up in the catering business.* **+ as** ▶ *John used the money he inherited to set up as a fashion designer.* **set up in business** (=start your own business) ▶ *a scheme that helps young people who want to set up in business*

2 set up sth, **set** sth **up**: to make the arrangements that are necessary for something to happen ▶ *I'll get my secretary to set up a meeting.*

3 set up, set up sth, **set** sth **up**: to prepare equipment so that it is ready to be used ▶ *I might need some help setting up my new computer.*

4 set up home: to start living in your own home and buy furniture etc for it ▶ *There's a shortage of housing for young people wanting to set up home.*

5 set up sth, **set** sth **up:** to put or build something somewhere ▶ *The police have set up roadblocks around the city.* ▶ *Napoleon set up a monument to honour his great army.*

6 set sb **up:** to deliberately make people think that someone has done something wrong or illegal when they have not ▶ *The four suspects claimed they had been set up by the police.*

    set-up N a dishonest plan that makes people think someone has done something wrong when they have not ▶ *Was he the victim of an elaborate set-up?*

7 set sb **up:** to give someone the money they need to start a business. **+ with** ▶ *Her parents set her up with her own bar in St John's Wood.* **set** sb **up in business** ▶ *After Pete graduated, his father set him up in business.*

8 set sb **up for life:** to provide someone with enough money to live well without having to work for the rest of their life ▶ *Ray grinned. "If this deal goes through, we'll be set up for life."*

9 set sb **up:** to arrange for two people to meet because you think they will be attracted to each other. **+ with** ▶ *Marty tried to set her up with a guy from work.*

SET UP AS →

set yourself up as sth: to make people believe that you have the right or the skill to do something, especially when this is not true ▶ *Politicians set themselves up as moral authorities, with the power to tell us how we should live our lives.*

SETTLE

SETTLE BACK →

settle back: to lean back in bed or in a chair, and relax and enjoy yourself ▶ *Jackie switched on the TV and settled back to watch the film.*

SETTLE DOWN →

1 settle down, settle sb **down:** to stop behaving in a noisy or excited way and become calm and quiet, or to make someone do this ▶ *Settle down please, class! Now turn to page 57 in your books.*

2 settle down: to start living in a place with the intention of staying there permanently, especially with a husband or wife ▶ *It's about time he settled down and got married.*

3 settle down: to start to feel happy and confident in a new situation, job, or school ▶ *It took him a while to get used to his new school, but I think he's settled down now.*

4 settle down: to start giving all of your attention to a job or activity. **settle down to** sth ▶ *I sorted out my mail and then settled down to some serious work.* **settle down to do** sth ▶ *John settled down to write her a letter explaining his behaviour.*

5 settle down: if a situation settles down, it becomes calmer and less busy ▶ *Things were really hectic during the sales, but it's settled down now.*

SETTLE FOR →

settle for sth: to accept something, even though it is not the best or not what you really want ▶ *They want £2500 for it, but they might settle for £2000.* ▶ *Obviously I'd like to get good grades, but I'll settle for a pass.* **not settle for (anything) less** (=refuse to accept something that is not the best) ▶ *Olivia wanted a flat in the most fashionable part of town and wouldn't settle for anything less.*

SETTLE IN, *also* **SETTLE INTO** →
settle in, settle into sth: to begin to feel happy and relaxed in a new situation, home, job, or school ► *How do you like your new home? Are you settling in OK?* **be settled in** ► *We'll wait till you're properly settled in before we come and visit you.*

SETTLE INTO →
settle into sth: to get used to a particular way of living or doing things ► *The baby soon settled into a routine of feeding and sleeping.*

SETTLE ON, *also* **SETTLE UPON** →
settle on/upon sth: to choose something, especially after discussing all the possibilities ► *They haven't settled on a date for the wedding yet.*

SETTLE UP →
settle up: to pay what you owe on an account or bill ► *We settled up and checked out of the hotel.* **+ with** ► *I'll settle up with the bartender and then we can leave.*

SETTLE UPON *see* **SETTLE ON**

SEW

SEW UP →
1 sew up sth, **sew** sth **up:** to close or repair something by sewing it ► *There's a hole in my coat that needs sewing up.*

2 sew up sth, **sew** sth **up:** to complete a business agreement or plan and get the result you want ► *Bob reckons the deal should be sewn up within a week.*

3 have sth **(all) sewn up:** to have control of a situation, and be sure to win or gain something ► *It seems like the Democrats have the election sewn up.*

SHACK

SHACK UP →
shack up: to start living with someone that you have a sexual relationship with but are not married to. **+ with** ► *Michael shacked up with his new girlfriend as soon as he divorced his wife.*

SHADE

SHADE IN →
shade in sth, **shade** sth **in:** to make part of a drawing or picture darker using a pencil or a darker colour ► *She started to shade in an outline of a tree with charcoal.*

SHADE INTO →
shade (off) into sth: if one thing shades into another, there is no clear division between them so that it is impossible to see where one stops and the other starts ► *The grey-blue sea shaded into the grey-blue sky.* ► *National pride can often shade into racism.*

SHAKE

SHAKE DOWN →
1 shake sb **down:** to use force or threats to make someone give you money ► *There is something wrong with a system that shakes the public down for more taxes every year.*
 shakedown N when someone gets money from someone else by using threats ► *After the thousand dollar shakedown, Eddie couldn't pay up any more.*

2 shake sb/sth **down, shake down** sb/sth: to search a person or place thoroughly ► *City authorities decided to shake down the area's prisons after 18 prisoners died.*

SHAKE OFF →
shake off sth, **shake** sth **off:** to get rid of an illness or something that is causing you problems ► *I've had this cold for weeks – I just can't seem to shake it off.* ► *It was 1949, and Europe was still trying to shake off the horror of World War II.*

S

SHAKE ON →

shake on sth: to agree on a decision or business agreement by shaking hands ▶ *"That's a deal," I said, and we shook on it.*

SHAKE OUT →

shake out sth, **shake** sth **out**, **shake** sth **out of** sth: to shake a cloth, bag, sheet etc, in order to make it smooth or to get rid of small pieces of dust or dirt ▶ *I went outside and shook the sand out of my sleeping bag.*

SHAKE OUT OF →

shake sb **out of** sth: to make someone change their mood, so that they stop feeling sad, upset, lazy etc ▶ *There was no one to help shake Lena out of her depression.* ▶ *"William!" The teacher's angry voice shook him out of his daydream.*

SHAKE UP →

1 shake sb **up, shake up** sb: to give someone a very unpleasant shock ▶ *Seeing that accident really shook me up.* ▶ *When he heard the news he was too shaken up to react immediately.*

2 shake up sth, **shake** sth **up**: to make big changes to a company or organization over a short period of time ▶ *A new director was brought in last year to shake things up.*

   shake-up N when big changes are made to a company or organization ▶ *a huge shake-up of the education system*

SHAPE

SHAPE UP →

1 shape up: to make progress and improve ▶ *The new recruits are shaping up nicely.* ▶ *You'd better shape up, John, or you'll be off the team.*

2 shape up: if a situation, activity, or struggle shapes up, it develops ▶ *Events were shaping up worse and*

faster than I could have expected. ▶ *Well, Sue, less than a week to go before the show! How's it all shaping up?*

3 shape up: to make yourself healthy and physically strong so that your body looks good ▶ *Here are 12 easy exercises to help you shape up for the summer.*

SHARE

SHARE OUT →

share out sth, **share** sth **out**: to divide something into smaller amounts, and give an amount to each person in a group ▶ *Take these cookies and share them out.* **+ between** ▶ *We've got three pizzas to share out between five people.* **+ among/amongst** ▶ *The profits are shared out among the company directors.*

SHARPEN

SHARPEN UP →

sharpen up sth, **sharpen** sth **up**: to improve something so that it reaches the necessary standard ▶ *We'll need a few more rehearsals to sharpen up the dance routine.*

SHAVE

SHAVE OFF →

shave off sth, **shave** sth **off**: to remove hair from your skin completely by shaving.

shave off your hair/beard etc ▶ *Dan shaved off his beard and bought a suit and tie.*

SHEAR

BE SHORN OF →

be shorn of sth: to have had your authority or power taken away from you ▶ *The king, shorn of more and more of his powers, had very little idea of what was happening.*

SHELL

SHELL OUT →

shell out, shell out sth: to pay a lot of money for something. **+ for** ▶ *We don't want to have to shell out for a Christmas disco again this year.* **+ on** ▶ *Kids these days shell out £30 or £40 on a computer game, without even thinking about it.*

SHIFT

SHIFT FOR →

shift for yourself: to look after yourself without any help from other people ▶ *Some children as young as seven or eight are left to shift for themselves on the streets.*

SHIN

SHIN DOWN →

shin down sth: to quickly climb down something such as a tree or pole ▶ *The thief must have climbed out of a back window and shinned down the drainpipe.*

SHIN UP →

shin up sth: to quickly climb up something such as a tree or a pole ▶ *A young man nimbly shinned up the tree and started to throw coconuts down.*

SHINE

SHINE THROUGH →

shine through, shine through sth: if a good quality that someone has shines through, it is easy to notice it ▶ *Kindness and humour shone through his letters.* ▶ *Gary's chess talents shone through at an early age.*

SHIP

SHIP IN →

1 ship sth **in, ship in** sth: to bring goods into a place in a ship or plane ▶ *Consumer goods such as videotapes and electric shavers are shipped in from abroad.*

2 ship sb **in, ship in** sb: to bring people to a place in order to work there ▶ *Because of the shortage of staff in our schools, teachers have to be shipped in from other parts of Europe.*

SHIP OUT →

ship sth/sb **out, ship out** sth/sb: to send goods or people somewhere in a ship or plane ▶ *Food and clothing will be shipped out to the disaster area within the next few days.*

SHOOT

SHOOT DOWN →

1 shoot sb/sth **down, shoot down** sb/sth: to make an enemy plane crash to the ground, by firing bullets or weapons at it ▶ *American war planes were shot down inside the no-fly zone.*

2 shoot down sb, **shoot** sb **down**: to kill or seriously injure someone by shooting them ▶ *Soldiers were accused of shooting down unarmed demonstrators.*

3 shoot sth/sb **down, shoot down** sth/sb: to say or show that someone's ideas or opinions are wrong or stupid ▶ *Officials shot down rumours of a merger between the two companies.*
shoot sth/sb **down in flames** (=completely destroy someone's ideas by showing that they are wrong or stupid) ▶ *The article was shot down in flames by government scientists.*

SHOOT FOR →

shoot for sth: to try to achieve a particular aim ▶ *Coach Bruce Corbett said he is shooting for a winning record this season.*

SHOOT OFF →

shoot off: to leave somewhere very quickly or suddenly ▶ *Every time I see* *him, he looks at his watch and shoots off to a meeting.*

SHOOT OUT →
shoot it out: to fight against someone with guns. **+ with** ▶ *The terrorists tried to shoot it out with the police before being overpowered.*

> **shoot-out** N a gun fight between two people or groups ▶ *At least two people at the prison were killed in a shoot-out with security forces.*

SHOOT UP →
1 shoot up: to increase very quickly ▶ *Some experts think that house prices will shoot up again this year.* **+ to** ▶ *Her weight shot up to fourteen stone after her children were born.*

2 shoot up: if a child shoots up, he or she grows taller very quickly ▶ *Chris has really shot up since I last saw him!*

3 shoot up, shoot up sth: to put harmful illegal drugs into your blood, using a special needle ▶ *Kids as young as ten are shooting up heroin.*

SHOP

SHOP AROUND →
shop around: to try to find the best price, quality, deal etc by comparing what various different shops or companies are offering ▶ *You can halve the cost of insuring your home, simply by shopping around.* **+ for** ▶ *Prices for sporting equipment vary enormously, and it's worth shopping around for the best buy.*

SHORE

SHORE UP →
1 shore up sth, shore sth up: to support something that is weak or likely to fail ▶ *a government attempt to shore up the ailing steel industry*

2 shore sth up, shore up sth: to support a wall or a building with large pieces of wood or metal ▶ *The tunnel was shored up with old wooden beams.*

SHOUT

SHOUT DOWN →
shout sb down, shout down sb: to shout loudly while someone is talking because you want to prevent them from being heard ▶ *One man stood up to protest, but was quickly shouted down.*

SHOUT OUT →
shout out sth, shout sth out, shout out: to suddenly shout something or say something in a loud voice ▶ *Someone in the audience shouted out "Get on with it!"*

SHOVE

SHOVE AROUND, *also* SHOVE ABOUT →
shove sb around/about: to tell someone what to do in a rude or unpleasant way ▶ *I left my old job because I was fed up with being shoved around.*

SHOVE OFF →
shove off!: used to tell someone rudely to go away ▶ *Shove off, Jerry. I don't want you here.*

SHOVE UP →
shove up!: used to tell someone to move a little in order to make space for someone else ▶ *If you shove up a bit, we can all get in the back seat.*

SHOW

SHOW AROUND, *also* SHOW ROUND →
show sb around/round sth, show sb around/round: to go around a place with someone to show them what is interesting or what they need to know ▶ *In the morning the Professor showed us around the university.* ▶ *A representative had arranged to meet us at the house and show us round.*

SHOW IN, *also* SHOW INTO →
show sb in, show sb into sth: to

polretely show a visitor the way into a room, building etc ▶ *A secretary showed Alison into a large office.*

SHOW OFF →

1 show off:
to behave in a way that you think makes you seem intelligent, skilful, rich etc to other people, but in fact is just

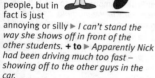

annoying or silly ▶ *I can't stand the way she shows off in front of the other students.* **+ to** ▶ *Apparently Nick had been driving much too fast – showing off to the other guys in the car.*

   show-off N ▶ *William was the youngest of ten children – a show-off and a class clown.*

2 show off sth/sb, **show** sth/sb **off:** to show something that you are very proud of to a group of people ▶ *She wanted to show off her new outfit at the party.*

SHOW OUT →

show sb **out, show out** sb: to politely show someone the way out of a room, building etc. **+ of** ▶ *Mr Burrows asked his secretary to show me out of the office.*

SHOW OVER →

show sb **over** sth, **show** sb **over:** to go around a place with someone in order to show them what is interesting or what they need to know ▶ *Lou showed her over the nearby castle and country houses.*

SHOW ROUND *see* SHOW AROUND

SHOW THROUGH →

show through, show through sth: if a quality or feeling that someone has

shows through, it is noticeable ▶ *The minister replied politely, but his irritation showed through.*

SHOW UP →

1 show up: to arrive, especially at a place where people are expecting you ▶ *We spent half an hour waiting for Martin to show up.*

2 show up: if a problem or fault shows up, it is easy to see or notice ▶ *In the sunlight, the decayed state of the house showed up quite clearly.*

3 show up sth, **show** sth **up:** to make a problem or fault easy to see or notice ▶ *These results have shown up serious faults in our examination system.*

4 show up sb, **show** sb **up:** to make someone feel embarrassed or ashamed ▶ *You can always rely on your children to show you up in public!*

5 show sb/sth **up, show** sb/sth: to show that someone or something is bad, unpleasant etc. **+ as** ▶ *By now the government had lost control and had been shown up as useless.* **be shown up for what it is** (=be shown to be something bad, unpleasant etc) ▶ *The idea was soon shown up for what it was: a waste of time and money.*

SHOWER

SHOWER ON, *also* SHOWER UPON →

1 shower sth **on/upon** sb: if you shower praise, honours etc on someone, you praise them a lot or give them a lot of honours ▶ *I didn't think it was a particularly good film, despite all the Oscars and awards that were showered on it.*

2 shower sth **on/upon** sb: to give a lot of money or gifts to someone in a very generous way ▶ *He had lot of weathy relatives who used to shower expensive presents on him.*

SHOWER WITH →

1 shower sb **with** sth: to give someone a lot of something, especially presents or praise ► *The senior officers were showered with medals and titles.*

2 shower sb **with** sth: to throw a lot of something over someone ► *Just then the bomb exploded, showering people with glass and debris.*

SHRINK

SHRINK AWAY →

shrink away: to move back and away from someone or something, because you do not want them to touch you.
+ from ► *"You're disgusting," Nell said, shrinking away from him and shuddering.*

SHRINK BACK →

shrink back: to move back and away from something or someone, especially because you are frightened or you do not want them to touch you.
+ against ► *"Well?" the teacher asked in a voice that made all four students shrink back against the wall.* **+ into** ► *As the men neared her hiding place, Tilly shrank back into the shadows.*

SHRINK FROM →

shrink from sth: to feel very unwilling to do something or deliberately avoid doing it ► *She never shrank from her duties as leader.* **shrink from doing** sth ► *He did not shrink from doing what he thought was right.*

SHRIVEL

SHRIVEL UP →

1 shrivel up:
if something
shrivels up, it
become smaller
and its skin
becomes
covered with
lines because it
is very dry or

old ► *The few unpicked apples on the top branches had shrivelled up and gone brown.*

2 shrivel up: to feel extremely embarrassed or frightened by something ► *When my mother brought out the baby photos, I just shrivelled up inside!*

SHROUD

BE SHROUDED IN →

1 be shrouded in mist/darkness etc: to be covered by mist, clouds etc, and difficult or impossible to see ► *It was very early in the morning, and the mountains were still shrouded in mist.*

2 be shrouded in mystery/secrecy etc: to be very strange and mysterious ► *For many years, the Rockwell incident has remained shrouded in mystery.*

SHRUG

SHRUG OFF →

shrug off sth, **shrug** sth **off**: to not worry about something and treat it as unimportant ► *She tried to shrug off his remarks, though they were very hurtful.* ► *Many people with the illness don't recognize the symptoms, or shrug them off as unimportant.*

SHUCK

SHUCK OFF →

1 shuck off sth, **shuck** sth **off**: to take off a piece of clothing in a quick and careless way ► *Michael shucked off his coat and hat and went to his room.*

2 shuck off sth, **shuck** sth **off**: to stop paying attention to an idea or feeling because you do not care about it or do not want to think about it ► *I tried to shuck off my worries and have a good time.*

SHUT

SHUT AWAY →

1 shut sb/sth **away**, **shut away**

sb/sth: to put someone or something n a place so that they are hidden or cannot leave ▶ *Should young criminals of fifteen or sixteen be shut away in adult prisons?* **keep sb/sth shut away** ▶ *Gina was puzzled as to why her father kept the diaries shut away.*

2 shut yourself away: to keep away from other people by staying in a room by yourself ▶ *I often had to shut myself away until two or three in the morning in order to get the work done.*

SHUT DOWN →

1 shut sth down, shut down sth, shut down: if a business, factory, shop etc is shut down or shuts down, it closes for a long time or permanently ▶ *In 1982 a series of strikes led to the airline being shut down.*

  shutdown N when a business, factory, shop etc closes for a long time or permanently ▶ *The power station has just re-opened following a prolonged shutdown for maintenance.*

2 shut sth down, shut down sth, shut down: if a machine shuts down, it stops working; if you shut down a machine, you turn it off to stop it working ▶ *Please wait while your computer shuts down.* ▶ *The pilot shut down the wrong engine by mistake.*

SHUT IN →

1 shut sb/sth in sth, shut in sb/sth: to prevent a person or an animal from leaving a place, by closing and often locking the door ▶ *The owners had gone away, leaving two dogs and a cat shut in on their own.*

2 shut yourself in (sth): to go into a room and shut the door so that no one else can get in ▶ *She ran upstairs and shut herself in her bedroom.*

3 be shut in: to be in a very small space, especially so that you feel that you cannot move or get out ▶ *Working*

down the mines meant being shut in all day without enough air or light.

SHUT OFF →

1 shut off sth, shut sth off: to turn off an engine, machine, power supply etc ▶ *Victor drew up outside his flat and shut off the engine.*

2 shut yourself off: to avoid meeting or talking to other people ▶ *After the initial shock of my husband's death, I realized that I couldn't shut myself off for ever.* **shut yourself off from the world/reality** ▶ *The old lady had unplugged the telephone, determinedly shutting herself off from the world.*

3 shut sth off, shut off sth: if a road, area etc is shut off, fences have been put round it and people are not allowed to go there ▶ *Parts of the city were shut off and traffic was being diverted.*

4 shut off sth, shut sth off: if something shuts off a view, the light etc, it prevents you from seeing it by getting in the way ▶ *A wall of mountains shuts off the view as you look south.*

SHUT OFF FROM →

be shut off from sth: to be completely separated from other people or things ▶ *The community was still living in the Middle Ages, having been shut off from the outside world for centuries.*

SHUT OUT →

1 shut sb out, shut out sb: to prevent someone from joining in an activity ▶ *At the moment some of the staff feel very shut out.* **+ of** ▶ *I knew there was something exciting going on, but I was shut out of it.*

2 shut sb out, shut out sb: to deliberately not tell someone about your thoughts and feelings ▶ *How can I help you if you keep shutting me out all the time?*

S

3 shut out sth, **shut** sth **out**: to deliberately stop yourself from thinking about something ▶ *I tried to sleep in an attempt to shut out my fears, but I couldn't.*

4 shut out sth, **shut** sth **out**: to prevent a sound, light etc from getting into a place ▶ *It was cool in the wood – the big green leaves shut out the sun.*

5 shut sb **out, shut** sth **out**: to prevent someone from entering a place, especially by closing a door ▶ *I tried to see him several times, but he shut me out by slamming the door in my face.*

SHUT UP →

1 shut up!: used to tell someone rudely or angrily to stop talking ▶ *"Shut up!" said Terry. "I don't care what you think."*

2 shut up, shut sb **up, shut up** sb: to stop talking, or to make someone stop talking ▶ *I can't stand that woman – she never shuts up.*

3 shut sb **up, shut up** sb: to keep a person or an animal somewhere and prevent them from leaving ▶ *Simply shutting more and more people up in prison doesn't solve the problem of crime.*

4 shut up sth, **shut** sth **up, shut up**: to close and lock a house, shop, room etc that you own ▶ *He was just shutting up his shop when four armed men burst in.*

SHY

SHY AWAY FROM →

shy away from sth: to avoid doing something because you are nervous about it. **+ from** ▶ *Some members of the party criticize the leadership in private, but shy away from a direct challenge.*

SIC

SIC ON →

sic sb/sth **on** sb: to tell someone or something to attack or catch someone ▶ *Get off my property or I'll sic my dog on you.*

SICKEN

SICKEN OF →

sicken of sth: to stop wanting to have or do something, because you have had or done enough of it already ▶ *After a few years, I began to sicken of political life.*

SIDE

SIDE AGAINST →

side against sb: to join together with other people in order to oppose someone else ▶ *A number of my colleagues sided against me at the last minute.*

SIDE WITH →

side with sb: to support a person, country, or group in an argument or fight ▶ *He was shocked to find that when he split up with his girlfriend, most of his friends sided with her.*

SIDLE

SIDLE UP →

sidle up: to walk towards someone or something quietly and a little nervously.
+ to ▶ *A woman with a baby in her arms sidled up to us and asked us for some money.*

SIFT

SIFT OUT →

sift out sth/sb, **sift** sth/sb **out**: to separate particular things or people from a group of others ▶ *We need to sift out the buyers that are really serious.* **+ from** ▶ *My job was bringing all the information together and* *sifting out the incorrect details from the rest.*

SIFT THROUGH →

sift through sth: to carefully examine a large number of things in order to find something that you are looking for ▶ *Police officers are sifting through thousands of items of information provided by the public.*

SIGN

SIGN AWAY →

sign away sth, **sign** sth **away**: to give property or a legal right to someone else, by signing an official document ▶ *Her husband had tricked her into signing away her rights to the house.*

SIGN FOR →

1 sign for sth: to sign a document to show that you have received a letter, package etc ▶ *Could you sign for the parcel here and print your name underneath?*

2 sign for Arsenal etc: to sign a contract agreeing to play for a particular football team ▶ *He signed for Leeds in the summer of 1998.*

SIGN IN →

1 sign in: to write your name in a book when you arrive somewhere that you are visiting ▶ *For security reasons, the company requires all visitors to sign in at reception.*

2 sign sb **in, sign in** sb: if you sign someone in at an office, club etc, you write their name in a book so that they are allowed to enter ▶ *He met me on the steps of his London club and signed me in.*

SIGN OFF →

1 sign off, sign off sth: to end an informal letter that you are writing, by giving your final message ▶ *Well, I'll sign off now. Many thanks again for having us to stay.*

2 sign off: to finish doing something, especially after you have been doing it for a long time ▶ *I'd been working hard all day so I decided it was time to sign off.*

3 sign sb **off, sign off** sb: if a doctor signs someone off, he or she gives them a note for their employer saying that they are ill and are not able to work ▶ *She had been signed off for two weeks suffering from work-related stress.*

SIGN ON →

1 sign on: to officially agree to work for someone or do a training course, usually by signing a contract or form. **+ with/ as** ▶ *I signed on as a volunteer at the homeless shelter.* **+ for** ▶ *She signed on for a course in Business Management.*

2 sign on, sign on sth: to claim the money given by the government to people who do not have a job ▶ *When we left college there were so few teaching jobs available that a lot of us had to sign on.* **sign on the dole** (=claim money from the government, because you do not have a job) ▶ *Mr Kelly signed on the dole in July, after his company went bust.*

SIGN OUT →

1 sign out: to write your name in a book when you leave somewhere that you are visiting ▶ *I waited while Dr Fraker collected his bags and signed out.*

2 sign out sth, **sign** sth **out**: to write your name on a form or in a book to show that you have taken or borrowed something ▶ *I'm afraid I can't find that file and there's no record of its being signed out.*

SIGN OVER →

sign sth **over, sign over** sth: to give property or a legal right to someone else, by signing an official document. **+ to** ▶ *When Julie and her husband split up, he signed over everything in* the house to her. ► The land has been signed over to his son.

SIGN UP →

1 sign up: to arrange to take part in an activity or a course of study, by writing your name down on a list ► *How many people have signed up to go on the theatre trip so far?* **+ for** ► *I'm thinking of signing up for an evening class in classical guitar.*

2 sign up: to sign a contract saying that you agree to work for someone. **+ with** ► *He's signed up with a major publishing company to write a book on Astronomy.*

3 sign sb **up, sign up** sb: to arrange for someone to sign a contract saying that they agree to work for you ► *Manchester United are very keen to sign him up.* **+ as** ► *An agency has now signed her up as a professional model.*

SILT

SILT UP →

silt up, silt sth **up, silt up** sth: if a river or lake silts up, or something silts it up, it fills with sand, mud or soil etc ► *In the 18th century, the San Diego River nearly silted up.*

SIMMER

SIMMER DOWN →

simmer down: to stop being angry and become calm again ► *Come on, Peggy, simmer down now.*

SING

SING ALONG →

sing along: to sing with someone else who is already singing or playing music ► *The crowd was dancing and singing along.* **+ with** ► *I always sing along with the radio when I drive.*

sing-along N an informal occasion when people sing songs together ► *Bring your guitar and we'll have a sing-along.*

SING OUT →

sing out, sing sth **out** sth: to sing loudly and clearly ► *Toby cheerfully sang out the birthday song as Ellen walked into the office.*

SING UP →

sing up: to sing more loudly ► *Don't be shy – sing up!*

SINGLE

SINGLE OUT →

single out sb/sth, **single** sb/sth **out**: to choose someone or something from among a group, especially in order to praise them or criticize them ► *She singled out Humphrey Bogart as her favourite actor.* **+ for** ► *Teachers should not single out students for special treatment.*

SINK

SINK BACK →

1 sink back: to sit or lie backwards into a comfortable, relaxing position ► *Inhaling deeply, Duvall sank back against the pillows.*

2 sink back: to return to a state that you were in before, or to return to a habit that you used to have. **+ into** ► *Eddie sank back into silence, apparently satisfied.*

SINK DOWN →

1 sink down: to let your body move or slide down to a sitting or lying position ► *I sank down next to her and looked at the photographs.*

2 sink down: to move downwards ► *The sun slowly sank down in the sky and disappeared.*

SINK IN →
sink in: if information, ideas, or facts sink in, you gradually understand them and realize their full meaning ▶ *Ron paused, as if to let the message sink in.* ▶ *Tears welled up in Nancy's eyes as the news of her father's death slowly sank in.*

SINK INTO →
1 sink sth **into** sth: to stick a knife or other sharp object into something ▶ *The man sank a knife into his brother's chest during an argument.*

2 sink money etc into sth: to provide a lot of money for a business or product, especially in order to make a profit later ▶ *Developers have already sunk millions of dollars into vacant Malibu land.*

SIPHON *also* SYPHON

SIPHON AWAY →
siphon away sth, **siphon** sth **away**: to take something that should have been given to another organization or person ▶ *Critics claim the plan would siphon money away from state schools.*

SIPHON OFF →
siphon off sth, **siphon** sth **off**: to illegally take something, especially money, from an organization or business ▶ *Billions of pounds have been siphoned off from government funds and placed in foreign bank accounts.*

SIT

SIT AROUND, *also* SIT ABOUT →
sit around/about, sit about/around sth: to spend a lot of time relaxing or not doing anything useful ▶ *They just sit around the house and gossip all day.* **sit around/about doing** sth ▶ *The men sat around drinking whisky and smoking cigars.*

SIT BACK →
1 sit back: to get into a comfortable sitting position and relax ▶ *Sit back and watch the movie.* ▶ *Just sit back and read the paper – I'll make dinner tonight.*

2 sit back: to wait for something to happen without making any effort to do anything about it yourself ▶ *You can't just sit back and expect customers to come to you.*

SIT BY →
sit by: to allow something to happen when you should be doing something to try to stop it ▶ *We can't just sit by and let our children's health be threatened.*

SIT DOWN →
1 sit down: to move into a sitting position after you have been standing ▶ *The old lady got onto the bus and sat down.* ▶ *"Mind if I sit down?" I asked.*

    sit-down meal/dinner etc N a sit-down meal, dinner etc is one in which you sit at a table and eat a meal ▶ *Are they having a buffet at the wedding reception, or a sit-down meal?*

    sit-down protest/strike etc N a protest, strike etc in which people sit down, especially to block a road or other public place ▶ *Several thousand people began a sit-down demonstration.*

2 sit sb **down**: to make someone move into a sitting position, or to ask someone to sit down ▶ *She picked up the child and sat him down on the sofa.*

SIT FOR →
sit for sb/ sth: to sit in a particular position so that someone can paint you, take a photograph of you etc ▶ *She used to sit for Stanley Spencer.*

S

SIT IN →

1 sit in: to be present at a class, meeting, discussion etc but watch or listen instead of taking part ▸ *Do you mind if I just sit in today? I'm not feeling very well.* **+ on** ▸ *Denny went back to UCLA and sat in on a few lectures.*

2 sit in: to take part in a protest in which people sit down, especially to block a road or other public place ▸ *Police arrived after protesters began sitting in at the state capitol building.*

> **sit-in** N a protest in which people sit down, especially to block a road or other public place ▸ *a sit-in organized by war protesters*

SIT IN FOR →

sit in for sb: to go to a meeting, do a job etc instead of the person who usually does it ▸ *Yvonne will be sitting in for me tomorrow while I'm at the conference.*

SIT ON →

1 sit on sth: to be very slow at dealing with something or to delay dealing with it ▸ *The bank sat on our loan application for two months.*

2 sit on sth: to be a member of an official group, committee etc ▸ *Roberta Smith is the first African-American woman to sit on the committee.*

3 sit on sth: to prevent someone from knowing a piece of information ▸ *A good journalist will know when to sit on a story and when to publish.*

SIT OUT →

1 sit out sth, **sit** sth **out**: to not take part in a game, competition, dance etc, because you are injured or tired ▸ *I think I'll sit this dance out.*

2 sit out sth, **sit** sth **out**: to wait until something is finished, even though it is boring or unpleasant ▸ *Sheila wanted to leave and go home, but her friend decided to sit the film out.*

SIT ROUND *see* SIT AROUND

SIT THROUGH →

sit through sth: to stay at a meeting, performance etc until it finishes, even though it is very long or boring ▸ *We had to sit through a whole day of boring talks about company sales.*

SIT UP →

1 sit up: to move into a sitting position after you have been lying down ▸ *Wendy sat up in bed and stretched.*

2 sit up: to make your back straighter when you are sitting ▸ *Sandie forced herself to sit up straight during the interview.*

3 sit up: to stay awake and not go to bed ▸ *They sat up late into the night talking about old times.*

4 sit up and take notice: to suddenly start paying attention to someone or something ▸ *People are starting to sit up and take notice about the dangers of genetically modified foods.*

SIZE

SIZE UP →

size up sb/sth, **size** sb/sth **up**: to look at or think about a person or situation in order to form an opinion about them ▸ *Rita has a talent for quickly sizing up people.* ▸ *He spent a few minutes sizing up the difficulty of the task which lay ahead.*

SKATE

SKATE AROUND, *also* SKATE OVER, SKATE ROUND →

skate around/over/round sth: to avoid talking about a problem or subject, or not give it enough attention ▸ *She skated around questions regarding her relationship with the minister.*

SKETCH

SKETCH IN →

sketch in sth, **sketch** sth **in**: to give

more information about a plan, idea etc ► *In his speech, the president sketched in his idea for reducing taxes.*

SKETCH OUT →
sketch out sth, **sketch** sth **out**: to describe something in a few words, giving only the basic details ► *The tour guide sketched out our programme for the first week.*

SKIM

SKIM OFF →
1 skim off sth, **skim** sth **off**, **skim** sth **off** sth: if you skim off money, you dishonestly take it from a larger amount and keep it for yourself ► *Public officials have been accused of skimming money off the county budget.*

2 skim off sth, **skim** sth **off**: to remove something that is on top of a liquid or surface ► *Skim off the excess fat from the pan before adding the rest of the ingredients.*

SKIM THROUGH →
skim through sth: to read something quickly in order to find the main facts or ideas in it ► *She tends to skim through novels, just to find out what happens at the end.*

SKIMP

SKIMP ON →
skimp on sth: to not spend enough money, time, effort etc on something, or to not use enough of something ► *Hospitals will not save money by skimping on patient care.* ► *He accused the company of skimping on safety tests and inspections.*

SKIRT

SKIRT AROUND, *also* SKIRT ROUND →
1 skirt around/round sth: to avoid an important or difficult problem, subject etc ► *If you continue to skirt round the problem, it will just get worse.*

2 skirt around/round sth: to go around the outside edge of a place ► *We skirted around the town, to avoid getting caught in traffic.*

SKIVE

SKIVE OFF →
skive off, skive off sth: to avoid work or school by staying away or leaving without permission ► *Do you fancy skiving off and going down to the pub?* ► *We used to skive off school to go to the beach.*

SLACK

SLACK OFF →
1 slack off: to become slower, weaker, or less busy ► *Economists predict sales will slack off after the holiday season.* ► *Air raids and bombings slacked off as the enemy retreated.*

2 slack off: to make less effort than usual, or become lazier ► *We've got a lot to get through this week, so no slacking off!*

SLACKEN

SLACKEN OFF →
slacken off: to become slower, weaker, or less busy ► *I expect business to slacken off over the summer.*

SLAG

SLAG OFF →
slag sb/sth **off, slag off** sb/sth: to talk about or to someone in a very critical way ► *I don't know why she doesn't break up with Dan. She's always slagging him off.* ► *Poor Lucy! She's always getting slagged off.*

S

SLAM

SLAM DOWN →
slam down sth, **slam** sth **down**: to hit something against a surface quickly and violently ► *I slammed my fist down on the table and told him I wouldn't be treated this way.*

SLAM INTO →
slam into sth/sb: to crash into something with a lot of force ► *The car's brakes failed and it mounted the pavement, slamming into a lamp-post.*

SLAM ON →
slam on the brakes: to suddenly put your foot hard on the brake in order to stop your car ► *The driver slammed on the brakes, but it was too late.*

SLAP

SLAP DOWN →
slap sb/sth **down**, **slap down** sb/sth: to rudely tell someone that their suggestions, questions, ideas etc are stupid or unreasonable ► *Margaret would immediately slap down anyone who argued with her.*

SLAP ON →
1 slap a tax/fine etc on sth: to suddenly order that something should be taxed, or that someone should pay a fine ► *In 1991 the government slapped a 50% tax on all luxury goods.*

2 slap sth **on** sth, **slap on** sth, **slap** sth **on**: to put or spread large amounts of paint, butter etc on a surface ► *Ellie rushed upstairs and hurriedly slapped on some make-up.*

SLATE

BE SLATED FOR →
be slated for sth: to be planned to happen at a particular time ► *The singer's debut is slated for the 17th of October.*

SLAVE

SLAVE AWAY →
slave away: to work very hard for a long time ► *While you've been out enjoying yourselves, we've been slaving away in the kitchen.*

SLEEP

SLEEP IN →
sleep in: to sleep later than usual in the morning ► *We usually sleep in on Sunday mornings.*

SLEEP OFF →
sleep sth **off, sleep off** sth: to sleep until you do not feel ill any more, especially after drinking too much alcohol ► *I suppose they're sleeping off the effects of last night's party.*

SLEEP ON →
sleep on sth: to delay making a decision about something until the next day or later. **sleep on it** ► *I'm going to sleep on it, and tomorrow I'll decide what to do.*

SLEEP OUT →
sleep out: to sleep outside ► *We used to sleep out under the stars on warm summer nights.*

SLEEP OVER →
sleep over: to sleep at someone else's house for a night ► *Is it okay if I sleep over at Jim's place tonight?*
   sleep-over N a party at which children or young people stay the night at someone's house ► *One night Mary Jo went to a sleep-over at a friend's house.*

SLEEP THROUGH →
sleep through sth: to continue sleeping while something is happening and not be woken by it ► *How did you manage to sleep through that storm last night?*

SLEEP TOGETHER →
sleep together: if two people are sleeping together, they are having a

sexual relationship with each other ▶ *When did you find out that Betty and your husband were sleeping together?*

SLEEP WITH →

sleep with sb: to have sex with someone ▶ *I'm not going to tell you how many women I've slept with.*

SLICK

SLICK BACK →

slick back sth, **slick** sth **back**: to push your hair back from your face and keep it in that style ▶ *His black hair was slicked back.*

SLICK DOWN →

slick down sth, **slick** sth **down**: to put water or another substance on your hair to keep it close to your head ▶ *He quickly straightened his tie and slicked down his hair with water.*

SLIM

SLIM DOWN →

1 slim down: to become thinner, especially in order to be healthier or more attractive ▶ *After three months on the diet she had slimmed down to a healthy 61 kilos.*

    slimmed-down ADJ a slimmed-down person has become thinner and more attractive ▶ *She showed off her new slimmed-down figure.*

2 slim down, slim down sth, **slim** sth **down**: if a company slims down or is slimmed down, it makes itself smaller by getting rid of some of its workers ▶ *Companies have been slimming down to improve their efficiency.*

SLIP

SLIP AWAY →

1 slip away: if someone's power or their chance of success slips away, it gradually disappears ▶ *With its power and prestige slipping away, the Party appealed for unity.* **+ from** ▶ *As the game went on I could feel the championship slipping away from us.*

2 slip away: to die peacefully ▶ *Tim lay there on his hospital bed and quietly slipped away.*

SLIP BY →

1 slip by: if time slips by, it seems to pass very quickly ▶ *The hours slipped by so quickly that he almost forgot about lunch.*

2 let a chance slip by also **let an opportunity slip by**: if you let a chance or opportunity slip by, you do not use it ▶ *Here was a chance to make some money, and he was not one to let such an opportunity slip by.*

SLIP IN →

slip in sth, **slip** sth **in**: to quickly mention something when you are talking or writing about something else ▶ *Writers of detective stories often slip in a tiny clue that most readers will miss.*

SLIP INTO →

1 slip into sth: to put on a piece of clothing in which you feel comfortable and relaxed ▶ *I'll just slip into something more comfortable.*

2 slip into unconsciousness/ a coma/ etc: to become unconscious or start to sleep ▶ *If brain damage is severe, the patient may slip into a coma.*

3 slip into sth: to start doing something or start behaving in a particular way, although you did not intend to ▶ *Without a job to go to, Kevin soon slipped into the habit of getting up at noon.*

S

SLIP OFF →
1 slip sth **off, slip off** sth: to take off a piece of clothing smoothly and easily ▶ *He slipped off his coat and hung it in the hall.*

2 slip off: to leave a place quickly and quietly, so that no one notices you going ▶ *"Where's Steve?" "I think he must have slipped off home."*

SLIP ON →
slip sth **on, slip on** sth: to put on a piece of clothing smoothly and easily ▶ *Just hop out of bed and slip on your dressing gown.*

SLIP OUT →
slip out: if a remark or a piece of information slips out, you mention it without intending to ▶ *I'm sorry, I shouldn't have said that – it just slipped out.*

SLIP OUT OF →
slip out of sth: to take off clothes or shoes quickly and easily ▶ *She slipped out of her swimsuit and wrapped a towel around her.*

SLIP OVER ON →
slip one over on sb: to deceive or trick someone by telling them something that is not true ▶ *It would be easy for a smooth talker like him to slip one over on these country boys.*

SLIP THROUGH →
slip through: if something that is incorrect or illegal slips through, it is accidentally not removed or changed ▶ *Even when a document has been given a computer spellcheck, some errors will inevitably slip through.*

SLIP UP →
slip up: to make a careless mistake ▶ *Your lawyer slipped up on an important detail – that's why the prosecution failed.*

slip-up N a careless mistake ▶ *I'm afraid there's been a bit of a slip-up over your contract.*

SLOB
SLOB AROUND →
slob around: to spend time doing nothing and being lazy ▶ *He was still slobbing around in his dressing gown at lunchtime.*

SLOG
SLOG AWAY →
slog away: to work hard at something for a long time ▶ *I'll go on slogging away until I've finished the job.* **+ at** ▶ *Randall spent the next few months slogging away at Russian grammar.*

SLOG OUT →
slog it out: to fight, compete, or argue with someone for a long time until one side wins ▶ *They're never going to agree, so it's best to leave them to slog it out.*

SLOG THROUGH →
slog through sth: to read or study something that is long and difficult ▶ *There was no alternative to sitting down and slogging through vocabulary lists.*

SLOP
SLOP AROUND →
slop around: to spend time being lazy and doing very little, wearing old, untidy clothes ▶ *I didn't really expect to find this famous scientist slopping around in old jeans and a dirty sweatshirt.*

SLOPE
SLOPE AWAY →
slope away: if the ground slopes away, it goes downwards ▶ *In front of the farmhouse the land slopes away towards the river.*

SLOPE OFF →
slope off: to leave somewhere quietly

S

nd secretly, especially to avoid work,
rouble etc ► *He must have sloped off*
ome when no one was looking.
► *Scenting our dogs, the wolf turned*
way and sloped off into the forest.

SLOSH

SLOSH AROUND →

be sloshing around: if there is a lot of
money sloshing around, there is more
of it available than is needed ► *Why*
an't some of that money sloshing
round in Europe be used to relieve
poverty in other countries?

SLOT

SLOT IN, also SLOT INTO →

slot sth/sb in, slot in sb/sth, **slot**
th/sb **into** sth: to find a time for
omething or someone in a carefully
planned programme of events ► *Dr*
Singh is extremely busy at present,
ut I could slot you in at 11.15
omorrow. ► *We could slot you into*
he afternoon session.

SLOUCH

SLOUCH AROUND, also SLOCH
ABOUT →

slouch around/about: to stand or
walk around slowly with your
houlders bent forward because you
re bored and have nothing to do
► *Bored youths were slouching around*
n street corners.

SLOUGH

SLOUGH OFF →

1 slough off sth, **slough** sth **off**: to get
id of a feeling, memory, or quality that
ou do not want ► *The company is now*
nxious to slough off its bad reputation.

2 slough off sth, **slough** sth **off**: if a
nake or other animal sloughs off its
ld dead skin, that skin comes off its
ody when a new skin grows ► *A*
attlesnake may slough off its skin up
o four times a year.

SLOW

SLOW DOWN →

1 slow down, slow down sb/sth, **slow**
sb/sth **down**: to start to move slowly
or to make someone or something do
this ► *Police are asking motorists to*
slow down and take extra care. ► *Ice*
on the road slowed us down
considerably.

2 slow down sb/sth, **slow** sb/sth
down, slow down: to start to work or
develop more slowly, or to make
someone or something do this ► *An*
industrial dispute has slowed down
production at the factory. ► *If business*
slows down, some of these workers
are going to lose their jobs.

3 slow down: if you slow down, you
become less active or work with less
energy than before ► *When you get to*
my age, it's time to slow down a little.

SLOW UP →

1 slow up, slow up sth/sb, **slow**
sth/sb **up**: to begin to move or work
more slowly or to make something or
someone do this ► *The car slowed up*
as it approached the gate.
► *Computing problems slowed us up a*
bit.

2 slow up sth, **slow** sth **up**: to make
something happen or develop more
slowly ► *The new legislation could*
slow up the whole election process.

SLUG

SLUG OUT →

slug it out: if two or more people,
teams, armies etc slug it out, they
fight, compete, or argue for a long
time until one side wins ► *Now we can*
watch our political leaders slugging it
out in live TV debates.

SMACK

SMACK OF →

smack of sth: to seem to contain some
of an unpleasant quality or attitude ► *I*

S

wouldn't want to be involved in anything that smacks of illegality.

SMARTEN

SMARTEN UP →

1 smarten up sth/sb, **smarten** sth/sb **up, smarten up**: to make yourself or something look neater and tidier ▶ *Barbara had smartened herself up ready for the interview.* ▶ *He had made up his mind to sell the old house after he had smartened it up a bit.*

2 smarten up your act *also* **smarten up your ideas**: to improve the way you think and work, so that you are more effective ▶ *You'd better smarten your ideas up if you want to keep your job here.*

3 smarten up: to become more wise and less stupid ▶ *Let's hope Barbara has smartened up since her last relationship.*

SMASH

SMASH DOWN →

smash down sth, **smash** sth **down**: to hit something such as a door or wall so violently that it falls to the ground ▶ *There were complaints that police had smashed down doors and destroyed furniture while searching the premises.*

SMASH IN →

smash sth **in, smash in** sth: to break something or make a hole in it, by hitting it violently ▶ *Someone had smashed his skull in with a baseball bat.* **smash sb's face/head in** (=hit someone hard in the face or on the head) ▶ *If he tries to mess me around, I'll smash his face in.*

SMASH UP →

smash up sth, **smash** sth **up**: to destroy something or damage it very badly by hitting it violently or crashing it ▶ *A gang of thugs came into the bar and smashed the place up.*

SMELL

SMELL OF →

smell of sth: to have a smell that is like a particular thing ▶ *The house still smells of paint.* ▶ *He came home smelling of whisky.*

SMELL OUT →

1 smell sth/sb **out, smell out** sth/sb: if an animal smells out something or someone, it finds them by using its sense of smell ▶ *A fox could hide in the woods, but our dogs would smell it out.*

2 smell out sth, **smell** sth **out**: to discover something that someone want to keep hidden or secret ▶ *They feared her because somehow she always smelt out their innermost secrets.*

SMILE

SMILE ON →

fortune is smiling on sb *also* **fate is smiling on** sb: used to say that someone is lucky because something good happens to them or they avoid something bad ▶ *Fortune must have been smiling on him – he arrived at the airport an hour late only to find that his flight had been delayed.*

SMOKE

SMOKE OUT →

1 smoke out sb, **smoke** sb **out**: to discover who is causing a problem and force them to make themselves known ▶ *The McCarthy trials were intended to smoke out Communist sympathizers and enemy agents.*

2 smoke out sb/sth, **smoke** sb/sth **out**: to force a person or animal to come out of a place by filling it with smoke ▶ *Beekeepers smoke out the bees and remove the honeycombs from the hive.*

SMOOTH

SMOOTH →

smooth away sth, **smooth** sth **away**: to get rid of any problems, worries, or difficulties ▸ *The two leaders met secretly to smooth away any obstacles to the peace agreement.*

SMOOTH DOWN →

smooth down sth, **smooth** sth **down**: to make the surface of something smooth and flat ▸ *Jenny got up and smoothed down her dress.*

SMOOTH OUT →

1 smooth out sth, **smooth** sth **out**: to make cloth or paper smooth and flat ▸ *He smoothed out the map, and began to plan their route.*

2 smooth out sth, **smooth** sth **out**: to make something happen in an even and regular way without any sudden changes or problems ▸ *The government wants to smooth out the business cycle, and stop the swings from boom to bust.*

3 smooth out sth, **smooth** sth **out**: to deal with any problems, difficulties, or disagreements, so that something can work effectively ▸ *The talks are intended to smooth out any practical problems which may get in the way of a settlement.*

SMOOTH OVER →

smooth over sth, **smooth** sth **over**: to make disagreements and other problems seem less serious by talking about them to the people involved ▸ *I was sure that I could smooth over our little misunderstanding.* **smooth things over** ▸ *Use this as an opportunity to smooth things over, to apologize again and make a fresh start.*

SMOTHER

SMOTHER IN, *also* SMOTHER WITH →

1 smother sth **in/with** sth: to cover the surface of something with a large amount of a substance ▸ *Before they set off for the beach they smothered themselves in suncream.*

2 smother sb **with kisses**: to kiss someone's face many times ▸ *She ran to meet him and smothered him with kisses.*

SNACK

SNACK ON →

snack on sth: to eat small amounts of a particular food between main meals or instead of a meal ▸ *I tend to snack on chocolate during the day when I'm working.*

SNAP

SNAP OUT →

snap out sth, **snap** sth **out**: to say something quickly or suddenly, especially when you are annoyed ▸ *Captain Vincent was furiously snapping out instructions to the crew.*

SNAP OUT OF →

1 snap out of sth, **snap** sb **out of** sth: to stop feeling unhappy or upset, and become more cheerful, or to make someone do this. **snap out of it** ▸ *Come on Fran, snap out of it! Things aren't really so bad.* **snap** sb **out of it** ▸ *Marie's been feeling really depressed recently, and I can't seem to snap her out of it.*

2 snap out of sth, **snap** sb **out of** sth: to suddenly stop thinking pleasant thoughts that make you forget about what is really happening, or to make someone do this ▸ *He was snapped out of his daydream by Rachel, who suddenly appeared by his side.*

S

SNAP UP →

1 snap up sth, **snap** sth **up**: to buy something quickly and eagerly before other people can buy it ► *All the tickets for the game were snapped up in less than two hours.*

2 snap up sth, **snap** sth **up**: to take an opportunity as soon as it becomes available ► *I'm sure if they offered him the job he'd snap it up straightaway.*

SNARL

SNARL UP →

1 snarl up, snarl up sth: if traffic snarls up or is snarled up, the cars cannot move freely because the road is blocked or too busy ► *Drivers were swearing as they got snarled up in the midday traffic.*

    snarl-up N when traffic cannot move freely because the road is blocked or there are too many cars ► *snarl-ups on the roads out of Paris*

2 snarl up, snarl up sth, **snarl** sth **up**: if a system or process snarls up or is snarled up, it stops working because there is too much work to deal with ► *The huge number of cases has snarled up the court process.*

SNATCH

SNATCH AWAY →

snatch away sth, **snatch** sth **away**: to suddenly take something away from someone ► *Marco tried to snatch the ring away from her.* ► *United snatched the championship away with an amazing goal from Payne.*

SNEAK

SNEAK ON →

sneak on sb: to tell someone such as an employer, parent, or teacher that another person has done something wrong ► *She didn't want the other girls to think that she was sneaking on them.*

SNEAK UP →

sneak up: to come near to someone very quietly, so that they do not hear or see you until you reach them ► *Kate sneaked up behind him and put her hands over his eyes.* **+ on** ► *A couple of kids sneaked up on him in a dark alley and took all his money.*

SNEEZE

SNEEZE AT →

not to be sneezed at: used to say that something is so good that you should definitely consider it ► *£5000 a week was not to be sneezed at.*

SNIFF

SNIFF AROUND, *also* SNIFF ROUND →

sniff around, sniff around sth: to try to find out information about someone or something, especially information that they want to hide ► *It won't be long before the tax office starts sniffing around.* ► *Of course she'll keep quiet. She won't want the police sniffing around her place.*

SNIFF AT →

1 not to be sniffed at: used to say that something is so good that you should definitely consider it ► *The price, however, is not to be sniffed at: £17.50!*

2 sniff at sth: to disapprove of something and think that it is not very good ► *The critics tended to sniff at his films, and dismiss them as being rather childish.*

SNIFF OUT →

1 sniff out sth, **sniff** sth **out**: to find out information that other people want kept secret, or to find something that may be useful or valuable ► *Journalists are trained to sniff out a good story.* ► *She had a talent for sniffing out bargains.*

2 sniff out
sth, **sniff** sth
out: if a dog
sniffs out
something,
for example
hidden drugs

or explosives, the dog finds it using its
sense of smell ▶ *A police dog sniffed
out over 400 pounds of cocaine in a
camper van.*

SNIFF ROUND *see* SNIFF AROUND

SNOW

BE SNOWED IN, *also* BE SNOWED
UP →

be snowed in: to be unable to leave
the place where you are because there
is so much snow on the ground
▶ *Many people are snowed in and
cannot get to work.* ▶ *We were
snowed up all week in a mountain
cabin.*

BE SNOWED UNDER →
be snowed under: to have so much
work, so many letters, phone calls etc,
that it is difficult to deal with
everything ▶ *I would have called you
earlier but I've been absolutely
snowed under.*

BE SNOWED UP *see* BE SNOWED IN

SNUFF

SNUFF OUT →

1 snuff out sth, **snuff** sth **out**: to end
something suddenly, especially
something that has been developing
or growing ▶ *Tanks were sent in to
control the protestors, and the
democracy movement was soon
snuffed out.*

2 snuff out sth, **snuff** sth **out**: to stop a
candle or flame from burning ▶ *He
turned over and snuffed out the
candle on his bedside table.*

SNUGGLE

SNUGGLE
DOWN →
**snuggle
down**: to
move into a
warm
comfortable

position in your bed, especially in
order to sleep ▶ *With a sigh, she
snuggled down under the quilt again.*

SNUGGLE UP →

1 snuggle up: to move into a warm
comfortable position lying or sitting
next to someone ▶ *It was a cold night
and the children snuggled up to keep
warm.* **+ to** ▶ *Tess snuggled up to him,
her head on his chest.*

2 be snuggled up: to be lying or
sitting in a warm comfortable position
▶ *She longed to be indoors, snuggled
up in bed with a good book.*

SOAK

BE SOAKED THROUGH →
be soaked through: to be completely
wet ▶ *By the time he got home, his
jacket was soaked through.*

SOAK UP →

1 soak up sth, **soak** sth **up**: to enjoy
experiencing or looking at something
in a place ▶ *You can stay in pretty
mountain villages and soak up the
scenery.* **soak up the sun** ▶ *Morocco is
an ideal place for soaking up the sun.*
soak up the atmosphere (=enjoy
watching and experiencing all the
interesting things that are happening
in a place) ▶ *I wanted to wander
around the old markets and soak up
the atmosphere.*

2 soak up sth, **soak** sth **up**: if
something soaks up a liquid, it takes
the liquid into itself ▶ *He used a towel
to soak up the blood.*

3 soak up sth, **soak** sth **up**: to learn a

lot of information and ideas about a subject by reading, listening to other people etc ▶ *I read a lot of books and tried to soak up as many new ideas as I could.*

4 soak up sth, **soak** sth **up**: to use a lot of money, especially an unreasonably large amount ▶ *The new satellite network soaked up more than £65 million of public money.*

SOBER

SOBER DOWN →

sober down: to stop being so excited, worried, or frightened, and become calm ▶ *When they'd all sobered down, he went on with his story.*

SOBER UP →

1 sober up, **sober** sb **up**, **sober up** sb: to gradually become less drunk or make someone less drunk ▶ *The next day, when she had sobered up, she came over to apologize for her behaviour.*

2 sober up, **sober up** sb, **sober** sb **up**: to behave in a more serious and sensible way, or make someone do this ▶ *The bombing helped to sober up a lot of people who had previously supported the terrorists.*

SOCK

SOCK TO →

1 sock it to sb: to hit someone very hard ▶ *Mike socked it to him with a left to his jaw.*

2 sock it to sb: to do something in a way that is very impressive and has a strong effect ▶ *The audience is waiting for you, Frank. Get out there and sock it to them.*

SOFTEN UP

SOFTEN UP →

1 soften up sb, **soften** sb **up**: to make someone more likely to do what you want, especially by praising them or being kind to them ▶ *I saw now she*

was trying to soften me up just to ask me a favour. ▶ *Buy her some flowers – that should soften her up a bit.*

2 soften up sth, **soften** sth **up**: to make something soft ▶ *The rain had softened up the ground.*

SOLDIER

SOLDIER ON →

soldier on: to continue doing something, even though it is difficult or unpleasant ▶ *He managed to soldier on until the end of the game in spite of his injuries.*

SORT

SORT OUT →

1 sort out sth, **sort** sth **out**: to successfully deal with a problem, a difficult situation, or a disagreement ▶ *She went to a counsellor to help sort out her marriage.* **get it sorted out** ▶ *I'll be glad when we've got everything sorted out.* **sort yourself out** also **sort out your life** (=deal with your personal problems) ▶ *You've got to try and stop drinking and sort yourself out.*

2 sort itself out: if a situation sorts itself out, it stops being a problem without anyone trying to do anything ▶ *Don't worry. I'm sure it'll all sort itself out in the end.*

3 sort out sth, **sort** sth **out**: to arrange or organize things so that they are no longer untidy or badly organized ▶ *Ally wanted me to help her sort out the house.* ▶ *We need to sort out our camping gear before we go away on holiday.*

4 sort out sth, **sort** sth **out**: to arrange to get something or to arrange for something to be done ▶ *Working mothers often have difficulty sorting out childcare.*

5 sort out sth, **sort** sth **out**: to make final decisions about something that is planned ▶ *Have you sorted out where you're going to live?*

6 sort out sth, **sort** sth **out**: to separate one type of thing from another ▶ *Steve had spotted the letter while sorting out his mail.*

SORT THROUGH →

sort through sth: to look for something among a lot of similar things ▶ *She sat down and sorted carefully through the files.*

SOUND

SOUND OFF →

sound off: to complain loudly and angrily about something. **+ about** ▶ *Here he is again, sounding off about the amount of sex and violence on TV.*

SOUND OUT →

sound out sb, **sound** sb **out**: to find out what someone thinks about a plan or idea ▶ *Government officials are trying to sound out the views of the public about the proposed ban.*

SOUP

SOUP UP →

soup up sth, **soup** sth **up**: to make changes to something in order to make it more powerful, effective, interesting etc than it was before ▶ *new software programs to soup up the office e-mail*

   souped-up ADJ something that is souped-up has been changed to make it more powerful, effective, interesting etc ▶ *a souped-up old Escort*

SPACE

SPACE OUT →

1 be spaced out: to be unable to think clearly, for example because of the effects of drugs or tiredness ▶ *That Saturday I was fine until the afternoon. Then I began to feel totally spaced out.*

2 space out: to stop paying attention and just look at something without thinking, especially because you are tired, bored, or have taken drugs ▶ *I totally spaced out during the meeting and didn't hear the details about our next project.*

SPARK

SPARK OFF →

spark off sth, **spark** sth **off**: to suddenly cause something to start, for example protests, violence, or interest in something ▶ *An apparently minor incident sparked off rioting which lasted for days.* ▶ *Her case did more than anything to spark off the civil rights movement.*

SPEAK

SPEAK FOR →

1 speak for sb: to express the opinions, thoughts, or feelings of a person or group of people ▶ *Shelley was a poet who spoke for the people.* ▶ *I'm sure I speak for everyone here when I say that it has been a pleasure to work with you.*

2 sth **speaks for itself**: used to say that something shows clearly that something is true ▶ *The fact that so many people are leaving teaching speaks for itself.*

3 sth **is spoken for**: if something is spoken for, someone else has already arranged to have it or use it ▶ *Sorry. This table's already spoken for.*

4 (you can) speak for yourself: used to say that you definitely do not have the same feelings or opinions as the person you are talking to ▶ *Speak for yourself. I don't have that kind of problem.*

5 let sb **speak for himself/ herself etc**: to let someone say what their opinion about something is, without having someone else to say it for them ▶ *I'll* *bring Mr Power in and let him speak for himself.*

6 speaking for myself: used before you say what your opinion about something is ▶ *Speaking for myself, I can't think of anything more boring!*

SPEAK OF →

1 speak of sth: to have qualities which make you think of something else ▶ *He wanted to create something that spoke of spring, that made people feel there was a celebration going on.*

2 speak of sth: to show clearly that something is true or exists ▶ *The decision to cancel the project speaks of a lack of confidence in the boardroom.*

SPEAK OUT →

speak out: to express your opinions publicly ▶ *People lived in constant fear of the police, and no one dared to speak out.* **+ against** ▶ *He was one of the few politicians who had the courage to speak out against the war.*

outspoken ADJ talking publicly about your opinions ▶ *an outspoken critic of the regime*

SPEAK UP →

1 speak up!: used to tell someone to speak more loudly ▶ *Speak up! I'm a little deaf!*

2 speak up: to express your opinions freely, especially to support or defend someone ▶ *The organization has been very active in speaking up on behalf of disadvantaged families.* ▶ *The victims of domestic violence are often afraid to speak up.*

SPEED

SPEED BY →

speed by: if time speeds by, it seems to pass very quickly ▶ *The weeks sped by and soon it was time to go back to school.*

SPEED OFF →

speed off: to leave somewhere quickly or suddenly ▶ *She watched them as they sped off into the night.*

SPEED UP →

speed up, speed up sth, **speed** sth **up**: to move, work, or happen more quickly, or make something do this ▶ *You'd better speed up Martin, or we'll never get this done.* ▶ *I'm sorry about the delay. I'll try and speed things up a bit.*

SPELL

SPELL OUT →

1 spell out sth, **spell** sth **out**: to explain something clearly and in detail ▶ *Television companies ran commercials spelling out the dangers of smoking.* ▶ *What they told you wasn't true. How many times do I have to spell it out for you?*

2 spell out sth, **spell** sth **out**: to say the letters of a word separately in their correct order ▶ *Jan spelled out his name, "F-A-H-E-R-T-Y".*

SPEW

SPEW OUT →

spew out sth, **spew** sth **out, spew out**: to send out something in large quantities, or to come out of something in large quantities ▶ *The four great chimneys to his left spewed out their fumes over the town.* ▶ *Tickertape was spewing out of the teleprinter.*

SPICE

SPICE UP →

spice up sth, **spice** sth **up**: to make something more interesting or exciting ▶ *She believes that adding real-life drama can spice up a history lesson.* ▶ *101 ways to spice up your love life*

SPILL

SPILL OUT →

1 spill out: to come or pour out of a container, usually by accident and in an untidy way ► *Half her clothes had spilled out of her suitcase.*

2 spill out: to come out of a place in large numbers, usually in a disorganized way ► *A coachload of tourists spilled out and hurried to the cliff-top to admire the view.*

SPILL OVER →

1 spill over:
if something in a container spills over, it pours over the edge, usually because the container is too full ► *The beer rose up the glass and began to spill over.*

2 spill over: if a problem or a bad situation spills over, it spreads and starts to affect other places, people etc. **+ into** ► *The fighting had spilled over into neighbouring countries.*
► *The effects of the recession spilled over into almost every aspect of people's lives.*

SPIN

SPIN AROUND, *also* SPIN ROUND →

spin around/round: to suddenly move quickly around, so that you are facing in a completely different direction ► *He spun around in his chair to face me.* ► *Someone tapped Davies on the shoulder and he spun round.*

SPIN OUT →

spin out sth, **spin** sth **out**: to make something continue for as long as possible, or make food, money etc last for as long as possible ► *She'd only prepared the first part of the class, so*

she tried to spin it out for as long as she could.

SPIN ROUND *see* **SPIN AROUND**

SPIRIT

SPIRIT AWAY →

spirit away sb/sth, **spirit** sb/sth **away**: to take someone or something away quickly and mysteriously ► *After the press conference, the royal couple were spirited away in a big black limousine.*

SPIT

SPIT OUT →

1 spit out sth, **spit** sth **out**: to make something come out of your mouth by blowing it, in order to get rid of it ► *He spat out a big watermelon seed.*

2 spit it out!: used to ask someone to tell you something that they seem too frightened or embarrassed to say ► *Come on man, spit it out!*

SPLASH

SPLASH DOWN →

splash down: if a spacecraft splashes down, it lands in the sea ► *The astronauts are due to splash down in the Pacific Ocean at around 4 pm.*
  splashdown N when a spacecraft lands in the sea ► *The crew managed to make radio contact just before splashdown.*

SPLASH OUT →

splash out: to spend a lot of money on something ► *I feel like splashing out a bit. Let's go to that new French restaurant.* **+ on** ► *The actor has splashed out £425,000 on a fourth home for himself and his wife.*

SPLIT

SPLIT OFF →

1 split off, split off sth, **split** sth **off**: if part of something splits off, or you split it off, it becomes separated from the rest ► *A group of white rocks had*

S

split off from the cliff. ▶ *Work is split off from people's family lives, and it has been so since the start of the Industrial Revolution.*

2 split off: to stop being members of a party or organization and form a new one ▶ *A small group split off and called themselves the Real Socialist Party.*

SPLIT ON →
split on sb: to tell someone in authority, for example a teacher, that someone has done something wrong ▶ *Don't worry. Robert won't split on us.*

SPLIT UP →
1 split up sth, **split** sth **up, split up**: to divide something into different parts or groups, or to separate into different parts or groups ▶ *None of us believed that it was right to split up the company.* ▶ *They all split up and went their own separate ways.* **+ into** ▶ *Many of the larger houses are being split up into flats.* **split up** sth **between** sb also **split up** sth **among** sb (=divide something so that each member of a group has part of it) ▶ *The former Soviet armed forces were split up between the new states.*

2 split up:
if two people split up, they end their romantic relationship or marriage ▶ *After her parents split up, she went off to live with her mother.* **+ with** ▶ *He split up with his wife after 18 years of marriage.*

3 split up: to stop performing or working together ▶ *Why do you think the Beatles split up?*

SPOIL

BE SPOILING FOR →
be spoiling for a fight also **be spoiling for trouble**: to want to have a fight or argument with someone and try to make this happen ▶ *Williams was obviously spoiling for a fight.*

SPONGE

SPONGE OFF, *also* SPONGE ON →
sponge off/on sb: to get money or other things from someone without paying them back or doing anything for them in return ▶ *He's sponged off his parents all his life.* ▶ *Millionaire executives are just sponging off the backs of ordinary workers.*

SPOUT

SPOUT ON, *also* SPOUT OFF →
spout on/off: to talk a lot about something in a boring way, especially without knowing a lot about the subject. **+ about** ▶ *a boring old man who kept spouting on about how young people have no sense of duty*

SPRAWL

SPRAWL OUT →
be sprawled out: to sit or lie with your arms or legs stretched out in a relaxed or careless way ▶ *He came in and sprawled out on the sofa in front of the TV.*

SPREAD

SPREAD OUT →
1 spread out sth, **spread** sth **out**: to open something that is folded and lay it flat on a surface ▶ *He spread a towel out on the sand and sat down.*

2 spread out sth, **spread** sth **out**: to arrange a group of things on a surface, so that you can look at them or use them ▶ *They put a rug down on the ground and spread the food out on it.*

3 spread out also **be spread out**: to

cover a large area ► *The wide sweep of the Bay of Naples spread out far below us.*

4 be spread out: if a group of people or things are spread out, they cover a wide area and are far apart from each other ► *Books and records were spread out all over the floor.*

5 spread out sth, **spread** sth **out**: to move your arms, legs, fingers etc, and stretch them so that there is a wide space between them. **spread out your arms/legs etc** ► *Diane leant back and spread out her arms along the back of the sofa.*

6 spread out: if a group of people spread out, they move apart from each other so that they cover a wider area ► *He ordered his men to spread out and search the surrounding fields.*

7 spread out, spread out sth, **spread** sth **out**: to move outwards and cover a wide area, or to make something do this ► *Shock waves spread out from the epicentre of the earthquake.*

8 spread out sth, **spread** sth **out**: to arrange for something to happen or be done in stages over a period of time. **+ over** ► *You can spread out the cost over a year and pay a little each month.*

SPREAD OVER →

spread sth **over** sth: to arrange for something to happen or be done in stages over a period of time ► *The tax increases will be spread over the next three years.*

SPRING

SPRING BACK →

spring back: if something that has been moved, pressed, or stretched springs back, it quickly returns to its original position or shape ► *The branch sprang back and hit him in the face.*

SPRING FOR →

spring for sth: to pay for something ► *I'll spring for a pizza if you go pick it up.*

SPRING FROM →

1 spring from sth: to come from or be caused by something ► *Many of her ideas spring from personal experience.*

2 where did you/he etc spring from?: used to show surprise when you suddenly see someone that you thought was somewhere else ► *Where did you spring from? I thought you had already left.*

SPRING ON →

1 spring sth **on** sb: to tell someone something that shocks or surprises them ► *Her family doesn't know about her engagement yet. She plans to spring it on them this weekend.*

2 spring sth **on** sb: to suddenly do something that shocks or surprises someone ► *Troops were forced to flee when rebels sprang an ambush on them.*

SPRING UP →

1 spring up: to suddenly appear or start to exist ► *Out-of-town shopping centres seem to be springing up everywhere these days.* ► *Beautiful flowers had sprung up on the barren hillside.*

2 spring up: to stand up suddenly ► *She sprang up from her seat and started shouting.*

SPROUT

SPROUT UP →

sprout up: to suddenly appear or start to exist, especially in large numbers ► *Businesses and factories have sprouted up on both sides of the border.*

SPRUCE

SPRUCE UP →
spruce up, spruce up sth, spruce sth up: to make yourself or something look tidier and more attractive ▶ *Paul went upstairs to spruce up a bit before dinner.* ▶ *Wealthier people moved into the area, and spruced up the old buildings.*

SPUR

SPUR ON →
spur sb on: to encourage someone to try harder in order to succeed ▶ *The course was really tough, but the desire to make her family proud of her spurred her on.* **spur** sb **on to do** sth ▶ *Recent discoveries are spurring us on to find a better treatment for the disease.*

SPY

SPY ON, *also* SPY UPON →
spy on/upon sb/sth: to watch someone or something secretly in order to get more information about them ▶ *Carey spied on US diplomats and military officials in Berlin.* ▶ *a children's novel about an 11-year-old girl who spies on her friends and neighbours*

SPY OUT →
spy out sth: to get more information about something by going and looking at it, often secretly ▶ *The soldiers immediately assumed that the men were there to spy out their defences.*

SPY UPON *see* SPY ON

SQUARE

SQUARE AWAY →
square sth away: to finish or make something ready, especially by adding final details ▶ *Peter needs another day to get things squared away at home.*

SQUARE OFF →
square off: to fight or play against someone in a sport ▶ *Arizona and Stanford square off in the Rose Bowl on Sunday.*

SQUARE UP →
1 square up: to pay someone money that you owe them ▶ *I'll pay for the drinks now and we can square up later.* **+ with** ▶ *Sandy had better square up with the credit card company soon.*

2 square up: to prepare to fight or compete with someone ▶ *Sixty schools are squaring up to compete in the Cricket Championships.*

SQUARE UP TO →
square up to sb/sth: to deal with a difficult situation or person in a determined way ▶ *Kathleen finally squared up to her brother and refused to lend him any more money.*

SQUARE WITH →
1a. square with: to seem right or similar when compared with something else ▶ *Denise's behaviour squares with her beliefs about animal rights.* ▶ *His story didn't square with the witnesses' statements.*

b. square sth **with** sth: to show that two things are right or similar when compared with each other ▶ *How can you square such violent actions with your religious beliefs?*

2 square sth **with** sb: to get someone to allow or agree to something ▶ *I'll take the day off if I can square it with my boss.*

SQUASH

SQUASH IN, *also* SQUASH INTO →
squash in, squash in sb/sth, **squash** sb/sth **in**, **squash** sb/sth **in** sth, **squash into** sth, **squash** sb/sth **into** sth: to push yourself or something else into a small space ▶ *He squashed in, sharing the back seat with his mother and sisters.* ▶ *Five of us*

squashed ourselves into one hotel room to save money.

SQUASH UP →

squash up: to move closer together in order to make space for someone or something else ▸ We can get four people on the back seat if you all squash up.

SQUEAK

SQUEAK BY →

squeak by, squeak by sb: to only just succeed in doing something or defeating someone ▸ My boyfriend scored incredibly high in the exam, but I just squeaked by. ▸ The Bears squeaked by the Spartans last season, winning 35-34.

SQUEAK THROUGH →

squeak through sth, **squeak through**: to only just succeed in doing something, for example passing a test or winning something ▸ Bradley squeaked through with 51 percent of the vote.

SQUEAL

SQUEAL ON →

squeal on sb: to tell someone in authority about something wrong or illegal that another person has done ▸ The cops found out about the robbery. Someone must have squealed on us.

SQUEEZE

SQUEEZE IN, also **SQUEEZE INTO** →

1 squeeze in sb/sth, **squeeze** sb/sth **in**, **squeeze** sb/sth **into** sth: to manage to do something or meet someone even though you are very busy or do not have much time ▸ On Wednesdays Allen can usually squeeze in a round of golf. ▸ She is able to squeeze workouts into her schedule by getting up early in the mornings.

2 squeeze in, squeeze in sb/sth, **squeeze** sb/sth **in**, **squeeze** sb/sth **in** sth, **squeeze** sb/sth **into** sth, **squeeze into** sth: to push or fit someone or something into a small space ▸ We were all squeezed into a tiny room. ▸ These jeans are a bit tight but I can still squeeze into them.

SQUEEZE OUT →

squeeze sb **out**: to prevent someone from taking part in a particular activity or business, or from staying in a particular area or job ▸ Big supermarkets are squeezing out smaller shops who can't offer such low prices. **+ of** ▸ Low-income families claim they are being squeezed out of the area by high rents.

SQUEEZE OUT OF →

squeeze sth **out of** sth/sb: to get something that you want from someone or something, especially when they do not want to give it to you ▸ Politicians find numerous ways of squeezing more money out of people.

SQUIRM

SQUIRM OUT →

1 squirm out: to only just succeed in escaping from a bad situation. **+ of** ▸ She squirmed out of every tough situation and managed to win the match.

2 squirm out: to avoid doing something that you do not want to do. **+ of** ▸ Dan squirmed out of the department meeting by claiming he had too much work to do.

SQUIRREL

SQUIRREL AWAY →
squirrel away sth, **squirrel** sth **away**: to save something and put it in a

safe or secret place so that you can use it at a later time ▶ *He had several million dollars squirrelled away in Swiss bank accounts.*

STACK

STACK UP →
1 stack up, stack sth **up, stack up** sth: to form into a neat pile, or to make something form into a neat pile ▶ *Stack up the chairs in your classroom before you leave.* ▶ *Boxes of food were stacked up in the warehouse, ready to be delivered to needy families.*

2 stack up: to gradually increase in number ▶ *Your phone messages really stacked up while you were on holiday.*

3 stack up: to be as good as or better than something else. **+ to/against** ▶ *Cable operators said satellite TV fails to stack up to cable in some areas.* **how** sth **stacks up** (=whether it is as good as other things of the same kind) ▶ *Parents want to know how their children's schools stack up against others.*

4 stack up: to happen in a particular way ▶ *How did the meeting stack up this afternoon?*

STAKE

STAKE ON →
stake sth **on** sth: to risk losing something that is valuable or important if a plan is not successful

▶ *He has staked his reputation and political career on this proposal.*

STAKE OUT →
1 stake out sth, **stake** sth **out**: if someone stakes out a building, they watch it to see who is coming and going or what is happening inside ▶ *Reporters have staked out her home and are offering £10,000 for an interview.*
    stakeout N when someone watches a building to see who is coming and going or what is happening inside ▶ *Detectives were on stakeout for armed robbers.*

2 stake out a claim: to say publicly that you think you have a right to something ▶ *The tribes have both staked out their claim to the territory.*

3 stake out sth, **stake** sth **out**: to mark or enclose an area to show that it belongs to you or that you plan to use it ▶ *We staked out a spot on the beach and sat down.*

4 stake out sth, **stake** sth **out**: to publicly explain your opinion on a particular subject ▶ *Coles has firmly staked out his policies.*

STAMMER

STAMMER OUT →
stammer out sth, **stammer** sth **out**: to say something with difficulty, for example because you are nervous ▶ *Manson began to stammer out excuses, hoping Kelly would believe him.*

STAMP

STAMP ON →
1 stamp on sb/sth: to use your authority to stop someone doing something or to stop something happening ▶ *Our boss stamped on every suggestion we made, and then decided to cancel the project.*

2 stamp sth **on** sth: if you stamp your

S

style or character on something, you influence it in your own personal way ▶ *The two designers have stamped their unique style on the room.*

STAMP OUT →

stamp out sth, **stamp** sth **out**: to completely get rid of something bad ▶ *Police believe they have nearly succeeded in stamping out drug dealing in the neighbourhood.* ▶ *an attempt to stamp out corruption in the Civil Service*

STAND

STAND AROUND, *also* STAND ABOUT →

stand around/about: to stand somewhere and not do anything ▶ *A group of press photographers were standing around outside the airport.*

STAND AGAINST →

stand against sb: to compete with someone for a political position ▶ *Republicans are unsure who will stand against the Democratic candidate in November's election.*

STAND APART →

stand apart: to be different from or better than others of a similar type ▶ *Excellent service will make our company stand apart.*

STAND ASIDE →

1 stand aside: to move so that someone can go past you ▶ *Stand aside, please, and let the runners pass.*

2 stand aside: to decide not to become involved in an argument, fight, or difficult situation ▶ *We can't just stand aside and do nothing while people are starving.*

3 stand aside: to leave your job and let someone else have it ▶ *Edgar was pressured to stand aside after the bribery scandal.*

STAND BACK →

1 stand back: to move backwards so that you are a short distance away from someone or something ▶ *From time to time, the artist stood back and admired his painting.*

2 stand back: to think about a situation in the way a person who is not directly involved in it would think about it, in order to solve it or understand it better ▶ *I think we should stand back and give this issue some long, calm thought.*

3 stand back: to decide not to take action or become involved in a situation ▶ *How can people just stand back when so many families need help?*

STAND BETWEEN →

stand between sb **and** sth: if something stands between you and something else, it stops you from achieving it or from getting into a situation ▶ *Welfare payments are the only thing standing between millions of our people and starvation.*

STAND BY →

1 stand by: to allow something to happen when you should be doing something to try to stop it ▶ *Several people stood by and did nothing to stop the robbery.*

> **bystander** N someone who sees something such as a crime happening, but does not get involved in it ▶ *Bystanders watched as a young man threatened to jump from the 110-storey building.*

2 stand by sth: to not change your mind about something you previously said ▶ *He stands by his story and denies any involvement in the murder.* ▶ *The president will probably stand by his earlier decision.*

3 stand by sb/sth: to continue to give someone help and support when they are in a difficult situation ▶ *Kate and Louie agreed to stand by their son Matt as he recovered from his drug addiction.*

4 stand by: to be ready to help someone or do something ▶ *Operators are standing by, ready to take your order.* **stand by to do** sth ▶ *Buses were standing by to take hotel guests to the airport.*

STAND DOWN →
stand down: to agree to leave your job or official position, so that someone else can do it instead ▶ *I'm prepared to stand down in favour of another candidate.*

STAND FOR →
1 stand for sth: to represent a word, phrase, or idea ▶ *What does 'UNHCR' stand for?* ▶ *For centuries in literature, the swan has stood for purity and virtue.*

2 stand for sth: to support a particular set of ideas, principles, or values ▶ *Martin Luther King stood for justice for all Americans.*

3 not stand for sth: to refuse to accept a situation without complaining or trying to change it ▶ *You can't ban cars from the city centre – people wouldn't stand for it.* **sb won't/ wouldn't stand for** sth ▶ *"I won't stand for swearing in my house," said Peggy indignantly.*

4 stand for sth: to try to be elected to a political or official position ▶ *He first stood for Parliament in the 1983 election.*

STAND IN →
stand in: to do someone else's job for a short period of time. **+ as** ▶ *Who's standing in as chairperson while Meg's away?* **+ for** ▶ *Teachers are getting fed up with having to stand in for absent colleagues.*

STAND OFF →
stand off sb/ sth: to prevent someone or something from coming close enough to attack you ▶ *The gunman stood off police for about two hours before surrendering.*

   standoff N a situation in which neither side in a battle or argument can get an advantage ▶ *Police surrounded the building and a standoff continued until shortly before 7 a.m.*

STAND OUT →
1 stand out: to be very easy to see or notice ▶ *The ads are meant to stand out and catch people's attention.*

+ against ▶ *Theresa's bleached blond hair stands out against her dark clothing.* **stand out a mile** (=used to emphasize that something stands out) ▶ *Of course he's rich – it stands out a mile!*

2 stand out: to be clearly better than other similar things or people ▶ *There are some interesting paintings in the exhibition, but one artist's work really stands out.* **+ as** ▶ *Darren always stood out as an athlete.* **+ from** ▶ *Her experience in management made Holly stand out from 50 other qualified candidates.*

STAND OUT AGAINST →
stand out against sth: to publicly say that you are strongly opposed to something ▶ *Am I the only person who is willing to stand out against the budget cuts?*

STAND OVER →
stand over sb: to stand very close to someone and watch as they do

S

something ▶ *I can't work with you standing over me like that.* ▶ *Mum always stood over us, making sure we ate everything on our plates.*

STAND ROUND *see* **STAND AROUND**

STAND TOGETHER →
stand together: if people or groups stand together, they are loyal to each other and work together to achieve the same things ▶ *Politicians from all parties have promised to stand together and protect our national security.*

STAND UP →
1 stand up: to move into a standing position after you have been sitting or lying down ▶ *A drunken fan sitting near me suddenly stood up and started yelling.* ▶ *I stood up and started putting on my coat.*

2 stand sb **up**: to fail to meet someone after promising that you would, especially someone that you were starting a romantic relationship with ▶ *It's not like Gina to just stand us up and not call.* ▶ *Looks like I've been stood up again.*

3 stand up: if something stands up, it can be proved to be true or correct.
+ under ▶ *I believe your story – but how will it stand up under police questioning?* **stand up in court** (=be successfully proved in a court of law) ▶ *Is there enough evidence to make the accusations stand up in court?*

4 stand up: to stay healthy in a difficult environment or stay in good condition after being used a lot ▶ *The trees stood up pretty well during the snowstorms this winter.*

5 stand up and be counted: to clearly say what you think about something, even though doing this could cause trouble ▶ *If we don't stand up and be counted, we're going to suffer the consequences.*

STAND UP FOR →
stand up for sb/sth: to support or defend a person, idea, or principle ▶ *"We're here standing up for freedom against our oppressors," one demonstrator declared.* **stand up for yourself** ▶ *You have to stand up for yourself and refuse to let your employer take advantage of you.*

STAND UP TO →
1 stand up to sth: to be strong enough not to be harmed or changed by something ▶ *How well will this light-coloured carpet stand up to dirt and spills?*

2 stand up to sb/sth: to defend yourself and refuse to let someone else treat you badly ▶ *Standing up to an abusive boss can be risky.* ▶ *It took a lot of courage for one man to stand up to the tobacco industry.*

STARE

STARE DOWN, *also* **STARE OUT** →
stare sb **down/out, stare down/out** sb: to look into someone's eyes for a long time so that they start to feel uncomfortable ▶ *Although he was frightened, Fenton stood tall and stared out the gunmen.*

START

START BACK →
1 start back: to begin the journey back to the place where you started from ▶ *Shouldn't you start back before it gets dark?* **+ to** ▶ *We waved goodbye to Uncle Rick and started back to the village.*

2 start back: to suddenly move backwards away from something because you are frightened or surprised ▶ *She started back as the mouse ran across the kitchen floor.*

START FOR →
start for sth: to begin going to a particular place ▶ *"I've got to go," Laura said, starting for the door.*

S

START IN →

1 start in: to begin criticizing or complaining about someone or something ▶ *Don't start in again, Jeff, or I'll leave right now.* **+ on** ▶ *Before I knew it, my mother had started in on my wife.*

2 start in: to begin eating something. **+ on** ▶ *Marge started in on her seven-layer rum cake.*

START IN ON →

start in on sth: to begin doing or dealing with something ▶ *When I arrived at work, Kent had already started in on our project.*

START OFF →

1 start off, start off sth, **start** sth **off**: to begin doing something in a particular way. **start off (sth) by doing** sth ▶ *I'd like to start off by thanking my friends and family.* **start off (sth) with** sth ▶ *Start your weekend off with a gourmet dinner and a bottle of California's finest wine.*

2 start off: to begin your life or career in a particular way ▶ *How sad for a child to start off in life with such a cruel father and a weak mother.* **+ as** ▶ *She started off as an English teacher and later became a writer.*

3 start off: to begin in a particular way. **+ as** ▶ *What had started off as a joke soon became a very serious matter.* **start off on the wrong foot** (=begin to do something in a way that is likely to make you unsuccessful) ▶ *My boss has never liked me – I think I definitely started off on the wrong foot here.*

4 start off: to begin a journey, or to begin moving in a particular direction ▶ *The bus started off down the road, leaving Kate behind.*

5 start sb **off, start off** sb: to help someone begin an activity ▶ *Danielson starts the students off with stretching exercises.*

6 start off, start sb **off**: to begin laughing or crying a lot, or begin talking a lot about something, or to make someone do this ▶ *Don't mention Tammy's name to Martin – you'll only start him off.*

START ON →

1 start on sth: to begin doing or dealing with something ▶ *Let's get started on the campfire before it gets dark.*

2 start on sth: to begin eating or drinking something, or to begin taking a drug ▶ *Most smokers started on cigarettes when they were teenagers.*

3 start sb **on** sth: to make someone start doing something regularly, especially because it is good for them ▶ *We started Ellen on solid foods when she was four months old.*

4 start on sb: to begin criticizing someone or complaining to someone about something ▶ *After shouting at me for leaving the kitchen in a mess, Mum started on Gary for coming home late.*

START OUT →

1 start out: to begin to go somewhere ▶ *We started out at 10 o'clock in the morning.* ▶ *My father and I started out for the church, as we did every week.*

2 start out: to begin your life or career in a particular way ▶ *It's easy to make mistakes when you're first starting out.* **+ as** ▶ *He started out as a singer in small clubs.*

3 start out: to begin to exist in a particular way. **+ as** ▶ *Jose's taco shop originally started out as a fast food take-out restaurant.*

4 start out to do sth: to intend to do something from the beginning ▶ *I didn't start out to be a model, I did it once, and then more work just kept coming.*

START OVER →
start over, start sth over: to do something again from the beginning ▶ *Slow down and start over, please. I can't understand a word you're saying.*

START UP →
1 start up sth, **start** sth **up, start up**: to begin to exist and operate, or to make something do this ▶ *Do you have the money to start up your own business?*

start-up ADJ relating to beginning and developing a new business, organization, programme etc ▶ *Start-up costs for the new recycling programme are expected to be about £60,000.*

2 start up sth, **start** sth **up**: if you start up an engine, car, machine etc, or it starts up, it begins to work ▶ *Arthur got into the car and started it up without any problems.*

3 start up, start up sth, **start** sth **up**: if a sound, event, or activity starts up, or someone starts it up, it begins to exist or happen ▶ *The hunting season starts up again in August.*

STARVE
STARVE FOR →
be starving for sth also **be starved for** sth: to want something very much because you have not had it for a long time ▶ *Most depressed patients are starving for human contact.* ▶ *I was away in the army and always starved for news from home.*

STARVE OF →
starve sb/ sth **of** sth: to prevent someone or something from having something that they need for a long time ▶ *He was a cold hard man, who had been starved of love as a child.* ▶ *Radio broadcasting has been starved of funds in recent years.*

STARVE OUT →
starve out sb, **starve** sb **out**: to force

people to leave a place by preventing them from getting food ▶ *The government blockaded the island and tried to starve out the rebels.*

STASH
STASH AWAY →
stash sth **away, stash away** sth: to put something in a safe or secret place ▶ *He had millions of dollars stashed away in a Swiss bank account.*

STAVE
STAVE IN →
stave sth **in, stave in** sth: to hit or kick something so violently that it is completely broken or crushed. ▶ *The door had been staved in, and torn half off its hinges.*

STAVE OFF →
stave off sth, **stave** sth **off**: to prevent something bad or unpleasant from happening, or delay it ▶ *Nowadays there are various ways to stave off the effects of ageing.*

STAY
STAY AWAY →
1 stay away: to deliberately not go to a place ▶ *During the strike, up to 90% of the workers were reported to have stayed away.* **+ from** ▶ *Local authorities have warned people to stay away from the river as a health precaution.*

2 stay away: to deliberately avoid seeing someone or trying to form a relationship with them. **+ from** ▶ *Jack warned her to stay away from Derek.*

STAY AWAY FROM →
stay away from sth: to avoid doing or getting involved in something, especially something that is not good for you ▶ *I had hoped that my children would stay away from acting as a profession.*

S

STAY BEHIND →
stay behind: to remain somewhere when other people have left ▶ *As a punishment, several of the children had to stay behind after school.*

STAY IN →
stay in: to remain at home, especially in the evening ▶ *Let's stay in tonight and watch TV.*

STAY OFF →
1 stay off sth, **stay off**: to not drink, eat, or take something that is bad for you ▶ *He's trying very hard to stay off drugs now.*

2 stay off: if weight stays off after you have succeeded in losing it, you do not get fatter and heavier again ▶ *I can lose weight quite easily, but it never stays off.*

3 stay off sth: to avoid talking about a particular subject ▶ *I think we'd better try and stay off politics.*

STAY ON →
1 stay on: to stay in a place longer than other people or longer than you planned ▶ *Lesley decided to stay on in Greece and try to find a teaching job.*

2 stay on: to continue working for longer than expected or planned ▶ *James's contract was finished, but he agreed to stay on for a further six months.*

3 stay on: to continue to study at school or university instead of leaving to get a job ▶ *I wish I'd stayed on and gone to university but my family didn't encourage it.*

STAY OUT →
1 stay out: to not come home at night, or to come home late ▶ *Phil had never stayed out without phoning me before.*

2 stay out (on strike): if workers stay out, they continue to refuse to work because of an argument with their employer ▶ *Teachers in some places stayed out on strike for several weeks.*

STAY OUT OF →
stay out of sth: to not become involved in a situation, activity, discussion etc ▶ *This is a very unpleasant business, and if I were you I'd stay out of it.*

STAY OVER →
stay over: to spend the night at someone else's house instead of going home ▶ *I'm staying over at a friend's house tonight.*

STAY UP →
stay up: to go to bed later than usual ▶ *When we were kids, we were only allowed to stay up on special occasions.* **stay up late** ▶ *It was Saturday night and we decided to stay up late and watch the horror movie.*

STAY WITH →
stay with: to continue to use, do, have etc a particular thing ▶ *It's a very long book, but stay with it – it's really worth reading.* ▶ *It's important to stay with a fitness programme long enough to feel the benefits.*

STEADY

STEADY ON →
steady on!: used to tell someone that what they are saying is too extreme, especially when they are criticizing someone ▶ *Steady on, Mark! You're talking about my best friend, you know.*

STEAL

STEAL AWAY →
1 steal away: to leave a place quietly, so that no one will notice you or try to stop you ▶ *Katherine listened at the door for a few minutes, before stealing away back to her bedroom.*

2 steal away sth/sb, **steal** sth/sb **away**: to take something or someone away, especially in a quiet, secret way

▶ *She was terrified that someone might try to steal her baby away.*

STEAL OVER →

1 steal over sb: if a feeling steals over you, you gradually feel it more and more ▶ *When he began to sing, I felt a warm deep pleasure steal over me.*

2 steal over sb's face: if an expression steals over someone's face, it gradually becomes more and more noticeable ▶ *An expression of contempt stole over her face.*

3 steal over sth: if sound or light steals over a place, you gradually hear or see it more and more ▶ *The first rays of daylight stole over the mountains.*

STEAL UP →

steal up: to move quietly towards someone or something until you are very near them ▶ *a leopard stealing up in silence through the darkness.* **+ on** ▶ *Carrie stole up on him from behind and threw her arms round his neck.*

STEAM

STEAM OFF →

steam off sth, **steam** sth **off**: to use steam to remove something that is stuck onto a surface ▶ *I used to steam off stamps that came from abroad.*

STEAM UP →

1 steam up
also **get steamed up**:
if a glass surface steams up or gets steamed up, it becomes covered with steam ▶ *It was so hot inside that my glasses began to steam up.*

2 get steamed up: to become very annoyed, angry, or excited about

something ▶ *There's no point in getting steamed up – there's nothing we can do.* **be steamed up** ▶ *Some of the nurses at the hospital were really steamed up about the news.*

STEEP

BE STEEPED IN →

be steeped in sth: to have been very strongly influenced or affected by something, so that it cannot be avoided or becomes a part of a situation, place etc ▶ *a culture steeped in corruption and violence.*
be steeped in history/tradition
▶ *Oxford is a beautiful city, steeped in history and tradition.*

STEER

STEER AWAY FROM →

steer away from sth/sb, **steer** sb **away from** sth/sb: to avoid talking about a particular subject or becoming involved with someone or something, or to make someone do this ▶ *As a writer, she preferred to steer away from political messages.* ▶ *His father subtly steered him away from anyone who might question the family's religious beliefs.*

STEM

STEM FROM →

stem from sth: to develop as a result of something ▶ *Many of the problems stemmed from a lack of communication between managers and staff.*

STEP

STEP ASIDE →

step aside: to leave your job or an official position, especially so that someone else can do it instead ▶ *Many people felt that the old King should step aside and give his son a chance.*

STEP BACK →

step back: to think about a problem or a situation in a new way, especially with less emotion, so that you are able to understand it and deal with it better ▶ *It's not always easy to step back when it's your own family involved.*

STEP DOWN →

step down: to leave an important job or official position ▶ *In 1990, she announced that she was stepping down as party leader.*

STEP FORWARD →

step forward: to offer to help ▶ *Fortunately, plenty of volunteers stepped forward to provide the necessary support.*

STEP IN →

step in: to try to help or stop the trouble when a situation is difficult, especially when people are arguing or fighting ▶ *Gary stepped in to calm things down between the boys.*

STEP ON →

step on it *also* **step on the gas**: to hurry and drive faster ▶ *If you don't step on it, we'll miss the plane!*

STEP OUT →

step out: to go out for a short time ▶ *I just stepped out for a cigarette.*

STEP UP →

step up sth, **step** sth **up**: to increase the amount of effort, pressure etc, or increase the speed of something ▶ *In the second half, United stepped up the pressure and took the lead.*

STICK

STICK AROUND →

1 stick around: to stay in a place ▶ *If you stick around for a while, I'm sure you'll find some sort of job.* ▶ *It looked like there was going to be trouble, but I didn't stick around to watch.*

2 stick around: to stay in the same job, or with the same boyfriend or girlfriend ▶ *What you need is someone who you know will stick around.*

STICK AT →

1 stick at sth: to continue to work hard at something, even if it is difficult. **stick at it** ▶ *You'll never be good at anything unless you stick at it.* ▶ *Mark hated the course but he stuck at it, eventually passing his exams with honours.*

2 stick at sth: to stop at a particular amount or number instead of increasing or decreasing ▶ *The club proposes to stick at around fifty members.*

3 be stuck at sth: to stop at a particular point or level and be unable to make any more progress ▶ *A lot of women get stuck at a lower level within the company.*

4 stick at nothing: to be willing to do anything, even if it is illegal, in order to achieve something. **+ to do** sth ▶ *We were dealing with corrupt officials, who would stick at nothing to preserve their privileges.*

STICK BY →

1 stick by sb: to continue to give support or help to someone when they have got problems ▶ *I promise I'll stick by you, whatever happens.* **stick by** sb **through thick and thin** (=stick by someone, even in very difficult situations) ▶ *His wife had stuck by him through thick and thin.*

2 stick by sth: to choose not to change a decision, opinion, or statement ▶ *I made that decision a long time ago, and I intend to stick by it.* ▶ *The newspaper says it is sticking by its story.*

STICK IN, *also* STICK INTO →

get stuck in *also* **get stuck into** sth: to start doing something with a lot of enthusiasm ▶ *All right, everyone. Roll* *your sleeves up and get stuck in!* ▶ *By the time I got there I was too exhausted to get stuck into the debate.*

STICK OUT →

1 stick out:
if something sticks out, it points outwards or upwards, beyond the end of something

▶ *He'd be quite good-looking if his ears didn't stick out so much.* **+ of** ▶ *a log was sticking out of the water*

2 stick your tongue out *also* **stick out your tongue**: to push your tongue out of your mouth, especially as a rude sign to someone ▶ *When she asked him to help her, he just stuck out his tongue and laughed.*

3 stick sth **out, stick out** sth: to push part of your body away from the rest of your body ▶ *Stand up straight and don't stick your stomach out.*

4 stick out: to be very clear and noticeable ▶ *The thing that sticks out is that there are no women involved in the project.* **stick out a mile** (=used to emphasize that something stands out) ▶ *Look, Terry, it sticks out a mile that something's worrying you – what is it?*

5 stick out like a sore thumb: to be very noticeable because of looking very different to the other people or things that are around ▶ *The new building stuck out like a sore thumb.* ▶ *Any stranger here sticks out like a sore thumb.*

6 stick sth **out**: to continue doing something that is difficult or unpleasant. **stick it out** ▶ *I hated law school, but Dad said that I had to stick it out for at least a year.*

7 stick your neck out: to take a risk by giving your opinions about something when you know you may be wrong or people may disagree ▶ *I quickly realized that it would be better not to stick my neck out in meetings.*

STICK OUT FOR →

stick out for sth: to continue demanding something until you get it ▶ *The City of London, which owns the land, stuck out for a rent that was three times the market value.*

STICK TO →

1 stick to sth: to continue doing what you have decided or promised to do ▶ *He says he intends to stick to his plan of retiring early next year.* ▶ *You need to make a decision to stop smoking and stick to it.*

2 stick to sth: to limit yourself to doing one particular thing or having only a particular amount ▶ *If I have to drive, I always stick to only one glass of wine.* **stick to doing** sth ▶ *It'll be quicker if we stick to using the main roads as much as possible.*

3 stick to your guns: to refuse to change your mind about something, even though people are opposing you ▶ *Amelia stuck to her guns although it made her very unpopular for a while.*

4 stick to your story: to not change what you have already said and continue to say that it is true ▶ *He's still sticking to his story that he was at home when the crime was committed.*

5 stick to the rules: to do exactly what you are expected to do or what is allowed ▶ *Women were expected to stick to the rules – get married, have children, grow old.*

STICK TOGETHER →

stick together: if people stick together, they continue to support each other even when they are in a difficult situation ▶ *In the old days*

S

families stuck together no matter what happened.

STICK UP →

1 stick up: if something sticks up, it points upwards or above the surface of something ▶ *Gordon was still in his pyjamas, his hair sticking up at all angles.* **+ out of/through/from** ▶ *In the river, islands of rock stuck up out of the water.*

2 stick 'em up!: used when threatening someone with a gun and telling them to put their hands up in the air ▶ *Stick 'em up! You're under arrest!*

STICK UP FOR →

1 stick up for sb: to defend or support someone, especially when they are being criticized ▶ *Thanks for sticking up for me the other day.* **stick up for yourself** ▶ *I was determined to be more confident and more able to stick up for myself.*

2 stick up for sth: to defend or fight for something that is important ▶ *You must stick up for what you believe in.*

STICK WITH →

1 stick with sth: to continue doing or using something as before ▶ *An enormous number of new products are available, but most people prefer to stick with what they know.*

2 be stuck with sb/sth: to be unable to change or get rid of something or someone ▶ *We're stuck with heavy traffic going right past out front door.*

3 stick with sth: to continue doing something even though it is difficult or there are problems ▶ *I think I'll*

stick with the job for another year at least.

4 stick with sb: to stay close to someone ▶ *If you don't want to get lost, you'd better stick with me.*

5 stick with sb: if something sticks with you, you remember it clearly for a long time ▶ *One thing he said then has stuck with me ever since.*

6 stick with sb: to support someone when they are in a difficult situation or have problems ▶ *I have some close friends who will stick with me.*

STING

STING FOR →

sting sb **for** sth: to charge someone a lot of money for something, especially an unreasonably large amount ▶ *Last time I took my car in for a service, they stung me for about £400.*

STIR

STIR IN, *also* **STIR INTO →**

stir in sth, **stir** sth **in**, **stir** sth **into** sth: to mix one substance with another, using a spoon to move them around together ▶ *Mr Blakey sat at the table stirring sugar into his tea.*

STIR UP →

1 stir up sth, **stir** sth **up**: to deliberately cause trouble, especially between other people ▶ *He has been accused of stirring up anti-government feeling in the South.*

2 stir up sth, **stir** sth **up**: to cause people to have a particular strong feeling or emotion ▶ *The huge statue of the leader was designed to stir up emotions of awe and respect.*

3 stir up controversy/debate etc: to make people argue about something or spend a lot of time discussing it ▶ *The report stirred up fierce controversy when it was published.*

4 stir up memories: to make you remember events in the past,

especially from a long time ago
▶ *Seeing Simon again had stirred up so many memories from her youth.*

STITCH

STITCH UP →

1 stitch up sth/sb, **stitch** sth/sb **up**: to sew the edges of a wound together, to help it heal ▶ *The nurse cleaned the wound, then the cut was stitched up.*

2 stitch up sth, **stitch** sth **up**: to sew pieces of material together in order to make or repair something ▶ *I've split these trousers – can you stitch them up for me?*

3 stitch up sb, **stitch** sb **up**: to make someone seem guilty of a crime by deliberately giving false information to the police or someone else in authority ▶ *You stitched me up, you rat – I got two years for something you did yourself!*

   stitch-up N when someone deliberately gives false information to make a person seem guilty of a crime ▶ *It was a stitch-up – he didn't do it!*

4 stitch up sb, **stitch** sb **up**: to deceive someone, especially in order to gain money from them ▶ *We got really stitched up – we trusted him with our savings and lost the lot!*

STOCK

STOCK UP →

stock up: to buy a lot of something to keep for when you need it. **+ on** ▶ *We'll stock up on wine and beer while we're abroad.* **+ for** ▶ *Supermarkets were busy with people stocking up for Christmas.* **+ with** ▶ *Residents stocked*

up with provisions as the hurricane headed towards them.

STOKE

STOKE UP →

stoke up sth, **stoke** sth **up**: to encourage people's anger, hate, or disagreement to grow and become stronger ▶ *Stories in the press have stoked up anti-government feeling.*

STOOP

STOOP TO →

stoop to sth: to do something that you know is bad or wrong in order to achieve something ▶ *The news editor must be short of good stories to stoop to this level of reporting.* **stoop to doing** sth ▶ *I don't believe she would stoop to lying.*

STOP

STOP AT →

stop at nothing: to be willing to do anything, even if it is cruel, dishonest, or illegal, in order to get what you want. **stop at nothing to do** sth ▶ *Drug addicts will stop at nothing to get money for their next fix.*

STOP BACK →

stop back: to come back to a place a short time later ▶ *Can you stop back later? I'm kind of busy right now.*

STOP BEHIND →

stop behind: to stay in a place after the other people have gone ▶ *I'll stop behind for a couple of hours after school to get this marking finished.*

STOP BY →

stop by, **stop by** sth: to visit a person or place for a short time ▶ *I want to stop by and see Tracy on the way home.* **stop by (sth) to do** sth ▶ *In the morning, Kim stopped by the post office to check the mail.*

STOP IN →

stop in: to visit a person or place for a

short time ► *She often used to stop in for a chat.* **+ at** ► *Stop in at the Coffee Plantation for Tucson's smoothest jazz!*

STOP OFF →

stop off: to stop somewhere before continuing a journey ► *On the way home, he stopped off to look at a house he was thinking of buying.* **+ at/in etc** ► *Boats will take you up and down the river, stopping off at Richmond, Kew, and Greenwich.*

  stop-off N a short visit that you make during a journey ► *The flight takes 14 hours with a stop-off in Singapore.*

  stop-off ADJ a stop-off point or place is a place where you stop during a journey ► *a useful stop-off point on the route across the mountains*

STOP ON →

stop on: to stay somewhere, especially longer than you had planned or longer than other people ► *Harry would leave next day for London, and I would stop on here for another month.*

STOP OVER →

1 stop over: to stay somewhere for a night or a few days during a long journey ► *The Foreign Minister will stop over in Paris on his way to the conference.*

  stopover N a short stay somewhere for a night or a few days during a long journey ► *There are no direct flights, so we'll have a two-day stopover in Delhi.*

2 stop over: to sleep at someone else's house when you have been visiting them ► *Malcolm and the kids came for a meal on Saturday and stopped over.*

STOP UP →

1 stop up sth, **stop** sth **up**: to fill a hole and prevent anything coming out or going in ► *There's a hole in this pipe. I need something to stop it up with.*

2 stop up: to not go to bed at the normal time and stay up late. **stop up to do** sth ► *I stopped up to watch the football and it went on until after twelve.*

STORE

STORE AWAY →

store away sth, **store** sth **away**: to put things in a safe place and keep them until you need them ► *All the data is stored away on the computer's back-up disk once a week.*

STORE UP →

1 store up sth, **store** sth **up**: to collect and keep a supply of something so that you can use it in the future ► *Squirrels store up nuts for the winter.* ► *At the beginning of the war, people started storing up goods for emergencies.*

2 store up sth, **store** sth **up**: to remember things so that you can use them or tell someone about them later ► *Writers store up these experiences for use in their novels.* ► *If you make a mistake, he'll store it up and use it against you later.*

3 store up problems etc (for the future): to do something that will cause problems in the future ► *Reducing interest rates now will only store up problems for the future.*

STOW

STOW AWAY →

1 stow away: to hide on a ship, plane etc in order to travel without paying ► *At the age of*

thirteen, Bill stowed away on a ship bound for New York.

stowaway N a person who hides on a ship, plane etc in order to travel without paying ▶ *Sam had been a stowaway on a ship from Shanghai to San Francisco.*

2 stow away sth, **stow** sth **away**: to put or pack something somewhere carefully and neatly until you need it again ▶ *When Dad had got all the bags stowed away in the car, we set off.*

STRAIGHTEN

STRAIGHTEN OUT →

1 straighten out sth/sb, **straighten** sth/sb **out**: to successfully deal with a problem, disagreement, or confused situation ▶ *It was a misunderstanding – I'm sorry I didn't get it straightened out at the time.*

2 straighten sb **out**, **straighten out** sb: to deal with someone's bad behaviour or personal problems ▶ *I told him that until he got his life straightened out I wasn't going to see him again.*

3 straighten out sth, **straighten out** sth, **straighten** sth **out**: to become straight or to make something straight ▶ *The road is narrow and very twisting for about a mile and then it straightens out.*

STRAIGHTEN UP →

1 straighten up, **straighten yourself up**: to stand upright again after bending down, or to make your back completely straight ▶ *She bent over to pick something up and couldn't straighten up again.*

2 straighten up sth, **straighten** sth **up**, **straighten up**: to make a place tidy ▶ *I made a feeble attempt to straighten things up, tossing clothing into the laundry bag and clearing dishes.*

3 straighten up: to begin to behave well after behaving badly ▶ *If you don't straighten up, we'll go home right now!*

STRAIN

STRAIN AT →

strain at sth: to pull hard at something that is holding you back ▶ *The bear pawed the air in fury, straining at the massive steel collar round its neck.*

STRAP

STRAP IN, *also* STRAP INTO →

strap in sb, **strap** sb **in**, **strap** sb **into** sth: to fasten someone into a seat in a car, plane etc using a strong belt, in order to help to keep them safe ▶ *Make sure your passengers are all strapped in before you set off.* **strap yourself in** ▶ *He took one of the two pilot seats and began to strap himself in.*

STRETCH

STRETCH AWAY →

stretch away: if an area of land stretches away, it continues for a long distance ▶ *To the west the Great Plains stretched away across Wyoming to the Rocky Mountains.*

STRETCH OUT →

1 stretch (yourself) out: to lie down in a relaxed way with your legs straight. **+ on** ▶ *He stretched himself out on the bed and closed his eyes.* **be stretched out** ▶ *When I got home, Paula was stretched out on the sofa, watching TV.*

2 stretch out sth, **stretch** sth **out**: to move your arms or legs away from your body and make them straight ▶ *He sat down by the fire and stretched his legs out.*

3 stretch out: if an area of land stretches out, it continues for a very long distance ▶ *hills that stretched out towards the Mustang Mountains*

S

4 stretch out: if a period of time stretches out in front of you, it seems to be going to continue for a long time. **stretch out before** sb ▶ *He felt he could see his whole life stretching out before him – years and years of the same old routine.*

5 stretch sth **out, stretch out** sth: to make something last for a longer period of time than is usual or necessary ▶ *The lawyers could stretch this case out for ten years or more.*

STREW

BE STREWN WITH →

1 be strewn with sth: to be covered with a lot of things in an untidy way ▶ *There was a small desk, strewn with books and papers.*

2 be strewn with sth: to be affected by a lot of problems or unpleasant things ▶ *His injury is the latest disaster in a career strewn with misfortune.*

STRIKE

STRIKE AT →

strike at sth/sb: to have a harmful effect on something or someone ▶ *This law strikes at the most vulnerable groups in our society.* **strike at the (very) heart of** sth ▶ *an issue that strikes at the heart of our democracy*

STRIKE BACK →

strike back: to attack or criticize someone after they have attacked or criticized you ▶ *United scored early in the second half, but Rangers struck back with two spectacular goals.* **+ at** ▶ *Government officials struck back at their critics.*

STRIKE DOWN →

1 strike down sb, **strike** sb **down**: if someone is struck down by something, they are killed or badly injured by it ▶ *The following morning he was dead, struck down by a massive heart attack.*

2 strike down sb, **strike** sb **down**: if someone is struck down by an illness, they are suddenly affected by it, usually severely ▶ *Thousands of people have been struck down by the mystery illness.*

3 strike down sth, **strike** sth **down**: if a court strikes down a law, it decides not to allow it ▶ *The Supreme Court struck down the Act because it violates the U.S. constitution.*

BE STRUCK OFF →

1 be struck off (sth): if a doctor, lawyer etc is struck off, they are no longer allowed to continue in their profession because they have done something wrong ▶ *The doctor was found guilty and struck off for professional misconduct.*

2 strike off: to start moving in a particular direction, especially in a confident or determined way. **+ along/ towards etc** ▶ *"This way" he called back, striking off towards the village.*

STRIKE ON →

strike on sth: to suddenly think of an idea or a solution to a problem ▶ *Richard eventually struck on a plan for solving his financial difficulties.*

STRIKE OUT →

1 strike out: to start moving in a particular direction, especially in a confident or determined way. **+along/ towards etc** ▶ *Picking up our bags, we struck out towards the mountains.*

2 strike out: to try to hit someone, using a sudden, violent movement ▶ *He grasped my collar. I struck out and hit him across the chest.* **+ at** ▶ *Without warning, he struck out at Davis, knocking him to the ground.*

3 strike out: to start to do something new and exciting in a confident independent way. **strike out on your**

own ▶ *In 1981, Tony left the company and struck out on his own.*

STRIKE UP →

strike up a conversation/friendship etc: to start a conversation or friendly relationship with someone ▶ *a story about a boy and a dog who strike up a friendship.* **+ with** ▶ *I struck up a conversation with the man sitting beside me.*

STRING

STRING ALONG →

string sb **along**: to deceive someone for a long time, especially by pretending that you love them or that you will help them ▶ *"She had no intention of marrying him, then?" "No, she was just stringing him along."*

STRING OUT →

1 string out sth, **string** sth **out**: if something is strung out somewhere, it is spread there in a long line ▶ *Tables had been set up in the field and lights strung out in the trees.*

2 string out sth, **string** sth **out**: to make something last for a longer period of time than is wanted or necessary ▶ *There was no point in stringing the relationship out – she would just tell him that it was over.*

STRING TOGETHER →

1 string together sth, **string** sth **together**: to join things together, adding one thing after another ▶ *a series of computer commands that are strung together on a single line*

2 string words together also **string a sentence together**: to succeed in saying something that other people can understand ▶ *I used to speak really good Spanish, but I don't think I could string two words together now.*

STRING UP →

1 string up sth, **string** sth **up**: to fasten something in a high position, especially something that forms a long line ▶ *Workmen were busy stringing up the Christmas lights in the centre of town.*

2 string up sb, **string** sb **up**: to kill someone by tying a rope around their neck and making them hang from it ▶ *If he's the bomber, they ought to string him up!*

STRIP

STRIP AWAY →

1 strip away sth: to remove something that prevents you from seeing what someone or something is really like ▶ *TV cameras have stripped away the mystery around the royal family.*

2 strip away sth: to get rid of rights or traditions that have existed for a long time ▶ *Women's human and civil rights were stripped away, and they were forbidden to leave their homes.*

STRIP DOWN →

strip down sth, **strip** sth **down**: to separate an engine or piece of equipment into pieces in order to clean or repair it ▶ *Nigel spent the weekend stripping down his motorbike.*

STRIP DOWN TO →

strip down to your underwear etc: to quickly take off all your clothes except your underwear etc ▶ *Paul stripped down to his swimming trunks and jumped into the lake.*

STRIP OF →

1 strip sb **of** sth: to take away something important from someone, especially as a punishment ▶ *Captain Evans was found guilty of fraud and stripped of his rank.*

2 strip sth **of** sth: to remove a lot of something from something else ▶ *a simplified form of religious worship that is stripped of all ritual*

S

STRIP OFF →

1 strip off sth, **strip** sth **off, strip off**: to quickly take off clothes that you are wearing or that someone

else is wearing ▶ *Boris loosened his tie and stripped off his clothes.* ▶ *Jack stripped off and jumped into the shower.*

2 strip off sth, **strip** sth **off**: to remove the surface of something or remove a layer of something that is covering a surface ▶ *Strip off all the old wallpaper and repair any holes in the plaster.*

STRIP OUT →

strip out sth, **strip** sth **out**: to take everything out of a room or building so that you can paint it or change it ▶ *They stripped out the interior of the building and completely redesigned it.*

STRUGGLE

STRUGGLE ON →

struggle on: to continue doing something even though it is very difficult ▶ *The two climbers struggled on, despite the severe weather conditions.*

STUB

STUB OUT →

stub out sth, **stub** sth **out**: to stop a cigarette from burning by pressing the end of it against something hard ▶ *She stubbed out her half-smoked cigarette in the ashtray.*

STUMBLE

STUMBLE ACROSS →

stumble across sth/sb: to find something or someone when you did not expect to ▶ *One day, she stumbled across an old diary of her father's.*

STUMBLE ON, *also* STUMBLE UPON →

stumble on/upon sth: to discover something, especially something important or interesting, when you did not expect to ▶ *Almost by accident, he had stumbled upon one of the greatest discoveries of the century.*

STUMP

BE STUMPED FOR →

be stumped for ideas/an answer etc: to be unable to think of an idea, a reply etc ▶ *The author seemed somewhat stumped for an answer to such an unusual question.*

STUMP UP →

stump up, stump up sth: to pay money, especially when you do not want to ▶ *That's ten pounds you owe me. Come on, stump up.* **+ for** ▶ *Those wishing to join the club will have to stump up £2,000 a year for membership.*

SUBJECT

SUBJECT TO →

1 subject sb **to** sth: to force someone to experience something very unpleasant ▶ *She was subjected to years of abuse before she finally divorced her husband.*

2 subject sth **to tests/scrutiny etc**: to test something or examine it carefully ▶ *Drugs are subjected to rigorous testing before they can be marketed.*

3 be subjected to sth: to be affected by physical forces such as heat, light, energy etc ▶ *When rocks are subjected to very high temperatures, structural changes occur.*

SUBMIT

SUBMIT TO →

submit to sth/sb: to accept the

authority of someone or something, and do what they want ▶ *If we submit to threats of violence now, we will only encourage further aggression.*

SUBSCRIBE

SUBSCRIBE TO →

1 subscribe to sth: to agree with an idea or opinion ▶ *The government employed only those teachers who subscribed to the official version of history.* **subscribe to the view/theory that** ▶ *I have never subscribed to the view that animals' rights are equal to humans'.*

2 subscribe to sth: to pay for regular copies of a newspaper or magazine to be sent to you, or to pay for a television, telephone, or Internet service ▶ *More and more people are subscribing to digital TV channels.* ▶ *She subscribes to the Guardian International.*

SUCCEED

SUCCEED IN →

succeed in sth: to do what you have been trying to do. **succeed in doing** sth ▶ *I finally succeeded in persuading her to come with us.* ▶ *Very few people who go on diets succeed in losing weight and keeping it off.* **succeed in** sth ▶ *In 1999, she succeeded in her ambition to climb Kino Peak.*

SUCK

GET SUCKED IN, *also* GET SUCKED INTO →

get sucked into sth: to gradually become more and more involved in a bad situation or harmful activity ▶ *John got sucked into a world of petty crime and drug abuse as a teenager.*

SUCK UP TO →

suck up to sb: to try to make someone in authority like you by being nice to them, in a way that is not sincere

▶ *She's always sucking up to the boss – it makes me sick.*

SUFFER

SUFFER FROM →

1 suffer from sth: to have an illness, especially a serious one ▶ *He was admitted to hospital, suffering from severe malnutrition.* ▶ *Deborah suffered from periods of deep depression.*

2 suffer from sth: to have a particular disadvantage ▶ *The region generally suffers from high unemployment and lack of investment.*

SUIT

SUIT TO →

1 be suited to sth: to be the right person or thing for a particular purpose, job, or situation ▶ *a holiday package suited to the needs of single parents and children.* **be suited to doing** sth ▶ *I don't think I'm really suited to working in an office.*

2 suit sth **to** sth: to make something exactly right for something else ▶ *Most teachers use a variety of approaches, suiting them to the needs of each student.*

SUM

SUM UP →

1 sum up sth, **sum** sth **up**: to describe something using only a few words ▶ *Vanessa summed up the evening in a single word: "Hell".*

2 sum up, sum sth **up, sum** sth **up**: to state the most important points of a speech, lesson, report etc again ▶ *There's a paragraph at the end of each chapter that sums up the main points.* **to sum up** (=used before summing up at the end of a speech or report) ▶ *So, to sum up, we need to concentrate on two things – better training and improved communication.*

summing-up N a statement giving the most important facts of something, especially made by a judge at the end of a trial ▶ *This afternoon, Judge O'Connor will begin his summing-up.*

3 sum up sb/sth, **sum** sb/sth **up**: to show the most typical qualities of someone or something ▶ *Andy Warhol's pictures seemed to sum up the new consumer society of the 1960s.*

SUMMON
SUMMON UP →

1 summon up sth: to try very hard to find something such as courage, energy, or strength in yourself ▶ *Bob summoned up all his powers of concentration and looked down at the exam paper.* **summon up the courage/ strength etc to do** sth ▶ *She lay there for a while, trying to summon up the strength to move.*

2 summon up sth: to make you remember something or think of something else ▶ *The smell of the sea summoned up memories of childhood holidays.*

SUSS OUT
SUSS OUT →

suss out sb/sth, **suss** sb/sth **out**: to discover what someone or something is really like, or how to do something ▶ *It didn't take me long to suss her out.* **+ what/ how etc** ▶ *I'm just trying to suss out how this program works.*

SWALLOW
SWALLOW UP →

1 swallow up sth, **swallow** sth **up**: if a large country, company, or organization swallows up a smaller one,

the smaller one becomes part of the larger one ▶ *A lot of the small publishing firms have been swallowed up by huge multinationals.*

2 swallow up sth, **swallow** sth **up**: if something swallows up a large amount of money, it uses all of it ▶ *I got a pay rise, but it was swallowed up by the increase in train fares.*

SWAP *also* SWOP
SWAP AROUND,
also SWAP ROUND →

swap sth **around/round**: to move two or more things so that each one is in the place the other one was in before ▶ *Jake swapped their two glasses around when she wasn't looking.*

SWAP OVER →

swap over: if two people swap over, one starts doing the thing that the other one was doing before ▶ *We shared the driving – I drove the first part of the journey, and then we swapped over.*

SWARM
SWARM WITH →

be swarming with sth: if a place is swarming with people or insects, it is full of large numbers of them moving around ▶ *The museum was swarming with tourists – you couldn't really see anything properly.* ▶ *The room was hot and stuffy, and swarming with flies.*

SWATHE
BE SWATHED IN →

be swathed in sth: to be wrapped or covered in layers of cloth or clothing ▶ *The Emperor sat on his throne, swathed in a golden robe of richly embroidered silk.* ▶ *Carter was lying on a stretcher, his head swathed in bandages.*

S

SWEAR

SWEAR BY →

swear by sth: if you swear by something, you are certain that it always works well and tell other people to use it ▶ *Margaret swears by vitamin C pills – she says she never gets colds.*

SWEAR IN →

1 be sworn in: to make an official promise in a special ceremony that you will be loyal to your country, profession etc, and do your job as well as you can. **+ as** ▶ *Only hours after Kennedy's death, Lyndon Johnson was sworn in as President.*

2 be sworn in: to give an official promise in a court of law, before you take part in a trial ▶ *After every member of the jury has been sworn in, the judge introduces the lawyers.*

SWEAR TO →

1 swear to sth: to be willing to say that something is true because you are sure about it ▶ *A man recognized you, Mark. He saw you take the money and will swear to it.* **I can't swear to it** ▶ *I think it was Sue I saw, but I couldn't swear to it.*

2 be sworn to secrecy *also **be sworn to silence***: if you are sworn to secrecy or silence, you have promised someone that you will not tell their secret ▶ *"What's Julia planning for my birthday?" "I can't tell you – I've been sworn to secrecy."*

SWEAT

SWEAT OFF →

sweat off sth, **sweat** sth **off**: to get rid of an illness by sweating a lot ▶ *You've got a fever – stay in bed and sweat it off.*

SWEAT OUT →

1 sweat it out: to work hard and continuously for long periods,

especially in hot conditions ▶ *The men had been sweating it out in the blistering heat from 6 am until 9 pm every day.* **sweat your guts out** (=work with a lot of effort) ▶ *We've been sweating our guts out trying to get this job finished on time.*

2 sweat it out: to wait anxiously for news that is very important to you ▶ *Pat sweated it out in a police cell while the jury decided his fate.*

SWEEP

BE SWEPT ALONG →

be swept along (by sth): to be very excited by something, so that you are persuaded to do something without thinking about it carefully enough ▶ *She was swept along by the excitement of the crowd.*

SWEEP ASIDE →

1 sweep aside sth, **sweep** sth **aside**: to refuse to consider something that someone says, and treat it as unimportant ▶ *Jamie swept all his protests aside.*

2 sweep aside sth, **sweep** sth **aside**: to get rid of something very quickly in order to replace it with something else ▶ *Whole forests have been swept aside to grow crops for western consumers.*

SWEEP AWAY →

1 sweep away sth, **sweep** sth **away**: to get rid of laws, beliefs, or traditions because they are considered to be old-fashioned or wrong ▶ *People celebrated in the streets as the last remnants of the old regime were swept away.*

2 be swept away: to be so excited by someone or something, that you forget about other things ▶ *I think she was swept away by his wealth and power.* ▶ *Giselle danced, swept away by the music.*

S

SWEEP UP →

1 sweep up, sweep up sth, **sweep** sth **up**: to clean dust and dirt from a floor using a special brush ▶ *The guests had all gone, and the cleaner was sweeping up.* ▶ *The barman scowled as he swept up the broken glass.*

2 sweep sb/sth **up, sweep up** sb/sth: to pick someone or something up with one quick movement ▶ *Gillian swept up the coins and put them in her pocket.*

3 be swept up in sth: to become involved in a dangerous situation that you cannot avoid or escape ▶ *The vast majority of the victims were innocent people, swept up in the dictator's campaign of terror.*

SWEETEN

SWEETEN UP →

sweeten up sb, **sweeten** sb **up**: to try to persuade someone to do what you want by being nice to them ▶ *Take him out to lunch – try to sweeten him up.*

SWELL

SWELL UP →

1 swell up: if part of your body swells up, it becomes larger and rounder than usual because of an injury or illness ▶ *His ankle's swollen up, but it's not broken.* ▶ *Joyce felt her top lip swell up and she tasted blood.*

2 swell up: to gradually increase in size ▶ *The beans will swell up if you soak them overnight.*

SWERVE

SWERVE FROM →

not swerve from sth: to be determined that nothing will stop you from trying to achieve an aim or follow a plan ▶ *We will not swerve from our programme of economic reform.*

SWILL

SWILL OUT →

swill out sth, **swill** sth **out**: to clean the inside of something by moving water around in it quickly ▶ *Mike poured the soup into bowls then quickly swilled out the pan.*

SWIM

BE SWIMMING IN →

be swimming in sth: to contain a lot of something or be surrounded by a lot of something ▶ *The main courses were swimming in cream and butter.*

SWING

SWING AROUND, *also* SWING ROUND →

1 swing around/round: to suddenly turn around so that you are facing the opposite direction ▶ *Bill heard a sound and swung around, startled.*

2 swing around/round: to change your opinion completely, so that you support something that you used to oppose, or oppose something that you used to support ▶ *American public opinion is gradually swinging around in favour of tougher gun-control laws.*

SWING AT →

swing at sb: to try to hit someone by swinging your arm in their direction ▶ *Jack swung at the man, but missed.*

SWING BY →

swing by, swing by sth: to visit a place or person for a short time before going somewhere else ▶ *I'll swing by the grocery store on my way home from work.*

SWING ROUND *see* SWING AROUND

SWIPE

SWIPE AT →

1 swipe at sb: to try to hit someone by swinging your arm ▶ *He tried to swipe at her but lost his balance and fell back.*

2 swipe at sb/sth: to criticize someone or something ▶ *a black comedy movie which mercilessly swipes at American youth culture*

SWITCH

SWITCH AROUND, *also* SWITCH ROUND →

switch sb/sth **around/round**: to move two or more things or people so that each one is in the place that the other was in before, or is doing what the other was doing before ▶ *Claudia dropped the sleeping pills into her own mug and then rapidly switched the mugs round.*

SWITCH OFF →

1 switch off sth, **switch** sth **off, switch off**: to make something stop working by using a switch ▶ *Sylvie switched the lights off and went to bed.* ▶ *People who object to sex scenes on TV can always switch off.*

2 switch off: to stop listening or paying attention to what someone is saying ▶ *You shouldn't make your speech too long, or people will switch off.*

3 switch off: to stop thinking about your work or problems, and relax ▶ *Sometimes she can't get to sleep, because she just can't switch off.*

SWITCH ON →

switch on sth, **switch** sth **on, switch on**: to make something start working by using a switch ▶ *Can you switch the light on?* ▶ *My sister switched on the radio, and began to dance around the kitchen.*

SWITCH OVER →

1 switch over: to change from one method, system, product etc to a different one. **+ to** ▶ *I've switched over to telephone banking because it's more convenient.* **+ from** ▶ *A new high-speed rail service would*

encourage passengers to switch over from air travel.

2 switch over: to change from one television or radio station to another ▶ *There's a film on the other channel – does anyone mind if I switch over?*

3 switch over: if two people switch over, they each start doing what the other one was doing before ▶ *If you get tired of driving we can always switch over.*

SWITCH ROUND *see* SWITCH AROUND →

SWIVEL

SWIVEL AROUND, *also* SWIVEL ROUND →

1 swivel around/round: to turn around, so that you face the opposite direction ▶ *Dr Schmidt swivelled around in his chair to face the window.*

2 swivel around/round: if something swivels around, or if you swivel it around, it turns around a fixed central point ▶ *She swivelled the camera around and scanned the room.*

SWOOP

SWOOP DOWN →

1 swoop down: if a bird or plane swoops down, it suddenly moves down towards the ground ▶ *The gull swooped down and plucked a fish out of the water.*

2 swoop down: if a group of soldiers, police officers etc swoop down, they make a sudden surprise attack. **+ on** ▶ *The police swooped down on them in a dawn raid, and all five gang members were arrested.*

S

SWOP *see* SWAP

SWOT

SWOT UP →

swot up, swot up sth, **swot** sth **up**: to learn as much as you can about a subject, especially before an exam.
+ on ▶ *I've got to swot up on French verbs for tomorrow's test.*

SYPHON *see* SIPHON

Tt

TACK

TACK ON, *also* **TACK ONTO** →
tack sth **on, tack on** sth, **tack** sth **onto** sth: to add something new to something that is already complete, especially in a way that spoils the original thing ▶ *a beautiful old stone house with a cheap modern extension tacked on at the back*

TAG

TAG ALONG →
tag along: to go somewhere with someone, especially when they have not asked you to go with them ▶ *If you're going into town, do you mind if I tag along?* **+ with** ▶ *He was a popular guy – there was always a crowd of people wanting to tag along with him.*

TAG ALONG BEHIND →
tag along behind, tag along behind sb: to follow behind someone when they are going somewhere ▶ *Madeleine always used to tag along behind her older brother and his friends.*

TAG ON →
be tagged on: to be added to the end of something that is said or written ▶ *On the occasions that he did remember to say thank you, it was usually just tagged on as an afterthought.*

TAIL

TAIL AWAY *see* **TAIL OFF**

TAIL BACK →
tail back: if traffic tails back, a long line of it forms and moves very slowly ▶ *Traffic tailed back for twelve miles after an accident on the M40.*

tailback N a long line of traffic that is moving very slowly or not moving at all ▶ *a five-mile tailback*

TAIL OFF, *also* **TAIL AWAY** →
tail off/away: to gradually become less, smaller etc, and often stop or disappear completely ▶ *After a few years the number of visitors coming to the park began to tail off.* ▶ *The old lady's voice tailed away into silence.*

TAILOR

TAILOR TO →
tailor sth **to** sb/sth: to make something so that it is exactly right for what a particular person, organization etc needs or wants ▶ *a personal development programme that is tailored to the requirements of the individual*

TAKE

BE TAKEN ABACK →
be taken aback: to be surprised or shocked ▶ *Philip seemed slightly taken aback by this sudden request.* ▶ *I was quite taken aback when I found myself on the front page of the morning paper.*

TAKE AFTER →
take after sb: to be like your mother, father, grandfather etc ▶ *Becky's really pretty. She takes after her mother.* ▶ *"Are you a good cook Paul?" "Of course he is. He takes after his Dad."*

TAKE AGAINST →
take against sb: to start to dislike someone, especially without a good reason ▶ *For some reason his mother took against his girlfriend and refused to speak to her.*

TAKE ALONG →
take along sb/sth, **take** sb/sth **along**: to take someone or something with you when you are going somewhere ▶ *The company sometimes lets*

employees take their spouses along on business trips.

TAKE APART →

1 take sth **apart**: to separate something into the different parts that it is made from ▶ *Danson was taking his gun apart so that he could clean it.*

2 take sb **apart**: to attack someone and cause them serious injuries ▶ *If you don't get out of here, mister, we're going to take you apart.*

3 take sth **apart**: to look in every part of a building, room etc because you are searching for something ▶ *The police came and took the place apart, but they didn't find anything.*

4 take sth **apart**: to carefully consider and criticize the ideas in a speech, piece of writing etc ▶ *Our teacher took our essays apart one by one, in front of the whole class.*

5 take sb **apart**: to criticize someone very strongly ▶ *He got taken apart by the press after his affair, and had to leave politics.*

TAKE AROUND, *also* **TAKE ROUND** →
take sb **around/round, take around/round** sb: to walk around a place with someone and show them the most interesting and important things there ▶ *A guide took us round the palace and gardens.*

TAKE ASIDE →

take sb **aside**: to separate someone from the rest of a group, so that you can talk to them without the other people hearing ▶ *After the meeting she took Paula aside and proposed a deal.*

TAKE AWAY →

1 take away sth, **take** sth **away**: to remove something from where it is ▶ *Cans and glass bottles are taken away for recycling.* **+ from** ▶ *She took her hands away from her eyes and looked again.*

2 take away sth, **take** sth **away**: to remove something that someone needs or wants ▶ *Building a new shopping centre would take away one of the last remaining green spaces in the town.* **+ from** ▶ *By cutting pensions, the government is taking money away from those who need it most.*

3 take away sb, **take** sb **away**: if someone takes you away, they force you to go somewhere with them when you do not want to go ▶ *The police came in the middle of the night and took him away.*

4 take sb **away**: to take someone with you when you go to stay in another place ▶ *I'm taking the kids away for a few days.*

5 take away sth, **take** sth **away**: to make a feeling or taste disappear ▶ *The nurse gave him something to take away the pain.*

6 take away sth, **take** sth **away**: if you take one number away from a second one, you reduce the second one by that number ▶ *253 take away 30 is 223.* **+ from** ▶ *Take £40 away from the total.*

7 take away sb, **take** sb **away**: if something takes you away from a place or activity, it stops you from being in that place or doing that activity. **+ from** ▶ *My Dad's job took him away from home a lot.*

8 take away sth, **take** sth **away**: to learn something from an experience, so that it helps you in the future ▶ *One thing I did take away from my time at* *university was a great love of English literature.*

9 to take away: if you buy food in a restaurant to take away, you buy it to eat somewhere else ▶ *Two burgers and two teas to take away, please.*

takeaway N **1** a hot meal that you buy in a shop or restaurant and eat somewhere else ▶ *I can't be bothered to cook – let's get a takeaway.*

2 a shop that sells hot food that you take and eat somewhere else ▶ *I'm going to the Chinese takeaway – do you want anything?*

TAKE AWAY FROM →
take away from sth: to make something seem less good, less impressive, less real etc ▶ *Being a film critic does somehow take away from the enjoyment of going to the movies.*

TAKE BACK →
1 take back sth, **take** sth **back**: to return a book or something else to the place that you borrowed it from ▶ *Can you take my library books back for me?* ▶ *I've got to take these videos back to the shop before they close.*

2a. take back sth, **take** sth **back**: to return something to the shop that you bought it from, because it is unsuitable or of bad quality ▶ *These trousers are a bit small – I'll have to take them back.*

b. take back sth, **take** sth **back**: if a shop takes back goods that you have bought there, they agree to give you your money back because the goods are unsuitable or of bad quality ▶ *They'll take it back if you've still got the receipt.*

3 take back sth, **take** sth **back**: to admit that you were wrong to say something ▶ *"I hate you!" she cried, and immediately wished she could take it back.*

4 take sb **back**: to make you remember a period of time in the past ▶ *That song 'Lili Marlene' takes me back a bit – we used to sing it during the war.* **+ to** ▶ *The prosecutor took her back to that terrible day once more.*

5 take sb **back**: if a story, film etc takes you back to a time in the past, it is about events that happened at that time ▶ *The latest film from Merchant Ivory takes us back to 18th century France.*

6 take back sb, **take** sb **back**: if you take someone back after an argument or after separating from them, you agree to let them live or work with you again ▶ *She once said that if Reggie ever left her for another woman, she'd never take him back.*

7 take back sth, **take** sth **back**: if you wish that you could take something back, you wish that you had not done it ▶ *That one play lost us the game. I wish I could take it back.*

TAKE DOWN →
1 take down sth, **take** sth **down**: to remove something that is fixed to a wall ▶ *We have to take the Christmas decorations down today.*

2 take down sth, **take** sth **down**: to remove a temporary structure by separating it into pieces ▶ *Can you help me take the tent down?*

3 take down sth, **take** sth **down**: to write down something, especially something that someone is saying ▶ *Let me take down your name and phone number.*

TAKE FOR →

1 take sb **for** sth: to think that someone is something that they are not ▶ *I wondered if the tourists took me for a New Yorker.*

2 take sb **for a fool** *also* **take** sb **for an idiot**: to treat someone as if they are stupid ▶ *Do you expect me to believe that? You must take me for an idiot!*

3 what do you take me for?: used to show that you are offended because someone has treated you as if you are very stupid or bad ▶ *What do you take me for? Do you think I'd leave a child to drown?*

TAKE IN →

1 take in sth, **take** sth **in**: **a.** to understand and remember something ▶ *The guide told us a lot about the place, but it was too much to take in.* **b.** to understand news or information and realize its meaning and importance ▶ *I had cancer. I sat staring into my cup, trying to take it in.*

2 be taken in: to be completely deceived by someone or something so that you believe a lie ▶ *We were completely taken in by his charming confident manner.*

3a. take in sb, **take** sb **in**: to let someone live in your home in return for payment ▶ *She couldn't afford to pay the mortgage any more, so she took in a lodger.* **b. take in** sb, **take** sb **in**: to let someone stay in your home or in your country when they have nowhere else to stay ▶ *Germany took in over 10,000 refugees.*

4 take in sth, **take** sth **in**: to include something – use this especially about the places visited on a trip, or the activities of a business ▶ *The bike ride will take in some of the loveliest parts of the county.*

5 take in sth, **take** sth **in**: to notice all the details or qualities of something when you look at it ▶ *She was too preoccupied to take in much about her surroundings.*

6 take in a film/show etc: to go to see a film, play etc ▶ *On Saturday night we can take in a film and maybe get a pizza afterwards.*

7 take in sth, **take** sth **in**: to collect or earn an amount of money ▶ *How much did the store take in today?*

8 take in sth, **take** sth **in**: to make a piece of clothing narrower so that it fits you ▶ *I've got a skirt that's quite nice, but it needs taking in.*

9 take in sb, **take** sb **in**: if the police take you in, they make you go to a police station to ask you questions ▶ *He was taken in by the police and charged with armed robbery.* **take** sb **in for questioning** ▶ *Mrs Burroughs was taken in for questioning at Royal Hill police station.*

10 take in air/food: if people or animals take in air or food, it goes into their bodies ▶ *Jellyfish take in air through their skin.*

    intake N the amount of food, drink etc that you take into your body ▶ *Lower your intake of fat and alcohol to improve your health.*

11 take in sb, **take** sb **in**: to accept someone as a student, patient, customer etc ▶ *The college plans to take in more overseas students next year.*

    intake N the people who are accepted by an organization at a particular time ▶ *This year's intake on the diploma course is particularly good.*

TAKE INTO →

take sb **into** sth: if something takes you into a particular job or activity, it makes you decide to start doing it

▶ *What took you into acting in the first place?*

TAKE OFF →

1 take off sth, **take** sth **off**: to remove something that you are wearing ▶ *She took her clothes off and got into bed.* ▶ *I forgot to take off my make-up last night.*

2 take off: if a plane or bird takes off, it leaves the ground and rises into the air ▶ *The plane took off into the night sky.* ▶ *The ducks took off and flew over the park.*

take-off N when a plane rises into the air at the beginning of a flight ▶ *We have to check in at least one hour before take-off.*

3 take sth **off**: to arrange to spend some time away from your normal work ▶ *Why don't you take some time off? You need a break.* **take a day/week etc off** ▶ *I take two weeks off every summer to go canoeing.*

4 take off: to suddenly start being successful ▶ *Handler was a young actor whose career was just about to take off.*

5 take off: to leave somewhere suddenly, especially without telling anyone ▶ *What's wrong with Ian? He just took off without saying goodbye.*

6 take sb **off**: to move someone away to a place, or make them go there with you. **+ to** ▶ *Two people had been dug out of the snow by rescuers, and taken off to hospital.*

7 take sb **off**: to copy the way that someone speaks or behaves in order to make people laugh ▶ *Peter's really*

good at taking people off. He does the Prime Minister brilliantly.*

take-off N when someone copies the way that someone else speaks or behaves in order to make people laugh ▶ *Donna did a brilliant take-off of the principal.*

8 take yourself off: to go somewhere ▶ *I took myself off for a walk, hoping to forget about my problems.*

9 take sb **off** sth: to stop someone from doing a particular type of work, usually because they are doing it badly ▶ *Detective Williams was taken off the case, and is suspected of taking bribes.*

10 take off sth, **take** sth **off**, **take** sth **off** sth: to take a particular amount or number from a total ▶ *Will the examiner take points off for spelling mistakes?*

11 take sth **off**: to no longer be performed or broadcast ▶ *The play failed to attract a big enough audience, and was taken off after only a few nights.*

TAKE ON →

1 take on sth/sb, **take** sth/sb **on**: to agree to do some work or to accept a responsibility ▶ *Don't take on too much work – the extra cash isn't worth it.* ▶ *a school that takes on difficult students*

2 take on sb, **take** sb **on**: to start to employ someone ▶ *We're taking on 50 new staff this year.*

3 take on sth: to begin to have a particular quality or appearance ▶ *Matt's face took on a worried look.*

4 take on sb, **take** sb **on**: to compete against someone or start an argument or fight with someone, especially someone who is likely to defeat you ▶ *Harlow Town FC will take on the league champions on Saturday.* **+ at** ▶ *It was always a mistake to take my brother on at Scrabble.*

5 take on sth, **take** sth **on**: to start having a debt by borrowing money ▶ *The banks are always looking for ways to encourage customers to take on more debts.*

6 take it on yourself to do sth *see* TAKE UPON

TAKE OUT →

1 take out sth, **take** sth **out**: to remove something from a bag, box, your pocket etc ▶ *Scott felt in his pocket and took out a bunch of keys.* ▶ *She took out a packet of cigarettes and tried to light one.*

2 take sb **out**: to take someone to a place such as a restaurant, theatre, club etc, or show them a place that they do not know ▶ *I had to take their son out and show him around.* **+ to** ▶ *It was Mother's Day, so we took Mum out to lunch.* **+ for** ▶ *He took her out for a meal in a French restaurant.*

3 take out a loan/insurance policy etc: to arrange to start using a financial service provided by a bank or insurance company ▶ *I just took out a £100,000 loan to buy a new boat.*

4 take out sth, **take** sth **out**: to get money from your bank account ▶ *I took out £300 to spend on holiday.*

5 take out sth, **take** sth **out**: to borrow a book from a library ▶ *You can't take more than six books out at once.*

6 take out sb/sth, **take** sb/sth **out**: to kill someone or destroy something ▶ *Our orders were to take out the sentries guarding the bridge.*

7 take out sb, **take** sb **out**: to hit someone and make them become unconscious ▶ *Lewis was a big guy, who looked as if he could take a man out with one punch.*

8 take sth **out**: to spend some time not working or not doing what you usually do. **take time out** ▶ *Why don't*

you take a little time out to be with the children? **take a year out** (=spend a year travelling or doing jobs, between leaving school and starting a university course) ▶ *Andy's thinking of taking a year out and travelling round Europe.*

9 take out sth: to go to a court of law and make an official complaint about someone, or get a legal decision made ▶ *His wife took out a court order to keep him away from her.*

TAKE OUT OF →

1 take it out of sb *also* **take a lot out of** sb: to make you feel very tired ▶ *Starting a new job takes a lot out of you.* ▶ *Looking after kids all day can really take it out of you.*

2 take sb **out of himself/herself**: to stop someone from thinking about their problems and feeling unhappy ▶ *Reading a good book is a great way of taking you out of yourself.*

3 take sth **out of** sth: to make an activity less difficult, less boring, less enjoyable etc. **take the worry/strain** etc **out of** sth ▶ *Comprehensive travel insurance takes the worry out of holidaying abroad.*

TAKE OUT ON →

take sth **out on** sb: to treat someone badly because you are angry and upset, even though it is not their fault. **take it out on** sb ▶ *Don't take it out on me – it's not my fault you've had a bad day.* **take your anger/frustration** etc **out on** sb ▶ *Well, whatever's happened, for God's sake stop taking your frustrations out on me.*

TAKE OVER →

1 take over, **take over** sth, **take** sth **over**: to start being responsible for something or doing a job that someone else was responsible for before you ▶ *We'll stop halfway, and I'll take over the driving.* **+ as** ▶ *She*

will take over as party leader if they
lose the next election.

2 take over sth, **take** sth **over**: to get
control of a company by buying it or
by buying most of its shares ▶ *They
have taken over five smaller banks in
the past two years.*

   takeover N when a company gets
control of another company by
buying most of its shares
▶ *Following its takeover of the car
manufacturer, the company plans to
shed over 1000 workers.* **takeover
bid** (=an attempt to get control of a
company) ▶ *a £1.8 billion takeover
bid.*

3 take over, take over sth, **take** sth
over: to get control of a place or a
political organization, especially by
using force ▶ *Communists took over
control of the Central Committee.*

4 take over sth, **take** sth **over**: to
appear in large numbers in a place,
especially so that other people or
things cannot continue normally
▶ *Every summer the town is taken over
by tourists.*

5 take over, take over sth: to start to
have a very big effect on you, so that
you do not think about anything else
▶ *When you run your own company,
it's easy to let work take over
completely.* **take over your life** ▶ *Once
the baby is born, it will completely
take over your life.*

6 take over: if a feeling takes over, you
start to feel it strongly and it controls
your behaviour ▶ *She knew she had to
stay calm – she mustn't allow panic to
take over.*

7 take over sth, **take** sth **over**: to start
living in or using a house or other
building ▶ *Stacey's bookshop is
expanding, and taking over a larger
building on Market Street.*

8 take over, take over sth: to start to

control what other people are doing,
in an annoying way ▶ *This was a nice
place to work until she came along
and started trying to take over.*

TAKE OVER FROM →

take over from sth/sb: to become
more successful, popular, or important
than something or someone else
▶ *Digital cameras will eventually take
over from conventional cameras.* **+ as**
▶ *London is taking over from Paris as
Europe's fashion capital.*

TAKE ROUND *see* TAKE AROUND

TAKE THROUGH →

take sb **through** sth: to show someone
how something is done by explaining
all the different parts or stages to
them ▶ *The dance teacher took her
class through a new routine.*

TAKE TO →

1 take to sb/sth: to start to like a
person or place, especially when you
first meet them or first go there ▶ *I
took to Paul as soon as I met him.*
▶ *Mel never took to country life, and
always longed to go back to the city.*

2 take to sth: to start doing something
regularly. **take to doing** sth ▶ *A group
of us took to meeting in a bar called
Harry's every evening.* **take to
drink/drugs** (=start drinking a lot of
alcohol or using drugs) ▶ *He took to
drink in a big way after his wife left
him.*

3 take to sth: to enjoy and be good at
doing something, especially the first
time you try it ▶ *She took to horse
riding like a natural.* **take to** sth **like a
duck to water** (=learn how to do
something very easily because you are
naturally good at it) ▶ *He took to show
business like a duck to water.*

4 take to sth: to go into or on to
something. **take to the hills/lifeboats
etc** (=in order to escape from danger)
▶ *Villagers were fleeing their homes in*

T

terror and taking to the hills. **take to the streets** (=in order to protest) ▶ *An estimated half a million protesters took to the streets.* **take to your bed** (=because you are ill) ▶ *My fever returned and I took to my bed.* **take to the road/air etc** (=start a journey by road or air etc) ▶ *There was a distant roar as a squadron of jet fighters took to the air.*

TAKE UP →

1 take up sth, **take** sth **up**: to start doing a particular activity or kind of work ▶ *When did Bryan take up golf?* ▶ *The government is trying to encourage more graduates to take up teaching.*

2 take up sth, **take** sth **up**: to start to have a new position of responsibility ▶ *He's leaving the company to take up a new directorship in Brussels.*

3 take up sth, **take** sth **up**: to use a particular amount of time, space, or effort ▶ *A new baby will take up all your time and energy.* ▶ *I had an essay to write, which took up most of the weekend.*

4 take up an offer/challenge: to accept an offer, challenge etc ▶ *So far a quarter of UK schools have taken up the offer of half-price computers.* ▶ *Each year more and more amateur runners take up the challenge of the New York Marathon.*

5 take up sth, **take up** sth: to try to make people pay attention to a problem or an unfair situation ▶ *The priest took up the issue of land reform on behalf of peasant farmers.* **+ with** ▶ *I'm going to take the matter up with my lawyer.*

6 take up a suggestion/ recommendation: to do what someone suggests or advises ▶ *No one has taken up our suggestion that the working week should be* cut to 30 hours from next year.

7 take up sth, **take** sth **up**: to start to use ideas, designs, or ways of doing things that someone else has developed ▶ *Keynes's economic theories were taken up by governments throughout Europe.*

8 take up a position: to move to the place where you are supposed to be or where you usually are ▶ *The flower sellers took up their positions in the market square.*

9 take up sth, **take** sth **up**: to continue a story or activity that was started by someone else, or that you started before ▶ *Last October pollution reached record levels. Our environment correspondent now takes up the story....* **take up where** sb **left off** ▶ *After the war I returned to college, hoping to take up where I'd left off.*

10 take up sth, **take** sth **up**: if a plant or animal takes up a substance, that substance goes into it ▶ *As we get older our bodies become less efficient in taking up some nutrients.*

TAKE UP ON →

1 take sb **up on** sth: to accept an offer that someone has made ▶ *"I'll cook you dinner if you like." "I might just take you up on that."*

2 take sb **up on** sth: to argue with or ask questions about what someone has said, because you disagree with them ▶ *Let me take you up on one or two of those points.* ▶ *He was quick, she noticed, to take her up on any casual remark.*

TAKE UP WITH →

1 be taken up with sth: to be very busy doing something and give it all of your attention ▶ *Jo's completely taken up with work at the moment.*

2 take up with sb: to become friendly with someone and spend a lot of time with them ▶ *He's taken up with a group of lads from college.*

TAKE UPON, *also* **TAKE ON** →
take it upon/on yourself to do sth: to decide to do something without asking anyone for permission or approval ▶ *A junior official had taken it upon himself to hand my report to the press.*

TALK

TALK AROUND, *also* **TALK ROUND** →
talk around/round sth: to discuss a subject in a general way without really dealing with the important parts ▶ *They wasted a whole hour talking around the problem, and never coming to the point.*

TALK AT →
talk at sb: to talk to someone without giving them a chance to speak or without listening to what they are trying to say ▶ *We teachers spend a lot of time talking at children. We ought to spend much more time listening.*

TALK BACK →
talk back: to answer your parent, teacher, manager etc rudely. **+ to** ▶ *I'd never let a child of mine talk back to me like that.*

TALK DOWN →
talk sth **down, talk down** sth: to talk in a way that makes something seem less good or successful than it really is ▶ *The Prime Minister accused his critics of talking Britain down.*

TALK DOWN TO →
talk down to sb: to talk to someone as if you believe that they are less intelligent than you are

▶ *My father always explained things and never talked down to me.*

TALK INTO →
talk sb **into** sth: to persuade someone to do something by explaining to them why they should do it ▶ *I should never have let you talk me into this crazy scheme.* **talk** sb **into doing** sth ▶ *If Louis tries to talk you into investing in his business, just say no.*

TALK OUT →
talk sth **out, talk out** sth: to discuss a problem with someone thoroughly in order to agree on a way of solving it ▶ *We needed time to talk things out and decide what was best for the future.* **+ with** ▶ *If there was a problem, she could always talk it out with her mother.*

TALK OUT OF →
talk sb **out of** sth: to persuade someone not to do something that they were intending to do ▶ *If you're still determined to leave, don't let them talk you out of it.* **talk** sb **out of doing** sth ▶ *She had to talk me out of sending a furious email to the boss.*

TALK OVER →
talk sth **over, talk over** sth: to discuss a problem or situation calmly with someone ▶ *If you're worried about your work, come and see me and we'll talk it over.* **+ with** ▶ *It's often helpful to talk things over with a professional counsellor.*

TALK ROUND *see also* **TALK AROUND** →
talk sb **round:** to persuade someone to change their opinion and agree with you ▶ *Dad doesn't like the idea of us going away together, but I'm sure I can talk him round.* **+ to** ▶ *We could never talk the girl round to our way of thinking.*

TALK THROUGH →
1 **talk** sth **through, talk through** sth: to

discuss all the details of a problem, idea, plan etc in order to understand it better and decide what to do ▶ *I'm sure if we sit down and talk things through, we can come to some sort of agreement.* **+ with** ▶ *Before you make your final decision, talk it through with someone you trust.*

2 talk sb **through** sth: to explain something slowly and carefully to someone ▶ *If you have a problem with the software, just phone us and we'll talk you through it.* ▶ *Dr Cameron spent some time talking me through the operation, so that I would know exactly what to expect.*

TALK TO →

talk to sb: to speak to someone severely and tell them that their behaviour, work etc is not good enough ▶ *I'm going to have to talk to Barry. He was late again this morning.*

talking-to N if you give someone a talking-to, you speak to them severely and tell them that their behaviour, work etc is not good enough ▶ *If you ask me, what that girl needs is a good talking-to.*

TALK UP →

talk up sth, **talk** sth **up**: to keep saying how good or successful something is ▶ *Travel agencies have been talking the place up as a great new tourist resort.*

TAMPER

TAMPER WITH →

tamper with sth: to make changes to something in a way that is dangerous, illegal, or has a bad effect ▶ *Someone had tampered with the brakes of the car.* ▶ *The police were accused of tampering with the evidence.*

TANGLE

TANGLE UP IN →

1 get tangled up in sth: to become caught or trapped in something such as branches, ropes, or wires ▶ *Dolphins often get tangled up in nets used for tuna fishing.*

2 get tangled up in sth: to become involved in a situation that it is difficult to get out of ▶ *I managed to get myself tangled up in a real mess!* **be tangled up in** sth ▶ *Don't you realize that you're tangled up in something that will probably end in disaster?*

TANGLE WITH →

tangle with sb/sth: to argue or fight with someone or something ▶ *I wouldn't tangle with him if I were you – he's a dangerous man.*

TAP

TAP FOR →

tap sb **for** sth: to persuade someone to give you money or information ▶ *I re-read the article and thought about who I could tap for more information.*

TAP IN →

tap in sth, **tap** sth **in**: to put information, numbers etc into a computer or other machine, by pressing the buttons on it ▶ *Tap in your personal identification number.*

TAP INTO →

1 tap into sth: to use energy, information, money etc that comes from a large supply ▶ *The new software allows consumers to tap into the Internet via their phones.*

2 tap into sth: to use a computer to illegally get into other people's computer systems ▶ *The court was told that he had managed to tap into computers at universities all over the world.*

TAP OUT →

1 tap out sth, **tap** sth **out**: to produce a series of sounds by hitting a surface lightly and regularly ▶ *As he played he tapped out the rhythm with his foot.*

2 tap out sth, **tap** sth **out**: to write words or numbers on a typewriter, computer, or other machine ▶ *The secretary grabbed the phone and began tapping out the number.*

3 tap out sb, **tap** sb **out**: to use all someone's energy or money so that they are unable to fight against you any longer ▶ *It's part of their strategy to keep us in court and tap us out.*

TAPER

TAPER OFF →

1 taper off: to gradually become less in amount, strength, size etc ▶ *Oil production tapered off and the country was forced to find new sources of income.*

2 taper off: if something tapers off, it becomes narrower at one end ▶ *The road was narrower here, and it eventually tapered off into a track.*

TART

TART UP →

tart sth **up, tart up** sth: to try to make a place look more attractive or more modern ▶ *The hotel's been tarted up now, and has lost a lot of its charm.*

TATTLE

TATTLE ON →

tattle on sb: to tell a person in authority about something wrong that someone has done ▶ *I suppose you'll go and tattle on me!*

TAX

TAX WITH →

tax sb **with** sth: to say that someone has done something wrong, and ask them for an explanation ▶ *Critics have taxed the government with failing to carry out a proper investigation.*

TEAM

TEAM UP →

team up: to join together with another person or organization in order to do something together ▶ *The parties teamed up and between them got 75% of the vote.* **+ with** ▶ *The explorers teamed up with a group of native travellers.*

TEAR

TEAR APART →

1 tear sth **apart, tear apart** sth: to make people argue or fight with each other, so that a relationship ends, or a family, group, country etc becomes divided ▶ *For years the country had been torn apart by civil war.* ▶ *The stresses and strains of modern life are tearing families apart.*

2 tear sth **apart, tear apart** sth: to make something break into pieces by pulling it violently in different directions ▶ *The fox is torn apart by the hounds in a matter of seconds.*

3 tear sth **apart, tear apart** sth: to destroy a building or a room completely and often violently ▶ *The factory was torn apart by a huge explosion.*

4 tear sth **apart, tear apart** sth: to criticize an idea, piece of work etc very severely ▶ *The book was torn apart by the critics when it first came out.*

5 tear sb **apart**: to make someone feel very upset and worried ▶ *Kelly couldn't bear to think of him with another woman. It was tearing her apart.*

T

TEAR AT →

tear at sth/sb: to pull violently at something or someone ▶ *She leapt at him in a fit of rage, tearing at his face.*

TEAR AWAY →

tear sb away: to make someone stop doing something, when they are so interested in doing it that they do not want to stop ▶ *Once he's in front of the TV, it's practically impossible to tear him away.* **tear yourself away** ▶ *Do you think you could tear yourself away from that computer for just one minute and listen?*

BE TORN BETWEEN →

be torn between sth: if you are torn between two things, it is difficult for you to choose one of them or to decide which one is more important to you ▶ *For a long time Clarissa had been torn between her family and her career.*

TEAR DOWN →

tear sth down, tear down sth: to deliberately destroy a building, wall etc because it is not needed any more or is not safe ▶ *The church had been so badly damaged that it had to be torn down and rebuilt.*

TEAR INTO →

tear into sb/sth: to criticize someone or something very severely and often unfairly ▶ *After the game the manager really tore into the team.*

TEAR OFF →

tear off sth, **tear** sth **off**: to take off a piece of clothing as quickly as you can ▶ *Ben tore off his jacket and dived into the river.*

TEAR UP →

1 tear sth **up, tear up** sth: to tear something made of paper or cloth into a lot of small pieces because you want to destroy it ▶ *Jason read the letter quickly, then tore it up and threw it on the fire.*

2 tear sth **up, tear up** sth: to destroy or damage something such as an area of land ▶ *Huge areas of rainforest are being torn up every day by logging companies.*

TEE

TEE OFF →

1 tee off: to hit the ball for the first time at the beginning of a game of golf ▶ *David Miller had just teed off at the fifteenth hole in the competition.*

2 tee off: to begin an event or activity ▶ *The celebration teed off with a round of champagne.*

3 tee sb **off, tee off** sb: to make someone angry ▶ *It really tees me off that he never helps with the housework!*

TEEM

TEEM DOWN →

teem down: to rain very heavily ▶ *At that moment the rain began teeming down, and we all ran for shelter.*

TEEM WITH →

teem with sth/sb: to be very full of people or animals ▶ *This apparently empty landscape is in fact teeming with wildlife.*

TELL

TELL AGAINST →

tell against sb: to make someone less likely to succeed in something ▶ *I badly wanted the job, but I knew that my age would probably tell against me.*

TELL APART →

tell sb/sth **apart**: if you can tell people or things apart, you can see the difference between them ▶ *The twins looked so alike that only their parents could tell them apart.*

TELL FROM →

tell sth/sb **from** sth/sb: if you can tell one person or thing from another, you can see or realize the difference between them ▶ *The two types of mushroom look very similar and it's difficult to tell one from the other.* ▶ *By this age most children will be able to tell right from wrong.*

TELL OFF →

tell sb **off, tell off** sb: to speak angrily to someone about something wrong that they have done ▶ *Miss McHale will tell you off if she sees you doing that!* **be told off** also **get told off** ▶ *Hurry up – I don't want to be told off for being late again!*

telling-off N when someone speaks to a child angrily about something wrong that they have done ▶ *I've already had one telling-off from Dad today.*

TELL ON →

1 tell on sb: to tell someone in authority such as a teacher or a parent about something wrong that someone has done – used especially by children ▶ *I'll tell on you if you don't give me my pen back.*

2 tell on sb: to have a bad effect on your health, or make you feel very tired ▶ *All those years of heavy drinking were starting to tell on her.*

TEND

TEND TO →

tend to sb/sth: to look after someone or something ▶ *Anna was in her greenhouse, tending to her plants.*

TEND TOWARDS, *also* **TEND TOWARD** →

tend towards sth: to usually have a particular type of attitude or behave in a particular way ▶ *He tends towards the right wing of the party.*

TENSE

TENSE UP →

1 tense up: to become nervous or worried and unable to relax ▶ *Every time the phone rang, she tensed up, not knowing whether to answer it or not.*

2 tense up, tense up sth, **tense** sth **up:** if your muscles tense up or you tense them up, they become hard and tight, for example because you are angry or nervous ▶ *I could feel the muscles in the back of my neck tensing up.*

TEST

TEST OUT →

1 test out sth, **test** sth **out:** to test a new product or idea in order to see whether it works well or will be popular ▶ *A group of children were asked to test out the new computer game for a local newspaper.* **+ on** ▶ *The drug still hasn't been tested out on humans.*

2 test sb **out:** to do or say something deliberately in order to find out what someone's reaction is ▶ *He was testing me out, leaving all that cash lying about. He wanted to see if I was honest.*

TESTIFY

TESTIFY TO →

testify to sth: to show clearly that something is definitely true ▶ *The growing number of empty shops in the High Street testify to the depth of the recession.*

THAW

THAW OUT →

1 thaw out, thaw sth **out, thaw out**

sth: if frozen food thaws out, or you thaw it out, it becomes warmer and no longer frozen ▶ *Keep the freezer door shut can you, or the food will start to thaw out.*

2 thaw out, thaw out sth, **thaw** sth **out**: to become warmer or make your body warmer after being outside and getting very cold ▶ *I put my fingers over the stove and tried to thaw them out.*

THIN

THIN OUT →

thin out: if people, cars, houses etc thin out, there starts to be fewer of them ▶ *The crowd had thinned out now, and only a few people were left in the square.* ▶ *I don't usually go home until after 5.30, when the traffic begins to thin out.*

THINK

THINK AHEAD →

think ahead: to think carefully and plan for what might happen or what you might do in the future ▶ *A lot of these problems could be prevented by thinking ahead and taking action early.* **+ to** ▶ *We are now thinking ahead to the third phase of the development plan.*

THINK BACK →

think back: to think about things that happened to you in the past. **+ to** ▶ *Think back to your first day at school.*

THINK OF →

1 think of sth: to find a new idea, suggestion etc by thinking about it ▶ *I'll have to think of some way of showing them how grateful I am.* ▶ *That's a brilliant idea – I hadn't thought of that before!*

2 think of doing sth: to consider doing something soon or in the future ▶ *I'm thinking of retiring next year.*

3 what do you think of ...?: used to ask what someone's opinion is about something ▶ *I'll ask Simon what he thinks of the idea.*

4 think of sth/sb: to think of someone or something in a particular way or as a particular thing. **+ as** ▶ *She still thought of Scotland as her home.*
think of sb/sth **in that way** ▶ *You're an adult now, and it's time you learnt to think of yourself in that way.*

5 think of sth/sb: to remember someone or something that you knew in the past ▶ *Lynn remembered the hotel clearly, but she couldn't think of its name.*

6 think of sb: to consider the needs or wishes of someone else ▶ *I can't just please myself, you know. I have a family to think of too.*

7 think of sb: to think about someone at a particular time, especially when they are unhappy or doing something difficult ▶ *Good luck in the exam – I'll be thinking of you.*

8 be well thought of also **be highly thought of**: if someone or something is well thought of or highly thought of, other people have a good opinion of them ▶ *She is well thought of throughout the industry.*

9 what was sb **thinking of ...?**: used to ask why someone did something stupid ▶ *"What were you thinking of?" Larry asked in horror. "You know we haven't got that much money!"*

THINK OUT →

1 think sth **out, think out** sth: to plan something carefully before you do it ▶ *It was clear that the thieves had thought it all out in advance, and knew exactly what they were doing.*

2 think sth **out, think out** sth: to think carefully about a situation, problem, plan etc, and think especially about what might happen as a result of it

▶ "You're much too young to get married," my mother said. "You haven't thought it out properly."

THINK OVER →
think sth **over, think over** sth: to think very carefully about an idea or plan before you make a decision about it ▶ *Government ministers are still thinking over the unions' demands.*
think it over ▶ *It was undoubtedly a good offer, so I agreed to think it over for a couple of days.*

THINK THROUGH →
think sth **through, think through** sth: to think carefully about a situation, problem, plan etc, and think especially about what might happen as a result of it ▶ *The article suggested that the UN was taking action without fully thinking through the consequences.*

THINK UP →
think up sth, **think** sth **up**: to find a new idea, suggestion etc by thinking about it and using your imagination or intelligence ▶ *Everyone in the room was told to try and think up a new and exciting name for the book.*

THIRST

THIRST FOR, *also* **THIRST AFTER →**
thirst for/ after sth: to want something very much ▶ *He was clearly thirsting for revenge.*

THRASH

THRASH ABOUT, *also* **THRASH AROUND →**
thrash about/ around: to move from side to side and move your arms around in a violent and uncontrolled way ▶ *I could just make out someone thrashing around in the water below.*

THRASH OUT →
thrash out sth, **thrash** sth **out**: to decide or agree about something by discussing it in detail and for a long

time ▶ *The two sides met in an attempt to thrash the matter out.*

THRIVE

THRIVE ON →
1 thrive on sth: to enjoy or be successful in a particular situation or condition ▶ *Some companies have great difficulty coping with change, while others seem to thrive on it.* ▶ *governments which thrive on secrecy and paranoia*

2 thrive on sth: to grow well with a particular food or in particular conditions ▶ *All he eats is junk food, but he seems to thrive on it!*

THROW

THROW ASIDE →
throw aside sth, **throw** sth **aside**: to suddenly get rid of an old idea, belief, or feeling that you had ▶ *We must throw aside the old prejudices and learn to live with our former enemies.*

THROW AT →
throw yourself at sb: to try very hard to get someone's attention and show them that you think they are attractive ▶ *She'd thrown herself at that man and made a complete fool of herself.*

THROW AWAY →
1 throw away sth, **throw** sth **away**: to get rid of something that you do not want or need ▶ *I shouldn't have thrown away the receipt.* ▶ *Do you want to keep these catalogues, or shall I throw them away?*

2 throw away sth, **throw** sth **away**: to waste an opportunity or lose an advantage ▶ *This could be the best* *chance you've ever had – don't throw it away.*

THROW BACK AT →
throw sth **back at** sb, **throw back** sth **at** sb: to criticize someone by reminding them of something wrong or embarrassing that they did in the past ▶ *I know I said some stupid things, but I wish you'd stop throwing them all back at me.*

BE THROWN BACK ON →
be thrown back on sth/sb: to be forced to depend on something or someone because of a change in your situation ▶ *Homeless and jobless, Joss was thrown back on what little support his parents could offer.*

THROW DOWN →
throw down a challenge *also throw down the gauntlet*: to invite someone to argue, fight, or compete against you ▶ *After lunch Marcie threw down the gauntlet and challenged me to a game of tennis.*

THROW IN →
1 throw in sth, **throw** sth **in**: to include more things with the thing that you are selling to someone, without increasing its price ▶ *The person selling the house may offer to throw in carpets and curtains as part of the deal.*

2 throw in sth, **throw** sth **in**: to add something to a performance, a story, an idea etc in order to improve it ▶ *We could throw in a song or two to liven up the play.*

3 throw in your lot with sb *also throw your lot in with* sb: to decide to support someone and work with them, so that your success depends on theirs ▶ *former socialists who had thrown their lot in with the conservatives*

4 throw in sth, **throw** sth **in**: if you throw in a job, you leave, especially when you are not going to start another job ▶ *She threw in a good job with an insurance company just so she could follow her boyfriend out to Hawaii.*

THROW INTO, *also* THROW IN →
throw sb **into/in** sth: to put someone in something. **be thrown into/in prison** *also be thrown into jail* ▶ *Many of the rioters were arrested and thrown into prison.*

THROW INTO →
1 throw sb **into confusion/panic etc**: to make people feel very confused, afraid etc ▶ *Within days the people were in revolt and the leadership was thrown into panic.*

2 throw sth **into turmoil** *also throw* sth *into chaos*: to suddenly make something very confused and badly organized ▶ *A failure of the computer system threw London's ambulance service into chaos.*

3 throw sth **into doubt** *also throw* sth *into question etc*: to suddenly make people uncertain whether something is true, or whether something will happen ▶ *These shocking events throw into doubt the whole future of the Olympic Games.*

4 throw yourself into sth: to start doing an activity or job eagerly and with a lot of effort ▶ *Now Julia threw herself into her work, staying up late every night.*

THROW OFF →
1 throw off the yoke of sth *also throw off the shackles of* sth: to get free from something that has been limiting your freedom ▶ *nations that were struggling to throw off the yoke of colonial rule*

2 throw off sth, **throw** sth **off**: to succeed in getting rid of an illness that is not very serious ▶ *I've had this cold for several weeks and I can't seem to throw it off.*

T

3 throw off sth, **throw** sth **off**: to succeed in getting rid of a problem or an unpleasant feeling ▶ *The city has been making great efforts to throw off its negative image.*

THROW ON →
throw on sth, **throw** sth **on**: to put on a piece of clothing quickly and carelessly ▶ *Throwing on a dressing-gown, I stumbled downstairs to open the door.*

THROW OUT →
1 throw out sth, **throw** sth **out**: to get rid of something that you do not want or need ▶ *We threw out lots of stuff when we moved house.* ▶ *I hope you haven't thrown out yesterday's paper – there was something I wanted to read.*

2 throw sb **out**, **throw out** sb: to force someone to leave a house, school, job etc ▶ *We can't throw him out in this kind of weather – he's nowhere else to go.* **+ of** ▶ *Wayne was thrown out of school for taking drugs.* **be thrown out of work** (=lose your job) ▶ *Hundreds of men were thrown out of work when Smith's shipyard closed.*

3 throw out sth, **throw** sth **out**: to refuse to officially accept or approve a plan, suggestion etc ▶ *The judge threw out the case, saying that the police had made up evidence.*

THROW TOGETHER →
1 throw sth **together**, **throw together** sth: to produce something quickly without planning it carefully, using whatever things are available ▶ *I'm afraid it isn't much of a meal – just something I threw together while you were unpacking.* ▶ *Charlie had thrown the show together at very short notice.*

2 throw sb **together**, **throw together** sb: if a situation throws people together, it causes them to meet and get to know each other ▶ *Because there were no other kids in the*

neighbourhood, Jimmy and I were thrown together a lot.

THROW UP →
1 throw up sth, **throw** sth **up**: to produce new problems, people, ideas etc ▶ *The report throws up some interesting questions.*

2 throw up, **throw** sth **up**, **throw up** sth: to bring up food from your stomach because you are ill ▶ *I've been throwing up all morning.*

3 throw up sth, **throw** sth **up**: to quickly build or make something such as a wall or fence ▶ *Citizens threw up barricades around the Kremlin.*

4 throw up sth, **throw** sth **up**: to suddenly leave a job or a course of study ▶ *You have a brilliant future to look forward to. It would be crazy to throw it all up now.*

THRUST

THRUST ASIDE →
thrust aside sth, **thrust** sth **aside**: to refuse to consider something, especially someone's complaints, protests etc ▶ *All our complaints were thrust aside and ignored.*

THRUST ON, *also* THRUST UPON →
thrust sth **on/upon** sb: if something is thrust on you, you are suddenly forced to deal with it or accept it ▶ *Fame was thrust upon Edward at an early age.*

THUMB

THUMB THROUGH →
thumb through sth: to turn the pages of a book, magazine etc, but not read it carefully ▶ *She sat in the dentist's waiting room thumbing through an old copy of Vogue.*

TICK

TICK AWAY →
1 tick away, **tick away** sth: if a clock or watch ticks away it makes regular sounds as time passes ▶ *The old*

T

grandfather clock ticks away the hours and minutes.

2 tick away: if time ticks away, it passes ▶ *The last few seconds of the game were ticking away.*

TICK BY →

tick by: if time ticks by, it passes ▶ *The days were ticking by, and I still hadn't found the courage to call her.*

TICK OFF →

1 tick off sth, **tick** sth **off**, **tick** sth **off** sth: to mark things on a list to show that they are finished or have been dealt with ▶ *The guests' names were ticked off as they arrived.*

2 tick sb **off**, **tick off** sb: to tell someone that they should not have done something – used especially about parents, teachers etc talking to children ▶ *Mrs. Brownfield ticked us off for talking in class.*

    ticking off N when a parent, teacher etc speaks to a child and tells them angrily that they should not have done something ▶ *Unless you want a ticking off from your Mum, you'd better get home.*

3 tick sb **off**, **tick off** sb: to annoy someone ▶ *I wish he wouldn't do that. It really ticks me off.*

TICK OVER →

tick over: to continue to operate without any problems, but without producing very much, without making a lot of progress etc ▶ *The firm had enough work to keep it ticking over for the next few months.*

TIDE

TIDE OVER →

tide sb **over**: if you have enough money or food to tide you over, you have enough of it to last until a later time ▶ *My Dad lent me some money to tide me over until I get paid.*

TIDY

TIDY AWAY →

tidy sth **away**, **tidy away** sth: to put things back in the place where they should be ▶ *Anthea looked at her watch and began to tidy her papers away.*

TIDY UP →

1 tidy up, **tidy up** sth, **tidy** sth **up**: to make a place look neater by putting things in their proper places ▶ *Would you mind tidying up a bit before the guests arrive?* **tidy up after** sb (=make a place look neater after someone has made it untidy) ▶ *She got fed up with tidying up after her husband all the time.*

    tidy-up N when you make a place look neater by putting things in their proper places ▶ *I'll just give the kitchen a quick tidy-up and then we can go out.*

2 tidy yourself up: to make yourself look tidier or cleaner ▶ *Janine went upstairs to tidy herself up before her date.*

3 tidy up sth, **tidy** sth **up**: to make a few small changes to something, especially a piece of written work, in order to improve it or finish it ▶ *I just want to tidy up a few things and then you can read it.*

TIE

TIE BACK →

tie back sth, **tie** sth **back**: to fasten your hair or something that hangs down so that it is pulled back ▶ *Her long hair was tied back in a red scarf.*

TIE DOWN →

1 tie sb **down**: to stop someone from being free to do what they want to do ▶ *He said he loved her, but he didn't want to be tied down.*

2 tie down sth/sb, **tie** sth/sb **down**: to tie a thing or a person onto something, so that they cannot move ➤ *Make sure all the boxes are securely tied down.* **+ to** ➤ *The kidnappers kept him tied down to a chair with a sack over his head.*

3 tie sb down: to make someone promise or agree that they will definitely do something. **+ to** ➤ *You need to tie him down to a definite date for the wedding.*

TIE IN WITH →

tie in with sth: to be similar to or connect well with something else ➤ *What you're saying doesn't tie in with what other people say about him.* ➤ *These findings tie in with recent research in the field of genetics.*

TIE UP →

1 tie up sb,
tie sb **up**:
to tie a
person or
animal to
something so
that they
cannot escape ➤ *Police said the man tied up two shop assistants before taking money from the safe.* ➤ *I tied my horse up and walked to the top of the hill.*

2 tie up sth, **tie** sth **up**: to fasten something together using a string or rope ➤ *We tied up the newspapers and took them to the recycling centre.*

3 be tied up: to be very busy, with the result that you cannot see someone or do something ➤ *Sorry, I couldn't see you earlier – I've been tied up in a meeting all morning.* ➤ *Can I call you later? I'm a bit tied up at the moment.*

4 get tied up: if you get tied up, something happens which prevents you from going somewhere or doing something ➤ *Sorry I'm late. I got tied up.*

5 tie up sth, **tie** sth **up**: to finish

arranging or dealing with all the details of something ➤ *Make sure you tie up the travel arrangements by the weekend.*

BE TIED UP WITH →

be tied up with sth: to be closely connected with something ➤ *A lot of his emotional problems are tied up with his childhood.*

TIGHTEN

TIGHTEN UP →

1 tighten up sth, **tighten** sth **up**, **tighten up**: to make a rule, law, or system more strict ➤ *plans to tighten up laws on tax evasion.* **+ on** ➤ *Airlines are tightening up on security after warnings of terrorist attacks.*

2 tighten up, tighten up sth, **tighten** sth **up**: if your muscles tighten up, or you tighten up your muscles, they become stiff ➤ *The muscles in my leg suddenly tightened up and I had to stop swimming.*

3 tighten up sth, **tighten** sth **up**: to turn something, such as a screw, so that another thing is firmly held in place ➤ *Tighten up the screws to keep the axle from slipping forward.*

4 tighten up, tighten up sth, **tighten** sth **up**: to work together, or make people work together, in a more effective way ➤ *Milan have tightened up their defence and will be a hard team to beat.*

TINKER

TINKER AROUND, *also* TINKER ABOUT →

tinker around / about: to make small changes to something such as a machine or system in order to repair or improve it. **+ with** ➤ *He spent all morning tinkering around with the engine.*

TINKER WITH →

tinker with sth: if you tinker with

something such as a machine or a system you make small changes to it in order to repair or improve it ▶ *My Dad used to like tinkering with cars.* ▶ *The government should stop tinkering with the educational system and let teachers get on with their jobs.*

TIP

TIP DOWN →
be tipping down: used to say that it is raining very hard ▶ *It's been tipping down all morning.*

TIP OFF →
tip off sb, **tip** sb **off**: to secretly tell or warn someone about something ▶ *The drug dealers were arrested after police were tipped off by local residents.*
+ about ▶ *Someone must have tipped off the press about her visit.*
    tip-off N a secret warning or message about something that is happening ▶ *Acting on an anonymous tip-off, police raided the house.*

TIP OVER →
tip over, tip over sth, **tip** sth **over**: if an object tips over, or if you tip it over, it falls on its

side ▶ *Bud was so mad he tipped his chair over.* ▶ *The boat tipped over and they were all thrown into the sea.*

TIP UP →
1 tip up sth, **tip** sth **up**: if you tip up a container, you move it so that its contents start to pour out ▶ *Stevens tipped up the wheelbarrow and emptied the rocks out onto the ground.*

2 tip up, tip up sth, **tip** sth **up**: if an object tips up, or if you tip it up, one end goes down and the other end goes up ▶ *A fat man sat down at one*

end of the bench, and the whole thing tipped up.

TIRE

TIRE OF →
1 tire of sth/sb: to become bored with something or someone ▶ *His parents kept buying him toys, but he soon tired of them.* **tire of doing** sth ▶ *Voters were beginning to tire of hearing the same old promises from politicians.*

2 sb never tires of doing sth: used to say that someone does something so much that it annoys you ▶ *Dan never tired of telling people what an excellent basketball player he was.*

TIRE OUT →
tire sb **out, tire out** sb: to make someone very tired ▶ *A full day of shopping tired us out.* ▶ *James has so much energy – he always tires me out.*
tire yourself out (=work so hard or do something so much that you become tired) ▶ *Take a rest, kid. You'll tire yourself out.*

TOIL

TOIL AWAY →
toil away: to work very hard for a long period of time ▶ *In the past, men and women toiled away in the fields all day.*

TONE

TONE DOWN →
1 tone down sth, **tone** sth **down**: to make something such as a speech, performance, or piece of writing less extreme, offensive, or critical ▶ *TV bosses have told them to tone the show down, claiming there are too many sex scenes and too much bad language.*

2 tone down sth, **tone** sth **down**: to make a colour less bright ▶ *Makeup can be used to help tone down a reddish complexion.*

TONE IN →

tone in: to look good and suitable when put together with something else. **+ with** ▶ *Choose a colour scheme for the curtains that will tone in with the rest of the room.*

TONE UP →

tone up sth, **tone** sth **up, tone up**: to make your body or muscles firmer and stronger by doing physical exercises ▶ *Aerobics really tones up your muscles.*

TOP

TOP OFF →

1 top off sth, **top** sth **off**: to finish something that has been very successful or enjoyable by doing one last thing. **+ with** ▶ *We topped off the evening with a meal in one of my favourite restaurants.*

2 to top it (all) off: used when you want to mention one final thing, especially something very surprising or annoying ▶ *She spent the whole evening telling me about her previous boyfriends. Then to top it all off, she suggested we go and visit one of them!*

3 top off: if prices of something top off at a particular level, that is the most expensive price. **+ at** ▶ *Tickets topped off at £75.*

4 top off sth, **top** sth **off**: to fill a partly empty container with liquid ▶ *Let me top off your drink.*

TOP OUT →

top out: to reach the highest level possible ▶ *Monday's temperature should top out at 40 degrees.*

TOP UP →

1 top up sth, **top** sth **up**: to fill a partly empty container with liquid ▶ *I'll just top up the coffee pot.*

2 top up sth, **top** sth **up**: to increase an amount of something so that it

reaches the level you want ▶ *I took an extra job in the evenings to top up my wages.*

TOPPLE

TOPPLE OVER →

topple over, topple sth **over**: to become unsteady and fall over, or to make something do this ▶ *The dishes were piled so high they looked as if they were going to topple over any moment.*

TOSS

TOSS AROUND, *also* TOSS ABOUT →

1 toss sth **around/about, toss around/about** sth: to move or shake something in a rough and often violent way ▶ *The little boat was tossed around by the waves.*

2 toss sth **around/about, toss around/about** sth: to talk about a plan, idea, or suggestion, usually without considering it in a serious way ▶ *We tossed around the idea of visiting Thailand this summer, but in the end decided we couldn't afford it.*

3 toss sth **around/about, toss around/about** sth: to use a word or phrase without thinking carefully about what it means ▶ *People often toss around words like "genius" and "living legend", but in his case they're all true.*

TOSS BACK →

1 toss back sth, **toss** sth **back**: to drink something very quickly, especially alcohol ▶ *His friends had been tossing back beers all day.*

2 toss back your head: to move your head backwards suddenly, because you are laughing or upset ▶ *Tossing her head back defiantly, Tina refused to admit she was wrong.*

TOSS FOR →

toss for sth, **toss** sb **for** sth: to decide

who can do or have something by throwing a coin in the air. The person who guesses which side the coin will land on can have or do the thing they want. ▶ *The two teams tossed for the kick-off.* ▶ *"Who gets the last piece of cake?" "I'll toss you for it."*

TOSS OFF →
toss off sth, **toss** sth **off**: to produce something quickly and without much effort ▶ *Some writers seem to be able to toss off a new book every few months.*

TOSS UP →
toss up: to decide who will do or have something by throwing a coin in the air. The person who guesses which side the coin will land on can do or have the thing they want. ▶ *They tossed up to see who would play first.* ▶ *Why don't we toss up for it? If you win, you get to keep the money.*

TOT

TOT UP →
tot up sth, **tot** sth **up**: to add together numbers or amounts of money in order to find the total ▶ *At the end of the game we'll tot up the points to find the winner.*

TOTAL

TOTAL UP →
total up sth, **total** sth **up**, **total up**: to add together numbers or amounts of money in order to find the total ▶ *Could you mark each other's work, please, and then total up your scores.*

TOUCH

TOUCH DOWN →
touch down: if a plane touches down, it lands on the

ground, especially at an airport ▶ *Margaret closed her book as the plane touched down at Istanbul airport.*

  touchdown N when a plane lands on the ground, or a spacecraft lands somewhere ▶ *Touchdown was only half a second later than predicted.*

TOUCH ON, *also* TOUCH UPON →
touch on/upon sth: to mention something for a short time and without giving very many details ▶ *She briefly touched on what happened at the conference, but then passed on to other things.*

TOUCH UP →
touch up sth, **touch** sth **up**: to improve something by changing it a little or adding more to it ▶ *She looked in the car mirror and touched up her lipstick.*

TOUCH UPON *see* TOUCH ON

TOUGH

TOUGH OUT →
tough it out: to deal with a difficult situation or strong opposition by being very determined and refusing to give up ▶ *Despite all the protests, the deposed leader tried to tough it out, thinking that the US would support him.*

TOUGHEN

TOUGHEN UP →
1 toughen up sth, **toughen** sth **up**: to make rules or laws stricter and more effective ▶ *We want the government to toughen up regulations on animal experiments.*

2a. toughen sb **up**, **toughen up** sb: to make someone become physically or emotionally stronger, and more able to deal with difficult situations ▶ *His parents sent him to survival school last summer to toughen him up a bit.*

b. toughen up: to become physically or emotionally stronger, and more able to deal with difficult situations ▶ *You'll have to toughen up a bit if you're serious about being a doctor.*

TOUT

TOUT FOR →

tout for business etc: to try to persuade people to buy the goods or services you are offering ▶ *Unlicensed taxis cruised the streets, touting for business.*

TOWER

TOWER OVER, *also* TOWER ABOVE →

1 tower over/ above sb/ sth: to be much taller than someone or something else ▶ *Roy was already over 6 feet tall, and towered over his classmates.*

2 tower over/ above sb/ sth: to be much better, more important etc than other people or organizations. **tower over/ above (all) the rest** ▶ *Just one of these writers seems to tower over the rest.*

TOY

TOY WITH →

1 toy with sth: to think about it and consider something, but not very seriously ▶ *Len's not sure what to study at university – he's been toying with various possibilities.* **toy with the idea of (doing)** sth ▶ *I had been to France several times, and was toying with the idea of buying a house there.*

2 toy with sth: to keep touching something or moving it around ▶ *We sat there toying with our food and trying to be polite to each other.*

3 toy with sb: to treat someone in a way that is not sincere or fair and is likely to upset them ▶ *Rod was not what he seemed – he had been toying with her that day on the river.*

TRACE

TRACE OUT →

trace out sth, **trace** sth **out**: to mark or write something carefully and clearly ▶ *I got out the map and traced out the route that we would have to take.*

TRACK

TRACK DOWN →

track down sb/ sth, **track** sb/ sth **down**: to manage to find someone or something after trying very hard ▶ *Police have managed to*

track down thirty people who were in the town centre when the attack occurred.

TRADE

TRADE DOWN →

trade down: to sell an expensive house, car etc, in order to buy one that is cheaper ▶ *Many homeowners decide to trade down in late middle-age, in order to get cash for retirement.*

TRADE IN →

trade sth **in**, **trade in** sth: to give a car, piece of equipment etc that you own as part of the payment for a new one you are buying. **+ for** ▶ *We traded our old van in for a smaller, more modern one.*

TRADE OFF →

1 trade off sth, **trade** sth **off**: to compare one thing with another when you are trying to decide what is the best thing to do. **+ against** ▶ *You have to trade off the increased viewing charges against the number of new channels you can watch.*

trade-off N an acceptable balance between two or more opposing things ► *the trade-off between leisure and work*

2 trade off sth, **trade** sth **off**: to give something up, or accept something you do not want in order to have something that is more important ► *They may have to trade off some of their newly acquired territory in order to secure a lasting peace.*

trade-off N something that you have to accept in order to have something else that is more important ► *He tolerates inflation as a trade-off for healthy economic growth.*

TRADE ON, *also* TRADE UPON →
trade on/upon sth: to use something in order to get an advantage for yourself ► *The newspapers accused her of trading on her relationship with the Prince.*

TRADE UP →
trade up: to sell a cheap house, car etc in order to buy one that is more expensive ► *Our car's getting a bit old now, so we're thinking of trading up and getting something a bit sportier.*

TRADE UPON *see* TRADE ON

TRAFFIC

TRAFFIC IN →
traffic in sth: to buy and sell illegal goods, especially drugs ► *The government has increased the penalties for trafficking in drugs and firearms.*

TRAIL

TRAIL OFF, *also* TRAIL AWAY →
trail off/away: if a person's voice trails off, it gradually becomes quieter and then stops ► *"I know I should have told you ..." At that point he trailed off and stared down at his feet.*

TRAIN

TRAIN ON, *also* TRAIN UPON →
train sth **on/upon** sb/sth: to aim a gun, camera etc at someone or something and keep it pointing at them ► *All the TV cameras and microphones were trained on him, but he refused to comment.*

TRAIN UP →
train sb **up, train up** sb: to teach someone a particular job, skill, or subject, until they reach the necessary standard ► *The company takes new graduates, and trains them up over a period of two years.*

TRAIN UPON *see* TRAIN ON

TRAMPLE

TRAMPLE ON, *also* TRAMPLE UPON →
trample on/upon sb/sth: to treat someone badly and unfairly, ignoring their rights or feelings ► *Don't try to be nice to everyone all the time – you'll just end up getting trampled on.*

TRESPASS

TRESPASS ON, *also* TRESPASS UPON →
trespass on sb's hospitality/ generosity etc: to use more than you should of someone else's time, help etc ► *She would have liked to stay longer but she felt that she must not trespass on his hospitality.*

TRICKLE

TRICKLE DOWN →
trickle down: if money, advantages, profits etc trickle down from the richest people in society to the poor, some of the money etc passes slowly to the poor people ► *The idea is that if tax breaks are given to the wealthy, the benefits will trickle down to lower income groups.*

TRIFLE

TRIFLE WITH →

trifle with sb/sth: to treat a person or their feelings without respect ▶ *He was not a man to be trifled with.*

TRIGGER

TRIGGER OFF →

trigger off sth, **trigger** sth **off**: to make something start ▶ *the events which triggered off the First World War* ▶ *Stress can trigger off a number of illnesses, such as heart disease or diabetes.*

TRIM

TRIM OFF →

trim off sth, **trim** sth **off**: to cut small pieces off something because they are not needed ▶ *Cut the chicken into thin strips and trim off any fat.*

TRIP

TRIP OUT →

trip out, trip sb **out**: if you trip out, or something trips you out, it seems very strange or surprising to you ▶ *I started saying some things in Russian, and she just tripped out.* ▶ *The whole thing is so weird, it really trips me out.*

TRIP OVER →

trip over sth, **trip over**: to fall or nearly fall because you hit your foot against something on the ground ▶ *Lily lost her balance, tripped over and landed in a pile of leaves.*

TRIP UP →

1 trip up, trip sb **up, trip** sb **up**: to fall or nearly fall, especially because you hit your foot against something on the ground, or to make someone do this ▶ *The path's very uneven – careful you don't trip up.*
▶ *Someone put out a foot and tripped the boy up as he was trying to escape.*

2a. trip sb **up, trip up** sb: to deliberately cause someone to make a mistake, especially

by making them say something that they did not intend to say ▶ *I wondered why the police had asked me that again. Were they trying to trip me up?*

b. trip up: to make a mistake, especially by saying something that you did not intend to say ▶ *Sally realized that she would have to be more careful, or she could easily trip up.*

TRIUMPH

TRIUMPH OVER →

triumph over sth/sb: to succeed in defeating something or someone ▶ *In 1984 Detroit triumphed over their main rivals, the San Diego Padres.*

TROT

TROT OUT →

trot out sth, **trot** sth **out**: to repeat something without thinking about it and without being sincere ▶ *I couldn't believe it when she trotted out the same old excuse again.*

TRUMP

TRUMP UP →

trump up sth, **trump** sth **up**: to invent information or facts in order to make someone seem guilty of a crime ▶ *The whole thing was trumped up by the authorities in order to shut him up.*

> **trumped-up** ADJ invented in order to make someone seem guilty of a crime ▶ *trumped-up charges*

TRUST

TRUST IN →
1 trust in sb: to feel confident that you can trust someone ▶ *You know you can trust in me.*

2 trust in sth: to feel confident that something is good, right etc and will be successful ▶ *None of us know what the future will be like, but we have to trust in our own ability to deal with it.*

TRUST TO →
trust to sth: to depend on something to help you do something ▶ *It is important to check the information first and not trust to memory.*

TRUST WITH →
trust sb **with** sth: to depend on someone to look after something carefully or deal with it in a sensible way ▶ *I could never trust Jeff with money – he just went out and spent it all on beer.*

TRY

TRY ON →
1 try sth **on, try on** sth: to put on a piece of clothing to see if it fits you or to see if you like it ▶ *I spent two hours trying on every coat in the shop, but none of them were just right.*

2 try it on: to deliberately behave in a way that you know is not acceptable, in order to see whether someone will try to stop you ▶ *Jake turned up uninvited at the last party, and he might try it on again this time.* **+ with** ▶ *Kids always try it on with a new teacher – so don't worry about that.*

TRY OUT →
1 try out sth, **try** sth **out**: to use something for the first time in order to see whether it works well, or whether you like it ▶ *Doctors are trying out a new vaccine which it is claimed may help prevent cancer.* **+ on** ▶ *The recipe sounded delicious, so I thought I'd try it out on my boyfriend.*

2 try out sth, **try** sth **out**: to practise something in order to try to improve it ▶ *If we went to France, it would give you the opportunity to try out your French.*

3 try sb **out, try out** sb: to get someone to do some work for you for a short time before deciding whether to employ them permanently ▶ *We'll try you out for a couple of weeks, and if you work well you can stay.*

4 try out: to compete or perform in front of a group of people who decide who should be chosen for a team, play, performance etc. **+ for** ▶ *She's currently trying out for a part in the new James Bond film.*

TUCK

TUCK AWAY →
1 be tucked away: to be in a quiet area where very few people go ▶ *The hotel is tucked away in a quiet little side street.*

2 be tucked away: to be kept hidden somewhere secret ▶ *The key to the cellar was kept tucked away behind some old books.*

3 tuck sth **away, tuck away** sth: to put something in a safe or secret place ▶ *His fingers touched the wallet, now tucked away in his inner pocket.*

TUCK IN →
1 tuck sb **in**: to make someone, especially a child, feel comfortable in bed by pulling the  sheets and blankets firmly around them ▶ *Adam took the little girl back to bed, tucked her in and kissed her goodnight.*

2 tuck sth **in, tuck in** sth: to push the

end of a piece of clothing, sheet, blanket etc inside or under something, in order to make it look tidy or stay in place ▶ *He stood up, tucking his shirt in at the waist and reaching for his tie.*

3 tuck in: to start eating something with enjoyment ▶ *The waiter brought our meal and we all tucked in.* **tuck in!** (=used when you want to tell people to start eating) ▶ *Come on, everyone, tuck in!*

TUCK INTO →

tuck into sth: to start eating something with enjoyment ▶ *We tucked into a delicious meal of steak, chips, and ice-cream.*

TUCK UP →

tuck sb **up**: to make someone, especially a child, feel comfortable in bed, by pulling the sheets etc firmly around them. **be tucked up in bed** ▶ *When all the children were tucked up in bed, we sat down and opened a bottle of wine.*

TUG

TUG AT →

1 tug at sth: to pull something quickly and strongly ▶ *We all tugged at the rope, but the boat refused to move an inch.*

2 tug at sb's **sleeve** also **tug at** sb's **arm**: to pull someone's clothes or arm several times to try and attract their attention ▶ *"Mister," Willie said tugging at Tom's coat sleeve, "Mister, what's that?"*

3 tug at sb's **heart** also **tug at** sb's **heartstrings**: to have a strong effect on someone's emotions ▶ *a very sad story that really tugs at your heartstrings.*

TUMBLE

TUMBLE DOWN →

1 tumble down: if a wall or building tumbles down, it falls to the ground

and is destroyed. **come tumbling down** ▶ *Do you remember the excitement there was when the Berlin Wall came tumbling down?*

tumbledown ADJ a tumbledown building is old and in such bad condition that parts of it are falling down ▶ *There was a tumbledown shed at the bottom of the garden.*

2 tumble down: to be destroyed or fail, and no longer exist. **your world is tumbling down** (=a lot of bad things happen to you and you feel very shocked or upset) ▶ *She felt her world was tumbling down around her.* **come tumbling down** ▶ *Many old prejudices came tumbling down in the 1960s.*

TUNE

TUNE IN →

1 tune in: to listen to or watch a particular programme on radio or television ▶ *More than 3.5 billion people are expected to tune in for the opening of the Olympic Games.* **+ to** ▶ *If it's Saturday afternoon, he'll probably be tuned in to the football on TV.*

2 be tuned in: to understand what other people are thinking or feeling ▶ *As a character, John is very sensitive and tuned in.* **+ to** ▶ *We must be more tuned in to our customers' needs.*

3 tune in: if you tune in to other people's feelings, ideas, needs etc, you have a good understanding of them. **+ to** ▶ *The best way to encourage your child is to tune in to his or her interests.*

TUNE INTO →

1 tune into sth: to listen to or watch a particular programme on radio or television ▶ *Last week, 4.3 million people tuned into "The Late Show".*

2 be tuned into sb/sth: to understand someone's feelings or ideas very well

▶ *It can be difficult for society to stay tuned into the needs of young people.*

TUNE OUT →

tune out sth, **tune** sth **out**, **tune out**: to ignore something or stop listening to it ▶ *We hope that people won't start tuning out warnings about the virus because they've heard it all before.*

TUNE UP →

tune up, tune up sth, **tune** sth **up**: to prepare to play a musical instrument by making changes to it until it produces the correct notes ▶ *The band were tuning up their guitars backstage, getting ready for the concert.*

TURF

TURF OUT →

turf sb **out**, **turf** sth **out**: to force someone to leave a place or an organization ▶ *If you don't get out of bed soon, I'll come and turf you out!* **+ of** ▶ *At half past eleven the landlord turfed us out of the pub.*

TURN

TURN AGAINST →

1 turn against sth/sb: to stop liking or supporting someone or something ▶ *He was never sure why the man had turned against him.* ▶ *By now it was clear that public opinion had turned against the Republicans.*

2 turn sb **against** sb/sth: to influence a person so that they do not like or support someone or something any more ▶ *If you give kids books that are too advanced, it can turn them against reading for life.*

TURN AROUND, *also* **TURN ROUND** →

1 turn around/round, turn sb/sth **around/round**: to turn so that you are facing in the opposite direction, or to make something do this ▶ *Simpson turned around in his chair and looked*

out of the window. ▶ *Can you help me turn the sofa round?*

2 turn sth **around/round, turn around/round** sth: to make a business, organization, economy etc successful again after it has been unsuccessful ▶ *A new management team was brought in to turn the company around.* **turn things around** ▶ *I'm sure if we get the right sort of financial backing we can turn things round.*

3 turn around/round and ...: used to say that someone suddenly does something that is unexpected or unreasonable ▶ *You can't tell other people what to do, and then turn around and say that you aren't going to do it yourself.*

4 turn sth **around/round**: to consider something in a different way ▶ *You can of course turn the whole idea around and look at it from another angle.*

5 turn around/round sth, **turn** sth **around/round**: to complete the process of making a product or providing a service ▶ *We guarantee we can turn your order around in under a month.*

TURN AWAY →

1 turn sb **away, turn away** sb: to not allow someone to enter a place ▶ *The guy at the desk turned me away because I didn't have a membership card.*

2 turn sb **away, turn away** sb: to refuse to help someone when they ask for help ▶ *When a member of your own family asks you for money, you can't just turn them away.*

TURN AWAY FROM →

1 turn away from sth/sb: to stop supporting someone, or stop using or being interested in something ▶ *A lot of teachers are turning away from traditional teaching methods.*

2 turn sb away from sth/sb: to make someone stop supporting someone or stop using or being interested in something ► *It was feared that foreign influences might turn the people away from their religion.*

TURN BACK →

1 turn back: to start going back in the direction that you came from ► *The Captain had been advised to turn back, due to very bad weather conditions.*

2 turn sb back, turn back sb: to make someone go back in the direction they came from ► *Police used tear gas to turn back demonstrators who marched towards the Palace.*

3 turn back: if you cannot turn back, you cannot change your plans and do something different. **can't turn back** ► *We've already spent so much money that we can't turn back.* **there's no turning back** ► *Stubbs nervously accepted the offer, realizing that there was no turning back now.*

4 turn back the clock also **turn the clock back**: to try to go back to past ways of doing things or to the attitudes that existed in the past ► *He was accused of wanting to turn back the clocks to the 1950s, when most women didn't work outside the home.*

5 turn back sth, **turn** sth **back**: to fold over one part of a piece of paper or material ► *Mel turned back the corner of the page, closed the book and lay down.*

TURN DOWN →

1 turn sth **down, turn down** sth: to reduce the amount of sound, heat etc produced by a machine such as a radio or a cooker ► *Could you turn that music down – we can't hear ourselves speak!* ► *After half an hour, turn the oven down to a low heat.*

2 turn down sth/sb, **turn** sth/sb **down**: to decide not to accept an offer or an opportunity to do something ► *Nowadays some men are turning down promotion in order to give more time to their families.*

3 turn down sb/sth, **turn** sb/sth **down**: to refuse to do what someone asks or suggests ► *At the end of the evening the committee voted on the proposal and turned it down.*

TURN IN →

1 turn in sth, **turn** sth **in**: to give something to a person in authority so that they can deal with it ► *The security forces arrested three hundred rebels and ordered them to turn in their weapons.*

2 turn in sb, **turn** sb **in**: to tell the police where a criminal is, or to take a criminal to the police ► *One of the other gang members turned him in.* **turn yourself in** (=go to the police and admit that you are responsible for a crime) ► *Smithson finally turned himself in, saying he deeply regretted what he had done.*

3 turn sth **in, turn in** sth: to give a finished piece of work to a teacher or manager ► *Only 17 students turned their papers in on time.*

4 turn in: to go to bed ► *Well, I think I'll turn in now – I have to get up early tomorrow.*

TURN INTO →

1 turn into sth/sb: to change and become a different type of thing or person ► *It started off as a dream, but quickly turned into a nightmare.* ► *When I saw him again, he'd lost a lot of weight and turned into a really good-looking boy.*

2 turn sth **into** sth: to change something so that it becomes a different thing or is used in a different way ► *The old barn next to the manor house had been turned into flats for old people.*

3 turn sb into sb: to change someone's life so that they become a different type of person ▶ *The film turned him into a huge star overnight.*

TURN OFF →

1 turn off sth, turn sth off: to make a light, machine, or engine stop working, or to stop a flow of gas, water, or electricity ▶ *Don't forget to turn off all the lights when you go to bed.* ▶ *Can you turn the tap off for me?*

2 turn off sth, turn off: to leave the road or path that you are going along, and start going along another ▶ *Stephen turned off the main road into an almost empty side-street.* ▶ *I'm sure we should have turned off at the last exit.*

turn-off N a road which leads off another, usually bigger, road ▶ *Go slowly or we'll miss the turn-off.*

3 turn sb off, turn off sb, turn sb off sth: to make someone decide that they do not like something or are not interested in it ▶ *I loved the house from the outside, but the decoration inside really turned me off.*

turn-off N something that you do not like, because you find it boring or unpleasant ▶ *Having to learn all the history of the place was a real turn-off.*

TURN ON →

1 turn on sth, turn sth on: to make a light, machine, or engine start working, or start the flow of gas, water, or electricity ▶ *I turned on the radio and listened to the six o' clock news.* ▶ *Could you turn the oven on, if you're going in the kitchen?*

2 turn on sth, turn sth on: to start using a particular way of speaking or behaving, especially when you are not being sincere. **turn it on** ▶ *Craig's brilliant at entertaining people – he*

can turn it on whenever he wants. **turn on the charm** ▶ *"Come in, have a drink," he said, smiling at her and turning on the charm.*

3 turn sb on, turn on sb: to interest or excite someone ▶ *Crime fiction just doesn't turn me on.*

TURN ON, *also* TURN UPON →

1 turn on/upon sb: to suddenly attack someone, either physically or with unpleasant words, especially when it is very unexpected ▶ *We watched in horror as the dog turned on the little girl.* ▶ *Peter turned on Rae, screaming, "Get out of my sight!"*

2 turn on/upon sth: to depend on something in order to be successful or work well ▶ *The whole future of the company turns on the success of this one product.*

3 turn sth on/upon sb: to suddenly aim something such as a gun, a light, or an angry look at someone ▶ *I was terrified she would turn the gun on me.*

TURN ON TO →

turn sb on to sth: to make someone start to like something or become interested in it ▶ *It was a neighbour of mine, a professor, who turned me on to modern art.*

TURN OUT →

1 turn out the light *also* turn the light out: to make an electric light stop working, by pressing a switch ▶ *Don't forget to turn out the lights when you come to bed.*

2 turn out: to happen in a particular way or have a particular result. **turn out fine/well** ▶ *Don't worry about the interview, it'll all turn out fine.* **turn out to be** ▶ *The holiday turned out to be the best we've ever had.*

3 turn out: if something turns out to be true, it is true, although this is surprising. **it turns out (that)** ▶ *It* *turned out that every one of the students in the room had tried cannabis.* **as it turned out** ► *As it turned out, Jane knew all about the affair anyway.*

4 turn out: if a child turns out in a particular way, that is the type of person they become ► *The Hedges were such an odd family, but all of the children had turned out perfectly normal.* **turn out to be** ► *Although very shy as a child, he eventually turned out to be a natural leader.*

5 turn out: if people turn out for an event, they go to watch it or take part in it ► *On Saturday only a few hundred people turned out to see the game.*

turn-out N the number of people who come to watch an event or take part in it ► *The turnout for the election was about 70%.*

6 turn out sth, **turn** sth **out**: to make or produce something, especially in large quantities ► *The new factory will turn out 100,000 pick-up trucks a year.*

7 turn sb **out**, **turn out** sb: to force someone to leave a place, especially a place where they are living ► *The building was sold, and hundreds of homeless people were turned out on to the streets.* **+ of** ► *Many farm workers lived in fear of being turned out of their homes.*

8 turn out sth, **turn** sth **out**: to empty a pocket, a cupboard, or other container in order to clean it or see what is in it ► *The teacher told us to turn out our pockets.*

9 be well/beautifully etc turned out: to be wearing attractive, neat, or expensive clothes ► *The music was wonderful and the choir was beautifully turned out.*

TURN OVER →

1 turn over, turn over sb, **turn** sb **over**: to move so that you are facing in a different direction when you are lying down, or to move someone so that they do this ► *Patrick turned over in bed and switched off the light.* ► *The nurses gently turned her over and straightened out the sheets.*

2 turn over sth, **turn** sth **over**: to move something so that you can use, look at, or listen to the other side of it ► *Could you turn over the cassette?*

3 turn over, turn sth **over**: to change to a different programme on the television, by pressing a button ► *The film was so boring that we turned over half way through.* ► *Do you mind if I turn the TV over to watch the news?*

4 turn over sb, **turn** sb **over**: to take a criminal to the police, or to tell the police where a criminal is. **+ to** ► *The FBI caught Rostov and turned him over to the CIA.*

5 turn sth/sb **over, turn over** sth/sb: to give something or someone to a person in authority so that they can deal with them or be responsible for them. **+ to** ► *The government seems to want to turn much of public health care over to the private sector.*

6 turn over sth, **turn over** sth: to give something such as a business or a piece of property to someone. **+ to** ► *I expect Mr Busby will turn the shop over to his son when he retires.*

7 turn over sth, **turn** sth **over**: if a business turns over an amount of money, it makes that amount in a particular period of time ► *The new company turned over £500,000 in its first year.*

turnover N the total amount of money made by a business in a particular period of time ▶ *an annual turnover of £5.6 million*

8 turn sth **over, turn over** sth: to think carefully about something in order to understand it better. **turn** sth **over in your mind** ▶ *I turned his final words over in my mind, unsure of what he had meant.*

9 turn sth **over**: to search a place thoroughly, or to steal things from it ▶ *The police went in and turned the whole house over to see if there were any drugs.* **turn the place over** ▶ *We came back from holiday to find the place had been turned over.*

TURN OVER TO →

turn sth **over to** sth, **turn over** sth **to** sth: to start to use a building or a piece of land for a particular purpose ▶ *From that time on, more and more of the land was turned over to sugarcane production.*

TURN ROUND *see* TURN AROUND

TURN TO →

1 turn to sb: to go to someone for advice, sympathy, or help ▶ *I felt very alone at that time – there was no one I could turn to.* **turn to religion** ▶ *Many people turn to religion during difficult periods in their lives.*

2 turn to drugs/crime etc: to start doing something bad ▶ *The scheme could give jobs to thousands of youngsters who might otherwise turn to crime.*

3 turn to sth: to start a new type of work or habit ▶ *Apparently more and more people are turning to vegetarianism each year.*

4 turn to sth, **turn** sth **to** sth: to start talking, thinking, or writing about a particular subject ▶ *The speaker then turned to other aspects of society, including the home and family.* **turn**

your attention/efforts etc to sth ▶ *She turned her attention to the paper on her desk.* **a conversation turns to** sth (=it starts to be about a particular subject) ▶ *Eventually the conversation turned to the subject of money.*

TURN UP →

1 turn up sth, **turn** sth **up**: to increase the amount of sound, heat etc produced by a machine such as a radio, heater, or cooker ▶ *It's really cold in here. Can you turn up the heating?* ▶ *She was in the bathroom with the radio turned up to full volume.*

2 turn up: to arrive somewhere, especially when you are expected ▶ *Rachel knew that Ross would be very worried if she didn't turn up.* **+ for** ▶ *In the end, only nineteen competitors turned up for the race.*

3 turn up: if something that is lost or missing turns up, someone finds it ▶ *I haven't found your watch yet, but I'm sure it will turn up sooner or later.*

4 turn up sth, **turn** sth **up**: to find something by searching thoroughly for it ▶ *A search by the state police and FBI failed to turn up anything suspicious.*

5 turn up: if a job or an opportunity turns up, it becomes available ▶ *Don't worry, I'm sure a job will turn up soon.*

TURN UPON *see* TURN ON

TYPE

TYPE IN, *also* TYPE INTO →

type in sth, **type** sth **in**, **type** sth **into** sth: to put information into a computer by typing ▶ *Pulman sat down at his computer and quickly typed in his name.*

TYPE OUT →

type out sth, **type** sth **out**: to produce a copy of something that you have written, by typing it on a computer or a typewriter ▶ *Michael had typed the poem out and sent it to me, asking for my comments.*

TYPE UP →

type up sth, **type** sth **up**: to produce a neat or complete copy of something that someone has written by typing it on a computer or a typewriter ▶ *It was my job to attend all the meetings and to type up my notes from them afterwards.*

T

Uu

URGE

URGE ON →

urge sb **on, urge on** sb: to encourage someone to keep on making an effort or to keep on doing something ▶ *He heard Sarah's voice above the noise of the crowd, urging him on.* ▶ *Congress, urged on by Human Rights groups, was once again debating the abolition of the death penalty.*

URGE ON, *also* URGE UPON →

urge sth **on/upon** sb, **urge on/upon** sb sth: to try to persuade someone that they must do something or must behave in a particular way ▶ *UN advisors were urging caution upon those countries preparing for war.*

USE

USE UP →

use up sth, **use** sth **up**: to use all of something so that there is none left ▶ *I had already used up the film in both my cameras.* ▶ *We used up all our money in the first week of the holiday.*

USHER

USHER IN →

usher in sth: to cause something new to start, or to exist at the start of something new ▶ *The discovery of oil ushered in a new era of employment and prosperity.*

U

Vv

VAMP

VAMP UP →

vamp up sth, **vamp** sth **up**: to try to make something seem new or more exciting by changing it or adding things to it ▶ *songs from the sixties that have been vamped up for today's audiences* ▶ *Writers have been told to vamp up the story line, or the show will be scrapped.*

VEER OFF

VEER OFF →

veer off: to suddenly go in a completely different direction ▶ *At that point the road veered off towards the left.*

VEG

VEG OUT →

veg out: to relax and do nothing when you are feeling lazy or very tired ▶ *When I go home after work I normally just veg out in front of the TV.*

VERGE

VERGE ON, *also* VERGE UPON →

verge on/upon sth: to be almost the same as an extreme feeling, quality, or situation ▶ *He thought her behaviour was verging on insanity.* **be verging on the impossible/ridiculous etc** (=be very close to being impossible, ridiculous etc) ▶ *Property prices here are verging on the ridiculous.*

VEST

BE VESTED IN →

be vested in sb/sth: if power is vested in a person or group, they officially or legally have that power ▶ *Executive authority is vested in a Governor, who is elected for a four-year term.*

VISIT

VISIT ON, *also* VISIT UPON →

visit sth **on/upon** sb/sth: to cause something very unpleasant or harmful to happen to someone or something ▶ *the terrible suffering that was being visited upon the people*

VISIT WITH →

visit with sb: to spend time talking to someone in a friendly way ▶ *Joe had a chance to visit with his old friend Logan while he was in Maryland.*

VOTE

VOTE DOWN →

vote sth **down**, **vote down** sth: to decide not to accept an idea or plan by voting ▶ *The proposal to build a sports stadium on the site was voted down.*

VOTE IN, *also* VOTE INTO →

vote sb/sth **in**, **vote in** sb/sth, **vote** sb/sth **into**: to give someone enough votes in an election for them to win an official position of power ▶ *The Democrats were voted in by a big majority.* **be voted into office** ▶ *He soon gained the support of the electors and was voted into office.*

VOTE OUT →

vote sb/sth **out**, **vote out** sb/sth: to not give someone enough votes in an election for them to stay in their official position of power ▶ *She was voted out as director, after a disagreement with the management board.* **be voted out of office** ▶ *He was voted out of office on February 25th.*

VOTE THROUGH →

vote through sth, **vote** sth **through**: to officially approve a law or plan by voting to accept it ▶ *The law, banning traffic from the city centre, was voted through six days ago.*

V

VOUCH

VOUCH FOR →

1 vouch for sth: to say that you know for certain that something is true, real, or of a high standard ▶ *Les knows the builders personally and can vouch for their reliability.* ▶ *Several people were prepared to vouch for what Becky was saying.*

2 vouch for sb: to say that you know someone personally and can promise that they have a good character ▶ *John was refused entrance to the club, until somebody arrived who could vouch for him.*

Ww

WADE

WADE IN →
wade in: to become involved in a situation, especially in a way that annoys people ▶ *I can't just wade in there and start telling her how she should bring up her own children.*

WADE THROUGH →
wade through sth: to spend a lot of time reading or dealing with something that seems very long and boring ▶ *You have to wade through pages and pages of advertisements before you can find anything interesting to read.*

WAFFLE

WAFFLE ON →
waffle on: to talk or write using a lot of words, without saying anything important ▶ *I asked for a pay rise, but he just waffled on without giving me a straight answer.* **+ about** ▶ *What's he waffling on about now?*

WAIT

WAIT AROUND, *also* **WAIT ABOUT →**
wait around / about: to stay in the same place and do nothing while you are waiting for something to happen, someone to arrive etc ▶ *We had to wait around for hours at the airport while they got the plane ready.* ▶ *Sorry to keep you waiting around. I'll be back in a minute.*

WAIT BEHIND →
wait behind: to stay somewhere after the other people have left ▶ *Jonathan asked her to wait behind after the meeting.*

WAIT IN →
wait in: to stay at home and wait for

someone to arrive ▶ *They said they'd deliver the computer yesterday. I waited in all day but no one came.*

WAIT ON →
1 wait on: to bring someone everything they want or need, or do everything for someone ▶ *The princess was accustomed*

to being waited on by a team of maids and servants. **wait on** sb **hand and foot** (=bring someone everything they want) ▶ *My last boyfriend expected to be waited on hand and foot.*

2 wait on sb: to serve food and drink to someone, especially in a restaurant ▶ *Tammy was waiting on a group of noisy teenagers.*

3 wait on sb: to sell goods to someone in a shop ▶ *For five years he waited on customers in the family grocery store.*

4 wait on sth: to wait for a result or decision, especially before deciding what to do next ▶ *We're still waiting on the results of the blood test.*

WAIT OUT →
wait out sth, **wait** sth **out:** to wait until something unpleasant has finished ▶ *Jim and Huck waited out the storm in a cave on Jackson's island.*

WAIT UP →
1 wait up: to wait and not go to bed until someone comes back home ▶ *We waited up all night, but she didn't appear till the following day.* **+ for** ▶ *Don't wait up for me. I'll probably be late.*

2 wait up!: used in order to tell someone to stop because you want to talk to them or go somewhere with

W

them ▶ *"Wait up!" Howard called to his sister. "Can I come too?"*

WAIT UPON →

1 wait upon sb: to bring someone everything they want or need ▶ *While we were guests, the Emperor's servants waited upon us, and obeyed our slightest wish.*

2 wait upon sth: to wait for a result or decision, especially before deciding what to do next ▶ *Congress must wait upon the decision of the Supreme Court before taking any further action.*

WAKE

WAKE UP →

1 wake up: to stop sleeping ▶ *I woke up at six o'clock this morning.* ▶ *She woke up to find that he had gone.*

2 wake up
sb, **wake** sb **up**:
to make
someone stop
sleeping, or
make someone
feel less sleepy
▶ *Can you wake*

me up at 7.30? ▶ *He was woken up by the sound of traffic outside his window.*

3 wake up: to start to listen or pay attention to something ▶ *Wake up! You almost hit that car!*

WAKE UP TO →

wake up to sth: to start to realize that something is important and pay attention to it ▶ *Employers are finally waking up to the fact that it's actually more productive to let people work from home.*

WALK

WALK ALL OVER →

walk all over sb: to treat someone ??ly, especially by always making ?? do what you want them to do ?? need to be quite firm with kids ??'ll walk all over you.

WALK AWAY →

1 walk away: to leave a bad situation and not stay and try to make it better ▶ *She can't just walk away after 15 years of marriage.* **+ from** ▶ *It's easy for you – you can just walk away from all this. I actually have to live here.*

2 walk away: to leave after an accident without having any serious injuries ▶ *Amazingly, both drivers walked away with only minor injuries.*

WALK AWAY WITH →

walk away with sth: to easily win a prize or competition ▶ *Most people thought last year's winner would walk away with the championship.*

WALK INTO →

1 walk into sth: to get a job very easily ▶ *People think that if you've been to Oxford University you can just walk into any job you want.*

2 walk into sth: to become involved in an unpleasant or dangerous situation without intending to ▶ *Without realising it, they had walked into a fight between two rival drug gangs.*

WALK OFF →

walk off, walk off sth: to walk away and leave a person or place, especially in a way that shows you are annoyed ▶ *She turned and walked off without saying goodbye.* ▶ *He walked off the court in protest at the umpire's decision.*

WALK OFF WITH →

1 walk off with sth: to win something easily, for example a prize or competition ▶ *Our cricket team walked off with the championship.*

2 walk off with sth: to steal something or take something from someone without asking their permission ▶ *Someone's just walked off with my drink.*

W

WALK OUT →

1 walk out: to leave a performance or meeting before the end, because you do not like it or because you feel annoyed about something ▶ *Several people walked out halfway through the film because they thought it was too violent.* **+ of** ▶ *He walked out of talks with the club manager after an argument over money.*

2 walk out: to stop working in order to protest about something ▶ *Twenty staff walked out yesterday when a colleague was fired.*

    walk-out N when a group of workers stop working in order to protest about something ▶ *Car workers staged an unofficial walk-out in protest at the company's 2% pay offer.*

3 walk out: to leave your wife, boyfriend etc suddenly and end your relationship with them ▶ *His wife walked out after 20 years of marriage.*

WALK OUT ON →

1 walk out on sb: to leave your wife, boyfriend etc and end your relationship with them ▶ *Dorothy's first husband walked out on her, leaving her with three children.*

2 walk out on sb/sth: to not do something that you have agreed with someone to do ▶ *You're not going to walk out on the deal, are you?* ▶ *We'd be completely stuck if she decided to walk out on us now.*

WALK THROUGH →

walk sb **through** sth: to explain something to someone slowly and carefully so that they understand it completely ▶ *The software has a beginner's tutorial that will walk you through the basic techniques and processes.*

WALL

WALL IN →

1 wall in sth, **wall** sth **in**: to surround an area with a wall ▶ *Part of the garden had been walled in to make a sheltered spot.*

2 wall in sth/sb, **wall** sth/sb **in**: to surround an area or person ▶ *The grey tower blocks walled in the space completely.*

WALL OFF →

1 wall off sth, **wall** sth **off**: to separate an area from another area with a wall ▶ *The garden was walled off to protect it from the wind.*

2 wall off sb/sth, **wall** sb/sth **off**: to keep someone or something completely separate from other people, things, countries etc ▶ *It had clearly been Dad's intention to wall off his past entirely.*

WALL UP →

wall up sth, **wall** sth **up**: to fill an entrance, window etc with bricks, stone etc so that it is completely blocked ▶ *The only doorway had been walled up long ago.* ▶ *Two of the windows were walled up, and there was very little natural light.*

WALLOW

WALLOW IN →

1 wallow in self-pity/misery etc: to seem to enjoy feelings of great self-pity, unhappiness etc ▶ *I'd feel more sympathy for her if she'd stop wallowing in her own self-pity.*

2 wallow in luxury etc: to enjoy being in a place that is very comfortable and expensive ▶ *I was sheltered from the more unpleasant aspects of city life, wallowing in the luxury of the Savoy Hotel.*

WALTZ

WALTZ OFF WITH →

waltz off with sth: to take something

W

without the owner's permission
▶ *While they were at the airport someone had waltzed off with their guitars.*

WALTZ THROUGH →
waltz through sth: to succeed in doing something very easily, especially passing a test, course etc ▶ *The first women Royal Marines recruits have waltzed through their military training.*

WANDER

WANDER OFF →
wander off: to leave the place where you are supposed to be, or the person you are with, without saying where you are going ▶ *Sometimes he just wanders off for days on end and we have no idea where he is.*

WANT

WANT FOR →
not want for anything *also* **want for nothing**: to have everything that you need ▶ *I have worked long and hard to make sure that my children want for nothing.* **not want for money/food etc** ▶ *The girl won't want for money – her wealthy uncle will see to that.*

WANT OUT →
1 want out: to want to stop being involved in something you are already involved in ▶ *Three months after Josh joined the gang, he wanted out.* **+ of** ▶ *Brown says he wants out of the Boston team.*

2 want out: to want to leave a place ▶ *Excuse me, I want out, please.* **+ of** ▶ *I want out of this bar – it's way too crowded in here!*

WARD

WARD OFF →
ward off sth, **ward** sth **off**: to prevent something from harming you, or prevent a disease from affecting you ▶ *masks are used to ward off evil*

spirits. ▶ *He takes aspirin daily to ward off heart disease.*

WARM

WARM TO, *also* **WARM UP TO** →
1 warm to sth, **warm up to** sth: to become more interested in something, be more williing to do something, be more attracted to something etc ▶ *Mark soon warmed to the task and continued with renewed confidence.* ▶ *Voters are starting to warm up to the idea.*

2 warm to sb, **warm up to** sb: to start to like someone ▶ *I was nervous about meeting his kids at first, but I warmed to them immediately.*

WARM THROUGH →
warm sth **through**: to heat food gently until it is warm ▶ *Stir for 5 minutes until the vegetables are warmed through.*

WARM UP →
1 warm up, warm up sb/sth, **warm** sb/sth **up**: to become warmer, or make something or someone warmer ▶ *In spring the weather soon starts to warm up.* ▶ *I tried running down the road to warm myself up.*

2 warm up sth, **warm** sth **up, warm up**: to heat food, especially food that has already been cooked, so that it is hot enough to eat, or to become hot enough to eat ▶ *She put the lasagne in the oven to warm it up.* ▶ *Do you want me to warm up some soup for you?*

3 warm up: to do gentle physical exercises to prepare your body just before playing a sport, dancing etc ▶ *The athletes are warming up for the race.*

W

warm-up N when you do gentle physical exercises to prepare your body just before playing a sport, dancing etc ▶ *The players were doing some stretching exercises as a warm-up.*

4 warm up, warm up sth, **warm sth up:** if an engine, computer, machine etc warms up, or you warm it up, it starts to be ready to work properly ▶ *He waited for the photocopier to warm up.*

5 warm up, warm up sth, **warm sth up:** to practise something for a short time before a performance ▶ *The band had very little time to warm up before they went on stage.*

warm-up N when musicians, singers, or performers practise just before a performance ▶ *After a quick warm-up the guys were ready to go on stage.*

6 warm up: if a situation or an event such as a party warms up, it becomes more exciting, enjoyable, etc ▶ *After midnight, things started to warm up and the party really got going.*

WARM UP TO *see* WARM TO

WARN

WARN AGAINST →
warn against sth, **warn sb against** sth: to tell someone that they should not do something because it may be dangerous or cause something bad to happen ▶ *Her financial adviser warned her against such a risky investment.*
warn (sb) against doing sth
▶ *Pregnant women have been warned against using the drug.*

WARN OFF →
1 warn off sb, **warn sb off:** to tell people that they should not go near something, especially because it may be dangerous ▶ *The army had put up signs warning people off.* ▶ *Some*

animals mark their territory to warn off rivals.

2 warn sb **off, warn** sb **off** sth, **warn off** sb: to tell someone that they should not do something because it may be dangerous or harmful ▶ *The actor has been warned off alcohol after a health scare.* **warn** sb **off doing** sth ▶ *Doctors should have warned people off using the drug much earlier.*

WASH

WASH AWAY →
wash away sth, **wash sth away:** if water washes something away, it carries it away, usually with a lot of force ▶ *The water rushed down the narrow streets, washing away cars like matchsticks.*

WASH DOWN →
1 wash down sth, **wash sth down:** to clean all of the surface of something, for example a car or a wall, using water ▶ *He washed the car down, dried it, and then waxed it.*

2 wash sth **down, wash sth down** sth: to drink something with or after food, or with medicine to help you swallow it ▶ *They ate pasta, washed down with several bottles of cheap Italian wine.*

WASH OFF →
a. wash off sth, **wash sth off, wash sth off:** to remove dirt or other unwanted substances from the surface of something using water ▶ *Your hands are covered in oil – you'd better go upstairs and wash it off.*
b. wash off: if something such as dirt or a mark on the surface of something washes off, it is removed by washing ▶ *Don't worry about the stain. It'll easily wash off.*

WASH OUT →
1 wash out sth, **wash sth out:** to quickly wash the inside of a cup or a container in order to clean it ▶ *Hannah*

washed out the vases and filled them with fresh flowers.

2 wash out, wash out sth, **wash** sth **out**: if something such as dirt or a mark washes out or if you wash it out, it is removed by washing ▶ *Emulsion paint can easily be washed out.*

3 be washed out: if a game or other event is washed out, it cannot take place because of rain ▶ *England's first match against Australia was washed out.*

washout N when a game or other event cannot take place or continue because of rain ▶ *The first day at Wimbledon was a washout.*

4 be washed out: to be very tired and have no energy ▶ *You'd better sit down and have a rest. You look washed out.*

WASH OVER →

1 wash over sb: if a feeling washes over you, you suddenly feel it very strongly ▶ *A sudden wave of anger washed over her.*

2 let sth **wash over you**: if you let something wash over you, you relax and enjoy it ▶ *She lay back and closed her eyes, letting the music wash over her.*

WASH UP →

**1 wash up,
wash up** sth,
wash sth **up**: to wash plates,
dishes, knives
etc, especially
after a meal

▶ *Since you made lunch, I'll wash up.* ▶ *Ruth was helping behind the bar, washing up the glasses.*

washing-up N if you do the washing-up, you wash plates, dishes, knives etc, especially after a meal ▶ *Susan was in the kitchen doing the washing-up.*

2 wash up: to wash your hands, especially before eating ▶ *Go wash up, boys. It's almost dinner time.*

3 wash up sth, **wash** sth **up**, **wash up**: if the sea washes something up, it carries it to the shore and leaves it there ▶ *Her body was found washed up on a Moroccan beach.*

4 be washed up: if someone is washed up, they are no longer successful in their life or their job ▶ *The former star said he knew he was washed up when no one seemed to recognize him anymore.*

WASTE

WASTE AWAY →

1 waste away: to become very thin and weak ▶ *By this time she couldn't stand or walk. She was wasting away.* ▶ *I'm only allowed one meal a day on this diet. I'm wasting away!*

2 waste away: to feel very bored and unhappy because your skills and abilities are not being used ▶ *One unemployed man said "It's not just the money. Work gives you something to do. I feel I'm just wasting away."*

3 waste away: to gradually become smaller or weaker and disappear ▶ *If you don't use your muscles, they begin to waste away.*

WATCH

WATCH FOR →

watch for sth: to pay attention in order to notice something if or when it happens ▶ *The police hid in the bushes, watching for drug smugglers trying to cross the border.*

WATCH OUT →

watch out: to be careful and pay attention because something bad may happen ▶ *"Watch out!" whispered Daniel, as their teacher appeared at the door.*

W

WATCH OUT FOR →

1 watch out for sth/sb: to be careful to notice something or someone because they could be dangerous, could cause problems etc ▶ *Watch out for thieves when you're travelling on the underground.*

2 watch out for sth: to be careful to notice something because it may be interesting, exciting, or useful ▶ *Watch out for the band's new record, which is climbing up the UK charts.*

WATCH OVER →

1 watch over sb/sth: to guard or take care of someone or something ▶ *The two policemen took it in turns to watch over him.*

2 watch over sb/sth: to watch and make sure that someone behaves properly or something happens in the correct way ▶ *Today there was no boss to watch over him, and he could do what he liked.*

WATER

WATER DOWN →

1 water down sth, **water** sth **down**: to change a plan, system, statement etc so that it is much less effective or powerful ▶ *The proposed reforms were watered down by the next parliament.*

2 water down sth, **water** sth **down**: to add water to alcoholic drinks and make them weaker ▶ *The bar staff aren't very friendly, and I'm sure they water down the beer.*

WAVE

WAVE ASIDE →

wave aside sth, **wave** sth **aside**: to refuse to accept what someone says, especially because you do not think it is important ▶ *The judge waved all their objections aside and sentenced them to three months in jail.*

WAVE DOWN →

wave down sth/sb, **wave** sth/sb

down: to make a vehicle stop by waving your arms at the driver ▶ *He raised his hand to wave the driver down.*

WAVE OFF →

wave sb **off**, **wave off** sb: to wave goodbye to someone as they leave ▶ *We all went down to the airport to wave her off.*

WAVE ON →

wave sb **on**, **wave on** sb: to wave your hands to tell someone to continue moving forwards ▶ *The guard looked at his papers, then waved him on.* ▶ *Police were waving the other drivers on.*

WAVE THROUGH →

wave sb **through**, **wave through** sb: to wave your hands to tell someone that they can go through or enter a place ▶ *The customs officer at the airport waved them straight through.*

WEAN

WEAN OFF →

wean sb **off** sth: to make someone stop using something that is harmful, by gradually reducing the amount that they can have ▶ *Dr Rossdale said he tried to wean her off the sleeping tablets.* ▶ *It is extremely difficult to wean a child off junk-food.*

BE WEANED ON →

be weaned on sth: to be strongly influenced by something because you experience it regularly when you are young ▶ *a generation weaned on TV and computer games*

WEAR

WEAR AWAY →

wear sth **away**, **wear away** sth, **wear away**: if something wears away or is worn away, it becomes thinner and gradually disappears because it has been used a lot or rubbed a lot ▶ *The mountain path has been worn away by*

W

tourists over the years. ► *The paint on the doors and windows has gradually worn away.*

WEAR DOWN →

1 wear sb **down, wear down** sb: to gradually make someone feel tired and less able or less determined to do something ► *Being constantly criticized really wears you down.*

2 wear down sth, **wear** sth **down, wear down**: if something is worn down, or wears down, it becomes thinner and smoother because something has been rubbing against it ► *Both my shoes have worn down at the heel.*
+ to ► *He was driving on a tyre that was worn right down to the bare canvas.*

WEAR IN →

wear in sth, **wear** sth **in**: to wear new boots or shoes for short periods of time until they become more comfortable ► *I'm not going on any long walks till I've worn in my new boots.*

WEAR OFF →

wear off: if a feeling or the effect of something wears off, it gradually becomes weaker and disappears ► *The effects of the anaesthetic were starting to wear off.* **the novelty wears off** (=you stop feeling excited about something because it is no longer new) ► *Would she become bored with married life once the novelty wore off?*

WEAR ON →

wear on: if a period of time wears on, it seems to pass very slowly ► *The night wore on, and still there was no sign of him.*

WEAR OUT →

1 wear out sth, **wear** sth **out, wear out**: if you wear out clothes, materials,

equipment etc, or if they wear out, they gradually become weak or damaged by being used a lot ► *After only a month Terry had worn out the soles of his shoes.* ► *When the motor wears out, it is easy to replace.*

  worn-out ADJ worn-out things have been used so much that they have become weak or damaged ► *the cost of replacing worn-out equipment*

2 wear sb **out, wear out** sb: to make someone feel extremely tired ► *Long hours of working in the hotel kitchen had worn her out.* **wear yourself out** ► *You must take a break sometimes – you'll wear yourself out.*

  worn out extremely tired ► *Come in and sit down. You look absolutely worn out.*

WEAR THROUGH →

wear through, wear through sth, **wear** sth **through**: if a piece of material wears through, or is worn through, a hole is gradually made in it ► *The soles of her boots were completely worn through.* **+ to** ► *In one place the carpeting had worn right through to the floorboards.*

WEASEL

WEASEL OUT →

weasel out: to not do something that you had agreed to or should do ► *Don't try to weasel out and say you don't remember the deal.* **+ of** ► *Fife is trying to weasel out of £25 million in debts.*

WED

BE WEDDED TO →

be wedded to sth: to believe strongly that a particular idea or way of doing something is right ► *The church remains firmly wedded to traditional moral values.*

WEDGE

BE WEDGED IN →

be wedged in: to be firmly stuck in a

small space ▶ *The injured driver was wedged in behind the steering-wheel.*

WEED

WEED OUT →
weed out sb/sth, **weed** sb/sth **out**: to get rid of unsuitable or unwanted people or things from a group ▶ *A committee was established to weed out corrupt party officials.* ▶ *First we need to weed out any data that is no longer valid.*

WEIGH

WEIGH AGAINST →
weigh sth **against** sth: to consider carefully whether one thing is more important or better than another, before making a decision ▶ *The potential benefits of nuclear power must be weighed against the risks.*

WEIGH DOWN →
1 weigh sb **down, weigh down** sb: if you are weighed down with something you are carrying, you cannot move easily because it is very heavy. **be weighed down with** ▶ *Sue and Brian staggered home, weighed down with shopping bags.*

2 weigh sb **down, weigh down** sb: if you are weighed down by problems, responsibilities etc, they make you feel very worried or unhappy ▶ *the terrible feeling of hopelessness that had been weighing her down ever since Howard died*

3 weigh down sth, **weigh** sth **down**: to prevent something from growing and being successful ▶ *a banking crisis that was weighing down the whole economy*

WEIGH IN →
1 weigh in: to add your own opinions, advice, suggestions etc to a discussion. **+ with** ▶ *Everyone weighed in with their own suggestions of who should captain the team.*

2 weigh in: to provide support in order to help make something successful. **+ with** ▶ *The striker weighed in with two fine goals to secure victory for Rovers.*

WEIGH INTO →
1 weigh into sb: to criticize someone very strongly ▶ *The senator's critics weighed into him with allegations about his business interests.*

2 weigh into sth: to start to take part in a discussion or argument by expressing your opinion very strongly ▶ *Churchill weighed into the debate with a speech that silenced all opposition.*

WEIGH ON →
1 weigh on sth: to have the effect of reducing prices, profits, values etc ▶ *Forecasts for warmer weather weighed on heating oil and gas prices.*

2 weigh on sth: to have the effect of making something less successful or less effective ▶ *Jack is so dedicated to his job that it's weighing on his marriage.*

WEIGH ON, *also* **WEIGH UPON** →
weigh on/upon sb: to make someone feel very worried ▶ *The question of her children's future constantly weighed on her.* **weigh on sb's mind** ▶ *Lisa's very quiet – I'm sure there's something weighing on her mind.*

WEIGH OUT →
weigh out sth, **weigh** sth **out**: to weigh an exact amount of something ▶ *I watched as he weighed out 200 grams of coffee beans.*

WEIGH UP →
1 weigh up sth, **weigh** sth **up**: to compare the advantages and disadvantages of a

W

situation, so that you can make a decision ▶ *After carefully weighing up the costs and benefits of using solar energy, the committee gave its approval.*

2 weigh sb **up, weigh up** sb: to pay attention to and think about someone carefully in order to form an opinion about them ▶ *I think we spent a little time weighing each other up before we became friends.*

WEIGH UPON *see* WEIGH ON

WELCH

WELCH ON, *also* WELSH ON →
welch on sth/sb: to not do something that you have promised to do ▶ *Clients are accusing them of welching on deals they had agreed on the telephone.*

WELL

WELL UP →

1 well up: if tears well up in your eyes, they come into your eyes ▶ *He turned away so that Anne would not see the tears that were welling up in his eyes.*

2 well up: to suddenly feel an emotion more strongly ▶ *Anger welled up inside him.*

3 well up: if liquid wells up, it rises to the surface with sudden force ▶ *Pools of crude oil welled up from the ground.*

WELSH

WELSH ON *see* WELCH ON

WHALE

WHALE ON →

whale on sb: to hit someone many times or criticize them strongly ▶ *Darren threw his sister to the ground and began whaling on her.*

WHEEL

WHEEL AROUND, *also* WHEEL ROUND →
wheel around/round: to turn around

suddenly, especially because you are angry or surprised ▶ *Hearing a voice behind him, Henry wheeled around.*

WHEEL OUT →

1 wheel out sth/sb, **wheel** sth/sb **out**: to use someone or something to support your opinion or in order to persuade people that you are right ▶ *A number of scientific experts were wheeled out to support the government's assurances about safety.*

2 wheel out sth/sb, **wheel** sth/sb **out**: to use the same things or people that you have often used before, in a way that is boring ▶ *Christmas television is so tedious – they wheel out the same old films year after year.*

WHEEL ROUND *see* WHEEL AROUND

WHILE

WHILE AWAY →
while away sth, **while** sth **away**: if you while away a period of time, you spend it in a pleasantly relaxing way ▶ *We whiled away the long afternoon over a game of cards.*

WHIP

WHIP INTO →
whip sb **into a frenzy/fury**: to make people feel very excited or angry about something, especially by talking to them ▶ *a speaker who had the power to whip his audience into sheer fury*

WHIP OUT →
whip out sth, **whip** sth **out**: to quickly bring something out from your pocket, bag etc ▶ *On a sudden impulse, I whipped out my cheque book and wrote out a donation of £500.*

WHIP THROUGH →
whip through sth: to do a piece of work or read something very quickly ▶ *Louise managed to whip through the rest of her routine paperwork before lunch.*

WHIP UP →
whip up sth/sb, **whip** sth/sb **up**: to make a lot of people feel interested, excited, or angry about something ▶ *a propaganda campaign designed to whip up support for the war effort* ▶ *They were accused of trying to whip up anti-American feeling.*

WHISK
WHISK AWAY, *also* WHISK OFF →
whisk sb **away/off**, **whisk away/off** sb: to take someone quickly away from a place ▶ *Immediately after the show, the new Miss America was whisked away in a limousine.*

WHISTLE
WHISTLE BY, *also* WHISTLE PAST →
whistle by/past sth/sb, **whistle by/past**: to move very quickly past something or someone and often very close to them ▶ *A bullet whistled past his ear.*

WHISTLE FOR →
he/she can whistle for sth: used to say that someone cannot have something because you are not going to give it to them ▶ *If he's coming here to ask me for money, he can whistle for it.*

WHISTLE PAST *see* WHISTLE BY

WHISTLE UP →
whistle up sth/sb: to arrange for something or someone to appear quickly ▶ *The government seems to be able to whistle up a crowd of demonstrators at a moment's notice.*

WHITTLE
WHITTLE AWAY (AT) →
whittle away sth, **whittle** sth **away**, **whittle away at**: to gradually reduce the amount, value, or effectiveness of something ▶ *The power of the monarchy was gradually whittled away by successive parliaments.*

WHITTLE DOWN →
whittle down sth, **whittle** sth **down**: to gradually reduce the size of a number, amount, or group by taking parts away ▶ *The original list of 25 competitors has been whittled down to six finalists.*

WHOOP
WHOOP UP →
whoop it up: to enjoy yourself by having a lot of noisy fun with other people ▶ *We spent the whole summer whooping it up at the nightclubs on Corfu.*

WIG
WIG OUT →
wig out, **wig** sb **out**: to be very anxious, upset, or frightened, or to make someone feel like this ▶ *The thought of seeing Mick again really wigs me out.*

WIMP
WIMP OUT →
wimp out: to decide not to do something that you had intended to do, because you are too frightened to do it ▶ *He said he'd give a speech at the wedding, but then he wimped out at the last minute.*

WIN
WIN AROUND *see* WIN ROUND

WIN BACK →
win back sth/sb, **win** sth/sb **back**: to succeed in getting back something or someone that you had in the past ▶ *The girl's mother went to the European Court in an attempt to win back her child.*

WIN OUT →
1 win out: to succeed or defeat others after a long struggle or debate ▶ *In the end, the environmentalists won out and the nuclear plant was not built.*

2 win out: to be stronger than another feeling or quality ▶ *In the end, my curiosity won out and I had to read the letter.*

W

WIN OVER →

win over sb, **win** sb **over**: to persuade someone to support you, or to get them to like you ▶ *We'll be working hard over the next ten days to win over the undecided voters.* ▶ *The jury were obviously completely won over by her performance in the witness box.*

WIN ROUND, *also* WIN AROUND →

win sb **round / around, win round / around** sb: to persuade someone to agree with you or do what you want ▶ *After a long debate, he finally succeeded in winning Harris round to his own way of thinking.*

WIN THROUGH →

win through: to finally succeed in achieving something or dealing with a difficult situation ▶ *We are confident that we will win through in the end and get what we want.*

WIND

WIND BACK →

wind sth **back, wind back** sth: to make a tape upon which something is recorded move backwards quickly ▶ *Could you wind back the video to the beginning?*

WIND DOWN →

1 wind down, wind down sth, **wind** sth **down**: if a company or organization winds down, or is wound down, it gradually does less and less work, produces less etc before it is closed completely ▶ *The original mill is winding down after over a hundred years in textile production.*

2 wind down, wind down sth, **wind** sth **down**: if something that people are doing winds down, or if someone winds it down, they gradually do less of it before stopping completely ▶ *Keller said he would be winding down his involvement in sport in the summer.* ▶ *The football season is winding down now, with only three weeks to go.*

3 wind down: to gradually relax after you have been working or after you have been worried ▶ *Have a drink – you look as if you need to wind down.* ▶ *After a tough day it's great to wind down in front of the TV.*

4 wind down sth, **wind** sth **down**: to open a car window by making the glass move down ▶ *She wound down her window and called to me across the street.*

WIND FORWARD →

wind sth **forward, wind forward** sth: to make a tape upon which something is recorded move forward quickly ▶ *I wound the tape forward until I found the song I wanted to hear.*

WIND ON →

wind sth **on, wind on** sth: to make a tape upon which something is recorded move forward to a later point ▶ *I wound the tape on to the next song.*

WIND UP →

1 wind sth **up, wind up** sth, **wind up**: to end, or to end something ▶ *Palmer wound up the debate with an extremely clever and amusing speech.* ▶ *With a bit of luck, the meeting should wind up by about four o'clock.*

2 wind sth **up, wind up** sth: to reduce the activity of a business, organization etc until it closes completely ▶ *The department is being wound up and its staff laid off.*

3 wind up: to get into a particular situation or place at the end of a long series of events ▶ *That's enough for one night or you'll wind up drunk.* ▶ *If the situation continues, some doctors could wind up losing their jobs.*

4 wind sb **up, wind up** sb: to deliberately say or do something that you know will annoy or worry someone ▶ *Don't pay any attention to him! He's just winding you up!*

5 be wound up: to feel tense and anxious and unable to relax. **+ about** ▶ *Sarah's very wound up about her interview next week.*

6 wind sth **up, wind up** sth: to make a clock, watch, or machine work, by turning a handle or key ▶ *It's a lovely old watch, but you have to remember to wind it up every day.*

7 wind sth **up, wind up** sth: to close a car window by making the glass move upwards ▶ *Tell me if you're cold in the back and I'll wind up the window.*

WINKLE

WINKLE OUT →

winkle out sth, **winkle** sth **out**: to succeed in getting something from someone that they do not want to give you, especially information. **+ of** ▶ *Mrs Fulton finally managed to winkle the truth out of him.*

WIPE

WIPE DOWN →

wipe down sth, **wipe** sth **down**: to clean the surface of a table, wall, shelf etc using a wet cloth ▶ *Polly wiped down the cooker and the work surfaces.*

WIPE OFF →

wipe sth **off, wipe off** sth, **wipe** sth **off** sth: to reduce the price or value of something by a particular amount ▶ *The recession wiped 62% off the company's pre-tax profits.*

WIPE OUT →

1 wipe out sth, **wipe** sth **out**: to destroy or get rid of something completely ▶ *Whole villages were wiped out and towns abandoned.* ▶ *We're going to use the money to wipe out all our debts and start again.*

2 wipe out sb, **wipe** sb **out**: to defeat

someone easily in a competition, election etc ▶ *The party was completely wiped out at the last general election.*

3 wipe sth **out, wipe out** sth: to clean the inside of something, using a wet cloth ▶ *I emptied all the drawers and wiped them out with a cloth.*

4 be wiped out: to be extremely tired ▶ *By the end of the week I was completely wiped out.*

WIPE UP →

1 wipe up sth, **wipe** sth **up**: to remove liquid or dirt from a surface using a cloth ▶ *Someone's got to wipe up this mess!*

2 wipe up, wipe up sth, **wipe** sth **up**: to dry plates, glasses etc that have been washed, using a cloth ▶ *It'll take me hours to wipe up all these glasses!*

WIRE

BE WIRED IN, *also* BE WIRED INTO →

be wired in sth / **be wired into** sth: to be very involved in and know a lot about a particular subject, job etc ▶ *Albers was wired into the art world both at home and in the United States.*

WIRE UP →

wire sth / sb **up, wire up** sth / sb: to connect something or someone to a piece of electrical equipment by using wires.

+ to ▶ *The house is wired up to a very expensive alarm system.* ▶ *I spent the whole day in hospital, wired up to various machines for tests.*

WISE

WISE UP →

wise up: to understand something

W

better or realize the truth about something, or to make someone do this ▸ *You'd better wise up, Mattie, and listen to what they're saying.* **wise** sb **up to** sth ▸ *If he doesn't know what's wrong with their marriage, someone had better wise him up to it.*

WISH

WISH AWAY →
wish sth **away, wish away** sth: to hope that a problem will disappear easily without you having to do anything about it ▸ *Poverty is a serious problem in our society, and you can't just wish it away.*

WISH FOR →
1 wish for sth: to want something very much and hope that you will get it ▸ *There was no escape now – the only thing they could do was wish for a miracle.* ▸ *As a child, Jenna had everything she could possibly wish for.*

2 couldn't wish for more/ better etc: used to emphasize that something or someone is as good, nice etc as they could possibly be ▸ *"Everyone has been so good to me," John said. "I couldn't wish for better friends."*

WISH ON, *also* WISH UPON →
wouldn't wish sth **on anyone** *also* **wouldn't wish** sth **on your worst enemy**: used to emphasize that a situation is extremely bad or unpleasant, and you would not want it to happen even to someone you dislike ▸ *You don't know what it's like to watch your brother die; I wouldn't wish it on anyone.*

WITHER

WITHER AWAY →
1 wither away: to gradually become weaker and finally stop existing ▸ *In the end most protest movements lose support and wither away.*

2 wither away: if plants wither away,

they become dry and start to die ▸ *I got back from holiday to find that all my plants had withered away.*

WITTER

WITTER →
witter on: to keep talking for a long time in a boring way, about unimportant things ▸ *I tried to smile and nod politely as he wittered on.*
+ about ▸ *We had to sit and listen to him wittering on about his love life all evening.*

WOLF

WOLF DOWN →
wolf down sth, **wolf** sth **down**: to eat food very quickly, especially because you

are very hungry ▸ *When dinner finally came, we wolfed it down in five minutes.*

WONDER

WONDER AT →
wonder at sth: to feel very surprised by something because it is so unusual, special, or difficult to understand ▸ *Eileen wondered at her sister's ability to know exactly what she was thinking.* ▸ *I sometimes wonder at the stupidity of these people.*

WORK

WORK AGAINST →
work against sb/ sth: to make it harder for someone to achieve something ▸ *In those days the company career structure tended to work against women.*

WORK AROUND, *also* WORK ROUND →
work around/ round sth: to organize

what you are doing so that you are able to do it in spite of things that might stop you ▶ *I agree that this is a major problem, but we'll just have to work around it.*

WORK AROUND TO, *also* **WORK ROUND TO** →
work around/round to sth: to very gradually prepare yourself or other people for something that you are going to say or do ▶ *It was a difficult subject to talk about with my boss, and I knew that I must work around to it gradually.*

WORK AT →
work at sth: to try hard to improve or achieve something ▶ *Budd always had a terrible temper, and really had to work at self-control.* **work at it** ▶ *If you work at it, your reading will improve over time.* **work at doing** sth ▶ *This year we've worked hard at expanding the business.*

WORK AWAY →
work away: to keep working hard for a long time ▶ *Engineers and technicians were working away in the control room.* **+ at** ▶ *I went round the back and found Jake working away at a table he was making.*

WORK IN →
1 work sth **in, work in** sth: to rub a soft substance into a surface until it disappears completely ▶ *Using a cloth, work the wax in well, and allow it to dry.*

2 work sth **in, work** sth **in:** to cleverly include something in a speech or a piece of writing ▶ *During the interview he managed to work in a reference to his new book.*

WORK INTO →
1 work sth **into** sth: to add one substance to another and mix them together thoroughly ▶ *Gradually work the remaining flour into the dough.*

2 work sth **into** sth: to rub a soft substance into a surface until it disappears completely ▶ *Work the cream gently into your skin.*

3 work sth **into** sth: to cleverly include something in a speech or a piece of writing ▶ *He managed to work a few jokes into his talk.*

4 work yourself into a state/rage etc: to become very upset or angry about something ▶ *She's worked herself into a real state about her electricity bill.*

WORK OFF →
1 work off sth, **work** sth **off:** to get rid of an unpleasant feeling by doing something that uses a lot of energy ▶ *If I feel aggressive and frustrated at the end of the day, I go and work it off in the gym.*

2 work off sth, **work** sth **off:** to do something that uses energy after you have eaten a lot, in order to stop yourself getting fat or so that you feel less full ▶ *Physical exercise is good for working off those extra calories.*

3 work off sth, **work** sth **off:** to pay back a debt by earning the money you owe, or by working without pay for the person who lent you the money ▶ *I'm not taking out another loan – it took me years to work off the last one.*

WORK ON →
1 work on sth: to work in order to produce or achieve something ▶ *At the time of her death she was working on a new novel.* ▶ *Are you working on any films at the moment?*

2 work on sth: to spend time trying to improve something in order for it to be successful ▶ *Chris is a very strong player, but he still needs to work on his technique.*

3 work on sth: to spend time working to repair something ▶ *He spends most of his weekends working on his motorbike.*

4 work on sb: to keep trying to persuade or influence someone ▶ *I've been working on my mum to let me have a computer for ages now.*

WORK OUT →

1 work out sth, **work** sth **out**: to calculate the answer to a problem that involves numbers, amounts, prices etc ▶ *Francis sat down to work out how much of his salary he would have to save each year.*

2 work out sth, **work** sth **out**: to think carefully about something in order to decide what you should do or how you should do it ▶ *Rod's spent over an hour working out the best route to take.* **+ what/ how etc** ▶ *We know what we're aiming at, but we still have to work out how to put it into practice.*

3a. work out sth, **work** sth **out**: to succeed in understanding something by thinking carefully about it. **+ what/ how etc** ▶ *There was obviously something wrong, but I couldn't work out what it was.*

b. work sb **out**: to understand someone's character or why they behave as they do ▶ *Don looked at her, puzzled. He was still trying to work this girl out.* **can't work** sb **out** ▶ *I can't work Geoff out, one day he's friendly and the next he ignores me completely.*

4 work out: if the cost of something works out at a particular amount, that is what it costs when you calculate the figures. **+ at** ▶ *At the end of the evening, the meal worked out at £15 each.* **+ to be** ▶ *The total cost of advertising works out to be about £900 million annually.*

5 work out: to be successful ▶ *The marriage didn't work out, and we split up after two years.*

6 work out: if a situation works out in a particular way, it happens or develops in that way. **work out well/**

badly etc ▶ *Financially, things have worked out very well for us.* ▶ *The situation seemed hopeless, but in the end it all worked out fine.*

7 work out: to do physical exercises in order to make your body fit and strong ▶ *I've started to work out in the gym two or three times a week.*

workout N a period of physical exercise or training ▶ *A good workout always relaxes me.*

8 work itself out: if a problem or a difficult situation works itself out, it gradually becomes less and less difficult until it stops existing ▶ *There are always problems when you start something like this, but they usually work themselves out in time.*

WORK ROUND *see* WORK AROUND

WORK ROUND TO *see* WORK AROUND TO

WORK THROUGH →

1 work through sth, **work** sth **through**: to deal with a problem by discussing it in detail until you find a solution ▶ *We have a good relationship, which should help us work through any differences.*

2 work through sth, **work** sth **through**: to deal with strong feelings of anger, sadness, guilt etc by talking or thinking about them ▶ *Tom's fear of relationships had to be explored and worked through.*

3 work through, work through sth: if the result of something works through, it gradually has an effect ▶ *The educational reforms will work through the system slowly, over several years.*

WORK TOWARDS, *also* WORK TOWARD →

work towards/ toward sth: to try hard to achieve something that can only be achieved gradually ▶ *The two sides*

have been working toward an agreement for several months.

WORK UP →

1 work up sth, **work** sth **up**: if you work up a feeling such as courage, interest, or sympathy, you try to make yourself feel it, especially with difficulty ▶ *We'd already lost one game, and couldn't work up any enthusiasm for another.* **work up the courage/energy to do** sth ▶ *I'm so tired I can't even work up the energy to go to bed.*

2 work up an appetite/thirst: to make yourself feel hungry or thirsty, for example by taking some exercise ▶ *We went for a brisk walk along the beach to work up an appetite.*

3 be worked up: to feel very angry, excited, or upset about something ▶ *Jill seemed to be very worked up about something.* **get worked up (about** sth**)** ▶ *Tim's always late, so there's no point in getting worked up about it.*

4 work sb **up**: to make someone feel upset, worried, or excited. **+ into** ▶ *He knew exactly how to work his audience up into a state of eager excitement.* **work yourself up** ▶ *Stop working yourself up over nothing and let's have a drink.*

5 work up: to gradually increase the amount of something that you do or take regularly ▶ *In general with this drug, it's best to start with a low dose and then work up.* **+ to** ▶ *Start with ten minutes of exercises each day and work up to half an hour.*

WORK UP TO →

work up to sth, **work** sb **up to** sth: to gradually get ready to do something that seems difficult ▶ *She suddenly realized that Tim was working up to a proposal of marriage.* **work yourself up to doing** sth ▶ *They've been working themselves up to asking for a pay rise, but I don't think they'll get it.*

WORM

WORM OUT →

worm sth **out of** sb: to succeed in getting information from someone although they do not want to give it ▶ *Nobody knows who his new girlfriend is yet, but I'm going to try and worm it out of him.*

WRAP

WRAP IN →

wrap sth/sb **in** sth: to fold paper, cloth etc around something or someone ▶ *Wrap the meat in foil and cook it for an hour in a hot oven.* ▶ *The baby had been left outside the police station, wrapped in a blanket.*

WRAP UP →

1 wrap sth **up, wrap up** sth: to fold a piece of paper or cloth around something so that it is completely covered ▶ *She gave me a box of chocolates, beautifully wrapped up in silver paper.*

2 wrap up sth, **wrap** sth **up**: to complete a job, agreement, or an activity in a successful way ▶ *They hope to have the deal all wrapped up in a couple of days.*

3 wrap (yourself) up: to put on warm clothes before going outside when it is cold ▶ *It's icy out there tonight. You'd better wrap up.*

4 be wrapped up in sth/sb: to give so much of your attention, thought etc to something or someone that you have no time for anything else ▶ *Nowadays many people are too wrapped up in work and money to really enjoy life.*

5 be wrapped up in sth: to be so involved in something that you do not notice what is happening around you ▶ *He was so wrapped up in his book that I had to repeat my question three times.*

WRESTLE

WRESTLE WITH →

1 wrestle with sth: to try very hard to deal with a difficult problem, and find an answer to it ▶ *Mathematicians had been wrestling with this problem for centuries.*

2 wrestle with your conscience: to try very hard to decide whether it is right for you to do something ▶ *After wrestling with my conscience for some days, I decided to tell her what her son had done.*

3 wrestle with sth: to have great difficulty controlling or holding something that is very large or heavy ▶ *The airport was full of passengers, all wrestling with their luggage.*

WRIGGLE

WRIGGLE OUT OF →

wriggle out of sth: to avoid doing something that you should do, by finding excuses for not doing it ▶ *You promised you'd help me this evening, so don't try to wriggle out of it now!*

WRING

WRING FROM, *also* **WRING OUT OF** →

1 wring sth **from/out of** sb: to get information, money, an agreement etc from someone, but only with great difficulty ▶ *Carla was determined to wring every dollar she could out of her ex-husband.*

2 wring sth **from/out of** sb: to deliberately behave in a way that causes a particular emotion in someone else ▶ *Nigel felt annoyed with her for trying to wring sympathy out of him in this way.*

WRING OUT →

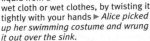

wring out sth, **wring** sth **out**: to remove the liquid from a wet cloth or wet clothes, by twisting it tightly with your hands ▶ *Alice picked up her swimming costume and wrung it out over the sink.*

WRING OUT OF *see* **WRING FROM**

WRITE

WRITE AWAY →

write away: to write a letter to a company or an organization asking them to send you something. **+ for** ▶ *I've just written away for their catalogue.*

WRITE BACK →

write back: to reply to a letter that someone sent you, by writing a letter to them ▶ *I wrote back immediately, thanking them for their kind invitation.* **+ to** ▶ *Ally sent him letters every week, but he never once wrote back to her.*

WRITE DOWN →

write down sth, **write** sth **down**: to write something on a piece of paper ▶ *This is the address – do you want to write it down? I wrote down the number on the back of an envelope.*

WRITE IN →

1 write in: to write a letter to an organization in order to give an opinion, ask for information etc ▶ *A lot of people have written in recently criticizing the programme.*

2 write sb **in, write in** sb: to add someone's name to the official list on the voting form, to show that you want to vote for them ▶ *The campaign to write in Johnson for governor failed.*

W

WRITE IN, *also* WRITE INTO →

1 write in sb/sth, **write** sb/sth **in**, **write** sth/sb **into** sth: to add a new character or scene to a book, play, film etc ▶ *When the book was made into a film a lot was changed and new scenes were written in.*

2 write in sth, **write** sth **in**, **write** sth **into** sth: to include or add something in a contract, agreement etc ▶ *It was written into his contract that he had to make five records a year.*

WRITE OFF →

1 write off: to write a letter to a company or an organization asking them to send you something. **+ for** ▶ *I've written off for more details of the offer.*

2 write off sb/sth, **write** sb/sth **off**: to decide that someone or something is not likely to be successful, or that they are not very good or interesting ▶ *At the time, everyone was writing the team off.* **+ as** ▶ *After six months of work, we eventually wrote the project off as a non-starter.*

  write-off N a complete failure or something that is not worth doing, considering etc ▶ *The whole idea was a write-off from the start.*

3 write off sth, **write** sth **off**: to crash a vehicle and damage it so badly that it is not worth repairing it ▶ *He's never let me drive his car since I wrote off his old one last year.*

  write-off N if a vehicle is a write-off, it has been so badly damaged in a crash that it is not worth repairing it ▶ *Doug's motor-bike was a complete write-off and he felt lucky to be alive.*

4 write off sth, **write** sth **off**: to officially say that a debt no longer has to be paid, for example because it is impossible to get the money back ▶ *The Inland Revenue wrote off £900 million in unpaid taxes last year.* ▶ *The US government agreed to write off debts worth billions of dollars.*

5 write off sth, **write** sth **off**: to make an official record of the amount of money that you have spent in order to reduce the amount of tax that you have to pay. **write off** sth **against tax** ▶ *The costs of setting up the business can be written off against tax.*

WRITE OUT →

1 write out sth, **write** sth **out**: to write something on paper, especially in a very complete, detailed, or neat way ▶ *The children were asked to choose a poem and write it out in their best handwriting.*

2 write out a cheque/bill etc: to write the necessary information on a cheque, bill etc ▶ *We waited while the girl at the desk wrote out our bill.*

3 write sb **out, write out** sb: to remove a character from a play or a television or radio series, by making him or her leave or die in the story. **+ of** ▶ *It was revealed last week that Jody is being written out of the series.*

WRITE UP →

1 write up sth, **write** sth **up**: to write a report, article etc in its final form ▶ *I took notes during the meeting, but I haven't had a chance to write them up yet.*

2 write sth **up, write up** sth: to write something on a wall, board etc where people can see it ▶ *The teacher repeated the word, and wrote it up on the board.*

3 write sb **up, write up** sb: if someone in authority writes you up, they make an official report about your bad behaviour ▶ *My supervisor wrote me up for being late three days in a row.*

W

X
X OUT →
x out sth, **x** sth **out**: to write an X on something to show that it is a mistake or should not be included in a piece of writing ▶ *Someone had xed out my name from the list.*

Yy

YEARN

YEARN FOR →

yearn for sth: to have a very strong desire for something ▶ *The people yearned for peace and a chance to rebuild their shattered lives.*

YELL

YELL OUT →

yell out sth, **yell** sth **out**: to shout something very loudly, especially because you are very excited, angry, or frightened ▶ *If you know the answer to the question, don't just yell it out, wait until you're asked.*

YIELD

YIELD TO →

1 yield to sth/sb: to agree to do something that someone is trying to make you do, even though you do not want to ▶ *There is no question of our party yielding to terrorists.* **yield to pressure (to do sth)** ▶ *The Prime Minister criticized the strikers, and said that the government would not yield to pressure.* **yield to demands** ▶ *There is little sign that the US will yield to the demands of the protestors.*

2 yield to sth: to finally do something that you have been trying not to do ▶ *"Are you married?" she asked, yielding to her curiosity.* **yield to temptation** ▶ *Dexter yielded to temptation, and lit a cigarette.*

YIELD UP →

yield up sth, **yield** sth **up**: to show or produce something that was hidden, unknown, or difficult to find ▶ *New research into the functioning of the human brain has yielded up some surprising discoveries.*

Y

Zz

ZERO

ZERO IN ON →

1 zero in on sth: to quickly direct all your attention towards something ► *He immediately zeroed in on the weakest part of her argument.*

2 zero in on sth/sb: to move quickly and directly towards something in order to attack it ► *missiles capable of zeroing in on a target thousands of miles away*

ZIP

ZIP UP →

1 zip up sth, **zip** sth **up**: to fasten a piece of clothing, a bag etc using a zip ► *Can you zip up my dress for me?* ► *This bag's useless – everytime I try to zip it up, the zip gets stuck.*

2 zip up: if a piece of clothing, a bag etc zips up, it can be fastened together using a zip ► *The jacket zips up at the front.*

zip-up ADJ a zip-up piece of clothing, bag etc fastens together using a zip ► *zip-up boots*

ZONE

ZONE OUT →

zone out: to stop thinking about things and not pay attention to anything ► *Larry's medication makes him zone out.* ► *When Tom gets home from work he just zones out in front of the TV.*

zoned out ADJ unable to think clearly about anything, especially because of the effects of drugs ► *Her daughter's zoned out on pills all the time.*

ZONK

ZONK OUT →

zonk out: to go to sleep quickly and completely because you are very tired ► *I was so exhausted that I just wanted to zonk out on the sofa.*

ZOOM

ZOOM IN →

zoom in: if a camera zooms in, it makes the person or thing that you are photographing or filming seem bigger and closer ► *The camera zoomed in for a close-up of his face.* **+ on** ► *You can stop the video and zoom in on anything on the screen.*

ZOOM OFF →

zoom off: to leave somewhere quickly and suddenly ► *Mark jumped in his car and zoomed off without even saying goodbye.*

ZOOM OUT →

zoom out: if a camera zooms out, it makes the person or thing you are photographing or filming seem smaller and further away ► *The camera zoomed out to show the whole of the city.*

Z

IRREGULAR VERBS

verb	past tense	past participle
abide	abided, abode	abided
be	was/were	been
bear	bore	borne
beat	beat	beaten
become	became	become
bend	bent	bent
bet	bet, betted	bet, betted
bind	bound	bound
bite	bit	bitten
blow	blew	blown
break	broke	broken
bring	brought	brought
build	built	built
burn	burned, burnt	burned, burnt
burst	burst	burst
bust	bust, busted	bust, busted
buy	bought	bought
cast	cast	cast
catch	caught	caught
choose	chose	chosen
cling	clung	clung
come	came	come
creep	crept	crept
cut	cut	cut
deal	dealt	dealt
dig	dug	dug
dive	dived	dived
do	did	done
draw	drew	drawn
dream	dreamed, dreamt	dreamed, dreamt
drink	drank	drunk
drive	drove	driven
dwell	dwelt, dwelled	dwelt, dwelled
eat	ate	eaten
fall	fell	fallen
feed	fed	fed
feel	felt	felt
fight	fought	fought
find	found	found
fling	flung	flung
fly	flew	flown
freeze	froze	frozen
get	got	got
give	gave	given
go	went	gone

verb	past tense	past participle
grind	ground	ground
grow	grew	grown
hang	hung, hanged	hung, hanged
have	had	had
hear	heard	heard
heave	heaved, hove	heaved, hove
hew	hewed	hewn, hewed
hide	hid	hidden, hid
hit	hit	hit
hold	held	held
keep	kept	kept
kneel	knelt, kneeled	knelt, kneeled
knit	knitted, knit	knitted, knit
know	knew	known
lay	laid	laid
lead	led	led
lean	leaned (*also* leant)	leaned (*also* leant)
leap	leapt, leaped	leapt, leaped
leave	left	left
lend	lent	lent
let	let	let
lie	lay	lain
light	lit, lighted	lit, lighted
lose	lost	lost
make	made	made
meet	met	met
mow	mowed	mown, mowed
partake	partook	partaken
pay	paid	paid
put	put	put
read	read	read
rid	rid, ridded	rid, ridded
ride	rode	ridden
ring	rang	rung
rise	rose	risen
run	ran	run
saw	sawed	sawn, sawed
say	said	said
see	saw	seen
seek	sought	sought
sell	sold	sold
send	sent	sent
set	set	set
sew	sewed	sewn, sewed
shake	shook	shaken
shave	shaved	shaved
shear	sheared	shorn, sheared
shine	shone, shined	shone, shined

verb	past tense	past participle
shoot	shot	shot
show	showed	shown, showed
shrink	shrank, shrunk	shrunk
shut	shut	shut
sing	sang	sung
sink	sank, sunk	sunk
sit	sat	sat
sleep	slept	slept
smell	smelt, smelled	smelt, smelled
sneak	sneaked	sneaked
speak	spoke	spoken
speed	sped, speeded	sped, speeded
spell	spelt, spelled	spelt, spelled
spill	spilt, spilled	spilt, spilled
spin	spun, span	spun
spit	spat	spat
split	split	split
spoil	spoiled, spoilt	spoiled, spoilt
spread	spread	spread
spring	sprang	sprung
stand	stood	stood
steal	stole	stolen
stick	stuck	stuck
sting	stung	stung
strew	strewed	strewn, strewed
strike	struck	struck
string	strung	strung
swear	swore	sworn
sweep	swept	swept
swell	swelled	swollen, swelled
swim	swam	swum
swing	swung	swung
take	took	taken
tear	tore	torn
tell	told	told
think	thought	thought
thrive	thrived, throve	thrived
throw	threw	thrown
thrust	thrust	thrust
wake	woke, waked	woken, waked
wear	wore	worn
wed	wedded, wed	wedded, wed
win	won	won
wind	wound	wound
wring	wrung	wrung
write	wrote	written